P9-DTP-016

BORLAND C++
TECHNIQUES AND UTILITIES

PLEASE NOTE—USE OF THE DISK(S) AND THE PROGRAMS INCLUDED ON THE DISK(S) PACKAGED WITH THIS BOOK AND THE PROGRAM LISTINGS INCLUDED IN THIS BOOK IS SUBJECT TO AN END-USER LICENSE AGREEMENT (THE "AGREEMENT") FOUND AT THE BACK OF THE BOOK. PLEASE READ THE AGREEMENT CAREFULLY BEFORE MAKING YOUR PURCHASE DECISION. PURCHASE OF THE BOOK AND USE OF THE DISKS, PROGRAMS, AND PROGRAM LISTINGS WILL CONSTITUTE ACCEPTANCE OF THE AGREEMENT.

BORLAND C++ TECHNIQUES AND UTILITIES

Kaare Christian

Ziff-Davis Press
Emeryville, California

Development Editor	Valerie Haynes Perry
Copy Editor	Jan Jue
Technical Reviewer	William Roetzheim
Project Coordinator	Bill Cassel
Proofreader	Sylvia Townsend
Cover Design and Illustration	Carrie English
Book Design	Peter Tucker
Screen Graphics Editor	Dan Brodnitz
Technical Illustration	Cherie Plumlee Computer Graphics & Illustration
Word Processing	Howard Blechman and Cat Haglund
Page Layout	M. D. Barrera and Bruce Lundquist
Indexer	Ted Laux

This book was produced on a Macintosh IIfx, with the following applications: FrameMaker®, Microsoft® Word, MacLink® Plus, Aldus® FreeHand™, Adobe Photoshop™, and Collage Plus™.

Ziff-Davis Press
5903 Christie Avenue
Emeryville, CA 94608

Copyright © 1993 by Ziff-Davis Press. All rights reserved.
PART OF A CONTINUING SERIES
Ziff-Davis Press, ZD Press, and Techniques and Utilities are trademarks of Ziff Communications Company.

All other product names and services identified throughout this book are trademarks or registered trademarks of their respective companies. They are used throughout this book in editorial fashion only and for the benefit of such companies. No such uses, or the use of any trade name, is intended to convey endorsement or other affiliation with the book.

No part of this publication may be reproduced in any form, or stored in a database or retrieval system, or transmitted or distributed in any form by any means, electronic, mechanical photocopying, recording, or otherwise, without the prior written permission of Ziff-Davis Press, except as permitted by the Copyright Act of 1976 and the End-User License Agreement at the back of this book and except that program listings may be entered, stored, and executed in a computer system.

EXCEPT FOR THE LIMITED WARRANTY COVERING THE PHYSICAL DISK(S) PACKAGED WITH THIS BOOK AS PROVIDED IN THE END-USER LICENSE AGREEMENT AT THE BACK OF THIS BOOK, THE INFORMATION AND MATERIAL CONTAINED IN THIS BOOK ARE PROVIDED "AS IS," WITHOUT WARRANTY OF ANY KIND, EXPRESS OR IMPLIED, INCLUDING WITHOUT LIMITATION ANY WARRANTY CONCERNING THE ACCURACY, ADEQUACY, OR COMPLETENESS OF SUCH INFORMATION OR MATERIAL OR THE RESULTS TO BE OBTAINED FROM USING SUCH INFORMATION OR MATERIAL. NEITHER ZIFF-DAVIS PRESS NOR THE AUTHOR SHALL BE RESPONSIBLE FOR ANY CLAIMS ATTRIBUTABLE TO ERRORS, OMISSIONS, OR OTHER INACCURACIES IN THE INFORMATION OR MATERIAL CONTAINED IN THIS BOOK, AND IN NO EVENT SHALL ZIFF-DAVIS PRESS OR THE AUTHOR BE LIABLE FOR DIRECT, INDIRECT, SPECIAL, INCIDENTAL, OR CONSEQUENTIAL DAMAGES ARISING OUT OF THE USE OF SUCH INFORMATION OR MATERIAL.

ISBN 1-56276-054-8

Manufactured in the United States of America
10 9 8 7 6 5 4 3 2 1

≡ Contents at a Glance

◼ TABLE OF CONTENTS

13. Assembling an OWL Application   341

14. Painting the Window   379

Acknowledgments

ALL OF US WHO WORK WITH C++ GRATEFULLY ACKNOWLEDGE THE LARGE contribution of Bjarne Stroustrup, who created the language. At Ziff-Davis Press, Cindy Hudson, publisher, and Valerie Haynes Perry, development editor, were always helpful and supportive, and Bill Roetzheim provided insightful technical advice. Michael Hyman at Borland answered technical questions and helped with other matters. And at home, my wife Robin Raskin and my children Kari, Arli, and Reed cheerfully helped me through another long project.

Portions of Borland's C++ Class Libraries reprinted by permission of Borland International, Inc. All rights reserved.

INTRODUCTION

MOST QUESTIONS ABOUT PC SOFTWARE ARE TOUGH TO ANSWER. TYPICALLY A client or friend asks what sounds like a simple question, and then I respond with a barrage of questions. Sorry, I just can't automatically tell which solution is best. It depends on who you are, what you're doing, who's helping you, which hardware and software you have already, which vendors look strong, what's going to happen next month or next year, and so on. But when the topic is software *development,* the answer's always Borland. For DOS development, use Borland's Turbo Vision application framework. For high programmer productivity, use Borland's user-supportive tools. For high code quality, use the new optimization built into Borland's compilers. For Windows, use OWL, an object-oriented library. And for general-purpose software development, use C++, in which Borland is the undisputed leader. I wish things were always this simple.

My purpose in writing this book was to help people move to the new object-oriented software development paradigm. I believe that I'm a good guide for you because I've been doing object-oriented development for over five years. When I first started, I made a lot of mistakes. That's why there is so much advice, and so many warnings, scattered throughout this book. But as my work matured, I learned what worked, and I became a very strong believer in the technique. Objects provide a great leap forward. They make it possible to create better solutions to most problems, they make it easier to reuse and extend code, and they make it easier to handle complex situations.

If you've been reading about PC software recently, I'm sure you've seen all the hype about objects. My first reaction was that such a load of hype must have been hiding a cartload of manure. But that's not the case. Yes, there are many false prophets trying to make big bucks by gluing the word *object* onto one thing after another. But I'm not a prophet; I'm simply a good guide for people who want to learn object-oriented programming so that they can increase their productivity, improve the reliability of their code, and get more enjoyment from programming.

Who This Book Is For

This book is written for people who are serious software developers. There is a strong emphasis on Windows development, because that's where demand is the greatest. I'm assuming that you already are a competent C programmer, and that you now want to become an accomplished C++ programmer. I'm assuming that you want to create industrial-strength applications, so I haven't shied away from the details, and I don't oversimplify.

My belief that you are a serious developer has guided my omissions. I'm not going to show you how to use Borland's integrated development environment (IDE), Resource Workshop (RW), debugger, or other tools. These tools are probably familiar to you from your Borland C programming experience, but even if you haven't previously used Borland C, I'm assuming that you can pick up these topics on your own. Few creators of software have much trouble using software, especially software that is as well designed as Borland's. I'm also omitting all discussion of the C programming language and the standard C library. If you're not already a C programmer, then this isn't the book for you.

How This Book Is Organized

This book is organized into four parts. Part 1 introduces object-oriented programming and C++. The pace is fast and demanding, but my coverage of both topics is thorough and complete. My assumption is that you want to understand the language as quickly and as thoroughly as possible.

Part 2 of the book moves directly into getting the most from C++, using Borland's class library. The class library, which is applicable to both DOS and Windows programs, lets you create complex data structures based on C++ templates. This capability, which is undoubtedly the best way to create flexible and extensible arrays, stacks, sets, and the like, is currently available only in Borland's implementation of C++. I show how you can use the library to solve complex problems and how you can customize the library to provide new facilities.

Part 3 of the book shows how you can use the object-oriented paradigm to create DOS applications using Borland's Turbo Vision application framework class library. Turbo Vision makes it easy to create interactive, multiwindow, menu-based, dialog-based DOS applications—applications that look like Borland's own DOS products, such as the Borland C++ IDE or Borland's Turbo Debugger. DOS development may not be the hottest topic in the early '90s, but there are about 100 million PCs that can run these applications, and they are surprisingly easy to build.

Part 4, the longest section of this book, shows how you can use Borland's Object Windows Library (OWL) to create Windows programs. OWL makes it easier to create Windows programs. It helps you respond to Windows messages, it simplifies management of dialog boxes, and it helps you organize your application. Windows development using OWL is simply superior to the timeworn native C approach.

If you've never programmed in Windows before, Part 4 of this book will be ideal to get you started. I'm not interested in repeating the standard references, but I'm very interested in showing, in detail, how to program using Borland C++ and OWL. If you work through the examples in Part 4, which includes over 3000 lines of code, you'll be ready for your own Windows development projects.

The Disk Accompanying This Book

This book is accompanied by a disk that contains the full source code for all of the Turbo Vision and OWL Windows examples, plus significant additional source code from the first two parts of the book. This source is a valuable resource, because it lets you extend and modify the book's examples. Each application is in its own directory, and each contains a project file so it's easy to build. There is also a batch file that will compile all the examples, so that you'll have a complete set of .EXE files.

The most important utility on the disk is the Find Files application, which is the principal example at the beginning of Part 4. Find Files is a useful Windows utility that lets you locate files by name, size, or content. What's better, you can further develop Find Files so that it can use alternate search criteria. The other major utility on the disk, winlsys, is recreational. It's a fun graphics program that lets you play with L-systems, an exciting graphical modeling scheme. See Appendix C, "What's on the Disk."

PART 1

Introducing Object-Oriented Programming

$\mathit{1}$ THE C++ PERSPECTIVE

C++ IS AN OBJECT-ORIENTED EXTENSION OF C. C++ COMBINES C'S POWER AND economy of expression with breakthrough features for object-oriented programming. This best-of-both-worlds language is fast becoming the standard for professional development, especially in cutting-edge applications for Microsoft Windows.

The major advantages of C++ are increased productivity and reliability. Both grow from the idea of an *object*, which in essence is a traditional data structure that has behaviors. Objects make it easier to reuse code, both because they are richer and more complete than traditional subroutine libraries, and because they are extensible. All of these advantages will be covered in much greater detail throughout this book.

Borland C++ 3.1 is the market-leading C++ compiler on the PC platform. While Zortech C++ was the first native code C++ compiler for the PC, Borland is the first C++ compiler to achieve the following results:

- Attain large volume on the PC

- Address both DOS and Windows with comprehensive class libraries

- Availability in a low-cost version suitable for home and school use

Throughout this book the focus is on Borland's extraordinary C++ compiler and its super-useful class libraries.

The Origin of C: Back to the '70s

C dates back to the very early 1970s, when Dennis Ritchie joined in Ken Thompson's work on the primordial version of the UNIX operating system. By 1973 the majority of the UNIX system had been rewritten in Dennis Ritchie's new programming language, C. Rewriting the UNIX system in C made it portable, which was a huge breakthrough.

The B Language: Comparing B to C

In both the alphabet and the history of programming languages, B comes before C. B is a primitive systems programming language developed by Ken Thompson. The central feature of B was its lack of data types; there were only two—words and pointers to words. On the other hand, C has been criticized as a Spartan, low-level language, but it is luxurious compared with B. C built on B's simple conceptual framework, providing a much richer environment.

3

Here's a brief list of similarities between B and C. Both are

- Designed to get the most out of a machine
- Strongly influenced by the needs of systems programmers
- Designed to stay out of the way, freeing the programmer from artificial constraints
- Lean and mean, dangerous, but effective

C Shortcomings: Too Low-Level?

C was an appropriate language for its time. Its emphasis on efficiency was appreciated, because machines of the early '70s—even those shared by dozens of users—were often slower than the PC on your desktop. C has sometimes been faulted for being too low-level; but I think the more appropriate reaction is *praise* for being so much *higher* in level than assembly language. Typical C users weren't mainframe COBOL users looking for more efficiency; rather, they were assembly language programmers looking for more convenience without sacrificing efficiency.

C's Deemphasis of Safety

Assembly language programmers are a hardy group. In assembly, nothing prevents you from obtaining the utmost from a machine, but likewise nothing stands between you and failure. To early C users, safety wasn't an issue, because they were accustomed to systems with even fewer safeguards. But over time C has become a widely used applications development language and its lack of safety has steadily become more of an issue.

There are many examples of C's deemphasis of safety; foremost is the standard I/O library. This library uses the printf( ) function for formatted output, which is a typeless and checkless function; it is an exercise in flexible but dangerous software design. Other examples are the assumption that subroutines return ints, the illusion of a character data type, the weak enum data type, and overuse of the C preprocessor.

Safety has been squarely addressed by the American National Standards Institute (ANSI) standardization effort, which has back-fitted numerous C++ safety features onto C. For example, ANSI C compilers now perform much stricter function argument checking because of function prototypes, and C pointer usage has been tightened. ANSI C is discussed later in this chapter.

Large Libraries: Does Bigger Mean Better?

I remember that when I first used C, I was very impressed by its large and capable library. It seemed like a lot to learn, but well worth it because of the functionality. For its time the standard C library was an accomplishment, but the concept hasn't scaled well to the far more demanding '90s environment.

The C library routines typically take one or two parameters, do something useful, and then return a value. There is, obviously, a large domain where this is appropriate, but there are even larger domains where richer behavior is needed. For example, to interact with the UNIX operating system, the C library has a few routines that use C data structures. This provides a richer interface, because more information can be conveyed. But it also is a more rigid interface, because applications programs evolve to rely on parts of the data structure that should be private and implementation dependent.

The Dual Track '80s

During the '80s the C language steadily gained in usage. At the beginning of the decade, C was too big a language to find widespread use on the early personal computers. But by the end of the decade the focus of the computing scene had switched to the desktop; the machines were far more powerful and the C language had emerged as the most widely used professional development tool in that arena.

ANSI C: The Importance of Standardization

One sign of C's importance was ANSI standardization, which started in the late '80s. The ANSI standard in part codified existing C syntax and practices, and in part adopted new ideas from the then experimental C++ language.

Standardization was important partly because it narrowed the range of interpretations. C, like all languages, is imperfectly defined. And C, even more than most other languages, is honest about leaving some behavior implementation dependent. For example, the sizes of the data types depend upon the implementation, the char type is either signed or unsigned, depending upon the implementation, and so on.

The ANSI effort was also important because it ratified the C language. The standardization effort said, clearly and forthrightly, that C is an important language, one with a future. This was especially important for C, because of its unorthodox, informal origins. After ANSI, C couldn't be dismissed as a hacker's language.

Cox's Objective C

At the same time that C was ascending to widespread use, preparations were under way to develop a successor language. Two main efforts emerged. The first was a language called *Objective C*, which was developed by Brad Cox. Objective C extends C in the direction of Smalltalk. The most important implementation of Objective C is on the NeXT machine, which adopted Objective C as its primary programming language. Objective C has been widely admired, but until it became available on the NeXT machine it was an expensive language to adopt. Also, in many ways Objective C is more ambitious than C++; it looks and feels less like C than C++ and presents more of an initial learning curve than C++. All of these barriers have kept Objective C from becoming as widely used as C++.

The other effort to extend C into new territory was led by Bjarne Stroustrup working at AT&T Bell Laboratories and is covered next.

Stroustrup's "C with Classes"

Stroustrup, a Dane, was strongly influenced by *Simula*. Simula is not often seen in the United States, but it is an influential language that is widely used in Scandinavia. Stroustrup began his work in the early 1980s, and by 1983 he had published a paper describing "C with Classes." C with Classes evolved into C++; C++ continued to evolve during the late '80s.

The Evolution of C++ Stage 1: cfront

C++ grew during the mid and late '80s. The first widely used version was AT&T's *cfront*, which compiled C++ into C. AT&T supplied cfront at a low cost to universities and licensed cfront to numerous computer vendors who adapted it to their hardware. Many commercial C++ products are still based on cfront, which AT&T has upgraded continually to reflect the latest version of the language.

As Stage 1 of the evolution of C++, cfront is important historically, but its active role is diminishing. In addition to the obvious overhead of adding another phase to the compilation process, there are many secondary problems associated with cfront. For example

- Errors emitted by the second-stage C compiler are often baffling to the programmer because the C compiler is working with a source that has been transformed.

- Translation makes it hard for debuggers and other tools to relate smoothly to the original source.

- Many C compilers just aren't up to the job of handling C++.

Stage 2: Native Code Generation   The emerging C++ trend, which is exemplified by Borland C++, is *native code generation*. This means that the C++ language is compiled directly to machine or assembly language. Ultimately more satisfying, native code generation makes it easier to produce integrated environments, such as Borland's Programmer's Platform, and to produce tightly coupled debuggers, such as Borland's Turbo Debugger.

In the beginning of the '90s C++ has clearly become the object-oriented language of choice for most business and professional programmers. Many programmers will continue to use earlier tools, and research into even more powerful alternatives will continue. But for practical programmers moving on to the next generation, C++ is without question the best solution.

C++: An Enriched C

Knowing C cuts two ways when you're learning C++. Certainly your familiarity with C syntax, the C library, and various bits of C arcana can be helpful. But C may also have caused you to develop bad habits; and C has certainly not prepared you for the object-oriented ideas that you must embrace if you want to be productive in C++.

Before moving on to the object-oriented parts of C++, the Borland compiler, and the rich Borland class libraries, in this section I would like to cover some basic C++ enhancements. These features aren't, of themselves, object-oriented. Rather they serve to create a better base upon which C++'s object-oriented superstructure can be erected. If you've followed the ANSI C standardization effort, some of these features may be familiar because of their adoption by the ANSI C committee.

Comparing References to Pointers

A *reference* is a type of variable that serves only to access some existing variable. References are similar to pointers, but there are important differences, which are described here:

References Compared to Pointers

More transparent. When a reference is created it must be initialized to *refer* to something; from that point forward the reference is a perfect alias for whatever it refers to. No operations pertain. You cannot assign a value, increment, or get the address of a reference.

Pointers Compared to References

More flexible. A pointer to a double can point at one double now and then point at another one later.

References are declared similarly to pointers, except that a reference must always be initialized. Visually, the chief difference is that an & is used instead of an * in the declaration, as shown next:

```
int x;        // declare an int named x
int& rx = x;  // declare rx to refer to x
```

The reference named rx is, in all respects, just like x. For example, the expression &x, which represents the address of x, has the same value as the expression &rx. Similarly, the expression rx == x is always true, and so forth.

Using References as Function Parameters   The previous example is probably the least common form of reference—all it accomplishes is renaming. The original variable named x gains a pseudonym, rx. References are much more useful as function parameters when they have reference members of classes. Such references are very effective because in more fluid situations there are more occasions to use a new name for a variable. For example, here is a function that has two reference parameters and returns a reference to a double:

```
double& max(double& d1, double& d2)
{
    return d1 > d2 ? d1 : d2;
}
```

Because the max( ) function returns a reference to a double, it can be used anywhere that a double can be used. If x and y are doubles, then we can use max( ) to increment the greater double by 1:

```
max(x,y)  += 1.Ø;
```

A max function similar to the one just shown can be written with pointers, as could anything using references, but pointers are much clumsier. Here is the pointer version of max( ):

```
double* pmax(double* d1, double* d2)
{
    return *d1 > *d2 ? d1 : d2;
}
```

And here is how the pmax() routine could be used:

```
*pmax(&x, &y)  += 1.Ø;
```

Although the notational advantage of references is important, it's not the only advantage. Because references are always initialized, and because they always point to just one thing during their lifetime, there are often opportunities for a compiler to generate better code.

The void and void* Data Types

C++ introduced the void and void* data types to remedy several subtle deficiencies in C. The void type is the easiest; it is used to escape from C's expression-based design in which everything has a value. There are just a few situations where void is used. The first is declaring the return type of a function. Any function declared to return void is known not to return a value. This gives C the ability to distinguish between functions that return a value and those that do not.

NOTE In Pascal and several other languages a routine that doesn't have a return value is called a procedure, but in C the word procedure is used more loosely to refer to any collection of statements that can be called.

Any procedure that doesn't return a value should be declared void, as shown here:

```
void hi()
{
    printf("Hello\n");
}
```

Another use of void is to indicate that a value should be discarded. For example, in the previous procedure, the printf() routine returns 6 bytes—the number of bytes that were output. C and C++ will happily ignore an unused return value, but you can also cast the return value to void to indicate very explicitly that the return value is ignored, as shown here:

```
void hi()
{
    (void) printf("Hello\n");
}
```

NOTE   The primary value of casting the return value to void is documentation. This operation clearly states that discarding the return value was a choice, not an omission.

The Virtues of const Values

Some values don't change, others change unexpectedly. Unchanging values should be declared *const*; variables altered by interrupt handlers and the like should be *volatile*. (The volatile type is covered in the next section.)

In C the preprocessor #define statement was used to create named constant values. The #define mechanism is obviously still available, but it should only be used to create preprocessor constants for use in #if and #ifdef statements.

Any C++ variable can be declared const, which means it must be initialized and its value cannot be altered, as illustrated here:

```
const int ArrayLen = 100;
const int MaxString = 200;
```

There are several advantages to const:

■ const items are true *datums*, which means they are accessible to debuggers, participate in all type checking, appear in symbol tables, and so on.

■ const can be applied to arrays and data structures, a task far beyond the power of #define.

■ Procedure pointer and reference parameters can be const, which guarantees that the procedure will not alter the addressed data.

The volatile Type

The volatile type is somewhat the opposite of const. As mentioned in the previous section, a variable marked as volatile may change unexpectedly. This is usually because the variable is modified by an interrupt handler, a graphics call back routine, or the like. It is important to identify volatile variables to the compiler, so that correct code can be generated. The classic case is a flag variable that is set by an interrupt handler. For example, assume that there is a flag variable

Generic Pointers

Traditional C pointers always point to some particular data type. For example, a double* pointer points to a double. The reason for associating types with pointers is to make sense of dereference expressions.

If p is a pointer to a double, then *p *is* a double. An important part of C's long march to type safety is increased rigor in checking pointer types. But in the C language, when you have rules, you also need to have escapes, because C and C++ continue to be languages that stand aside when necessary. Thus C++ introduced the idea of a void* pointer, which is a *generic pointer* that doesn't point to a specified type. The void* type has been adopted from C++ by ANSI C, so you may already be familiar with the concept.

The most familiar example of a generic pointer is probably the pointer returned by malloc(), which is just a pointer to a region of storage. Traditionally malloc() returns the char* type, but that is a convenient fib because malloc() is unaware of how the storage will be used. Now, with the void* type, malloc() can tell the truth.

Unlike the void type, which denotes the lack of values, the void* type denotes a generic pointer value. It is acceptable to declare void* pointers and to use them in expressions, as shown here:

```
void *pv;
. . .
pv = &x;    // x is a variable
```

Any pointer expression, such as the expression &x used above (which is the address of some variable), can be trivially converted to void*. But the opposite *is not* true: A pointer value stored in a void* pointer variable can't be converted to some other type without a cast. Observe the following:

```
double *pd;
void *pv;
. . .
pv = pd; // trivial: anytype* to void* conversion
. . .
pd = (double*)pv;  // explicit conversion
```

The reason for requiring an explicit cast is safety. The compiler is relying on the programmer to ensure that the value in the void* pointer addresses the proper type. The explicit cast is the programmer's pledge that the operation is necessary and correct.

called intDone that is set to TRUE at the conclusion of a hardware interrupt service routine. Observe this sample code:

```
void waitForDone()
{
        extern volatile int intDone;
        while (!intDone)
            ;
}
```

If the intDone variable weren't declared volatile, the compiler would likely load it into a register the first time through the loop, and never again read from memory to pick up a fresh copy. Such behavior would make a nice infinite loop, but wouldn't satisfy the goal of waiting until the Interrupt Service Routine (ISR) set the intDone flag. The volatile keyword notifies the compiler that intDone is somehow special, implying that a fresh copy should be loaded from memory each time it is used.

The volatile type is a good example of how C and C++ have adapted over time. Years ago, few compilers were smart enough to keep variables in registers. Now such optimizations are common, a need that has been answered by the volatile type.

Mixing const and Pointers: Proceed with Caution

You need to be careful when you mix pointers and const, because there are three possibilities:

- **Pointer to a const**—the item that the pointer addresses can't be changed

- **const pointer**—the pointer itself can't be changed

- **const pointer to const**—both the pointer and the item that the pointer addresses can't be changed

Observe the first case—a pointer to a const:

```
const int *ptr2const;    // pointer to a const
```

You can assign a value to ptr2const to make it point at something else, or you can assign it NULL to indicate that it doesn't point at anything. But you cannot change what it points to. Thus the expression (*ptr2const)++ is not allowed.

The previous sample code also shows C++'s new comment type, which starts with // and continues to the end of the line. Ordinary C comments—which start with /* and continue until */—are still available. New comments can be placed inside old, and vice versa, although old style comments still cannot be nested.

Observe the second case—a const pointer:

```
int n = Ø;
int *const constptr = &n;    // const pointer
```

You can't write the expression constptr++ because constptr is a constant. It can't be assigned a new value; for its whole lifetime it will point to n. But you *can* write the expression (*constptr)++ because the int it points to isn't constant.

Observe the third and last case—a const pointer to const:

```
int m = Ø;
const int *const constptr2const = &m;   // const pointer to const
```

The constptr2const pointer is read only in the extreme. You can't alter the pointer, you can't alter what it points to.

If you've been following this very carefully, you may have noticed that it's okay for a pointer to const to point at something that isn't const. In the previous code snippet, it's okay to write m++, because m isn't const. But it's *not* okay to write (*constptr2const)++, because constptr2const can't be used to change what it points to. You need to keep in mind that an ordinary pointer isn't allowed to point at a const, as shown in this sample code:

```
const int ArrayLen = 100;
int *p = &ArrayLen;     // not allowed, ArrayLen is const
```

The reason that ordinary pointers can't address consts should be obvious; what would prevent using the pointer to alter the const?

Using const to Declare Procedure Parameters

In C++ programming, const is often used to declare procedure parameters, indicating that they are not altered. This has some value in ordinary value parameters, because it means that inside the procedure the parameter must be treated as a const. The following routine is okay, because no attempt is made to modify nDoubles.

```
double sum(double *vals, const int nDoubles)
{
    double sum = Ø.Ø;
    for(int i = Ø; i < nDoubles; i++)
        sum += *vals++;
    return sum;
}
```

But the next, more compact, version, which is a gutsier coding style adopted by many C experts, wouldn't be allowed, because it modifies nDoubles.

```
double sum(double *vals, const int nDoubles)
{
    double sum = 0.0;
    while(nDoubles--)      // not allowed, nDoubles is const
        sum += *vals++;
    return sum;
}
```

People who are familiar with C++'s const type will probably be surprised by the previous sum() example, because const parameters aren't normally used with simple types such as int. The reason for this is that a const int parameter only controls how that parameter is used inside the function. Even though sum()'s second parameter is a const int, the second argument to sum() could be either a constant or a variable; it doesn't matter because both are compatible with const int.

The more common use of const parameters is with pointer and reference parameters. For example, here is a version of sum() that pledges not to alter any of the items in the vals[] array:

```
double sum(const double *vals, const int nDoubles)
{
    double sum = 0.0;
    for(int i = 0; i < nDoubles; i++)
        sum += *vals++;
    return sum;
}
```

If we had a const array of doubles, its address could be passed to the sum() whose first parameter is const double*, but not to the version of sum() whose first parameter is a double*.

Function Overloading: Same Name, Different Argument

We've all run out of names at one time or another. For example, in "Using References as Function Parameters" earlier in this chapter, I introduced a tiny procedure named max() to return the maximum of two doubles.

```
double& max(double& d1, double& d2)
{
    return d1 > d2 ? d1 : d2;
}
```

But what about the maximum of two longs, or of a long and a double, and so on? Truly, we could need many different versions of max. In C the solution would be to #define max as a macro, or to create a series of max( ) functions, each with its own name. However, neither of these two solutions should be used in C++, which allows overloaded functions. *Overloaded functions* are functions that have the same name, but different argument types. Here is a max( ) for longs:

```
long& max(long& d1, long& d2)
{
    return d1 > d2 ? d1 : d2;
}
```

The version of max( ) for longs doesn't conflict with the version for doubles, or for any other version that uses different argument types. When you use the max( ) function, the compiler looks at the arguments that you are using, it browses through all of the max( ) routines that it has encountered, and it picks the best match. For example, if you have two longs named l1 and l2, and you write the expression max(l1,l2)++, then the compiler will use the long version of max.

The main thing to avoid is creating a dilemma for the compiler. For example, if d1 is a double and l1 is a long, then the compiler will choke on the expression max(d1,l1)++. The problem is that the double version of max is best for the first argument, while the long version is best for the second argument.

Creating Inline Subroutines

There's always a need to go faster, to push the limits. One speedup option is assembly language, but using assembly language should be reserved for extreme cases. A simpler intermediate solution is *inline functions*. Inline functions avoid the overhead of a subroutine call in certain short but important routines. The best known example is probably the getc() facility in the C standard I/O library, which is commonly provided as a #define style macro. The getc() routine needs to be fast, because it is usually called once for each character of input.

C++ has the same facility, but it is provided within the framework of the language, not as a macro definition feature of the preprocessor. The advantages of sanctioned, supported inline subroutines are much the same as the advantages of const. Inline subroutines obey the ordinary rules of subroutines, not the rules of macros, and inline subroutines are available to debuggers and other tools, which can be a great help.

You can request an inline subroutine simply by writing the word **inline** in front of the function header. Here is the max() specified as an inline function:

```
inline long& max(long& d1, long& d2)
{
    return d1 > d2 ? d1 : d2;
}
```

The word inline is a hint to the compiler. If your inline subroutine is too large or too complex, the compiler will ignore your request and create an ordinary callable subroutine. In this respect, inline is similar to the register specifier, which will be ignored if registers aren't available. But if your inline subroutine is simple and compact, its code will be wired in directly where it is needed, saving the time and expense of a procedure call.

NOTE In Borland C++ the inline facility is ordinarily turned off when debugging is turned on, so that debugging will be simplified. You can defeat inline subroutine generation by using the -vi- command-line option, or you can enable inline generation even when debugging using the -vi command-line switch.

Another aspect of Borland C++ that relates to inline functions is its set of intrinsic inlines. About 20 subroutines in the standard C library—primarily the strn...() routines and some mem...() routines—can benefit from inlining. The execution time of these routines, especially when they operate on short strings or short memory blocks, can be dominated by the function call overhead. If you specify the -Oi optimization switch, or if you use the -O2 switch to turn on all of the speed optimizations, the Borland compiler will automatically generate inline versions of the functions shown in Table 1.1. You can also use the Borland #pragma directive to selectively enable or disable inline generation for specific functions. For example, the following will turn on inline generation for the strlen() function.

```
#pragma intrinsic strlen
```

The contrary is also easy; the following pragma will disable inlining of strlen:

```
#pragma intrinsic -strlen
```

TABLE 1.1

Borland Library Functions That Are Inlined Using the -Oi Compilation Option

rotl()	memcmp()	strcmp()	strncmp()	strlen()
rotr()	memcpy()	strcpy()	strncpy()	strcat()
fabs()	memset()	stpcpy()	strnset()	strncat()
alloca()	memchr()	strchr()		strrchr()

Type Safe Linking:
Solving the Incorrect Linkage Problem

Anyone with some experience in C has had the following ordeal: Your program has compiled and linked without complaint even though some subroutine is called with wildly wrong arguments. The problem shows up, disastrously, during execution. This sort of difficulty is only possible because C doesn't require function prototypes that describe the available functions. Unlike more protective languages, C doesn't insist upon knowing exactly how each function should be used. C also assumes, unless told otherwise by a function declaration, that all functions return an int.

One part of the solution to the incorrect linkage problem is *type safe linking*. Type safe linking ensures that each C++ function is exactly what was advertised by the function prototype in the header file. For example, earlier in this chapter I defined two max( ) procedures, one that requires two double parameters, and one that requires two longs. The max( ) procedure's argument type information is encoded in the function name, so the linker can check that everything is correct.

Using Ellipses with Variable Arguments

C's lax attitude was once thought to be a good idea, because it was flexible. Without the original latitude, the standard I/O library's printf( ) routine would be impossible. But printf( ) is the exception; the majority of functions have fixed argument lists. Today most people agree that the language shouldn't be bent asunder because of printf( ). C++ has a solution for procedures such as printf( ) that take variable argument lists, denoted by an *ellipsis* (three periods). When an ellipsis is encountered in a function prototype, it means that any arguments are acceptable. Ellipses reinstate the original "take no prisoners" style of C. Here is the function prototype of printf( ) from the stdio.h header file:

```
int _Cdecl printf(const char _FAR *format, ...);
```

The previous prototype specifies that printf( ) must have at least one argument—a pointer to char—possibly followed by additional unspecified arguments.

Another contribution of C++ to the problem of guaranteeing correct linkage is to require complete function prototypes. C++ considers it an error to try to use a function, say strlen( ), without first providing a function prototype. This guarantees that C++ knows what arguments are required for each function that you use. This rule applies to your own functions as well as to those you pull in from libraries, so you had better make sure the prototypes in your header files are in good shape.

Linkage Specification and Enhanced Compatibility

One of Stroustrup's most important design goals was for C++ to be compatible with C. In a few small areas (compared to the language as a whole), C++ is slightly different from C, but overall, considering how far C++ has extended C, the compatibility is remarkable. Most C programs can be passed through a C++ compiler without much difficulty. Most problems will result from C++'s much tighter type checking, which will require more precise function declarations, and more attention to details.

But there is one major area where C++'s improvements have had a major impact on compatibility—the type safe linkage system. Although the C++ standard doesn't specify how type safe linkage should work, the most common method is to decorate function names with type information. Thus the max() routine that takes two double arguments might be named _max_dd and the version that takes two long arguments might be named _max_ll. These compiler-enhanced names enable type safe linkage, which is a good thing, but the system is totally incompatible with traditional C compilers. The opposite problem also exists; if a C++ compiler is looking for a strlen() procedure that accepts a char* argument, it will expect the name to be something like _strlen_pc, not the _strlen that is present in the standard C library.

The solution is to use a linkage specification to tell the C++ compiler that a given function or set of functions obeys the naming and possibly the calling conventions of a foreign language. All C++ compilers are required to implement C linkage, if only to enable use of the standard C library.

A linkage specification consists of the word *extern* followed by a quoted string naming a language. For example, here is one way to indicate that strlen() is a function with C linkage:

```
extern "C" size_t strlen(char *s);
```

But usually it's better to indicate that a group of functions has C linkage, as shown here:

```
extern "C" {
    size_t strlen(char *s);
    char * strcat(char *dest, const char *src);
    // and so on
}
```

The problem with placing extern "C" in a header file is compatibility with C. (Many header files, such as the header files for the standard C library, must be compatible with both C and C++ compilers.) When a C++ compiler sees extern "C", it knows this is a linkage specification, and treats it accordingly. But a C compiler reports an error when it encounters the keyword extern followed by "C" (a constant string). The solution, which you'll see in all of Borland's C and C++ header files, is to conditionally compile the extern "C" specification based on the identifier __cplusplus. During a C++ compilation, the __cplusplus identifier will be defined; it is undefined during a C compilation. Thus the preceding example becomes

```
#ifdef __cplusplus
extern "C" {
#endif
    size_t strlen(char *s);
    char * strcat(char *dest, const char *src);
    // and so on
```

```
#ifdef __cplusplus
}
#endif
```

Borland's include files for the C library have been adapted so that they are compatible with both C and C++, which means that they already contain C linkage specifications, and they are const correct for most pointer and reference parameters. But you may be using a third-party library or one of your own C header files that you want to use in a C++ module. One solution was shown in the previous sample code. Another solution is to surround the include directive with a linkage specification, as shown here:

```
extern "C" {
#include "myproj.h"
}
```

As you might suspect, linkage specifications can be nested.

Using the Operators for Memory Allocation

When you look at C, there are two key places where it is impossible to be type correct. We've already looked at one of these situations—the printf() subroutine. C++'s solution for routines like printf() that require variable argument lists is ellipses in the argument list. The other place where C programming inexorably leads to type-lax programming is malloc(), the standard C library routine for allocating heap memory.

The malloc() routine fits well with C's idea of moving functionality out of the compiler and into the library. But malloc() returns a generic pointer. Historically malloc()'s return type was char*, but now with the addition of the void type, malloc() has been redefined to return a void* pointer.

The problem with returning a generic pointer is that you never allocate voids. Here's a typical invocation of malloc():

```
double *pd = (double *)malloc(sizeof(double) * 100);
```

The cast on malloc()'s result is necessary, because malloc()'s return type is void*, not double*.

The C++ solution for type-safe memory allocation is to move memory allocation back into the compiler using the new operator. Here's how you can allocate an array of 100 doubles in C++ with full type safety:

```
double *pd = new double[100];
```

Because the compiler knows about the new operator, it knows that the "type" of new depends on what it is allocating. In the previous example, new's type is double*, which is of course compatible with the type of pd. If we make a mistake, such as the following,

```
char *pd = new double[100];
```

then the compiler will notice and complain.

In very simple situations, such as in the previous example, the type checking has little value. But in more complex situations, and complex situations are unavoidable, the type checking performed by new is invaluable.

The other half of allocation—*deallocation*—is handled in C++ by the delete operator. For example, the following will deallocate the memory pointed to by pd:

```
delete pd;
```

It's okay to delete the memory indicated by pd, because it was allocated with new. But be sure to avoid *free()*ing memory allocated with new, or *delete*ing memory allocated with malloc().

In the previous discussion I've indicated that C++'s introduction of the new and delete operators was motivated by the need for type safety. Type safety is a central concern of C++, but it is only part of the reason for new and delete. The other part of the reason for using new and delete is that class objects must be initialized when they are created. Moving allocation into the domain handled by the compiler lets the compiler make sure that initialization always follows allocation for class objects. Thus you should always use new to allocate space for objects; if you malloc() your class objects, they won't be initialized. Either the new operator or the malloc() routine can be used to allocate space for built-in types, although my recommendation is to always use the new operator in new code.

2. AN OVERVIEW OF OOP

OBJECT-ORIENTED PROGRAMMING (OOP) IS A NEW WAY OF THINKING ABOUT software development. This chapter will introduce the OOP paradigm and most OOP terminology using a simple example: a DOS program to display several types of files on the screen. The point here isn't to produce the ultimate file viewer, but rather to work with a simple example that illustrates the basic concepts.

Even though this chapter focuses on the ideas behind object-oriented programming, it also contains numerous fragments of C++ code. At this point in the book you shouldn't worry about all the details of C++ syntax. Those details will be covered in Chapters 3 and 4, and after reading those chapters you'll have mastered the syntax. In this chapter you should attend to the Big Picture and let the details slide.

Classes Are Object Blueprints

The word "object" has become marketing magic, like motherhood and apple pie. But in this book, marketing slogans must be checked at the door. The confusion about "object" comes in part from the fact that it has two technical meanings. The first sense of object is as a high-level principle, a concept that lets us think about organizing software. The term "object-oriented programming" speaks to this first meaning (see Figure 2.1).

The second sense of object is more specific. An object is a region of storage in an executing program that obeys a set of user-defined rules. In a mathematical program that has matrices and arrays, each matrix and array in memory would be an object. Conceptually, the software developer would have thought about what features would be necessary in an array object; in a running program each array that is created in memory is an object. *Instance* is another term for an object in memory; it comes from the term *instantiate*, which is a technical description of bringing an object to life by creating a place for it in memory and then initializing that memory according to the object's rules.

The preceding two paragraphs have described objects as a concept and objects as memory regions. It should be clear that we create objects as a concept by thinking. But how do we create objects as storage regions? Or to say it another way, what programming language feature lets us specify and build objects? The answer is the *class*, which in most object-oriented languages, including C++, is a user-defined data type for creating objects. Classes are like blueprints—they specify exactly how an object can be built and how it will

FIGURE 2.1

Objects and classes

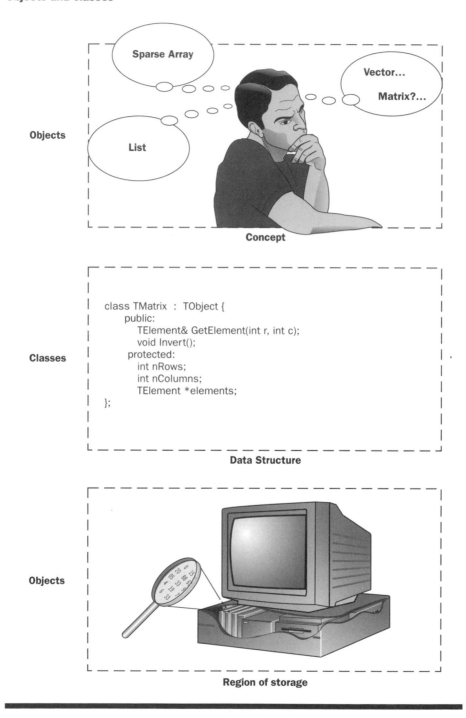

Objects

Concept

Classes

```
class TMatrix  :  TObject {
    public:
        TElement& GetElement(int r, int c);
        void Invert();
    protected:
        int nRows;
        int nColumns;
        TElement *elements;
};
```

Data Structure

Objects

Region of storage

behave. Classes are discussed throughout the remainder of this chapter, and are covered extensively next.

Calling Member Functions

A class *definition* specifies the data members and member functions that comprise the class. Because class syntax in C++ is taken largely from struct syntax in C, we can predict how to access class data members. For example, consider a class named TTextView that has a data member named fin. If we have a TText-View object named oTTV, we can access the fin data member by using standard C notation:

```
if (oTTV.fin == NULL)
    . . .
```

Similarly, if we have a pointer named pTTV that points at a TTextView object, we would use standard C pointer notation to access the data member.

```
if (pTTV->fin == NULL)
    . . .
```

But what about the member functions? In C we can pass a struct pointer to a function so that the function can use the struct. I'm sure you're familiar with this technique from the C standard I/O library, which passes FILE * pointers to most of the functions. In C++ there is a much closer coupling between functions and data; functions are full members of classes. Thus there is a special syntax for calling class member functions. The TTextView class mentioned above has a member function called AddLine(). For a TTextView object named oTTV we can call AddLine() to manage that object using the following notation:

```
oTTV.AddLine();
```

oTTV is the object name, the dot (period) has its usual "member of" meaning, AddLine is the name of a member function, and the parentheses are standard C function call indicators. Everything is standard—it is only the combination that is unfamiliar. I would pronounce the above statement as "The oTTV object's AddLine() member function is called."

Class member functions can also be called using a pointer to an object, such as the pTTV pointer mentioned earlier.

```
pTTV->AddLine();
```

However it is called, inside the AddLine() member function the members of the calling object are directly available.

The Major Tools in the Object-Oriented Kit

The three most important concepts in object-oriented programming are *abstraction*, *inheritance*, and *polymorphism*. Introduced here, these three fundamentals of OOP will appear throughout this book and be vital to all your work with C++.

In OOP we design software by using component parts, which are called *objects*. Objects are comprised of data members plus a set of routines to manipulate the data, which are called *member functions*. The combination of data with routines makes objects robust and complete, so that they can perform their role in various environments. But having procedures glued onto data structures is only part of what OOP can offer. Other characteristics, which are best understood by analogy to characteristics of physical objects, contribute to the OOP tool chest.

For example, physical objects often have an external interface that hides their internal complexity. Information hiding (and creating boundaries in information space) is often called *abstraction* by software designers. To be more concrete, consider an architect designing a house. The architect can make basic plans for the house's heating system without worrying about how the heating system works (see Figure 2.2). He or she only needs to consider the heating plant's physical requirements, such as its floor space, its power consumption, its fuel requirement, its ventilation requirement, and so on. The architect needn't study internal combustion, and the boiler designer needn't study art or architecture. Instead there is a well-defined interface that lets the architect take advantage of the work of the boiler designer. Yes, this sounds mundane and obvious, but it is very different from how most software has been designed.

Another aspect of physical objects is that they can be extended to create new objects. In OOP terminology, this is called *inheritance* and we say that one object is derived from another. Again we can be more concrete. An architect can modify existing plans for a house to add a two-car garage and sun room. Such additions would require some adjustment to the house's floor and window plans, but the basic design of the house would remain the same. Again, this sounds mundane and obvious, but again this is not how software has been designed.

A third characteristic of physical objects is that very different objects often operate the same way. In OOP this is called *polymorphism*. Consider motor vehicles, from go carts to automobiles to tractor-trailer trucks. All are operated using a gas pedal, a brake pedal, and a steering wheel. In this range of vehicles, very different mechanisms are used for, say, the brakes. But in all cases the brake pedal is a uniform interface to the underlying mechanism. Mundane and obvious, certainly, but innovative in the world of software technology.

Designing a File Viewer

To DOS, a file is a file is a file. All that DOS knows about a file is its size, date, and location on the disk. To get the full meaning from most files, we need to use a specific applications program—for example, 1-2-3 for .WKS files, a paint program for .PCX files, CorelDraw for .CDR files, and so on. In between DOS, with its profound ignorance, and applications programs, which fully understand the

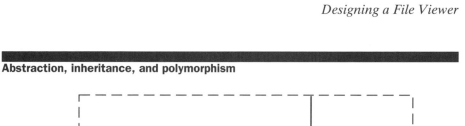

FIGURE 2.2

Abstraction, inheritance, and polymorphism

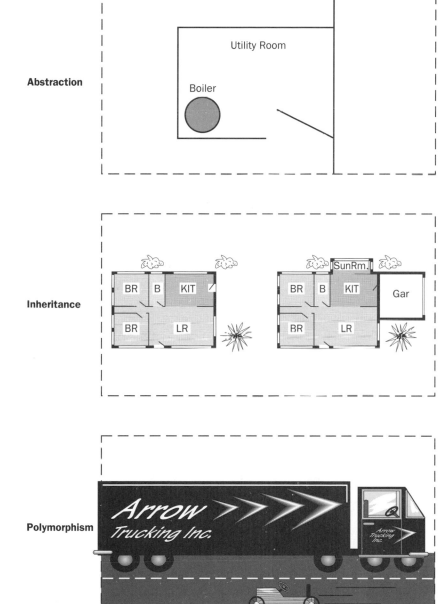

Abstraction

Inheritance

Polymorphism

various file types, are *file viewers*, which know enough about some file types to display them on screen. Many DOS shells include file viewers. My favorite file viewer is the viewer supplied with Norton Desktop for Windows, which understands more than a dozen file formats.

Like most programming tasks, developing a file viewer program could be approached from a traditional perspective or from an object-oriented perspective. There are a few advantages to the traditional approach. One is that the traditional approach is likely to be the most comfortable one for many people, and many developers will already have some code pearls that they can reuse in a file viewer. People often tout OOP for managing the complexity of huge applications, but a file viewer is not a huge application.

However, there are also many advantages on the OOP side. OOP software is designed from the outset for extension, and a file viewer naturally demands extension as new file formats become popular. Also, in this example I'm not going to worry about a user interface, but an OO (object-oriented) file viewer "engine" is a natural complement to any of several OO user interface libraries, such as Borland's TurboVision and OWL libraries.

Yet to me the most important motivation for an object-oriented approach is that an object-oriented coding style can clearly reflect the structure of the task. The set of DOS file types falls naturally into several broad categories—document files, spreadsheet files, database files, bitmapped graphics files, and vector graphics files—and we could create a file viewer application with a corresponding internal structure.

To make this a manageable example, I want to concentrate on just a few file types. I'm going to omit all consideration of graphics, spreadsheets, and databases, and instead concentrate on a few simple file types. Although I'm certainly trying to create an extensible structure, for now I'm not going to extend it very far. I'll leave that to your imagination and tinkering. I'm also not going to worry at all about a user interface. Let's first do something small but useful to get started in object-oriented programming, and then we'll work on some larger problems.

First, let me state a few basic requirements for our small file viewer.

- The viewer should be developed using object-oriented techniques so that it is extensible.

- The viewer should be able to move forward through a file one line of text at a time. The definition of a line of text will vary from one file type to another. Graphical file formats will not be considered.

- The viewer should retain a full page of text, discarding old lines as new ones are read in. This makes it compatible with systems such as Windows that may ask an application, at any time, to redraw the screen. Each line of the page should be easily accessible, and the page size (number of lines, width of each line) should be specified when the object is created.

- The viewer should make as few assumptions about the environment as possible. The C stdio library should be used for file I/O. No other libraries may be used.

Next let's specify the basic file types that should be displayed:

- **Text Files** Each line of text is delimited by a newline character. Lines too long to fit in the specified page width should be truncated, not wrapped.

- **Document Files** Each paragraph of text is delimited by a newline. The viewer should collect words from the paragraph to fill lines.

- **Directory Files** Directory entries should be formatted to detail one file on each line. This gives the viewer a capability similar to DOS's DIR command.

Creating Families of Classes by Using Inheritance

Inheritance is the key to creating organized, extensible, reusable families of classes. In broad strokes, the file viewer application should use a generic *base class* that meets the four requirements that were already mentioned, and then use *derived classes* to manage each specified type of file. The base class, which will be called TViewer, will be responsible for managing storage, storing status information, and presenting a uniform interface. The derived classes, which will be called TTextView, TDocView, and TDirView, are responsible for managing the details for their specified file types. This simple organization is shown in Figure 2.3.

FIGURE 2.3

The file viewer class diagram

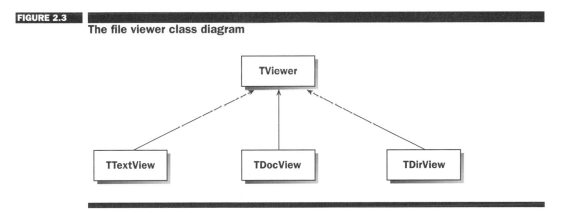

I'm deliberately keeping the viewer simple, so that the ideas don't get lost in the details. But let's digress for a moment to think about how a more capable file viewing engine might be organized. As I mentioned earlier, there are several families of file types, such as spreadsheet files. Spreadsheets, for example, would have much in common, so it would be natural to create a class that addressed that commonality. From the generic spreadsheet class we would derive the specialized classes to manage each kind of spreadsheet file. The same would hold true for database files, graphics files, and the like. This richer organization is sketched in Figure 2.4.

FIGURE 2.4

A class diagram for a hypothetical file viewer

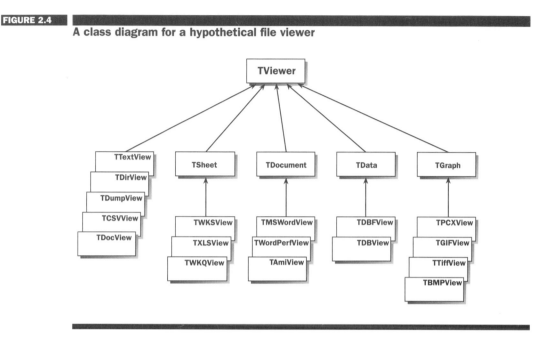

Even though Figure 2.4 is somewhat complex, it reflects the nature of the file viewer task with clarity. When I think about DOS's myriad file types, my mental image loosely matches Figure 2.4. What liberation to be able to organize software in a similarly obvious manner. One of my criteria for a good class is that it should be easy to describe its role. You can pick any class pictured in Figure 2.4 and understand its role, based only on its name and its position in the diagram. Certainly it would be a lot of work to create all the classes so simply sketched in this figure, but the task would be organized and directed, because the design captures the essence of the problem.

Because Figures 2.3 and 2.4 are the first class diagrams in this book, let me briefly describe the conventions. An arrow is used to indicate an inheritance relationship. The arrow from TDocView to TViewer in Figure 2.3 means that TDocView is derived from TViewer. When one class is derived from another, the original class—TViewer in this example—is called the *base class* and the other class is called the *derived class*. Some OO languages use the confusing terminology parent and child, but most C++ programmers prefer the more explicit terms base class and derived class. When a group of classes is shown overlapped, as in Figure 2.4, all of the classes are at the same level, and an arrow from the group means that all the classes in the group are derived from a common ancestor. Thus in Figure 2.4 the classes TWKSView, TXLSView, and TWKQView are all derived from the TSheet class.

Figure 2.4 also shows that a class may be both a derived class and a base class. Consider TSheet. In the relationship between TViewer and TSheet, TSheet is the derived class. But when you are considering TSheet and TWKSView, then TSheet is the base while TWKSView is the derived class.

Another element in Figures 2.3 and 2.4 is the standard naming convention introduced by Borland and used by me in this book. Class names, because they define new types, usually start with the letter T and use mixed case. This convention isn't part of C++ itself, but it is commonly followed by people using Borland C++ simply because it works well with the supplied class libraries.

What Is *is a*?

What is *is a*? It's a relationship between two classes. A derived class often has an *is a* relationship with its base class. For example, TTextView is a TViewer because it is *publicly derived* (explained in the next section) from TViewer. An *is a* relationship means that the derived class can be used in any way that the base class can be used. Because a TTextView object is a TViewer object, we know that TTextView has all the same members as TViewer, that it can be passed to any function that expects a TViewer object, and so on.

You need to be careful here for two reasons. First, an *is a* relationship works only one way. When public derivation is used, a derived class has an *is a* relationship with its base class. But a base class never has an *is a* relationship with its derived class. A TViewer object is not a TTextView; TTextView is a more specialized class, and it may have additional data members or member functions.

The humble sounding *is a* relationship is actually the key to creating a family of classes that share common traits. In the specification for the file viewer application, I mentioned four major requirements. These four requirements are addressed by the TViewer class, which provides specific member functions to address the second (line by line access) and third (retain a full page of information) requirements. (The first requirement—an OO approach—is met by the overall design approach, and the fourth requirement—minimize environmental assumptions and use the C stdio library—is met both by the overall design and by the coding practices used in individual member functions.) Because the derived classes are all publicly derived from TViewer, they each have an *is a* relationship with TViewer and they each contain the specified capabilities.

Let me be more specific. TViewer, whose class definition is shown in Listing 2.1, contains a GetLine() member function so that individual lines in the current page can be accessed. The GetLine() member function is defined in TViewer, but because of the *is a* relationship it works equally well in any class that is publicly derived from TViewer, such as the TTextView class. Also note that you don't have to place any code in a derived class to get this functionality; all the buffering is managed by the TViewer class and the GetLine() supplied by TViewer suffices for all the derived classes.

LISTING 2.1

The TViewer class

```
//
// file viewer base class
//
class TViewer {
public:
    enum eStatus { END, OK, BAD };   // status constants
                                     // fetch stored line
    virtual const char *GetLine(int n);
    virtual void AddLine() = 0;      // get next line
    inline eStatus Status();         // get error status
protected:
    int nRows, nCols, nCurRow;       // stats
    eStatus curStatus;               // error status
    char **pszLines;                 // page buffer
    void Scroll();                   // discard oldest
    TViewer(int rows, int cols);     // constructor
    virtual ~TViewer();              // destructor
};
```

The other major public member function of the TViewer class is AddLine(), which is called to advance to the next line of the input file. As mentioned earlier, the definition of "line" is left up to the individual derived classes. For the TText-View class, a "line" is the amount of text up to the next newline character. For a TDocView class a "line" is as many words as will fit from the current newline-delimited paragraph. In the TDirView class a "line" is a directory entry. The TViewer class supplies the prototype of the AddLine() member function, but it doesn't actually supply any code for AddLine(). Each derived class is responsible for providing a suitable version of AddLine(). Even though TViewer doesn't define an AddLine() function, the *is a* relationship between the derived classes and TViewer compels the derived classes to provide this functionality.

To create the desired *is a* relationship, specialized classes to view specific file types should be publicly derived from TViewer. For example, the TTextView class, shown in Listing 2.2, is publicly derived from TViewer. Derivation is indicated in the heading of a class definition. The heading of the TViewer class (shown in Listing 2.1), which is not a derived class, simply says "class TViewer" followed by the brace-enclosed class definition. The heading of TTextView is more complex because it is a derived class. The TTextView heading, which literally is "class TTextView : public TViewer," would be pronounced "the TText-View class is publicly derived from the TViewer class."

Although public derivation is the most common derivation, and although it is required for creating an *is a* relationship, it is not the only type of derivation. C++ also allows both protected and private derivation, although both are little used. They will be discussed further in the next chapter.

LISTING 2.2

The TTextView class

```
//
// View a text file (\n delimits lines)
//
class TTextView : public TViewer {
public:
    TTextView(int r, int c, char *filename);
    void AddLine();
    ~TTextView();
protected:
    FILE *fin;
};
```

Hiding the Details with Abstraction

Classes always exist to do something; classes should be active. But classes usually have an additional role: They should hide something. Classes should create an *abstraction*. An abstraction is something that captures a general idea, something that catches the essence of some more complicated thing.

There are several features of C++ that help you create classes that provide powerful abstractions. The first is the fact that a class definition, such as the definition of the TViewer class shown in Listing 2.1, collects all the important information about a class into a single place. The class definition shows the data members, it gives prototypes for the function members, and it defines local types, such as the eStatus type in TViewer. The class definition omits function bodies, except for some inline functions, so that you can concentrate on the abstraction, not on the details.

The second feature of C++ that aids abstraction is the ability to segregate a class into public, protected, and private regions:

- The public part of a class is its general interface; the public part of a class is universally available. Most users of a class need only be concerned with its public interface. For example, as a user of the TViewer class, you would need to use and understand only the eStatus enumeration type and the GetLine(), AddLine(), and Status() member functions.

- The protected part of a class is its interface for derived classes. Only authors of derived classes and authors of friend classes (explained later in this chapter) need to understand a class's protected part.

- The private part of a class defines class elements that are only used by the class itself or by friends of the class.

In a class definition, the labels "public:," "protected:," and "private:" control accessibility. After one of these access keywords is encountered, the specified accessibility is in force until the next access keyword is encountered. Thus in the TViewer class (see Listing 2.1) the initial four elements are public, while the last eight elements are protected. The TViewer class does not have any private elements.

Creating Uniform Interfaces Using Polymorphism

Polymorphism comes from the Greek, meaning having or taking many forms. In object-oriented programming *polymorphism* refers to a runtime mechanism in which a member function is selected that is appropriate for a given type of object.

Polymorphism is demonstrated by the file viewer application's AddLine() member function. If you examine the view.h (see Listing 2.3) or view.cpp (see Listing 2.4) files shown at the end of this chapter, you will notice that all three of the specialized file viewer classes, TTextView, TDocView, and TDirView, contain an AddLine() member function. If you have a TDocView object and you use it to call the AddLine() member function, then the TDocView class's version of AddLine() will be used. This sounds pretty mundane until you start to realize that the selection of the correct version of AddLine() can occur during runtime.

This is best illustrated by the main() routine that I have supplied to exercise the TViewer family classes. In broad brush summary, the main() routine performs three chores. It

1. Creates either a TTextView, TDocView, or TDirView object, based on command-line options

2. Outputs the first screenful of text

3. Outputs any remaining text interactively until either EOF or user abort

The full source code to the sample main() routine is shown in Listing 2.5 at the end of the chapter.

The first chore, creation of a file viewer object, doesn't involve polymorphism. This is always true; when you create an object, you must create a specific type of object, and polymorphism is not involved. But what is interesting about the object creation in the file viewer's main() routine is that a pointer to the new object, which is either a TTextView, a TDocView, or a TDirView object, is stored in a type TViewer pointer named tv. Remember that the whole reason for defining the TViewer class was to define the interface to a family of classes. This lets us access all of the common derived class behaviors using the TViewer pointer.

```
tv->AddLine();          // polymorphic member call
```

If tv is pointing at a TTextView object, then the TTextView class's version of AddLine() will be called, and so forth. This marvelous capability is the heart of polymorphism. It means we can create a family of classes, define a basic interface to that family in the base class (TViewer in this example), and then use objects from the family interchangeably. The objects themselves will, in the words of Spike Lee, "do the right thing."

The TViewer family of classes shows the mechanics of polymorphism, but not its importance. In the TViewer family, there are only three specialized classes and only one polymorphic member function. This is hardly a den of complexity. But imagine a more realistic file viewer, containing 20 or more specialized viewer classes, and imagine a richer interface, containing a half dozen polymorphic member functions. As complexity grows, the value of polymorphism grows even faster.

Pragmatic Object-Oriented Design

Object-oriented design is an approach to developing software that can be followed in many ways. Of course the emphasis in this book is on the C++ language's object-oriented solutions. The first part of this chapter has already discussed the three cornerstones of any object-oriented programming language: inheritance, abstraction, and polymorphism. Now I want to turn to three topics that are less central to the object-oriented paradigm, even though they are an important part of C++'s object-oriented technology.

These three features of C++ are *constructors*, which allow you to control how objects are created; *templates*, which let you create classes that have the same code but for different types; and *friends*, which relax the C++ access rules. These three topics are important C++ capabilities that have a major impact on all C++ object-oriented software designs.

Constructing Classes

Many electronic devices, such as televisions and VCRs, have a brief warm-up period. Thankfully, you don't have to do anything during this period; once a TV is turned on it automatically does whatever is necessary to move to the standard operational state.

Similarly, objects also often need a brief warm-up period. In traditional software this is usually called *initialization*, but in object-oriented terminology the "warm up" is often called *construction*. An object is constructed by a special member function called a *constructor*. Objects may have several constructors, so long as they each have different argument lists. The job of a constructor is to initialize all the data members. But because constructors may have arguments, objects can be constructed with a specified initial value.

The TViewer class has a constructor that takes two arguments, the height and width of the display "page." Constructors are member functions that have the same name as the class, so a constructor for the TViewer class is the TViewer() member function. The two principal tasks of the TViewer class are to establish the interface for the family of file viewer classes and to manage the text buffer. It is this second task, managing the text buffer, that concerns the constructor. The constructor, based on the required height and width of the buffer, allocates storage using the C++ *new* operator. If an allocation failure occurs, the object's status flag is set to indicate an error, so that other member functions won't attempt to use the broken buffer.

The point of construction is to ensure that necessary initialization chores are performed when an object is created. This prepares an object for use, so that it is ready to go. Note that it is your job, as a class designer, to decide just what must be done in a constructor. As a general rule, one with many exceptions, you should perform only mandatory, simple chores in a constructor. Making a constructor do too much reduces your flexibility. If your constructors are becoming too complicated, leave the simple, fail-safe code in the constructor and then create an ordinary member function to handle the more complex, more failure-prone initialization.

Duplicating Code with Templates

One of the most powerful routines in the standard C library is qsort(), which implements the quick sort algorithm. To use qsort() you must supply a pointer to the array of items to be sorted, the number of elements in the array, the size of each element, and a routine to compare two elements. Because all the necessary information is supplied to qsort(), it can be used to sort any array.

However, there are several drawbacks to qsort()'s approach. The first is that qsort(), like printf(), is a typeless function. All the pointers it uses are generic (void *), and it forces you to provide a comparison function in which it is mandatory to use casts to restore type information. Qsort() is useful, but it is a serious gash in the type system.

A second problem with qsort() is inefficiency. Not the efficiency of the quick sort algorithm, which is well known to have a running time proportional to N log(N), but the efficiency of the implementation. For each comparison of two items qsort() must perform a function call because qsort() doesn't know what type of data it is sorting. As I noted already, qsort() has a type-free interface. For sorting arrays of numbers or other sorts in which the comparison is trivial, the cost of approximately N log(N) function calls dominates the time of the sort.

The C++ solution for this and many similar problems is a *template*. A template lets you specify classes or functions without filling in all the type information. Later, you can create a class or function for a specific type. Templates let you stamp out code just like a cookie cutter lets you stamp out cookies. A cookie cutter is used with different flavors of dough to make different kinds of cookies; a template is used with different data types to build corresponding classes or functions (see Figure 2.5). For example, you could create a quick sort function template, and then you could create specific versions of that function to sort doubles, strings, dates, and so on. Templates give you the ability to create generic solutions, like qsort(), but with the advantage of having strongly typed interfaces and high efficiency.

Making Friends

The C++ public, protected, and private access restrictions provide two benefits. First, they are a conceptual aid. For example, identifying the public part of a class guides the reader to the public parts; the access keywords promote readability. But more importantly, the access rules prevent unwanted access, so that a class can enforce restrictions and rely on its own conventions. Classes sometimes provide access to non-public members by using public access functions, which give a class control over how its non-public members are used.

FIGURE 2.5

Templates

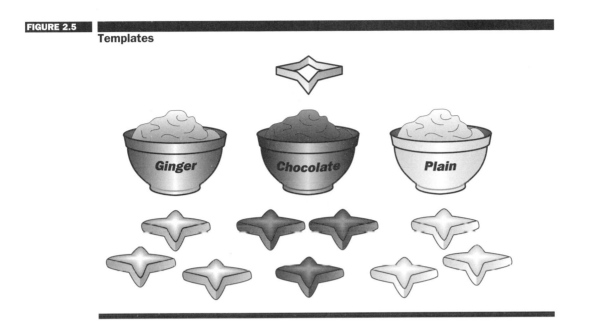

For example, in the TViewer class the buffer that stores the current page of text, which is accessed using the pszLines pointer, is protected. This ensures that the buffer can only be accessed directly by derived classes. To allow public access, the TViewer class provides a GetLine() member function that returns a pointer to an individual line. To maintain the buffer's integrity, the GetLine() access function returns a pointer to const, so the buffer can't be modified.

These rules, while admirable and useful, are sometimes too restrictive. For example, you may design a class that has a legitimate need to access another class's non-public members. One solution is obviously to publicize the necessary members, so that the access will be permitted. This path, followed very far, destroys the access system because soon everything is public. The better choice is friendship, which lets one class grant access either to another class, or to a specific function. Figure 2.6 illustrates friendship using a private club analogy. The club has three front entrances: a public entrance for anyone, a protected entrance for members of derived (related!) clubs, and a private entrance for club members. Friendship bypasses the access system, providing direct access to the specified friends.

Friendship relaxes the rules, it lets us state that certain class members are non-public, but that there is an exception. In some ways friendship is like type casting, because both are used to circumvent the standard rules. But there is one important difference. When casts are used, they are often used expediently, because a need has arisen that is most easily handled by a cast. Friendship works from the opposite point of view. A class designer grants friendship because one class has a legitimate need for enhanced access to another.

The friend capability of C++ has been criticized because it bypasses the standard access rules. If friendship were granted too often, this would be a more significant criticism. In my experience, friendship is a lightly used, valuable aspect of C++.

FIGURE 2.6

Friends

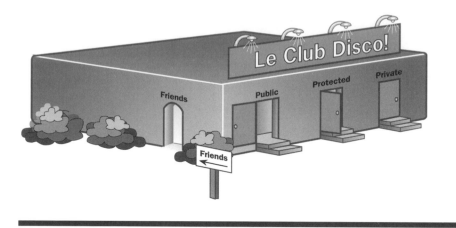

Object-Oriented Design Guidelines

The essence of object-oriented design is to conceive of a set of objects, which you can realize as a set of classes, that solve the given problem. In large part, expertise in object-oriented design can only be acquired by experience with object-oriented development and by considerable knowledge of the problem domain. I don't have an easy answer to what is obviously a difficult problem, but I do have a brief list of suggestions that may shorten your learning time.

- Objects should be active. Make sure each of your objects does something.

- Objects should correspond to some significant entity in the problem domain.

- Objects should do enough so that they are significant and important, but not so much that they are too large or complex. Objects should address a manageable portion of the problem.

- Objects should have a role that is easy to explain to someone who is not a software developer.

- Objects should be designed to be reusable.

- Objects should be self-reliant. You should minimize unnecessary environmental dependencies.

- Objects should be complete. An object should store, to the degree practical, all information that is necessary for its correct operation.

- Objects should use access controls to publicize their public interfaces and to hide their internal data and interfaces.

- Objects should use inheritance and polymorphism to create families of specialized objects.

- In C++, objects should define constructors, so that objects are always properly initialized.

- In C++, objects should define *destructors*, which should usually be polymorphic, that reclaim all storage and perform all other necessary cleanup tasks.

- In C++, you should pay extra attention to the default constructor, the copy constructor, and the operator=() member function. The characteristics of these three members have a major impact on an object's correct operation. (Default constructors, copy constructors, and the operator=() member functions will be discussed in the next chapter.)

My last suggestion is so important that I can't in good conscience call it a mere guideline. *Objects should be correct.* Perfection isn't of this world, but if an object meets most or all of the above criteria, then you should be able to state, with conviction, that your object works as specified.

DOS File Viewer Source Code

If this is your first pass through the book and you don't already know C++, then the following code may look like C gone sour. Nevertheless, the file viewer example is discussed in this chapter, so this is where the source code belongs. If you return to this source code after learning C++, it will make much more sense.

To compile the file viewer, you can either run *make* in the viewer directory, which will use the supplied makefile, or you can load the viewer.prj project file into the Borland C++ IDE and use that environment. In either case you will produce an executable file called viewer.exe.

As promised, viewer.exe has a minimal user interface. To start the program, you must use one of three command-line options. The viewer.exe usage message, which is displayed if you don't use the specified command-line syntax, says it best:

```
Usage: view -d|-t|-f filename
 -d - view a document file
 -t - view a text file
 -f - view a file's directory entry (wild cards ok)
```

For example, to use viewer to get a directory listing of the current directory you would enter the command

```
view -f *.*
```

If you entered the above command in the viewer directory just following a build of viewer.exe, you would see the following:

```
VIEW.OBJ    8124 Mon Jun 08 19:48:42 1992
MAIN.CPP    1559 Mon Jun 08 09:54:24 1992
VIEW.H      1384 Mon Jun 08 19:47:48 1992
```

```
DATA.DOC        626 Thu Jun Ø4 Ø4:5Ø:Ø4 1992
MAIN.OBJ       3822 Mon Jun Ø8 19:48:48 1992
VIEW.CPP       4254 Mon Jun Ø8 1Ø:Ø7:ØØ 1992
VIEW.EXE      19Ø26 Mon Jun Ø8 1Ø:Ø7:18 1992
MAKEFILE         94 Mon Jun Ø8 1Ø:Ø7:Ø4 1992
VIEWER.EXE    28829 Mon Jun Ø8 19:48:52 1992
VIEWER.PRJ     5361 Mon Jun Ø8 19:49:14 1992
VIEWER.DSK      846 Mon Jun Ø8 19:49:36 1992
```

In the above case, viewer has less than a full screen of output, so it simply formats the requested information and exits. If more than one screenful of input is available, the supplied main() routine provides a tiny user interface:

```
Strike Enter to scroll down one line.
Strike Ctrl-C or Ctrl-Break to quit.
Strike anything else to scroll down one half screen.
```

Listings 2.3–2.6 display source code for view.h, view.cpp, main.cpp, and makefile.

LISTING 2.3

view.h

```cpp
//
// file viewer base class
//
class TViewer {
public:
    enum eStatus { END, OK, BAD };  // status constants
                                    // fetch stored line
    virtual const char *GetLine(int n);
    virtual void AddLine() = Ø;      // get next line
    inline eStatus Status();         // get error status
protected:
    int nRows, nCols, nCurRow;       // status
    eStatus curStatus;               // error status
    char **pszLines;                 // page buffer
    void Scroll();                   // discard oldest
    TViewer(int rows, int cols);     // constructor
    virtual ~TViewer();              // destructor
};


//
// View a text file (\n delimits lines)
//
```

LISTING 2.3

view.h (Continued)

```
class TTextView : public TViewer {
public:
    TTextView(int r, int c, char *filename);
    void AddLine();
    ~TTextView();
protected:
    FILE *fin;
};


//
// View a document file (\n delimits paragraphs)
//
class TDocView : public TViewer {
public:
    TDocView(int r, int c, char *filename);
    void AddLine();
    ~TDocView();
protected:
    FILE *fin;
};


//
// View a directory
//
class TDirView : public TViewer {
public:
    TDirView(int r, int c, char *filename);
    void AddLine();
protected:
    int First;
    struct find_t dirent;
    char *pszFiles;
};

inline TViewer::eStatus TViewer::Status()
{
    return curStatus;
}
```

LISTING 2.4

view.cpp

```cpp
#include <stdlib.h>
#include <stdio.h>
#include <string.h>
#include <conio.h>
#include <ctype.h>
#include <dos.h>
#include <time.h>
#include <sys/stat.h>
#include "view.h"

//
// class TViewer constructor
//
TViewer::TViewer(int rows, int cols) :
    nRows(rows),
    nCols(cols),
    nCurRow(-1),
    curStatus(OK)
{
    typedef char *pc;
    pszLines = new pc[nRows];
    if (!pszLines) {    // alloc failure
        curStatus = BAD;
        return;
    }
    for(int i = 0; i < nRows; i++) {
        // width + nl + null
        pszLines[i] = new char[nCols+1+1];
        if (!pszLines[i]) {
            curStatus = BAD;
            return;
        }
        *pszLines[i] = '\0';
    }
}


// destructor
TViewer::~TViewer()
{
    return;
}
```

LISTING 2.4

view.cpp (Continued)

```cpp
const char *TViewer::GetLine(int n)
{
    if (curStatus != OK)
        return "";
    if (n < 0 || n >= nRows)
        return "";
    return pszLines[n];
}

void TViewer::Scroll()
{
    if (curStatus != OK)
        return;
    if (nCurRow < (nRows-1))
        nCurRow++;
    else {
        char *tmp = pszLines[0];
        for(int i = 1; i < nRows; i++)
            pszLines[i-1] = pszLines[i];
        pszLines[nRows-1] = tmp;
        *tmp = '\0';
    }
}

// constructor
TTextView::TTextView(int r, int c, char *filename) :
    TViewer(r,c)
{
    if (curStatus == BAD)
        return;
    fin = fopen(filename, "r");
    if (fin == NULL) {
        curStatus = BAD;
        return;
    }
}

// destructor
TTextView::~TTextView()
{
    if (fin != NULL)
        fclose(fin);
}
```

LISTING 2.4

view.cpp (Continued)

```cpp
void TTextView::AddLine()
{
    Scroll();
    if (curStatus != OK)
        return;
    if (fgets(pszLines[nCurRow], nCols, fin) == NULL)
        curStatus = END;
    int len = strlen(pszLines[nCurRow]);
    if (pszLines[nCurRow][len-1] != '\n') {
        while(1) {   // skip to end of line
            int ch = getc(fin);
            if (ch == EOF) {
                curStatus = END;
                break;
            } else if (ch == '\n')
                break;
        }
    } else
        pszLines[nCurRow][len-1] = '\0';
}


//
// TDocView constructor
//
TDocView::TDocView(int r, int c, char *filename) :
    TViewer(r,c)
{
    if (curStatus == BAD)
        return;
    fin = fopen(filename, "r");
    if (fin == NULL) {
        curStatus = BAD;
        return;
    }
}


TDocView::~TDocView()
{
    if (fin != NULL)
        fclose(fin);
}


void TDocView::AddLine()
{
```

LISTING 2.4

view.cpp (Continued)

```cpp
        if (curStatus != OK)
            return;
        Scroll();

        // read text into buffer
        // reset restartpos each time whitespace is encountered.
        int ch;
        char *line = pszLines[nCurRow];
        char *restartch = line;
        long restartpos = ftell(fin);
        int n = 0;
        while(n < nCols) {
            ch = getc(fin);
            if (ch == EOF) {
                line[n] = '\0';
                curStatus = END;
                return;
            }
            if (ch == '\n') {
                line[n] = '\0';
                return;
            }
            line[n] = ch;
            if (isspace(ch)) {
                restartch = line + n;
                restartpos = ftell(fin);
            }
            n++;
        }
        if (restartch == line)  // huge word, break arbitrarily
            line[nCols] = '\0';
        else {  // retreat to last white space for a better break;
            *restartch = '\0';
            fseek(fin, restartpos, SEEK_SET);
        }
}

TDirView::TDirView(int r, int c, char *filename) :
    TViewer(r,c),
    First(1)
{
    // store filename
    pszFiles = new char[strlen(filename)+1];
    if (pszFiles)
```

LISTING 2.4

view.cpp (Continued)

```cpp
            strcpy(pszFiles, filename);
        else
            curStatus = BAD;
    }

    void TDirView::AddLine()
    {
        if (curStatus != OK)
            return;
        Scroll();

        // get the next entry
        if (First) {
            if (_dos_findfirst(pszFiles, _A_NORMAL, &dirent))
                curStatus = END;
            First = 0;
        } else {
            if (_dos_findnext(&dirent))
                curStatus = END;
        }

        // format dir entry
        struct stat statbuf;
        char buf[50];
        char buf2[30];
        stat(dirent.name, &statbuf);
        strcpy(buf2, ctime(&statbuf.st_mtime));
        buf2[24] = 0;
        sprintf(buf, "%12s %7ld %s",
            dirent.name, dirent.size, buf2);
        strncpy(pszLines[nCurRow], buf, nCols);
        pszLines[nCurRow][nCols] = 0;
    }
```

LISTING 2.5

main.cpp

```cpp
    //
    // File viewer sample main()
    //
    #include <stdlib.h>
    #include <stdio.h>
    #include <dos.h>
```

LISTING 2.5

main.cpp (Continued)

```cpp
#include <conio.h>
#include "view.h"

int usage()
{
    printf("Usage: view -d|-t|-f filename\n");
    printf(" -d - view a document file\n");
    printf(" -t - view a text file\n");
    printf(" -f - view a file's directory entry"
        "(wild cards ok)\n");
    return -1;
}

void main(int c, char **v)
{
    const int Rows = 24;
    const int Cols = 80;
    TViewer *tv;
    if (c == 3) switch(v[1][1]) {
        case 't':
            tv = new TTextView(Rows, Cols, v[2]);
            break;
        case 'd':
            tv = new TDocView(Rows, Cols, v[2]);
            break;
        case 'f':
            tv = new TDirView(Rows, Cols, v[2]);
            break;
        default:
            exit(usage());
    }
    else
        exit(usage());

    int i;
    for(i = 0; i < Rows; i++) {          // initial output
        tv->AddLine();
        if (tv->Status() != TViewer::OK)
            break;
        printf("%s\n", tv->GetLine(i));
    }
    // interactive output
    while(tv->Status() == TViewer::OK) {
        int c = getch();
```

LISTING 2.5

main.cpp (Continued)

```cpp
        int n;
        if (c == '\r')
            n = 1;
        else if (c == Ø3)    // ctrl c
            break;
        else
            n = Rows/2;
        for(int i = Ø; i < n; i++) {
            tv->AddLine();
            if (tv->Status() == TViewer::OK)
                printf("%s\n", tv->GetLine(Rows-1));
            else
                break;
        }
    }
}
```

LISTING 2.6

makefile

```
view.exe: view.obj main.obj
    bcc view.obj main.obj
view.obj: view.h
main.obj: view.h
```

OBJECTS AND CLASSES

THERE ARE MYRIAD SMALL CHANGES THAT MAKE C++ A BETTER C, BUT THERE is only one big change—classes, which are used to build objects. To become a productive C++ developer you need a thorough knowledge of classes. That's exactly the point of this chapter and the next, to tell you everything you need to know about classes.

This chapter concentrates on all of the features and characteristics that make C++ classes a fertile resource. Some of the most important information about classes is condensed into Figure 3.1.

The only major aspect of classes that isn't covered here is *inheritance*. The reason is that inheritance, one of the pillars of object-oriented development, is such a rich topic that it is covered by itself in Chapter 4.

Action! Member Functions

Classes, as you must be tired of hearing, are about action. Classes should do something; they should have active member functions that form their primary interface. You've already seen classes in Chapter 2 that contained member functions, but let's now approach member functions more slowly and systematically.

First, let's create a TPlace class that stores x and y positions. This class will represent positions, such as the position of something on a display screen. What actions are appropriate for such an object? Well, movement comes to mind.

```
class TPlace {          // C++ TPlace definition
  public:
    void MoveTo(int newx, int newy);
    void MoveBy(int dx, int dy);
    int x;
    int y;
};
```

The TPlace class definition contains two members functions, MoveTo() and MoveBy(). Most readers will suspect, because of the function names, that MoveTo() specifies a position, whereas MoveBy() specifies a translation by amounts dx and dy.

FIGURE 3.1

Anatomy of a class

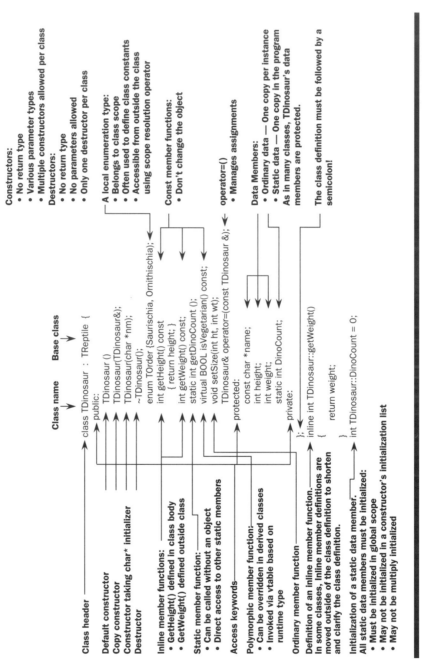

The TPlace definition contains only the function prototypes of MoveTo() and MoveBy(), not their full function definitions. The usual organizational strategy is to place class definitions in a .H header file and to place the class's member function definitions in a .CPP source file. For the TPlace class, we might put the TPlace class definition into place.h, and then put the function definitions into place.cpp. And of course place.cpp will contain an include directive to pull in the place.h header file.

The reason we partition C++ classes into header files and source files is the same reason that header files are used with the traditional C library. The .H header file contains the information that is needed to use something; it will likely be included into many source code files that use the class. The class's corresponding .CPP source code file contains all the details; it will be compiled separately into a .OBJ file and linked into the program. Typical partitioning of a class into .H files and .CPP files is shown in Figure 3.2.

FIGURE 3.2

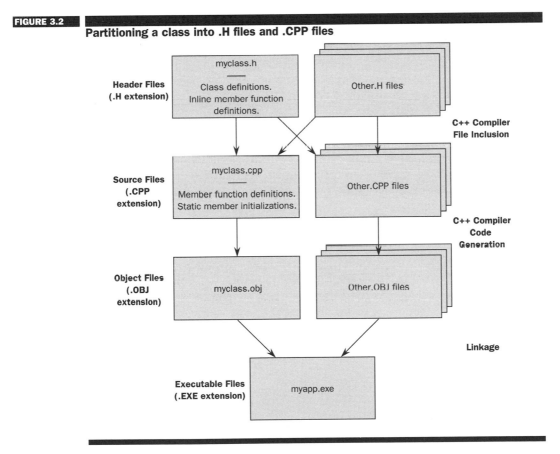

Partitioning a class into .H files and .CPP files

Here's the place.cpp file that defines the TPlace member functions:

```
// TPlace member functions
void TPlace::MoveTo(int newx, int newy)
{
    x = newx;
    y = newy;
}
void TPlace::MoveBy(int dx, int dy)
{
    x += dx;
    y += dy;
}
```

The most surprising part of the two function definitions is probably the TPlace:: prefix to the function names. In C++, the :: is called the *scope resolution operator* and it lets you specify a context. In the above function definitions, the TPlace:: prefix tells the compiler that you are defining entities from the TPlace class. This is necessary because the MoveBy() and MoveTo() functions are member functions; to fully define them the compiler must know their class affiliation.

The second surprising part of the function definitions may be the use of the variable names x and y within the functions. Remember that x and y are members of the TPlace class. Within a class's member functions, all the member variables are directly available. Careful here, because a program may have many, many TPlace objects. For example, the following declarations create 52 TPlace objects.

```
TPlace PlaceList[5Ø];
TPlace a, b;
```

So which object do x and y refer to? The answer is the x and y members of whichever object you use. Whenever you invoke a member function, you must specify an object. Here's how you would invoke the MoveBy() function to operate on the tenth element in the PlaceList[] array.

```
PlaceList[9].MoveBy(-1, -1);
```

When MoveBy() is called using the PlaceList[9] object, as in the preceding example, then inside MoveBy() the variables x and y refer to the x and y components of the PlaceList[9] object. That's the whole point of member functions. They are called to do something for a specific object; inside the member function you can easily refer to that object's members.

Efficient Inline Member Functions

Perhaps the most touted aspect of object-oriented programming is abstraction. Objects do something, and you can use an object without worrying about the details, just as you can drive a car without understanding internal combustion, gearing, or metallurgy. If I may extend the analogy just a bit further, let me point out that car designers spend a lot of time making their cars as robust as possible. You must do the same for your objects. As you design an object, you must constantly be thinking about how it might be broken, and you must strive to prevent such failures.

Your major tool for bullet-proofing your objects is control. Objects must control their own destiny, which is a fancy way of saying that objects must control their key data values. How? Principally by making most data elements protected or private, so that users of an object can't modify them directly. Of course there are exceptions, but most of an object's data should be protected.

The way to provide access to private or protected data members is to use access functions. They allow clients to have controlled access to the data. Sometimes all an access function does is make a data member read-only, by returning its value. Other times an access function does some sanity checking, to make sure that reasonable values are being assigned to a data member.

The problem is, yes, efficiency. Do we really want the time overhead of a function call each time we access some simple value in an object? No, of course not. The solution is to use inline member functions, so that function call overhead is usually eliminated. There are two simple ways to create inline member functions. Let me show both in a slightly revised version of TPlace.

```
class TPlace {          // C++ TPlace definition
  public:
    void MoveTo(int newx, int newy);
    void MoveBy(int dx, int dy);
    int GetX() { return x; }  // inline definition
    int GetY();
  protected:
    int x;
    int y;
};
inline int TPlace::GetY()           // definition
{
    return y;
}
```

In the TPlace class, both GetX() and GetY() are inline member functions that provide read-only access to TPlace's x and y components. If a user of TPlace wants to assign a value to the x and y components, he or she must use the MoveTo() or MoveBy() member functions, which should provide any necessary bounds checking. If a user of TPlace wants to access the x or y components, he or she must use GetX( ) or GetY( ).

The GetX( ) inline member function shows the most straightforward way to provide an inline member—simply provide the function body inside the class definition. The advantage is simplicity and directness. But the disadvantage is that a large class with many inline members will soon become cluttered and overwhelmed by the mass of function bodies.

The alternative is illustrated by the GetY( ) member function. Inside the class definition all you need do is declare the function. If you want, you can declare the function as inline using the inline keyword, but it isn't necessary. The advantage is keeping the class definition relatively uncluttered, which is important for improving the readability of large classes. Following the class, but still in the header file, you provide the inline function body. Note that I said in the header file. It's tempting to put inline function bodies with other function bodies; keeping likes together is as applicable to programming as to organizing your kitchen. But the compiler can't generate inline code unless it sees the body of the inline function before it encounters a call of the function.

Compilers differ in their ability to use inline functions. For example, Borland C++ can't use inline functions that contain loops. If you include a loop in an inline function, Borland C++ will issue a warning message and then implement an ordinary (out of line) function.

Inlines save you execution time, but often at the expense of space. If you have an inline function that expands to 40 bytes of machine code, and you use that function 100 times in a large application, that's 4,000 bytes of code, versus about 800 bytes of code (the exact amount depends on memory model, optimization level, and so on) if function calls are used. My suggestion is to use inline only for very short functions, or only for larger functions whose time overhead is critically important. Don't overuse inline.

Steady const Member Functions

One of the major innovations of C++ is the const type modifier, which allows us to create data values that don't change. const is a huge and welcome step away from the preprocessor. It is yet another tool in C++ that allows us to say what we mean.

const, however, is not without problems. Foremost is the problem of our own programming habits. Most of us aren't used to thinking about what is constant versus what varies. It's hard to use const here and there in a program. If you use const at all, you must use it consistently, or you'll get rafts of compiler errors.

Another difficulty with const is that it has many ramifications. For example, consider a const TPlace that, say, stores the position of the center of the screen:

```
const TPlace MidScreen(320, 240);
```

Please accept, for just a moment, that a TPlace can be initialized. (The secret to initialization is a *constructor,* which will be discussed soon. Let's assume, for now, that our TPlace has a suitable constructor.) Because Mid-Screen is a const object, it can't be altered. Thus we should be able to call the GetX() and GetY() member functions, to fetch x and y values, but we should be prevented from calling MoveTo() or MoveBy(), because those functions alter the x and y values.

The solution is to identify those member functions that don't modify the object, making them const member functions. At first guess you might suspect that we could do this simply by inserting the word const in front of the function name. But that creates a member function whose return value is a const, while what we want is a const member function, one that doesn't alter its object. The answer is to place the word const at the end of the member function's header. Here is the TPlace class definition from the preceding section, now enhanced to indicate that GetX() and GetY() are const member functions:

```
class TPlace {          // C++ TPlace definition
  public:
    void MoveTo(int newx, int newy);
    void MoveBy(int dx, int dy);
    int GetX() const { return x; } // const member fn
    int GetY() const;              // const member fn
  protected:
    int x;
    int y;
};
inline int TPlace::GetY()          // definition
{
    return y;
}
```

Declaring a member function to be const has two effects. The first is that the compiler will make sure that the member function behaves as you claim; the compiler will prohibit you from assigning values to member variables, and it will prohibit calls to non-const member functions. Thus if either MoveBy() or MoveTo() had been declared const, the compiler would have objected to the assignments to the x and y member variables.

The second effect is that the compiler will allow you to invoke a const member function for a const object.

```
const TPlace MidScreen(320,240);  // const object
int xMid = MidScreen.GetX();      // ok
MidScreen.MoveTo(50,50);          // error
```

The error occurs because a non-const member function is being invoked using a const object.

Of course the compiler will also allow you to invoke a const member function for a non-const object. If the MidScreen object in the above code fragment had been non-const, then both member function calls would have been okay.

Volatile Member Functions

Volatile member functions exist so that a member function can be invoked for a volatile object. As I discussed in the first chapter, a volatile datum is one that may change unexpectedly, usually because of something that happens asynchronously, such as a hardware interrupt. The volatile attribute exists to tell the compiler that the value may change unexpectedly, so that correct code can be generated.

If you mark a member function as volatile, by writing the keyword volatile at the end of the function's header, then the compiler will generate very conservative code for the member function. If you have a volatile object, then you will only be able to call volatile member functions. Of course the compiler will allow you to invoke a volatile member function for a non-volatile object.

Polymorphism and Virtual Member Functions

Polymorphism is one of the major advances of object-oriented programming. Polymorphism allows the user of an object to invoke standard behavior, without knowing exactly what type of object is being used. This lets us craft families of objects that share certain traits, while also exhibiting their own personalities.

In C++ you must identify all member functions that will have polymorphic behavior. For polymorphic member functions, runtime object typing is used to determine which function to call. If a member function is not polymorphic, then static typing is used to determine which function to call.

The virtual keyword is used to specify that a member function is polymorphic. Like the inline specifier, the virtual specifier appears in front of the function header. We first encountered virtual in the definition of the TViewer class in Chapter 2. Here are the prototypes of the two public polymorphic member functions of the TViewer class.

```
virtual const char *GetLine(int n);
virtual void AddLine() = 0;
```

The full TViewer class definition was shown in Listing 2.3 (view.h).

In the TViewer family, TDocView, TTextView, and TDirView all define their own AddLine() member function. If AddLine() is called for an object type that is known in advance, static typing, which is done during the compilation process, can be used. Here is an example of static typing.

```
void main()
{
    const int Rows = 24;
    const int Cols = 80;
```

```
    TDocView oDoc(Rows, Cols, "file.doc");
    TTextView oTxt(Rows, Cols, "file.txt");
    TDirView oDir(Rows, Cols, "*.*");

    // static typing, call TDocView::AddLine()
    oDoc.AddLine();

    // static typing, call TTextView::AddLine()
    oTxt.AddLine();

    // static typing, call TDirView::AddLine()
    oDir.AddLine();
}
```

Polymorphism isn't used in the above example, because all the types are known in the compiler.

Polymorphism is used when the compiler can't determine the types in advance. For example, the original TViewer example used runtime typing. Here is a sketch of that example. (For full source code see Listing 1.3.)

```
void main(int c, char **v)
{
  TViewer *tv  // pointer to any TViewer family object

  //
  // Create either a TDocView, TTextView, or TDirView
  // object, depending on command-line arguments.
  //
  tv = new ...

  //
  // Display the file
  //
  while ...
    tv->AddLine();  // Runtime Typing, call appropriate AddLine()
}
```

Polymorphism is used in Listing 1.3, because the compiler can't know in advance what type of object will be used. That choice is made by the user each time the program is executed. So instead runtime typing is used to ensure that the correct version of AddLine() is called.

The GetLine() member function is an ordinary virtual function. A definition is provided, but derived classes are free to implement their own version of GetLine(). In the DOS file viewer application, GetLine() was made virtual because I foresaw the possibility that a derived class might want to manage its own storage. In the DOS file viewer presented in Chapter 2, none of the derived classes manages its own storage, and none redefines GetLine().

The AddLine() member is also a virtual function, but it differs from GetLine() because it is a *pure* virtual function. A pure virtual member function needn't be defined, which is why you won't find a definition of AddLine() for the TViewer class in Listing 2.4 (view.cpp). Syntactically, you indicate that a virtual member function is pure by writing = 0 after the function header. The = 0 notation brings to mind assigning null to a pointer, which reminds us that the body of the function might not exist.

A class that contains a pure virtual function is called an *abstract class*. You can't create an object of an abstract class, although pointers to the class are permissible. Abstract classes by themselves aren't very useful; they are only valuable as base classes. An abstract class's pure virtual functions serve as placeholders. They indicate that a certain facility is not provided in the base class, but that it will be provided by the offspring.

Descendent classes of an abstract class will also be abstract, unless they provide a definition for each of the pure virtual functions in the base class. In the TViewer class hierarchy, each of the derived classes provides its own AddLine() function. Thus none of the derived classes is abstract; only the TViewer class is abstract.

The GetLine() and AddLine() polymorphic member functions illustrate the full range of possibilities. GetLine() is polymorphic, but only because it is possible to imagine that a derived class will want to take over its role. At the other extreme, AddLine() is quintessentially polymorphic; it must be redefined in all (ultimate) base classes. In between these extremes lie the majority of polymorphic member functions, which are often but not invariably redefined in derived classes.

Static Members

The static keyword should be rewarded for its patience in handling so many different roles in C and C++. In traditional C, static already has two meanings. Inside a function, the static keyword is used to specify that a datum will be retained for the life of a program. The data will be allocated statically, instead of on the stack. The second usage of static is to declare externs, either data or procedures, which have local linkage. Something declared static cannot be accessed directly by a procedure from outside the current file.

C++ retains these two meanings of static, and then adds two more. The first additional usage in C++ is to declare static data in a *class*. Like static data in a procedure, a class's static data exists for the life of the program. A class's ordinary data is the basis of each class object; there is one copy of the ordinary class data in each class object. However, a program always has exactly one copy of a class's static data, no matter how many objects exist.

```
class TChair {
public:
    TPlace Position;
```

```
    BOOL Occupied;
    static int NumChairs;
};
```

The TChair class has three data members: two ordinary data members and the NumChairs static data member. In some ways, NumChairs is like a global variable: It exists for the life of the program, and it is initialized by a value in the program's load image. But NumChairs is very much a part of the TChair class: Its access is governed by class access rules, and it is directly accessible by TChair member functions.

Static class members must be explicitly initialized. Here's how you would initialize NumChairs:

```
int TChair::NumChairs = 0;
```

The initialization uses the TChair:: prefix to specify NumChairs's class. Remember that NumChairs belongs to the TChair class; it isn't a global variable but rather a class's static member variable.

C++'s second new usage of static is to identify static class member functions. A *static* member function is like an ordinary member function, but it doesn't need to be invoked for a particular object. Instead, somewhat like an ordinary global function, it can simply be invoked. But like a static class variable, a static member function must be invoked using the class's name.

Inside a static member function, you can directly access all of the static class elements (variables and functions), but you don't have direct access to non-static members. Here's the earlier TChair example, slightly enhanced to include a static member function.

```
class TChair {
public:
    TPlace Position;
    BOOL Occupied;
    static int GetNumChairs();
protected:
    static int NumChairs;
};
```

The GetNumChairs() member function can be invoked either with or without a TChair object. If you have a TChair object, say DadsChair, then GetNumChairs() can be invoked using standard notation:

```
int n = DadsChair.GetNumChairs();
```

Even though you can do the above, I consider it bad style. The object DadsChair is simply used to identify a particular class, it has no specific role in invoking GetNumChairs( ), and its data members aren't made available to GetNumChairs( ). For all these reasons I prefer to use the class name followed by the scope resolution operator to invoke a static member function.

```
int n = TChair::GetNumChairs();
```

To me, this alternative notation states clearly that a static member function is being called.

Life and Death with Constructors and Destructors

Classes let us create our own types. They let us move beyond the limiting idea that memory contains either numbers or text, to a more liberating idea that memory contains objects that have behaviors. In the older, simpler world of text and numbers, initialization consisted solely of installing some initial value. But for objects, it is often better to think of an initial state, not an initial value, and it is insufficient to simply flood an object's storage region with some bit pattern.

Although there are simple objects that do little more than encompass one or two values, it is more useful to think of objects as small machines. Like physical machines, an object is more than the sum of its parts. The parts must be assembled correctly so that they relate to each other.

A *constructor* is a special member function that initializes an object. In C++, constructors have the same name as the class. Constructors are called automatically when an object is created.

- For static objects, the constructor is called before the application proper starts to execute.

- For automatic objects in a function (stored on the stack), the constructor will be called automatically when the function is entered.

- For dynamically allocated objects (allocated using new), the constructor will be called after memory has been allocated.

You may have several constructors for a class, although each must have a different argument list.

Constructors are considered to be special member functions because they play a key role in object creation. But they are also special because there are numerous restrictions that you must observe:

- Constructors may not return a value. You may not declare a return type, not even void.

- Constructors may not be static or virtual.

- Constructors may not be const or volatile, although they can be invoked to construct const or volatile objects.

- You may not take the address of a constructor.

It's important to know the order in which the components of a class will be constructed. If the class is a derived class, its base class construction will occur first. Then if the class has member objects that have constructors, those constructors will execute next. Finally the class's own constructor will execute last. Thus within the body of the constructor you can rely on correct operation of the member objects. Order of construction and destruction is diagrammed in Figure 3.3.

FIGURE 3.3

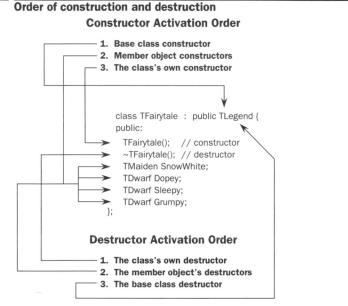

Order of construction and destruction
Constructor Activation Order

1. Base class constructor
2. Member object constructors
3. The class's own constructor

```
class TFairytale : public TLegend {
public:
    TFairytale();   // constructor
    ~TFairytale();  // destructor
    TMaiden SnowWhite;
    TDwarf Dopey;
    TDwarf Sleepy;
    TDwarf Grumpy;
};
```

Destructor Activation Order

1. The class's own destructor
2. The member object's destructors
3. The base class destructor

Several aspects of constructors are illustrated by the TDonut class.

```
class TDonut {
  public:
    enum TFlavor
      { Plain, Chocolate };
    enum TFilling
      { None, VanCream, ChocCream, Jelly };
    // constructors
    TDonut();                // default constructor
    TDonut(TDonut &d);       // copy constructor
    TDonut(TFlavor f);       // TFlavor constructor
                             // TFlavor,TFilling constr.
    TDonut(TFlavor flav, TFilling fill);
    ~TDonut();               // destructor
  protected:
```

```
        const TFlavor Flavor;
        const TFilling Filling;
        static int DonutCount;
    };
```

TDonut's public members are two enumeration types, four constructors, and a destructor. The protected part of TDonut contains two const enumeration values that store the donut's characteristics, and a static int that keeps track of how many donut objects have been created.

The four constructors provide the following four ways to declare a TDonut object:

```
// use default constructor
TDonut plain;
// use Tflavor constructor
TDonut choc(TDonut::Chocolate);
// use TFlavor,TFilling constructor
TDonut cream(TDonut::Plain, TDonut::VanCream);
// use copy constructor
TDonut myfavorite(choc);
```

The choc, cream, and myfavorite TDonut objects have been initialized using the new C++ initialization style that suggests a function call. You can instead use the traditional C style declaration that resembles an assignment statement. Here are these three declarations rewritten in the more traditional C style:

```
TDonut choc = TDonut::Chocolate;
TDonut cream = TDonut(TDonut::Plain, TDonut::VanCream);
TDonut myfavorite = choc;
```

I prefer the new style because the equal sign in an initialization seems misleading to me.

As you can see, using these mouth-watering constructors is easy, so let's move to the richer topic of writing your own constructors.

Initializing Members

While you are using C++ you need to carefully distinguish between *initialization*, which happens to a datum just once when it is created, and assignment, which may occur routinely during a variable's lifetime. The most important reason for this distinction is that C++ contains const and reference types that can only be initialized, not assigned. Actually, the rule is even stronger. Consts and references must be initialized; it is not permissible to omit the initial value for consts and references. (Assignment is discussed later in this chapter under "Details of Specific Operator Functions.")

Syntactically, there is a careful distinction between initialization and assignment. When you are declaring a datum and you supply a value, that's initialization. Similarly, when procedure parameters attain their value during a procedure call, or when a value is returned from a procedure, that's initialization. When you have an expression statement and an lvalue (an lvalue is something that can be assigned a value; it is so named because it can appear to the left of an equal sign) appears to the left of an equal sign, that's an assignment. Classes can control assignment using an operator=() member function, which will be discussed later in this chapter.

A constructor is a class member function, so it generally follows the same rules as other member functions. But there are a few exceptions, such as the ability of a constructor to initialize class data members. Here is the TDonut class constructor that requires a single TFlavor argument.

```
TDonut::TDonut(TFlavor f) :
    Flavor(f),      // initialize Flavor
    Filling(None)   // initialize Filling
{
    DonutCount++;
}
```

In a constructor, and only in a constructor, you can place an *initialization list* between the function header and the function body. The initialization list is introduced by a colon, the elements are separated by commas, and each element of the list is the name of a class member followed by a parenthesized initial value. In the TDonut constructor just shown, the Flavor member is initialized by the parameter f, and the Filling member is initialized by the enumeration constant None.

In the TDonut class, both Flavor and Filling are const values. This means that they must be initialized by each constructor. It is not permissible to assign a value to either Flavor or Filling in the body of the constructor; remember, they are consts.

In a constructor's initialization list,

- You must initialize all const or reference members.

- You should initialize all member objects of classes that have constructors. If you don't initialize a member object, its default constructor will be invoked.

- You are not allowed to initialize static class members.

For completeness, let me show you the constructor that lets you specify both the donut's flavor and filling.

```
TDonut::TDonut(TFlavor flav, TFilling fill) :
    Flavor(flav),
```

```
    Filling(fill)
{

    DonutCount++;
}
```

The Default Constructor

A constructor that doesn't have any arguments (or one that has only a default argument) is called a *default constructor*. The default constructor will be used whenever you don't supply an initial value. We've already seen one way to invoke the default constructor:

```
TDonut plain;
```

There are several other situations in which a default constructor will be used. For example, if you don't supply enough initializers for a static array, the default constructor will be used in place of the missing initializers:

```
TDonut batch[5] = {
    TDonut(),
    TDonut(TDonut::Chocolate),
    TDonut(TDonut::Chocolate, TDonut::ChocCream)
};
```

In the batch array, the default constructor is explicitly invoked to construct batch[0], and it is used implicitly for batch[3] and batch[4].

The default constructor will also be used when you dynamically allocate an array of objects:

```
TDonut *pDonut = new TDonut[5];
```

pDonut will point to an array of five dynamically allocated TDonut objects, and each TDonut object in the array will be initialized using the default constructor.

Here is the default constructor for the TDonut class:

```
TDonut::TDonut() :
    Flavor(Plain),
    Filling(None)
{

    DonutCount++;
}
```

The default constructor is special in part because it is used automatically in the situations mentioned above. But it is also special because it can be generated automatically by the compiler. If you create a class but you don't define any constructors, the compiler will, if necessary, generate a default constructor. The generated constructor will be public, and it will construct each of its member objects.

- If you supply any constructors, then the compiler will not generate a default constructor.

- If you supply any constructors but don't supply a default constructor, then the compiler will issue errors for any situation that requires a default constructor.

I consider it bad practice to let the compiler create constructors. If your class needs a default constructor, you should write that constructor; don't ask the compiler to write it for you.

Controlling Copies with the Copy Constructor

A *copy constructor* is a constructor that is called with a reference to an existing object of the same type. For example, a TDonut constructor that takes a TDonut& argument is a copy constructor for the TDonut class. Although you are free to do whatever you like when you write a copy constructor, the usual meaning of a copy constructor is to give a new object the same value as the existing object. That's exactly what the TDonut class's constructor does:

```
TDonut::TDonut(TDonut &d) :
    Flavor(d.Flavor),
    Filling(d.Filling)
{
    DonutCount++;
}
```

Copy constructors, like default constructors, can be generated automatically by the compiler. If you don't supply a copy constructor, the compiler is free to generate one. Thus you should always, in my opinion, write your own copy constructor. Writing your own lets you control copying, by making your own copy constructor protected or private. Writing your own also lets you take care of related business, such as the TDonut copy constructor, which increments the DonutCount static variable to keep track of the number of TDonut objects.

Converting Types with Conversion Constructors

Any constructor that uses a single argument of one type to produce another type is called a *conversion constructor*. For example, the TDonut constructor that uses a TFlavor enumeration value to build a TDonut object is a conversion constructor.

You need to know about conversion constructors because they may be used by the compiler to patch up type mismatches. For example, let's assume that we have a function called Eat( ) that takes a TDonut argument. Here's the function prototype for Eat( ):

```
void Eat(TDonut d);
```

You would expect that Eat( ) would require an actual TDonut object as its argument. For example, if myfavorite is a TDonut object, then you could call Eat( ) as follows:

```
Eat(myfavorite);
```

Many people would assume that the following is an error, because TDonut::Plain is a type TDonut::TFlavor enumeration constant.

```
Eat(TDonut::Plain);
```

But it is actually not an error, because the compiler will use the TDonut(TFlavor) conversion constructor to convert TDonut::Plain into a temporary TDonut object, which will be passed to Eat( ). In some situations, this is natural behavior that you want to perform easily. In other situations, the conversion is unintended and unwanted.

I think it would be too harsh to suggest that you avoid single argument constructors just because they may be used (unexpectedly) by the compiler to perform conversions. But you should be very aware of the hazard. Be especially careful when you create conversion constructors for the built-in types int, char, char*, and double, because these conversions can occur in innumerable ways.

The End: Destructors

Although there may be many ways to construct a class object, each class has only one way to disassemble a class object, which is called *destruction*. *Destructors* should perform cleanup chores, storage reclamation, and other operations required when an object terminates. Destructors don't take arguments and they don't return values.

- For a dynamically allocated object, the destructor is called when the object is deleted.

- For an automatic object (local to a procedure), the destructor is called when the object goes out of scope because the procedure returns.

- For a global object (an object declared static inside a procedure or class, or any object declared at file scope), the destructor is called when the program terminates.

- Destructors may also be called explicitly, although this is rarely necessary.

Note that dynamically allocated objects that are never deleted are never destroyed, and also note that an abnormal program termination can cause many destructor calls to be skipped.

In C++, the destructor's name is a tilde (~) followed by the class name. For example, ~TDonut( ) is the destructor for the TDonut class.

```
TDonut::~TDonut()
{
    DonutCount--;
}
```

For the TDonut class, the destructor's only chore is to decrement the DonutCount static variable, so that the count of TDonut objects is correct.

In classes that may serve as base classes, destructors should usually be virtual. This ensures that any derived class's destructor will be called, even if the object is being accessed using a pointer to its base class. Notice the asymmetry between constructors and destructors:

- A class may have multiple constructors; a class may have only one destructor.

- Constructors may not be virtual; destructors for base classes should usually be virtual.

I mentioned earlier that classes are constructed in a specific order: First the base class is constructed, then member objects are constructed, and finally the class's own constructor is activated. Destruction happens in the opposite order: First the class's own destructor is activated, then the member object's destructors, and finally the base class destructor.

Better Notation Using Operator Functions

A part of the breakthrough in C++ is its expressive power. C++, far more than C, lets you say what you mean. An important part of this expressive power is the ability to define operator functions. An operator function is much like an ordinary function, except that it can be invoked using algebraic notation instead of using traditional function call notation. This lets us write expressions that are translated by the compiler into a series of function calls.

For example, if we add operator functions to the TPlace class, then we will be able to manipulate TPlace objects using algebraic notation:

```
TPlace a(100,100);
TPlace b(10,10);
a = b;      // assignment, call operator=()
a += b;     // add sum, call operator+=()
```

Without operator functions we would need to explicitly call functions to perform these operations. Understand that the advantage is only notational. In the preceding example, the statement a = b will be performed by calling the operator=() function, and the statement a += b will be performed by calling the operator+=() function. No time is saved using operator notation, but the code is easier to read and understand than the corresponding code written using explicit function calls.

In some fields, operator notation has little value, and operator functions are rarely used. In other areas, such as scientific and mathematical software, operator notation is heavily used.

Almost all of the C and C++ operators can be overloaded, which means you can write your own operator functions for them. However, there are several limitations to C++ operator functions:

- You cannot write operator functions for any of the preprocessor operators.

- You cannot write an operator function for the ?: (ternary), . (member of), .* (pointer to member), or :: (scope resolution) operators.

- You cannot invent new operators (wouldn't that be nice!).

- You cannot change the associativity, precedence, or kind (unary or binary) of the current set of operators.

Table 3.1 shows the operators that can be overloaded.

TABLE 3.1

Overloadable Operators

->	->*	()	[]	new	delete
+	–	*	/	%	,
+=	–=	*=	/=	%=	=
^	&	|	<<	>>	++
^=	&=	|=	<<=	>>=	– –
<	<=	==	!=	>=	>
&&	||	!	~		

Let me continue by showing how we can add a few operator functions to the TPlace class. Then I'll discuss several operator functions that need to be examined individually.

The TPlace class is a good candidate for adding operator functions, because it is easy to think of places mathematically. One position can be added to or subtracted from another, you might want to know the distance between two places, or you might want to assign one place to another. All these constructs are naturally expressed using operator notation, which suggests using operator functions with the TPlace class.

Class Member Operator Functions

The first thing to decide is whether you want to create operator functions that are members of the TPlace class, or whether you want to write stand-alone operator functions. The major difference is how the first operand is handled. Here are the rules for operator functions written as class member functions:

- *Unary Operators*   The member function takes no argument. The single operand is the object used to invoke the member function.

- *Binary Operators*   The member function takes one argument. The left-hand operand is the object used to invoke the member function; the right-hand operand is the member function's argument.

- *Both Unary and Binary Operators*   The operator function must be invoked by an object of the correct type. The compiler will not apply any conversions to the left (for binary operators) or sole (for unary operators) operand. The usual rules for conversions apply to the right operand (for binary operators).

Listing 3.1 shows the TPlace class definition, extended to contain three operator functions: assignment, assign sum, and unary minus. I've also removed the MoveTo( ) and MoveBy( ) functions, because they are now superfluous. Listing 3.2 shows the definitions of the TPlace member functions.

LISTING 3.1 ▮▮▮▮▮▮▮▮▮▮▮▮▮▮▮▮▮▮▮

tplace.h

```
// C++ TPlace definition using operator functions
class TPlace {
  public:
    TPlace();                // default constructor
    TPlace(TPlace& p);       // copy constructor
    TPlace(int ix, int iy); // TPlace(int,int) constr.
    TPlace& operator=(const TPlace &rhs);  // assignment
    TPlace& operator+=(const TPlace &rhs); // assign sum
    TPlace operator-() const;             // unary minus
    int GetX() const { return x; }
    int GetY() const { return y; }
  protected:
    int x;
    int y;
};
```

LISTING 3.2

tplace.cpp

```cpp
TPlace::TPlace() :          // default constructor
  x(0),
  y(0)
{
  return;
}
TPlace::TPlace(TPlace& p) : // copy constructor
  x(p.x),
  y(p.y)
{
  return;
}
TPlace::TPlace(int ix, int iy) :
  x(ix),
  y(iy)
{
  return;
}
TPlace& TPlace::operator=(const TPlace &rhs)
{
  x = rhs.x;
  y = rhs.y;
  return *this;
}
TPlace& TPlace::operator+=(const TPlace &rhs)
{
  x += rhs.x;
  y += rhs.y;
  return *this;
}
TPlace TPlace::operator-() const
{
  TPlace p(-x, -y);
  return p;
}
```

Let's first examine assign sum, which is a binary operator. Assign sum, whose symbol is +=, is handled by the operator+=() function. (Under the usual rules for C and C++ identifiers, the symbol += is an operator, and the text "operator+=" would be interpreted as the word "operator" followed by the operator "+=". But in an operator function, the symbol is incorporated into the name. Thus "operator+=" is interpreted as an identifier.) If a and b are TPlace objects, and TPlace has an operator+=( ) function, then the following expression will use that operator function:

```
a += b
```

Object a is the left operand and object b is the right operand. If you have an operator+=( ) function that is a class member, then the compiler will take the above expression and produce code that corresponds to the following:

```
a.operator+=(b)
```

I would read this aloud as "the a object is used to invoke its operator assign-sum member function, giving it the argument b." Here is the definition of the TPlace class's operator+=( ) function:

```
TPlace& TPlace::operator+=(const TPlace &rhs)
{
    x += rhs.x;
    y += rhs.y;
    return *this;
}
```

Because the left operand, the one that gets modified, is used to invoke the operator+=( ) function, it is the directly accessible members x and y that are modified. The right operand is passed to the function, and is accessible inside the operator+=( ) function via the rhs (right-hand side) parameter. The rhs parameter is a reference, for efficiency, and it's a const, so that it can be used with either const or ordinary TPlace objects.

The last statement in the function, return *this;, returns a reference to the current object. In a class member function, you can always use a pointer named this to access the current object. Let me digress for one moment to explain this (pun intended) further.

We have already seen that you call a class member function to operate on a specific object. If o is an object of a class C that has a member function named fn(), then the expression o.fn() will call the member function named fn(). Inside fn() you will be able to access all of the members of class C. The mechanism that lets you access the members is quite simple; the compiler passes a hidden argument named this to fn() that points to the calling object o. Inside fn(), when you use one of the class members, the compiler actually uses the hidden this pointer to access that member.

This scheme usually works automatically, and you don't have to worry about the details. But occasionally you want to refer to the current object directly using this. For example, the TPlace operator+=( ) function wants to return the current object. Since this pointer points to the current object, *this is the current object. Thus the statement return *this; is C++ idiom to return the current object. You'll see this idiom often in operator functions. The other common use of the this pointer is in derived classes when you want to access an overridden function from the base class. If you cast this, whose type is a pointer to derived, to be a pointer to base, you can easily access otherwise inaccessible base class members.

Stand-alone Operator Functions

My natural inclination is to make everything that is part of a class, a member of that class. Thus my first thought for operator functions is usually to make them class member functions. But operator functions can also be *stand-alone functions*. Here are the major reasons you should consider making operator functions stand-alone instead of making them class members:

- For binary operators, stand-alone operator functions behave symmetrically. Both the left and the right operand are subject to the usual conversions, and the left operand needn't be an object. For example, you can write a stand-alone operator function to add a double (left operand) and a complex object (right operand). You can't do this with member operator functions because the left operand must be an object. Thus with member operator functions you would only be able to add a complex object (left operand) to a double (right operand).

- You can write stand-alone operator functions for classes that you don't own.

However, not all operator functions are allowed to be stand-alone. The following operator functions may be written only as class member functions: operator=(), operator()(), operator[](), and operator–>().

It is easy to change the TPlace class to use stand-alone functions for operator+=() and operator–(). Only two changes are required. First, in the class definition you should delete the prototypes for the operator+=() and operator–() member functions, and instead insert the following two friend declarations into the TPlace class:

```
friend TPlace& operator+=(TPlace& lhs, const TPlace& rhs);
friend TPlace operator-(const TPlace& opnd);
```

These declarations state that the two operator functions are friends of the TPlace class, which allows them direct access to all the TPlace members. This somewhat simplifies writing the operator functions, but it isn't strictly necessary. GetX() and GetY() could be used to fetch the values, the TPlace(int,int) constructor could be used to build new TPlace values, and the operator=() member could be used for assignment.

The second thing you must do is replace the original operator member function definitions with the following two stand-alone function definitions:

```
TPlace& operator+=(TPlace& lhs, const TPlace& rhs)
{
    lhs.x += rhs.x;
    lhs.y += rhs.y;
    return lhs;
}
TPlace operator-(const TPlace& opnd)
{
    TPlace p(-opnd.x, -opnd.y);
    return p;
}
```

If you compare these two stand-alone functions with the original member functions, you'll notice a few small changes:

- Each function has gained an additional argument. As class member functions, each function received an implicit this argument. Now that they are stand-alone functions, that argument is explicit.

- The operator+=() function returns its first argument, instead of returning *this.

- There is no implicit access to any object. Each access to an object member refers to an explicitly declared object.

For the TPlace class, I prefer to write the operator functions as member functions, because in TPlace there is little advantage to the stand-alone versions. But for classes that have more interactions with other types and that demand symmetrical operator usage, stand-alone operator functions are often preferred.

Selecting Argument Types and Return Types

The operator functions in the TPlace class illustrate several aspects of member function argument types and return types. In my experience, most programmers don't have much trouble choosing argument and return types for ordinary member functions, because ordinary member functions are directly analogous to the global functions that we have been working with for many years. But operator functions are different, because they are embedded in expressions. Not only do operator functions need to perform their own computations, they need to return values for use by other elements in an expression.

First let's examine the argument types. For efficiency, it is usually best to deliver arguments by reference. If an argument is not going to be modified, make sure you state that in the parameter declaration. Passing arguments by value should usually be avoided, unless they really are simple values such as integers, doubles, or pointers.

Selecting operator function return types is a more complicated decision. Here are some guidelines that apply to small objects, such as TPlace:

- Operators that modify their left operand, such as the assignment operators, should usually return a reference to their left operand.

- Operators that select or deliver operands, such as [] (element of), * (indirection), –> (member access), and () (procedure call), should usually return a reference to the selected value.

- Operators that compute a new value, but that don't modify their operands, such as the binary logical, bitwise, and arithmetic operators (+, –, *, /, %, &, |, ^, &&, ||); unary minus and plus (–, +); and unary not and bitwise insert (!, ~); should usually return a copy of a locally allocated object.

- The pre-increment and pre-decrement operators should usually return a reference to their operand.

- The post-increment and post-decrement operators should usually save a copy of their operand, modify the operand, and then return the copy.

If you want to create operator functions for large objects, such as arrays, matrices, or database tables, you will need to develop an efficient and comprehensive strategy that's appropriate for your data.

Details of Specific Operator Functions

I was initially surprised that most of the operator function capability is provided within the ordinary rules of C++ functions and member functions. The special part is mostly the fact that the compiler recognizes the specific operator function names, and then uses them accordingly in expressions. But there are a few operator functions that have more specific requirements detailed in the following table.

		May Be Inherited?	Member or Friend?	May Be Virtual?	Return Value
Assignment	operator=()	no	member	yes	any

Assignment is a fundamental operation that has broad implications for how a class behaves. That's why assignment is the only operator function that will be generated automatically by the compiler. However, I recommend that you not rely on the compiler generated assignment operator, and instead that you write your own.

Assignment is also the only operator function that is not inherited. The reason is that derived classes are usually larger than their base classes, which suggests that an inherited operator=() would rarely do a complete job. For example, consider a T3DPlace class that was derived from TPlace. It would likely have a z component. If T3DPlace inherited TPlace's operator=() function, then you could assign one T3DPlace object to another using that operator, but the operator wouldn't copy the z value. Not nice! (A compiler generated operator=( ) for a T3DPlace class would use the base class operator=( ) to assign the base class part, and it would then assign the additional z member.)

The assignment operator may return anything. The two most common choices are to specify the void return type, and to return a reference to the assigned object. The void return type prohibits chained assignment statements such as x = y = z;, which is a prohibition that some class designers favor. Returning a reference to the assigned value does just the opposite: it enables chained assignment statements.

		May Be Inherited?	Member or Friend?	May Be Virtual?	Return Value
Pre-increment	operator++( )	yes	either	yes	any
Pre-decrement	operator--	yes	either	yes	any
Post-increment	operator++(int)	yes	either	yes	any
Post-decrement	operator--(int)	yes	either	yes	any

Increment and decrement are unary operators, but they are unusual because they can either be prefix or postfix operators. This capability causes a problem for the usual operator function scheme because it doesn't have a way to distinguish between the prefix and postfix version. This was a problem in early versions of C++, but now a dummy argument is used to identify the postfix version of these operators. You can easily remember that it is the postfix operator that has the extra dummy argument, because these are the only unary postfix operators in the language. Prefix increment and decrement, like other unary prefix operators, don't have a dummy argument.

Here is a short example:

```
class incdemo {
  public:
    incdemo& operator++()        // prefix
      { val++; return *this; }
    incdemo operator++(int) {  // postfix
      incdemo tmp;
      tmp.val = val;
      val++;
      return tmp;
    }
  protected:
    int val;
};
```

Notice that the prefix operator++() can simply modify the current object and return (a reference to) that object. The postfix operator++() has much more work. It first saves a copy of the current object into the tmp object. Then it increments the current object, and returns (by value) the tmp object. It is important that tmp be returned by value; it is a bad (and common) error to return a reference to (or a pointer to) a local variable.

		May Be Inherited?	Member or Friend?	May Be Virtual?	Return Value
Subscripting	operator[]()	yes	member	yes	any
Member Access	operator–>()	yes	member	yes	restricted
Function Call	operator()()	yes	member	yes	any

The subscript operator lets you use array access syntax to access a class. This lets you create bounds-checked arrays, sparse arrays, virtual arrays, associative arrays, and the like. The subscript operator is a binary operator. The left operand must be an object. The right operand must be a type specified in the function declaration, and the right operand is delivered to the operator function as an argument.

Here is a simple example class that contains an array of ints whose indices are a..z (or equivalently A..Z):

```
// an array of ints indexed by letters
class subscriptdemo {
  public:
    int& operator[](char c) {
      if (islower(c)) return val[c-'a'];
      else if (isupper(c)) return val[c-'A'];
      else return x;
    }
  protected:
    int val[26];
    int x;  // error (don't care) bucket
};
```

Here's how you might use the subscriptdemo class to count characters from the standard input:

```
#include <stdio.h>
void main()
```

```
{
  subscriptdemo counts;
  int ch;
  while((ch = getchar()) != EOF)
     counts[ch]++;
  for(ch='a'; ch<='z'; ch+=2)
     printf("%c %4d    %c %4d\n",
        ch, counts[ch],
        ch+1, counts[ch+1]);
}
```

The member access operator lets you create smart pointers, access gates, and the like. Somewhat surprisingly, the member access operator is considered a unary operator of its left operand. What looks like the right operand is not delivered to the operator function. In fact, what looks like the right operand is the name of a class, struct, or union member. The return value of the member access operator must be one of the following:

- An object for which operator[]() is defined. (But not the original type of object.)

- A true pointer to a class, struct, or union that contains the member mentioned to the right of the –> symbol.

Note that the member access operator is the only way to attain this type of functionality, because the . (member of) operator is not overloadable.

Here is an example of the member access operator in which a class TAccess is used to gain entry to a class called TSecure. TSecure has a public data value, private constructors, and a friend class TAccess.

```
class TSecure {
  friend class TAccess;
  public:
    int val;
  private:
    TSecure() {}        // default constructor
    TSecure(TSecure&) {} // copy constructor
};
class TAccess {
  public:
    TAccess() { p = new TSecure; }
    TSecure *operator->() { return p; }
  protected:
    TSecure *p;
};
```

If you create a TAccess object, its constructor will allocate a TSecure object and store a pointer to that object. Then you can use the operator–>( ) member of TAccess to access the value stored in the TSecure object:

```
TAccess a;
a->val = 1; // assign to val memb. of TSecure obj.
```

In a more realistic example, there would be more meaning to this mechanism. The TAccess and TSecure classes show only the mechanics of using operator–>( ).

The function call operator lets you use a function-call-like syntax with class objects. It is unique because it can have multiple "right" operands. The types of the right operands must match the types mentioned in the operator( )( ) function declaration. Here is a tiny example:

```
class calldemo {
  public:
    void operator()(char, int, double);
};
```

You can invoke the function call operator as follows (assume c is a calldemo object):

```
c('a', 1, 1.Ø);
```

I'm not a fan of the procedure call operator. I see little advantage to using the procedure call operator over simply defining a member function that does the same thing. For example, you could place the following function declaration in the calldemo class:

```
void fn(char, int, double);
```

And then you could invoke fn by writing

```
c.fn('a', 1, 1.Ø);
```

I suggest that you use ordinary named member functions in preference to using the function call operator.

		May Be Inherited?	Member or Friend?	May Be Virtual?	Return Value
new	operator new( )	yes	static member	no	void*
delete	operator delete( )	yes	static member	no	void

The new and delete operators are used to allocate and free memory. It is occasionally useful to write your own versions of these functions to gain control of memory allocation. The two most common reasons to micromanage allocation are to generate debugging or performance monitoring information, or to speed up allocation for classes with well-defined needs. For example, a class that is constantly allocating and freeing small chunks of memory might best be served by having its own allocator that manages a small pool of memory. In most cases, special-purpose memory allocators can operate more efficiently than general-purpose allocators.

The major restrictions on your own versions of new and delete are that they must be static member functions, operator new( ) must return a pointer to void, and operator delete( ) must have return type void. Operator new( ) is handed the size of the requested memory, which is a size_t type. (size_t is defined in <stddef.h>.) It should return a pointer to a region of memory, or 0 to indicate an allocation failure. Operator delete is given a pointer to an allocated memory block (version 1) or a pointer to an allocated memory block plus the size of that block (version 2). You may only declare one of these two versions of delete.

Cloning Code with Templates

Classes are important because they are the basis of code reuse. The most important way to reuse a class is *inheritance*. Starting with a class that does most of what you want, inheritance allows you to specialize and extend the class, while maintaining much of its original functionality. Inheritance has proven to be a major advance in software technology. It is, other than the class itself, the most important new feature of C++.

But there are some important problems that aren't helped much by inheritance. For example, consider a class to manage a list of objects. Such a class would have a way to move forward and backward through the list, functions to add and remove elements, and perhaps functions to search for a specific element. What we would like to do is create a generic list class, and then create specific versions that implement lists of points, lists of windows, lists of menus, lists of doubles, and so forth. Unfortunately, inheritance doesn't help, because all of the functions in a list need to know the type of element comprising the list.

Two solutions have been used in the past. The first is to create list classes whose elements are generic (void *) pointers. This allows you to have a list of anything, but it has drawbacks:

- No type safety.

- Because of the lack of type information, operations such as sorting and searching are extremely clumsy and inefficient.

The other historical solution is to use the preprocessor to build a specific list class from a generic list class prototype. This approach actually works pretty well, other than the bother of creating huge macros, each line terminated by a backslash. One drawback is that the preprocessor isn't part of the language proper, which can lead to subtle problems. Another difficulty is portability, because the preprocessor's capacity varies significantly from system to system. I once created some large macros using one compiler, and then discovered that they exceeded the capacity of another.

A better solution, which has only recently become a part of C++, is to use *templates*. A template is a parameterized blueprint. The parameters are either types or values. Templates allow you to fill in the blueprint, specifying the types of the materials, the positions of the utilities, and so forth. With templates you can code an algorithm just once, and then create implementations of that algorithm for specific types.

Templates are usually used to implement *container classes*. A container class is used to store something. There are many types of container classes because of the multitude of storage requirements. In brief, containers are commonly used to implement vectors (arrays) that are optimized for indexed access; lists that are optimized for sequential access and flexible insertion/extraction; trees for flexible multidimensional structures; stacks for last-in, first-out storage; queues for first-in, first-out storage; and so forth. Borland C++ contains a comprehensive, template-based container class library that addresses these issues, which I will cover in Chapter 5.

Templates apply to both classes and functions. First I'm going to present a short example of template classes, which will demonstrate the syntax and mechanics. Then I'll complete the discussion with a brief example of a function template.

I worked hard to think of a template example that didn't overlap with the template code in the Borland class library. Thus I considered the traditional container classes, lists, queues, and such, to be off-limits. I finally arrived at the following, which was inspired by the conglomeration of plastic milk crates that my six-year-old son uses to store his treasures. When we ask Reed to clean up, things are deposited into these crates. When Reed plays, bits and pieces of once-expensive toys emerge in seemingly random order. Some toys enter the crates but never leave. The software analog is the TBlackHole container class, which lets you deposit, but randomly returns things when you withdraw.

The TBlackHole class is, like most of the short examples in this part of the book, primarily oriented toward demonstrating the language feature. For more realistic examples of templates you should examine the Borland class libraries, which make extensive use of templates to build the container class library.

The TBlackHole template class contains three public members: a default constructor, a PutIn( ) member function to insert items, and a TakeOut( ) member function to withdraw things. The constructor creates an array of values and initializes a few housekeeping variables. The PutIn( ) member fills the array slots in order. When the end is reached, it circles back to the beginning and starts over. Yes, values are overwritten, but so what? This is a black hole! The TakeOut( ) member function randomly picks one of the deposited entries and returns it.

It is easy to be put off and intimidated by the syntax for declaring a template class. Unfortunately, there is a lot of information for you to convey to the compiler, and this leads to lots of keystrokes and a dense look. Let me try to go through it slowly, because once you understand it you'll find it's not so bad.

First, remember that templates are also called *parameterized classes,* and they work very similarly to parameterized #define macros. If you were to fake a template using a #define macro, it would look something like this:

```
#define MyNewClass(MyType,siz)  \
  class MyClass ## MyType {      \
  .  .  .                        \
  MyType val[siz];               \
  .  .  .                        \
  body of class                  \
  .  .  .                        \
  };
```

The first line of this fakery introduces the parameter, which is called MyType, the second line builds a class name using preprocessor token concatenation, and then the subsequent lines define the body of the class.

Template class definitions are organized similarly. Here is the template class definition for the TBlackHole class:

```
template <class T, unsigned max = 100>
class TBlackHole {
public:
  TBlackHole();
  ~TBlackHole() { if (!bad) delete Vals; }
  void PutIn(const T& newval);
  const T& TakeOut();
protected:
  T *Vals;
  const int maxVals;
  int nVals;
  int putIndex;
  int bad;
};
```

The first line sets the scene and details the parameters, and then the following lines define the class blueprint. Inside the class definition, the identifier T refers to a user-supplied type, and the identifier max refers to a user-supplied unsigned value, whose default value is 100.

One misleading aspect of template declarations is how the word "class" is used in the first line. The syntax for a template declaration is the following:

```
template < template-argument-list > declaration
```

Inside the template-argument-list, you should interpret the word "class" to mean "type." The parameter T refers to any user-supplied type, not just to class types. On the second line, "class TBlackHole {", the word class has its usual meaning.

All three TBlackHole member functions are shown in Listing 3.3.

LISTING 3.3

TBlackHole

```
//
// TBlackHole member functions
//
template <class T, unsigned max>
TBlackHole<T,max>::TBlackHole() :
  maxVals(max),
  putIndex(Ø),
  nVals(Ø),
  Vals(new T[max]),  // T needs default constructor
  bad(Ø)
{
  if (!Vals)
    bad++;
}

template <class T, unsigned max>
void TBlackHole<T,max>::PutIn(const T& newval)
{
  if (bad)
    return;
  if (putIndex >= maxVals)
    putIndex = Ø;  // back to beginning
  if (nVals < maxVals)
    nVals++;
  Vals[putIndex++] = newval;
}

template <class T, unsigned max>
const T& TBlackHole<T,max>::TakeOut()
{
  static T x;
  if (bad || nVals == Ø)
    return x;
  return Vals[rand() % nVals];
}
```

Let me go over one of the TBlackHole member functions in more detail. Here is the simplest TBlackHole member function, TakeOut():

```
template <class T, unsigned max>
const T& TBlackHole<T,max>::TakeOut()
{
    static T x;
    if (bad || nVals == Ø)
        return x;
    return Vals[rand() % nVals];
}
```

The first line consists of the keyword "template" followed by the template-argument-list. This line is the same as the first line of the TBlackHole template class definition, except that the default value for max is purposely omitted. The reason for this line is to tell the compiler and the reader that we are starting a template declaration, and to introduce the parameters for that declaration.

The second line is a somewhat ordinary header for a member function definition. Remember that ordinarily a member function header specifies the return type, followed by class-name::, followed by the function name and argument list. If you look carefully, you'll see that's exactly what is present, although the template parameterization makes it a bit murky. Here are the elements one by one:

- **Function return type—const T&**   T refers to the user-supplied type. This is the essence of using templates. The TakeOut() function will return whatever type you want. You can build a TBlackHole class to store any type; its TakeOut() member will return that type.

- **Class-name::—TBlackHole<T,max>::**   When you are defining a template-class member function, you must use the generic name for the template class, which consists of your own class name (TBlackHole in this example) followed by the argument list.

- **Function-name()—TakeOut()**

Listing 3.4 shows a small main() that creates a couple of black holes.

Here is the declaration that creates a black hole object named sink to store integers:

```
TBlackHole<int,1Ø> sink;
```

The desired black hole size could have been omitted if you wanted to accept the default of 100.

Typedef statements are often used with templates to ease the syntax burden. Here is a typedef statement that creates a simple type name for the integer black hole:

```
typedef TBlackHole<int> IntBlackHole;
```

LISTING 3.4

Using the TBlackHole template class

```c
#include <stdio.h>
#include <math.h>
void main()
{
  // build a black hole for ints
  TBlackHole<int,10> BlkHole;
  int i;
  for(i=0; i<10; i++)
    BlkHole.PutIn(i*i);
  for(i=0; i<10; i++)
    printf("%d %d\n", i, BlkHole.TakeOut());

  // build a black hole for doubles
  TBlackHole<double,20> dblBlkHole;
  for(i=0; i<10; i++)
    dblBlkHole.PutIn(pow(10.0*i, 2));
  for(i=0; i<10; i++)
    printf("%d %g\n", i, dblBlkHole.TakeOut());
{
```

Templates for functions are very similar. Here is a template that lets you clone swap( ) functions:

```c
template <class T>
void swap(T& v1, T& v2)
{
  T tmp;
  tmp = v1;
  v1 = v2;
  v2 = tmp;
}
```

If you call swap(d1, d2) where d1 and d2 are doubles, then the compiler will create a double version of swap, and use it to swap the two values.

One small caveat is that the compiler performs minimal type promotion on templates that it builds implicitly. This is to avoid subtle errors. So if c is a char and i is an int, the call swap(c,i) will produce an error, because the compiler will refuse to promote the char to an int. You can avoid this difficulty by explicitly telling the compiler about specific versions of the function that you want it to generate. For example, you could follow the above template declaration of swap( ) with this line, to tell the compiler to build an integer version of swap( ):

```c
void swap(int, int);
```

Because you have explicitly requested an integer version of swap(), the compiler will use standard promotions with that version. This will allow you to swap, say, an int and a char.

You can also provide your own versions of a template function, so that you can take over in those situations that don't fit the mold. Simply define the desired function, and the compiler will use your explicit version in preference to building one with the same signature from the template.

If you think a little bit about what is happening when the compiler creates specific functions and classes from your template blueprints, you might wonder about multiple definitions. If you put the swap() template into a header and build swap(int,int) in multiple source files, the compiler will create a swap(int,int) in each. With ordinary functions, this would be a big problem. But the Borland C++ linker allows multiple definition of template functions and classes; it will discard the superfluous instances. You can get this default behavior using the -Jg compiler switch.

Sometimes it is preferable to use a more traditional architecture, in which you have a single file that generates the template instances, and other files refer to those instances. This alternative architecture is enabled by using the -Jgd compiler switch to compile the file containing the template instances, and using -Jgx to compile your other files to refer to those templates.

Structs, Classes, and Pointers to Them

C's data structure is the struct, while C++ has both structs and classes. (Both have unions, which are more a data storage shortcut than a proper data structure.) In C++, classes and structs are almost the same, but you must know the few differences. And one other thing: You must understand the difference between how C and C++ interpret *struct tags*. Those are the topics of the next few sections.

Struct Tags, C versus C++

In C we might declare a simple struct named COMPLEX to store values that have real and imaginary components:

```
struct COMPLEX {          /* C or C++ COMPLEX definition */
    double real;
    double imag;
};
```

In C, the word COMPLEX in the struct definition is called a tag, and it is used to declare individual instances of a COMPLEX:

```
struct COMPLEX p, q[10];  /* C declaration of
                             a COMPLEX p and an
                             array of 10 COMPLEX q's */
```

A tag in C isn't a true type name, which explains why you have to write "struct COMPLEX" to declare individual COMPLEX items.

The main difference in C++ is that both struct and class definitions create new types. So in C++ the above definition of COMPLEX, which is a perfectly valid C++ struct definition, creates a new type called COMPLEX. Once the definition of COMPLEX has been encountered, C++ allows you to use the word COMPLEX (by itself!) to declare COMPLEX objects.

```
COMPLEX m, n[1Ø];        // C++ declaration of
                         // 11 COMPLEX objects
```

C++, Structs versus Classes

C++ classes are based on C structs, and they are declared similarly to C structs. For example, the preceding definition of the COMPLEX struct can be recast as a C++ class:

```
class TComplex {         // C++ TComplex definition
    double real;
    double imag;
};
```

In C++, there are two main differences between a struct and a class. Yes, only two. The first is technical: Members of a struct are public by default, while members of a class are private by default. Both structs and classes allow you to use access specifiers (the private, protected, and public keywords) to control access, although in practice they are rarely used in structs. Thus the preceding TComplex class isn't equivalent to the COMPLEX struct, because TComplex's members are private. Here is the exact equivalent.

```
class TPubComplex {   // C++ TPubComplex definition
  public:
    double real;
    double imag;
};
```

The other difference between classes and structs is more philosophical. Classes should be used to create objects, entities that encompass both data and procedures. Structs should be reserved for their traditional role, collecting related data items into a single package. C++ won't prevent you from adding a gaggle of member functions to a struct, and it won't force you to make a class active. But you should use structs for data and use classes for objects, so that others will understand your work.

Pointing to Classes

If you build a sparkling new class, you're likely to also want pointers to that class, references to that class, and so on. That's why Borland C++ contains the _CLASSDEF macro. If you examine Borland's C++ header files, you'll notice that each class is preceded by the _CLASSDEF macro. For example, if you were creating a header file containing the above TPubComplex class, you would place the following line above the TPubComplex definition:

```
_CLASSDEF(TPubComplex)
```

Note that _CLASSDEF is a macro; don't use a terminating semicolon!

The _CLASSDEF macro uses typedef statements to create the following type names:

Type Name	Use
PTPubComplex	Pointer (P) to a TPubComplex object
RTPubComplex	Reference (R) to a TPubComplex object
RPTPubComplex	Reference to a pointer (RP) to a TPubComplex object
PCTPubComplex	Pointer to a constant (PC) TPubComplex object
RCTPubComplex	Reference to a constant (RC) TPubComplex object

As you can see, the _CLASSDEF macro affixes a character or two to the beginning of the class name to form the type name. Here's how you might use some of the type names created by the _CLASSDEF macro.

```
TPubComplex Root;              // TPubComplex object
RTPubComplex rRoot = Root;     // reference
PTPubComplex pRoot = &rRoot;   // pointer
void Solve(RCTPubComplex p);   // function taking
                               // reference to const
```

When you see type names such as PTWindowsObject in Borland header files, you should pay particular attention to the prefixes: P for pointer, R for reference, C for const, and T for TYPE.

INHERITANCE

IN 1866 GREGOR MENDEL, AN AUSTRIAN MONK AND SCHOLAR, PUBLISHED A paper describing how plants inherit traits from their ancestors. This seminal work, whose importance wasn't recognized for about 30 years, revolutionized the study of biology. Today similar ideas are being applied to software development, so that new data types can be created by inheriting from existing data types.

In biology, inheritance lets organisms specialize in order to better survive in their habitat. Similarly, in software development we use inheritance to create more specialized classes that meet our needs better than existing classes. As in nature, inheritance in software development lets us make fine adjustments; it lets us adapt working systems.

Deriving Classes

The easy part of learning about inheritance is learning the mechanics of deriving one class from another by using C++; the hard part is learning how to apply this new technique to your own work. Let me start with the easy part through a fanciful example that demonstrates the basic language features for inheritance. Throughout the rest of this book I'll address the harder subject, learning how and when to use inheritance to improve your code and your productivity.

Let's start with a simple base class and then use it to derive a new class. The base class is TThing, which represents something that might be found in a grade B horror flick.

```
class TThing {
  public:
    TThing(); // default constructor
    void Growl();
    void OozeIck();
    void PlayDead();
  protected:
    int gallonsOfIck;
    int deadTime;
  private:
    char thoughts;
};
```

Grade B horror flicks rarely have only a single unpleasant thing, rather there are usually many slightly different dreadful things. Here's how we can derive a TLoudGreenThing from a TThing.

```
class TLoudGreenThing : public TThing {
  public:
    TLoudGreenThing();   // constructor
    void Shriek();
  protected:
    int pitch;
};
```

You can tell that TLoudGreenThing is a derived class from its header. The header starts normally, the word class followed by the class name, but then there is a phrase that specifies the derivation: first a colon, then the word "public," and then finally the name of the base class.

The word public in the header specifies public derivation, which is the normal form of derivation. Public derivation means that the derived class can be used in place of the base class, and it means that public and protected base class members remain public and protected in the derived class. C++ also supports protected and private derivation, which are used much less often. The derivation defaults to private if none is specified explicitly, so remember to write public when you want the usual public derivation.

A TLoudGreenThing can do anything a TThing can do, plus it can Shriek(). Each TLoudGreenThing object stores the same information as a TThing object, plus it stores the pitch of the Shriek. These characteristics are shown more concretely by the following example.

```
void Scene1()
{
  TThing oscar;
  TLoudGreenThing gomez;
  oscar.OozeIck(); // a TThing can ooze ick
  gomez.OozeIck(); // so can a TLoudGreenThing
  gomez.Shriek();  // Only a TLoudGreenThing can shriek
}
```

Inheritance is a shorthand. It lets you state that a derived class is the same as its base class, except for a set of additions and changes. But this marvelous shorthand, like all shorthands, can only be understood if you know the code. For example, the statement "call bg tom am" only makes sense if you know that call means make a telephone call, bg is a person, tom means tomorrow, and am means morning. Similarly the statement "class TLoudGreenThing : public TThing" means that TThing is a part of TLoudGreenThing. To fully understand a derived class (for example, TLoudGreenThing) you must understand its base class (for example, TThing), the base class's base classes, and so on.

Public Derivation: The *is a* Relationship

The most common form of derivation is public derivation, because it expresses the most frequently desired relation between derived and base classes, the *is a* relation. When you use public derivation, the derived class has an *is a* relationship with the base class. This means a derived object can be used anywhere a base object can be used; a derived object can be assigned to a base object, a pointer to a derived object can be used wherever a pointer to a base object can be used, and so on. In short, although a derived class may have its own characteristics that go beyond those of the base class, it still has all the base class characteristics and can be used in the same way as a base class.

Here is an example that shows a few ways in which a derived object is used where a base class object is required. (It uses the TThing and TLoudGreenThing classes from the previous example.)

```
void Scene2(TThing *p);   // param: pointer to TThing
void Scene3(TThing t);    // param: TThing
void Scene4(TThing& rt);  // param: reference to TThing
void Scene5()
{
  TThing toth;
  TLoudGreenThing tven;
  Scene2(&tven);    // is a
  Scene3(tven);     // is a
  Scene4(tven);     // is a
  toth = tven;      // is a
}
```

Remember that the *is a* relation only works in one direction. A derived object *is a* base object, but not the converse. This follows from simple logic. The derived class is likely to have members not present in the base, so there is no way for a base object to substitute for a derived object. For example, in the Scene5() function you couldn't write

```
tven = toth;      // illegal, base is not a derived
```

The problem is that toth, a TThing object, *is not* a TLoudGreenThing. The toth object can't be used in a situation, such as on the right side of a TLoudGreenThing assignment, where a TLoudGreenThing is required.

Even though a base can't be used in place of a derived, there are times when what looks like a base is actually a derived. In those occasional instances it is safe to explicitly use a cast to convert base to derived, as shown in this example.

```
void TakeTwo()
{
  TThing *pThing = new TLoudGreenThing;
  TLoudGreenThing pLGT = new TLoudGreenThing;
  *pLGT = *(TLoudGreenThing *)pThing;
}
```

Remember, when you cast from base to derived, it is your responsibility to ensure that the cast makes sense. It will only work when what looks like a base really is a derived.

Table 4.1 shows that in public derivation the public and protected members of a base class retain their accessibility in the derived class. However, the private members of the base class are not accessible from a derived class member function. Table 4.1 first introduces the idea of inaccessible members. You can't declare a member to be inaccessible—what would be the point of that? But in a derived class the private members of the base are inaccessible, as are any already inaccessible members of the base class.

TABLE 4.1

Accessibility of Base Class Members

Base Class Access	Accessibility in a Privately Derived Class	Accessibility in a Protected Derived Class	Accessibility in a Publicly Derived Class
Inaccessible	Inaccessible	Inaccessible	Inaccessible
Private	Inaccessible	Inaccessible	Inaccessible
Protected	Private	Protected	Protected
Public	Private	Protected	Public

This is the key difference between private and protected members.

- Private members are only accessible to a class's own member functions and to friend classes or functions; they are not accessible to member functions of a derived class.

- Protected members are accessible to a class's own member functions, to member functions of derived classes, and to friend classes or functions.

Private and Protected Derivation:
The *composed of* Relationship

Although public derivation is by far the most common, C++ also supports both private and protected derivation. There are two key differences between public derivation and the other two forms of derivation.

- In protected and private derivation the base class members are less accessible than in public derivation. Table 4.1 summarizes the differences. This means that public base class members are accessible to member functions of the derived class, but they are not a part of the derived class's public interface.

- In protected and private derivation the derived class has a *composed of* (not an *is a*) relation with the base class.

The *composed of* relationship means that the derived class has a copy of the base, and it contains all of the functionality of the base, but derived class objects can't be used anywhere that base class objects are required. Again, simple logic is the key to understanding the rules. In a privately derived class the public base class members are private. But if there were an automatic conversion to base (that is, an *is a* relationship), then in any place where a conversion had occurred the base's public members would be public! To avoid this contradiction, automatic conversion from derived to base is not allowed for classes created using private and protected derivation.

Virtual Functions: Enabling Polymorphism

Polymorphism is a class's best form of self-expression. Polymorphism lets a class state that it has the same interface as a base class, but that the derived class's behavior is different than the base class's behavior. What's more, if you call a member function using a derived object, then the derived class's function will be invoked even if the function is invoked via a pointer (or reference) to base. Polymorphism means each derived type can have its own behavior. The *is a* relationship means that the common interface (the base class's interface) of a family of classes can be invoked using base class pointers or base class references.

Polymorphism is enabled by declaring a base class function to be *virtual*. Then in the derived class, any function with the same name and signature will also be virtual, whether or not it is declared virtual.

Listing 4.1 shows a brief program that demonstrates polymorphism. The program contains a base class named TDice and three derived classes. The base class contains two polymorphic member functions, Roll() and Title(). Each of the derived classes in Listing 4.1 implements a different type of random number generator. The TDice2 class implements a coin, the TDice4 class implements a tetrahedron, and the TDice6 class implements a standard six-sided die. Each of the derived classes in this example happens to define both Roll() and Title() member functions, although there is no requirement for a derived class to define a virtual base class function. If a derived class doesn't define a base class's virtual function, it simply picks up the base class's behavior.

LISTING 4.1

The Dice Program

```c
#include <stdlib.h>
#include <stdio.h>
#include <time.h>
//
// Dice base class
//
class TDice {
  public:
    virtual int Roll() { return Ø; }
    virtual const char *Title() { return ""; }
};
//
// two sided device (a coin)
//
class TDice2 : public TDice {
  public:
    int Roll() { return rand() % 2; }
    const char *Title() { return "Flip a coin"; }
};
//
// four sided device (a tetrahedron)
//
class TDice4 : public TDice {
  public:
    int Roll() { return rand() % 4; }
    const char *Title() { return "Tumble a t'hedron"; }
};
//
// six sided device (a die)
//
class TDice6 : public TDice {
  public:
    int Roll() { return rand() % 6; }
    const char *Title() { return "Roll a dice"; }
};
//
// use an object of a class derived from the TDice class
//
void main()
{
  TDice *dice;  // pointer to base
  // allocate a derived object
  srand((unsigned) time(NULL));
```

LISTING 4.1

The Dice Program (Continued)

```
switch(rand()%3) {
  case 0: dice = new TDice2; break;
  case 1: dice = new TDice4; break;
  case 2: dice = new TDice6; break;
}
printf("%s: ", dice->Title());
for(int i = 0; i < 10; i++)
  printf("%d ", dice->Roll());
printf("\n");
}
```

The main() routine in Listing 4.1 demonstrates the polymorphic behavior of the Roll() and Title() functions. At the beginning of main(), a switch statement randomly creates one of the specified types of object. Thus there is no way for the compiler to know in advance what type of object will be used at the bottom of main(), when the object's Roll() and Title() member functions are invoked. When the program is executed, the appropriate versions of Roll() and Title() are invoked, based on the runtime object type.

Pure Virtual Functions: Enabling Abstract Classes

In many class families, the base class is a useful and functional class, and the derived classes simply refine and extend the base class's behavior. In this type of class hierarchy, it is reasonable to create objects of the base class type and of the derived types. But there are also situations in which the base class is simply a skeleton or a framework, and only the derived classes are useful and functional. For example, in the preceding Dice example (Listing 4.1) the TDice base class doesn't implement a specific random generator. Instead the TDice base class outlines the shape of the class, and then the derived classes implement the functionality.

As written in Listing 4.1, the TDice base class supplies generic function bodies for the Title() and Roll() member functions. Here's the TDice class definition to refresh your memory:

```
class TDice {
  public:
    virtual int Roll() { return 0; }
    virtual const char *Title() { return ""; }
};
```

There are a couple of problems with this TDice definition:

■ The Roll() and Title() functions have actions (function bodies), even though they are not intended to be called.

■ The TDice class can be used normally, even though the intent is obviously to use only TDice's derived classes.

Basically, TDice isn't expressing itself well. It is intended to be used only as a base class, but as written it is a perfectly good class by itself. The solution is to recast TDice's functions as *pure virtual functions*, which by implication makes TDice an *abstract class*.

```
class TDice {
  public:
    virtual int Roll() = 0;
    virtual const char *Title() = 0;
};
```

The notation "= 0;" following the virtual member function names makes them pure virtual functions. A pure virtual is a virtual function that doesn't need a body; it serves as an interface to derived class functionality. Each derived class must either define all of the base class's pure virtual functions, or the derived class itself will be an abstract class.

An abstract class is either a class that contains a pure virtual function, or a class that inherits a pure virtual function and doesn't define that function. You can't create an instance of an abstract class, although it is okay to have pointers to an abstract class or references to an abstract class. Thus all of the following declarations are allowed for the abstract TDice class:

```
// pointer to TDice family object
TDice *pDice;
// function taking a reference to a TDice family object
void RollOne(TDice& rDice);
```

The pDice pointer can't really point at a TDice object, instead it will always point at an object from one of TDice's derived classes. Similarly the RollOne() function won't be called with an actual TDice object, but with an object from one of TDice's derived classes. What's not allowed is to do anything that creates a true TDice object. Thus both of the following are not allowed:

```
// illegal: can't create a TDice
TDice *pDice = new TDice;
// illegal: can't pass a TDice object
void RollTwo(TDice dice);
```

There are two reasons to make a class abstract. The first is to avoid writing useless function bodies, and the second is to prevent users from creating instances of the class. When you're creating a family of classes, and only the derived classes should be instantiated, consider using pure virtual functions in the base class.

To be complete, there's one small additional point that needs to be discussed. It is possible to create a function body for a pure virtual function. In the class definition you use the standard "= 0;" notation to specify that a function is pure virtual, but then you are allowed separately to specify the function's body. The class will still be abstract, derived classes will still be required to define the function (or they will be abstract), and any calls of the function will be passed to a derived class. The only way to call a defined pure virtual function is to use the scope resolution operator. Even though defining the body of a pure virtual is allowed by the C++ language definition, it is a C++ feature that I don't recommend because it is confusing. Once I've noticed that a base class function is pure virtual, I expect any calls of that function to invoke a derived class version. If you need a base class function that does something, don't make it a pure virtual.

Using Base Class Constructors

If a base class has a default constructor, and the derived class wants to use that constructor, then you don't need to do anything explicitly. The compiler will ensure that, in the absence of other instructions from you, the base class's default constructor will be invoked. But often you want to use a base class constructor other than the default constructor. For example, the TDonut class from Chapter 3 defines four constructors. Here is a repeat of the TDonut class definition:

```
class TDonut {
  public:
    enum TFlavor
      { Plain, Chocolate };
    enum TFilling
      { None, VanCream, ChocCream, Jelly };
    // constructors
    TDonut();             // default
    TDonut(TDonut &d);    // copy
    TDonut(TFlavor f);
    TDonut(TFlavor flav, TFilling fill);
    // destructor
    ~TDonut();
  protected:
    const TFlavor Flavor;
    const TFilling Filling;
    static int DonutCount;
};
```

My friend Jasmine invented a new type of donut that is bigger and richer than a standard donut. Like ordinary donuts, Jasmine's bigger donuts have both a flavor and a filling. Here is a class definition for Jasmine's bigger donuts. Like the TDonut class, the TBigDonut class has four constructors. The TBigDonut constructors, like the TDonut constructors, consist of a default constructor, a copy constructor, a constructor that requires a TFlavor argument, and a constructor that requires both a TFlavor and a TFilling constructor.

```
class TBigDonut : public TDonut {
  public:
    // constructors
    TBigDonut()             // TBigDonut default constr.
      { return; }
    TBigDonut(TBigDonut &d) : // TBigDonut copy constr.
      TDonut(d)             // TDonut copy constructor
      { return; }
    TBigDonut(TFlavor f) :
      TDonut(f)             // TDonut(TFlavor) constructor
      { return; }
    TBigDonut(TFlavor flav, TFilling fill) :
      TDonut(flav, fill) // TDonut(TFlavor, TFilling)
      { return; }
    // destructor
    ~TBigDonut()
      { return; }
};
```

The default TBigDonut constructor doesn't explicitly invoke a base class constructor, so the compiler will automatically use the default TDonut base class constructor. The other three TBigDonut constructors use their initialization lists to specify which base class constructor should be used. Note that when you use a constructor initialization list to initialize a data member, you use that member's name in the list. However, for a base class, you use the base class type name in the initialization list.

I mentioned that you don't have to explicitly ask to use a default base class constructor, because by default the compiler will use it if it exists and you haven't specified another constructor. But I'm in favor of being as clear as possible, so let me show how you explicitly invoke the base class constructor in a derived class. Here is the default TBigDonut constructor, slightly rewritten to explicitly invoke the default base class constructor.

```
class TBigDonut : public TDonut {
  public:
    // constructors
    TBigDonut() :      // TBigDonut default constr.
      TDonut()         // TDonut default constructor
      { return; }
```

```
    . . .  // remainder unchanged
  };
```

I am comfortable with allowing the compiler to invoke a default constructor, so I usually write derived class constructors as shown in the first version of TBigDonut. But if you prefer to be super-explicit, use the second version.

Multiple Inheritance

The beginning of this chapter has discussed *single inheritance*, which means each derived class inherits traits from a single base class. *Multiple inheritance* extends this capability so that a derived class can inherit traits from more than one base class. This lets a derived class combine, blend, and extend the characteristics of several base classes. Multiple inheritance lets a derived class have an *is a* relationship with several public base classes. Thus the derived class can be used in place of any of its public base classes, just as in the single inheritance case.

The syntax for multiple inheritance is a simple extension of the syntax for single inheritance. Instead of writing a single base class in the derived class's header, place a comma-separated list of base classes in the header. For each base class you should specify public, protected, or private. If you omit the specifier, private will be used by default.

Listing 4.2 shows a simple example of multiple inheritance. The two base classes are TDice, which is the same as TDice from Listing 4.1 except that the member functions are pure virtual, and TLog, which is a simple event-logging class that records times and event ID numbers each time the Record() member function is called. The TLog class also has a Show() member function to print the event log.

LISTING 4.2 ▇▇▇▇▇▇▇▇▇▇▇▇▇▇▇▇▇▇▇▇▇▇▇▇▇▇▇▇▇▇▇▇

The Dice2 Program

```
#include <stdlib.h>
#include <stdio.h>
#include <time.h>
#include <arrays.h>
#include <dos.h>
#include <string.h>
//
// Logging base class
//
class TLog {
  public:
    TLog() :    // constructor
      times(49, Ø, 5Ø),
      events(49, Ø, 5Ø)
    { return; }
```

LISTING 4.2

The Dice2 Program (Continued)

```
      void Record(char eventId) {
        times.add(time(NULL));
        events.add(eventId);
      }
      void Show();
    protected:
      BI_ArrayAsVector<long> times;
      BI_ArrayAsVector<char> events;
};
//
// show the event log
//
void TLog::Show()
{
  char buf[3Ø];
  int i;
  for(i = Ø; i < times.getItemsInContainer(); i++) {
    strcpy(buf, ctime(&times[i]));
    buf[24] = Ø; // strip nl
    printf("Event %d, %s: %d\n", i, buf, events[i]);
  }
}
//
// Dice base class (abstract)
//
class TDice {
  public:
    virtual int Roll() = Ø;          // pure virtual
    virtual const char *Title() = Ø; // pure virtual
};
//
// two sided device (a coin)
//
class TDice2 : public TDice, public TLog {
  public:
    int Roll()
    {
      int val = rand() % 2;
      Record(val);
      return val;
    }
    const char *Title() { return "Flip a coin"; }
};
```

LISTING 4.2

The Dice2 Program (Continued)

```
//
// use a TDice2 class object
//
void main()
{
  TDice2 dice;
  printf("%s\n", dice.Title());
  for(int i = 0; i < 10; i++) {
    sleep(rand()%3);
    dice.Roll();
  }
  dice.Show();
}
```

The TDice2 class in Listing 4.2 is derived from both TDice and TLog. Because TDice2 is derived from TDice, it defines its own Roll() and Title() member functions. And because TDice2 is derived from TLog, it has direct use of TLog's Record() and Show() member functions. All of these features of TDice2 are shown in the main() routine in Listing 4.2. An inheritance diagram of these classes is shown in Figure 4.1.

FIGURE 4.1

Inheritance of TDice2

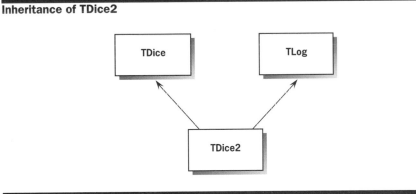

One final note on Listing 4.2. The TLog class member functions use the array template container classes from the Borland container class library. These classes will be discussed fully in Chapter 5, and further examples of their use will be shown in Chapter 6.

Virtual Base Classes

Multiple inheritance adds significant complexity to C++ in various subtle ways. It is so difficult an area that single inheritance was a part of the language for many years before multiple inheritance was introduced. Although many of the difficulties of multiple inheritance can be relegated to the people who write the compiler, a few difficulties must be faced directly by you, the software developer. This section and the next two present the three principal issues that you must face if you choose to use multiple inheritance in your work, or if you choose to use class libraries that use multiple inheritance.

The first issue is how to handle a base class that appears in an inheritance diagram more than once. Consider the following simple example:

```
class A { } ;
class B1 : public A { } ;
class B2 : public A { } ;
class D : public B1, public B2 { } ;
```

Classes B1 and B2 are derived from A, and class D is derived from B1 and B2. This relationship is diagrammed in Figure 4.2.

FIGURE 4.2

Class D inheritance, using two copies of Class A

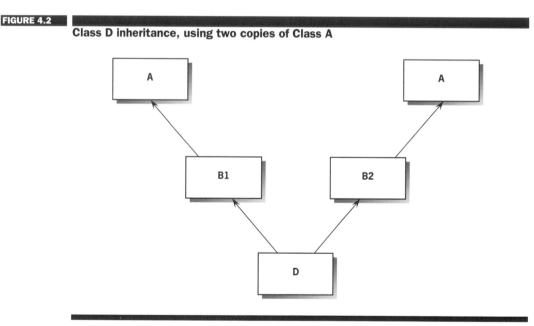

What you should notice in Figure 4.2 is that class A appears twice, once via each of class D's base classes. Sometimes this is just what you want. For example, if class A is an integral part of B1, and an integral part of B2, then you probably want two copies of A in class D. But at other times it makes more sense to have only a single copy of A, as shown in Figure 4.3.

The key to achieving the relationship shown in Figure 4.3 is to make A a virtual base class. When the compiler is building a class, it takes all of the virtual instances of a class and coalesces them into a single instance. Here is how we would change the preceding example to make A a virtual base of B1 and B2.

```
class A { } ;
class B1 : public virtual A { } ;
class B2 : public virtual A { } ;
class D : public B1, public B2 { } ;
```

FIGURE 4.3

Class D inheritance, using a single copy of Class A

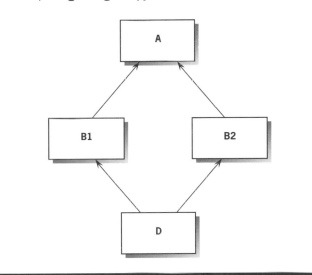

It is also possible for a class to be included in both virtual and non-virtual versions. When this happens, all of the virtual instances are combined into a single instance, while all of the non-virtual instances are treated normally and included individually.

Casting and Virtual Base Classes

Virtual base classes solve one problem, but they quickly introduce another. Normally, a pointer to a base class can be cast to be a pointer to a derived class, because often a base class pointer is actually pointing at a derived class. But when a base class is virtual, it is very hard for a compiler to know how to perform this cast. The basic difficulty is that a compiler needs great freedom to rearrange the layout of virtual base classes. This freedom conflicts with the usual way that a compiler implements a cast from base to derived, which is to know exactly how they are stored in memory.

The following example illustrates the difficulty.

```
class A { };
class B1 : public virtual A { };
```

```
void goo()
{
  B1 *pb = new B1;   // a B1* pointing at a B1
  A *pa = new B1;    // an A* pointing at a B1
  *pb = *(B1 *)pa;   // illegal, can't cast from
                     // virtual base to derived
}
```

If A weren't a virtual base, then the cast in the last line of goo() would be legal, because the compiler would know the class layout and would know how to make the cast. But because A in the example is a virtual base, the layout is problematic and the cast is not allowed.

Constructors and Virtual Base Classes

When a class is an ordinary base, not a virtual base, then the constructors of the derived control which base class constructors are invoked. That's the usual situation. But when a class is a virtual base, things are much less straightforward because there are many derived classes, each with equal claim on the base class. Since the virtual base should only be initialized once, we need a rule to specify which derived class actually controls the activation of a virtual base's constructor. The solution adopted by C++ is to let the class of the actual object, sometimes called the most derived class, be in charge.

For example, if Z has, via many twisty turns, a virtual base called A, then it is up to Z's constructors to control which of A's constructors are invoked. If A has a default constructor and a Z constructor doesn't explicitly refer to A in its initialization list, then A's default constructor will be used. However—and here's the surprise—if A only has argument-taking (non-default) constructors, then Z must explicitly select one of A's constructors. This can be very surprising, especially if Z and A are widely separated in the inheritance tree.

Although the rule is that the most derived class is in control, by implication every derived class's constructors must specify which of A's constructors to use, because you can't know which of the derived will actually be created during run-time. Thus, if A has only argument-taking constructors, every class having A as a virtual base—no matter how distant—must explicitly provide constructors that invoke A constructors in their initialization lists.

The last surprise follows directly from all the others. If you have a class hierarchy with A as a virtual base, then only the initialization of A specified by the most derived class will be used; all the others will be skipped. I'm uncomfortable with this feature of C++ because when you look at the code, you see initializations that may or may not be performed. If a B object is created, then its initialization of virtual base A will be used. But if class C is derived from B, and a C object is created, then B's initialization of virtual base A will be skipped, and C's will be used instead. You must understand this feature to use the Turbo Vision library, because it contains several virtual base classes that require arguments.

PART 2
Borland Container Classes

THE BORLAND CLASS LIBRARY

IMPROVED CODE REUSE IS THE FUNDAMENTAL CLAIM OF OBJECT-ORIENTED development. Abstraction, inheritance, and polymorphism are wonderful ideas, but if they don't lead to extensive code reuse, then all we have is a palace coup, not a true revolution.

Code reuse has two components. The first is reuse of your own code. While you are developing your application, you should be thinking of ways in which your current work can be used in your future projects. Within any software domain, one program is much like another, except for the details. Design your classes for reuse, so that future projects can benefit from today's work.

The second aspect of code reuse is learning to use standard components in your designs.

- Don't build, buy.

- Don't reinvent, reuse.

Three major class libraries are supplied with Borland C++. Two of these libraries, OWL (Object Windows Library) and Turbo Vision, are application frameworks. They can help you with the user-interface aspect of your application, and they will be discussed in Parts 3 and 4 of this book.

The other class library supplied by Borland is simply called the *container class library,* although its title is a misnomer because it has more than just container classes. The container class library is stored in the classlib subdirectory of your \borlandc directory. Unlike Turbo Vision and OWL, the container class library is supplied with all versions of Borland C++.

Debugging Using Preconditions and Checks

Before I talk about the class libraries proper, let me touch upon the library's debugging aids. The Borland class libraries all include a file called checks.h that defines two macros named PRECONDITION and CHECK. You can use these macros to insert runtime checks in your code, so that you can take some action when an error occurs.

The PRECONDITION macro is intended to be used at the start of a function, to ensure that the function has been called properly. For example, if you try to pop() something from an empty stack, the PRECONDITION macro should jump in, print an error message, and exit. Here's a sketch of how you would achieve this in a function called pop( ):

```
someType pop()
{
    PRECONDITION(!isEmpty());
    // pop code goes here
    return value;
}
```

The CHECK macro also takes a single argument, and it also will print an error message and exit if the value of the argument is zero. The difference is that CHECK is intended to search for failures inside a routine. CHECK should be placed so that it looks for errors other than the error of calling a function erroneously.

As a general rule, you can disable CHECKs in a module once you are convinced that each routine in that module is working correctly. Usually you should enable the PRECONDITIONs somewhat longer, to guard against interface errors.

The CHECK and PRECONDITION macros are enabled and disabled by the __DEBUG preprocessor identifier. You should

- Define __DEBUG as 2 to enable both macros.

- Define __DEBUG as 1 to enable only the PRECONDITION macro.

- Define __DEBUG as 0 to disable both macros.

If you use the Borland class library, be very careful to give some value to the __DEBUG preprocessor identifier, because the checks.h file defines it as 2 if you don't define it! Using the IDE, specify __DEBUG=0 (or 1 or 2) in the Defines control of the Options-Compiler-CodeGeneration dialog. Using BCC, specify -D__DEBUG=0 on the command line. Or you can simply put a #define directive in your source, although you must remember to place it above your #include that pulls in any Borland class library header file.

Setting __DEBUG yourself is especially important if you use the template versions of the classes, because template code is actually compiled when you build your own code. Thus if you build a container using a template (details shortly) but don't set __DEBUG, you'll build a full debug version. This is often not what you want. This problem is much less severe with the non-template classes, because they are in libraries that were compiled with debugging off. (There is also a version of the library files compiled with PRECONDITIONs on, although you won't link to them unless you specifically request it.)

Both CHECK and PRECONDITION (and assert from the standard C library) call a subroutine called __assertfail( ) to actually output the failure message and abort the program. You can supply your own __assertfail( ) if you want to take over failure control. Listing 5.1 shows a small example that demonstrates how to write your own __assertfail( ) function.

LISTING 5.1

check.cpp

```
#define __DEBUG 2
#include <checks.h>
#include <stdio.h>
#include <stdlib.h>
//
// a custom __assertfail()
//
extern "C"
void _Cdecl __assertfail( char _FAR *__msg,
    char _FAR *__cond,
    char _FAR *__file,
    int __line)
{
    printf(__msg, __cond, __file, __line);
    printf("Now I'm going to exit . . .\n");
    exit(-1);
}
void checkers(char *s)
{
    PRECONDITION(s != NULL); // check argument
    printf(s);
}
void main()
{
    checkers(∅);                    // cause a failure
      }
```

There is a strong coupling between the container class library's CHECK and PRECONDITION macro, and the standard library's assert macro—they all call __assertfail( ) when the condition is false. This coupling, fortunate or unfortunate depending upon your point of view, must be addressed if you use all three macros in your code. Also, keep in mind that the assert macro's operation is controlled by the NDEBUG preprocessor identifier, while the CHECK and PRECONDITION macros are controlled by the __DEBUG identifier. (Simply defining NDEBUG prevents assertions.)

Borland's String Class

The String class, which is defined in <strng.h> in the class library include directory, makes it easier to manage strings. It automatically allocates and deallocates storage for the string, and provides assignment and comparison operators. The major facilities of Borland's String class are summarized below.

Constructors:	String(const char *); String(const String &);
Operators:	String& operator=(const String &); operator const char *( );

Member Functions:	int isEqual(const Object &);
	int isLessThan(const Object &);
	classType isA( );
	char *nameOf( );
	hashValueType hashValue( );
	void printOn(ostream &);

Using the Borland String class is simple. Here's a tiny example program:

```
#include <stdio.h>
#include <strng.h>
void main()
{
  String s;
  s = "Hello Philippe\n";
  printf(s);
}
```

To use the IDE to compile this or any other program that uses the container class library, you must set the Options-Environment-Directories dialog so that \borlandc\classlib\include is one of the include directories, and so that \borlandc-\classlib\lib is one of the library directories. (Of course path names on your system may differ.)

The above tiny example program illustrates several interesting things about String classes. The first is that the String class clearly presents a better abstraction of a string than the native C support for character strings. The assignment statement causes the String class's operator=() member function to set aside storage for the string, and then copies it into its own buffer. This is what we usually want, and the ability to graft this functionality onto the language is part of the attraction of C++.

Another interesting aspect of the String class is its operator const char*() operator function. Notice that this cast operator returns a const char * pointer, not an ordinary char * pointer. The reason is that the String class wants control of its destiny, meaning control of its buffer. If it gave out a pointer that could be used for writing the buffer, then the buffer might be overwritten. Instead it gives out a read-only pointer. Because it returns a pointer to const char, the compiler will object if you try the following:

```
strcpy(s, "A new message");
```

As you can see, const can be an important tool that helps a class protect itself.

The operator const char *() member function will be used automatically when the compiler deduces that a conversion to const char * is necessary. For example, the cast is used automatically to code the printf(s); statement, because printf() is prototyped to require a const char * first argument. If instead you had wanted to supply s as a later argument to printf(), you would have to supply the cast explicitly, because printf()'s prototype leaves later arguments undefined. (Printf()'s prototype is int printf(const char *, ...);.)

```
printf("My greeting today is: %s", (const char *)s);
```

While Borland's String class is a big step forward from native string support, it can easily be improved. Its biggest problem is that it makes too much use of malloc() to allocate memory. Consider the code I presented above. The assignment statement in that code was

```
s = "Hello Philippe\n";
```

To implement this assignment statement, malloc() is used twice. Let me show you how. First, the compiler realizes that there is no assignment operator to assign a native string (a const char * type) to a String object. So the compiler uses the String(const char *) constructor to build a temporary String object, and then it uses the operator=() function to perform the assignment. Conceptually, the compiler converts the above statement to the following:

```
String tmp("Hello Philippe\n"); // construct
s.operator=(tmp);               // assign
tmp.~String();                  // destruct
```

This explains the two malloc()s. The first is in the constructor that creates tmp, the second in the operator=() member function. The construction of tmp (and one of those expensive malloc()s) could be avoided if the String class had an operator=() that assigned a native string to a String object.

Another example of excessive use of malloc() is shown by the following:

```
String Short("A short string.");
String Long("A somewhat longer string.");
Long = Short;
```

The problem is that the buffer originally allocated for the Long object is large enough to store the Short string. But in the String class, the buffer is always exactly the length of the string; there is no way to store a ten-character string in a 20-character buffer. Thus the statement Long = Short is implemented by deleting Long's existing buffer, allocating a shorter buffer, and then copying in the string. I would prefer a String class that did less malloc()ing and used its buffer more intelligently.

Well, this is the world of C++, and if you don't like something, fix it! I created a new class, called QString, that remedies these shortcomings. QString is derived from String, so most of the existing String facilities can be used unchanged. What I added was a new operator=() for char* right operands, a smarter operator=() for String& right operands, new constructors (usually necessary when you derive a class), and a member variable called bufferlen that stores the size of the buffer. Qstrng.h is shown in Listing 5.2.

LISTING 5.2 ▰

Qstrng.h

```
#include <strng.h>
//
// Strings with improved buffer management and
// better efficiency
//
class QString : public String {
  public:
    QString(const char _FAR * = "");
    QString(const QString _FAR &);
    QString(int buflen, const char _FAR * = "");
    QString& operator = (const String _FAR &);
    QString& operator = (const char _FAR *);
  protected:
    int bufferlen;
      };
```

The key change in the QString class is its improved buffer management. By storing the buffer length, it is able to avoid unnecessary memory allocation. In addition to the original constructors, I added a constructor that allows you to specify the buffer length. This is useful if you know that you are going to use a QString with strings of a given length. For example, if you are reading strings from a file and you let the buffer adapt dynamically, you might allocate successively longer buffers 10 or 20 times until you eventually encountered the longest string in the input. This could be avoided by specifying a large enough value at the outset using the QString(int, char*) constructor. Avoiding extraneous allocation isn't just a speed issue, the memory fragmentation caused by excessive allocation can lead to problems in programs that use extensive dynamic memory allocation.

I encountered one unexpected difficulty while building the QString class. In Borland's String class, its member variables were declared private. This made it impossible to access them, even in my derived QString class. Therefore I took the liberty of editing Borland's strng.h file, to change the accessibility of the two member variables to protected.

NOTE Be very careful when you change a header file but don't recompile the class libraries. In Borland C++ I knew that changing the accessibility wouldn't change the class layout, but on a different implementation it could change the layout. Other changes, like making a function virtual, changing data types, or changing the order of the members, will cause problems in all C++ implementations.

Also, the operator=( ) member function and the copy constructor operate most efficiently if they can access the len member variable of their argument. I could instead have used strlen( ) (from the C library) to figure out the length, but why add to the burden? Therefore I made the QString class a friend of String.

The source code for QString is shown in Listing 5.3. If you look at Borland's supplied source code for the String class, you'll discover that it looks very similar to my code. In case you were worrying that Borland lifted my source code, please be at ease. They didn't. Instead, I used their code as a model for my own. In my version the details are different, because my buffer management is somewhat smarter, but the flavor of the original is present.

LISTING 5.3

QString.cpp

```
//
// Strings with improved buffer management and
// better efficiency
//
// QString(const char *) constructor
//
QString::QString(const char *ptr) :
    String(ptr)
{
    bufferlen = len;
    return;
}
//
// copy constructor
//
QString::QString(const QString& sourceString)
{
    len = bufferlen = sourceString.len;
    theString = new char[len];
    CHECK(theString != 0);
    strcpy(theString, sourceString.theString);
}
//
```

LISTING 5.3

QString.cpp (Continued)

```
// QString(int, char*) constructor, explicit buffer allocation
//
QString::QString(int buflen, const char _FAR *ptr)
{
    if (ptr == Ø)
      ptr = "";
    len = strlen(ptr) + 1;
    bufferlen = buflen > len ? buflen : len;
    theString = new char[bufferlen];
    CHECK(theString != Ø);
    strcpy(theString, ptr);
}
//
// operator = for String& r.h.s.
//
QString& QString::operator =(const String& sourceString)
{
    if (*this != sourceString) {
        if (bufferlen < sourceString.len) {
            delete theString;
            bufferlen = sourceString.len;
            theString = new char[bufferlen];
            CHECK(theString != Ø);
        }
        len = sourceString.len;
        strcpy(theString, sourceString.theString);
    }
    return *this;
}
//
// operator = for char* r.h.s.
//
QString& QString::operator =(const char *ptr)
{
    int srclen = strlen(ptr) + 1;
    if (bufferlen < srclen) {
        delete theString;
        bufferlen = srclen;
        theString = new char[bufferlen];
        CHECK(theString != Ø);
    }
    len = srclen;
    strcpy(theString, ptr);
    return *this;
    }
```

Object Classes versus BIDS Classes

A *collection* is a group of data elements, which are stored and accessed according to a program's need. For example, a stack collection stores data in such a way that the most recently deposited element will be the next element that is retrieved. Other common collection types are arrays, bags, sets, queues, and double-ended queues.

Programs have various needs for collections. For example, sometimes efficient access is important, other times storage flexibility is paramount. Because there are so many different requirements for collections, it's not practical to build generic support for collections into a programming language. Like most programming languages, C and C++ have one built-in collection type, the array. The built-in array is limited by having only numeric indices, and each array has a fixed size. Other collection needs have traditionally been met by building collection support into the data element that is being collected, or by implementing flimsy universal collections, in which data elements are accessed indirectly using generic (void*) pointers.

Borland C++ version 3 and above contain two complete container class libraries—the Object class library and the Borland International Data Structures (BIDS) class library. The Object class library was supplied first with Borland C++ version 2, while the BIDS library, which relies on the new C++ template capability, was first supplied in version 3.

A class named Object is the ultimate base class of the Object class library. The Object class defines facilities for runtime typing, comparison, and output. Some classes derived from Object define the individual collections, such as the Array class that implements an array collection. Collection members must themselves be objects from classes that are derived from the Object class. Thus the Object class library isn't able to manage a collection of a built-in type such as double, unless you wrap the double into a simple Object-based class.

The other difficulty with the Object library is that it is typeless. Each member of a collection must be an object of a type derived from the Object class. There is no other requirement. This is sometimes exactly what you want, because there are many uses for heterogeneous collections. But at other times this is much too loose, and it would be better to have a collection of a particular type, enforced by the compiler.

Many existing programs use the Object library, so it will likely be supported by Borland for a long time. But newer software should be written using the BIDS library, which uses templates to form collections. In the BIDS library, individual collections are defined by template classes. You create a specific BIDS collection by expanding the collection template for a given type. You can use BIDS to create collections whose members are any type, including the built-in types. BIDS is exactly as type-safe as you want it to be. If you create a collection of doubles, then only doubles can be added to the collection. But BIDS can also have the same behavior as the Object class. If you create a collection of pointers to a base class (such as the Object class), then objects from that whole family of classes are eligible for membership.

One of the interesting aspects of the BIDS container classes is their ability to mimic or nearly mimic the Object classes. For total compatibility, Borland supplies the TC (Turbo C) version of the BIDS templates. Like the Object classes, most member functions of the TC version of BIDS are virtual. This was essential to the Object library, but is less so to BIDS because of its use of templates. Virtual functions are flexible, but they impose a small performance burden. Therefore Borland also supplies a similar set of classes, the O classes (BIDS naming will be explained in the next section). O classes have the same set of member functions as the Object classes, but the member functions aren't virtual, yielding somewhat higher performance.

In this book I'm going to cover only the BIDS container classes. There are several reasons for this choice. Foremost, BIDS is the future. You should use BIDS containers for all of your new development. Secondly, BIDS is a superior library. It has higher performance, higher type safety, and increased flexibility. The disadvantage of my approach is that there are a few classes in the Object library—B-Trees and priority queues—that aren't supplied in the BIDS library.

BIDS Container Classes

The BIDS container classes are arranged into two layers. The bottom layer consists of the three Fundamental Data Structures (FDS) that are listed in Table 5.1. The FDS template classes reflect how data is stored in a computer. They encompass the fundamental possibilities: Data can be stored in sequential locations (a vector), or each element can have a pointer to the next element (a list), or there can be two sets of pointers, so that the list can be traversed in either direction (a double list). The three storage organizations of the Borland FDS template classes are diagrammed in Figure 5.1.

TABLE 5.1

BIDS Fundamental Data Structures

Type of Structure	Description
Vector	Each element is stored successively in memory, and each is accessed using a numeric index. The lowest index is always zero.
List	Each element has a pointer to the subsequent element.
DoubleList	Each element has a pointer to the preceding and following elements.

The FDS classes may occasionally be useful to you directly, but more often they will serve as a foundation for building an Abstract Data Type (ADT) class. An ADT class is a usage-oriented data collection. It has a set of characteristics that correspond to how we want to use the collection. The Borland C++ ADT Template classes, which comprise the top layer of the BIDS library, are listed in Table 5.2.

We often need stack collections in which the most recently deposited element should be the next element retrieved. If additionally you need a stack that can grow, you can implement a stack using a list. If instead you need more efficient operation but you can tolerate a fixed size, then you can implement a stack as a vector. The Borland ADTs do exactly that, they give you a choice. The BIDS library has a template for a stack that uses the vector FDS to manage the storage, plus it also has a template for a stack that uses a list FDS to manage the storage.

FIGURE 5.1

Storage methods of Borland FDS template classes

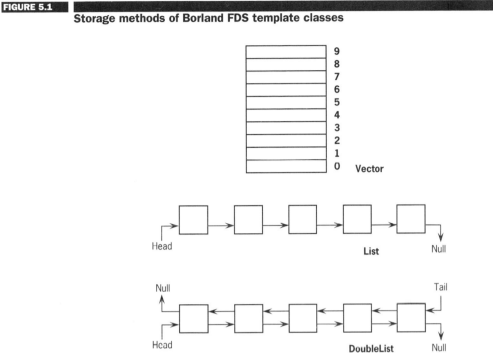

TABLE 5.2

BIDS Abstract Data Types

Abstract Data Type	Description
Array	A single dimensional indexed data structure.
Stack	A last-in, first-out (LIFO) data structure.
Queue	A first-in, first-out (FIFO) data structure.
Deque	A double-ended queue.
Bag	A data structure that contains things. Unordered, and duplicates are allowed.
Set	A data structure that contains things. Unordered, and no duplicates allowed.

I don't want to dwell on the FDS classes in the Borland library. Most users, I suspect, will never use them directly. If you do need to use them to create a new ADT, you probably need to read the source code to glean the details that are beyond the scope of this book.

Introducing the BIDS ADTs

The major characteristics of the ADT template classes supplied in the Borland library are shown in Table 5.3. In the Fundamental Operations column of that table I have listed only the member functions that, in my opinion, are basic to the given abstraction. For example, the sorted array ADT contains an addAt() member, but to me it makes little sense to add a member to a specific position of a sorted array. Instead most people will use the add() member, which searches through the array for the correct position to add the new element.

TABLE 5.3

BIDS Abstract Data Types

Abstract Data Type	Fundamental Operations	Allow Duplicates	Sorted	Fixed/ VariableSize	Indexed Access
Array	add(); addAt(); operator[]()	Yes	No	Either	Yes
Sorted Array	add(); operator[]()	Yes	Yes	Either	Yes
Bag	add(); hasMember(); findMember();	Yes	No	Variable	No
Set	add(); hasMember(); findMember();	No	No	Variable	No
Stack (as Vector)	push(); pop(); top();	Yes	No	Fixed	No
Stack (as List)	push(); pop(); top();	Yes	No	Variable	No
Queue (as Vector)	get(); put();	Yes	No	Fixed	No
Queue (as Double-List)	get(); put();	Yes	No	Variable	No
Dequeue (as Vector)	getLeft(); putLeft(); peekLeft(); getRight(); putRight(); peekRight();	Yes	No	Fixed	No
Dequeue (as Double-List)	getLeft(); putLeft(); peekLeft(); getRight(); putRight(); peekRight();	Yes	No	Variable	No

Table 5.3 tries to show how each ADT is different from the others. For example, the table shows that sets and bags differ only in that sets don't allow duplicates. Similarly, a queue as a vector is the same as a queue as a double list except that a queue as a double list can grow, while a queue as a vector has a fixed size.

Table 5.4 shows the exact template names used in the BIDS libraries, and it shows the name of the include file that defines each template. Note that all of the BIDS library include file names are plural. The older Object library uses singular names.

TABLE 5.4

BIDS Template Names

Abstract Data Type	Standard Template Name	Template to Emulate the Object Container Library	Include File
Array	BI_ArrayAsVector<T> BI_IArrayAsVector<T>	BI_OArrayAsVector<T> BI_TCArrayAsVector<T>	arrays.h
Sorted Array	BI_SArrayAsVector<T> BI_ISArrayAsVector<T>	BI_OSArrayAsVector<T> BI_TCSArrayAsVector<T>	arrays.h
Bag	BI_BagAsVector<T> BI_IBagAsVector<T>	BI_OBagAsVector<T> BI_TCBagAsVector<T>	bags.h
Set	BI_SetAsVector<T> BI_ISetAsVector<T>	BI_OSetAsVector<T> BI_TCSetAsVector<T>	sets.h
Stack	BI_StackAsVector<T> BI_IStackAsVector<T> BI_StackAsList<T> BI_IStackAsList<T>	BI_OStackAsVector<T> BI_TCStackAsVector<T> BI_OStackAsList<T> BI_TCStackAsList<T>	stacks.h
Queue	BI_QueueAsVector<T> BI_IQueueAsVector<T> BI_QueueAsDoubleList<T> BI_IQueueAsDoubleList<I>	BI_OQueueAsVector<T> BI_TCQueueAsVector<T> BI_OQueueAsDoubleList<T> BI_ICQueueAsDoubleList<T>	queues.h
Dequeue	BI_DequeAsVector<T> BI_IDequeAsVector<T> BI_DequeAsDoubleList<T> BI_IDequeAsDoubleList<T>	BI_ODequeAsVector<T> BI_TCDequeAsVector<T> BI_ODequeAsDoubleList<T> BI_TCDequeAsDoubleList<T>	dques.h

It's usually convenient to use the typedef statement to create a name for a template. For example, suppose you are building a calculator that needs a stack for results, a stack for operands, and a scratch stack, all of doubles. One way to declare these stacks is the following:

```
BI_StackAsVector<double> results(5Ø);
BI_StackAsVector<double> operands(5Ø);
BI_StackAsVector<double> scratch(5Ø);
```

Perhaps a better way is to use typedef, so you have a more convenient and meaningful name for your stack type:

```
typedef BI_StackAsVector<double> StackOfDouble;
StackOfDouble results(5Ø);
StackOfDouble operands(5Ø);
StackOfDouble scratch(5Ø);
```

Borland emphasizes that you can simply change a typedef in order to change the underlying implementation of the stack. For example, you could change the preceding typedef so that StackOfDouble was formed from a BI_StackAsList<double>. Unfortunately, things aren't quite that simple. The problem with the typedef switch is that a stack based on a vector should have its size specified at the outset, otherwise you'll pick up the default size. A stack built on a list FDS may not have a specified initial size.

The BIDS classes are Borland's first classes that use a conservative naming convention. The naming convention, which simply means placing the BI_ on the front of the names, reduces the likelihood that you'll encounter a third-party library that uses the same name. If you're developing a library for widespread distribution, you should consider adopting a similar convention.

After the BI_ is an optional prefix to indicate the type of the class:

I   Indirect collection. The collection stores pointers to the elements.

O   Object library compatibility, but without virtual functions.

TC   Object library compatibility, including virtual functions.

I'm not going to discuss the O and TC versions of the classes, since they will primarily be used by people who are already using the Object container library. You can use these classes automatically to implement Object library functionality by setting the preprocessor identifier TEMPLATES before including any of the Object library header files.

Indirect Containers

The BIDS library can house things either directly or indirectly. *Direct storage* is what corresponds closest to our conception of a container. The container actually stores the item. For direct storage to work, the contained item must either be a built-in type, or it must be a class that has a default constructor and a meaningful operator=() member function. Direct storage is best for objects of small or moderate size. More specifically, direct storage is generally best for classes that are tens of bytes to several hundred bytes.

Indirect storage is the preferred storage method for classes that don't copy well, either because they are large or because copying has side effects that should be avoided. Indirect storage means that you hand a pointer to an object to the container class. Thus object creation is under your control, and object copying doesn't occur.

We're all aware that containers are used in many different ways. In some cases, containers are treated like banks, and they have complete control of their deposits. In other situations, containers are more like a stock brokerage, which does your bidding, but never pretends to own your stocks.

These concerns aren't relevant to the direct storage collections, because in direct storage collections each element of the collection is, unambiguously, owned by the collection. If a direct storage collection is deleted, it will in turn delete each of its elements. But in indirect collections ownership is problematic, which is why Borland bases all of its indirect BIDS collections on the TShould-Delete class. The TShouldDelete class contains a public constructor, two public member functions, and an enumeration. Here are the public members of TShouldDelete:

```
enum DeleteType { NoDelete, DefDelete, Delete };
TShouldDelete(DeleteType dt = Delete);   // constr.
int ownsElements();                      // get
void ownsElements(int del);              // set
```

The ownsElements( ) member functions are available in all of the BIDS indirect container classes.

The TShouldDelete constructor automatically specifies deletion, so if you want to "own" the elements of an indirect collection, you must use the second form of ownsElements( ) to specify a "no delete" policy. For example, consider an indirect container object named cabinet. By default, cabinet would delete its members on exit. You can reverse that policy as follows:

```
cabinet.ownsElements(TShouldDelete::NoDelete);
```

Also note that the three enumeration constants in the TShouldDelete class are used throughout the BIDS library (in the detach( ), destroy( ), and flush( ) member functions) to control object deletion.

BIDS Arrays

The BIDS array templates let you create one-dimensional arrays to store any given type of data. Like the native arrays, BIDS arrays are accessed using a numeric expression. But unlike native arrays, BIDS arrays support the following capabilities:

- Automatically resizing the array

- Searching for individual elements

- Removing individual elements, causing later elements to move down one position

■ Using the supplied iterators to search the array without writing a loop

■ Having a non-zero bottom index

■ Finding out how many elements have been deposited

Table 5.5 shows the member functions of the BIDS array templates. I'm not going to provide a detailed reference for each function because most are self-explanatory, and the others can be understood by reading about the similarly named function in the Object container library function reference provided by Borland.

TABLE 5.5

BIDS Array Template Class Member Functions

The BI_ArrayAsVector Class The BI_SArrayAsVector Class	The BI_IArrayAsVector Class The BI_ISArrayAsVector Class
Constructors:	Constructors:
BI_ArrayAsVector(int upr,int lwr = 0,int delta = 0);	BI_IArrayAsVector(int upr,int lwr = 0,int delta = 0);
BI_SArrayAsVector(int upr,int lwr = 0,int delta = 0);	BI_ISArrayAsVector(int upr,int lwr = 0,int delta = 0);
int lowerBound();	Same
int upperBound();	Same
sizeType arraySize();	Same
void add(T t);	void add(T *t);
void addAT(T t, int loc);	void addAt(T *t, int loc);
void detach(T t, DeleteType dt = NoDelete);	void detach(T *t, DeleteType dt = NoDelete);
void detach(int loc, DeleteType dt = NoDelete);	Same
void destroy(int i);	Same
void flush(DeleteType dt = DefDelete);	Same
int isFull();	Same
int isEmpty();	Same
int hasMember(T t);	Same
	int find(T *t);
countType getItemsInContainer();	Same
T& operator[](int loc);	T* operator[](int loc);
void forEach(void (*f)(T &, void*), void *args);	Same
T* firstThat(int (*f)(const T &, void*), void *args);	Same
T* lastThat(int (*f)(const T &, void*), void *args);	Same
	int ownsElements();
	void ownsElements(int del);

The array constructors all require from one to three arguments. The first argument is the upper bound. To create an N element array, specify N–1 as the upper bound. The second argument is used if you want to create an array that isn't zero based. Simply supply the high index as the first argument, and the low index as the second. For example, the following could create an array of doubles with indices from the ordinal value of 'a' to that of 'z':

```
BI_ArrayAsVector<double> c('z', 'a');
```

The third argument, usually called *delta,* specifies whether the array can grow. By default, the value is zero, which means the array will have a fixed size. If the third argument is non-zero, then that many new elements will be added each time you try to add elements past the current end of the array. Be aware that growing an array is an expensive proposition, because a new array will be allocated, existing elements will be copied individually, and then the original array will be deleted. If you want to have arrays that can grow dynamically, you should pick a delta that strikes a careful balance between wasting memory (delta is too large) and calling malloc() too often (delta is too small). If you want an array to be able to grow in an emergency, but you don't think that growth is very likely, then you might want to pick a very small delta. You should understand that growing by one or two elements hundreds or thousands of times is a "wait till the cows come home" proposition.

For a graphical application that I'll cover in more detail in Chapter 6, I needed an array of characters that could grow. I didn't need string facilities like those in Borland's String class, so it seemed more appropriate to start with a growable array, rather than start with a non-growable String.

The basic characteristics that are necessary for this application are

- The character array must be able to grow.

- There must be facilities for appending strings or single characters to the array.

- There must be sequential read access.

- There must be indexed read access.

I attained these characteristics using the CharArray class shown in Listing 5.4. At one point I considered deriving the CharArray class from the BI_Array-AsVector<char> class. This would have given my CharArray class all of the facilities of the standard BIDS classes. I decided instead to make a BI_ArrayAs-Vector object a member of the class, just to avoid having all of the standard BIDS interface be part of my class. As a general-purpose foundation, the rich BIDS facilities are ideal. But in a class designed for a specific purpose, it is usually preferable to supply functionality that precisely fits that purpose.

Listing 5.5 shows the member functions of the CharArray class. It should be obvious that there is little work to do because most of the work is handled by the data member, the BIDS array. My CharArray class puts a new face on a BIDS data structure, and that's not a very hard task.

LISTING 5.4

charray.h

```
#include <arrays.h>
//
// expandable character arrays
//
class CharArray {
  public:
    CharArray(int len0, int delta = 100);  // constr.
    CharArray(CharArray&);              // copy constr.
    char operator[](int n) const;       // indexed access
    int getch()                         // sequential read
      { return curChar < len ? data[curChar++] : -1; }
    void rewind()                       // reset read pos.
      { curChar = 0; }
    void operator+=(const char *s);     // append string
    void operator+=(char ch);           // append char
                                        // assignment
    const CharArray& operator=(const CharArray&);
    void flush();                       // reuse array
    unsigned getLength() const          // array length
      { return len; }
  protected:
    BI_ArrayAsVector<char> data;        // data storage
    unsigned len;                       // length
    unsigned curChar;                   // read position
};
```

LISTING 5.5

charray.cpp

```
//
// standard constructor
//
CharArray::CharArray(int len0, int delta) :
  data(len0-1, 0, delta),
  len(0),
  curChar(0)
{
  return;
}
//
// copy constructor
//
CharArray::CharArray(CharArray& rhs) :
  data(rhs.data),
  len(rhs.len),
  curChar(0)
{
  return;
```

LISTING 5.5

charray.cpp (Continued)

```cpp
}
//
// indexed access
//
char CharArray::operator[](int n) const
{
  CHECK(n>=0 && n < len);
  return data[n];
}
//
// append string
//
void CharArray::operator+=(const char *s)
{
  while (*s)
    operator+=(*s++);
}
//
// append char
//
void CharArray::operator+=(char ch)
{
  len++;
  CHECK(len < 65000);
  data.add(ch);
}
//
// assignment
//
const CharArray& CharArray::operator=(const CharArray& rhs)
{
  data = rhs.data;
  len = rhs.len;
  curChar = 0;
  return *this;
}
//
// reset an array so it may be reused
//
void CharArray::flush()
{
  data.flush();
  len = 0;
  curChar = 0;
    }
```

Listing 5.6 contains a tiny main() routine that shows how the CharArray class might be used. This main() calls a function called replace() that performs a replacement operation on the data. The data consists of strings formed from a's and b's. Inside replace() the a's are replaced with one string, while the b's are replaced with another. When this operation is performed, new patterns emerge.

LISTING 5.6

Code to exercise the CharArray class

```
#include <stdio.h>
#include "charray.h"
void replace(CharArray& orig, CharArray& repl,
  const char *aStr, const char *bStr)
{
  orig.rewind();
  int ch;
  while((ch = orig.getch()) != -1)
    if (ch == 'a')
      repl += aStr;
    else if (ch == 'b')
      repl += bStr;
    else
      repl += ch;
}
void print(CharArray& s)
{
  s.rewind();
  int ch;
  while((ch = s.getch()) != -1)
    putchar(ch);
  putchar('\n');
}
void main()
{
  CharArray a(200, 100);
  CharArray b(200, 100);
  char aStr[] = "bba";
  char bStr[] = "bab";
  const int nIterations = 3;
  const char *titles[nIterations] = {
    "first: ", "second: ", "third: " };
  a += "<abba>"; // seed
  printf("seed: ");
  print(a);
  for(int i = 0; i < nIterations; i++) {
    replace(a, b, aStr, bStr);
    a = b;
    b.flush();
    printf(titles[i]);
    print(a);
  }
}
```

Here is the output of running the test main( ) routine:

```
seed: <abba>
once: <bbababbabbba>
twice: <babbabbbababbbababbabbbababbabbbabbba>
thrice: <babbbabababbabbbababbabbabbbababbbabab
babbabbbabababbbababbabbbababbabbabbbababbbabab
babbbababbabbbababbabbabbbba>
```

Printed as sequences of a's and b's these strings are deadly dull. But when interpreted graphically, as they will be in Chapter 6, they spring to life.

BIDS Bags and Sets

Bags and *sets* are collections of members. Their member functions are listed in Table 5.6. Sets and bags have no ordering, and no direct access. The only difference between a bag and a set is that a bag permits duplicates. By default, sets and bags will grow as needed, but they only grow one element at a time. You must be very careful to create an initial size that is large enough to meet your needs. Otherwise, performance will be very poor.

An *iterator* is a collection member function that you can use to access collection members. For each member of the collection, the iterator will call a function that you supply. The Borland container classes supply three iterators:

- forEach( )—Access every member.

- firstThat( )—Access members starting at the beginning until the user-supplied function returns true.

- lastThat( )—Access members starting at the end, working backward, until the user-supplied function returns true.

The iterators all require two arguments: a pointer to the function that will be called for each member, and a pointer to that function's argument or argument list. The user-supplied function for the firstThat( ) and lastThat( ) iterators return an int, while the user-supplied function for forEach( ) has no return value.

For uniformity, the container library supplies the iterators for each collection class. Collections that have easy direct access to members, such as the Array collection, offer a built-in alternative to the iterators. But collections that don't provide direct access, such as bags and sets, rely heavily on the standard iterators.

I made a simple example that uses sets to store the membership list of a club. The Member class, which is quite unremarkable, is shown in Listings 5.7 and 5.8. It simply stores the member's name, the date of entry to the club, and most importantly, whether the dues payments are up to date. Because the Member class is going to be used in a collection, I was careful to supply a default constructor, an assignment operator, and an equality operator. Without these standard members you will get compilation errors when Borland C++ tries to expand the template definitions.

TABLE 5.6

BIDS Bag and Set Template Classes Member Functions

The BI_BagAsVector Class The BI_SetAsVector Class	The BI_IBagAsVector Class The BI_ISetAsVector Class
Constructors:	Constructors:
BI_BagAsVector(unsigned sz);	BI_IBagAsVector(unsigned sz);
BI_SetAsVector(unsigned sz);	BI_ISetAsVector(unsigned sz);
void add(T t);	void add(T *t);
void detach(T t, DeleteType dt = NoDelete);	void detach(T *t, DeleteType dt = NoDelete);
void flush(DeleteType dt = DefDelete);	Same
int isFull();	Same
int isEmpty();	Same
int hasMember(T t);	Same
T findMember(T t);	T* findMember(T *t);
int getItemsInContainer();	Same
void forEach(void (*f)(T &, void*), void *args);	Same
T* firstThat(int (*f)(const T &, void*), void *args);	Same
T* lastThat(int (*f)(const T &, void*), void *args);	Same
	int ownsElements();
	void ownsElements(int del);

LISTING 5.7

The Member.h file

```cpp
#include <strng.h>
#include <ldate.h>
class Member {
  public:
    Member();
    Member(String& nm, Date& dt);
    Member& operator=(const Member& m);
    int operator==(const Member& m) const;
    const String& nameOf() const
      { return name; }
    const Date& dateOf() const
      { return date; }
    int paidUp() const
      { return paid; }
```

LISTING 5.7

The Member.h file (Continued)

```
    void paidUp(int p)
      { paid = p; }
    void print() const;
  protected:
    String name;
    Date date;
    int paid;
};
```

LISTING 5.8

The Member.cpp file

```cpp
#include "member.h"
#include <stdio.h>
#include <string.h>
//
// default constructor
//
Member::Member() :
  name(""),
  date(),
  paid(0)
{
  return;
}
//
// the usual constructor
//
Member::Member(String& nm, Date& dt) :
  name(nm),
  date(dt),
  paid(1)
{
  return;
}
//
// operator =
//
Member& Member::operator=(const Member& m)
{
  name = m.name;
  date = m.date;
  paid = m.paid;
```

LISTING 5.8

The Member.cpp file (Continued)

```
    return *this;
  }
  //
  // operator ==
  //
  int Member::operator==(const Member& m) const
  {
    return name == m.name;
  }
  //
  // print (using printf)
  //
  void Member::print() const
  {
    printf("%12s %d/%d/%d\n", (const char *)name,
      date.Month(), date.Day(), date.Year());
  }
```

The code related to sets is in Listing 5.9. At the beginning of main( ) a set of Members named EastchesterBayYC is declared and five Member objects are deposited. The interesting parts are the middle and last thirds of main( ), which use the supplied iterators. In the middle of main( ), the firstThat( ) iterator is used to find the Member object whose name element is "rudy." The firstThat( ) iterator calls a function named findMember( ) to look at each member of the set. FindMember( ) returns true when the specified member is encountered, causing firstThat( ) to return a pointer to that member of the set. In main( ), rudy's paidUp status is altered to reflect his poor dues paying habits.

LISTING 5.9

The Sets.cpp file

```
#include <sets.h>
#include "member.h"
//
// iterator function to find a member (by name)
//
int findMember(const Member &m, void *s)
{
 if (!strcmp(m.nameOf(),(char *)s))
   return 1;
 return 0;
}
```

LISTING 5.9

The Sets.cpp file (Continued)

```
//
// iterator function used with forEach()
//
void printPaid(Member &m, void *)
{
  if (m.paidUp())
    m.print();
}
void main()
{
  BI_SetAsVector<Member> EastchesterBayYC;
  EastchesterBayYC.add(Member(String("malcolm"), Date(5,2,1984)));
  EastchesterBayYC.add(Member(String("alison"), Date(6,12,1987)));
  EastchesterBayYC.add(Member(String("rudy"), Date(9,1,1992)));
  EastchesterBayYC.add(Member(String("bruce"), Date(8,3,1991)));
  EastchesterBayYC.add(Member(String("sylv"), Date(6,30,1990)));
  // rudy is behind in his dues
  Member *m = EastchesterBayYC.firstThat(findMember, "rudy");
  if (m)
    m->paidUp(Ø);
  // print list of paid-up members
  EastchesterBayYC.forEach(printPaid, Ø);
}
```

The second iterator in main() prints a list of all Members who have paid their dues. The iterator function is called printPaid() and it simply calls print() to print each fully paid member. The printPaid() iterator function is called from the forEach() iterator. Unlike firstThat() (and lastThat()), forEach() always traverses the entire list.

BIDS Stacks

A *stack* is a LIFO data structure. The fundamental operations on a stack are to push something onto the stack, and to pop the top item off of the stack. The BIDS collection classes present two underlying data structures for a stack—vectors and lists. A vector-based stack has good performance but a fixed size, while a list-based stack has variable size but relatively poor performance. If you can estimate the maximum size that will ever be needed, or if you can somehow adapt to running out of stack space, then the vector-based stack is probably preferable. The stack member functions are listed in Table 5.7.

I created the calculator program in Listing 5.10 to demonstrate some simple stack usage. The calculator is a basic four-function unit that uses reverse Polish notation (RPN). In RPN you enter the operands (numbers) followed by the operators. RPN is easy to use, once you get used to it! In the main() routine of the calculator, each number that is encountered is pushed onto the stack, and each operator causes two numbers to be popped off the stack and used in an expression.

TABLE 5.7	BIDS Stack Template Class Member Functions

The BI_StackAsVector Class The BI_StackAsList Class	The BI_IStackAsVector Class The BI_IStackAsList Class
Constructors:	Constructors:
BI_StackAsVector(unsigned sz);	BI_IStackAsVector(unsigned sz);
BI_StackAsList();	BI_IStackAsList();
void push(T t);	void push(T *t);
T pop();	T* pop();
T top();	T* top();
int isFull();	Same
int isEmpty();	Same
void flush(DeleteType dt = DefDelete);	Same
int getItemsInContainer();	Same
void forEach(void (*f)(T &, void*), void *args);	Same
T* firstThat(int (*f)(const T &, void*), void *args);	Same
T* lastThat(int (*f)(const T &, void*), void *args);	Same
	int ownsElements();
	void ownsElements(int del);

LISTING 5.10	

Calc.cpp

```
#include <stdio.h>
#include <stdlib.h>
#include <ctype.h>
#include <stacks.h>
enum TokenType { Error, Eof, Plus, Minus,
  Times, Divide, Number };
//
// read a token (an operator or number) from the input
//
TokenType gettoken(double *val)
{
  int ch;
  char word[5Ø];
  do { // skip whitespace
    ch = getchar();
  } while(ch != EOF && isspace(ch));
  if (isdigit(ch)) {  // read a number
    word[Ø] = ch;
    int i = 1;
    do {  // read digits, Es, and .s
      ch = getchar();
```

LISTING 5.10

Calc.cpp (Continued)

```
      word[i++] = ch;
    } while(ch != EOF &&
    (isdigit(ch) || ch == 'e' || ch == 'E' || ch == '.'));
    ungetc(ch, stdin);   // we read one too far
    word[--i] = 0;
    *val = atof(word);
    return Number;
  }
 switch(ch) {
   case '+': return Plus;
   case '-': return Minus;
   case '*': return Times;
   case '/': return Divide;
   case EOF: return Eof;
   default: return Error;
  }
}
//
// pop two operands off the stack
//
int pop2(BI_StackAsVector<double>& stk, double& d1, double& d2)
{
  if (!stk.isEmpty())
   d1 = stk.pop();
  else {
   printf("empty stack\n");
   return 1;
  }
  if (!stk.isEmpty())
   d2 = stk.pop();
  else {
   printf("empty stack\n");
   return 1;
  }
  return 0;
}
void main()
{
   BI_StackAsVector<double> stack(50);
   while(1) {
     double val, val2;
     switch(gettoken(&val)) {
       case Error:
         printf("Illegal input.\n");
         break;
       case Eof:
        return;
       case Plus:
         if (pop2(stack, val, val2)) break;
         printf("%g\n", val2 + val);
         break;
       case Minus:
         if (pop2(stack, val, val2)) break;
```

LISTING 5.10

Calc.cpp (Continued)

```
        printf("%g\n", val2 - val);
        break;
    case Times:
      if (pop2(stack, val, val2)) break;
      printf("%g\n", val2 * val);
      break;
    case Divide:
      if (pop2(stack, val, val2)) break;
      if (val == 0.0)
        printf("Can't divide by zero\n");
      else
        printf("%g\n", val2 / val);
      break;
    case Number:
      if (!stack.isFull())
        stack.push(val);
      else
        printf("stack overflow\n");
      break;
  }
 }
}
```

BIDS Queues

BIDS's queues and double-ended queues are usually used to pass information from producers to consumers. They expand and collapse as necessary, allowing the producer and consumer to operate more independently. In the BIDS library, the chief difference between the single-ended queues and the double is that the single version has but a single set of put( ) and get( ) routines, while the double-ended version has putLeft( ) and putRight( ), plus getLeft( ) and getRight( ). The member functions of the BIDS queue and double-ended queue templates are listed in Table 5.8. The queues are available based either on a vector FDS or on a double list FDS. As with stacks, the vector-based implementation is more efficient, but has a fixed size. The single-ended version is defined in the queues.h header file, and the double-ended version is defined in deques.h.

Date and Time

Borland's Date and Time classes are simple encapsulations of date and time values. They provide a few simple ways to manipulate date and time information, but overall they are too simplistic to be very useful. For example, there is no built-in way to convert a type time_t time value (which is seconds since Jan 1, 1970) into a Time object. Similarly, DOS's packed time information (returned by getftime( ) or stored in an ffblk struct) can't easily be used with a Time object. And their output functions work only with the iostream library (Chapter 7), making them of little value to programs that don't use iostreams.

TABLE 5.8

BIDS Queue and Dequeue Template Class Member Functions

The BI_QueueAsVector Class **The BI_QueueAsDoubleList Class**	**The BI_IQueueAsVector Class** **The BI_IQueueAsDoubleList Class**
Constructors:	Constructors:
BI_QueueAsVector(unsigned sz);	BI_IQueueAsVector(unsigned sz);
BI_QueueAsDoubleList();	BI_IQueueAsDoubleList();
T get();	T *get()
void put(T t);	void put(T *t);
The BI_DequeAsVector Class **The BI_DequeAsDoubleList Class**	**The BI_IDequeAsVector Class** **The BI_IDequeAsDoubleList Class**
Constructors:	Constructors:
BI_DequeAsVector(unsigned sz);	BI_IDequeAsVector(unsigned sz);
BI_DequeAsDoubleList();	BI_IDequeAsDoubleList();
T peekLeft(); T peekRight();	T *peekLeft(); T *peekRight();
T getLeft(); T getRight();	T *getLeft(); T *getRight();
void putLeft(T t); void putRight(T t);	void putLeft(T *t); void putRight(T *t)
The BI_QueueAsVector Class **The BI_QueueAsDoubleList Class** **The BI_DequeAsVector Class** **The BI_DequeAsDoubleList Class**	**The BI_IQueueAsVector Class** **The BI_IQueueAsDoubleList Class** **The BI_IDequeAsVector Class** **The BI_IDequeAsDoubleList Class**
int isFull();	Same
int isEmpty();	Same
void flush(DeleteType dt = DefDelete);	Same
int getItemsInContainer();	Same
void forEach(void (*t)(T &, void*), void *args);	Same
T* firstThat(int (*t)(const T &, void*), void *args);	Same
T* lastThat(int (*f)(const T &, void*), void *args);	Same
	int ownsElements(); void ownsElements(int del);

Both the Date and Time classes are derived from classes, called baseDate and baseTime, that actually do much of the work. The only member function in Date and Time that makes a contribution is the printOn( ) function, which outputs a Date or Time object in text form to an ostream connection. The reason for this organization is to allow you to write different derived classes that output date and time information in different formats. In Borland's organization the underlying class manages most of the details, while the derived class manages the output formatting. The Date and Time classes are detailed below.

The header file for using the Date class is ldate.h, and the header file for the Time class is ltime.h. A simple example of using the Date class is shown in Listings 5.7 and 5.8.

The Borland Date Class (Including the baseDate Members)

Constructors:	Date();
	Date(unsigned char Mon, unsigned char Day, unsigned Year);
	Date(const Date &);

Member Functions:	unsigned Month();	// get values
	unsigned Day();	
	unsigned Year();	
	void SetMonth(unsigned char);	// set values
	void SetDay(unsigned char);	
	void SetYear(unsigned);	
	int isEqual(const Object &);	// standard functions
	int isLessThan(const Object &);	
	classType isA();	
	char *nameOf();	
	hashValueType hashValue();	
	void printOn(ostream &);	

The Borland Time Class (Including the baseTime Members)

Constructors:	Time();
	Time(unsigned char Hour, unsigned char Minute, unsigned char Sec, unsigned char Hundredths);
	Time(const Time &);

The Borland Time Class (Including the baseTime Members) (Continued)

Member
Functions:

unsigned hour();	// get values
unsigned minute();	
unsigned second();	
unsigned hundredths();	
void SetHour(unsigned char);	// set values
void SetMinute(unsigned char);	
void SetSecond(unsigned char);	
void SetHundredths(unsigned char);	
int isEqual(const Object &);	// standard functions
int isLessThan(const Object &);	
classType isA();	
char *nameOf();	
hashValueType hashValue();	
void printOn(ostrcam &);	

6 Using and Extending the Class Library

AS I MENTIONED AT THE BEGINNING OF THE PREVIOUS CHAPTER, INCREASED source code reuse is the true test of object-oriented programming. In this chapter I'm going to show two examples of using the Borland container classes to simplify program development. In the first example, an *L-system graphic*, I take one of the standard abstract data types (ADTs) and use it to store an L-system. In the second example I take a fundamental data structure (FDS) and use it to build a new priority queue ADT.

Both examples demonstrate specialization, but there are important differences, which are outlined below:

- **L-system graphic**—A generic ADT gets a new interface, so that it is optimized for storing L-system graphics. The specialization leads directly to the end result.

- **Priority queue**—An FDS is used as the basis for a new ADT. Like other ADTs, the priority queue ADT is a generic data structure, one that will be used in many different programs. The specialization leads to a result that is designed to be the root of further specialization.

Creating L-system Graphics

L-systems were invented by theoretical biologist Aristid Lindenmayer to model the growth of plants. L-systems are a substitution system. Growth occurs in stages. In each stage, certain elements are replaced by new elements. In just a few generations, extremely simple L-systems can produce very beautiful and rich patterns, which can be interpreted graphically.

L-systems are related to several other emerging branches of mathematics and physics. For example, many fractal patterns can be produced using L-systems, and the notion of self-similarity is common to both fractal geometry and to L-systems. Similarly, there are many commonalities in the study of the grammar of L-systems and the more formal studies of grammar by linguists such as Chomsky.

Let me show you how L-systems work before I discuss the code that uses the Borland class library to create L-system graphics. Consider simple strings that may be composed of the letter F, pluses, and minuses. Here is an example:

```
F++F++F
```

We can adopt the *rule* that each time we see an F in a string, we will replace it with

```
F-F++F-F
```

If the first generation, called the *seed*, is the preceding F++F++F, then the next generation will be

```
F-F++F-F++F-F++F-F++F-F++F-F
```

Figure 6.1 shows a more graphic way to see how we use the seed and the rule to form the first generation.

FIGURE 6.1

Forming the first generation

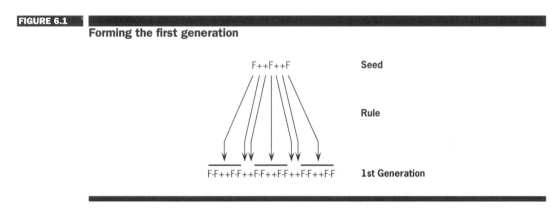

This process can be repeated as many times as you like, each time forming more complicated patterns.

Although there are many variations and improvements that can be made, the preceding paragraphs have covered the basics of L-systems. Given a seed (a starting point) and a rule, you can successively apply the rule to form new generations of the system.

L-systems start to be more fun when they are interpreted graphically. This is easily done using a set of conventions reminiscent of *turtle graphics*. In turtle graphics a "turtle" is instructed to move forward, turn right, and so on, all the while drawing a pattern. Turtle graphics is present in many forms and places, but is perhaps most widely known as an important part of the Logo programming language.

Using the basic idea of turtle graphics, we can interpret an F as a command to move forward a fixed amount, a – means turn right a fixed angle, and a + means turn left. If the amount to turn is 60°, the string F++F++F is interpreted graphically as a triangle (see Figure 6.2).

The replacement rule should also be interpreted graphically, as shown in Figure 6.3. In the replacement that I mentioned previously, a single line segment (an F) is replaced by the series of four line segments (F–F++F–F) shown in Figure 6.3. Notice that this particular replacement rule preserves direction (that is, the last line segment is pointing in the same direction as the first one), because it has as many right turns as it has left turns. If the replacement rule is applied to our seed (the triangle), you produce the more interesting shape in Figure 6.4A. If you repeat the replacement, you get 6.4B, one more repetition will produce 6.4C, and so on.

FIGURE 6.2

The L-system F++F++F produces a closed triangular shape when + is interpreted as a 60° left turn. The standard turning angle is called delta (δ)

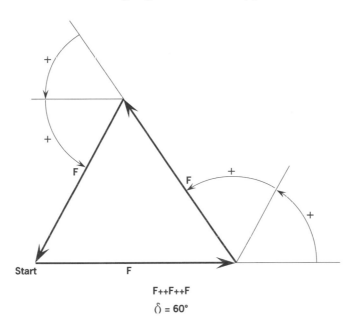

F++F++F

δ = 60°

FIGURE 6.3

The L-system F–F++F–F, drawn with a δ of 60°

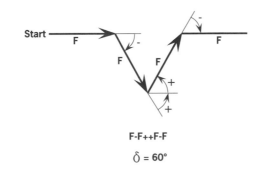

F-F++F-F

δ = 60°

FIGURE 6.4

The first, second, and third generations of the L-system F++F++F produced by following the rule F–F++F–F; δ is 60°

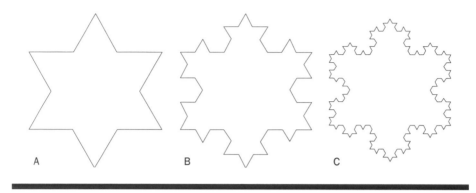

People who are familiar with fractals should recognize that Figure 6.4C is the beginning of a *Koch snowflake*, which is generally regarded as one of the earliest examples of a fractal shape. A few more generations of the L-system would produce a Koch snowflake that would be as detailed as possible given the resolution of the printer used for this book. Of course you would need infinitely many generations of the L-system to produce a Koch snowflake with a truly fractal dimension.

Let me introduce just one more simple idea, *branching.* Many plants, such as flowers and trees, have a branched structure. We can model branching in an L-system by adding brackets to our notation. The [(left bracket) symbol means start a branch, and the] (right bracket) means return to the most recent branch point. If you like to think of things in terms of a stack machine, the [means push the current position and direction, while] means pop.

An example L-system using this notation is

```
F[-F][+F-F]
```

which is shown in Figure 6.5. The [–F] is the branch to the right, and the [+F–F] branch leads off to the left.

For further reading, Lindenmayer's seminal paper on L-systems is "Mathematical Models for Cellular Interaction in Development, Parts I and II," in the *Journal of Theoretical Biology*, 18:280–315, 1968. Since then over 100 papers have been published relating to L-systems. My primary reference is the beautiful book *The Algorithmic Beauty of Plants*, by Przemyslaw Prusinkiewicz and Aristid Lindenmayer, Springer-Verlag, 1990.

FIGURE 6.5

The branching L-system F[−F][+F−F], drawn with a δ of 60°

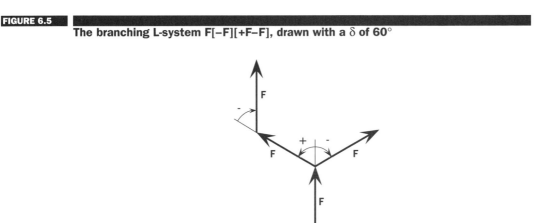

F[-F][+F-F]

δ = 60°

First-cut LSystem Class

I wanted to create a general-purpose L-system class that would make it easy to play with L-systems. Obviously such a class should be able to store a seed and a rule, and it should be able to create successive generations of the L-system by following the rule a specified number of times. But should the class also be able to display an L-system? The problem with adding graphics to an L-system class is that there are so many graphics environments. Under DOS we can use the BGI (Borland's Graphics Interface) facility, then there is Windows, there are printers, and so on. Any class that includes graphical operations is immediately tuned for some particular environment.

I decided to compromise. My LSystem class contains a draw() routine, but the only graphical operation that it uses is line(). I assumed that in all graphics environments I would be able to find some function to draw a line. Other than line(), the class is easily portable to any environment that supports the Borland container class libraries.

The first way that Borland's container class libraries are involved in my LSystem class is storing the L-system text. This is an important task because L-systems can grow quickly. Each generation is usually much larger than the previous. The easy solution is the CharArray class, which has already been discussed in Chapter 5. The CharArray class lets you create an expandable array of characters, and it has operator+=() member functions so that you can append strings or characters to the array.

The other way that the Borland container class library can help an L-system class is in storage of the seed and rule using the String class. The String class isn't nearly as much of a time saver as the CharArray class, but it is still quite useful.

The combination of the CharArray class, which is a slightly enhanced Array-AsVector<char> from the Borland class library, plus the String class, lets my LSystem class concentrate on L-systems. If you look at the code for the LSystem class in Listings 6.1 and 6.2, you'll notice that it is a straightforward implementation of the L-system rules that I've already introduced.

LISTING 6.1

Lsys.h

```cpp
//
// L-Systems
//
#include <strng.h>
#include "charray.h"
class LSystem {
  public:
    LSystem();
    void setDrawing(double th0, double d, int dx);
    void setRules(char *_seed, char *_rule);
    void rewrite(int iterations);
    void draw(int x0, int y0);
    int length() const
      { return system.getLength(); }
  protected:
    void rewrite();
    void graph(int x, int y, double theta); // recursive
    double theta0;
    double delta;
    int dist;
    CharArray system;
    String seed;
    String rule;
};
```

LISTING 6.2

Lsys.cpp

```cpp
//
// L-System implementation
//
#include <graphics.h>
#include <math.h>
#include "lsys.h"
inline double degreesToRadians(double degrees)
{
  return M_PI * degrees / 180.0;
}
//
// Constructor
//
LSystem::LSystem() :
  theta0(0.0),
  delta(0.0),
```

LISTING 6.2

Lsys.cpp (Continued)

```cpp
    dist(1),
    system(200, 200),
    seed(""),
    rule("")
{
  return;
}
//
// Set the drawing parameters
//
void LSystem::setDrawing(double th0, double d, int dx)
{
  // d in degrees, delta in radians
  theta0 = degreesToRadians(th0);
  delta = degreesToRadians(d);
  dist = dx;
}
//
// Set the seed and rule
//
void LSystem::setRules(char *_seed, char *_rule)
{
  seed = _seed;
  rule = _rule;
}
//
// public Rewrite
//
void LSystem::rewrite(int iterations)
{
  system.flush();
  system += seed;
  while(iterations--)
    rewrite();
}
//
// Draw
//
void LSystem::draw(int x0, int y0)
{
  system.rewind();
  graph(x0, y0, theta0);
}
//
// protected rewrite - build next generation
//
void LSystem::rewrite()
{
  CharArray newsys(200, 200);
  int ch;
  system.rewind();
  while((ch = system.getch()) != -1) {
    if (ch == 'F')
```

LISTING 6.2

Lsys.cpp (Continued)

```cpp
          newsys += rule;
      else
          newsys += ch;
    }
    system = newsys;
}
//
// Graph a branching L-system
//
void LSystem::graph(int x, int y, double theta)
{
    int ch;
    int x1, y1;
    while((ch = system.getch()) != -1) {
      if (ch == 'F') { // step and draw
        x1 = x + dist * cos(theta);
        y1 = y - dist * sin(theta);
        line(x, y, x1, y1);
        x = x1;
        y = y1;
      } else if (ch == '-')
        theta -= delta;
      else if (ch == '+')
        theta += delta;
      else if (ch == '[')
        graph(x, y, theta);
      else if (ch == ']')
        return;
    }
}
```

The two most important procedures in the LSystem class are rewrite() and graph. Rewrite() has the task of transforming the seed according to the rule, for a specified number of generations. There are actually two rewrite() functions in the LSystem class. The public version of rewrite() is the user interface to L-system rewriting. Its parameter is the number of iterations (generations), and its chore is to call the protected rewrite() to do the work. The protected rewrite() reads the current L-system character by character using the getch() facility. Each time an F is encountered, the current rule is appended to a temporary L-system, while other characters are simply appended. The final action is to copy the temporary L-system to the current system.

The graph() member function, which is protected, is reponsible for drawing the current L-system. It is invoked by the draw() function, the public interface to drawing. Graph() goes through the L-system text and performs the appropriate actions. For every F, it draws a line from the current position to the next position. For each [in the input it calls itself recursively, and for every] it returns. The + and – symbols change the current direction.

I created the Lsysmain.cpp file, shown in Listing 6.3, to draw some example L-systems. Lsysmain uses the BGI for graphics.

LISTING 6.3

Lsysmain.cpp

```cpp
#include <graphics.h>
#include <conio.h>
#include <stdio.h>
#include <stdlib.h>
#include "lsys.h"
void main(int c, char *argv[])
{
  int n = (c == 2) ? atoi(argv[1]) : 1;
  int GraphDriver = DETECT;
  int GraphMode;
  char *driverPath = "c:\\borlandc\\bgi";
  if (getenv("BGI"))
    driverPath = getenv("BGI");
  initgraph(&GraphDriver, &GraphMode, driverPath);
  int ErrorCode = graphresult();
  if (ErrorCode != grOk) {
    printf("Graphics System Error: %s\n",
      grapherrormsg(ErrorCode));
    exit(1);
  }
  int maxcolor = getmaxcolor();
  int maxx = getmaxx();
  int maxy = getmaxy();
  LSystem sys;
  sys.setRules("F", "FF-[-F+F+F]+[+F-F-F]");
  sys.rewrite(4);
  for(int i = 1; i <= n; i++) {
    sys.setDrawing(90.0, 22.50,
      (maxy+1)/120 + rand()%(maxy/120) );
    // draw last in WHITE, mid screen; others randomly placed.
    setcolor(i == n ? WHITE : (1 + rand() % maxcolor));
    int x = i == n ? (maxx/2) : (maxx/8 + rand()%(6*maxx/8));
    int y = maxy - (i == n ? (maxy/16) : (rand()%(maxy/8)));
    sys.draw(x, y);
  }
  getch();
  closegraph();
}
```

You can supply a command-line parameter to specify how many trees will be displayed; the default is one. Figure 6.6 shows a single Lsystem tree image, while Figure 6.7 shows a small grove of these trees. These L-system figures are drawn on screen in several colors, but in Figures 6.6 and 6.7 they are shown in shades of gray. A grove of slightly different trees, produced by another L-system, is shown in Figure 6.8.

FIGURE 6.6

A tree figure produced by an L-system. Seed: F; Rule: FF–[–F+F+F]+[+F–F–F]; δ 22.5°; 4 iterations. The parameters come from *The Algorithmic Beauty of Plants*, Prusinkiewicz and Lindenmayer, Springer-Verlag 1990

FIGURE 6.7

A grove of trees produced from the L-system in Figure 6.6

The only difficult code in Lsysmain.cpp occurs in the drawing loop, which places the figures in random positions. Initial x values are chosen to be in the middle three-quarters of the screen, while starting y positions are computed to fall in the bottom eighth of the screen. The formulas try to take into account different screen resolutions; this code was considerably easier to understand before I tried to support resolutions other than 640x480.

FIGURE 6.8

A grove of trees. Seed: F; Rule F[+F]F[–F][F]; δ 20°; 5 iterations. Parameters suggested by Prusinkiewicz and Lindenmayer, op cit.

Improving the LSystem Class

The LSystem class I've been discussing can produce interesting figures, but there are some obvious improvements that should be made. Let me discuss a few of these shortcomings, and then present an improved LSystem class.

The first difficulty is speed. Display speed wasn't my main criterion, but faster is almost always better than slower. The most obvious chance for improvement is in the inner drawing loop, in which the sin() and cos() functions are called to calculate the endpoints of each line segment. Calling a transcendental function in the inner loop of a graphics application is something that should be avoided, if possible. Fortunately, in most L-systems there are only a few angles that will be needed, so it is easy to precompute most of the sines and cosines. Because spiral L-systems don't follow the pattern of revisiting a small set of precomputed angles, I ensured that the program would compute the necessary values for any angles that fell outside the cached range.

Another difficulty is the trade-off between speed and accuracy. The LSystem class in Listing 6.1 uses integer positions, primarily to avoid the time overhead of floating point. But when you use integers for positions, closed paths don't close, because of the truncation errors. Thus in some cases it is better to use floating-point coordinates, to avoid truncation errors. Since there are two reasonable data types for the coordinates, I decided that a better LSystem class should be a template class, so that the appropriate coordinate type could be user specified.

These two improvements are shown in Listing 6.4, Lsys2.h. Because the improved LSystem class is a template, I had to move all of the function definitions from Lsys.cpp into Lsys2.h. Thus Lsys2.h is now quite long, and it doesn't need a separate file containing the function bodies. When I measured the speed of the new version, I found that drawing time was cut in half.

LISTING 6.4

Lsys2.h

```
#include <strng.h>
#include "charray.h"
//
// L-System template class
//
template <class T, int CacheSize = 10>
class LSystem {
   // T int (drawing speed)
   // T double (positional accuracy)
  public:
    LSystem();
    void setDrawing(double th, double d, double dx);
    void setRules(char *_seed, char *_rule);
    void rewrite(int iterations);
    void draw(T x0, T y0);
    int length() const
       { return system.getLength(); }
  protected:
    void rewrite();
    void graph(T x, T y, int theta); // recursive
    double theta0;
    double delta;
    double dist;
    CharArray system;
    String seed;
    String rule;
  private:
    // sine, cosine cache
    double sinDist[CacheSize * 2 + 1];
    double cosDist[CacheSize * 2 + 1];
};
//
// L-System implementation
//
#include <graphics.h>
#include <math.h>
inline double degreesToRadians(double degrees)
{
  return M_PI * degrees / 180.0;
}
//
// Constructor
//
template <class T, int CacheSize>
LSystem<T, CacheSize>::LSystem() :
  theta0(0),
  delta(0.0),
  dist(1),
```

LISTING 6.4

Lsys2.h (Continued)

```
    system(200, 200),
    seed(""),
    rule("")
{
    return;
}
//
// Set the drawing parameters
//
template <class T, int CacheSize>
void LSystem<T, CacheSize>::setDrawing(double th0, double d, double dx)
{
    // parameters in degrees, convert to radians
    delta = degreesToRadians(d);
    theta0 = degreesToRadians(th0);
    dist = dx;
    // precalculate some needed sines and cosines
    // use indices 0..CacheSize into table for angles
    // (CacheSize is middle, i.e., initial angle)
    for(int i = -CacheSize; i <= CacheSize; i++) {
        sinDist[i+CacheSize] = dist * sin(theta0 + ((double)i * delta));
        cosDist[i+CacheSize] = dist * cos(theta0 + ((double)i * delta));
    }
}
//
// Set the seed and rule
//
template <class T, int CacheSize>
void LSystem<T, CacheSize>::setRules(char *_seed, char *_rule)
{
    seed = _seed;
    rule = _rule;
}
//
// public Rewrite
//
template <class T, int CacheSize>
void LSystem<T, CacheSize>::rewrite(int iterations)
{
    system.flush();
    system += seed;
    while(iterations--)
        rewrite();
}
//
// Draw
//
template <class T, int CacheSize>
void LSystem<T, CacheSize>::draw(T x0, T y0)
{
    system.rewind();
    graph(x0, y0, CacheSize);
```

LISTING 6.4

Lsys2.h (Continued)

```cpp
}
//
// protected rewrite - build next generation
//
template <class T, int CacheSize>
void LSystem<T, CacheSize>::rewrite()
{
  CharArray newsys(200, 200);
  int ch;
  system.rewind();
  while((ch = system.getch()) != -1) {
    if (ch == 'F')
      newsys += rule;
    else
      newsys += ch;
  }
  system = newsys;
}
//
// Graph a branching L-system
//
template <class T, int CacheSize>
void LSystem<T, CacheSize>::graph(T x, T y, int theta)
{
  int ch;
  T x1, y1;
  while((ch = system.getch()) != -1) {
    if (ch == 'F') { // step and draw
      if (theta >= 0 && theta <= 2*CacheSize) {
        x1 = x + cosDist[theta];
        y1 = y - sinDist[theta];
      } else {
        // not in cache -- do calculation
        double th = theta0 + (theta-CacheSize) * delta;
        x1 = x + dist * cos(th);
        y1 = y - dist * sin(th);
      }
      line(x, y, x1, y1);
      x = x1;
      y = y1;
    } else if (ch == '-')
      theta--;
    else if (ch == '+')
      theta++;
    else if (ch == '[')
      graph(x, y, theta);
    else if (ch == ']')
      return;
  }
}
```

To celebrate my improved LSystem class, I wrote an interactive program called Lsysintr for displaying L-systems. This interactive program suffers from an old-fashioned question-and-answer style user-interface dialog, but at least it lets me play with L-systems without running the compiler to change each parameter. The Lsysintr.cpp program file is shown in Listing 6.5, and some L-systems produced using Lsysintr are shown in Figures 6.9A and 6.9B.

LISTING 6.5

Lsysintr.cpp

```cpp
#include <graphics.h>
#include <conio.h>
#include <stdio.h>
#include <stdlib.h>
#include "lsys2.h"
typedef LSystem<double, 10> LSys;
//
// input L-system parameters
//
void getrules(LSys& sys)
{
  static char seed[80] = "F";
  static char rule[80] = "F[+F]F[-F]F";
  static double theta0 = 90;
  static double delta = 20.0;
  static double len = 1.6;
  static int iter = 5;
  char tmp[100];
  int ch;
  int mode = getgraphmode();
  restorecrtmode();

  do {
    printf("\n\n\nEnter seed <%s>: ", seed);
    fgets(tmp, sizeof(seed), stdin);
    tmp[strlen(tmp)-1] = 0; // strip off newline
    if (*tmp) strcpy(seed, tmp);

    printf("Enter rule <%s>: ", rule);
    fgets(tmp, sizeof(rule), stdin);
    tmp[strlen(tmp)-1] = 0; // strip off newline
    if (*tmp) strcpy(rule, tmp);

    printf("Enter iterations <%d>: ", iter);
    fgets(tmp, sizeof(tmp), stdin);
    if (*tmp != '\n') iter = atoi(tmp);

    printf("Enter theta0 (degrees) <%g>: ", theta0);
    fgets(tmp, sizeof(tmp), stdin);
    if (*tmp != '\n') theta0 = atof(tmp);

    printf("Enter delta (degrees) <%g>: ", delta);
    fgets(tmp, sizeof(tmp), stdin);
    if (*tmp != '\n') delta = atof(tmp);
```

LISTING 6.5

Lsysintr.cpp (Continued)

```cpp
      printf("Enter segment length (pixels) <%g>: ", len);
      fgets(tmp, sizeof(tmp), stdin);
      if (*tmp != '\n') len = atof(tmp);

      printf("\n\nSeed %s\n", seed);
      printf("Rule: %s\n", rule);
      printf("Iterations %d, Theta0 %g, Delta %g, Length %g\n",
        iter, theta0, delta, len);
      printf("\nOK? Y to continue, N to reenter: ");
      ch = getch();
   } while(ch != 'y' && ch != 'Y');

   printf("\nCalculation . . .\n");
   sys.setRules(seed, rule);
   sys.rewrite(iter);
   sys.setDrawing(theta0, delta, len);
   printf("System is %u bytes\n", sys.length());
   printf("Press any key to go back to graphics..." );
   getch();

   setgraphmode(mode);
   settextjustify(LEFT_TEXT, TOP_TEXT);
   int y = 10;
   sprintf(tmp, "Seed: %s", seed);
   outtextxy(10, y, tmp);
   y += textheight(tmp) + textheight(tmp)/2;
   sprintf(tmp, "Rule: %s", rule);
   outtextxy(10, y, tmp);
   y += textheight(tmp) + textheight(tmp)/2;
   sprintf(tmp, "Iterations %d, Theta0 %g, Delta %g, Length %g",
       iter, theta0, delta, len);
   outtextxy(10, y, tmp);
}
//
// Play with L-systems
//
void main()
{
  int GraphDriver = DETECT;  // The Graphics device driver
  int GraphMode;             // The Graphics mode value
  char *driverPath = "c:\\borlandc\\bgi";
  if (getenv("BGI"))
    driverPath = getenv("BGI");
  initgraph(&GraphDriver, &GraphMode, driverPath);
  int ErrorCode = graphresult();
  if(ErrorCode != grOk){
    printf("Graphics System Error: %s\n",
      grapherrormsg(ErrorCode));
    exit(1);
  }
  LSys sys;
  while(1) {
```

LISTING 6.5

Lsysintr.cpp (Continued)

```
    getrules(sys);
    setcolor(GREEN);
    sys.draw(getmaxx()/2, getmaxy()-10);
    outtextxy(10, getmaxy()-2*textheight(""),
      "<ESC> to exit, other key to continue.");
    if (Ø33 == getch())
      break;
  }
  closegraph();
}
```

FIGURE 6.9

Two L-systems drawn using the lsysintr program. The L-system parameters are shown in the upper-left corner of each screen

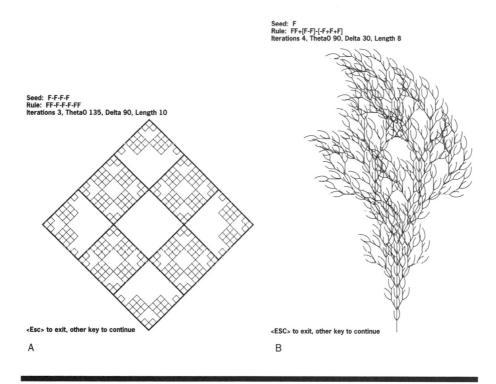

Seed: F
Rule: FF+[F-F]-[-F+F+F]
Iterations 4, Theta0 90, Delta 30, Length 8

Seed: F-F-F-F
Rule: FF-F-F-F-FF
Iterations 3, Theta0 135, Delta 90, Length 10

<Esc> to exit, other key to continue

<ESC> to exit, other key to continue

A   B

The Lsysintr program illustrates the general rule that interactive software must be bulletproof. On several occasions I specified a high number of iterations, and found that the machine was frozen. After some investigation, I discovered there were two somewhat related problems.

The first problem was that Borland's vectimp.h file occasionally allocates memory without checking for success. I added the CHECK macro to check for allocation failures in two places in vectimp.h: in the constructor of BI_VectorImp (line 52), and in the resize() member of BI_VectorImp<T> (line 176). These changes may be in slightly different places in your version of vectimp.h, or they may be unnecessary, as I presume that Borland will eventually fix this problem.

The second problem is that Borland's container classes can only be used to hold a maximum of 65,535 items, because the container classes all use 16-bit unsigned ints as their indices. This problem won't arise with most collections, but it could certainly arise with my CharArray class pushed hard to store a large L-system. I solved this problem by placing a CHECK into the CharArray's operator+=(char) member function to limit CharArray objects to 65,000 characters. Now instead of silent hangs, a request to build too large an L-system causes an abort with a somewhat informative error message. A better solution, which is left for the reader, would be to take over the __assertfail() procedure, and simply continue with user input to produce the next L-system.

Another size issue is that using a CharArray object with a capacity of 50,000 or more characters is only possible if you compile using the compact, large, or huge model. In small and medium model programs, the Borland container classes allocate space from the 64k near heap. Because ArrayAsVector<> classes grow by allocating a larger object and then copying in the existing object, the near heap size of 64k (in small and medium programs) will limit your total collection size to a theoretical maximum of about 32k. But reality (that is, memory fragmentation) intrudes, and about 20k is a more realistic upper bound on collection size in small and medium model programs.

Building a Priority Queue

A *priority queue* is like an ordinary queue, except that when items are placed in the queue they are positioned according to priority. Thus items may be deposited in any order, but withdrawals will always be ordered according to priority. Priority queues are often used like ordinary queues to provide a loose coupling between producers and consumers, but a priority queue adds the ability to handle prioritized messages. The BIDS container class library doesn't contain a priority queue ADT, although Borland's Object Library does contain one. Priority queues represent the more traditional approach to extending class libraries, as compared to creating L-system graphics.

The BIDS container class library contains all of the components for assembling a priority queue. Basically, any sorted (ordered) FDS can be used to build a priority queue ADT. The BIDS library contains two sorted FDS containers, Lists and Vectors. I decided to base a priority queue on a sorted List, because Lists easily supports additions and deletions of elements anywhere in the list. If you prefer to use a Vector as the implementation, simply build it using the recipe presented in this section.

I built the priority queue shown in Listing 6.6 by reworking the QueueAs-DoubleList<T> source code supplied with the BIDS library. I had to change all the references to the DoubleList FDS to refer instead to the SList FDS, and I had to change the logic in several places to accommodate the differences between a DoubleList and an SList. Because I wanted my priority queue to have the same interface as an ordinary queue, I was careful not to change any of the public function names, parameters, or return types.

LISTING 6.6

Priqueue.h

```
//
// Priority queue
//   code stolen from deques.h (by kc)
//   and adapted to use an SListImp
//
#include <listimp.h>
template <class Lst, class T> class _CLASSTYPE BI_PriqueAsListImp
{
  public:
    BI_PriqueAsListImp() :
      itemsInContainer( 0 )
    {
    }
    T peek()
    {
      PRECONDITION( !isEmpty() );
      return data.peekHead();
    }
    T get()
    {
      PRECONDITION( !isEmpty() );
      T t = data.peekHead();
      data.detach( t, 0 );
      itemsInContainer--;
      return t;
    }
    void put( T t )
    {
      data.add( t );
      itemsInContainer++;
    }
    void flush( int del )
    {
      data.flush( del );
      itemsInContainer = 0;
    }
    int isFull() const
    {
      return 0;
    }
    int isEmpty() const
    {
      return itemsInContainer == 0;
    }
    int getItemsInContainer() const
    {
      return itemsInContainer;
    }
```

LISTING 6.6

Priqueue.h (Continued)

```
protected:
  Lst data;
  int itemsInContainer;
};
/*-------------------------------------------------------------------*/
/*                                                                   */
/*  template <class T> class BI_PriqueAsList                         */
/*                                                                   */
/*  Implements a priqueue of objects of type T, using an SLi         */
/*  as the underlying implementation.                                */
/*                                                                   */
/*-------------------------------------------------------------------*/
template <class T> class _CLASSTYPE BI_PriqueAsList :
    public BI_PriqueAsListImp<BI_SListImp<T>,T>
{
  public:
    friend class _CLASSTYPE BI_PriqueAsListIterator<T>;
    void forEach( void (_FAR *f)(T _FAR &, void _FAR *), void _FAR *args )
    {
      data.forEach( f, args );
    }
    T _FAR *firstThat( int (_FAR *f)(const T _FAR &, void _FAR *),
            void _FAR *args ) const
    {
      return data.firstThat( f, args );
    }
    T _FAR *lastThat( int (_FAR *f)(const T _FAR &, void _FAR *),
            void _FAR *args ) const
    {
      return data.lastThat( f, args );
    }
};
template <class T> class _CLASSTYPE BI_PriqueAsListIterator :
    public BI_ListIteratorImp<T>
{
public:
    BI_PriqueAsListIterator( const BI_PriqueAsList<T> _FAR & s ) :
    BI_ListIteratorImp<T>(s.data)
    {
    }
};
/*-------------------------------------------------------------------*/
/*                                                                   */
/*  template <class T> class BI_IPriqueAsList                        */
/*                                                                   */
/*  Implements a priqueue of pointers to objects of type T,          */
/*  using a double-linked list as the underlying implementation.     */
/*                                                                   */
/*-------------------------------------------------------------------*/
template <class T>
class _CLASSTYPE BI_IPriqueAsList :
    public BI_PriqueAsListImp<BI_ISListImp<T>,T _FAR *>,
    public virtual TShouldDelete
```

LISTING 6.6

Priqueue.h (Continued)

```
{
  public:
    friend class _CLASSTYPE BI_IPriqueAsListIterator<T>;
    T _FAR *peek() const
    {
      PRECONDITION( !isEmpty() );
      return (T _FAR *)BI_PriqueAsListImp<BI_IListImp<T>,T _FAR *>::peek();
    }
    T _FAR *get()
    {
      return (T _FAR *)BI_PriqueAsListImp<BI_IListImp<T>,T _FAR *>::get();
    }
    void put( T _FAR *t )
    {
      BI_PriqueAsListImp<BI_IListImp<T>,T _FAR *>::put( t );
    }
    void flush( TShouldDelete::DeleteType dt = TShouldDelete::DefDelete )
    {
      BI_PriqueAsListImp<BI_IListImp<T>,T _FAR *>::flush( delObj(dt) );
    }
    void forEach( void (_FAR *f)(T _FAR &, void _FAR *), void _FAR *args )
    {
      data.forEach( f, args );
    }
    T _FAR *firstThat( int (_FAR *f)(const T _FAR &, void _FAR *),
            void _FAR *args ) const
    {
      return data.firstThat( f, args );
    }
    T _FAR *lastThat( int (_FAR *f)(const T _FAR &, void  FAR *),
            void _FAR *args ) const
    {
      return data.lastThat( f, args );
    }
};
template <class T> class _CLASSTYPE BI_IPriqueAsListIterator :
    public BI_IListIteratorImp<T>
{
  public:
    BI_IPriqueAsListIterator( const BI_IPriqueAsList<T> _FAR& s ) :
    BI_IListIteratorImp<T>(s.data)
    {
    }
};
```

One slight difficulty that I encountered was that in a List (or SList) you have direct access only to the list head, which contains the least-valued elements. You have two choices. One is that you can decide that the lowest numerical value is the "highest" priority (a common choice of many computer hardware designers). Or you can reverse the sense of the comparison operator for the contained class (this solution doesn't work if you are containing a built-in type, because you can't redefine comparision of built-ins).

Pqmain, shown in Listing 6.7, demonstrates the major features of a priority queue. In pqmain the queue holds Jobs objects. The Jobs class is a simple class that contains just two data elements, a text field and a priority. It also contains all of the members necessary to support inclusion in a sorted list, including a default constructor, an assignment member function, and an operator<() member function.

LISTING 6.7

pqmain.cpp

```cpp
#include <stdio.h>
#include <stdlib.h>
#include <strng.h>
#include "priqueue.h"
//
// simple class to store job priorities and
//  descriptions. Contains default constructor,
//  operator<() and operator=() functions so it
//  can be used in a sorted list
//
class Jobs {
  public:
    // default constructor
    Jobs() :
      priority(Ø),
      task()
    {
      return;
    }
    // copy constructor
    Jobs(Jobs& j) :
      priority(j.priority),
      task(j.task)
    {
      return;
    }
    // constructor
    Jobs(int i, char *p) :
      priority(i),
      task(p)
    {
      return;
    }
    // destructor
    ~Jobs()
      { return; }
    // assignment operator
    Jobs& operator=(const Jobs& j)
    {
      priority = j.priority;
      task = j.task;
```

LISTING 6.7

pqmain.cpp (Continued)

```
          return *this;
        }
        // comparison operator
        int operator < (const Jobs &rhs) const
        {
          return priority > rhs.priority;
        }
        // equality operator
        int operator == (const Jobs &rhs) const
        {
          return
            (priority == rhs.priority) &&
            (task -- rhs.task);
        }
        // access functions
        const char *getTask() const
          { return task; }
        int getPriority() const
          { return priority; }
  protected:
        int priority;
        char *task;
};
int findPriority(const Jobs &j, void *prio)
{
  if (j.getPriority() == *(int*)prio)
    return 1;
  return 0;
}
void main()
{
  Jobs j;
  Jobs trash(1, "Take out trash");
  Jobs school(10, "Go to school");
  Jobs quitsmoking(5, "Quit smoking");
  Jobs remodel(2, "Remodel the kitchen");
  Jobs exercise(4, "Jane's 20 minute workout");
  Jobs shopping(3, "Buy groceries");
  BI_PriqueAsList<Jobs> pqueue;
  pqueue.put(trash);
  pqueue.put(school);
  pqueue.put(quitsmoking);
  pqueue.put(remodel);
  pqueue.put(exercise);
  pqueue.put(shopping);
  printf("%d items in container.\n", pqueue.getItemsInContainer());
  int five = 5;
  Jobs *p5 = pqueue.firstThat(findPriority, &five);
  if (p5)
    printf("First Priority 5 Job: %s\n", p5->getTask());
  while (!pqueue.isEmpty()) {
```

LISTING 6.7

pqmain.cpp (Continued)

```
    j = pqueue.get();
    printf("%3d %s\n", j.getPriority(), j.getTask());
  }
}
```

Pqmain creates a group of Jobs objects, copies them into a priority queue, searches the queue for the first element whose priority is five, and then drains and prints the queue. The output from pqmain is

```
6 items in container.
First Priority 5 Job: Quit smoking
 10 Go to school
  5 Quit smoking
  4 Jane's 20 minute workout
  3 Buy groceries
  2 Remodel the kitchen
  1 Take out trash
```

The priority queue template that I developed shows the value of Borland's FDS/ADT architecture for the BIDS library. Developing the priority queue class was painless, and I have great confidence in its correct operation because it is based on the SList class supplied (and tested!) by Borland.

THE IOSTREAM CLASS LIBRARY

THE IOSTREAM LIBRARY IS A CLASS LIBRARY FOR TEXT INPUT AND OUTPUT that was developed at AT&T Bell Laboratories. It is a response to the long-recognized deficiencies of printf(), plus the new opportunities presented by C++ (strong type checking, operator overloading). It is available with all current implementations of C++, which makes it ideal for applications that must be portable to several computer platforms.

The iostream library should be considered for code that performs file I/O and for programs that use a traditional line-by-line (dumb terminal) style of interaction. I often use it for simple programs whose "user-interface" consists of the command-line arguments. I don't believe that the iostream library is useful, other than for file I/O, in Windows programs, or in most sophisticated character-mode DOS programs.

The iostream library has two main advantages. The first is type safety; the compiler uses data types to ensure that the correct conversion operations are performed. This is a big advantage over printf(), which is not type safe. We've all made the mistake of writing a printf() output statement in which the argument list doesn't match the conversions specified in the format string. Nonsense output is the only diagnostic. Iostream's type safety prevents this and other absurd errors.

The second advantage is that the iostream library is extensible. You can write your own conversion routines to output or input your own class data types. Again this is a big advantage over printf(), which can't be extended to support user-defined types.

The two main advantages of the iostream library, type safety and extensibility, are somewhat offset by a few disadvantages. The first disadvantage is the bulk of the library. The iostream include files are about 1,000 lines long, which slows every compilation that uses iostreams, and the .OBJ part of iostreams adds some weight to each program that uses iostreams.

The second disadvantage is performance. The iostream architecture is very general, but at the price of generating more function calls than would the equivalent operation using printf(). Much I/O code isn't performance-sensitive, either because it works at human speeds, or because it doesn't handle very much data. But you should be careful with iostreams in performance-sensitive settings.

The final disadvantage, which is more subjective, is the appearance of the I/O code. Newcomers to C often found printf()'s format string difficult and unattractive, but with time it has become second nature to most C programmers.

The iostream library uses a different approach, in which each element to be input or output is a separate expression, and the expressions are separated by >> or << operators. This gives the code a much sparser appearance, which can make it hard to see what is happening.

Text Streams

The iostream library is based on the idea of a text stream, which is a sequence of characters. Output operations, which are called *insertions*, place text onto an output stream, while input operations, which are called *extractions*, take text from an input stream.

A pure stream doesn't allow you to specify a position for read or write operations. For example, a keyboard is a pure stream; it doesn't make sense to talk about position in the keyboard input stream. However, files do have positions, and it is helpful to be able to move (seek) the read/write position when streams are connected to files. The iostream class library has a set of classes with features, such as positioning, that support streams connected to files.

Another variety of stream connects an iostream to a memory buffer, so that operations are performed in core. Such streams are called *string streams*, although they needn't follow the standard C conventions for strings. The final type of stream is a *stdio stream*, which uses the C standard I/O library for its I/O mechanism. Stdio streams are most often used when new C++ code must work with existing C code that already makes extensive use of stdio operations.

Insertion

Insertion pours information into an output stream. Here's the classic Hello World program using the iostream library.

```
#include <iostream.h>
void main()
{
  cout << "Hello world" << endl;
}
```

To use the iostream library you must include one of the appropriate header files, which are listed in Table 7.1.

The single statement in the body of main() contains the iostream library output statement. Let me go through each symbol in the statement:

cout is the name of the predefined iostream library output connection. The other predefined connections are cin for input, cerr for error output, and clog for logging output.

<< is normally called the shift left operator, but in an iostream expression it should be called the insertion operator. The iostream library contains overloaded operator<<() functions that output their right operand. Output appears in the natural left to right order because the << operator groups left to right.

"Hello world" is a string that is output by the iostream library.

<< is another insertion operator.

endl is an iostream library manipulator, which is a function that performs some action on a stream. The endl manipulator outputs an end of line character code.

; is the normal statement terminator.

TABLE 7.1

Iostream Class Library Header Files

Header File	Includes	Usage
iostream.h	mem.h	Stream connections to the standard input and output; definitions of the standard stream connections.
fstream.h	iostream.h	Stream connection to files.
strstrea.h	iostream.h	Stream connections to strings (memory buffers).
stdiostr.h	iostream.h stdio.h	Stream connections using the C stdio library for I/O.
constrea.h	iostream.h iomanip.h conio.h	Stream connection to the PC console using direct console I/O. Borland C++'s console stream class contains iostream extensions to support simple windowing and other facilities. Available only in Borland C++; don't use console streams if your code must be portable to UNIX or other environments.
iomanip.h	iostream.h generic.h	Input/Output manipulators. Numeric formatting, line and string terminators, width control, and so on.

Output is managed by the ostream class, or by a class derived from ostream. The ostream class is derived from ios, which contains things like status functions that are used by both output streams and input streams. The ios class and its descendants are diagrammed in Figure 7.1.

The ostream operator<<() functions (inserters) all output their right operand, and then return their left operand. This characteristic makes the iostream library work, because it enables complex output expressions such as the following:

```
cout << "Send " << nWidgets << " widgets, at $" << dCost
    << ", to the " << szCity << "branch.";
```

The above io statement is bulkier than the printf() equivalent, but in many ways it is easier to understand. For example, you don't have to look up the types of the variables nWidgets, dCost, or szCity to understand the statement. The dCost variable might be a double, which is a type that iostream knows how to output. But dCost might also be a user-defined TDollars class object. If the TDollars class has an iostream inserter, the preceding statement will work fine.

FIGURE 7.1

The ios class and its descendants

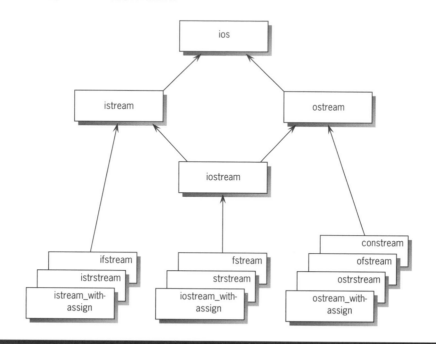

The built-in insertion operators are listed in Table 7.2 and the important public functions of the ostream class are listed in Table 7.3.

Each of the built-in ostream insertion operators (shown in Table 7.2) is demonstrated in the ios program, which is shown in Listing 7.1.

TABLE 7.2

The ostream Class's Built-in Insertion Operators

signed char	unsigned char	
short	unsigned short	
int	unsigned int	
long	unsigned long	
float	double	long double
const signed char *	const unsigned char *	void *
streambuf *		

TABLE 7.3

The ostream Class's Public Member Functions

Function	Description
ostream& seekp(streampos);	Seek to the specified position.
ostream& seekp(streamoff, ios::seek_dir);	Seek by the specified amount in the specified direction.
streampos tellp();	Get the current position.
ostream& put(char);	Insert a single character.
ostream& write(const char *, int);	Insert data without conversion.
int opfx();	Output prefix. It should be called at the beginning of all insertion functions, and the stream should only be used if opfx() returns true.
void osfx();	Output suffix. Should be called at the end of all insertion functions.

LISTING 7.1

Ios.cpp

```
#include <iomanip.h>
void main()
{
  const int wid = 23;
  cout << setw(wid) << "Signed char: "
       << (signed char)'A' << endl;
  cout << setw(wid) << "Unsigned char: "
       << (unsigned char)'B' << endl;
  cout << setw(wid) << "Short: "
       << (short)1 << endl;
  cout << setw(wid) << "Unsigned short: "
       << (unsigned short)2 << endl;
  cout << setw(wid) << "Int: "
       << (int)3 << endl;
  cout << setw(wid) << "Unsigned int: "
       << (unsigned int)4 << endl;
  cout << setw(wid) << "Long: "
       << (long)5 << endl;
  cout << setw(wid) << "Unsigned long: "
       << (unsigned long)6 << endl;
  cout << setw(wid) << "Float: "
       << (float)7.1 << endl;
  cout << setw(wid) << "Double: "
       << (double)8.2 << endl;
```

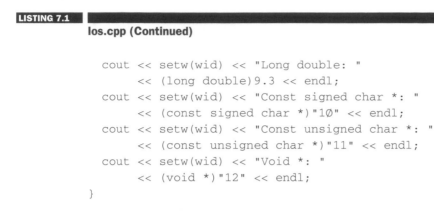

LISTING 7.1

Ios.cpp (Continued)

```
    cout << setw(wid) << "Long double: "
         << (long double)9.3 << endl;
    cout << setw(wid) << "Const signed char *: "
         << (const signed char *)"10" << endl;
    cout << setw(wid) << "Const unsigned char *: "
         << (const unsigned char *)"11" << endl;
    cout << setw(wid) << "Void *: "
         << (void *)"12" << endl;
}
```

When you execute the program in Listing 7.1, you generate the following output:

```
        Signed char: A
      Unsigned char: B
              Short: 1
     Unsigned short: 2
                Int: 3
       Unsigned int: 4
               Long: 5
      Unsigned long: 6
              Float: 7.1
             Double: 8.2
        Long double: 9.3
 Const signed char *: 10
Const unsigned char *: 11
             Void *: 0x017f
```

There are several small things to notice in Listing 7.1. The first is that I used the setw() manipulator to specify the width of the string labels. That's why the first column of the output is a uniform width. All the manipulators will be discussed later in this chapter. The other thing to notice is that the string whose type was cast to void* was output as a hexadecimal number, not as a string. When you supply a char* pointer, the iostream library outputs it as a string, but any other type of pointer will be converted to void* by the compiler and then output as a hexadecimal number. In the above output, the value 0x017f is the address of the string "12". The final thing you might notice is that the output formatting in Listing 7.1 is extremely primitive. Output formats are easy to control using iostream manipulators, discussed shortly.

Extraction

Extraction is taking information from an istream, or from a stream whose class is derived from istream. The general approach is the same as for insertion, except that the expressions in an extraction statement must all be lvalues. Otherwise, extraction is unremarkable. The data types for which the istream class defines an operator>>() member function are listed in Table 7.4, and the other public members of the istream class are listed in Table 7.5. Listing 7.2 shows the ios2.cpp program, which is a simple extraction demonstration.

TABLE 7.4

The istream Class's Built-in Extraction Operators

signed char&	unsigned char&	
signed char *	unsigned char *	
short&	unsigned short&	
int&	unsigned int&	
long&	unsigned long&	
float&	double&	long double&
streambuf *		

TABLE 7.5

The istream Class's Public Member Functions

Function	Description
istream& seekg(streampos);	Seek to the specified position.
istream& seekg(streamoff, ios::seek_dir);	Seek in the specified direction by the specified amount.
streampos tellg();	Get the current stream position.
istream& get(char& ch);	Get a single character from the stream.
istream& get(char *buf, int n, char delim = '\n');	Get characters until buffer is full or delimiter character is encountered. The buffer is null terminated, the delimiter is not read from the stream and is not placed into the buffer.
istream& getline(char *, int n, char delim = '\n');	Same as get, except the delimiter is read from the stream and placed in the buffer.
istream& read(char *buf, int n);	Read n characters into the buffer.
int peek();	Peek at, but don't extract, next character.
int get();	Get the next character.
istream& putback(char ch);	Put a single character back into the stream.
istream& ignore(int n = 1, char delim = EOF);	Read and discard at most n characters, or until the delim character is encountered.

TABLE 7.5

The istream Class's Public Member Functions (Continued)

Function	Description
int ipfx(int n = 0);	Input prefix statement. Should be the first statement called in all extraction functions. The ipfx() function flushes the tied stream, and skips whitespace if n is zero. Whitespace isn't skipped if n is 1, or if the stream's state has been set to not skip whitespace. Returns true if stream is okay, 0 if an error is encountered.
int ipfx0();	Same as ipfx(0).
int ipfx1();	Same as ipfx(1).

LISTING 7.2

Ios2.cpp

```cpp
#include <iomanip.h>
void main()
{
    char string[50];
    double d;
    long double ld;
    long l;
    char ch;
    cout << "Iostream demo, "
        "press <Enter> after each entry." << endl;
    cout << "Enter a string: ";
    cin >> setw(sizeof(string)) >> string;
    cout << "Enter a double: ";
    cin >> d;
    cout << "Enter a long double: ";
    cin >> ld;
    cout << "Enter a long: ";
    cin >> l;
    cout << "Enter a single character: ";
    cin >> ch;
    cout << "  -- Values --" << endl;
    cout << "String:     " << string << endl;
    cout << "Double:     " << d << endl;
    cout << "LongDouble: " << ld << endl;
    cout << "Long:       " << l << endl;
    cout << "Char (hex): " << ch << " (0x"
        << hex << (int)ch << ")" << endl;
}
```

There are two lessons in Listing 7.2. The first is that you have to be very careful when extracting into a string. You should always use the setw() manipulator to tell the iostream library the size of the string buffer, so that you won't overrun the buffer. This is the only use of setw() during extraction. When you use setw(), for either insertion or extraction, its effect only lasts until the next operation. Thus if you are extracting into an array of strings, each the same length, you must call setw() with the length before each extraction.

The other lesson, which is probably easiest to understand if you run the program, is the problem caused by lack of error checking. Any program that reads data must be very zealous about input errors. Whether your data comes from a keyboard or a data file, you are likely to encounter illegal entries. The ios2 program in Listing 7.2 has several problems related to error checking:

- Illegal input, such as entering nonnumeric text where a number is expected, causes the program to silently fail. Once an input error occurs, the subsequent input operations are not performed.

- Multiple words on a line cause problems. The second word will be used to satisfy the subsequent input. For example, if you type "A String" when prompted for a string, the word "String" will be used as the entry for the following double, causing the program to fail. Or if you type "1 2" when asked for a double, the 1 will be used for the double, and then the 2 will be used as the input for the following long double.

- No recovery is made following illegal input. Erroneous input should be detected, and some appropriate action should be taken.

One of the strengths of the iostream library is its ability to detect errors so that you can write more reliable programs. Table 7.6 lists the status information that is maintained by all iostream connections, and Table 7.7 lists the iostream member functions that are available to test and set the status information.

Some of the capabilities of Table 7.3 are used in the ios3.cpp program, which is shown in Listing 7.3.

TABLE 7.6

Iostream Status Information

Condition	Recoverable	Meaning
EOF	No	End of file has been encountered.
FAIL	Yes	An input failure, such as alphabetic input where numeric input is expected, has occurred. The stream is usable once the FAIL condition is reset.
BAD	No	An unrecoverable failure has occurred.
HARD	No	A hard error has occurred.

TABLE 7.7

Iostream Status Functions

Function	Action
good()	Returns true if !(FAIL I BAD I HARD I EOF), otherwise returns false.
bad()	Returns BAD I HARD.
fail()	Returns FAIL I BAD I HARD.
eof()	Returns EOF.
operator!()	Returns FAIL I BAD I HARD.
operator void *()	Returns 0 if FAIL I BAD I HARD, otherwise returns this pointer.
rdstatus()	Returns FAIL I BAD I HARD I EOF. (The status bitmask.)
clear()	Clears the status bitmask.
clear(int newstat)	Sets the status bitmask to newstat.

LISTING 7.3

Ios3.cpp

```cpp
#include <iomanip.h>
#include <checks.h>
void main()
{
  double d = Ø;
  long double ld = Ø;
  do {
    if (cin.fail()) {
      cin.clear();
      cin.ignore(1ØØ, '\n');
    }
    cout << "Enter a double: ";
    cin >> d;
    CHECK(!cin.eof());
    if (cin.fail()) {
      cout << "Bad entry. Should be numeric." << endl;
      continue;
    }
    cin.ignore(1ØØ, '\n');
    cout << "Enter a long double: ";
    cin >> ld;
    CHECK(!cin.eof());
    if (cin.fail()) {
      cout << "Bad entry. Should be numeric." << endl;
```

LISTING 7.3

Ios3.cpp (Continued)

```
        continue;
      }
      cin.ignore(100, '\n');
   } while(cin.fail() && !cin.bad());
   cout << "  -- Values --" << endl;
   cout << "Double:     " << d << endl;
   cout << "LongDouble: " << ld << endl;
}
```

The ios3 program checks for failures after every input. If a failure occurs, the data input loop is repeated, until valid input is entered. I've written several programs that have the overall structure of the ios3 program. Here is a brief sketch of that structure, using an istream named *in*.

```
do {
   if (in.fail()) { // true when loop repeats
      in.clear();     // clear error condition
      . . .           // other recovery stuff
   }
   // read something
   in >> . . . ;
   if (in.eof())      // unexpected end of file
      . . .           // handle eof
   if (in.fail()) { // bad input
      . . .           // failure management
      continue;
   }
   //
   // other inputs here
   //
// following condition repeats the loop so long as
// data failure, but while stream still usable
} while ( in.fail() && !in.bad() );
```

There are two key points. The first is that there are checks after every input statement. In a throwaway program you might omit the checks, but in long-lived code it is mandatory to check for errors after each input. The second point is that further input is attempted only if the error is a simple failure. If either in.eof() or in.bad() returns true, then the stream is unusable and you can't attempt further input. The standard test for a stream that has had a conversion error but is otherwise okay is in.fail() && !in.bad(), which is the test made in the condition of the do statement. The condition in.eof() should usually be tested separately, because premature end of file is a different type of problem.

In the ios3 program the input is presumed to occur one value per line. There are several ways to enforce this constraint. One way is shown in the ios3 program, which uses the ignore() member function, which can skip to the end of a line. The first argument to ignore() is the maximum number of characters to skip, and the second is the sentinel character. The ignore() function will gobble up characters from its input stream until either the maximum number has been encountered, or until the sentinel character has been encountered. Another way would be to use one of the unformatted input statements, such as get(), to read input until a newline is encountered. A third way is to read the input a line at a time, perhaps using the get() or getline() member functions of the istream class, and then use the input line with an istrstream (input string stream) object for the actual input. This last method is somewhat like the standard C trick of reading input lines using gets() or fgets() and then extracting the information from those lines using sscanf().

Manipulators

A *manipulator* is a function that is called within an iostream expression to modify the operation of a stream. Some manipulators perform standard chores, such as inserting an end of line into an output stream, others are used to control output format. We've already seen two manipulators—the endl manipulator, which inserts an end of line character, and setw, which specifies an input or output width. All of the Borland C++ manipulators are listed in Table 7.8.

TABLE 7.8

Iostream Library Manipulators

Manipulator	Use in an istream	Use in an ostream	Action
dec	Yes	Yes	Set the conversion radix to decimal.
oct	Yes	Yes	Set the conversion radix to octal.
hex	Yes	Yes	Set the conversion radix to hexadecimal.
ws	Yes	No	Skip whitespace.
ends	No	Yes	Add a null to a stream; usually used to null-terminate a string stream.
endl	No	Yes	Add an end of line sequence to a stream.
flush	No	Yes	Flush a stream so that all stored output is sent to the final destination.
setfill(int ch);	Yes	Yes	Set the fill character to ch.
setprecision(int np);	Yes	Yes	Set the floating-point precision to np.

TABLE 7.8

Iostream Library Manipulators (Continued)

Manipulator	Use in an istream	Use in an ostream	Action
setw(int n);	Yes	Yes	Set the width to n. On output, w is the minimum field width. On input, w is the size of a char array for storing a string. The width setting only applies to the immediately following conversion.
setbase(int b);	Yes	Yes	Set the conversion base to b, which should be 0, 8, 10, or 16. 0 means output in decimal and input using the C numeric conventions (see Table 7.9 discussion of dec, oct, hex flags).
setiosflags(long f),	Yes	Yes	Set the ios flag bits that are true in f.
resetiosflags(long f);	Yes	Yes	Reset the ios flag bits that are true in f.

The setiosflags() and resetiosflags() manipulators in Table 7.8 let you manually manage the conversion flags that are maintained for each stream. This is especially important for controlling floating-point output, because the supplied manipulators don't provide full control over floating fields. The flags are stored in individual bits in a status word, and the ios class contains an enumeration that defines constants for all the bits. The enumeration constants are listed in Table 7.9. The default setting for cin is ios::skipws and the default for cout is ios::skipws and ios::unitbuf.

TABLE 7.9

Iostream Library Format Constants

Format	Usage
skipws	Skip whitespace before extractions.
left, right	Right or left justification. The default is right justification.
internal	Internal justification, which means that numeric values are padded to field width in between the prefix (sign, 0x for hex) and the digits.
dec, oct, hex	Set the conversion base for integral types to decimal, octal, or hexadecimal. If not specified, output is in decimal and input is according to C conventions: first digit is 0 for octal; first digit is 1..9 for decimal; first digits are 0x for hexadecimal.
showbase	Output integral values with a leading 0 for octal output or a leading 0x for hexadecimal output.
showpoint	Include a decimal point in floating-point output.
uppercase	Output hex digits in uppercase.
showpos	Output positive integral values with a leading +.
scientific	Output in scientific notation: n.mmmEnn. The number of digits after the decimal point is governed by the precision() member function.

TABLE 7.9

Iostream Library Format Constants (Continued)

Format	Usage
fixed	Output in fixed-point notation: nnn.mmm. The number of digits after the decimal point is governed by the precision() member function.
unitbuf	Flush all streams after each insertion.
stdio	Flush stdout and stderr after each insertion.

It is easy to make your own manipulators. Manipulators without parameters are the easiest. For example, here are two manipulators that let you set the justification to right and left.

```
#include <iomanip.h>
ostream& left(ostream &s)
{
  s << resetiosflags(ios::right)
    << setiosflags(ios::left);
  return s;
}
ostream& right(ostream &s)
{
  s << resetiosflags(ios::left)
    << setiosflags(ios::right);
  return s;
}
```

For a parameterless manipulator, all you need to write is a function that returns a reference to a stream, takes a reference to a stream, and that does something to that stream in the function body. The stream should be an ostream for an output-only manipulator, an istream for an input-only manipulator, or ios for either type of stream.

You use the manipulator by placing a pointer to the function, not a call of the function, into an insertion or extraction expression.

```
cout << left << setw(5) << 1Ø << 2Ø << endl;
```

The ostream class contains an operator<<() function for operands that are pointers to functions taking a reference to an ostream and returning a reference to ostream. Because left has the recognized signature, it is called by the operator<<() function, which gives it a chance to manipulate the stream.

Manipulators with parameters are harder. The basic idea is to create a class that stores a pointer to a function and a parameter to send to that function. Inside an extraction or insertion expression you can create an object of that class, and then the iostream library will be responsible for calling the function to do the manipulation. Yes, this is a circuitous path, but the macros in the iomanip.h file make it easier than you might expect.

You need to create two functions when you create a parameterized manipulator. The first function is the actual manipulator. It should take a reference to the stream plus its own parameter, and it should return a reference to the stream. The second function should build a class object that stores a pointer to the true manipulator and the manipulator's parameter. The class itself is created using macros from iomanip.h. Here's an example, which allows you to choose left or right justification using a variable (1 for right, 0 for left).

```
#include <iomanip.h>
// parameterized manipulator
ostream& _setjust(ostream& s, int just)
{
  if (just) // right
    s << resetiosflags(ios::left)
      << setiosflags(ios::right);
  else      // left
    s << resetiosflags(ios::right)
      << setiosflags(ios::left);
  return s;
}
// build a class object to call _setjust() manipulator
OMANIP(int) setjust(int just)
{
  OMANIP(int) obj(_setjust, just);
  return obj;
}
```

The macro OMANIP(int) is the name of a class that is defined by a gaggle of complicated macros in iomanip.h. To build a manipulator for an istream you would use the IMANIP macro, and to build a manipulator for either type direction of stream you would use the SMANIP. The iomanip.h header file has already created all of the necessary classes for int and long parameters. If you want to use another type of parameter, you would use the IOMANIPdeclare-(type) macro to build all the pieces.

Here's how you could use the parameterized setjust() manipulator.

```
int i = rand() % 2;
cout << setjust(i) << setw(10) << 10 << endl;
```

In the above insertion expression, setjust(i) calls the setjust() function. The setjust() function constructs an OMANIP(int) type of object, initialized with a pointer to _setjust() and with the supplied value, and returns it. The ostream class knows that an OMANIP(int) object should be inserted by calling the function whose address is stored in the object with the parameter that is also stored in the object. This tortuous process completes with the call of _setjust() to actually manipulate the stream.

PART 3

Turbo Vision Class Library

TURBO VISION TUTORIAL

TURBO VISION IS AN APPLICATION FRAMEWORK FOR CREATING DOS CHARACTER-mode applications. Turbo Vision is in part a user-interface toolkit. It has components that let you construct dialog boxes, overlay windows, build menu-based applications, and the like. But in addition Turbo Vision specifies how these components, plus components that you supply, will work together to form a full application. Turbo Vision is more than just a set of widgets, it's a way of constructing applications.

But what about Windows? If you need to develop Windows applications, and you have no interest in DOS, you should skip ahead to Part 4 and learn about OWL, Borland's class library for Windows. DOS development isn't as glamorous right now as Windows development, but many more PCs can run DOS than can run Windows. DOS development also continues to be far easier than Windows development. With Turbo Vision, it is much simpler to create DOS applications that have the same ease of use as Windows applications.

The advantages of DOS-based Turbo Vision compared with Windows development include

- Applications can run on a wider range of machines because character-mode user interface requires less horsepower.

- Applications require less development effort, which makes it easier to recoup your costs even when you target a niche market.

- Turbo Vision is an ideal upgrade path for improving the interface of existing DOS character-mode applications.

Turbo Vision is a C++ class library, and it fully uses C++ capabilities. There is no way to use Turbo Vision without thoroughly knowing C++. If you're a C programmer who has bypassed the first part of this book hoping to jump right into your first Turbo Vision application, then think again. None of it will make sense until you are proficient in C++.

Turbo Vision is supplied with Borland's Turbo C++ for DOS and with Borland C++ with Application Frameworks. I don't understand why it isn't part of ordinary Borland C++, but if you have Borland C++ and want to write sophisticated DOS applications, you need to upgrade to Borland C++ with Application Frameworks. You shouldn't use Turbo Vision if your code must be portable to other environments or compilers. One final caveat: Turbo Vision has little in common with Borland's Object Windows Library, so don't expect to maintain one set of sources to create both DOS and Windows versions of your application.

My aim for this chapter and the next is to help you become proficient in using the Turbo Vision class library. More specifically, I have three goals. My first goal is to introduce you to the key ideas of Turbo Vision, so that you have a basic understanding of how the major components are used. The second is to introduce you to the basic components of Turbo Vision, so that you can start to explore the library. The third goal is to cover several more advanced topics, so that you can start to see how professional applications are developed using Turbo Vision. One final point: I'm not going to duplicate the reference material that is in Borland's *Turbo Vision for C++* manual. Use the manual as a reference when you need more detailed information.

Zen and the Art of Turbo Vision

Just as you need to understand a few ideas and concepts before learning C++, so also should you understand a few things before you start to learn the mechanics of Turbo Vision. For some, Turbo Vision's message-based, object-based methodology will seem very natural and familiar. But to far more people the approach taken by Turbo Vision will seem awkward, almost as if things were all done upside down.

The first Turbo Vision axiom is that you use Turbo Vision by extending it. To many, this is very unfamiliar territory, because extending a library isn't practical with a traditional library of functions. But Turbo Vision is a library of classes, many of which are designed to be extended. Turbo Vision is literally just a framework. It's up to you to flesh it out to form a complete application.

The next axiom is that Turbo Vision is an event-driven system. All of the individual elements in a Turbo Vision application perform their chores in response to events. There are three main types of events: keyboard events, mouse events, and message events, plus a placeholder event, the nothing event. One of the most important roles of the Turbo Vision framework is to package events into messages, and then route the messages to the appropriate elements. Some messages are handled automatically, but most message handling is your domain; much of the work of crafting a Turbo Vision application is managing and responding to messages.

A third axiom is that everything that appears on the screen is a view, which is represented by the TView class. TView is the fundamental class in the Turbo Vision hierarchy. It is the base class for anything that can be seen on the screen. Although there are other important and fundamental classes, TView has the central role. The second most important class is probably TGroup, because it is the basis for building collections of views. But to underline TView's primacy, consider that TGroup is itself an offspring of TView.

Turbo Vision is, fundamentally and inescapably, an object-oriented environment. In a Turbo Vision application, everything of importance is an object. Things happen by creating objects, those objects create further objects, and so on. Turbo Vision accepts and encourages a dynamic applications structure, one that is created on-the-fly in response to interactive demands. The key to this flexibility is heavy use of the heap, in which most Turbo Vision objects are created. This contrasts with a traditional procedural library, where the stack is the locus of activity. Turbo Vision's use of the heap makes it easy to have many contexts, each full and rich and self-sufficient.

The TVNull Application

A tiny do-nothing Turbo Vision application named TVNull is shown in Figure 8.1, and its source code is presented in Listing 8.1. TVNull defines an application class named TNullApp and it contains a brief main() routine to create and then activate an object from the TNullApp class.

FIGURE 8.1

TVNull

LISTING 8.1

The TVNull application

```
#define Uses_TApplication
#include <tv.h>

class TNullApp : public TApplication {
  public:
    TNullApp();  // constructor
};

TNullApp::TNullApp() :
  TProgInit(initStatusLine, initMenuBar, initDeskTop)
{
  return;
}
```

LISTING 8.1

The TVNull application (Continued)

```
void main()
{
  TNullApp myApp;
  myApp.run();
}
```

The TVNull application has a standard appearance and built-in functionality. The screen display in Figure 8.1 shows the three standard elements of the Turbo Vision screen: an empty menu line at the top, an empty desktop in the middle, and a simple status line at the bottom. The built-in functionality is the ability to exit, either by using the mouse to click the status line "Alt-X Exit" label, or by pressing Alt-X.

Let me go through Listing 8.1 and explain all the elements. Then in the remainder of this chapter I'll show how several of the features of TVNull can be expanded to create a more interesting application.

The first line of TVNull is a #define statement that defines a preprocessor identifier named Uses_TApplication. Each time you use a Turbo Vision class or other major element, you must insert a corresponding "uses" definition above the line that includes <tv.h>. This ensures that the correct header files will be included in your application. Note that you only need to have "uses" definitions for the classes that you use directly and not for their parents. For example, if you specify that you are using the TApplication class, tv.h will automatically include TApplication's parents and any other required files. If you use a class but omit its "uses" definition, you will get compilation errors. Placing extra "uses" clauses into a program is harmless, but it will slow compilation because unnecessary header files will be processed.

The second line includes tv.h, which must be included into all modules that use Turbo Vision classes. The tv.h header file contains logic to include other Turbo Vision header files, based on the "uses" clauses that you have specified.

The TVNull application derives a class named TNullApp from TApplication that contains only a constructor. The TNullApp class hints at the standard technique, which is to derive an application-management class from TApplication, but TNullApp itself is missing all of the common elements that create an application's character. Usually the application class derived from TApplication is the major initiator and organizer of an application. It specifies the menus and status bar appearance of an application, and it usually has an event handler that creates most of the top-level functionality.

The TNullApp class constructor's only role is to specify three function-pointer arguments to the TProgInit constructor. This is the only required action of a class derived from TApplication. The three arguments to TProgInit are pointers to functions that create the status line, menu bar, and desktop, respectively. Nearly all applications define their own status line and menu bar, although the default desktop is often sufficient. The TNullApp class chooses to specify the default functions, defined in the TApplication class, to perform these initializations. As you can see from Figure 8.1, the default menu bar is an empty menu bar, and the default status line contains a single label and key combination for exiting the program. What you can't see in Figure 8.1 is that there are three additional key combinations, which I'll discuss later in this chapter under "Setting the Status Line."

The main() routine in the TVNull application is actually quite representative of many Turbo Vision applications. Because the Turbo Vision library is strongly object oriented, the only standard role of main() is to create an application object and then call that object's run() member to start the application. If you have initialization or cleanup chores that must be performed before or after the interactive phase of execution, you can place those chores inside main().

One of the main ideas of Turbo Vision is that things are built dynamically. For example, a menu is built by creating a linked list of submenus, and each submenu is a linked list of menu items. The desktop works the same way; it contains a linked list of the items on the desktop. We can convert the TNullApp program into a more traditional "Hello" application by inserting some text onto the desktop. Because Turbo Vision must be in control of everything at all times, we can't just printf() some text onto the screen. Instead we must create an object that knows how to display text, and then insert that object onto the screen. The easiest object to use is one defined by the TStaticText class. The TStaticText class is most often used to provide labels in a dialog, but it may also be used in other ways, such as on the desktop. Figure 8.2 shows the appearance of the program, and Listing 8.2 shows the slightly modified program. (For those who don't recognize the surrogate for "Hello World," it is a quote from the rock opera *Tommy* by the Who.)

FIGURE 8.2

TVHi

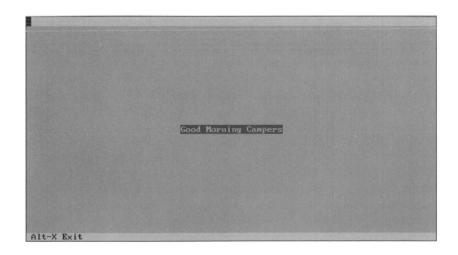

LISTING 8.2

The TVHi application

```cpp
#define Uses_TApplication
#define Uses_TStaticText
#define Uses_TRect
#include <tv.h>
#include <string.h>

class THiApp : public TApplication {
  public:
    THiApp();  // constructor
  protected:
    void centerText(TRect& r, char *msg);
};

THiApp::THiApp() :
  TProgInit(initStatusLine, initMenuBar, initDeskTop)
{
  char *Msg = "Good Morning Campers";
  centerText(getExtent(), Msg);
}

void THiApp::centerText(TRect& r, char *msg)
{
  int len = strlen(msg);
  TRect msgRect;
  // calculate center for the message
  msgRect.a.y = r.b.y / 2;
  msgRect.b.y = msgRect.a.y + 1;
  msgRect.a.x = r.b.x / 2;
  msgRect.a.x -= len / 2;
  msgRect.b.x = msgRect.a.x + len;
  // build and insert a static text object
  TStaticText *txtObj = new TStaticText(msgRect, msg);
  insert(txtObj);

  return;
}

void main()
{
  THiApp myApp;
  myApp.run();
}
```

Listing 8.2 shows that it is easy to add elements to a Turbo Vision application; simply initialize the object and then insert it into position. Most objects are much more complex than a static text object, but the principle is the same.

Before moving into more interesting territory, I want to mention the mechanics of building a Turbo Vision application. Because Turbo Vision itself is large, you must always use the large memory model. (The two applications presented above, which are almost as small as possible, are each about 170k.) Another point is that you must link to the Turbo Vision library (by checking off the Turbo Vision box in the Options-Linker-Libraries dialog of the IDE, or by specifying -tv.lib on the bcc command line), and you also must make sure that the compiler and the linker search the Turbo Vision include and lib directories.

Making Menus—The TVMenu Program

Turbo Vision menus are built by the TApplication class as the application springs to life. In the TVHi and TVNull applications discussed in the preceding section, a TApplication member function named initMenuBar() created an empty menu bar. Now it is time to see how you can write your own function to create a more interesting menu bar.

First let's settle the terminology. The menu line at the top of the screen is called a *menu bar*. Each title on the menu bar is the name of a *submenu*. Most submenu titles have a highlighted character, which, when combined with Alt, will pop up that submenu. For example, the F in the word File in most applications' File submenu is usually highlighted to indicate that you can press Alt-F to pop up the File submenu. Alternatively you can click on a submenu title with the mouse to pop up a submenu. Submenus are composed of *menu items*.

Several conventions apply to menu items:

- Menu item titles often have a highlighted character that can be typed to select that item. The menu item must be visible to use the shortcut.

- An accelerator for a menu item is often listed to the right of a menu item title. The menu item need not be visible to use the accelerator. (Accelerators are covered later in this chapter.)

- Menu item titles often are followed by ... (an ellipsis) to indicate that they lead to a dialog box.

- Some menu items lead to further submenus, which is indicated by a right pointing arrow following the menu title.

- Menu items are usually associated with a command message that is transmitted when the menu is selected.

The TVMenu program in Listing 8.3 creates an application that lets you select a few well-known television programs. The TVMenu program is mostly the same as TVNull, except for the addition of an initMenuBar() function to build a menu bar.

LISTING 8.3

The TVMenu program

```
//
// The TVMenu application
//

#define Uses_TApplication
#define Uses_TRect
#define Uses_TMenu
#define Uses_TMenuBar
#define Uses_TSubMenu
#define Uses_TMenuItem
#define Uses_TKeys
#include <tv.h>

// command constants
const cmMyKids   = 100;  // Daytime menu
const cmYourKids = 101;
const cmSearch   = 102;
const cmWorld    = 103;
const cmThirty   = 110;  // Evening menu
const cmSimpson  = 111;
const cmCheers   = 112;
const cmLetter   = 120;  // Late menu
const cmArsenio  = 121;
const cmJohnny   = 122;
const cmJay      = 123;

//
// Application class
//
class TMenuApp : public TApplication {
  public:
    TMenuApp();  // constructor
  protected:
    static TMenuBar *initMenuBar(TRect r);
};

//
// TMenuApp constructor
//
TMenuApp::TMenuApp() :
  TProgInit(initStatusLine, initMenuBar, initDeskTop)
{
  return;
}
```

LISTING 8.3

The TVMenu program (Continued)

```
//
// create a menu bar
//
TMenuBar *TMenuApp::initMenuBar(TRect r)
{
  // manually build sub-submenu for the Tonight Show
  TMenuItem *tonight - new TMenuItem("~J~ohnny",
    cmJohnny, kbNoKey);
  tonight->append(new TMenuItem("J~a~y",
    cmJay, kbNoKey));

  r.b.y = r.a.y + 1; // menu location

  return new TMenuBar(r,
    // DAYTIME submenu
    *new TSubMenu("~D~ayTime", kbAltD)
    + *new TMenuItem("All ~M~y Kids",
            cmMyKids, kbF1, hcNoContext, "F1")
    + *new TMenuItem("All ~Y~our Kids",
            cmYourKids, kbF2, hcNoContext, "F2")
    + *new TMenuItem("~S~earch (but only for tomorrow)",
            cmSearch, kbF3, hcNoContext, "F3")
    + *new TMenuItem("~A~s the World Turns",
            cmWorld, kbF4, hcNoContext, "F4")

    // EVENING submenu
    + *new TSubMenu("~E~vening", kbAltE)
    + *new TMenuItem("~3~0 ??", cmThirty, kbNoKey)
    + *new TMenuItem("~S~impsons", cmSimpson, kbNoKey)
    + *new TMenuItem("~C~heers", cmCheers, kbNoKey)

    // LATE NIGHT submenu
    + *new TSubMenu("~L~ate Night", kbAltL)
    + *new TMenuItem("~T~onight Show", kbNoKey,
        new TMenu( *tonight ) )
    + newLine()
    + *new TMenuItem("~L~etterman", cmLetter, kbNoKey)
    + *new TMenuItem("~A~rsenio", cmArsenio, kbNoKey)
  );
}

//
// main
```

LISTING 8.3

The TVMenu program (Continued)

```
//
void main()
{
  TMenuApp myApp;
  myApp.run();
}
```

Most of the initMenuBar() function is a return statement that is 24 lines long. Here's what the return statement would look like, if we stripped away all the details:

```
return new TMenuBar(r,
    submenuObj + menuitemObj + ...
    + submenuObj + menuitemObj + ...
    + submenuObj + menuitemObj + ... );
```

The return statement is returning a TMenuBar object, and the TMenuBar object is initialized with a linked list of TSubMenu and TMenuItem objects. The linked list is created by an overloaded operator+() function, which explains why the menu objects are separated by + symbols.

The first parameter for TMenuItem and TSubMenu constructors is the title. You should place tilde characters around the highlighted letter, so that Turbo Vision can help you build a keyboard interface to the menu. TMenuItem objects are followed by parameters for the value of the item's command code, the keyboard accelerator that can be used to generate that command code, and optionally a help context ID and the text for the right side of the menu. If you don't want a keyboard accelerator, you should specify the value kbNoKey, and if you aren't using help contexts, you should specify hcNoContext. A complete list of the symbolic key names can be found in the Turbo Vision include file tkeys.h. More information on help contexts can be found in the "Context-Sensitive Status Lines" section at the end of this chapter.

Another important role of the initMenuBar() function is to position the menu bar. The initMenuBar() function is given a TRect object for the entire screen, and from this it constructs a TRect for the top line. Then this new top-line rectangle is passed to the TMenuBar constructor, so the menu bar will be properly positioned. (A TRect object stores the character coordinates of a rectangular screen region. See the "Turbo Vision Coordinates" section of Chapter 9 for more information.)

The next four illustrations show the menus that are produced by the TV-Menu program. The DayTime submenu, which is the only menu that contains accelerators and accelerator legends, is shown here:

The Evening submenu looks like this:

The Late Night submenu is shown here:

The separator bar in the Late Night submenu is produced by the newLine() function. The Tonight Show menu item leads to a sub-submenu, shown here:

This Tonight Show menu was constructed manually at the beginning of the init-MenuBar() function, using the TMenuItem's insert() member function.

Messages and Message Handlers

The Turbo Vision menu discussed in the preceding section looks good, but it doesn't accomplish anything. Behind the scenes Turbo Vision is busily sending messages each time you make a menu selection, but I haven't specified how those messages should be handled. Now it's time to address that topic, so that you can see the ebb and flow of messages in a simple Turbo Vision application.

First let's talk about messages. Each message is coded by a number, which is stored in an unsigned short variable. Thus there are potentially 65,536 different messages, although no application is likely to handle even a small fraction of that number. Of these 65,000 messages, 256 are special because they can be enabled and disabled during execution. Thus it's slightly more accurate to say there are 255 first-class message seats, and about 65,000 additional message seats in second class. On screen, a disabled menu item is grayed and it can't be clicked on by using the mouse, or activated by typing its keyboard accelerator.

In the first-class section, Turbo Vision reserves messages 0 through 99, which is why the command numbers in the preceding TVMenu program started at 100. Of the second-class messages, Turbo Vision reserves numbers 256 through 999. These restrictions are summarized in Table 8.1.

TABLE 8.1

Turbo Vision Message Numbers

Numeric Range	Can Be Disabled?	Reserved by Turbo Vision
0..99	Yes	Yes
99..255	Yes	No
256..999	No	Yes
1000..65,535	No	No

Messages are acted upon by the handleEvent() member function from the TView class. The TView class's handleEvent() member function is virtual, because most classes derived from TView need to define their own handleEvent(). When you create your own application class, you invariably need to give it a handleEvent() member function that takes care of most of the main menu-bar commands. Listing 8.4 shows the TVMenu2 program, which has been enhanced to handle all of the messages generated by the menu bar.

LISTING 8.4

The TVMenu2 program

```
//
// The TVMenu application
//

#define Uses_TApplication
#define Uses_TRect
#define Uses_TMenu
#define Uses_TMenuBar
#define Uses_TSubMenu
#define Uses_TMenuItem
#define Uses_TKeys
#define Uses_TEvent
#define Uses_MsgBox
#include <tv.h>
```

LISTING 8.4

The TVMenu2 program (Continued)

```
// command constants
const cmMyKids    = 100;   // Daytime menu
const cmYourKids  = 101;
const cmSearch    = 102;
const cmWorld     = 103;
const cmThirty    = 110;   // Evening menu
const cmSimpson   = 111;
const cmCheers    = 112;
const cmLetter    = 120;   // Late menu
const cmArsenio   = 121;
const cmJohnny    = 122;
const cmJay       = 123;
// first and last
const cmMenuFirst = 100;
const cmMenuLast  = 129;   // Indexed by a commandID—
                           // cmMenuFirst


// command id strings
static char *cmdNames[] = {
  // Daytime (100..109)
  "All My Kids", "All Your Kids",
  "Search for the Next Day", "As the World Spins",
  "", "", "", "", "",  "",  // placeholders
  // Evening (110..119)
  "Thirty More or Less", "Alan Simpson",
  "It's a Cheery Life",
  "", "", "", "", "", "", "",
  // Late Night (120..129)
  "David L.", "Arsenio H.",
  "Johnny C.", "Jay L.",
  "", "", "", "", "", ""
};


//
// Application class
//
class TMenuApp : public TApplication {
  public:
    TMenuApp();  // constructor
  protected:
    static TMenuBar *initMenuBar(TRect r);
    void handleEvent(TEvent& event);
};
```

LISTING 8.4

The TVMenu2 program (Continued)

```
//
// TMenuApp constructor
//
TMenuApp::TMenuApp() :
  TProgInit(initStatusLine, initMenuBar, initDeskTop)
{
  return;
}


//
// create a menu bar
//
TMenuBar *TMenuApp::initMenuBar(TRect r)
{
  // manually build sub-submenu for the Tonight Show
  TMenuItem *tonight = new TMenuItem("~J~ohnny",
    cmJohnny, kbNoKey);
  tonight->append(new TMenuItem("J~a~y",
    cmJay, kbNoKey));

  r.b.y = r.a.y + 1; // menu location

  return new TMenuBar(r,
    // DAYTIME submenu
    *new TSubMenu("~D~ayTime", kbAltD)
    + *new TMenuItem("All ~M~y Kids",
           cmMyKids, kbF1, hcNoContext, "F1")
    + *new TMenuItem("All ~Y~our Kids",
           cmYourKids, kbF2, hcNoContext, "F2")
    + *new TMenuItem("~S~earch (but only for tomorrow)",
           cmSearch, kbF3, hcNoContext, "F3")
    + *new TMenuItem("~A~s the World Turns",
           cmWorld, kbF4, hcNoContext, "F4")
    // EVENING submenu
    + *new TSubMenu("~E~vening", kbAltE)
    + *new TMenuItem("~3~0 ??", cmThirty, kbNoKey)
    + *new TMenuItem("~S~impsons", cmSimpson, kbNoKey)
    + *new TMenuItem("~C~heers", cmCheers, kbNoKey)
    // LATE NIGHT submenu
    + *new TSubMenu("~L~ate Night", kbAltL)
    + *new TMenuItem("~T~onight Show", kbNoKey,
        new TMenu( *tonight ) )
    + newLine()
```

LISTING 8.4

The TVMenu2 program (Continued)

```
        + *new TMenuItem("~L~etterman", cmLetter, kbNoKey)
        + *new TMenuItem("~A~rsenio", cmArsenio, kbNoKey)
    );
}


//
// application's main event handler
//
void TMenuApp::handleEvent(TEvent& event)
{
  TApplication::handleEvent(event); // give base a chance

  if (event.what == evCommand) {
    ushort& evCmd = event.message.command;
    switch(evCmd) {   // the evening shows are feuding
      case cmThirty:
        disableCommand(cmSimpson);
        break;
      case cmSimpson:
        disableCommand(cmCheers);
        break;
      case cmCheers:
        disableCommand(cmThirty);
        break;
    }
    if (evCmd >= cmMenuFirst && evCmd <= cmMenuLast) {
      messageBox(cmdNames[evCmd-cmMenuFirst],
        mfInformation);
      clearEvent(event);
    }
  }
}


//
// main
//
void main()
{
  TMenuApp myApp;
  myApp.run();
}
```

The handleEvent() member function is passed a reference to a TEvent structure. TEvent contains an unsigned short named *what* that indicates what type of event it contains. The event.h header file, which is included by tv.h whenever you #define Uses_TEvent, contains masks that should be used to interrogate the *what* element. Table 8.2 lists the event masks and their uses. The masks that cover a group of events should be ANDed with *what,* while those that dissect a single event may be compared for equality with *what.*

TABLE 8.2

Turbo Vision Event Masks

Mask	Usage
evMessage	Should be ANDed with *what;* TRUE indicates that the event is a command, broadcast, or user-defined message.
evCommand	Indicates a command message.
evBroadcast	Indicates a broadcast message.
evKeyboard	Should be ANDed with *what;* TRUE indicates a keyboard event.
evKeyDown	Indicates a key down event. (Currently the only type of keyboard event.)
evMouse	Should be ANDed with *what;* TRUE indicates a mouse event.
evMouseDown	Indicates mouse button press.
evMouseUp	Indicates mouse button release.
evMouseMove	Indicates mouse movement.
evMouseAuto	Indicates an auto event, which occurs periodically when a mouse button is held down.

The handleEvent() function in TVMenu2 only handles command events, which is typical for an application's top-level event handlers. Keyboard and mouse events are more likely handled by handlers inside individual windows. Most handleEvent() functions have a structure similar to that of TVMenu2. Usually there is a test at the top to make sure an event is the proper kind, followed by a switch statement to handle the individual messages of that kind.

```
void someClass::handleEvent(TEvent& event)
{
  // give base class first crack
  baseClass::handleEvent(event);

  // now handle locally
  if (event.what == evSomeType) {
    switch(event.someField) {
      case . . .
```

```
      case . . .
    }
    clearEvent(event); // only if handled!!
  }
}
```

In TVMenu2, the three messages pertaining to evening shows are handled by disabling the command of a competing evening show, using the disableCommand() member function from TView. The point of this is to have some code in handleEvent() that manages specific messages, and also to show how commands are enabled and disabled. The standard action for all commands in TMenuApp's handleEvent() function is to pop up a message box containing the title of the show. After each message has been handled, it should be cleared using clearEvent(). Be careful not to clear events that haven't been handled, but be sure to clear those that have been handled.

Setting the Status Line

The status line is a single line at the bottom of the screen that usually lists several keyboard shortcuts. You can invoke the status line commands either by pressing the indicated key, or by clicking on the status line text with the mouse. In addition, the status line can be used to display hints, which are extremely brief explanations of the current state of the program. The status line is also used as a device in Turbo Vision applications for creating keyboard accelerators that aren't listed on the status line.

As you might expect of a feature named "status line," the status line can change. You can craft a Turbo Vision application so that the status line changes dynamically, and without runtime intervention on your part, according to what the user is doing. I'm first going to show a very simple example that creates a staid, unchanging status line, but then I'll move to a more spirited example that shows how Turbo Vision can dynamically manage the status line.

The Turbo Vision example programs that you have already seen all use the default status line, which displays the text "Alt-X Exit." If you press Alt-X, the default status line will generate the cmQuit command, which normally causes the application to exit. The default status line also creates most of the other standard accelerators, which are listed in Table 8.3. (The default status line doesn't implement the F6 or Shift-F6 accelerators for activating the next or previous window.)

TABLE 8.3

Standard Turbo Vision Keyboard Accelerators

Key	Command	Usage
Alt-X	cmQuit	Exit from the application.
Alt-F3	cmClose	Close the active window.

TABLE 8.3

Standard Turbo Vision Keyboard Accelerators (Continued)

Key	Command	Usage
F5	cmZoom	Zoom the active window to full screen if not maximized; to previous size if maximized.
Ctrl-F5	cmResize	Move and resize the current window. The arrow keys move the window; the shifted arrows resize the window; the Enter key returns to normal operation.
F6	cmNext	Activate the next window.
Shift-F6	cmPrev	Activate the previous window.
F10	cmMenu	Activate the menu bar.

The status line is created and defined by a function whose address is passed to the TProgInit constructor by the constructor of your application class. You could use a global function to create the status line, but instead it is traditional to use a static member function from your application class. You can name the function at your discretion, but the traditional name is initStatusLine. The function must accept a TRect argument, and it must return a TStatusLine object that has been allocated dynamically.

Like the initMenuBar() function that we looked at in Listing 8.3, the initStatusLine() function in Listing 8.5 builds a linked list of objects by using an operator+() function. The individual items that comprise a status line are TStatusDef objects and TStatusItem objects. The TStatusDef object is a header for a group of TStatusItem objects that form a single status line. You can have multiple groups of TStatusItem objects so that each context in your application will have its own status line and its own set of accelerators.

LISTING 8.5

The TVMenu3 application's status line functions

```
//
// Application class
//
class TMenuApp : public TApplication {
  public:
    TMenuApp();  // constructor
  protected:
    static TMenuBar *initMenuBar(TRect r);
    static TStatusLine* initStatusLine(TRect r);
    void handleEvent(TEvent& event);
};

//
```

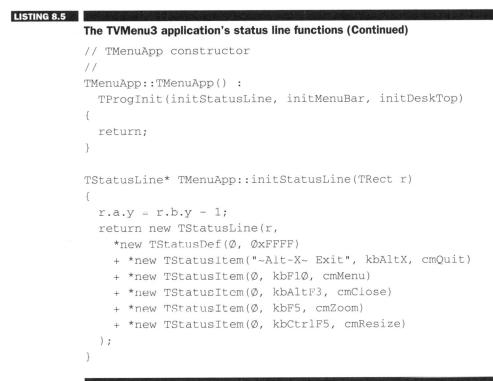

LISTING 8.5

The TVMenu3 application's status line functions (Continued)

```
// TMenuApp constructor
//
TMenuApp::TMenuApp() :
  TProgInit(initStatusLine, initMenuBar, initDeskTop)
{
  return;
}


TStatusLine* TMenuApp::initStatusLine(TRect r)
{
  r.a.y = r.b.y - 1;
  return new TStatusLine(r,
    *new TStatusDef(0, 0xFFFF)
    + *new TStatusItem("~Alt-X~ Exit", kbAltX, cmQuit)
    + *new TStatusItem(0, kbF10, cmMenu)
    + *new TStatusItem(0, kbAltF3, cmClose)
    + *new TStatusItem(0, kbF5, cmZoom)
    + *new TStatusItem(0, kbCtrlF5, cmResize)
  );
}
```

The TStatusDef class's constructor requires two arguments, which are used to define a range of help contexts. If you want a single status line to serve throughout an application, you should specify the full range (for an unsigned short) of 0 to 0xffff. Each element in a TStatusDef group is a TStatusItem object. The TStatusItem's constructor requires three arguments: a text label that will appear on the status line, the keyboard accelerator, and the command that will be sent when the accelerator is pressed or when the text label is clicked using the mouse. The keyboard constant should be one of the constants defined in Turbo Vision's tkeys.h file. Be sure to define Uses_TKeys if you use any of the keyboard constants. Simply use a null pointer (0) in place of the text label if you want to have an anonymous accelerator, one that isn't displayed on the status line.

Listing 8.5 shows only the status-line-related parts of TVMenu3, which is yet another variant of TVMenu. The parts of TVMenu3 that aren't shown are identical to TVMenu2. I chose to make the initStatusLine() function in TVMenu3 create a status line that does exactly the same thing as the default Turbo Vision status line. The only difference is who is in control, you or Turbo Vision. If you look at the initStatusLine() code in Listing 8.5, you'll see that there are five elements in the status line. The first, which establishes Alt-X as a way to generate the cmQuit command, is visible, while the remaining four elements implement the standard anonymous accelerators.

Context-Sensitive Status Lines

Turbo Vision makes it easy to build a status line that changes dynamically, and automatically, as the user interacts with an application. The key idea is that each view in an application should be identified, so that Turbo Vision always knows what status line to use. The identifiers are called help context identifiers, because they are also used to produce context-sensitive help.

Listing 8.6 shows the TVMenu4 program, which is the same as TVMenu3 but with a context-sensitive status line. To provide context sensitivity I created a group of context identifiers, and I made sure that each element in the program, which in this simple program means each menu item, was associated with a help context. If you don't specify help contexts, they default to hcNoContext, whose value is 0.

In Listing 8.6 I created help context ranges for each of the three menus on the menu bar. This organization is partly revealed near the top of Listing 8.6 where the help context identifiers are initialized. But it is much more clearly revealed in the return statement of the initStatusLine() function, which creates four groups of status line items. The first group is for help contexts ranging from 0 (the default) up to hcDaytime–1. It contains the standard Alt-X label on the status line, and it contains the four standard keyboard accelerators. The other three status line groups are for the three menu bar items. Each of these status lines provides the Alt-X shortcut, but the other accelerators aren't relevant during menu operations. Also, so you can see what is going on, each of the three status lines has a slightly different label for the Alt-X keyboard shortcut.

In addition to identifying accelerators on the status line, Turbo Vision allows you to display hints. Hinting is controlled by the TStatusLine class's hint() member function. Each time the context changes, hint() is called upon to output the hint for that context. The hint() member of TStatusLine always returns a pointer to an empty string, but hint() is a virtual function expressly to enable you to supply your own hints.

In Listing 8.6 I derived the class TMenuStatusLine from TStatusLine solely to provide my own hinting. The TMenuStatusLine class contains only two member functions, a constructor and hint(). The constructor simply passes its arguments to the base class constructor. The hint() member contains a switch statement that returns a particular hint. If the given context doesn't correspond to one of the hints in the switch statement, a pointer to a null string is returned.

You might expect that the number of hints would correspond to the number of status lines. Certainly there is a relationship, but it is easy to have many more hints than status lines. Each group of status lines corresponds to a range of help contexts, while each hint is for a specific help context. In the application in Listing 8.6 there are separate hints for the title of a submenu and for the submenu items. I could have provided a separate hint for each menu item, but instead I made one hint apply to all of the menu items in a submenu.

LISTING 8.6

The TVMenu4 program, demonstrating context-sensitive status lines and hinting

```
//
// The TVMenu application
//    (with status line and hints)
//

#define Uses_TApplication
#define Uses_TRect
#dcfine Uses_TMenu
#define Uses_TMenuBar
#define Uses_TSubMenu
#define Uses_TMenuItem
#define Uses_TKeys
#define Uses TEvcnt
#define Uses_MsgBox
#define Uses_TStatusLine
#define Uses_TStatusDef
#define Uses_TStatusItem
#include <tv.h>

// command constants
const cmMyKids    = 100;  // Daytime menu
const cmYourKids  = 101;
const cmSearch    = 102;
const cmWorld     = 103;
const cmThirty    = 110;  // Evening menu
const cmSimpson   = 111;
const cmCheers    = 112;
const cmLetter    = 120;  // Late menu
const cmArsenio   = 121;
const cmJohnny    = 122;
const cmJay       = 123;
// first and last
const cmMenuFirst = 100;
const cmMenuLast  = 129;

// command id strings
static char *cmdNames[] = {
  // Daytime (100..109)
  "All My Kids", "All Your Kids",
  "Search for the Next Day", "As the World Spins",
  "", "", "", "", "",  "",
  // Evening (110..119)
```

LISTING 8.6

The TVMenu4 program, demonstrating context-sensitive status lines and hinting (Continued)

```
    "Thirty More or Less", "Alan Simpson",
    "It's a Cheery Life",
    "", "", "", "", "", "", "",
    // Late Night (120..129)
    "David L.", "Arsenio H.",
    "Johnny C.", "Jay L.",
    "", "", "", "", "", ""
};

//
// a few help contexts for the status line
//
const hcDaytime    = 0x1000;
const hcDaytimeMenu = hcDaytime + 1;
const hcEvening    = 0x2000;
const hcEveningMenu = hcEvening + 1;
const hcLateNight = 0x3000;
const hcLateNightMenu = hcLateNight + 1;

//
// Application class
//
class TMenuApp : public TApplication {
  public:
    TMenuApp();   // constructor
  protected:
    static TMenuBar *initMenuBar(TRect r);
    static TStatusLine* initStatusLine(TRect r);
    void handleEvent(TEvent& event);
};

//
// Class for status line with hints
//
class TMenuStatusLine : public TStatusLine {
  public:
    TMenuStatusLine(TRect& r, TStatusDef& d) :
      TStatusLine(r, d)
    {
      return;
    }
    const char *hint(ushort u);
```

LISTING 8.6

The TVMenu4 program, demonstrating context-sensitive status lines and hinting (Continued)

```
};


//
// TMenuApp constructor
//
TMenuApp::TMenuApp() :
  TProgInit(initStatusLine, initMenuBar, initDeskTop)
{
  return;
}


//
// create a menu bar
//
TMenuBar *TMenuApp::initMenuBar(TRect r)
{
  // manually build sub-submenu for the Tonight Show
  TMenuItem *tonight = new TMenuItem("~J~ohnny",
    cmJohnny, kbNoKey);
  tonight->append(new TMenuItem("J~a~y",
    cmJay, kbNoKey));

  r.b.y = r.a.y + 1; // menu location

  return new TMenuBar(r,
    // DAYTIME submenu
    *new TSubMenu("~D~ayTime", kbAltD, hcDayTimeMenu)
    + *new TMenuItem("All ~M~y Kids",
            cmMyKids, kbF1, hcDaytime, "F1")
    + *new TMenuItem("All ~Y~our Kids",
            cmYourKids, kbF2, hcDaytime, "F2")
    + *new TMenuItem("~S~earch (but only for tomorrow)",
            cmSearch, kbF3, hcDaytime, "F3")
    + *new TMenuItem("~A~s the World Spins",
            cmWorld, kbF4, hcDaytime, "F4")

    // EVENING submenu
    + *new TSubMenu("~E~vening", kbAltE, hcEveningMenu)
    + *new TMenuItem("~3~0 ??",
            cmThirty, kbNoKey, hcEvening)
    + *new TMenuItem("~S~impsons",
            cmSimpson, kbNoKey, hcEvening)
```

LISTING 8.6

The TVMenu4 program, demonstrating context-sensitive status lines and hinting (Continued)

```
    + *new TMenuItem("~C~heers",
            cmCheers, kbNoKey, hcEvening)

    // LATE NIGHT submenu
    + *new TSubMenu("~L~ate Night", kbAltL, hcLateNightMenu)
    + *new TMenuItem("~T~onight Show", kbNoKey,
        new TMenu(*tonight), hcLateNight)
    + newLine()
    + *new TMenuItem("~L~etterman",
            cmLetter, kbNoKey, hcLateNight)
    + *new TMenuItem("~A~rsenio",
            cmArsenio, kbNoKey, hcLateNight)
  );
}


//
// Build status lines for the four main contexts
//
TStatusLine* TMenuApp::initStatusLine(TRect r)
{
  r.a.y = r.b.y - 1;
  return new TMenuStatusLine(r,
    // default help context
    * new TStatusDef(0, hcDaytime-1)
    + *new TStatusItem("~Alt-X~ Exit", kbAltX, cmQuit)
    + *new TStatusItem(0, kbF10, cmMenu)
    + *new TStatusItem(0, kbAltF3, cmClose)
    + *new TStatusItem(0, kbF5, cmZoom)
    + *new TStatusItem(0, kbCtrlF5, cmResize)
    // Daytime
    + *new TStatusDef(hcDaytime, hcEvening-1)
    + *new TStatusItem("~Alt-X~ Daytime Exit", kbAltX, cmQuit)
    // Evening
    + *new TStatusDef(hcEvening, hcLateNight-1)
    + *new TStatusItem("~Alt-X~ Evening Exit", kbAltX, cmQuit)
    // Late Night
    + *new TStatusDef(hcLateNight, 0xffff)
    + *new TStatusItem("~Alt-X~ LateNight Exit", kbAltX,
  cmQuit)
  );
}
```

LISTING 8.6

The TVMenu4 program, demonstrating context-sensitive status lines and hinting (Continued)

```cpp
//
// hints for status line
//
const char *TMenuStatusLine::hint(ushort h)
{
  switch(h) {
    case hcDaytime:
      return "Daytime shows";
    case hcDaytimeMenu:
      return "Menu of daytime shows";
    case hcEvening:
      return "Evening shows";
    case hcEveningMenu:
      return "Menu of evening shows";
    case hcLateNight:
      return "Late night shows";
    case hcLateNightMenu:
      return "Menu of late night shows";
    default:
      return "";
  }
}


//
// application's main event handler
//
void TMenuApp::handleEvent(TEvent& event)
{
  TApplication::handleEvent(event); // give base a chance

  if (event.what == evCommand) {
    ushort& evCmd = event.message.command;
    if (evCmd >= cmMenuFirst && evCmd <= cmMenuLast) {
      messageBox(cmdNames[evCmd-cmMenuFirst],
        mfInformation);
      clearEvent(event);
    }
  }
}
```

LISTING 8.6

The TVMenu4 program, demonstrating context-sensitive status lines and hinting (Continued)

```
//
// main
//
void main()
{
  TMenuApp myApp;
  myApp.run();
}
```

9 TURBO VISION TECHNIQUES

TURBO VISION'S MENUS AND STATUS LINE ARE IMPORTANT ASPECTS OF ANY Turbo Vision application, but they are not the central issue. Now that you have seen how simple Turbo Vision applications are constructed, it is time to move to the principal topic, how to construct the core of a Turbo Vision application.

As I stated earlier, the TView class is the central class in the Turbo Vision class library, but instead of starting with a discussion of the TView class, I'm going to start by showing how to make Turbo Vision dialogs. This will demonstrate a key facility of the Turbo Vision library, but it will also show many of the features of TView. Then I'll move directly to TView, so you can discover how to make your own classes from the TView class.

Creating a Dialog Box

Turbo Vision dialogs are built in the same style as other Turbo Vision elements. First you create a dialog box object, and then you insert controls into that object. The TDialog class is a descendant of TGroup, so it knows how to maintain a list of elements. Each control in a dialog box is implemented by one or more Turbo Vision objects. Simple controls, such as a text label or a button, are implemented by a single object, while more complex controls, such as radio buttons and check boxes, are implemented by sets of interacting objects, which are themselves a group.

Dialog boxes can be either modal or modeless. A modal dialog box, which is by far the most common form of dialog, grabs the focus and doesn't let go. It must be closed before any other window can be used. A modeless dialog box obeys the conventions of an ordinary dialog box—it usually has buttons, and so on—but it gets and releases the focus like an ordinary window.

Dialog boxes are created in four steps:

1. Create a TDialog object. You must specify the dialog box title and its size and location on the screen.

2. Create the individual dialog box controls and insert them into the dialog box.

3. Initialize the controls using the dialog box's setData() member function.

4. Activate the dialog box. For a modal dialog you should use the application's deskTop pointer to activate the desktop's execView() member function. For a modeless dialog you use the application's deskTop pointer to insert the dialog into the desktop.

Once activated, dialog boxes work autonomously. For most dialog boxes you don't need to attend to anything while the dialog box is active, although some dialogs need to display behavior that isn't built into Turbo Vision.

Dialog boxes are usually terminated by pressing the OK or Cancel button. When things go well and the user has made satisfactory choices, you should pick up the new settings from the dialog box by using the getData() member function. If the dialog is canceled, you should skip the call of getData().

Turbo Vision Coordinates

Turbo Vision uses a coordinate system that is very sensible and easy to use, but it is probably different from what you are used to. Instead of numbering each cell, Turbo Vision uses coordinates to refer to the points between the cells. As is usual in character environments, x values increase to the right, y values increase downward, and the origin is the top-left corner of the screen. Figure 9.1 shows the top-left corner of the coordinate system, in which the rectangle defined by the points (2,1) and (7,2) contains the text "Hello." The advantage of the Turbo Vision system is that sizes pop out naturally, without having to fudge by plus or minus one. In the example shown in Figure 9.1, the width of the text is five characters, which you can calculate by subtracting the x coordinates (seven minus two is five). Similarly the text height is one line, which can easily be calculated by subtracting the y coordinates. (In coordinate systems where coordinates refer to display locations, subtracting x- and y-coordinates produces widths and heights that are too small by 1.)

Coordinates in Turbo Vision applications are usually specified using a TRect object. You can construct a TRect object by using a pair of TPoint objects, but by far the more common way is to specify two pairs of (x,y) coordinates. Here is the declaration of a TStaticText object that could be inserted into a window to display "Hello" at the position shown in Figure 9.1.

```
TView *hi = new TStaticText(TRect(2,1,7,2), "Hello");
```

The other thing to remember about Turbo Vision coordinates is that everything is relative. When you create a dialog box, you specify its location in screen coordinates. But when you place objects inside the dialog box, you place them relative to the dialog box's own coordinate system, which originates in its own top-left corner.

Turbo Vision coordinates have their origin in the top-left corner, with x increasing to the right and y increasing down. The coordinates refer to the corners of the character cells, not to the cells themselves. The string "Hello" in the figure is in the region bounded by the points (2,1) and (7,2).

FIGURE 9.1

The Turbo Vision coordinate system

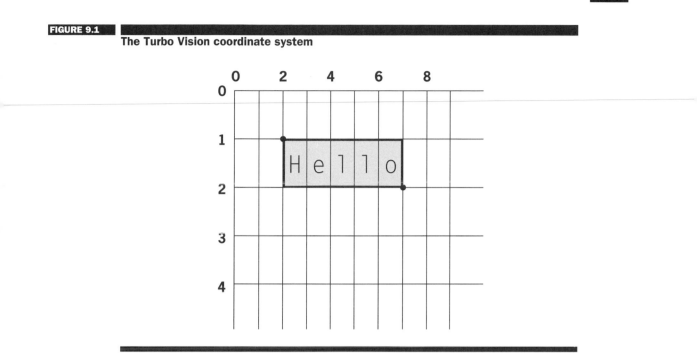

Starting a Dialog—Exploring TVDialog

A moderately complex dialog box is shown in Figure 9.2, and the source code to produce it is shown in Listing 9.1.

FIGURE 9.2

The TVDialog application

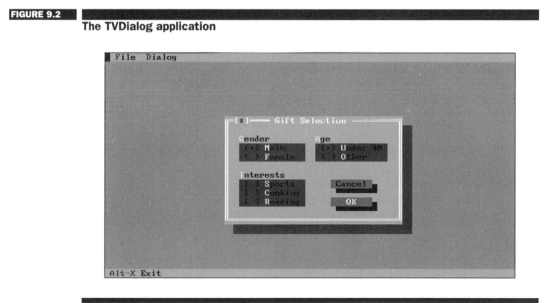

LISTING 9.1

The TVDialog application

```
//
// The TVDialog application
//

#define Uses_TApplication
#define Uses_TDeskTop
#define Uses_TRect
#define Uses_TMenu
#define Uses_TMenuBar
#define Uses_TSubMenu
#define Uses_TMenuItem
#define Uses_TKeys
#define Uses_TEvent
#define Uses_MsgBox
#define Uses_TDialog
#define Uses_TButton
#define Uses_TRadioButtons
#define Uses_TCheckBoxes
#define Uses_TLabel
#define Uses_TSItem
#include <tv.h>

// command constants
const cmDialog1 = 100;  // Run the dialog

//
// Store the dialog data
//
// N.B. -- Layout must match order of insertion
// in Dialog().
//
struct TDialogData {
  ushort nGender;
  ushort nInterests;
  ushort nAge;
  TDialogData() : // initialize
    nGender(0),
    nInterests(0),
    nAge(0)
    { return; }
};

//
// Application class
```

LISTING 9.1

The TVDialog application (Continued)

```
//
class TDialogApp : public TApplication {
  public:
    TDialogApp();   // constructor
  protected:
    static TMenuBar *initMenuBar(TRect r);
    void handleEvent(TEvent& event);
    void Dialog1();
    TDialogData dialogData;
};


//
// TDialogApp constructor
//
TDialogApp::TDialogApp() :
  TProgInit(initStatusLine, initMenuBar, initDeskTop)
{
  return;
}


//
// create a menu bar
//
TMenuBar *TDialogApp::initMenuBar(TRect r)
{
  r.b.y = r.a.y + 1; // menu location

  return new TMenuBar(r,
    *new TSubMenu("~F~ile", kbAltF)
    + *new TMenuItem("~Q~uit",
            cmQuit, kbAltX, hcNoContext, "Alt+X")
    + *new TSubMenu("~D~ialog", kbAltD)
    + *new TMenuItem("Dialog ~1~",
            cmDialog1, kbAlt1, hcNoContext)
  );
}


//
// application's main event handler
//
void TDialogApp::handleEvent(TEvent& event)
{
  TApplication::handleEvent(event); // give base a chance
```

LISTING 9.1

The TVDialog application (Continued)

```cpp
   if (event.what == evCommand) {
     ushort& evCmd = event.message.command;
     switch(evCmd) {
       case cmDialog1:
         Dialog1();
         break;
       default:
         messageBox("Unknown Command",
           mfInformation);
         break;
     }
     clearEvent(event);
   }
}

//
// Create a Gift Selection dialog box
//
void TDialogApp::Dialog1()
{
  TDialog *pd = new TDialog(TRect(23, 6, 58, 18),
    "Gift Selection");

  if (pd) {
    // GENDER
    TView *v1 = new TRadioButtons(TRect(3, 3, 16, 5),
      new TSItem("~M~ale",
      new TSItem("~F~emale", Ø))
    );
    pd->insert(v1);
    pd->insert(new TLabel(TRect(2, 2, 9, 3),
      "~G~ender", v1));

    // INTERESTS
    TView *v2 = new TCheckBoxes(TRect(3, 7, 16, 1Ø),
      new TSItem("~S~ports",
      new TSItem("~C~ooking",
      new TSItem("~R~eading", Ø)))
    );
    pd->insert(v2);
    pd->insert(new TLabel(TRect(2, 6, 12, 7),
      "~I~nterests", v2));

    // AGE
```

LISTING 9.1

The TVDialog application (Continued)

```
        TView *v3 = new TRadioButtons(TRect(18, 3, 32, 5),
          new TSItem("~U~nder 18",
          new TSItem("~O~ther", Ø))
        );
        pd->insert(v3);
        pd->insert(new TLabel(TRect(17, 2, 21, 3),
          "~A~ge", v3));

        // BUTTONS
        pd->insert(new TButton(TRect(2Ø, 7, 3Ø, 9),
          "Cancel", cmCancel, bfNormal));
        pd->insert(new TButton(TRect(2Ø, 9, 3Ø, 11),
          "O~K~", cmOK, bfDefault));

        // Run the modal dialog
        pd->setData(&dialogData);
        int cmd = deskTop->execView(pd);
        if (cmd != cmCancel)
          pd->getData(&dialogData);
          destroy(pd);
    }
}

//
// main
//
void main()
{
  TDialogApp myApp;
  myApp.run();
}
```

Much of the program in Listing 9.1 is the same as the simple menu examples from Chapter 8. The new aspect of the TVDialog application is concentrated in the Dialog1() function, which is called from the application's eventHandle() function whenever the cmDialog1 event occurs.

Let me go through the Dialog1() function slowly so you can see all the details. I'll use this as an opportunity to explain the four most common controls: TButton, TLabel, TRadioButtons, and TCheckList. Once you understand how the simple controls are used, it is easy to understand the other controls that are supplied with Turbo Vision.

Creating a Dialog Box Object

The first activity inside Dialog1() is to create a dialog box object.

```
TDialog *pd = new TDialog(TRect(23, 6, 58, 18),
  "Gift Selection");
```

The TDialog constructor requires two parameters, a TRect that specifies the dialog box's location on the screen, and the title for the dialog box, which will be centered on the top border of the dialog box. Note that creating a TDialog object doesn't cause anything to happen on the screen; all it does is create an object that can store controls, and that can later be instructed to display itself on the screen. Also note that the box is allocated dynamically using new; we must be careful to deallocate it at the end of Dialog1() so that its memory is released.

Creating the Controls

The next step is to create the controls. They must be created in tab order, which is the order in which you move the focus from one control to another using the Tab key. Ordinarily you want the tab to start in the top-left corner and then move through the box in a logical order. Here is the code that creates the TRadioButtons object that manages the set of radio buttons in the upper-left corner of the Gift Selection dialog box in Figure 9.2.

```
// GENDER
TView *v1 = new TRadioButtons(TRect(3, 3, 16, 5),
  new TSItem("~M~ale",
  new TSItem("~F~emale", 0))
);
```

The TRadioButtons constructor requires two arguments, the position of the radio buttons and a pointer to a list of TSItem objects. The position of the radio buttons includes the buttons and their text descriptions, but it doesn't include the TLabel object that identifies the group of radio buttons. If you look at the TRect that specifies the position of the radio buttons, you'll see that its upper-left corner is at (3,3), which is in the upper-left region of the dialog box, and you might also notice that the height of the buttons is two (five minus three), which corresponds to the two items in the list of TSItem objects.

The list of TSItem objects is used to supply labels for the individual radio buttons. The labels are "~M~ale" and "~F~emale." As in menu items, the tildes surround the highlighted letters, which lets you easily create keyboard shortcuts. Each TSItem constructor requires two arguments, a string that is used as a button label, and a pointer to the next item in the list. TSItem lists are usually created as shown in the preceding code, in which a pointer to the second item in the list is the argument to the first item, a pointer to the third item is the argument to the second, and so on. This can get unpleasant because of the nesting of the parentheses. In the preceding code, I placed the close parenthesis for the

TRadioButtons constructor on its own line, and then the last TSItem object needs to be followed by one parenthesis for each item in the list.

After creating a TRadioButtons object, you need to insert it into the dialog box, using the dialog box's insert() member function.

```
pd->insert(v1);
```

Creating a Label

The last step is to create a label to identify the group of radio buttons, because the preceding code has only created the buttons themselves and their individual labels. Labels for radio buttons, check boxes, input line boxes, and list boxes are all created using TLabel objects. The constructor for TLabel needs to know the position of the label, its text, and a pointer to the associated control.

```
pd->insert(new TLabel(TRect(2, 2, 9, 3),
  "~G~ender", v1));
```

When the label is activated, by typing its shortcut key or clicking it with the mouse, both the label and the associated control become active.

Additional Buttons and Check Boxes

The other radio buttons and check boxes in the TVDialog application's dialog box follow the same principles as the Gender radio buttons, so I'll skip over them. Of course the full code for the dialog box is shown in Listing 9.1.

The bottom-right corner of the dialog box contains two push buttons—an OK button and a Cancel button. Here is the code that creates those buttons.

```
// BUTTONS
pd->insert(new TButton(TRect(20, 7, 30, 9),
  "Cancel", cmCancel, bfNormal));
pd->insert(new TButton(TRect(20, 9, 30, 11),
  "O-K-", cmOK, bfDefault));
```

The constructor for a TButton object requires a location, the text of the button label, the command that will be broadcast when the button is pressed, and a button style constant. There are three button style constants: bfNormal for ordinary buttons, bfDefault for the default button, and bfLeftJust to left justify the button text. The bfLeftJust constant should be ORed with one of the other two button styles.

When placing a button, you should remember that it has a shadow that helps create its 3-D appearance, so that you get good visual feedback when you push the button. Thus you should make buttons two lines tall, and at least four characters wider than the text label. OK and Cancel buttons are often ten characters wide, both because it looks right and because it is the minimum width for Cancel.

Also note that nothing in the Cancel button is highlighted by tildes, because the cmCancel command automatically uses the ESC key for a shortcut. The OK button has its "K" surrounded by tildes. This is very conventional, and it is mostly for appearance, not so that K or Alt-K will be a shortcut. Another alternative is to avoid any shortcut/highlight; pressing Enter while in a dialog is already a shortcut for the cmDefault command, which activates the default button in a dialog, which is usually the OK button.

Executing the Dialog

The next-to-last thing you do with a dialog box object is to start it executing, so that it is visible and active. A part of this task is to specify the initial values for the controls. This is done with the setData() member function, covered in the next section. Next call the desktop's execView() function, giving it a pointer to the dialog object, to actually run the dialog. The return value from execView() tells you what command terminated the dialog, so that you can decide whether to fetch the final settings of the controls using getData(). Here is the code for this group of related chores.

```
// Run the modal dialog
pd->setData(&dialogData);
int cmd = deskTop->execView(pd);
if (cmd != cmCancel)
  pd->getData(&dialogData);
```

Destroying the Object

And now for the last thing that you do with a dialog: destroy the object and free all resources. For many objects that you create dynamically, all you need do to clean up is delete the object. But Turbo Vision objects are more complex, they often manage groups of other objects, and so on. So instead of using delete, you should call the destroy() member function.

```
destroy(pd);
```

The destroy() function does everything that delete does, plus it takes care of the fine points related to Turbo Vision, such as removing a view from the screen before it is deleted. When using Turbo Vision, don't delete, destroy().

Managing Dialog Box Data

People using dialog boxes usually expect that their selections will stick from one interaction to another. Therefore just before you call execView() to display a modal dialog box you should usually call setData() to set the controls to their proper values. Similarly, when a dialog is completed, you should, assuming the user hasn't canceled the box, call getData() to retrieve the settings of the controls. Of course there are occasional dialog boxes, such as those that only have buttons, in which this isn't necessary, but for most dialog boxes it is standard procedure.

Each control in a dialog box contains getData(), setData(), and dataSize() member functions. The dataSize() member returns the size of the data element that is used. It may return 0 to indicate that data exchange isn't used for a specific control type. The setData() member takes a void* pointer to a data structure, and uses that data to initialize the control. For example, the TRadioBoxes control interprets its void* pointer as a pointer to a ushort (a Turbo Vision unsigned short) and uses that ushort value as the index of the pressed radio button. The getData() function does the reverse; it fills in the indicated buffer with the requested information. Table 9.1 specifies what data types are used to interact with the standard dialog box controls.

TABLE 9.1

Dialog Box Controls setData()/getData() Types

Control	Data Element	Discussion
TStaticText		None.
TLabel		None.
TButton		None.
TRadioButtons	ushort curr;	A value from 0 to one less than the number of radio buttons, indicating which button is pressed.
TCheckBoxes	ushort mask;	A bitmask with bits set for checked check boxes. The state of the top check box is in bit 0, and so on.
TListBox	TCollection *pc; ushort curr;	The first element is a pointer to the collection; the second element records which member of the collection is current.
TInputLine	char buf[n];	n is the maximum length of the input line, as specified when the TInputLine was constructed.

So far I've described what the individual controls do, but if you looked closely at the end of the Dialog1() function in Listing 9.1, you might have noticed that I called the dialog box's setData() and getData() functions, not those of the individual controls. What happens is that the dialog box's getData() simply goes through its list of controls, calling each control's getData() to fully fill in the record.

In the TVDialog program, I passed a pointer to the following structure to getData() and setData().

```
struct TDialogData {
  ushort nGender;
  ushort nInterests;
  ushort nAge;
  TDialogData() : // initialize
    nGender(0),
```

```
        nInterests(Ø),
        nAge(Ø)
        { return; }
};
```

The dialog box in the TVDialog application contains eight controls, but only the two TRadioButton objects and the TListBox object have values that can be set or fetched. Thus the TDialogData structure has only three data elements. When the address of a TDialogData structure is passed to the dialog box's get-Data() or setData() function, that function interrogates each control, thereby filling all three fields of the structure.

You might be surprised that I supplied a constructor for the TDialogData structure. Yes, structs can have constructors. Actually they can have all of the accoutrements of classes. The only difference is that struct members default to public, whereas class members default to private. This was my reasoning: Because TDialogData was intended primarily for data storage, I made it a struct. But its initial value is critical, because it is used to initialize the dialog box radio buttons and check boxes. Instead of jamming an explicit initialization somewhere into the program, I provided a default constructor for TDialogData that ensured everything is set to zero each time a TDialogData struct is created.

Turbo Vision's getData()/setData() interface is, to be honest, ugly and unsafe. Nothing prevents error, no checking is performed, none is possible. The reason for the lack of safety is that getData() and setData() are actually TView member functions, which means they are built to be overridden in derived classes, and which means that they are forced to deal with all types of values. Furthermore, order is important, because the dialog box getData() and setData() functions cruise through the controls in order, calling their getData() and setData() functions. The data structure you hand to the dialog box must have exactly the right layout; the order of the elements in the structure must match the order of the controls, and each element must be the proper type and size.

Designing Dialog Box Layouts

Sharp, attractive dialog box design is a key part of designing an application. I don't want to dwell on the human factors aspect of dialog box design, but instead focus on the mechanics of realizing your design using Turbo Vision.

The best way to manage dialog box layout is to start with a paper layout, such as that shown in Figure 9.3. Admittedly, a first draft paper layout is not likely to be exact, but it can help you get controls in approximately the right location. Then you can iterate using the compiler, to fine-tune the positions. I've found it useful to remember that controls should usually be separated horizontally by two empty character cells, while a single empty row is usually enough vertical separation. However, buttons don't need to be separated by an empty row, because the drop shadow on the upper button appears to occupy only half of the row.

FIGURE 9.3

The graph paper sketch for the Gift Selection dialog box

```
   0  2  4  6  8  10 12 14 16 18 20 22 24 26 28 30 32 34
 0 ┌─────────────────── GIFT SELECTION ───────────────────┐
   │  ┌────────────┐              ┌───┐                    │
 2 │  │Gender      │              │Age│                    │
   │  │  (·)  Male  │             │  (·)  Under  18         │
 4 │  │  ( )  Female│             │  ( )  Other             │
   │  └────────────┘              └───┘                    │
 6 │  ┌──────────┐                                         │
   │  │Interests │            ┌─────────┐                  │
 8 │  │  [ ]  Sports          │ Cancel  │                  │
   │  │  [ ]  Cooking         └─────────┘                  │
10 │  │  [ ]  Reading         │   OK    │                  │
   │  └──────────┘            └─────────┘                  │
12 └──────────────────────────────────────────────────────┘
```

When you are making a sketch, you should refer to Table 9.2 to determine the size for each element. The TInputLine control's width, and the size of a TListBox can be adapted to fit the available space, because both of these controls are designed to work with data that is larger than the viewing surface. But the other controls are sensitive to their sizes, and things can go badly awry when you don't provide enough room for a control. If your dialog pops up garbled, make everything a bit larger, make the dialog box itself larger, and try again. It doesn't take long to isolate a control whose bounding box is too small. Borland should do more work in this area, so that undersized controls behave more predictably.

Although most of us work on color systems, Turbo Vision automatically provides for the rapidly disappearing MDA (Monochrome Display Adapter) video standard. When a Turbo Vision application is run on a system using an MDA, small arrows are used to highlight the current element, instead of the color highlighting that probably appears on your own screen. The space used for the arrows accounts for some of the extra width that I call for in Table 9.2. For example, on a color system when you select a TLabel object its text changes color to white. But on an MDA a tiny right arrow is drawn in the cell to the left of the label. That's why the allocated region for a TLabel object must start one position to the left of where you really want the label to appear, and why the width must be at least one wider than the text of the label. Somewhat the opposite problem occurs with buttons. To appear three-dimensional, buttons on a color screen are drawn with a drop shadow on the following line. This space isn't used on an MDA, but to make your programs operate on any screen you need to make your buttons two lines tall. Before releasing your application, you should run it on an MDA system to make sure that the dialogs function properly.

TABLE 9.2

Sizes of Turbo Vision Dialog Box Controls

Control	Width	Height
TStaticText	The minimum width is the width of the text.	The number of lines in the text.
TLabel	The minimum width is the width of the text plus 1.	Usually 1.
TButton	The minimum width is the width of the text, plus 4. Often groups of TButtons are made the same size; OK and Cancel buttons are often made 10 characters wide.	Should always be 2.
TRadioButtons	The width of the widest text label.	The number of buttons.
TCheckBoxes	The width of the widest text label plus 6 (5 to the left of the label and 1 to the right).	The number of check boxes.
TInputLine	The width of the field plus 2 lets you enter text without horizontal scrolling. If the width is less than the field width plus 2, the control will support horizontal scrolling.	Should be 1.
TListBox	The minimum width, assuming you must see all of each element in the list, is the width of the widest list element plus 2.	The number of lines in the list box.

Deriving Dialog Classes from TDialog

Borland's Turbo Vision documentation recommends that dialog boxes be crafted as shown in Listing 9.1. The dialog is created within a function that is a member of the program's application class. Each time the function is called, the dialog box object and all of the control objects are created, the dialog box is executed, and then everything is cleaned up just before the function returns.

I have two problems with Borland's suggestion. My first objection is that building a dialog box within a member function of your application class makes it hard to reuse the dialog box in a related application. I find it preferable to place the dialog box in its own source code file, with its own header, and then simply invoke the dialog from within the application class's handleEvent() function. This approach uses more files, and is a bit more work initially, but it makes code reuse easier.

My second objection is that Borland's approach doesn't easily allow you to customize the dialog box behavior by deriving a class from TDialog. Borland's documentation states that "you will rarely find it necessary to derive a class from TDialog." But in the example programs that are supplied with Borland C++, four of 12 dialogs are implemented by deriving a class from TDialog. And three of the dialog classes supplied with Turbo Vision—TColorDialog, TFileDialog, and TChDirDialog—are derived from TDialog. So deriving your own dialog class from TDialog is not a rarity, but rather an important and often-used technique.

To demonstrate this more sophisticated and powerful approach, deriving a dialog class from TDialog, I created a variant of the Gift Selection dialog application. There are several changes that I made to the original application to create the new version.

- I added a field to the box to show the current gift suggestion, based on the settings of the other controls. (In the original version, you could specify the traits of the gift recipient, but there weren't any suggestions.) The application itself is in the TVDial2.cpp file (Listing 9.2), and is managed using the TVDial2.prj project file.

- To support the Suggestion field, I derived a class from TDialog that updates the suggestion each time one of the controls changes. The main feature of the new TGiftDialog class is its eventHandle() member function. Also, I moved the dialog code into its own source and header files (Giftdial.h in Listing 9.3, and Giftdial.cpp in Listing 9.4).

- To implement a text field that can be changed dynamically, I derived the TDynamicText field from TStaticText. Because this is a potentially reusable control, I placed it in its own header and source file (Dynamict.h in Listing 9.5 and Dynamict.cpp in Listing 9.6).

- To provide the actual gift suggestions, I created a getSuggestion() subroutine that returns a suggestion based on the current control settings. The actual suggestions were provided by my wife, Robin, and my children (Gifts.h in Listing 9.7 and Gifts.cpp in Listing 9.8).

LISTING 9.2

The TVDial2.cpp file

```
//
// The TVDialog2 application
//

#define Uses_TApplication
#define Uses_TDeskTop
#define Uses_TRect
#define Uses_TMenu
#define Uses_TMenuBar
#define Uses_TSubMenu
#define Uses_TMenuItem
#define Uses_TKeys
#define Uses_TEvent
#define Uses_MsgBox
#define Uses_TStaticText
#define Uses_TDialog
#include <tv.h>
#include "dynamict.h"
```

LISTING 9.2

The TVDial2.cpp file (Continued)

```cpp
#include "giftdial.h"

// command constants
const cmDialog1 = 100;   // Run the dialog

//
// Application class
//
class TDialogApp : public TApplication {
  public:
    TDialogApp();   // constructor
  protected:
    static TMenuBar *initMenuBar(TRect r);
    void handleEvent(TEvent& event);
    TGiftDialog *pGiftDialog;
};

//
// TDialogApp constructor
//
TDialogApp::TDialogApp() :
  TProgInit(initStatusLine, initMenuBar, initDeskTop),
  pGiftDialog(new TGiftDialog)
{
  return;
}

//
// create a menu bar
//
TMenuBar *TDialogApp::initMenuBar(TRect r)
{
  r.b.y = r.a.y + 1; // menu location

  return new TMenuBar(r,
    *new TSubMenu("~F~ile", kbAltF)
    + *new TMenuItem("~Q~uit",
            cmQuit, kbAltX, hcNoContext, "Alt+X")
    + *new TSubMenu("~D~ialog", kbAltD)
    + *new TMenuItem("Dialog ~1~...",
            cmDialog1, kbAlt1, hcNoContext)
  );
}
```

LISTING 9.2

The TVDial2.cpp file (Continued)

```cpp
//
// application's main event handler
//
void TDialogApp::handleEvent(TEvent& event)
{
  TApplication::handleEvent(event); // give base a chance

  if (event.what == evCommand) {
    ushort& evCmd = event.message.command;
    switch(evCmd) {
      case cmDialog1:
        pGiftDialog->execute(deskTop);
        break;
      default:
        messageBox("Unknown Command",
          mfInformation);
        break;
    }
    clearEvent(event);
  }
}

//
// main
//
void main()
{
  TDialogApp myApp;
  myApp.run();
}
```

LISTING 9.3

The Giftdial.h file

```cpp
//
// Gift Dialog classes
//

#ifndef __DYNMTEXT_H
#error "Include dynmtext.h to use this file"
#endif

#if !defined(Uses_TDialog)   \
   || !defined(Uses_TDeskTop) \
```

LISTING 9.3

The Giftdial.h file (Continued)

```
  || !defined(Uses_TEvent)    \
  || !defined(__INC_DIALOGS_H)
#error "Define Uses_... (see above) and include tv.h\
 before including this file"
#endif


//
// Store the dialog data
//
// N.B. -- Layout must match order of insertion
// in Dialog().
//
struct TDialogData {
  ushort nGender;
  ushort nInterests;
  ushort nAge;
  TDialogData() : // initialize
    nGender(Ø),
    nInterests(Ø),
    nAge(Ø)
    { return; }
};


//
// A Gift Suggestion Dialog
//
class TGiftDialog : public TDialog {
  public:
    TGiftDialog();
    ushort getGender()
      { return dialogData.nGender; }
    ushort getAge()
      { return dialogData.nAge; }
    ushort getInterests()
      { return dialogData.nInterests; }
    void handleEvent(TEvent& ev);
    void execute(TDeskTop *d);
  protected:
    TDialogData dialogData;    // save control state
    TDynamicText *pSuggestion;  // handy pointers
    TView *pGender;            // to controls
    TView *pInterests;
    TView *pAge;
};
```

LISTING 9.4

The Giftdial.cpp file

```cpp
#define Uses_TDeskTop
#define Uses_TView
#define Uses_TDialog
#define Uses_TRadioButtons
#define Uses_TStaticText
#define Uses_TLabel
#define Uses_TCheckBoxes
#define Uses_TSItem
#define Uses_TButton
#define Uses_TEvent
#define Uses_TRect
#include <tv.h>
#include "dynamict.h"
#include "giftdial.h"
#include "gifts.h"

#include <mem.h>
#include <stdio.h>

//
// constructor
//
TGiftDialog::TGiftDialog() :
  TDialog(TRect(17, 6, 62, 18), "Gift Suggestion"),
  TWindowInit(&TDialog::initFrame),
  dialogData(),
  pSuggestion(0)
{
    // GENDER
    pGender = new TRadioButtons(TRect(3, 3, 16, 5),
      new TSItem("~M~ale",
      new TSItem("~F~emale", 0))
    );
    insert(pGender);
    insert(new TLabel(TRect(2, 2, 10, 3),
      "~G~ender", pGender));

    // INTERESTS
    pInterests = new TCheckBoxes(TRect(3, 7, 16, 10),
      new TSItem("~S~ports",
      new TSItem("~C~ooking",
      new TSItem("~R~eading", 0)))
    );
    insert(pInterests);
```

LISTING 9.4

The Giftdial.cpp file (Continued)

```cpp
    insert(new TLabel(TRect(2, 6, 12, 7),
      "~I~nterests", pInterests));

    // AGE
    pAge = new TRadioButtons(TRect(18, 3, 32, 5),
      new TSItem("~U~nder 18",
      new TSItem("~O~ther", 0))
    );
    insert(pAge);
    insert(new TLabel(TRect(17, 2, 21, 3),
      "~A~ge", pAge));

    // suggestion
    insert(new TStaticText(TRect(18, 6, 28, 7), "Suggestion"));
    pSuggestion = new TDynamicText(TRect(18, 7, 42, 8),
      getSuggestion(0,0,0));
    insert(pSuggestion);

    // BUTTONS
    insert(new TButton(TRect(19, 9, 29, 11), "O~K~",
      cmOK, bfDefault));
    insert(new TButton(TRect(32, 9, 42, 11), "Cancel",
      cmCancel, bfNormal));
}


//
// run the Gift Suggestion dialog
//
void TGiftDialog::execute(TDeskTop *desk)
{
    // Run the modal dialog
    setData(&dialogData);
    int cmd = desk->execView(this);
    if (cmd != cmCancel)
      getData(&dialogData);
}


void TGiftDialog::handleEvent(TEvent& ev)
{
  static TDialogData lastData;
  static TDialogData thisData;

  TDialog::handleEvent(ev);
```

LISTING 9.4

The Giftdial.cpp file (Continued)

```
    pGender->getData(&thisData.nGender);
    pInterests->getData(&thisData.nInterests);
    pAge->getData(&thisData.nAge);
    if (memcmp(&thisData, &lastData, sizeof(TDialogData))) {
      pSuggestion->setText(getSuggestion(thisData.nGender,
        thisData.nInterests, thisData.nAge));
      pSuggestion->drawView();
      lastData = thisData;
    }
}
```

LISTING 9.5

The Dynamict.h file

```
//
// dynamic text
//
// (( Include after tv.h.
//    Be sure to #define Uses_TStaticText. ))
//

#if !defined(Uses_TStaticText) \
 || !defined(Uses_TPalette)       \
 || !defined(__INC_DIALOGS_H)
#error "Define Uses_... (from above) and include tv.h\
 before including this file"
#endif

#ifndef __DYNMTEXT_H
#define __DYNMTEXT_H

//
// Dynamic text
//
class TDynamicText : public TStaticText {
  public:
    TDynamicText(TRect& r, const char *aText) :
      TStaticText(r, aText)
    {
      return;
    }
    void setText(const char *s)
    {
```

LISTING 9.5

The Dynamict.h file (Continued)

```
        if (text)
            delete (char *)text; // un const "text"
        text = newStr(s);
    }
    TPalette& getPalette() const;
};


#endif
```

LISTING 9.6

The Dynamict.cpp file

```
#define Uses_TPalette
#define Uses_TStaticText
#include <tv.h>
#include "dynamict.h"

//
// Color palette for dynamic text.
//     Same as Dialog box's InputLine normal
//
static const char *const cpDynamic = "\x13";

//
// getPalette
//
TPalette& TDynamicText::getPalette() const
{
    static TPalette palette(cpDynamic, sizeof(cpDynamic)-1);
    return palette;
}
```

LISTING 9.7

The Gifts.h file

```
//
// Store gift ideas
//

typedef unsigned short ushort;
```

LISTING 9.7

The Gifts.h file (Continued)

```cpp
struct GiftData {
  ushort Female;     // Ø male; 1 female
  ushort Interests;  // Ø none; 1 sports; 2 cooking
                     // 3 sports+cooking; 4 reading
                     // 5 read+sports; 6 read+cook
                     // 7 read+sports+cooking
  ushort Older;      // Ø <18; 1 >=18
  char *Suggestion;
};

char *getSuggestion(ushort female, ushort interests, ushort
older);
```

LISTING 9.8

The Gifts.cpp file

```cpp
#include "gifts.h"

GiftData gifts[] = {

// young males
{ Ø, Ø, Ø, "Movie Gift Certificates"},
{ Ø, 1, Ø, "Bow and Arrow"},
{ Ø, 2, Ø, "Meat Cleaver"},
{ Ø, 3, Ø, "GatorAde Recipes"},
{ Ø, 4, Ø, "Book: White Fang"},
{ Ø, 5, Ø, "Book: McEnroe Legend"},
{ Ø, 6, Ø, "Book: Chocolate Cookery"},
{ Ø, 7, Ø, "Book: Sports Cookery"},

// young females
{ 1, Ø, Ø, "Plaid Skirt"},
{ 1, 1, Ø, "Running Shoes"},
{ 1, 2, Ø, "Jello Molds"},
{ 1, 3, Ø, "Pasta Machine"},
{ 1, 4, Ø, "Book: Little Women"},
{ 1, 5, Ø, "Book: Navratilova!"},
{ 1, 6, Ø, "Book: Vegetarian Epicure"},
{ 1, 7, Ø, "Book: Fonda's Recipes"},

// older males
{ Ø, Ø, 1, "Cufflinks"},
```

LISTING 9.8

The Gifts.cpp file (Continued)

```
{ 0, 1, 1, "Yankee Tickets"},
{ 0, 2, 1, "Chef's Hat"},
{ 0, 3, 1, "Trail Mix (Gorp)"},
{ 0, 4, 1, "Book: 1 Minute Manager"},
{ 0, 5, 1, "Book: Tyson's Punch"},
{ 0, 6, 1, "Book: Zagatt's Guide"},
{ 0, 7, 1, "Book: Joggers Recipes"},

// older females
{ 1, 0, 1, "Scarf"},
{ 1, 1, 1, "Leotard"},
{ 1, 2, 1, "Food Processor"},
{ 1, 3, 1, "Picnic Basket"},
{ 1, 4, 1, "Book: The Second Sex"},
{ 1, 5, 1, "Book: Amelia Earhart"},
{ 1, 6, 1, "Book: Frugal Gourmet"},
{ 1, 7, 1, "Book: Outdoor Cookery"}
};

char *getSuggestion(ushort female, ushort interests, ushort
older)
{
  int i = sizeof(gifts) / sizeof(GiftData);

  while(i--)
    if (gifts[i].Female == female &&
        gifts[i].Older == older &&
        gifts[i].Interests == interests)
          return gifts[i].Suggestion;

  return "No idea!";
}
```

This new Gift Suggestion dialog box is shown in Figure 9.4. The layout has been slightly widened to accommodate the suggestion text, and the OK and Cancel buttons have been correspondingly repositioned in a horizontal arrangement. Each time the specification of the recipient's age, sex, or interests is changed, the text of the suggestion changes immediately.

The mechanism for keeping the suggestion up-to-date is to trap all of the events that are generated in the dialog box. Each time an event occurs I look for changed selections; if a selection has changed, then the suggestion is updated. This mechanism relies on intercepting all of the events, which is easy to do in a derived class (TGiftDialog) by writing your own handleEvent() virtual member function.

FIGURE 9.4

The TVDial2 application

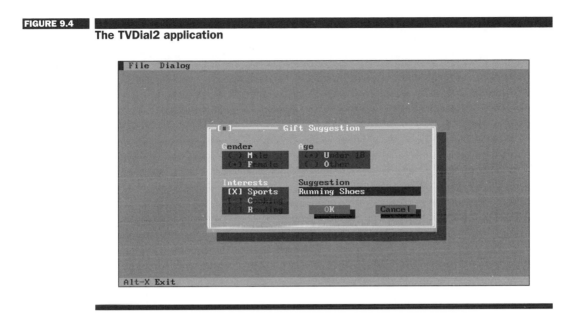

The TGiftDialog Class

The first action of the TGiftDialog class's handleEvent() function is always to pass the event to the TDialog class's handleEvent() function, where the standard work is performed. Then the TGiftDialog event handler interrogates the controls to discover if something has changed. If there has been a change, the event handler looks up the new gift suggestion by calling getSuggestion(), sends that suggestion to the TDynamicText object, and then finally asks the TDynamicText object to redraw itself. The logic for this, other than the creation of the TDynamicText class, is just a few lines. This is a very small price to pay for a customized dialog box.

One other difference between this version of the gift dialog and the previous one is that a TGiftDialog object is constructed when the application starts, and then is used whenever the dialog should be displayed. Thus the dialog needn't be constructed, from scratch, each time it is used. There are advantages and disadvantages to this strategy. For example, this approach simplifies memory allocation checking, because all the memory for the dialog is allocated when the application initializes. Another difference is that keeping the dialog object alive even when the dialog isn't on the screen makes it easy, at any time, to interrogate the dialog object to discover the control settings. If the dialog object is destroyed when the dialog box is closed, then the setting must be saved in an external data structure, which seems clumsy to me. (An alternative is to use static class members to store the dialog settings, so they can belong to the dialog class yet still exist when there isn't a dialog object.)

The TDynamicText Class

I created the TDynamicText class to make it easy to have a text label whose "text" could easily be changed. All of the hard part of the TDynamicText class is handled by Turbo Vision's TStaticText class, which I used as a base class. In the derived class all you need to do is provide a way to change the text, which I supplied in the setText() member function. I thought of having the setText() function also initiate the screen redraw of the control, but then I realized that in a dialog box with several TDynamicText objects you might want to have all of them redraw at the same time, so I refrained from calling drawView() from within setText(). It is up to the client to call drawView() each time the text is changed.

The other concern of the TDynamicText class is what color will be used for the control. Initially I didn't supply a color map for TDynamicText, which made it use the color map of its base class. But this didn't look right, because the dynamic text looked like a label, not like an active field. So instead I supplied a color map in the TDynamicText class, so that it could look like a text edit control. Visually, this was far superior because it drew attention to the field and made it look like something that might change, rather than look like a fixed label. I will explain the color palette aspect of the TDynamicText class in the next section on Turbo Vision palettes.

The TGiftDialog and the TDynamicText class are both implemented in the standard reusable style, using a .H file for the class definition and a .CPP file for the class implementation. Users of these classes need only include the .H file and link in the .OBJ file produced by compiling the .CPP file. Because the .H files for my classes use the Turbo Vision classes, they must be included after tv.h. But it is also important for there to be the correct #define Uses_... definitions, so that all of the required pieces will have been included by tv.h. Thus the beginning of a client program that uses the TDynamicText class will look something like

```
#define Uses_... // client "uses" list
#define Uses_...
#include <tv.h>
#include "dynamict.h"
```

But because the TDynamicText class is based on Turbo Vision's TStaticText class, the client program's Uses_... list must include a define of Uses_TStaticText. I decided, after forgetting this once or twice, to put some checks at the beginning of dynamict.h to ensure that the required Uses_... clauses had been defined, and also to ensure that tv.h itself had been included. The preprocessor statements to make these checks are ugly, and some of the preprocessor symbol names may be version dependent, but the checks make it much easier to use these header files.

The last major component of the TVDialog2 application is the list of gift suggestions. It consists of an array of GiftData structs and a getSuggestion() function to search the list for a specific suggestion. Because the list is short and unordered, getSuggestion() uses a simple linear search strategy. If the focus of this application were gift suggestions, they would have been implemented as a class with much smoother and more reliable functionality.

Palettes

A palette, to an artist or to Turbo Vision, is a set of colors. Turbo Vision keeps track of 64 color usages, and then maps those 64 color uses to the available colors on the user's display. Today many users work with a VGA display adapter, which supports 16 colors in the text display modes, but Turbo Vision can also accommodate monochrome adapters, EGA adapters, and so on.

Turbo Vision's color management is flexible and easy-to-use, but you need to understand the principles before you try to manage the details. The first principle is that the member functions that manage the color palettes are all virtual member functions. Thus each type of visible Turbo Vision object may elect to supply its own palette, or it may elect to use the palette of its base class.

The second principle is that each palette is an index into the palette of the containing view. For example, consider a TStaticText object that has been inserted into a TDialog object, which in turn has been inserted into the desktop, which is illustrated in Figure 9.5A. The TStaticText object palette contains indices that select entries in the TDialog object palette; the TDialog object palette contains indices into the TProgram palette; the TProgram palette contains indices into the display adapter's actual color map. If the TStaticText object had instead been inserted directly into the desktop (Figure 9.5B), then its palette would contain indices into the TProgram object's palette, not the TDialog palette.

Let's make this more concrete by looking at the TDynamicText class. The base class for TDynamicText is TStaticText, which contains a two-element color palette. Here is the declaration of the TStatic palette from the Turbo Vision source code.

```
#define cpStaticText "\x06"
```

The TStaticText class's palette is a single value, because TStaticText objects are drawn in a single color; they can't be highlighted, selected, and so on. Objects that have more colors will have a larger palette. Because TStaticText objects are customarily inserted into TDialog objects, we can make sense of this palette by looking at the TDialog palette. If you look up TDialog in the Turbo Vision reference, you'll discover that its sixth entry is called "Static Text" and it contains the value 0x25. Then if you look at the 37th (0x25 is 37 in decimal) entry of the TProgram palette, you will discover that it is also called "Static Text" and it contains the value 0x70, which will be used for the attribute byte in the display adapter's screen buffer.

Let's also look at what would happen if the TStaticText object were inserted directly into the desktop. In this case its index would refer to entry six of the TProgram object. The sixth entry is called "Disabled selection," and it has the value 0x24 on a color adapter/color monitor, 0x07 on a color adapter/black-and-white monitor, and 0x70 on a system using a monochrome adapter. Thus when

FIGURE 9.5

Turbo Vision color palettes

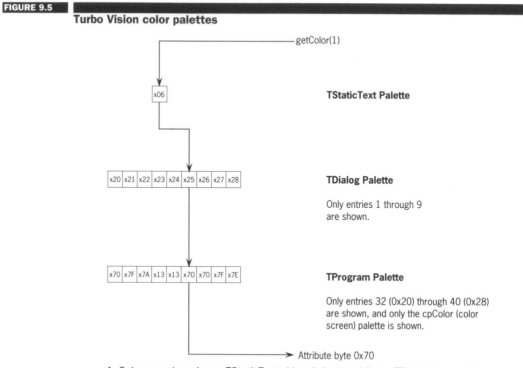

getColor(1)

x06   **TStaticText Palette**

| x20 | x21 | x22 | x23 | x24 | x25 | x26 | x27 | x28 |

TDialog Palette

Only entries 1 through 9
are shown.

| x70 | x7F | x7A | x13 | x13 | x70 | x70 | x7F | x7E |

TProgram Palette

Only entries 32 (0x20) through 40 (0x28)
are shown, and only the cpColor (color
screen) palette is shown.

Attribute byte 0x70

A. Color mapping when a TStaticText object is inserted into a TDialog box, which is
inserted into the desktop.

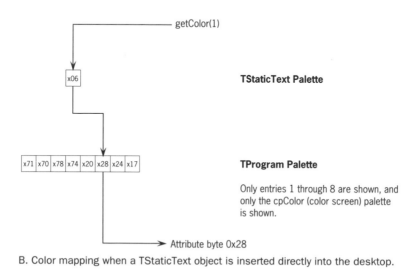

getColor(1)

x06   **TStaticText Palette**

| x71 | x70 | x78 | x74 | x20 | x28 | x24 | x17 |

TProgram Palette

Only entries 1 through 8 are shown, and
only the cpColor (color screen) palette
is shown.

Attribute byte 0x28

B. Color mapping when a TStaticText object is inserted directly into the desktop.

inserted onto the desktop, TStaticText would have the same color selections as disabled text.

When you create a Turbo Vision class, you need to consider its color palette. If you derive your class from one of the standard visible classes, you should supply a palette if your coloring will differ from the base class's.

Because C++ doesn't support the concept of "virtual data," palettes are implemented using virtual member functions. Classes that supply their own palette contain a virtual member function called getPalette() that returns a reference to a TPalette object. The size of the palette dictates the range of color indices supported by the object.

The TDynamicText class's getPalette() function is shown in Listing 9.6. The getPalette() function constructs a static TPalette object from a string, and returns a reference to that object. The palette data comes from a character string, which must be in binary. So be careful to code a hex 13 as "\x13" and not as "0x13"! The first value in the string is the value of the first color index, and so on up to the length of the string. When you supply a palette string to the TPalette class constructor, you must also supply the number of entries in the palette. You can either count them by hand, or you can use the expression sizeof(palString)–1 to calculate the number of entries.

Opening Windows and Views

The material presented so far has given us many glimpses of the TView class, but it hasn't been examined in detail. Now it is time to look at TView directly, so that you can learn what it has to offer, but also so that you can learn to use TView to construct the heart of your application, your application's main window.

The TView class is the center of the Turbo Vision class hierarchy. It establishes the size and shape of Turbo Vision, and it is a base class of all of the visible classes in the hierarchy. The TView class originates much of Turbo Vision's functionality. For example, TView contains the getPalette() function mentioned in the preceding section, it contains the getData() function that was discussed earlier when dialog boxes were examined, it contains the critical handleEvent() function, and so on. In more concrete terms, the TView class contains about 20 virtual member functions that form much of the central Turbo Vision functionality.

The other key class that helps you construct the main window or windows of your application is called TWindow. The TWindow class manages the standard features of a window, such as its border, title, sizing, moving, and so on. The TWindow class is derived from TGroup, which in turn is derived from TView. Thus a TWindow object is visible, it has all the characteristics of a TView, plus it has the characteristics of a TGroup, meaning things can be inserted into a window. Additionally, TWindow is derived from TWindowInit, which is concerned with the frame (border) that surrounds the window.

A complete window consists of the window frame and the other window features (maximize icon, size control, close icon, and so on) plus whatever is inserted into the interior of the window. Most of the window accoutrements are managed automatically by TWindow, leaving you the main chore, supplying the interior views. The interior views will usually be classes that you design to

LISTING 9.9

TVView.cpp

```cpp
//
// The TVMenu application
//

#define Uses_TApplication
#define Uses_TRect
#define Uses_TMenu
#define Uses_TMenuBar
#define Uses_TSubMenu
#define Uses_TMenuItem
#define Uses_TKeys
#define Uses_TWindow
#define Uses_TWindowInit
#define Uses_TView
#define Uses_TDeskTop
#include <tv.h>
#include "logo.h"

//
// Application class
//
class TViewApp : public TApplication {
  public:
    TViewApp();   // constructor
  protected:
    static TMenuBar *initMenuBar(TRect r);
};

//
// TViewApp constructor
//
TViewApp::TViewApp() :
  TProgInit(initStatusLine, initMenuBar, initDeskTop)
{
  deskTop->insert(new TLogoWindow(28, 5));
  return;
}

//
// create a menu bar
//
TMenuBar *TViewApp::initMenuBar(TRect r)
{
  r.b.y = r.a.y + 1; // menu location
```

LISTING 9.9

TVView.cpp (Continued)

```cpp
    return new TMenuBar(r,
      *new TSubMenu("~F~ile", kbAltF)
      + *new TMenuItem("~Q~uit",
              cmQuit, kbAltX, hcNoContext, "Alt+X")
    );
}


//
// main
//
void main()
{
  TVicwApp myApp;
  myApp.run();
}
```

LISTING 9.10

Logo.h

```cpp
#if !defined(Uses_TView)     \
  || !defined(Uses_TRect)    \
  || !dcfined(Uses_TWindow) \
  || !defined(Uses_TWindowInit)
#error "Missing #define Uses_..."
#endif

//
// class TLogoView
//
class TLogoView : public TView {
  public:
    TLogoView(TRect r);
    virtual void draw();
    static const int nHeight();
    static const int nWidth();
  protected:
    static const char * const strLogo[];
};

//
// class TLogoWindow
//
```

LISTING 9.10 ▓▓▓▓▓▓▓▓▓▓▓▓▓▓▓▓▓▓▓▓▓▓▓▓▓▓▓▓▓▓▓▓▓▓▓▓

Logo.h (Continued)

```cpp
class TLogoWindow : public TWindow {
  public:
    TLogoWindow(ushort x, ushort y);
};
```

LISTING 9.11 ▓▓▓▓▓▓▓▓▓▓▓▓▓▓▓▓▓▓▓▓▓▓▓▓▓▓▓▓▓▓▓▓▓▓▓▓

Logo.cpp

```cpp
#define Uses_TView
#define Uses_TRect
#define Uses_TWindow
#define Uses_TWindowInit
#include <tv.h>

#include "logo.h"

//
// class TLogoView constructor
//
TLogoView::TLogoView(TRect r) :
  TView(r)
{
  return;
}


//
// TLogoView draw() routine
//
void TLogoView::draw()
{
  TDrawBuffer buf;
  ushort color = getColor(2);
  for(int i = 0; i < size.y; i++) {
    buf.moveStr(0, strLogo[i], color);
    writeLine(0, i, size.x, 1, buf);
  }
}

const ushort ncHeight = 12;
const ushort ncWidth  = 26;

const char * const TLogoView::strLogo[ncHeight] = {
```

LISTING 9.11

Logo.cpp (Continued)

```
"                     ",
"  ZDZDZDZD   ZDZDZD   ",
"         ZD  ZD  ZD   ",
"        ZD   ZD   ZD  ",
"       ZD    ZD   ZD  ",
"      ZD     ZD   ZD  ",
"     ZD      ZD   ZD  ",
"    ZD       ZD   ZD  ",
"  ZD         ZD  ZD   ",
"  ZDZDZDZD   ZDZDZD   ",
"                     ",
"   P   R   E   S   S  ",
};

int TLogoView::nWidth()
{
  return ncWidth;
}

int TLogoView::nHeight()
{
  return ncHeight;
}

//
// class TLogoWindow constructor
//
TLogoWindow::TLogoWindow(ushort x, ushort y) :
  TWindow(
    TRect(x, y,
        x + TLogoView::nWidth() + 2,
        y + TLogoView::nHeight() + 2
    ),
    "Z I F F  D A V I S", wnNoNumber),
  TWindowInit(&TLogoWindow::initFrame)
{
  flags = wfMove; // disallow zoom, grow, close
  TRect r = getClipRect();
  r.grow(-1, -1);
  insert(new TLogoView(r));
}
```

The TLogoWindow's constructor initializes its base classes, and then it creates and inserts a TLogoView object into its interior. The base class initialization consists of telling the TWindow class (and eventually the TView class) what TRect is occupied by the window and the window title, and telling the TWindowInit class what function will supply the window's TFrame object. The TWindowInit class is a virtual base class, so it must be explicitly initialized in the most derived class in a hierarchy, just as TProgInit is a virtual base class of TProgram that must be initialized explicitly in your application class.

The body of the TLogoWindow constructor creates a TLogoView object and inserts it into its interior. The size of the TLogoView object is fixed, by the dimension of the logo. Thus the TLogoWindow object makes its size two characters larger than the logo, to allow room for the window frame, and then builds the TLogoView object with the correct size. The TLogoWindow with its TLogoView interior is shown in Figure 9.7.

FIGURE 9.7

The TVView application

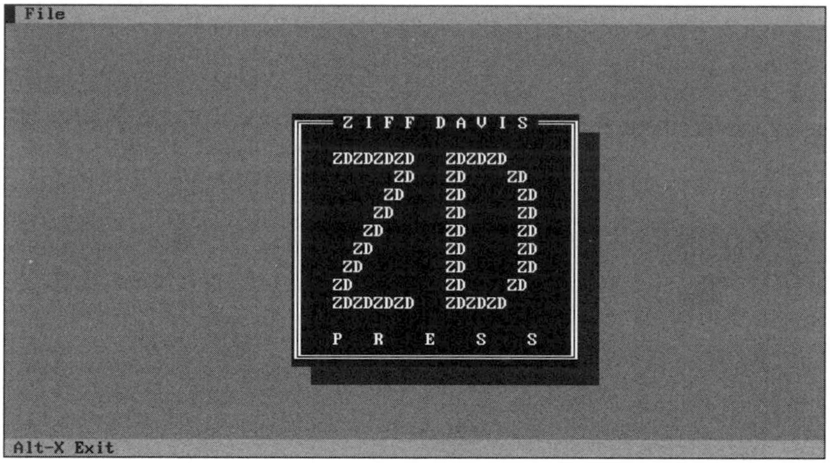

The draw() Routine

The work, such that it is, of the TVView application occurs in the draw() routine of the TLogoView object, which is shown in Listing 9.11. When you create a view, you must provide a draw() routine that will paint the view's surface, but you shouldn't ever call it directly. Instead, let Turbo Vision call your view's draw() routine as necessary to paint the window surface. If you know that something has changed and the view needs to be updated, call drawView(). This will inform Turbo Vision that the view needs to be redrawn, and Turbo Vision will then call draw() as necessary. Remember, views are often hidden, and only Turbo Vision knows all the details.

Although I said that draw() paints the view's surface, I should be more precise. What actually happens is that draw() tells Turbo Vision what should be presented on the view's surface, but it is up to Turbo Vision to perform the actual screen I/O. In a Turbo Vision application, you must never write directly to the screen. Instead you perform I/O using TView's writeStr(), writeLine(), writeChar(), and writeBuf() functions. These functions perform the necessary checking for overlapping windows, hidden windows, and the like, before performing the screen I/O. Also you may only use these functions inside a draw() function of a class derived from TView. Any other usage is likely to muddle the screen.

Turbo Vision uses TDrawBuffer objects to specify screen contents. In the TLogoView class, draw() first creates a TDrawBuffer object. Then it repeatedly fills the draw buffer with one line from the logo, being careful to fully paint the view's area. The draw() function uses the TDrawBuffer's moveStr() function, which moves a string into the buffer, and then it calls TView's writeLine() member function to write the line to the screen. Here is TLogoView's draw() function.

```
void TLogoView::draw()
{
  TDrawBuffer buf;
  ushort color = getColor(2);
  for(int i = 0; i < size.y; i++) {
    buf.moveStr(0, strLogo[i], color);
    writeLine(0, i, size.x, 1, buf);
  }
}
```

The draw() routine calls getColor(), a TView virtual member function, to get the requested color. Since I knew that the TLogoView would be in a TWindow object, I looked for a color mapping that would produce bright white text. The second TWindow entry is "Frame Active," which maps to entry 9 in TProgram, which is bright white.

The constructor of the TLogoWindow class sets the TWindow class's flags member variable to the value wfMove. This specifies that the window can be moved, by dragging its title bar with the mouse. However, because the mfGrow, wfClose, and wfZoom flag bits aren't set, the window can't be resized, closed, or zoomed.

Many other Turbo Vision objects have several modes of operation. For example, TView objects can be selectable or not selectable, framed or not framed, and so on. You usually manage these modes as shown in the TLogoWindow class, by setting the mode=control variables in the constructor of your derived class. The most important mode variables are the options, growMode, eventMask and dragMode data members of TView, and the flags data member of TWindow. The Turbo Vision reference has full details on all of these mode settings.

Active Views

The Ziff-Davis Press logo in the TVView application (Figure 9.7) is nice to look at, but it doesn't do anything. Yes, there are times you want a do-nothing view, but certainly that's the exception. More often views are active—they respond to mouse clicks, keyboard input, menu-generated commands, and the like. Turbo Vision is much more than a pretty face, it's a comprehensive system for bringing that pretty face to life.

As you should have already guessed, the handleEvent() function is the key player in providing behaviors for a view. In this and the previous chapter we've only seen handleEvent() used to respond to control messages. This is clearly an important role, but handleEvent() has even a broader role: It also responds to keyboard and mouse messages.

Let's start with some basic terminology. There are three broad classes of Turbo Vision events:

- *Positional events*, which are usually mouse events. Positional events are routed based primarily on what view contains the event's position. If there are several overlapping views at that spot, then the event is routed secondarily from top to bottom.

- *Focused events*, which are usually keyboard or command events. Focused events are routed according to the focus chain, which means from the desktop to the active window, to that window's active subwindow, and so on.

- *Broadcast events*, which are usually command events or user-defined events. Broadcast events are sent to all the subviews of the current modal view.

When an event occurs, the current modal view gets the first opportunity to handle it. After that, it is handled according to its classification—positional, focused, or broadcast.

I created the TVView2 application to show some simple event handling. The application displays a logo, just like the TVView application, but now you can manipulate the logo. If you strike F1 through F8, you can switch the logo's color index from 1 to 8, which will try all of the entries in the TWindow palette. And if you click the mouse on the logo, the line you have selected will either rotate right (if you click right of center) or left (if you click left of center). Also, I've created two logo windows in the TVView2 application, so that you can experiment with how the focus affects the way events are distributed. The TVView2 application is shown in Figure 9.8. As you can see from the figure, I've used the mouse to put a slant into the left logo, and I've split the right logo in two, shifting its top to the left and its bottom to the right.

The TVView2 application has the same basic structure as TVView. It consists of the file tvview2.cpp that contains the application class, plus the files logo2.h (Listing 9.11) and logo2.cpp (Listing 9.12) that contain the TLogoWindow and TLogoView classes. The tvview2.cpp file is exactly the same as the tvview.cpp file (Listing 9.9), except that the TMenuApp class's constructor is different, because it creates two TLogoWindow objects. Here is that constructor.

```
TMenuApp::TMenuApp() :
  TProgInit(initStatusLine, initMenuBar, initDeskTop)
{
  deskTop->insert(new TLogoWindow(45, 5));
  deskTop->insert(new TLogoWindow(6, 5));
  return;
}
```

FIGURE 9.8

The TVView2 application

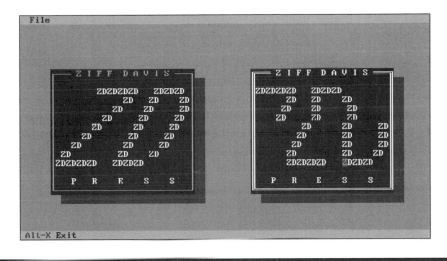

I inserted the windows in right-to-left order because I wanted the initial focus to be on the left window. Since the last inserted window initially gets the focus, I inserted them in this backwards order. Alternatively I could have inserted them in the left-to-right order and then used the select() member function to switch the focus to the left window. I'm not going to include the full code listing of tvview2.cpp, because of its similarity to tvview.cpp.

The handleEvent() function of the TLogoView class contains the code that lets the logo respond to the keyboard and mouse. If you look at handleEvent() in Listing 9.12, you'll see that the event handling is separated into two parts, handling of mouse events and handling of keyboard events. However, both of these code sections use the information provided in the TEvent struct, which contains full information about the event.

LISTING 9.12

Logo2.cpp

```cpp
#define Uses_TView
#define Uses_TRect
#define Uses_TWindow
#define Uses_TWindowInit
#define Uses_TEvent
#define Uses_TKeys
#include <tv.h>

#include <string.h>

#include "logo2.h"

const ushort ncHeight = 12;
const ushort ncWidth  = 26;

const char * const TLogoView::strLogo[ncHeight] = {
"                        ",
"   ZDZDZDZD    ZDZDZD   ",
"        ZD    ZD    ZD  ",
"       ZD    ZD     ZD  ",
"      ZD     ZD     ZD  ",
"     ZD      ZD     ZD  ",
"    ZD       ZD     ZD  ",
"   ZD        ZD     ZD  ",
"  ZD         ZD    ZD   ",
"   ZDZDZDZD    ZDZDZD   ",
"                        ",
"   P   R   E   S   S    ",
};

//
// class TLogoView constructor
//
TLogoView::TLogoView(TRect r) :
  TView(r),
  cIndex(2)
{
  typedef char *pc;
  options |= ofSelectable;
  myLogo = new pc[ncHeight];
  for(int i = Ø; i < ncHeight; i++)
    myLogo[i] = newStr(strLogo[i]);
}
```

LISTING 9.12

Logo2.cpp (Continued)

```cpp
void TLogoView::draw()
{
  TDrawBuffer buf;
  ushort color = getColor(cIndex);
  for(int i = 0; i < size.y; i++) {
    buf.moveStr(0, myLogo[i], color);
    writeLine(0, i, size.x, 1, buf);
  }
}

int TLogoView::nWidth()
{
  return ncWidth;
}

int TLogoView::nHeight()
{
  return ncHeight;
}

// rotate a string to the right
void ror(char *s)
{
  int n = strlen(s) - 1; // index of last char
  if (n < 1) return;      // too short to rotate
  char ch = s[n];
  // always use memmove for overlapping moves
  memmove(s+1, s, n);
  *s = ch;
}

// rotate a string left
void rol(char *s)
{
  char ch = s[0];
  int n = strlen(s) - 1;
  if (n < 1) return;
  memmove(s, s+1, n);
  s[n] = ch;
}

//
// handle mouse and kbd events
//
```

LISTING 9.12

Logo2.cpp (Continued)

```cpp
void TLogoView::handleEvent(TEvent& event)
{
  TView::handleEvent(event);

  if (event.what == evMouseDown) {
    if(mouseInView(event.mouse.where)) {
      TPoint spot = makeLocal(event.mouse.where);
      if (spot.x > ncWidth/2)
        ror(myLogo[spot.y]);
      else
        rol(myLogo[spot.y]);
    }
    clearEvent(event);
    drawView();

  } else if (event.what == evKeyboard) {
    int okKey = 1;
    switch (event.keyDown.keyCode) {
      case kbF1: cIndex = 1; break;
      case kbF2: cIndex = 2; break;
      case kbF3: cIndex = 3; break;
      case kbF4: cIndex = 4; break;
      case kbF5: cIndex = 5; break;
      case kbF6: cIndex = 6; break;
      case kbF7: cIndex = 7; break;
      case kbF8: cIndex = 8; break;
      default: okKey = Ø; break;
    }
    if (okKey) {
      clearEvent(event);
      drawView();
    }
  }
}

//
// class TLogoWindow constructor
//
TLogoWindow::TLogoWindow(ushort x, ushort y) :
  TWindow(
    TRect(x, y,
      x + TLogoView::nWidth() + 2,
      y + TLogoView::nHeight() + 2
    ),
```

LISTING 9.12

Logo2.cpp (Continued)

```
    "Z I F F   D A V I S", wnNoNumber),
  TWindowInit(&TLogoWindow::initFrame)
{
  flags = wfMove; // disallow zoom, grow, close
  TRect r = getClipRect();
  r.grow(-1, -1);
  insert(new TLogoView(r));
}
```

The management of the mouse event first determines whether the mouse event occurred within the current view. If so, the coordinates of the event are converted to local coordinates, because inside the view we always need to use local coordinates. Then the local coordinates are used to determine whether the mouse was clicked on the left half or the right half, and what line was clicked. Based on this information, either ror() or rol() is called to rotate the contents of the selected line. Then the event is cleared and drawView() is called to request a redraw.

The keyboard event is managed similarly. If one of the first eight function keys has been pressed, then the color index is set to the corresponding value, the event is cleared, and a redraw is requested. The only other aspect of handling the keyboard event is ensuring that the event is routed to the TLogoView class's handleEvent() function. By default, views are not selectable, which means they don't accept the focus, and thus don't get a chance to handle focused events (keyboard events, command events). Therefore I had to make sure that the TLogoView constructor set the ofSelectable flag in the options TView data member. When a view is selectable, Turbo Vision automatically sends it relevant focused events, focus moves to it via mouse clicks, and so on.

One small complication in this new version of the TLogoView class is that the rotation of the logo should be done to a local copy of the logo, not to the static copy of the logo. Therefore I added some code to the TLogoView constructor to make its own copy of the ZD logo text. This allows you to rotate the logo in one window without altering the logo in the other window.

10 TURBO VISION COMPONENTS

THE KEY ADVANTAGE OF TURBO VISION IS PRODUCTIVITY. TURBO VISION MAKES it much easier to build a program with an intuitive, multiwindow, menu-based, dialog-based user interface. Yes, you could always build it from scratch, but with a huge effort compared with the effort of learning Turbo Vision.

In the preceding chapters I've presented many of the basics of Turbo Vision, so that you can start to work with this powerful application framework. Now I would like to present several Turbo Vision components that I have developed for my own use. These components have been used in several applications, so they are time tested, and I've found them to be very useful. However, if my components don't themselves prove useful in your applications, the general approach that I've followed to identify and build these components will at least have educational value.

My own software makes heavy use of dialog boxes, so I've spent some time learning how to build reusable dialog box components. In addition, I've designed some of my own controls. In Chapter 9 you saw my TDynamicText control; in this chapter I'm presenting my TGrid control, which is a low-resolution XY input control. Also, users of my software have found it helpful to keep a log of what they've done, so I've built a log window that resembles the error message window found in Borland's DOS IDE.

Ready-made Cancel and OK Buttons

Nearly every dialog box contains a Cancel and an OK button. They really aren't very hard to produce, but placing each button in a dialog box requires a lot of typing. And each time you need to change their location, usually because the dialog box is growing as you add controls, you have to change the coordinates.

One day, as I was adding Cancel and OK buttons to my fifth or sixth dialog box that day, I realized that there had to be a better way. That's when I decided to build a subroutine to do most of the drudgery of inserting the Cancel and OK buttons into the box. Because there are two common layouts, vertical and horizontal, I actually made two subroutines. Each subroutine requires a pointer to the dialog box, and it needs to know the position of the top-left corner of the two buttons. Here are the prototypes of these two functions:

```
extern void cancelOKStdButtonsH(TDialog *dialog,
```

```
     int x, int y);
extern void cancelOKStdButtonsV(TDialog *dialog,
  int x, int y);
```

The actual code for these two functions is very straightforward. Here's the code for the horizontal version, cancelOKStdButtonsH().

```
void cancelOKStdButtonsH(TDialog *dialog, int x, int y)
{
    dialog->insert(new TButton(TRect( x+00, y, x+10, y+2),
        "Cancel", cmCancel, bfNormal));
    dialog->insert(new TButton(TRect( x+12, y, x+22, y+2),
        "O~K~", cmOK, bfDefault));
}
```

The source for the vertical version, cancelOKStdButtonsV(), is shown in stddial.ccp under "StdDialogs Source Code" later in this chapter. These routines are used in all of the dialog examples in this chapter.

AB Input Lines

Most of my recent software analyzes and enhances bitmapped graphical images. As you might imagine, there are many numerical parameters that the user enters to specify how the images should be manipulated. For example, one of my dialog boxes lets the user specify upper and lower thresholds for a masking operation. The first time I needed a pair of numeric input controls I simply created a pair of input lines, and a pair of labels, and then specified their positions in the dialog box. But after doing this several times I realized that numeric parameters often traveled in pairs, so I created a simple function to place the components for a pair of numeric controls into a dialog box.

Here is the function prototype for the abStdInputLine() function:

```
extern void abStdInputLine(TDialog *dialog,
  int x, int y, const char *s1, const char *s2);
```

The first two parameters for abStdInputLine() are the same as for the Cancel and OK std buttons function, a pointer to the dialog and the position of the controls. The two final parameters are the strings that are the labels for the two input line controls. If either string is null, then that control isn't inserted into the dialog.

Here's the source for the abStdInputLine() function:

```
const numLen = 10;  // strings used to store numbers
void abStdInputLine(TDialog *dialog, int x, int y,
    const char *s1, const char *s2)
{
  int y1 = y + 1;
  int x2 = x + 12;
  if (s1 && *s1) {
    TView *a = new TInputLine(TRect(x+3, y, x+11, y1),
      numLen);
    dialog->insert(a);
```

```
    dialog->insert(new TLabel(TRect(x,    y,  x+3,  y1),
      s1, a));
  }
  if (s2 && *s2) {
    TView *b = new TInputLine(TRect(x2+3, y, x2+11, y1),
      numLen);
    dialog->insert(b);
    dialog->insert(new TLabel(TRect(x2,    y, x2+3,  y1),
      s2, b));
  }
}
```

For my image processing software, the labels for my numeric input lines tend to be very short, such as X and Y, or W and H, or Θ and φ. Thus I've arranged the abStdInputLine() function to put a one- or two-letter label to the left of the input line. A more usual layout, which would allow longer labels, would be to place the label above the input line.

Here is an example dialog box function that uses a pair of numeric controls created by the abStdInputLine() function. (It also uses the cancelOKStdButtonsH() function from the previous section.) The dialog box produced by the dispTextDialog() function is shown in Figure 10.1.

```
static void dispTextDlg(void)
{
  static TextData data;
  TDialog *dialog = new TDialog(TRect(0, 0, 28, 14),
    "Display Text");
  dialog->options |= ofCentered;
  TInputLine *line =
    new TInputLine(TRect( 3, 3, 25, 4 ), 80);
  dialog->insert(line);
  dialog->insert( new TLabel(TRect( 2, 2, 15, 3),
    "~T~ext:", line));
  abStdInputLine(dialog, 2, 5, "~X~", "~Y~");
  TCheckBoxes *check =
    new TCheckBoxes( TRect( 3, 7, 25, 8 ),
      new TSItem( "~L~arge Font", 0 ));
  dialog->insert(check);
  TView *c;
  dialog->insert(c =
    new TInputLine(TRect(  3, 9, 13, 10), numLen));
  dialog->insert(
    new TLabel(TRect( 14, 9, 22, 10), "~C~olor", c));
  cancelOKStdButtonsH(dialog, 3, 11);
  dialog->selectNext(False);
  dialog->setData(&data);
  ushort result = TProgram::deskTop->execView(dialog);
  if (result == cmOK) {
    dialog->getData(&data);
    showMessage("Screen message: %s", data.sLine);
```

```
    write_str(atoi(data.sX), atoi(data.sY),
      data.sLine, data.nLarge, atoi(data.sColor));
  }
  TObject::destroy(dialog);
}
```

FIGURE 10.1

The Display Text dialog box

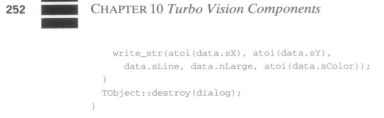

There are a couple of things in the dispTextDlg() function that might not be familiar. One is the write_str() function, which is a subroutine from my image processing collection that writes a string on the image display. Its operation is obvious. Another unfamiliar item is the TextData structure, which is used to declare a static variable called data, and is discussed in the next section.

Initializing Controls

In Chapter 9 I discussed the setData() and getData() functions, which are used to transfer data to/from the controls in a dialog box. Usually you create a structure whose fields correspond to the controls in the dialog box. But before the structure is used, it must be initialized. For a long time I initialized all of these structures manually, by assigning a value to each field. But that's too much work, so I adopted the following scheme. For each dialog box I create a similarly named struct. Here's the struct that houses the data for the Text Display dialog box.

```
struct TextData {
    char sLine[8Ø];
    char sX[numLen];
    char sY[numLen];
    ushort nLarge;
    char sColor[numLen];
    TextData(); // init
};
```

What's interesting here is the constructor. Yes, structs are allowed to have a constructor. Actually, a struct can have all the features that classes can have; the only difference is that a struct's members are public by default, while a class's are private. I advised you earlier in this book to use structs where you only store data, and to use classes where you have objects, that is, data plus actions. Yes, I stand behind that advice. That's why TextData is a struct; it doesn't do anything, its only role is to store the Text Display dialog box's data. But automatic initialization isn't so much a behavior as a godsend, and providing a constructor ensures that the struct will always be properly initialized, without my having to write a series of explicit initialization statements. Here's the constructor for the TextData struct.

```
TextData::TextData()
{
    memset(this, Ø, sizeof(TextData));
    *sX = 'Ø';
    *sY = 'Ø';
    nLarge = Ø;
    strcpy(sColor, "2ØØ");
}
```

I follow this system consistently, because it greatly simplifies management of dialog box data.

The File-Open Clan

Opening files is a key part of any program's user interface. Today, most users expect a lot of flexibility. They don't want to have to remember their file names; instead, they require a menu of files. Plus they expect to be able to navigate through the file system using a file-open dialog box. Yes, most of today's file-open dialogs have nearly as much functionality as early DOS shells.

Of course, Turbo Vision can greatly reduce the difficulty of providing a file-open dialog. At the simplest level, there is the TFileDialog class. It presents a standard file dialog box, complete with a scrollable window of file names, the ability to navigate through the file system, a history window to make it easier to recover already entered file names, and a configurable set of options and buttons. You can look up more complete information on the TFileDialog class in the Turbo Vision reference, or you can browse through Borland's source for the TVEdit application.

I just want to show a simple example of how the TFileDialog class might be used, and then show several variants that let you access file dialogs from within other dialogs. First the simple use. Here's the statement from one of my applications that creates a TFileDialog object to load in a color lookup table:

```
TDialog *d = new TFileDialog("*.lut", "Load Color Map",
    "~N~ame", fdOpenButton, 11Ø);
```

The parameters are the mask for the initial set of files that will be displayed, the title of the dialog box, the label for the input line that allows you to type in file names, a set of flags denoting what buttons will be displayed, and an ID for the history window. Figure 10.2 shows the file-open dialog box produced by the above statement.

FIGURE 10.2

A standard file-open dialog box

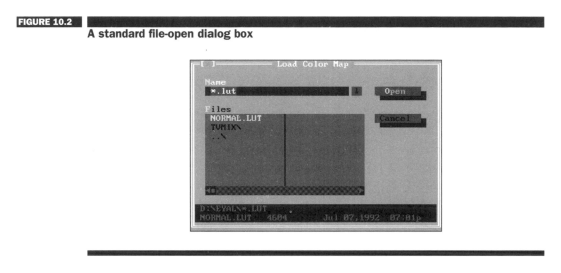

File-Open inside a Dialog

The Turbo Vision TFileDialog will work great for you if what you want is a generic file-open dialog. But what about file-open dialogs that have additional features? You really have two choices:

- Make your own file dialog, starting from the standard TFileDialog class, which contains your additional features. This approach is difficult because TFileDialog isn't designed to serve as a base class. Your only choice is to make a copy of Borland's code, and then add your own features.

- Invoke the standard Turbo Vision TFileDialog from within your own dialog. In your dialog you place all of your application-specific features, plus a TInputLine for the file name, plus a TButton to invoke the standard TFileDialog. This approach lets your own dialogs concentrate on things unique to your application, it lets you take advantage of the Turbo Vision file dialog, and it also lets you craft dialogs that reference several files.

I'm going to concentrate on the second approach, because it's what I've used in my own code. The basic approach is to have a TInputLine object and a TButton object work as a pair. I customarily place the button to the right of the input line, with a label above the input line, as shown in Figure 10.3. If the user simply wants to enter a file name, the TInputLine is ready and able. If, instead, the user prefers a file dialog, then he or she presses the FileDialog button, and a file dialog pops up. If the file dialog is terminated by something other than cm-Cancel, then the result is automatically copied into the input line.

FIGURE 10.3

A dialog box that can activate a file-open dialog

I've created a number of components that support this scheme, but let me start with the fundamental component, the fileInput() procedure. FileInput() is modeled on the standard dialog procedures that you've seen already. It takes a pointer to a dialog box, and a position in that box, and it inserts the requested components at those positions. However, there are a few small differences. One difference is that fileInput() needs to know the x position of both the TInput-Line control and the TButton control. Another is that fileInput() needs to know the text of the label for the TInputLine control, and it needs to know what command will be generated by the button. One other difference is the return value. The fileInput() function returns a pointer to the TInputLine control, because it is needed when the file-open dialog is activated. Here's the prototype for the fileInput() function:

```
extern TInputLine *fileInput(TDialog *dialog,
    char *sLabel,    // the label
    int cmCmd,       // for the button
    int xLine,       // where the input line starts
    int xButton,     // where the button starts
    int y);
```

The fileInput() procedure does roughly the same thing as the abStdInput-Line() and cancelOKButtonsH() functions that I've already shown. Of course the full source for fileInput() is shown in stddial.cpp under "StdDialogs Source Code," later in this chapter.

Popping up one dialog from within another is a bit tricky. What you want is for the file dialog to appear immediately when the button is pressed. One way to do this would be to create your own dialog class with its own handleEvent() function, so that you could quickly take over when the given button is activated. There's nothing wrong with this approach, other than that it requires some effort to create your own dialog class each time you want to activate a file dialog from within some other dialog.

The easier approach involves a small trick. The idea is to assign a command to the button that will terminate the original dialog, so that the file dialog can be invoked. This approach is feasible because there are two commands, other than cmOK and cmCancel, that will terminate a dialog: cmYes and cmNo. Thus whenever I want to have either one or two file name inputs in an application dialog, I follow this procedure:

1. Create an application dialog containing all application-specific controls.

2. Use fileInput() to add TInputLine and TButton controls for either one or two file input control pairs. The first uses the command cmYes and the second uses cmNo.

3. Use execView() as usual to activate the application dialog.

4. If the application dialog terminates with the return status of cmYes or cmNo, create and execute a TFileDialog.

   ■ If the TFileDialog returns with a status other than cmCancel, then copy its result into the TInputLine control. This shows the user the currently selected file.

   ■ Then use execView() again to restore the original application dialog, and return to step 4.

5. If the application dialog terminates with the return status of cmCancel or cmOk, perform the usual cleanup operations.

Let's now look at how this works in practice. Here's the code that produces the simple dialog box shown in Figure 10.3.

```
static void showIVHeaderDlg(void)
{
  static char fileName[MAXPATH] = "";
  TDialog *dialog = new TDialog(TRect(0, 0, 41, 8),
    "Show IV Info.");
  dialog->options |= ofCentered;
  TInputLine *inputLine = fileInput(dialog,
    "~F~ilename", cmYes, 2, 25, 2);
  inputLine->setData(fileName);
  cancelOKStdButtonsH(dialog, 16, 5);
  ushort result;
  while(1) {
    inputLine->select();
    result = TProgram::deskTop->execView(dialog);
    if (result == cmCancel) {
      break; // done
    } else if (result == cmOK) {
      // show the IV header
      inputLine->getData(fileName);
      showIVHeader(fileName);
      break; // done
    }
    else if (result == cmYes) {  // file dialog
      inputLine->getData(fileName);
      if (execDialog(new TFileDialog( "*.*", "Show IV Header",
        "~N~ame", fdOpenButton, 120 ), fileName) != cmCancel)
```

```
            inputLine->setData(fileName);
        }
    }
    TObject::destroy(dialog);
}
```

There are a couple of things in this code that might not be familiar in the showIVHeaderDlg() function. One is the showIVHeader() function, which is a routine from my image processing collection that displays the header of an IV format image file. Because I'm showing my working code, pure and unadulterated, I left it in, but its operation clearly doesn't concern us here.

The second unfamiliar element is the execDialog() function. The execDialog() function is a gem that Borland developed for their TVEdit demo application. It performs the usual steps for executing a dialog: it initializes the data using sctData(); it activates the dialog using execView(); if the dialog isn't canceled, it retrieves the dialog data using getData(); and then it calls destroy() to clean up. Borland's execDialog() function is very handy, and I use it in all my applications.

It's easy to not quite understand the final while loop in the showIVHeaderDlg() procedure. The loop implements steps 3, 4, and 5 from the list. The loop will repeat until either the cmCancel command or the cmOK command is returned from the dialog, which means until the Cancel or OK button is pressed. When the FileDialog button is pressed, the dialog terminates with the cmYes command, then a TFileDialog is run, and then the original dialog is restarted.

File-Open, Three or Four Times, inside a Dialog

As I've mentioned already, there are only four commands that will cause a dialog box to terminate: cmOK, cmCancel, cmYes, and cmNo. I've adopted the convention, for my own code, of using cmYes and cmNo for my file dialog buttons, so that I can start file dialogs whenever the file dialog buttons are pressed.

But what if I need more than two file dialog buttons in a single dialog box? The solution is to create an extended dialog box class, called TExtDialog, derived from TDialog, that will provide additional commands to close the dialog box. Half in jest, I've called these extra commands cmMaybe and cmPerhaps. Here's the class definition of the two new commands and that of the TExtDialog class.

```
const cmMaybe = 15;    // follows cmYes and cmNo
const cmPerhaps = 16;
class TExtDialog : public TDialog {
  public:
    TExtDialog(TRect r, const char *title) :
      TDialog(r, title),
      TWindowInit(TDialog::initFrame)
      { return; }
    void handleEvent(TEvent &ev);
};
```

As you can see, the only member functions of TExtDialog are the constructor and the handleEvent() function. Both of these member functions simply provide access to the same member of the base class, except that handleEvent() also manages the two commands that I've added to provide additional ways to close the dialog. Here's the simple source code for the TExtDialog class's handleEvent() function.

```
void TExtDialog::handleEvent(TEvent& e)
{
  TDialog::handleEvent(e);
  if (e.what == evCommand) switch (e.message.command) {
    case cmMaybe:
    case cmPerhaps:
      if ((state & sfModal) != 0) {
        endModal(e.message.command);
        clearEvent(e);
      }
      break;
  }
}
```

The TExtDialog class is a perfect example of how inheritance lets you enhance a class library. Borland's programmers never imagined, when they were writing the TDialog class, that I might need a couple of extra commands to terminate the dialog. But because the dialog is a class, it's easy for me to step in and add this capability, using inheritance. Imagine how much harder this would be if Turbo Vision were a subroutine library instead of a class library!

I'm going to illustrate use of the TExtDialog class using a dialog box (shown in Figure 10.4) from one of my image processing applications. This time I've decided to simplify the code slightly. To reduce the length, which originally was 72 lines, I've replaced some of the details with brief comments. I think this foreshortened subroutine better gives the flavor of how you can use the TExtDialog class, while still providing all of the important details.

FIGURE 10.4

A dialog box that can activate three file-open dialogs

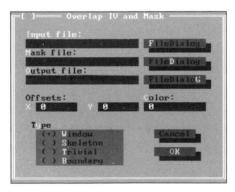

```
static void overlapDlg(void)
{
  TExtDialog *dialog =
    new TExtDialog(TRect(0, 0, 42, 19),
      "Overlap IV and Mask");
  dialog->options |= ofCentered;

  TInputLine *inputLine =
    fileInput(dialog, "~I~nput file:",
      cmYes, 2, 25, 2);
  TInputLine *maskLine =
    fileInput(dialog, "~M~ask file:",
      cmNo, 2, 25, 4);
  TInputLine *outputLine =
    fileInput(dialog, "~O~utput file:",
      cmMaybe, 2, 25, 6);

  // x, y, color, and type controls inserted here

  cancelOKStdButtonsV(dialog, 27, 13);

  // initialize dialog box data here
  inputLine->select();

  ushort result;
  while(1) {
    result = TProgram::deskTop->execView(dialog);
    switch(result) {

    case cmOK:
      //
      // getData() and do task here
      //
      /*nobreak*/
    case cmCancel:
      TObject::destroy(dialog);
      return; // the only way out

    case cmYes:    // input file dialog
      inputLine->getData(data.infileName);
      if (execDialog( new TFileDialog( "*.*",
        "Overlap Input IV File", "~N~ame", fdOpenButton,
        120), data.infileName) != cmCancel)
          inputLine->setData(data.infileName);
      inputLine->select();
      break;

    case cmNo:    // mask file dialog
      maskLine->getData(data.maskfileName);
      if (execDialog( new TFileDialog( "*.*",
        "Overlap Input Mask File", "~N~ame", fdOpenButton,
        120), data.maskfileName) != cmCancel)
          maskLine->setData(data.maskfileName);
      maskLine->select();
      break;
```

```
case cmMaybe:   // output file dialog
  outputLine->getData(data.outfileName);
  if (execDialog( new TFileDialog( "*.*",
    "Overlap Output IV File", "~N~ame", fdOpenButton,
    120), data.outfileName) != cmCancel)
      outputLine->setData(data.outfileName);
  outputLine->select();
  break;

default:
  errmsg("dialog end code %d", result);
  break;
  }
 }
}
```

Admittedly, even with the simplification this isn't a simple subroutine. But I would argue that the code is quite simple for what it does, and that the simple structure of the code makes it unlikely that there are hidden or subtle problems. You should keep in mind that this isn't just one dialog, but four: a base dialog and then the three file dialogs that it can invoke. Things look chatty because each of the file dialogs has its own title, parameters, and so on.

The point of all this isn't the low-level detail of how I built the dialog box in Figure 10.4 that can invoke three separate file-open dialog boxes. Frankly, few readers will ever need a dialog box exactly like that in Figure 10.4. What is important is the general approach. A good class library is clay, not stone. You can form and improve it, so that it does what you need it to do. Turbo Vision is an excellent class library because it is clay of exactly the right consistency. It is already well formed and useful, but it is still soft enough that I can mold it to my own purpose.

StdDialogs Source Code

In the preceding sections I've presented about half of the code that implements my standard dialog elements. Now I'd like to show that code in its entirety so you can see all of the details. Listing 10.1 shows stddial.h and Listing 10.2 shows stddial.cpp.

LISTING 10.1

Stddial.h

```
const numLen = 10;  // strings used to store numbers

extern void abStdInputLine(TDialog *dialog, int x, int y,
  const char *s1, const char *s2);

extern void cancelOKStdButtonsH(TDialog *dialog,
  int x, int y);
extern void cancelOKStdButtonsV(TDialog *dialog,
  int x, int y);
```

LISTING 10.1

Stddial.h (Continued)

```cpp
extern TInputLine *fileInput(TDialog *dialog,
  char *sLabel,   // the label
  int cmCmd,      // for the button
  int xLine,      // where the input line starts
  int xButton,    // where the button starts
  int y);

//
// an extended dialog--more button commands that
//   terminate the dialog
//
const cmMaybe = 15;   // follows cmYes and cmNo
const cmPerhaps = 16;
class TExtDialog : public TDialog {
  public:
    TExtDialog(TRect r, const char *title) :
      TDialog(r, title),
           TWindowInit(TDialog::initFrame)
      { return; }
    void handleEvent(TEvent &ev);
};
```

LISTING 10.2

Stddial.cpp

```cpp
#define Uses_TDialog
#define Uses_TButton
#define Uses_TInputLine
#define Uses_TView
#define Uses_TRect
#define Uses_TLabel
#define Uses_TEvent
#include <tv.h>
#include <dir.h>
#include <string.h>
#include "stddial.h"

//
// A pair of TInputLine controls
//
// Layout:
//
// S XXXXXXX    S XXXXXXX
```

LISTING 10.2

Stddial.cpp (Continued)

```cpp
void abStdInputLine(TDialog *dialog, int x, int y,
  const char *s1, const char *s2)
{
  int y1 = y + 1;
  int x2 = x + 12;

  if (s1 && *s1) {
    TView *a = new TInputLine(TRect(x+3, y, x+11, y1),
      numLen);
    dialog->insert(a);
    dialog->insert(new TLabel(TRect(x,    y, x+3,  y1),
      s1, a));
  }

  if (s2 && *s2) {
    TView *b = new TInputLine(TRect(x2+3, y, x2+11, y1),
      numLen);
    dialog->insert(b);
    dialog->insert(new TLabel(TRect(x2,    y, x2+3,  y1),
      s2, b));
  }
}


//
// Horizontal Cancel/OK buttons
//
void cancelOKStdButtonsH(TDialog *dialog, int x, int y)
{
  dialog->insert(
    new TButton(TRect( x+00,   y, x+10, y+2),
      "Cancel", cmCancel, bfNormal));
  dialog->insert(
    new TButton(TRect( x+12,   y, x+22, y+2),
      "O~K~", cmOK, bfDefault));
}


//
// Vertical Cancel/OK buttons
//
void cancelOKStdButtonsV(TDialog *dialog, int x, int y)
{
  dialog->insert(
    new TButton(TRect( x,   y+0, x+10, y+2),
      "Cancel", cmCancel, bfNormal));
```

LISTING 10.2

Stddial.cpp (Continued)

```cpp
    dialog->insert(
      new TButton(TRect( x,   y+2, x+10, y+4),
        "O~K~", cmOK, bfDefault));
}


//
// An input line and a file dialog button for simple
//   file name entry
//
// Layout:
//
// LLLLL.
// IIIIIIIIIIIIIIIII  BBBBBB
//
TInputLine *fileInput(TDialog *dialog,
  char *sLabel, // the label
  int cmCmd,    // for the button
  int xLine,    // where the input line starts
  int xButton,  // where the button starts
  int y)
{
  int y1 = y + 1;
  int y2 = y + 2;
  int y3 = y + 3;
  char *fd = "?";

  if (cmCmd == cmYes)
    fd = "~F~ileDialog";
  else if (cmCmd == cmNo)
    fd = "File~D~ialog";
  else if (cmCmd == cmMaybe)
    fd = "FileDialo~G~";
  else if (cmCmd == cmPerhaps)
    fd = "FileDia~L~og";

  TInputLine *i = new
    TInputLine(TRect(xLine+1, y1, xButton, y2), MAXPATH);
  dialog->insert(i);

  TLabel *l = new
    TLabel(TRect( xLine, y, xLine + strlen(sLabel), y1),
      sLabel, i);
  dialog->insert(l);
```

LISTING 10.2

Stddial.cpp (Continued)

```
  dialog->insert(
    new TButton(TRect( xButton, y1, xButton+14, y3 ), fd,
      cmCmd, bfNormal));
  return i;
}


//
// the extended dialog class
//
void TExtDialog::handleEvent(TEvent& e)
{
  TDialog::handleEvent(e);
  if (e.what == evCommand) switch (e.message.command) {
    case cmMaybe:
    case cmPerhaps:
      if ((state & sfModal) != Ø) {
        endModal(e.message.command);
        clearEvent(e);
      }
      break;
    }
}
```

Building a Lo-Res Position Control

Most of my image processing software works with images that have a resolution that is much lower than the resolution of the display screen. This is intentional, because we often want to have multiple images displayed next to each other, so that they can be compared. I originally provided this facility by allowing the user to specify the x and y position denoting where on the screen an image should be displayed. But this is far too clumsy, so instead I created a position control. The position control allows you to point the mouse at a region of the dialog box, to denote a region of the separate image display screen. Figure 10.5 shows a position control in the dialog box.

The position control is implemented by the TGrid class, which is publicly derived from the TView class. The data members of TGrid store the current row and column position of the selected cell, which I call the *hot spot*. The class contains member functions to handle events, draw itself, get and set data, and get a palette. I've also included the stream I/O functionality, so that the TGrid control can be archived in a file. More information on using Turbo Vision objects in streams can be found in the reference manual.

The TGrid class definition is shown in Listing 10.3, and the full source for the TGrid class is in Listing 10.4.

FIGURE 10.5

A dialog box that contains a position control

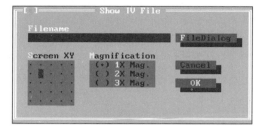

LISTING 10.3

TGrid.h

```cpp
#if !defined( __GRID_H )
#define __GRID_H
//
// implement a small rectangular grid
//    The class's "value" is the x/y
//    position of the selected cell.
//
class TGrid : public TView
{
public:
  TGrid( TRect& r );
  TGrid( StreamableInit ) : TView(streamableInit) { };
  virtual void draw();
  virtual void handleEvent( TEvent& event );
  void getData(void *v);
  void setData(void *v);
  ushort dataSize(void);
  TPalette& getPalette(void) const;
  static const char * const name;
  static TStreamable *build();
protected:
  ushort xHot, yHot;
  virtual void write( opstream& );
  virtual void *read( ipstream& );
private:
  virtual const char *streamableName() const
        { return name; }
};

inline ipstream& operator >> ( ipstream& is, TGrid& cl )
    { return is >> (TStreamable&) cl; }
```

LISTING 10.3

TGrid.h (Continued)

```cpp
inline ipstream& operator >> ( ipstream& is, TGrid*& cl )
    { return is >> (void *&) cl; }
inline opstream& operator << ( opstream& os, TGrid& cl )
    { return os << (TStreamable&) cl; }
inline opstream& operator << ( opstream& os, TGrid* cl )
    { return os << (TStreamable *) cl; }
#endif       // __GRID_H
```

LISTING 10.4

TGrid.cpp

```cpp
#define Uses_TRect
#define Uses_TEvent
#define Uses_TKeys
#define Uses_TDrawBuffer
#define Uses_TStreamableClass
#define Uses_TStreamable
#define Uses_TView
#define Uses_TWindow
#include <tv.h>
__link( RView )
__link( RWindow )
#include <string.h>
#include <stdlib.h>
#include <ctype.h>
#include <strstrea.h>
#include <iomanip.h>
#include "grid.h"

//
// TGrid functions
//
const char * const TGrid::name = "TGrid";

void TGrid::write( opstream& os )
{
    TView::write( os );
    os.writeBytes(&xHot, sizeof(xHot));
    os.writeBytes(&yHot, sizeof(yHot));
}

void *TGrid::read( ipstream& is )
{
```

LISTING 10.4

TGrid.cpp (Continued)

```cpp
        TView::read( is );
        is.readBytes(&xHot, sizeof(xHot));
        is.readBytes(&yHot, sizeof(yHot));
        return this;
}

TStreamable *TGrid::build()
{
        return new TGrid( streamableInit );
}

TStreamableClass RGrid( TGrid::name,
        TGrid::build,
        __DELTA(TGrid)
            );

TGrid::TGrid(TRect& r) :
  TView(r),
  xHot(Ø),
  yHot(Ø)
{
  options |= ofSelectable;
  setState(sfCursorIns, True);
}

void TGrid::draw()
{
  TDrawBuffer buf;
  char color = getColor(1);
  for(int y = Ø; y <= size.y-1; y++) {
    buf.moveChar(Ø, ' ', color, size.x);
    for(int x = Ø; x <= size.x-1; x++)
      if (x & Ø1) // odd are spaces
        buf.moveChar(x, ' ', color, 1);
      else if (y == yHot && x == 2*xHot)
        buf.moveChar(x, Øxb2, color, 1);
      else
        buf.moveChar(x, Øxf9, color, 1);
    writeLine(Ø, y, size.x, 1, buf);
  }
  showCursor();
}

const char cpGrid[] = "\x1Ø\x11\x12\x12";
```

LISTING 10.4

TGrid.cpp (Continued)

```cpp
TPalette& TGrid::getPalette(void) const
{
  static TPalette palette(cpGrid, sizeof(cpGrid) -1);
  return palette;
}

void TGrid::handleEvent(TEvent& event)
{
  TView::handleEvent(event);
  if (event.what == evMouseDown) {
    do {
      if(mouseInView(event.mouse.where)) {
        TPoint spot = makeLocal(event.mouse.where);
        setCursor(spot.x, spot.y);
        xHot = spot.x/2;
        yHot = spot.y;
        drawView();
      }
    } while (mouseEvent(event, evMouseMove));
    clearEvent(event);
  } else {
    if (event.what == evKeyboard) {
      int hit = 1;
      switch (event.keyDown.keyCode) {
        case kbHome:
          setCursor(0,0);
          break;
        case kbEnd:
          setCursor((size.x-1)&~01, size.y-1);
          break;
        case kbUp:
          if (cursor.y > 0)
            setCursor(cursor.x, cursor.y-1);
          break;
        case kbDown:
          if (cursor.y < size.y-1)
            setCursor(cursor.x, cursor.y+1);
          break;
        case kbLeft:
          if (cursor.x > 1)
            setCursor(cursor.x-2, cursor.y);
          break;
        case kbRight:
          if (cursor.x < size.x-2)
```

LISTING 10.4

TGrid.cpp (Continued)

```
                setCursor(cursor.x+2, cursor.y);
              break;
            default:
              if (event.keyDown.charScan.charCode == ' ') {
                xHot = cursor.x/2;
                yHot = cursor.y;
                drawView();
              }
              else
                hit = Ø;
              break;
          }
        if (hit)
          clearEvent(event);
      }
    }
}

ushort TGrid::dataSize(void)
{
  return 2 * sizeof(ushort);
}

void TGrid::setData(void *v)
{
  ushort *p = (ushort *)v;
  xHot = *p++;
  yHot = *p;
}

void TGrid::getData(void *v)
{
  ushort *p = (ushort *)v;
  *p++ = xHot;
  *p++ = yHot;
}
```

Most of the functionality for the TGrid class resides in two functions, handleEvent() and draw(). Let me start with a brief description of draw().

The draw() Function

The draw() function is responsible for drawing the TGrid control on the screen. It uses a TDrawBuffer object to do the actual output. Each position in the grid is signified by a dot, whose code in PC video adapters is 0xf9. The hot spot is shown by a rectangular character, whose code is 0xb2.

I originally implemented the TGrid control as a simple rectangular region that was directly addressed. For example, for a four by four TGrid control I simply used four rows and four columns on the screen. The problem with this simple approach was that characters are roughly twice as tall as they are wide, so a "square" four by four region looked tall and skinny. My solution was to insert blank spaces between the columns. Thus, in the final version, I implement a four by four TGrid control using four rows and seven columns on the screen. The seven columns are the four active columns plus the three filler columns. Yes, this visual improvement considerably complicates the code, because X coordinates need to be treated very carefully!

The handleEvent Member

The handleEvent() member of the TGrid class gives the control its behaviors. The TGrid class handles keyboard events and mouse events. Thus you are able to specify a position by using the cursor keys or using the mouse. Whenever possible, Turbo Vision applications should be operable by users who don't have (or who don't like to use) a mouse. In the TGrid control, you can use the keyboard to move the cursor to the desired hot spot position, and then you press the spacebar to actually move the hot spot to the current location. Much easier, in my opinion, is simply clicking on the desired position using the mouse.

The logic inside handleEvent() for mouse clicks is very simple. Mouse click coordinates are converted to local coordinates, the cursor is moved to the mouse click location, the new hot spot location is computed, and then the control is scheduled for a redraw by calling drawView().

The handleEvent() function's keyboard logic requires much more effort. Basically, all of the cursor motion keys are handled by computing a new cursor position, taking into consideration the bounds of the control and the fact that X positions must change by two. When the spacebar is pressed, the new hot spot is computed and the control is scheduled for redraw.

Let me conclude this chapter with a confession that is also a piece of advice. I didn't create the TGrid control from a blank slate. Instead, when I started to think about building a position control, I tried to think of similar things that could be adapted to create a position control. I realized that in Borland's TV-Demo program they have an ASCII chart window that had much of the logic that I needed. The ASCII chart allows you to select a character from the chart using either the cursor or the mouse. This is the heart of my TGrid control, although most of my details are different. Therefore I built my TGrid class by making a copy of Borland's TTable class, and then changing it bit by bit into a position control. Borland supplies a lot of useful code with Turbo Vision; get familiar with it so you can borrow from it as necessary.

PART 4

Object Windows Class Library

THE OWL APPLICATION FRAMEWORK

WE ARE LONG PAST THE POINT WHERE IT MAKES SENSE TO DEBATE THE course of PC desktop computing in the mid-90s. For commercial applications software, and increasingly for specialized corporate and departmental software, the future is Windows. This much is clear.

But knowing that the future is Windows doesn't make it any easier to develop Windows software. Windows is a complex, demanding environment that is both unforgiving and unyielding. Unfortunately, the difficulties of Windows itself have been compounded by the inadequacies of Microsoft's original Windows development tools, which were clearly deficient. Even worse, the original software development paradigm, the blueprint for all Windows applications, was substandard.

Today there are many alternatives that facilitate Windows development. Many of these alternatives are high-level software development environments, such as Microsoft's Visual Basic, Borland's ObjectVision, and Asymetrix's ToolBook, that address many of the most common development needs. But when you need to build a complex application from the ground up, there is only one language you should consider, C++. Once you've decided on C++, the next decision must be which class library to use. (Yes, I've skipped past the decision of whether you should use a class library. Use one.) There are many choices, and several of them are good, but I strongly advocate Borland's Object Windows (class) Library (OWL). OWL targets those aspects of Windows that can be improved using a class library, while skipping other areas that offer less room for improvement. And OWL is a proven library, due to its extensive use in Borland's own Windows product line.

OWL takes much of the sting out of Windows programming. This is partly a result of how OWL superimposes a somewhat higher-level interface onto Windows. But OWL's advantage mostly comes from the application of object-oriented techniques to Windows, which is inherently an object-oriented environment. Somewhat separate from OWL itself is the fact that Windows programming using Borland tools is easier and more productive than Windows programming using other tools.

My approach in these six OWL chapters is to provide a comprehensive introduction to OWL Windows programming. I'm not trying to replace the OWL reference manuals that come with the Borland compiler, so you'll often need to refer to the manuals for specific information. Similarly, I'm not writing a complete guide to Windows programming, so you'll need to refer to the standard

Windows references and guides as you learn about OWL programming. And finally, I'm not covering Borland's development tools, such as their stunning Resource Workshop and their powerful TDW Windows debugger. These tools are well described in the Borland manuals.

The Windows Paradigm

Although OWL is a wonderful mediator, there is a limit to its magic. This book is strongly directed toward OWL, but to understand OWL you need to understand basic Windows concepts. That's what I'll focus on in the next few pages. If you're already familiar with Windows, please skip ahead to the OWL paradigm section.

Event-Driven Programming

In a traditional number- or data-crunching application, the application itself is constantly in charge of its own destiny. The application performs a series of tasks, under its own control. This model works well for simulating the behavior of the stock market or for processing checks, but it is not very well suited to desktop applications, such as spreadsheets and word processors, because in desktop applications the user directs the application.

The problem with software for the desktop is that the user of the software has so many options. What's needed is a programming environment that reacts, in a natural way, to the user's actions. If the user clicks the mouse to push a button in a dialog, task x should be performed. If instead the user closes a window, task y should be performed. If the user switches to a second application, further input should go to the second application while the first lies idle. The main advantage of event-driven programming is that it addresses this need.

An event-driven program has an orientation that is the opposite of a traditional program. In an event-driven program, the program waits for a work order. If the user uses the mouse to push a dialog box button, the system (Windows) creates a message that describes the event, and then sends that message to the program. The application wakes up, receives the message, processes the message, and then waits for another message.

Another reason for using an event-driven programming model is that it helps Windows manage several independent applications. If an application asks Windows for the next message, then Windows knows that the application has finished its previous chore. This helps Windows allow some other application to operate. If Windows needs to obscure part of an application's visible window, it knows that it can later ask the application to redraw its window. Similarly, as the focus of user activity moves from one application to another, Windows simply routes the user-generated messages to the application managing the active window. Thus there are many reasons for using an event-driven programming model for desktop productivity applications.

Figure 11.1 shows a schematic of the event-driven Windows architecture. On the right are user input devices, which are the source of many of the Windows events. When these devices are used, the Windows device drivers manage the input/output operations. Input from devices such as mice and keyboards usually means, to Windows, composing and sending messages to the active application. Software applications, shown on the left of Figure 11.1, interchange messages with the Windows kernel.

FIGURE 11.1

The Windows event-driven architecture

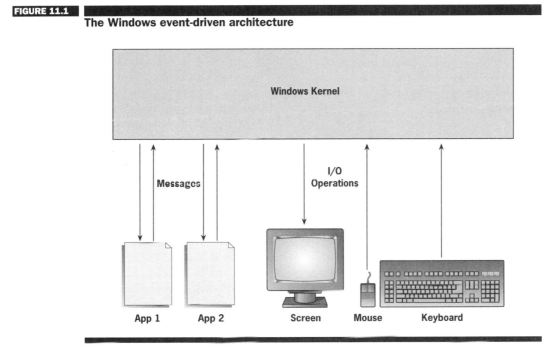

For the most part, applications receive messages, but they are also able to send messages. The display screen, shown in the middle of the figure, is responsible for much of the message traffic. One of Windows's most intricate jobs, and certainly its most visual task, is to manage the display. Because the display is often shared by several applications, changes made by one application sometimes affect another. For example, if the user enlarges the window of one application, it may partially obscure the window of another.

Even though Windows uses an event-based, message passing architecture, it also contains a traditional procedural interface. When messages arrive for an application to process, much of the response is likely to be a series of procedure calls to the Windows kernel. Some of these Windows kernel calls are replaced by functionality in OWL, but most OWL applications will continue to include many direct Windows calls.

In the traditional C language approach to message handling, which was used to produce all of the early Windows applications, a C switch statement was used to select a response for each message. There are many liabilities to using a C switch statement as a message router. The most obvious is that there are hundreds of messages, which can lead to huge, unwieldy code. A second obvious problem is that each case in a C switch statement doesn't have its own context, which means that the code for one case can easily stomp on the values used by another.

But the most important problem with using a C switch statement to route messages is that it doesn't support the idea of inheritance. There's no way in a C switch statement to say that Window B is like Window A, except that these one or two messages are handled differently. No way, that is, other than using the text editor to cut and paste vast hunks of C code.

There is, of course, a better way—objects. C++ lets you create objects that correspond to the major components of Windows. Thus in OWL there are classes that represent an application, classes that represent windows, classes that represent Windows controls, and so on. Each class provides member functions that handle specific messages. This provides an architecture that allows encapsulation—one function to handle one message—and inheritance to streamline Windows development.

Using Resources

In a traditional environment, such as DOS, the operating system really doesn't do very much for an application program. Instead the program is expected to fend for itself. But Windows is a tremendously rich environment that can help your program to manage resources such as windows (screen real estate), dialogs, menus, controls (buttons, lists, scroll bars, and so forth), fonts, images, and so on. In fact, it's Windows's management of these elements that is the impetus for writing Windows applications. If managing these elements were so easy, then each major software vendor might have written their own graphical environment. But instead these elements are complex, and it is Windows's built-in management of these elements that we find so attractive.

Resources are usually managed in three stages. In the first stage, a program asks Windows to access a resource. For example, a program might ask to use a certain icon, or to use a certain font. If the resource is available, Windows gives the program a handle to refer to the resource. In the second stage, the resource is used by the program, usually by passing its handle to a Windows function. Finally, in the third stage, the program releases the resource, again by using its handle.

Many resources are provided by Windows itself. For example, Windows comes with a useful selection of icons, a large set of fonts, and a number of useful cursors. But in addition, most programs bring their own resources to the party. For example, most programs provide their own icons, menus, and dialog boxes. In addition, many provide their own cursors, fonts, and other resources. Resources that are provided by an application for its own use are usually compiled into the application's .EXE file, and then are accessed by the application during program execution. (Font resources are an exception. They are usually installed into the Windows system directory and made available to all applications.)

Separating an application's executable code from its resources can be a boon to internationalization. If you want to provide foreign language versions of your application, you should strive to place all of your message text in resource files. This makes it relatively easy to add foreign language support, because the changes will be concentrated in just a few files. It also makes it possible for you to subcontract the job of adding foreign language support without providing full source code to the subcontractor.

Traditional Windows Tools and Organization

It might be possible to develop a Windows application by using just a C compiler, a linker, and an editor, but for practical work you need several other tools. Perhaps most importantly, you need a resource compiler that can put bitmaps, icons, fonts, menus, dialog box layouts, and the like, into an executable form that can be used in Windows. The resource "compiler" has sometimes been compared to an actual compiler, but it really works at a level much more comparable to assembly.

The raw materials for the resource compiler may be resources stored in the .RC script, which is to resources what your main .CPP file is to executable code. But especially in larger programs the resources will be stored in their own files. Most individual resource files, such as dialog .DLG files, are edited using a visual design tool. In the original Windows tool set this program was called the Dialog Editor, but in the Borland compiler all of the visual design tools are collected into the Resource Workshop program. Resource Workshop is a bit awkward in places, but it is a dream compared with what was available in the mid- to late 80s.

The traditional approach is outlined in Figure 11.2. The left side of the figure is similar to any diagram showing the compilation process for a high-level language, while the right side shows the elements that are specific to Windows. Figure 11.2 is actually somewhat forward-looking, because many of the early tools for working with dialog boxes, cursors, and icons worked directly with the .RES file, which is a binary file similar conceptually to an .OBJ file. But the trend has been to store resources in their own files, and then to move them into the .RES binary resource file during resource compilation.

The dotted line in Figure 11.2 from the .H files to the .RC file shows one of the common pitfalls of Windows development. Overall, the clean separation of the program code (the .CPP files, the .H files) from the resource files is a good thing. But there has to be some linkage, because the executing software needs to be able to access the resources. In Windows you can access some resources by using either a string or an ID number, while other resources are always tagged by ID numbers. The general approach is to create a header file that contains all of the resource identifiers, and then include that header in the necessary .C files and also in the .RC resource script. Unfortunately there are no compilation aids that can help you here, and it's easy to get things mixed up. Your two best defenses are to use good naming conventions for resource identifiers, so that errors jump out at you when you're looking at code, and to define all your resource identifiers in one place.

One unfamiliar file in Figure 11.2 is the .DEF file shown on the bottom right. The .DEF file is a module definition file that is used during the linkage process. It tells the linker about the program, the size of the heap, the size of the stack, the types of the segments, and so on. An application's .DEF file controls the characteristics of the application's .EXE file, but it isn't included in the .EXE, which is symbolized by the dotted line connecting the two files in Figure 11.2. In traditional Windows programs, each application needs its own .DEF file, but as we'll see later in this chapter, OWL manages these details for you, which means the OWL programs can almost always use Borland's supplied OWL.DEF.

FIGURE 11.2

The files used to build a traditional C language Windows application

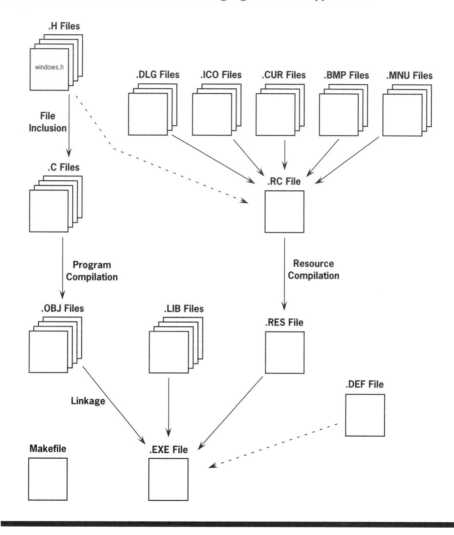

All Windows applications must include the windows.h header file, which is shown on top of the stack of include files in Figure 11.2. Windows.h defines all of the symbolic constants, data structures, and function prototypes used to work with Windows. It is a massive header file; the time spent pulling windows.h through C compilers has put constant pressure on Windows programmers to use machines at the cutting edge. The standard Windows manuals are improving, and indexes are provided, but you'll certainly run into occasional dilemmas that are best resolved by searching through windows.h.

The bottom-left corner of Figure 11.2 shows a makefile. Traditionally, the process of building a Windows application was neither fish nor fowl. Part of the process, such as designing dialog boxes or painting icons, was best done using

Windows tools. But other parts of the process, such as program compilation, resource compilation, and linking, were done by DOS software, usually controlled by a makefile. But that's history; today there are three main approaches that can be used for Windows program development using Borland C++:

- BCC, the DOS-based command-line compiler. This may be attractive to some, but to me the productivity gains from the IDE are so high that they are clearly worth learning. However, there are alternative IDEs that some people prefer, and these IDEs generally hook up to the Borland command-line tools.

- BC, the DOS-based IDE. This is my preference on a system that has only modest performance, because the DOS IDE has crisper performance than the Windows IDE. (A better solution is to get faster hardware!)

- BCW, the Windows-based IDE. My preference, provided your hardware is able.

With all three approaches you will probably use Borland's Resource Workshop to develop your visual elements, although it is also possible to use third-party design tools.

Figure 11.3 shows that the file organization used to build OWL Windows applications isn't fundamentally different from the standard C process. Because you'll usually use BCW or BC to build your application, Figure 11.3 shows the makefile replaced by a .PRJ file. Similarly, Figure 11.3 shows that you'll usually use OWL.DEF instead of a custom .DEF for each application. And of course the .C files have evolved into .CPP files.

The most striking change in Figure 11.3 is the addition of the OWL include files. All OWL-based applications need to include owl.h, and most need to include other OWL header files. These voluminous files, plus the weighty windows.h, ensure that even the smallest OWL module will force the compiler to slog through 10,000 to 12,000 lines of header code. I like to think of it as a bargain—someone else did all that work and I can use it with comparatively little effort.

What Figure 11.3 fails to convey is the difference in the quality of the tools. With Borland's magnificent BCW programming environment, their power-packed Resource Workshop, and their TDW debugger, you can develop fully within Windows. This environment offers complete on-line help, a consistent set of applications, and an object-oriented paradigm. These all add up to productivity.

The OWL Paradigm

The Object Windows Library doesn't fundamentally alter Windows's event-driven paradigm, but it clearly provides a much more convenient and trouble-free way to use the event-driven paradigm. There isn't just one advantage to using OWL, there are multiple advantages, which accumulate into a huge productivity increase once you've mastered the OWL class library.

FIGURE 11.3

The files used to build an OWL Windows application

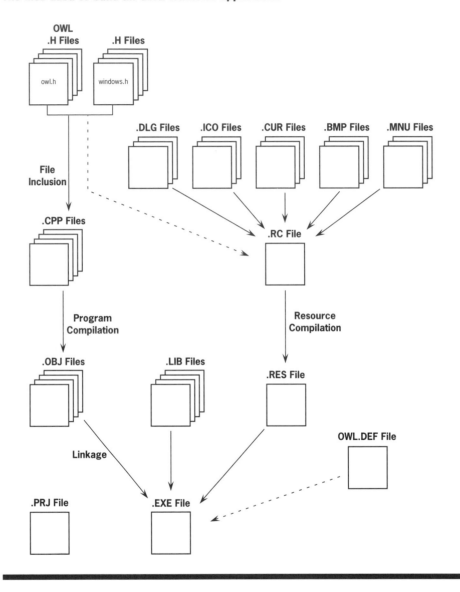

The OWL advantages include the following:

■ C++ provides much stronger type- and usage-checking than C, which is a tremendous boon in Windows programming. Even if you don't use the OWL class library, your Windows programming can be significantly boosted by running your code through Borland's skeptical C++ compiler, instead of through Borland's more trusting C compiler.

- The OWL library provides classes that relate directly to the major Windows concepts. There is a TWindow class for working with windows, various classes for the controls, a TDialog class for creating dialog boxes, and so on. These classes often take care of many details automatically, and they can all be used as base classes, which makes it easy for you to create specialized behavior.

- The OWL library lets you associate class member functions with individual messages. This eliminates the need for huge, unwieldy C switch statements, and conceptually it provides a far cleaner way to manage messages. Unfortunately the OWL message handling scheme uses a C++ language extension created by Borland, which means that OWL code isn't portable to other compilers. This is a limitation, but it's one that I'm willing to live with in exchange for the other benefits of OWL.

The price you pay for OWL is what it does to your .EXE files. They get bigger. I've never been very interested in having tiny .EXE files, so long as the application loads and works at acceptable speeds. And with the Windows architecture, which frees us from the 640k barrier, chubby .EXE files are a worry of the past for most applications.

Resource Workshop

Borland's Resource Workshop is a unified design tool for creating resources. Resource Workshop can create all of the standard resources: bitmaps, cursors, dialog boxes, fonts, icons, menus, and strings. Because Resource Workshop is such a complete tool, you don't need to know very much about the file formats used for Windows resources. Of course you'll occasionally need to refer to the Windows manuals for an arcane detail, but far less than when resources invariably need some hand-tuning to get them to be just right.

When I'm doing Windows development, I usually run both Resource Workshop (RW) and Borland C for Windows (BCW). This lets me easily switch back and forth, which helps keep the code (the .CPP files and the .H files) in sync with the resource files. I usually have Resource Workshop use an .RC file as its "project" file, and I place that same .RC file into my BCW project. (Resource files will be discussed further in the "Understanding Resource Files" section.) Thus the .RC file becomes the meeting point of the code and the resources.

Although there are many approaches, my usual style is to only keep the resources open in Resource Workshop while I'm actively using Resource Workshop. When I've finished editing a resource and I want to return to BCW, I use RW's File-CloseAll command to close the resources. This ensures that any build done in BCW will use the latest resources. Failure to close the resources before compiling can lead to confusion, because the changes you've just made in RW won't show in your latest BCW build.

OWL's Bedrock Classes

OWL consists of about 25 classes, but many of the classes are relatively simple, specialized classes. However, there are four classes—TWindowsObject, TApplication, TWindow, and TDialog—that have a broader role, and I would like to discuss each very briefly. You can consult Borland's *Object Windows for C++ Users' Guide*, which is included in your documentation package, for detailed information about these and other OWL classes. A very simplified diagram of these four classes is shown in Figure 11.4. For a more detailed diagram of the OWL library consult the Borland documentation.

FIGURE 11.4

A simplified diagram of the OWL class hierarchy

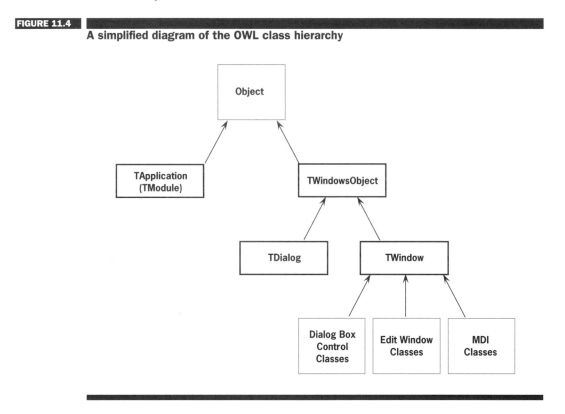

The TApplication Class

The TApplication class is the cornerstone of an OWL application. It's responsible for creating the main window of the application, it contains the standard Windows message loop that processes incoming messages, and it provides you with control over some of the fundamental aspects of how an application behaves.

The TApplication class is derived from the TModule class. When you are writing an ordinary OWL application, by which I mean you are not writing an OWL-based dynamic link library (DLL), then you should consider TApplication and TModule to be a single class. The reason for having two separate classes is that TModule only addresses those aspects of an "application" that are applicable in a dynamic link library.

Your own OWL applications will invariably contain an application class that is derived from TApplication. The main feature of your customized application will be to provide your own InitMainWindow() member function, which is responsible for creating the main window of your application.

How does your application object get created? Here are the steps that occur at the start of every OWL Windows application:

1. Windows starts the application by calling the WinMain() function. WinMain() is a holdover from the old C days, and I encourage you to do as little work as possible in WinMain().

2. Your WinMain() function uses the new operator to create your custom application object.

3. Your application object springs to life. Its constructor (actually the TApplication constructor) calls the InitMainWindow() virtual function.

4. Your application class's InitMainWindow() function uses the new operator to create your application's main window, which is usually a custom window class that you have derived from TWindow.

At the conclusion of step 4 you have a fully operational Windows application. If this four-part program seems like a lot of work, crack open a traditional C language guide to Windows and see what is involved in getting a C language Windows app up and running.

Sometimes you need to access your application object from a member function of one of the window classes. For example, to create a modeless or modal dialog box you need to use respectively the MakeWindow() or ExecDialog() functions of the TApplication (really the TModule) class. This is slightly tricky, because the TApplication class is in a separate branch of the class hierarchy from the window classes. From within a window class, the easiest solution is to use the GetApplication() member function, which is part of the TWindowsObject class. If you're in a class that's not a part of (or an extension of) the OWL hierarchy, you can always call the GetApplicationObject() function, which is a stand-alone function. Both GetApplication() and GetApplicationObject() return a pointer to the application object that you created in WinMain().

The TWindowsObject Class

The TWindowsObject class is the root of the window part of the OWL class hierarchy. Remember that in Windows, everything you see on the screen, all the visual elements, are windows. One of the surprises of Windows is just how many windows there are! For example, if you pop up a dialog box, each of the controls is at least one window, the title bar is composed of several windows, and so on. The most important of these windows, which means those that you need to control and manage, have counterparts in OWL, and all of the counterparts are derived either directly or indirectly from TWindowsObject.

You're not likely to derive a class directly from TWindowsObject, because most OWL programmers work from the more specialized descendants of

TWindowsObject. But you are very likely to use its member functions, because many of them are central to working with Windows.

The TWindow Class

The TWindow class is the first class in the OWL hierarchy that tackles the chores that most programmers envision when they think about a windowing environment. TWindow deals with menus, it defines the characteristics of a window, and it has member functions that respond to the common operations that are performed on windows, such as painting, resizing, and moving.

When you create your own window class, for example when you create a main window for an application, you'll usually derive your new class from TWindow. This lets you override those features that you want to change, and it lets you extend TWindow to have the behavior that you desire.

For example, if your application has a main menu, you'll need to derive a class from TWindow that contains member functions to handle each menu selection. If you want your application to output to the main window, you'll need to supply your own WMPaint() member function in your window class. The only applications that don't derive their own window class from TWindow are those that, like calculators and some games, use a dialog box as their main window.

The TDialog Class

The TDialog class is the only one of the four fundamental OWL classes that is a leaf. The other three classes that I've mentioned are all base classes within the OWL hierarchy; TDialog is the exception. But when you create dialog boxes, your dialog boxes will (for all but the most trivial dialogs) be handled by a class derived from TDialog.

Because dialog boxes are so intricate, Windows endows them with a lot of functionality. Windows contains a set of controls that you can place into dialog boxes, and these controls already have sophisticated behavior built in. The main role of TDialog is to help you get involved when a dialog box is created and when it closes. At both times, you are likely to need to interact with the controls, so you can establish their initial values and so that you can react to user selections. Classes derived from TDialog also often have member functions that respond to messages generated by button controls, although TDialog out-of-the-box is able to manage the OK and Cancel buttons that are found in most dialog boxes.

Dialog boxes and the TDialog class will be discussed in much more detail in Chapter 12. Now we're going to start building a Windows application, and just getting its skeleton up and running will be challenge enough for this chapter.

Find Files Stage 0: Planning an OWL Application

As a pragmatic introduction to OWL, I'm going to build a complete Windows application. The plan will be to start small, no, to start tiny, and then to add features until we have a useful, complete Windows application. I'm not planning to add much polish to this application, because as you will soon discover there is going to be a lot of code even without the polish. The polish is left to you, as an exercise.

The example that I've chosen is a program to find files by searching an entire file system. The program can perform three types of searches:

■ Search for specific file names, using DOS wildcard conventions. Thus by searching for *.DOC you could get a list of all the .DOC files anywhere on a disk.

■ Search for files by size. You can search for files of exactly the given size, or for files that are larger or smaller than the given size. For example, you could search your hard drive for files that are larger that 1,000,000 bytes, to discover where all that disk space is being used.

■ Search for files by content. You can search for files that contain a given snippet of text. Yes, this takes a while, especially on a large disk. For example, if you misplaced a letter you wrote to President Clinton, you could search every file on your disk for the text "Clinton".

Whenever you're designing a Windows application you should think about how it will look, because in Windows the appearance has a lot to do with how you will organize your code. For example, each dialog in your application is likely to translate into a class in your code. Similarly, multiple document interface (MDI) programs have a somewhat different structure than ordinary single-window programs.

My basic visual design for the Find Files program is to have a main window with menu selections to start each type of search. Each search will be managed using its own dialog box. In a more commercial version of this program you might want a single dialog to control all the searches, and you might want Boolean operations, such as "search for all .DOC files greater than 50,000 bytes," but in this version I'm trying, desperately, to keep it simple.

Another aspect of keeping it simple is to display the list of found files in a dialog box. There are other choices, but they involve more work. So in this initial design I'm going to build up the list of found files in a modeless dialog box. This lets me get under way by leveraging the existing capabilities of dialog boxes and of list box controls. Later, the list of found files can be placed elsewhere, such as in an MDI child window, without major impact on the program organization.

Figure 11.5 shows the sketches that I made to help guide my efforts. In this chapter we won't get much farther than building the main window and adding a menu, but it's very helpful to know, as much as possible, where we are going. You might also notice that, as much as possible, I've followed standard Windows design guidelines. For example, I put a File menu on the left of the menu bar, even though the only choice on that menu is Exit. People expect that they can go to the File menu to exit, so that's what Find Files provides. Similarly, I've placed the Help menu as the rightmost menu bar choice, and its only menu item pops up an About dialog box. Again, this is pretty standard for a Windows application.

I plan to create the Find Files application in a series of measured steps. With each step, Find Files will get closer to the goal of being a useful, complete Windows program. The individual steps are described here:

- Stage 1; Directory: find.1—Just get it running, with zero functionality.

- Stage 2; Directory: find.2—Add an icon, so at least it looks like we're making progress.

- Stage 3; Directory: find.3—Add a menu, so we can make selections that do absolutely nothing. Then add accelerators, more ways to do nothing.

- Stage 4; Directory: find.4—Hook up dialogs to the menu selections, so we have even more ways to do nothing.

- Detour; Directory: dosfind—Write a DOS program that can search for files. At the completion of this step we will have a beautiful Windows program that does nothing, and an ugly DOS program with great functionality.

- Stage 5; Directory: find.5—The wedding. Marry the DOS search engine to the Windows interface.

- Stage 5B; Directory: find.5b—The honeymoon. Convert the dialogs to Borland Windows Custom Controls (BWCC) style.

FIGURE 11.5

Sketches of the visual elements of the Find Files application

```
 ─┐            Find Files           ┌─┬─┐
  │                                 │▽│△│
 ─┴─────────────────────────────────┴─┴─┘
 File  Search  Help
┌──────────────────────────────────────┐
│                                        │
│                                        │
│                                        │
│                                        │
│                                        │
└──────────────────────────────────────┘
```

File Menu
    Exit Alt+F4

Search Menu
    For File by Name...   Alt + N
    For File by Size...   Alt + Z
    For File Containing Text...   Alt + T

Help Menu
    About...

FIGURE 11.5

Sketches of the visual elements of the Find Files application (Continued)

Search By Name Dialog

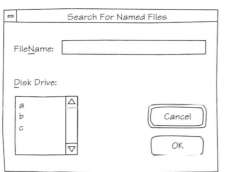

FoundFiles Modeless Dialog

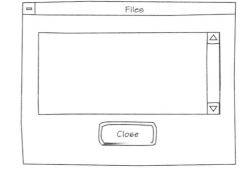

Search By Size Dialog

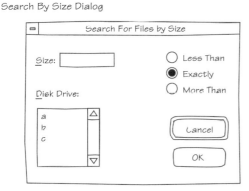

Cancel Search Modeless Dialog

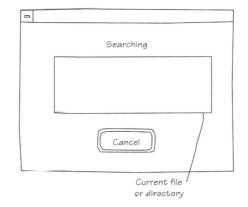

Search By Content Dialog

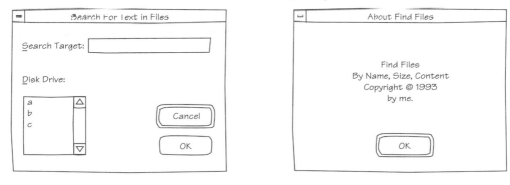

About Dialog

Only Stages 1 through 3 will be covered in this chapter. The last stages of the Find Files application will be covered in Chapters 12 and 13, and the detour will be covered in Appendix A.

Find Files Stage 1: Opening the Main Window

Doing nothing isn't easy, especially in Windows. Most any C programmer can instantly write down the standard, do-nothing C program for DOS: void main(){}. In the world of DOS, nothing can be accomplished in just 13 keystrokes, or merely eight if you omit the void declaration. Things aren't nearly that simple in Windows.

As I mentioned earlier, all Windows programs start with a call of Win-Main(), so we'll need to create a WinMain() function. To get OWL off the ground (see the list of initialization steps earlier in this chapter under "The TApplication Class") we need to have WinMain() create an application object, and the application object needs to create a main window. These steps will create a bare skeleton Find program. It will execute and have a window, but it won't have a menu, an icon, or any real functionality. But, it's a start.

In the remainder of this section I want to describe individually all of the elements of the \find.1\find.cpp program. (The source will be shown in its entirety under "Stage 1 Source Code," later in this chapter.) It's probably easiest just to go in order, so let me start with the first two lines of find.cpp:

```
#define STRICT
#define WIN31
```

The definition of WIN31 is necessary so that OWL knows what version of Windows to target. I'd recommend targeting Windows 3.1 if at all possible, because most users have upgraded from 3.0. If you must be compatible with 3.0, change the define. The definition of STRICT, which is only applicable to Windows 3.1, provides much better usage checking when you call Windows functions. You can't get the strong type checking provided by C++, because the Windows functions are really C functions, but STRICT provides some help. Since the above two definitions will be used in almost all of your OWL programming, you may want to define them in the Defines edit control of Borland's Options-Compiler-CodeGeneration dialog box. In my other work that's what I do, but for this book I like to show everything as explicitly as possible, so I've placed them in the code, which makes them visible in the book.

The next line includes the owl.h header file:

```
#include <owl.h>
```

Including owl.h is necessary in all OWL programs. The owl.h file will include many other header files, including the Windows granddaddy header file, windows.h.

The next element in the Stage 1 version of the find.cpp program is a class definition for an application class. The TFindApp class is derived from TApplication. The main task of the TFindApp class is to supply an InitMainWindow() member function, which will create the application's main window. But before we get to InitMainWindow(), let's look at the TFindApp class definition.

```
class TFindApp : public TApplication {
  public:
    TFindApp(LPSTR name, HINSTANCE hInstance, HINSTANCE hPrevInstance,
      LPSTR lpCmdLine, int nShow) :
      TApplication(name, hInstance, hPrevInstance, lpCmdLine, nShow)
    {
      return;
    }
  virtual void InitMainWindow();
};
```

The constructor for the TFindApp class has just one chore, to pass its arguments to the TApplication class's constructor. I'll discuss the arguments later, when I talk about WinMain(). Besides the constructor, the only member of the TFindApp class is its InitMainWindow() member function.

```
void TFindApp::InitMainWindow()
{
  MainWindow = new TWindow(NULL, "Find Files");
}
```

The only thing that InitMainWindow() does is allocate a generic TWindow object. In most applications you'll create your own window class, which will be derived from TWindow, but in this super-simple Stage 1 version of the Find Files application, we can use the TWindow class directly. If you look in the TWindow reference, you'll discover that its first argument to the constructor is a pointer to the parent window, while the second argument is the window title. Because this is the main window of an application, it doesn't have a parent window, so the first parameter is NULL. As you can see in Figure 11.6, this minimalist version of Find Files has few features, but its window does have the caption "Find Files" that was the second argument to the TWindow class constructor.

A pointer to the main window object is stored in the MainWindow data member of the TApplication class. This is an important linkage that allows the TApplication class (which is responsible for the message loop functionality of the application) to pass messages to the windowing part of the application.

The last part of this Stage 1 do-nothing version of Find Files is the Win-Main() routine. WinMain() is found in all Windows applications, because it is the routine to which Windows transfers control after loading the application into memory. I'm sure you are familiar with DOS conventions for passing the standard argument count and argument vector arguments to main(). Similarly, Windows passes four arguments to WinMain():

- A handle to the current instance of the application. This handle is occasionally used when you are requesting resources from Windows. This instance handle is, like all other Windows handles, simply a numeric value used to refer to something.

FIGURE 11.6

The Find Files Stage 1 application

■ A handle to an already executing (previous) instance of the program. If this is the only copy of the application that is executing, the previous instance handle is NULL. If it is non-null, then it can be used to refer to the previous instance. The previous instance handle is mostly used by applications, such as Microsoft's File Manager, that make sure that only one copy of the application is executing at a time.

■ A pointer to a string containing the command line. Command lines aren't used much in Windows, but they do exist, and if one is supplied, it is passed along to the application in this parameter. The Windows Program Manager lets you specify a command line for an application using the Program Item Properties dialog box, which is activated by the File-Properties menu selection.

■ A parameter denoting the initial visibility of the application. If you check the Run Minimized check box of Program Manager's Program Item Properties dialog box, then the show parameter will indicate that the application should initially be minimized. Otherwise the application will start as a visible window.

Here is the WinMain() function of the Find Files Stage 1 application:

```
int PASCAL WinMain(HINSTANCE hInstance, HINSTANCE hPrevInstance,
  LPSTR lpCmdLine, int nShow)
```

```
{
  TFindApp findApp("Find Application", hInstance, hPrevInstance,
    lpCmdLine, nShow);
  findApp.Run();
  return findApp.Status;
}
```

WinMain() simply passes its parameters to the TFindApp constructor, which in turn passes them to the TApplication constructor. Once the TFindApp object is fully constructed, MainWindow() calls its Run() member function. Run() calls InitApplication() and InitInstance(), and InitInstance() calls Init-MainWindow(), which builds the application's main window. Then Run() starts the message loop, which will continue for the duration of the application.

When the application terminates, the message loop will terminate, and Run() will complete, and then WinMain() will return the Status member from the application class.

Tuning BCW for OWL Development

I built the Stage 1 version of the Find Files application using BCW. I created a project for the application which contained just two items: find.cpp and owl.def (owl.def is in the /borlandc/owl/include directory). The owl.def file is used to specify exactly how the application should be linked. It's not concerned with things like what .OBJ modules to load, but rather with things like the heap size, the stack size, and the characteristics of the data and code segments. OWL applications usually can be linked according to the defaults in the owl.def module definition file. The other settings that I made with BCW to enable the compilation were as follows:

- Adding the OWL include and lib directories to the list of directories in the Options-Directories dialog box.

- Selecting the OWL library and the Container library to be statically linked in the Options-Linker-Libraries dialog.

- Selecting the Large model in the Options-Compiler-CodeGeneration dialog box.

- Selecting the precompiled headers option in the Options-Compiler-CodeGeneration dialog box. As I mentioned above, OWL Windows programming uses extensive header files, and compilation times decrease dramatically if you use precompiled headers. The only drawback is that megabyte-sized files are stored on your hard disk.

Most other options are not critical and can be adjusted to suit your preferences.

Stage 1 Source Code

Listing 11.1 shows the complete source code for Stage 1 of the Find Files application. At this early stage, the application is completely stored in one source file.

LISTING 11.1

Stage 1: find.cpp

```
#define STRICT
#define WIN31
#include <owl.h>

//
// application class
//
class TFindApp : public TApplication {
  public:
    TFindApp(LPSTR name, HINSTANCE hInstance, HINSTANCE hPrevInstance,
      LPSTR lpCmdLine, int nShow) :
      TApplication(name, hInstance, hPrevInstance, lpCmdLine, nShow)
    {
      return;
    }
  virtual void InitMainWindow();
};

//
// Initialize a generic main window
//
void TFindApp::InitMainWindow()
{
  MainWindow = new TWindow(NULL, "Find Files");
}

//
// WinMain
//
int PASCAL WinMain(HINSTANCE hInstance, HINSTANCE hPrevInstance,
  LPSTR lpCmdLine, int nShow)
{
  TFindApp findApp("Find Application", hInstance, hPrevInstance,
    lpCmdLine, nShow);
  findApp.Run();
  return findApp.Status;
}
```

Find Files Stage 2: Adding an Icon

Stage 1 of the Find Files application doesn't have its own icon. This means that the application defaults to using a rectangular icon supplied by Windows, the same plain icon that is often used to represent unknown DOS applications. You might think that simply adding an icon to the Find Files app should be easy. Well, the mechanics are easy but they introduce several new areas that should be explained thoroughly.

There are really two aspects to adding an icon to represent the application. The first is the issue of creating an icon, using Resource Workshop, and getting that icon into the application .EXE file so that it can be accessed while the program is running. If you haven't programmed Windows before, you might expect that that's all there is to it. Actually there is also an important second step. For every window, Windows keeps track of several characteristics, such as what cursor to use, and what icon to use. When you have a new window whose characteristics differ from existing windows, you must register a new window class. That's the second part of adding a new icon. I'll discuss each of these chores alongside the important new Stage 2 code that implements these two chores. Then I'll present the complete source code for the Find Files application under "Stage 2 Source Code," later in this chapter.

Understanding Resource Files

A resource file is a specification of visual and other user interface elements of a Windows application. It is analogous to a .C or .CPP source code file, but instead of specifying actions, resource files generally specify the appearances. The distinction is somewhat blurry, but generally true.

For example, in adding an icon to the Find Files application, the icon characteristics (size, shape, colors) need to be specified in the resource file, and then it is left to the source code files to ask Windows to use that icon. It is customary to use the file-name extension .RC for the main resource script of an application. You can store most resources directly in the .RC script, or you can store resources in individual files and then refer to them using #include directives in the .RC file.

Most resources can be referred to either by name (short text strings) or by number. In either case, you should use very consistent naming conventions. Most of the OWL routines that refer to resources are overloaded, so that you can either use a string or a number as an identifier. When referring to a named (as opposed to a numbered) resource in a .C or .CPP program, you must of course explicitly use quotes to specify to the compiler that you are using a string. For example, in the Find Files Stage 2 application I named the icon IDI_FindApp. In the C++ source to load the icon, I wrote a statement similar to

```
hIcon = LoadIcon(hInstance, "IDI_FindApp");
```

The quotes clearly identify IDI_FindApp as a string. But the convention is different in a resource file, where by default everything is a string unless it is known to be something else. So in the find.rc resource file, the introduction of the icon description is

```
IDI_FindApp ICON
```

In the resource file, the word IDI_FindApp is just assumed to be a string, because it hasn't been identified as anything else. If you wanted to use a numeric identifier, the best way is to create a header file, often called resource.h, use the #define mechanism to define IDI_FindApp to have some value (for example, 100), and then #include that file into both find.rc and into your .CPP files.

I'm emphasizing this somewhat trivial issue because, in my experience, it is a trap in which many Windows programmers are snared. It's easy to make mistakes, and the error checking, such as it is, is all during program execution. If resources aren't getting loaded correctly, first make sure that you understand clearly whether you are using numeric or text identifiers, and then make sure, absolutely sure, of the exact spelling of everything.

I created the icon for the Find Files application by starting Resource Workshop, specifying that I wanted to create a new project with the .RC file type, and then specifying that I wanted to create a new icon. A simple icon editor popped up, I painted the icon, and then saved my work. One small thing to watch out for in the Resource Workshop icon editor is to distinguish between the background color, a transparent background, and an inverted background. In some color schemes these icon backgrounds can look the same when you are painting, but behave very differently when an icon is displayed on top of something (for example, desktop wallpaper) that doesn't have that background color.

When I was done with painting, I used the Resource-Name dialog to specify a name for the icon. Since the name that I used (IDI_FindApp) wasn't recognized by Resource Workshop, the program asked me if I wanted to create an identifier. If I had said yes, the program would have created an identifier with a numeric value. I said no, which somewhat obscurely signaled my desire to use a string identifier. Then I saved my work into the .RC file and exited. You can see the find.rc file, exactly as it was created by Resource Workshop, later in this chapter under "Stage 2 Source Code." Figure 11.7 shows the Resource Workshop icon editor, my Program Manager group that contains all five stages of Find Files, an executing version of Find Files Stage 2 in the bottom-right quadrant, and an iconized Find Files Stage 2 on the bottom left.

So far I've described resource scripts, resource identifiers, and the icon creation process, but I haven't mentioned how the icon actually makes its way from the .RC file into the Find Files application's .EXE file. That is accomplished by specifying the .RC file in an application's project file. In Stage 1, the Find Files project mentioned just two files: owl.def and find.cpp. Now for Stage 2 I added find.rc to the project. BCW "knows" about the .RC file type, and if you mention an .RC file in your project, its resources will automatically be bound into the application .EXE file.

Registering a Window Class

Unfortunately, there don't seem to be enough words to describe all of the different concepts that software developers encounter. For example, the idea of an object has little (nothing?) to do with an object file. The word "window" is an equally good example. When you are working with Windows you have to carefully distinguish between a Windows window class, and a C++ class. C++ classes are, or at least should be, pretty easy. They are simply data structures created in a C++ program using the C++ class keyword.

FIGURE 11.7

The Find Files Stage 2 application

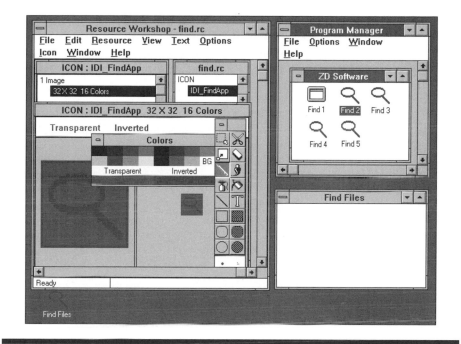

But Windows also uses the term class. Each window has its own class. Window classes are named, and for each window class there are a set of characteristics that Windows maintains. Each class contains handles for

- The application instance
- The window's cursor
- The window's icon
- The background brush (essentially the window's background color)

The window class also contains

- Information about the window's style
- The name of the window's menu

This information is all stored by Windows in the WNDCLASS struct.

If you want an application to have its own icon, what you need to do is to register a new window class that refers to the desired icon. The mechanics of this in OWL are pretty straightforward.

1. Derive your own window class (your own C++ class!) from OWL's TWindow class.

2. Define GetClassName() and GetWindowClass() functions for your own window class.

3. GetClassName() should simply return a string; the name of your window class is the conventional name but any unique name is acceptable.

4. GetWindowClass() should call the TWindow class's GetWindow-Class() function, and then it should modify any elements of its WND-CLASS struct argument.

That's all there is to it. Now let me show you the details individually. The full source for the Find Files Stage 2 application is shown in the next section.

As I just mentioned in the previous list, we need to derive a new window class and to supply definitions for the GetClassName() and GetWindowClass() member functions. Here is the definition of the TFindWindow class:

```
class TFindWindow : public TWindow {
  public:
    TFindWindow(PTWindowsObject pParent, LPSTR pTitle);
    LPSTR GetClassName() {
      return "TFindWindow";
    }
    void GetWindowClass(WNDCLASS& rWndClass);
};
```

The TFindWindow constructor simply passes its arguments along to the TWindow constructor, and the GetClassName() member function simply returns a constant string. Neither needs any further explanation.

The heart of registering a window class is found in the GetWindowClass() member function. Here is the Find Files application's GetWindowClass() function.

```
void TFindWindow::GetWindowClass(WNDCLASS& rWndClass)
{
  TWindow::GetWindowClass(rWndClass);
  rWndClass.hIcon = LoadIcon(GetApplication()->hInstance,
    "IDI_FindApp");
  if (rWndClass.hIcon == NULL) {
    MessageBox(HWindow, "Bad Icon Load", "icon", MB_ICONSTOP);
    rWndClass.hIcon = LoadIcon(0, IDI_APPLICATION);
  }
}
```

The body of the GetWindowClass() function would only be two lines long if I didn't check for the error return from LoadIcon(). Note that LoadIcon() is a Windows function, not an OWL function. Thus it needs to be supplied with standard Windows parameters. In the case of LoadIcon(), it wants the application's instance handle as its first argument, and the char* pointer to the icon identifier as its second argument.

I knew, when I created the IDI_FindApp icon, that I was going to access it using Windows's LoadIcon() function. Thus I made sure it could be accessed using a string identifier. But using a numeric identifier is only slightly harder. Let me spend a few paragraphs showing exactly how you can use numeric resource identifiers.

Let's suppose that I created a file named resource.h containing the statement

```
#define IDI_FindApp 100
```

If I included this file into find.rc, then the IDI_FindApp icon would have a numeric identifier. At the same time I would need to include resource.h into find.cpp, and then change the LoadIcon() statement to the following:

```
rWndClass.hicon = LoadIcon(GetApplication()->hInstance,
  MAKEINTRESOURCE(IDI_FindApp));
```

The MAKEINTRESOURCE macro is found in windows.h. It twists things around so that small integers are turned into something that looks like a string pointer. It's one of many ugly kludges that were forced into Windows by limitations in early-80s language technology. As I mentioned before, those parts of OWL that refer to resource identifiers that may either be strings or numbers use overloaded functions, so that you have one less detail to consider.

The last half of the GetWindowClass() function checks for an error return from LoadIcon(). If you look in the Windows function reference manual, you'll discover that LoadIcon() returns null if it can't find the icon. When this happens, GetWindowClass() uses the Windows MessageBox() function to display an error message. Like FindIcon(), MessageBox() is a windows function that requires that you supply traditional Windows parameters. For MessageBox(), the first parameter must be the handle of the window that owns the message box. The second parameter is a string that will appear in the box, the third is a string that will be the caption of the message box, and the fourth parameter is the style. There are many styles; for a complete list you should consult the MessageBox() entry in your Windows function manual.

Because the message box is being displayed from within a class derived from TWindow, TWindow is the first place to go to look for the window handle. If you look in the OWL documentation for TWindow, you won't find anything about a handle for the window, but if you then go to TWindow's base class, the TWindowsObject class, you'll quickly discover that it stores a member variable called HWindow that is the window's handle. This is what MessageBox() wants as its first argument. The other arguments are used to specify the message box's style and content.

When I was first programming for Windows, I often used message boxes as a simple debugging aid, so I could see what was happening. They are easy to use, and they can be #ifdef'd out in a production version of your application. Now that I'm more experienced, and now that I customarily use OWL, I find that I rarely place debugging message boxes in my code.

Stage 2 Source Code

You should examine Figure 11.8, which contains the class diagram for the Find Files Stage 2 application. In Stage 2 the class hierarchy is still quite simple, but I want to show it now so you can compare it with later stages. Listings 11.2 and 11.3 contain the complete source code for the Find Files Stage 2 application.

FIGURE 11.8

The Find Files Stage 2 class diagram. (The class hierarchy of OWL is not shown. The Find Files application's classes are shown shaded, while the OWL classes are unshaded.)

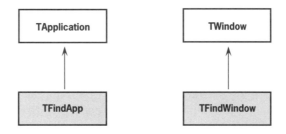

LISTING 11.2

Stage 2 find.cpp

```cpp
#define STRICT
#define WIN31
#include <owl.h>

//
// the Find App class
//
class TFindApp : public TApplication {
  public:
    TFindApp(LPSTR name, HINSTANCE hInstance, HINSTANCE hPrevInstance,
      LPSTR lpCmdLine, int nShow) :
      TApplication(name, hInstance, hPrevInstance, lpCmdLine, nShow)
    {
      return;
    }
  virtual void InitMainWindow();
};

//
// the Find Window Class
//
class TFindWindow : public TWindow {
  public:
    TFindWindow(PTWindowsObject pParent, LPSTR pTitle);
    LPSTR GetClassName() {
      return "TFindWindow";
```

LISTING 11.2

Stage 2 find.cpp (Continued)

```cpp
    }
    void GetWindowClass(WNDCLASS& rWndClass);
};

// Find App, create the main window
void TFindApp::InitMainWindow()
{
  MainWindow = new TFindWindow(NULL, "Find Files");
}
// Find Window, constructor

TFindWindow::TFindWindow(PTWindowsObject pParent, LPSTR pTitle) :
  TWindow(pParent, pTitle)
{
  return;
}

// create a window class for the Find Window
void TFindWindow::GetWindowClass(WNDCLASS& rWndClass)
{
  TWindow::GetWindowClass(rWndClass);
  rWndClass.hIcon = LoadIcon(GetApplication()->hInstance, "IDI_FindApp");
  if (rWndClass.hIcon == NULL) {
    MessageBox(HWindow, "Bad Icon Load", "icon", MB_ICONSTOP);
    rWndClass.hIcon = LoadIcon(Ø, IDI_APPLICATION);
  }
}

//
// WIN MAIN
//
int PASCAL WinMain(HINSTANCE hInstance, HINSTANCE hPrevInstance,
  LPSTR lpCmdLine, int nShow)
{
  TFindApp findApp("Find Application", hInstance, hPrevInstance,
    lpCmdLine, nShow);
  findApp.Run();
  return findApp.Status;
}
```

LISTING 11.3

Stage 2 find.rc

```
IDI_FindApp ICON
BEGIN
    'ØØ ØØ Ø1 ØØ Ø1 ØØ 2Ø 2Ø 1Ø ØØ ØØ ØØ ØØ ØØ E8 Ø2'
    'ØØ ØØ 16 ØØ ØØ ØØ 28 ØØ ØØ ØØ 2Ø ØØ ØØ ØØ 4Ø ØØ'
    'ØØ ØØ Ø1 ØØ Ø4 ØØ ØØ ØØ ØØ ØØ 8Ø Ø2 ØØ ØØ ØØ ØØ'
    'ØØ ØØ ØØ ØØ ØØ ØØ ØØ ØØ ØØ ØØ ØØ ØØ ØØ ØØ ØØ ØØ'
    'ØØ ØØ ØØ ØØ 8Ø ØØ ØØ 8Ø ØØ ØØ ØØ 8Ø 8Ø ØØ 8Ø ØØ'
    'ØØ ØØ 8Ø ØØ 8Ø ØØ 8Ø 8Ø ØØ ØØ 8Ø 8Ø 8Ø ØØ CØ CØ'
```

LISTING 11.3

Stage 2 find.rc (Continued)

```
'CØ ØØ ØØ ØØ FF ØØ ØØ FF ØØ ØØ ØØ FF FF ØØ FF ØØ'
'ØØ ØØ FF ØØ FF ØØ FF FF ØØ ØØ FF FF FF ØØ ØØ ØØ'
'ØØ ØØ ØØ ØØ ØØ ØØ ØØ ØØ ØØ ØØ ØØ ØØ ØØ ØØ ØØ ØØ'
'ØØ ØØ ØØ ØØ ØØ ØØ ØØ ØØ ØØ ØØ ØØ ØØ ØØ ØØ ØØ ØØ'
'ØØ ØØ ØØ ØØ ØØ ØØ ØØ ØØ ØØ ØØ ØØ ØØ Ø9 9Ø ØØ ØØ'
'ØØ ØØ ØØ ØØ ØØ ØØ ØØ ØØ ØØ ØØ ØØ ØØ 99 9Ø ØØ ØØ'
'ØØ ØØ ØØ ØØ ØØ ØØ ØØ ØØ ØØ ØØ ØØ Ø9 99 9Ø ØØ ØØ'
'ØØ ØØ ØØ ØØ ØØ ØØ ØØ ØØ ØØ ØØ ØØ 99 99 ØØ ØØ ØØ'
'ØØ ØØ ØØ ØØ ØØ ØØ ØØ ØØ ØØ ØØ Ø9 99 9Ø ØØ ØØ ØØ'
'ØØ ØØ ØØ ØØ ØØ ØØ ØØ ØØ ØØ ØØ 99 99 ØØ ØØ ØØ ØØ'
'ØØ ØØ ØØ ØØ ØØ ØØ ØØ ØØ ØØ Ø9 99 9Ø ØØ ØØ ØØ ØØ'
'ØØ ØØ ØØ ØØ ØØ ØØ ØØ ØØ ØØ 99 99 ØØ ØØ ØØ ØØ ØØ'
'ØØ ØØ ØØ ØØ ØØ ØØ ØØ ØØ Ø9 99 9Ø ØØ ØØ ØØ ØØ ØØ'
'ØØ ØØ ØØ ØØ ØØ ØØ ØØ ØØ 99 99 ØØ ØØ ØØ ØØ ØØ ØØ'
'ØØ ØØ Ø9 99 99 99 9Ø Ø9 99 9Ø ØØ ØØ ØØ ØØ ØØ ØØ'
'ØØ 99 99 99 99 99 99 99 99 ØØ ØØ ØØ ØØ ØØ ØØ ØØ'
'Ø9 99 99 99 99 99 99 99 9Ø ØØ ØØ ØØ ØØ ØØ ØØ ØØ'
'99 99 9Ø ØØ ØØ ØØ Ø9 99 99 ØØ ØØ ØØ ØØ ØØ ØØ Ø9'
'99 ØØ ØØ ØØ ØØ ØØ ØØ ØØ 99 9Ø ØØ ØØ ØØ ØØ ØØ 99'
'9Ø ØØ ØØ ØØ ØØ ØØ ØØ ØØ Ø9 99 ØØ ØØ ØØ ØØ ØØ 99'
'ØØ ØØ ØØ ØØ ØØ ØØ ØØ ØØ ØØ 99 ØØ ØØ ØØ ØØ ØØ 99'
'ØØ ØØ ØØ ØØ ØØ ØØ ØØ ØØ ØØ 99 ØØ ØØ ØØ ØØ ØØ 99'
'ØØ ØØ ØØ ØØ ØØ ØØ ØØ ØØ ØØ 99 ØØ ØØ ØØ ØØ ØØ 99'
'ØØ ØØ ØØ ØØ ØØ ØØ ØØ ØØ 99 ØØ ØØ ØØ ØØ ØØ ØØ 99'
'9Ø ØØ ØØ ØØ ØØ ØØ ØØ ØØ Ø9 99 ØØ ØØ ØØ ØØ ØØ Ø9'
'99 ØØ ØØ ØØ ØØ ØØ ØØ ØØ 99 9Ø ØØ ØØ ØØ ØØ ØØ ØØ'
'99 99 9Ø ØØ ØØ ØØ Ø9 99 99 ØØ ØØ ØØ ØØ ØØ ØØ ØØ'
'Ø9 99 99 99 99 99 99 99 9Ø ØØ ØØ ØØ ØØ ØØ ØØ ØØ'
'ØØ 99 99 99 99 99 99 99 ØØ ØØ ØØ ØØ ØØ ØØ ØØ ØØ'
'ØØ ØØ Ø9 99 99 99 9Ø ØØ ØØ ØØ ØØ ØØ ØØ ØØ ØØ ØØ'
'ØØ ØØ ØØ ØØ ØØ ØØ ØØ ØØ ØØ ØØ ØØ ØØ ØØ ØØ ØØ ØØ'
'ØØ ØØ ØØ ØØ ØØ ØØ ØØ ØØ ØØ ØØ ØØ ØØ ØØ ØØ ØØ ØØ'
'ØØ ØØ ØØ ØØ ØØ ØØ ØØ ØØ ØØ ØØ ØØ ØØ ØØ ØØ ØØ ØØ'
'ØØ ØØ ØØ ØØ ØØ ØØ ØØ ØØ ØØ ØØ ØØ ØØ ØØ ØØ FF FF'
'FF FF FF FF FF FF FF FF FF F9 FF FF FF F1 FF FF'
'FF E1 FF FF FF C3 FF FF FF 87 FF FF FF ØF FF FF'
'FE 1F FF FF FC 3F FF FF F8 7F FF FF FØ FF FF 8Ø'
'61 FF FC ØØ Ø3 FF F8 ØØ Ø7 FF FØ 7F 83 FF E3 FF'
'F1 FF C7 FF F8 FF CF FF FC FF CF FF FC FF CF FF'
'FC FF CF FF FC FF C7 FF F8 FF E3 FF F1 FF FØ 7F'
'83 FF F8 ØØ Ø7 FF FC ØØ ØF FF FF 8Ø 7F FF FF FF'
'FF FF FF FF FF FF FF FF FF FF FF FF FF FF'
```

END

Find Files Stage 3: Adding a Menu and Keyboard Accelerators

The menu bar at the top of a window is the primary user interface for most Windows programs. The menu is usually the passageway to an application's functionality. When you encounter a new Windows application, do you first pull down all the menu selections, to get a sense of the application's possibilities? I sure do.

Windows does a tremendous amount of behind the scenes work with menus, so that they are very easy for you (the developer) to manage. As with icons, you have two related chores. The first chore is to create a menu resource, probably using Resource Workshop. The menu resource specifies the text of the menu selections, and it specifies a numeric ID for each menu selection. The second chore is to tell Windows to use the menu resource for a specific window. Some applications, like the Find Files application, have a single menu, while other programs, especially MDI programs, have many menus that are managed dynamically to reflect the current chore.

When the user makes a menu selection, Windows generates a message and sends it to the active window. To act on each selection, your window class must have a member function to handle each menu item. Thus the Find Files application, which has a total of five menu items, has five message handler member functions.

Menu Resources

Menu resources are simple enough that you can easily create them with a text editor, but it is a lot more fun to use Resource Workshop. In Resource Workshop, you can see the menu as it is created and you can play with it as you work on it, which makes it easy to see if the menu is balanced and attractive.

My usual approach is to create all of the numeric menu identifiers beforehand and store them in a .H file. By convention, I call that file resource.h. The numeric values should be small integers, and they should be distinct. Then I manually edit the application's .RC file and insert the following include statement at the top of the file:

```
#include "resource.h"
```

Then when Resource Workshop loads in the .RC file, it immediately learns about all of my new menu item identifiers.

This preparation helps get me organized, and it lets me place comments in resource.h that identify how each identifier is used. You can have Resource Workshop build your .H file of resource identifiers, but it doesn't put in comments, and it only lets you work on one identifier at a time. (I find it easier to adopt productive naming conventions by working on all of the identifiers at once.) The resource.h file that I prepared for Find Files Stage 3 is shown later in this chapter under "Stage 3 Source Code."

When you use Resource Workshop to create a menu resource, all you need to do is to enter the text of each menu item and the identifier for each. The text for the menu items should follow these conventions.

- An & should be placed in front of a letter to indicate a shortcut key. For example, you would write &Open if you want the letter O to be a shortcut for making the Open menu item selection. (Shortcuts are keys that can be struck to move to a menu item after the menu has been popped up.)

- Menu items that lead to dialog boxes should be followed by ... (ellipses).

- Menu items that can be accessed using an accelerator key should mention the accelerator. Place \t (tab) after the menu text, and then place the description of the accelerator. Thus if Ctrl+S is an accelerator for the Save menu item, the menu item text should be

```
&Save\tCtrl+S
```

Windows will automatically find the longest menu text in the list of menu items, and then place a tab stop just past that, so that all of the accelerator key descriptions are aligned in a column.

- Arrange your menu selections in standard sequence. To the degree possible, have your menu selections resemble the menu structure of some of the common Windows applications. For example, if there is a File menu, it is always the leftmost menu bar selection, and is often followed by Edit or Search selections. In MDI applications there is usually a Window selection that is second from the right, and a Help menu selection is usually the rightmost choice. Within each of these standard menus, there is a common order to the selections. For example, in the File menu the Print choices are usually placed below the true "file" choices such as New, Open, Save, and Save As.

- Use separators (horizontal lines) to group related selections in a menu.

Figure 11.9 shows the Resource Workshop screen while I was working on the Find Files Stage 3 menu. The left part of the window lets you specify each menu item, the top right shows the menu in progress, while the bottom right shows the outline of the menu.

Binding a Menu to a Window

As usual, it isn't enough to create a menu resource. You must also tell Windows exactly how that resource will be used. In the Find Files application, we only have one window, which is represented by the TFindWindow class, and we only have one menu, which I've chosen to call the FindMenu. So all we have to do is make the linkage.

FIGURE 11.9

The Find Files Stage 3 application menu being created using Resource Workshop

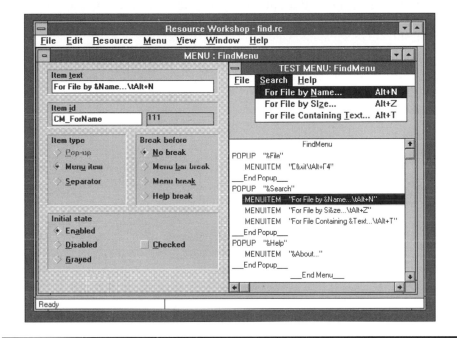

The customary OWL approach is to assign the menu to the window in the window class's constructor. Here is the body of the Stage 3 TFindWindow constructor:

```
TFindWindow::TFindWindow(PTWindowsObject pParent,
    LPSTR pTitle) :
      TWindow(pParent, pTitle)
{
   AssignMenu("FindMenu");
   return;
}
```

AssignMenu is a member of the TWindow class. It is an overloaded function, so you can supply either a string or a numeric argument, depending on whether your resource is defined using a string or numeric identifier.

Message Handlers

When the user activates a menu selection, Windows generates a message and sends that message to the application. It is your responsibility to make sure that the message is handled. This is yet another area where it is very easy for the resource side of the project and the code side of the project to get out of sync. Be careful, because the only checking is runtime checking.

For each message that a window's menu can generate, you should create a message handler member function. Here is the Stage 3 TFindWindow class definition, showing its five message handler member functions.

```
class TFindWindow : public TWindow {
  public:
    // constructor
    TFindWindow(PTWindowsObject pParent, LPSTR pTitle);
    // window class members
    LPSTR GetClassName() {
      return "TFindWindow";
    }
    void GetWindowClass(WNDCLASS& rWndClass);
    // message handlers
    virtual void CMQuit(RTMessage msg) =
      [CM_FIRST + CM_Quit];
    virtual void CMSrchForName(RTMessage msg) =
      [CM_FIRST + CM_ForName];
    virtual void CMSrchForSize(RTMessage msg) =
      [CM_FIRST + CM_ForSize];
    virtual void CMSrchForText(RTMessage msg) =
      [CM_FIRST + CM_ForText];
    virtual void CMAbout(RTMessage msg) =
      [CM_FIRST + CM_About];
};
```

What should jump out at you from the message handler declarations is that they use a Borland C++ language extension. After the declaration of the function header there is an equal symbol, and then a square-bracketed numeric expression. Note that the syntax of declaring a message handler is reminiscent of declaring a pure virtual function.

The value of the numeric expression indicates what message will be handled. You could declare a message handler by simply writing a constant value inside the brackets, such as

```
virtual void fn(RTMessage m) = [100];
```

However, what's actually done in practice is to compose the numeric constant by adding two symbolic constants. The first constant indicates what type of message is being handled, and the second is an identifier for a specific message. Table 11.1 shows the supplied OWL constants to indicate the message type. The table also shows how many messages of that type are available, which is important for child window messages and command messages, because the numeric identifiers that you create for these elements must be within the allowable range.

TABLE 11.1

OWL Message Ranges

OWL's Range Identifier	Range	Offset	Usage
WM_FIRST	(1)	A WM_ constant from windows.h	Standard Windows messages. You use these in any window or control class that must respond to the given message. For example, [WM_FIRST + WM_PAINT]
NF_FIRST	(1)	A BN_, CN_, LBN_, CBN_ message, or one of the SB variants of a scroll message	Notification messages. You use this range in control classes to create "smart" controls. For example, [NF_FIRST + BN_CLICKED]
ID_FIRST	0..3839	The ID of a control	Windows's child window messages. You use this message range in a parent window class to respond to all messages from a specific control. For example, [ID_FIRST + IDOK]
CM_FIRST	0..3839	A menu ID number	Command messages. You use this range in a window class to respond to menu selections. For example, [CM_FIRST + CM_SaveAs]

Note. Ranges are irrelevant for standard Windows messages and for notification messages, because the message identifiers are supplied in windows.h and they all fall within the supplied range.

Message handler functions should always have the void return type; have one argument that is a reference to a TMessage struct; and be virtual functions.

The TMessage struct is used to pass information to the message handler function. If you look up individual messages in the Windows API reference manual, you'll usually see references to values in wParam (WORD) and lParam (LONG). These values, plus other relevant information, can be acquired from the TMessage struct.

Here is the definition of the TMessage struct:

```
struct TMessage {
  HWND Receiver;        // the handle of the window
  WORD Message;         // the message
  union {
    WORD WParam;        // the message's WParam
    struct tagWP {
      BYTE Lo;
      BYTE Hi;
    } WP;               // WParam as two bytes
  };
```

```
union {
  DWORD LParam;       // the message's LParam
  struct tagLP {
    WORD Lo;
    WORD Hi;
  } LP;               // LParam as two words
};
long Result;          // a result code
};
```

The two anonymous unions in the TMessage struct house the WParam and LParam parameters. These fields are unions because some messages treat WParam as a pair of BYTE values, while other messages treat the LParam as a pair of WORDs. (In traditional Windows programming you use the HIWORD, LOWORD, HIBYTE, and LOBYTE macros to disassemble LONGs and WORDs into WORDs and BYTEs. These two unions remove most need for these macros.)

For example, the WM_LBUTTONDOWN message is sent whenever the left mouse button is depressed. The WM_LBUTTONDOWN message uses WParam to store information about the Ctrl key, the Shift key, and the other (middle, right) mouse buttons. It uses LParam to store the X and Y coordinates; X in the low word and Y in the high word. Here's the code that would extract the status information and the X and Y coordinates from a TMessage struct named msg:

```
WORD stat = msg.WParam;
WORD x = msg.LP.Lo;
WORD y = msg.LP.Hi;
```

Now that we've gotten past the background information, let's take a look at one of the actual message handlers from the Find Files Stage 3 application.

```
// handle CM_ForName menu selection
void TFindWindow::CMSrchForName(RTMessage /*msg*/)
{
  MessageBox(HWindow, "Search for named file",
    "FindFile", MB_ICONSTOP);
}
```

One thing to note is that the message dispatch code is only present in the class definition, not in the actual function definition. Another thing to note is that RTMessage is a type name that denotes a reference to a TMessage struct. The type RTMessage was declared in the Borland header files using the _CLASSDEF macro, which was discussed in the "Pointing at Classes" section of Chapter 3.

At this point in its genesis, the Find Files Stage 3 application's message handlers merely pop up a message box, so you can verify that they are being called. I'll add more functionality to these message handlers in Stages 4 and 5.

The one message handler that does something is the handler for the CM_-Quit menu selection:

```
// handle CM_Quit menu selection
void TFindWindow::CMQuit(RTMessage /*msg*/)
{
  PostQuitMessage(0);
}
```

There are several ways to terminate an OWL application, but my preference is to use the normal Windows mechanism, which is to send the application the WM_QUIT message. The easiest way to send the WM_QUIT message is to use the PostQuitMessage() Windows function. The parameter for the PostQuitMessage() function is the exit code, which is usually zero.

None of the message handlers in the Find Files application use the TMessage struct parameter. That's why the function definitions comment out the msg parameter. If the msg parameter weren't commented out, then the compiler would issue a warning that the parameter isn't used. Commenting out the parameter relies on the somewhat obscure C++ placeholder arguments feature. If we have a function that is called with an int, a double, and a char, but the double isn't used, the function definition can be written:

```
void fn(int i, double, char c)
{
  . . .
}
```

By omitting the name of the double parameter, you signal to the compiler (and to the reader) that it won't be used in the function body. Even better is to comment out the name of the unused parameter, so the reader can deduce its role from the name. OWL's stereotypical message handler functions, which supply an RTMessage parameter whether it is needed or not, illustrate the need for this feature.

Keyboard Accelerators

Keyboard accelerators are an important part of any Windows application, because they are a key aspect of providing a user interface for experienced users. This should be clear to you from your own experiences with Borland's programming environments, which provide consistent and useful keyboard accelerators.

When a user enters a key combination that is recognized as a keyboard accelerator, Windows generates a message and sends it to the application. The message has the same form as a message sent when a menu selection is made. If the keyboard accelerator ID code is the same as a menu selection ID code, Windows flashes that menu selection, to provide some visual feedback. Most keyboard accelerators invoke the same functionality that is present in your menu system, but it is also possible to provide features that are only available using accelerators, just as it is possible to have functionality that is only available using menu selections.

An application can have multiple accelerator tables, each with its own name. This lets you switch accelerators depending on what the user is doing, and it also addresses internationalization concerns. However, the Find Files application only has a single accelerator table, named ACCELTABLE.

The task of adding keyboard accelerators follows the now-familiar two-step process. Step one is to use Resource Workshop to add the keyboard accelerators to the resource file.

Here is the accelerator table for the Find Files Stage 3 application. It is also shown, in context, in the final section of this chapter, "Stage 3 Source Code."

```
ACCELTABLE ACCELERATORS
BEGIN
    VK_F4, CM_Quit, VIRTKEY, ALT
    "z", CM_ForSize, ASCII, ALT
    "n", CM_ForName, ASCII, ALT
    "t", CM_ForText, ASCII, ALT
END
```

The Find Files accelerator table illustrates the two most common ways to define accelerators. In both styles, you define what key you want to designate as an accelerator, you define the ID code that should be sent when that key is entered, and then you define the characteristics of the key.

The first style shown in the ACCELTABLE table is for a virtual key, which simply means a key that is not part of the ASCII set. Such keys are given symbolic names in windows.h. Here's the line that specifies that Alt+F4 is an accelerator that should send a message indicating the CM_Quit command.

```
VK_F4, CM_Quit, VIRTKEY, ALT
```

The ALT keyword at the end indicates that the Alt key must be depressed along with the F4 key. Other possible modifiers are CONTROL and SHIFT.

The second style is for keys that are part of the ASCII set. For example, the following entry indicates that Alt+z should send a message encoding the CM_-ForSize request:

```
"z", CM_ForSize, ASCII, ALT
```

Note that the "z" part is case sensitive. If you also want Alt+Z to be an accelerator, you would have to add this line to the accelerator table.

```
"Z", CM_ForSize, ASCII, ALT
```

Because the Ctrl key is so often used with ASCII keys, the special notation ^ is often used in accelerator tables to indicate that the following character is really Ctrl+char. Here is a line that indicates that Ctrl+t is an accelerator:

```
"^t", CM_ForText
```

Note that ASCII Ctrl+char codes aren't case sensitive; they can be specified in either case and the Shift key is ignored during user entry.

Step two of adding keyboard accelerators is to load the accelerator table during program execution. This should be performed in your application class's InitInstance() procedure. Here's the InitInstance() from the Find Files application:

```
void TFindApp::InitInstance()
{
  TApplication::InitInstance();
  HAccTable = LoadAccelerators(hInstance, "ACCELTABLE");
}
```

Note that the base class's InitInstance() is also called, so that its processing can be performed.

Stage 3 Source Code

Listings 11.4, 11.5, and 11.6 show the (almost) full source code for the Find Files Stage 3 application. The only thing missing is the definition of the icon. In Stage 2, the icon definition was present in the find.rc file, but for Stage 3 I've moved the icon source into its own file, and then used the include mechanism to pull it into find.rc.

The class diagram for Find Files Stage 3 is the same as for Stage 2, so I've chosen not to repeat Figure 11.8. But the organization of the application into source files is now rich enough to warrant its own diagram, which is shown in Figure 11.10. Find Files Stage 3 itself is shown in Figure 11.11.

As you can see, it takes a lot of work, meaning about 100 lines of code, to bring even the simplest application to life. What we've achieved is more than the sum of a few menu choices and a table of keyboard accelerators. What we've really constructed is a sturdy foundation. Now it's time to attend to the barn raising—Stages 4 and 5 of Find Files—which will be covered in Chapters 12 and 13.

LISTING 11.4 ▉▉

Stage 3 resource.h

```
//
// Find App Resource Constants
//

// Menu Items
```

LISTING 11.4

Stage 3 resource.h (Continued)

```
#define CM_Quit    101  // File menu
#define CM_ForName 111  // Search menu
#define CM_ForSize 112
#define CM_ForText 113
#define CM_About   114  // Help menu
```

LISTING 11.5

Stage 3 find.cpp

```cpp
#define STRICT
#define WIN31
#include <owl.h>
#include "resource.h"

//
// the Find App class
//
class TFindApp : public TApplication {
  public:
    TFindApp(LPSTR name, HINSTANCE hInstance, HINSTANCE hPrevInstance,
      LPSTR lpCmdLine, int nShow) :
      TApplication(name, hInstance, hPrevInstance, lpCmdLine, nShow)
    {
      return;
    }
    void InitInstance();
    virtual void InitMainWindow();
};

//
// the Find Window Class
//
class TFindWindow : public TWindow {
  public:
    // constructor
    TFindWindow(PTWindowsObject pParent, LPSTR pTitle);
    // window class members
    LPSTR GetClassName() {
      return "TFindWindow";
    }
    void GetWindowClass(WNDCLASS& rWndClass);
    // message handlers
    virtual void CMQuit(RTMessage msg) =
      [CM_FIRST + CM_Quit];
    virtual void CMSrchForName(RTMessage msg) =
      [CM_FIRST + CM_ForName];
    virtual void CMSrchForSize(RTMessage msg) =
      [CM_FIRST + CM_ForSize];
    virtual void CMSrchForText(RTMessage msg) =
      [CM_FIRST + CM_ForText];
    virtual void CMAbout(RTMessage msg) =
      [CM_FIRST + CM_About];
```

LISTING 11.5

Stage 3 find.cpp (Continued)

```cpp
};

// Find App, routine initialization
void TFindApp::InitInstance()
{
  TApplication::InitInstance();
  HAccTable = LoadAccelerators(hInstance, "ACCELTABLE");
}

// Find App, create the main window
void TFindApp::InitMainWindow()
{
  MainWindow = new TFindWindow(NULL, "Find Files");
}

// Find Window, constructor
TFindWindow::TFindWindow(PTWindowsObject pParent, LPSTR pTitle) :
  TWindow(pParent, pTitle)
{
  AssignMenu("FindMenu");
  return;
}

// create a Window class for the Find Window
void TFindWindow::GetWindowClass(WNDCLASS& rWndClass)
{
  TWindow::GetWindowClass(rWndClass);
  rWndClass.hIcon = LoadIcon(GetApplication()->hInstance,
    "IDI_FindApp");
  if (rWndClass.hIcon == NULL) {
    MessageBox(HWindow, "Bad Icon Load", "icon", MB_ICONSTOP);
    rWndClass.hIcon = LoadIcon(0, IDI_APPLICATION);
  }
}

// handle CM_Quit menu selection
void TFindWindow::CMQuit(RTMessage /*msg*/)
{
  PostQuitMessage(0);
}

// handle CM_ForName menu selection
void TFindWindow::CMSrchForName(RTMessage /*msg*/)
{
  MessageBox(HWindow, "Search for named file",
    "FindFile", MB_ICONSTOP);
}

// handle CM_ForSize menu selection
void TFindWindow::CMSrchForSize(RTMessage /*msg*/)
{
  MessageBox(HWindow, "Search for file by size",
    "FindFile", MB_ICONSTOP);
```

LISTING 11.5

Stage 3 find.cpp (Continued)

```
}

// handle CM_ForText menu selection
void TFindWindow::CMSrchForText(RTMessage /*msg*/)
{
  MessageBox(HWindow, "Search for text in file",
    "FindFile", MB_ICONSTOP);
}

// handle CM_About menu selection
void TFindWindow::CMAbout(RTMessage /*msg*/)
{
  MessageBox(HWindow, "Find File App",
    "FindFile", MB_ICONSTOP);
}

//
// WIN MAIN
//
int PASCAL WinMain(HINSTANCE hInstance, HINSTANCE hPrevInstance,
  LPSTR lpCmdLine, int nShow)
{
  TFindApp findApp("Find Application", hInstance, hPrevInstance,
    lpCmdLine, nShow);
  findApp.Run();
  return findApp.Status;
}
```

LISTING 11.6

Stage 3 find.rc

```
#include "resource.h"
#include "find.ico"

FindMenu MENU
BEGIN
    POPUP "&File"
    BEGIN
        MENUITEM "E&xit\tAlt+F4", CM_Quit
    END
    POPUP "&Search"
    BEGIN
        MENUITEM "For File by &Name...\tAlt+N", CM_ForName
        MENUITEM "For File by Si&ze...\tAlt+Z", CM_ForSize
        MENUITEM "For File Containing &Text...\tAlt+T", CM_ForText
    END
    POPUP "&Help"
    BEGIN
        MENUITEM "&About...", CM_About
    END
END

ACCELTABLE ACCELERATORS
```

LISTING 11.6

Stage 3 find.rc (Continued)

```
BEGIN
    VK_F4, CM_Quit, VIRTKEY, ALT
    "z", CM_ForSize, ASCII, ALT
    "n", CM_ForName, ASCII, ALT
    "t", CM_ForText, ASCII, ALT
END
```

FIGURE 11.10

The file organization of the Find Files Stage 3 application. Files that I created are shown in gray, while files provided with Borland C++ (for example, owl.h), or files produced by standard tools (for example, find.exe), are unshaded. (Standard include files are omitted from the diagram.)

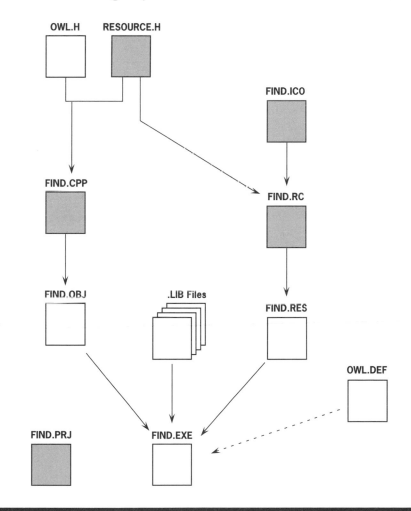

FIGURE 11.11

The appearance of the Find Files Stage 3 application. Two instances are executing. In the top window, Find Files is shown with the Search menu pulled down. In the bottom window, the Search for File by Size menu choice has just been selected.

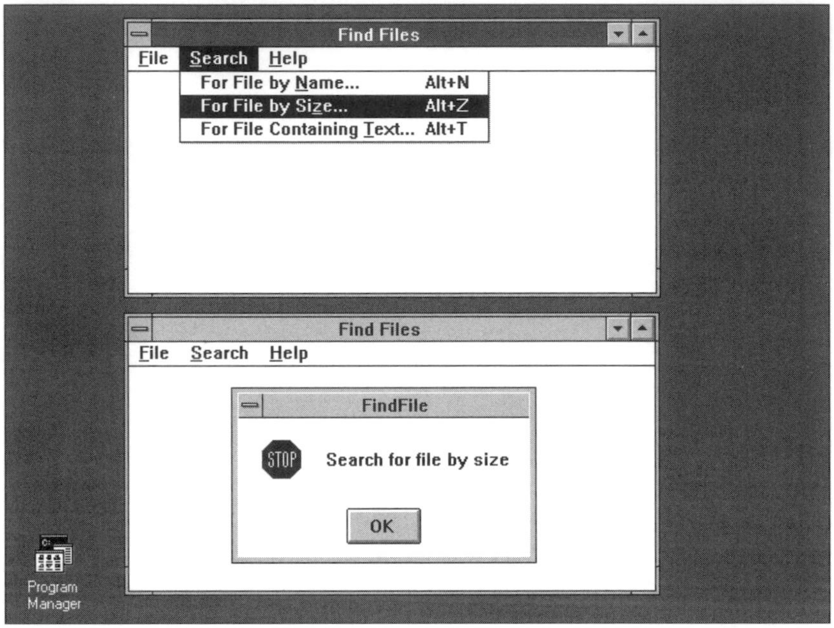

12 OWL DIALOG BOXES

DIALOG BOXES ARE A KEY ELEMENT OF THE USER INTERFACE FOR MOST WINdows programs. They can present an organized set of related choices, so that an entire issue can be addressed at one time. Dialog boxes can also be used simply to present information; the About box found in most Windows applications is the most common example.

Dialog box design is an important aspect of creating Windows applications. Keep the following points in mind when you are designing dialog boxes:

- Address a single topic and cover all of that topic. If there is too much information for a single dialog, provide buttons to pop-up secondary dialog boxes.

- Present the controls in a natural order. The progression from one control to the next using the Tab key should follow a reasonable order of selections.

- Choose labels and other text elements carefully so that the dialog box is self-explanatory.

- Incorporate keyboard shortcuts so that users aren't forced to use the mouse.

- Give dialog boxes a balanced, attractive appearance.

- By convention, follow the text of a menu item that invokes a dialog with an ellipsis (...).

Windows's straightforward treatment of dialog boxes has always been one of its strengths. Even in the bad old days of buggy, simplistic tools and DOS-based compilers, it was easy to see that building a dialog box within the Windows framework was far less work than rolling your own. Today dialog box creation is even more efficient, because the tools are so much better, and because the dialog and control classes of OWL provide more convenient access to dialog box functionality.

Before getting into the details, let's first go over who does what in the dialog box world. First, here's what native Windows provides:

- Display of a dialog based on a dialog box resource. This enables you to use a visual design tool to create the dialog, it frees you from thinking about coordinates and sizes, and it frees you from a lot of drudgery in positioning and displaying the controls.

- Functionality for standard controls, such as list boxes, combo boxes, edit windows, buttons (several styles), static text elements, and scroll bars.

- Most of the logic for the dialog box, such as the logic for switching the focus from one control to another.

OWL then addresses slightly higher-level tasks, so that dialog box programming is even easier:

- Convenient message handling, so that you can respond to control and dialog box messages by using message handler member functions.

- Derivation of custom dialog box classes from TDialog, so that you can meet specific needs.

- Saving and restoring values from controls, using transfer buffers.

- High-level interface to controls.

And there is one other big advantage, although it isn't related specifically to OWL. You can use the Borland Windows Custom Controls (BWCC) library to create a sculpted, textured dialog box appearance.

In this chapter I'll cover dialog boxes within the context of the Find Files application that I partially described in Chapter 11. This chapter will present Stage 4 in the evolution of Find Files.

By the end of this chapter I will have explained

- How to add dialogs to a Windows application

- How your C++ code relates to the dialog resource

- How to save and restore dialog control settings

Then Chapter 13 will complete the Find Files application by showing how the search engine is incorporated into the Find Files framework. Subsequent chapters will cover Windows's Graphic Device Interface (GDI) and Windows's Multiple Document Interface (MDI), and will present further complete applications.

Source code for Stage 4 can be found at the end of this chapter.

Find Files Stage 4: Adding Dialogs

Find Files is a relatively simple Windows program. When the user fills in one of the three search dialogs and clicks OK, the program searches for files according to the specified criteria. In this Stage 4 version of Find Files, I'm only going to do what's necessary to get the three main search dialogs, plus the About dialog, visible on the screen. I'm not (yet) going to worry about performing a file search when the user presses OK. However, I will take care of one detail—preserving the information in the dialog controls so that you don't have to start from scratch each time you start the dialog.

Modal and Modeless Dialogs

A *modal dialog* pops up, is used, and then is removed from the screen. This is by far the most common dialog type, and I'm sure it's what comes to your mind when you envision a dialog. In an ordinary modal dialog, you must complete the dialog before you continue with your application, but you are free to switch to another application. A slightly more restrictive dialog is a *system modal dialog*, which prevents you from switching to another application until the dialog is closed. System modal dialogs are used for things that must be addressed immediately, such as severe error messages, hardware failure messages, and the like.

A *modeless dialog* is a dialog that remains on the screen while you attend to other chores. One of the earliest examples is the Find dialog in Windows Write, which remains on the screen so that you can search for multiple text strings without revisiting the menu. Today there are many other examples of modeless dialogs, which are becoming increasingly popular because they bring functionality right to where it's needed.

From a programmer's perspective, there isn't much difference between a modal and a modeless dialog. There are really only two things to remember. The first is that you start a modal dialog by using OWL's ExecDialog() function, while you start a modeless dialog by using the MakeWindow() function. Both functions are accessible using a pointer to a TApplication object. The second thing to remember is that a modal dialog is automatically displayed when it is created, while a modeless dialog needs to be explicitly displayed.

Using Resource Workshop to Insert Controls in a Dialog

You should use Borland's Resource Workshop to create the resource for a dialog box. When you use Resource Workshop's Resource New menu command, select *dialog* from the list. You will be presented with an empty dialog box, which you can resize and fill with controls. Figure 12.1 shows the Resource Workshop screen while I was working on the Find Files application's About dialog box.

Once you've inserted a control into the dialog, you can double click the control to bring up a Style dialog to specify the details. Resource Workshop has a Style dialog for each general type of control: the Button Style dialog for buttons, the Edit Style dialog for edit boxes, the Static Style dialog for static controls, and so on. Resource Workshop also has a Window Style dialog that you can use to dictate the overall style of the dialog. Double click the dialog frame to activate the Window Style dialog.

For each control, you need to specify different information. If you don't understand some of the choices presented in a Style dialog, consult the Resource Script Statements of the Windows API reference supplied by Borland. You'll find that the choices outlined in each Style dialog closely follow the options outlined in the Windows API reference.

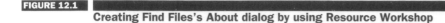

FIGURE 12.1

Creating Find Files's About dialog by using Resource Workshop

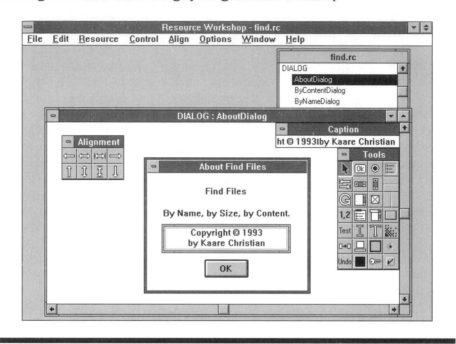

All of the Style dialogs let you enter a control ID. This is critically important, because the control IDs allow you to refer to and interact with specific controls. When you don't need to interact with a control, specify –1 as its ID. Usually, your software doesn't need to interact with static text controls, icon controls, rectangle controls, and frames. For these items you should usually specify –1 as the ID.

For other controls you should specify a small number. I usually prepare a set of identifiers in my resource.h script before using the dialog editor, so that I'm in charge of grouping, layout, and commenting of the resource.h header file.

I normally use the following naming conventions for dialog box controls:

- Control ID names start with IDD, which stands for ID Dialog.

- A two- or three-letter code for the control type: LB for list box, TE for text edit box, PB for push button, RB for radio button, CB for check boxes, HS and VS for scroll bars, CBB for combo boxes, ST for static text.

- A mixed-case description of the control.

Some examples of such names are IDD_LB_Drive for a list box containing a list of the system's disk drives, IDD_TE_Name for a file-name text edit box, and IDD_RB_Less for a radio button labeled Less.

Simple Dialog Boxes

Simple is almost always the best way to start. And in most applications, what is the simplest dialog? Usually it's the About dialog. Typical About dialogs present the application name, version information, and a copyright notice. What makes most About dialogs simple is that they have only one active control, an OK button.

The simplest dialog in the Find Files application is indeed its About dialog, which you've already glimpsed in Figure 12.1. Here is the resource statement that defines Find Files's About dialog. It is found in the find.rc file.

```
AboutDialog DIALOG 85, 47, 125, 91
STYLE DS_MODALFRAME | WS_POPUP | WS_CAPTION | WS_SYSMENU
CAPTION "About Find Files"
BEGIN
  CTEXT "Find Files", -1, 44, 10, 35, 8,
    WS_CHILD | WS_VISIBLE
  CTEXT "By Name, by Size, by Content.", -1, 12, 27, 100, 9,
    WS_CHILD | WS_VISIBLE
  CTEXT "Copyright \251 1993\nby Kaare Christian", -1,
    10, 42, 104, 18, WS_CHILD | WS_VISIBLE
  DEFPUSHBUTTON "OK", IDOK, 45, 67, 34, 14,
    WS_CHILD | WS_VISIBLE | WS_TABSTOP
END
```

To be honest, the above isn't exactly the resource definition that is produced by Resource Workshop. Resource Workshop wasn't designed to produce resource definitions for publication, and its output is considerably more cluttered than what I'm showing you. Also, Resource Workshop often uses the general CONTROL statement to define individual controls, but I've switched to the more readable, more specialized CTEXT and DEFPUSHBUTTON statements shown above. Since I've been using Resource Workshop, I've not found it necessary to know very much about the arcane syntax of dialog resource definitions, such as the About dialog that I've just presented. If you feel you need to know the details, consult the Resource Script Statements chapter of Borland's Windows API Guide.

As usual, creating a resource is only half the job. The second half is to activate the resource. Usually you will code individual dialog classes for each of your dialogs, and then you will create a custom dialog object to display the dialog on the screen. The advantage of crafting your own dialog class is to gain control over dialog creation and destruction, to store data used by the controls, and to give the dialog its own behavior and characteristics. But for a trivial About dialog you can use the standard TDialog class from the OWL library. You may recall from Find Files Stage 3 that the CM_About message is generated whenever the user clicks the About menu item. (In Stage 3 the message handler for CM_About simply popped up a message box.) Here's the Stage 4 CMAbout() message handler that displays the About dialog box. (The CMAbout() member function is found in the find.cpp file.)

```
void TFindWindow::CMAbout(RTMessage /*msg*/)
{
  GetApplication()->ExecDialog(new TDialog(this, "AboutDialog"));
}
```

Note that the TDialog constructor needs a pointer to the parent window object and the name of the dialog resource. Note also that you create a modal dialog using the ExecDialog() function, which is accessible using a pointer to the application object.

The About dialog in the Find Files application has only one active control, an OK push button. When the OK button is pressed, the dialog automatically closes. The mechanism that underlies this functionality is the Ok() message handler member function of the TDialog class, which is defined by the TDialog class to respond when the IDOK button control is pressed. (When you create the dialog resource, you must make sure that the ID of the OK button is the predefined Windows constant IDOK.) The other message handler of TDialog responds when an IDCANCEL button control is pressed. (The ID of the Cancel button must be IDCANCEL.) Both IDOK and IDCANCEL are constants defined in windows.h.

Transfer Buffers

One of the most important reasons for crafting your own dialog class is to initialize the controls. For most controls in most dialog boxes, the user expects that the controls will attain their former values each time the dialog is revisited. It is possible to tend to controls individually, but that's not the suggested technique. Instead you should create a transfer buffer, which is simply a struct containing the values for all the controls. When the dialog springs to life, initial values for the controls will come from the values in the transfer buffer. When the dialog is closed normally (not canceled) the control's settings will be stored in the transfer buffer.

You need to do several things to make transfer buffers work:

- Derive your own dialog class from TDialog.

- In your dialog class's constructor, you must create a control object for each control that will be initialized.

- Create a transfer buffer containing initializers for each control object that will be initialized. (See Table 12.1 for a list of data types for each control type.)

- In your dialog class's constructor, you must assign the address of your transfer buffer to the TransferBuffer data member of the TDialog class.

TABLE 12.1

Data Types for OWL Transfer Buffers

Control Type	Transfer Buffer Data Type
TButton	None.
TCheckBox	WORD.
TRadioButton	WORD.
TStatic	By default, transfer is not enabled for a static control. If you explicitly enable transfer by calling the EnableTransfer() member function, the data should be a buffer of TextLen characters, where TextLen is the length specified when the control is constructed.
TEdit	A buffer of TextLen characters, where TextLen is the length specified when the control is constructed.
TListBox	A pointer to a TListBoxData struct.
TComboBox	A pointer to a TComboBoxData struct.
TGroupBox	None.
TScrollBar	A pointer to a TScrollBarData struct.

The TListBoxData, TComboBoxData, and TScrollBarData structs are detailed in the OWL reference manual. Note that transfer buffers contain pointers to such objects, not the objects themselves. For TEdit (and TStatic, if transfer is enabled) the transfer buffer contains the storage for the string, not a pointer to the storage.

The transfer buffer can't be an ordinary data member of your dialog class, because it must continue to exist even when the dialog object doesn't exist. One possibility is to make the transfer buffer an ordinary global variable. I don't like this approach very much, because then the transfer buffer isn't seen as a member of your dialog class. Another solution is to make the transfer buffer a static local variable in the message handler that created the dialog class object. This addresses the need for locality, but it unfortunately prevents the transfer buffer data from being accessed outside of the procedure. A third, better solution is to make the transfer buffer a static class member. This lets you access the control values even when the dialog isn't visible, but it also makes the transfer buffer a class member. Thus you can make it private or protected, according to your needs.

Transfer buffers should be structs, because they simply store data; they don't have behaviors. However, I usually provide a constructor for a transfer buffer, so that I am assured that it will be initialized. Initialization is especially important for transfer buffers, because sometimes their data members are pointers to structs.

In the next section I'm going to discuss the Find Files application's TBySizeDialog class. The transfer buffer for the TBySizeDialog class is the TBySizeTransfer struct. Here's the definition of the TBySizeTransfer struct from the file dialog.h.

```
struct TBySizeTransfer {
  BOOL BtnLess;
  BOOL BtnSame;
  BOOL BtnMore;
  char FileSize[MAXPATH];
  PTListBoxData pListBox;
  TBySizeTransfer();        // constructor
};
```

If you look at the TBySizeDialog constructor, you'll see that the fields of the TBySizeTransfer struct match the order in which control objects are created in the TBySizeConstructor. This is important, because the transfer mechanism relies on the transfer buffer having the expected fields in the expected order. When you use the fields of the transfer buffer, you do so by name. But when the transfer buffer is used by the TDialog class, it is treated as a block of anonymous storage that is parceled out, in order, to the individual controls. There is no checking of any kind performed by the compiler, so be careful to get the details right.

The constructor for the transfer buffer simply initializes all of the members. It is found in the bysize.cpp file.

```
TBySizeTransfer::TBySizeTransfer()
{
  memset(FileSize, 0, MAXPATH);
  BtnLess = BtnMore = FALSE;
  BtnSame = TRUE;
  pListBox = new TListBoxData;
}
```

The controls are initialized by the constructor to have reasonable values. The radio button controls are initialized so that only one of them is TRUE; the character buffer is cleared; and the pointer to the TListBoxData object is initialized to point at a dynamically allocated TListBoxData object.

The TBySizeDialog Box Class

The Find Files application contains three similar dialog boxes that are used to specify a file search, but I'm only going to discuss the TBySizeDialog box in detail. The others are similar, actually simpler, and once you get the basic idea you will easily understand all three. You can find the source code for the TByContentDialog and TByNameDialog classes in the listings for bycontnt.cpp and byname.cpp, and you can find the definitions of all three dialogs in the dialog.h file. All three dialogs are shown in Figure 12.2.

FIGURE 12.2

(A) The Search for Named Files dialog box; (B) The Search for Files by Size dialog box; (C) The Search for Text in Files dialog box

A.

```
Search for Named Files

FileName:  *.bat

DiskDrive:

[-a-]
[-b-]                    Cancel
[-c-]
                           OK
```

B.

```
Search for Files by Size

                          ┌ Match ──────
FileSize:  1024           ⦿ Less Than
                          ○ Exactly
                          ○ More Than

DiskDrive:

[-a-]
[-b-]                    Cancel
[-c-]
                           OK
```

C.

```
Search for Text in Files

SearchTarget:  David

DiskDrive:

[-a-]
[-b-]                    Cancel
[-c-]
                           OK
```

The TBySizeDialog class contains a static TBySizeTransfer struct, plus a constructor, plus the SetupWindow() and CanClose() member functions. Here is the definition of the TBySizeDialog class:

```
class TBySizeDialog : public TDialog {
  public:
    TBySizeDialog(PTWindowsObject pParent); // constructor
```

```
    virtual void SetupWindow();
    virtual BOOL CanClose();
    static TBySizeTransfer BySizeData;      // transfer data
};
```

The role of the TBySizeDialog class's constructor is to create individual control objects for each control that will be involved in the transfer mechanism. As I mentioned before, the order in which the control objects are created must match the order of the fields in the TBySizeTransfer struct. Here's the body of the TBySizeDialog class's constructor, which is found in the bysize.cpp file:

```
TBySizeDialog::TBySizeDialog(PTWindowsObject pParent) :
  TDialog(pParent, "BySizeDialog")
{
  // order must match order of TForSizeTransfer struct
  new TRadioButton(this, IDD_RB_Less, 0);
  new TRadioButton(this, IDD_RB_Same, 0);
  new TRadioButton(this, IDD_RB_More, 0);
  new TEdit(this, IDD_TE_Size, MAXPATH);
  new TListBox(this, IDD_LB_Drive);
  TransferBuffer = &BySizeData;
}
```

If you understand the requirements of the transfer mechanism, I think you'll find few surprises in the body of the constructor. However, you might want to look closely at the constructor's initialization list. It invokes the base TDialog class's constructor, giving it the name of the dialog box resource. Placing the dialog resource name in the TBySizeDialog constructor's initialization list means that you don't have to refer to the resource name in find.cpp when you create the dialog. This is good organization, because it makes a link between the resource and the .cpp file that handles the dialog details. This placement of the resource name reduces the linkage between the dialog resource and the higher-level C++ code.

The dialog resource for the BySize dialog and the dialog resources for the ByContent and ByName dialogs are shown in the "Stage 4 Source Code" section. (The resource identifiers used in these dialog files are listed in resource.h.) I'm not going to repeat them here because they are similar to the About dialog resource that was shown in the "Simple Dialog Boxes" section. All three dialog box resources are included in find.rc using #include statements.

The SetupWindow() function is called just before the dialog box appears on the screen. Thus it provides an opportunity, at a later time than the constructor, for controlling the dialog box. Usually, a dialog class's SetupWindow() function is used to initialize controls. Note that Windows controls can't be initialized in the constructor, because during construction Windows hasn't yet created its internal version of the dialog. But by the time SetupWindow is called, Windows has done most of its own work and the dialog is about to pop up onto the screen. The TBySizeDialog class's SetupWindow initializes the list box that contains a list of your computer's disk drives. Windows contains a function called DlgDirList() that will load file-name lists into a list box, given a handle to the dialog, the ID of the list box control, plus some information about what files you want to list. Here's the SetupWindow() function of the TBySizeDialog class.

```
void TBySizeDialog::SetupWindow()
{
  TDialog::SetupWindow();
  DlgDirList(HWindow, "*.*", IDD_LB_Drive, 0, 0xc000);
}
```

The last parameter of DlgDirList() specifies what types of files you want to look at. Unfortunately, Windows doesn't contain symbolic constants for these values, although they are clearly tabulated in the DlgDirList() citation in the Windows API Guide supplied by Borland. The value 0xc000 is an OR of 0x4000 which looks for disk drives and 0x8000 which is the exclusive bit. When the exclusive bit is set, only the requested files are examined and ordinary files are omitted from the list.

Note that I'm explicitly initializing the disk drive selection list box; I'm not using the transfer mechanism to manage it. This makes sense for this control, because what I want is simply a list of all the available drives. The easiest thing is to let Windows fill it in. Note that this is the only control that I'm not initializing using the transfer mechanism.

The CanClose() member of the TBySizeDialog class is called when the user attempts to close the dialog, usually by clicking the OK button. CanClose() isn't called when the dialog is canceled. CanClose() is supposed to return TRUE if the dialog is in a state where it can be closed. CanClose() is the place to install sanity checks that prevent the user from closing a dialog box that hasn't been fully (or perhaps consistently) utilized. Here is the TBySizeDialog class's CanClose() member function:

```
BOOL TBySizeDialog::CanClose()
{
  if (TDialog::CanClose() == False)
    return False;

  PTEdit pEdit = (PTEdit)ChildWithId(IDD_TE_Size);
  if (pEdit == NULL) {
    MessageBox(HWindow, "Can't find edit control",
      "CanClose", MB_ICONEXCLAMATION);
    return True;
  }

  char buf[MAXPATH];
  *buf = 0;
  pEdit->GetText(buf, MAXPATH);
  if (*buf == 0) {
    MessageBox(HWindow, "Please enter a file size or Cancel",
      "", MB_ICONEXCLAMATION);
    return False;
  }

  if (!isdigit(buf[0])) {
    MessageBox(HWindow, "Size should be numeric",
      "", MB_ICONEXCLAMATION);
    return False;
  }
  return True;
}
```

The TBySizeDialog class's CanClose() function first checks the base class's CanClose() function. This is primarily a courtesy, as a generic TDialog will seldom have a reason not to close. However, in OWL programming a derived class's CanClose() should always call the base class's, and return False if False is returned by the base class. Next the TBySizeDialog function attends to the edit control. The idea is to return True only if the edit control contains a number. First a pointer to the edit control object is acquired using the ChildWithId() member of the TWindowsObject class. (The existence of the ChildWithId() member explains why the TBySizeDialog constructor didn't save the addresses of the control objects that it allocated.) Then CanClose() determines if the edit control is empty, and if it is not, whether its first character is numeric. A more exhaustive check might look at every character, but looking at the first finds most of the problems. If the control is empty or if it doesn't contain a number, then error messages are produced and CanClose returns False.

Stage 4 Source Code

This section contains the nearly complete listing of the source code of the Stage 4 Find Files application. These files are shown in Listings 12.1–12.12. All that is missing is the find.ico file, which contains the icon. (See Listing 11.3 for the text of the icon resource.)

Figure 12.3 shows the file organization of the Find Files Stage 4 application, and Figure 12.4 shows its class hierarchy. The parts of Figures 12.3 and 12.4 that have changed since Find Files Stage 3 relate to the dialog boxes: the new dialog box classes, and the new dialog box resources.

Now that the Find Files application has working dialog box code, it's time to attend to functionality. In Chapter 13, I'll show how you can take generic code that searches through a file system and insert it into the Find Files Stage 4 framework, to produce a working program.

LISTING 12.1

resource.h

```
//
// Find App Resource Constants
//
// Menu Items
#define CM_Quit    1Ø1  // File menu
#define CM_ForName 111  // Search menu
#define CM_ForSize 112
#define CM_ForText 113
#define CM_About   114  // Help menu
// Search Dialog IDs
#define IDD_LB_Drive 12Ø  // TListBox for all three
#define IDD_TE_Name  121  // TEdit filename for byName
#define IDD_TE_Size  122  // TEdit filesize for bySize
#define IDD_TE_Value 123  // TEdit search target for byContent
#define IDD_RB_Less  124  // TRadioButton < for bySize
#define IDD_RB_Same  125  // TRadioButton = for bySize
#define IDD_RB_More  126  // TRadioButton > for bySize
```

FIGURE 12.3

The file organization of the Find Files Stage 4 application. The application source files are shown shaded, while files supplied by Borland or created during compilation are shown unshaded.

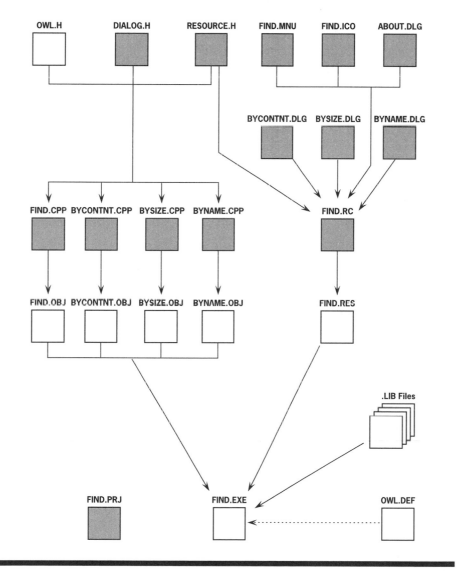

FIGURE 12.4

The class hierarchy of the Find Files Stage 4 application. The shaded classes were created for the Find Files application, while the unshaded classes are part of the OWL class library.

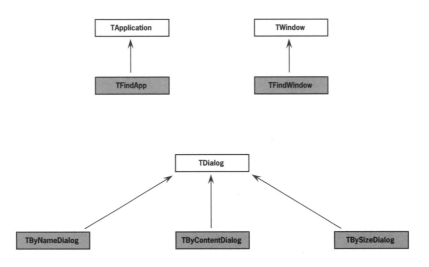

LISTING 12.2

dialog.h

```
//
// The dialogs for the find files app
//
#ifndef MAXPATH
#include <dir.h>
#endif

//
// Transfer Buffer for TByNameDialog
//
// N.B. Order must match order in TByNameDialog constr.
struct TByNameTransfer {
  char FileName[MAXPATH];
  PTListBoxData pListBox;
  TByNameTransfer();          // constructor
};

//
// Search By Name Dialog
//
class TByNameDialog : public TDialog {
  public:
    TByNameDialog(PTWindowsObject pParent); // constructor
    virtual void SetupWindow();
    virtual BOOL CanClose();
    static TByNameTransfer ByNameData;      // transfer data
};
```

LISTING 12.2

dialog.h (Continued)

```
//
// Transfer Buffer for TBySizeDialog
//
// N.B. Order must match order in TBySizeDialog constr.
struct TBySizeTransfer {
  BOOL BtnLess;
  BOOL BtnSame;
  BOOL BtnMore;
  char FileSize[MAXPATH];
  PTListBoxData pListBox;
  TBySizeTransfer();         // constructor
};


//
// Search By Size Dialog
//
class TBySizeDialog : public TDialog {
  public:
    TBySizeDialog(PTWindowsObject pParent); // constructor
    virtual void SetupWindow();
    virtual BOOL CanClose();
    static TBySizeTransfer BySizeData;     // transfer data
};


//
// Transfer Buffer for TByContentDialog
//
// N.B. Order must match order in TByContentDialog constr.
struct TByContentTransfer {
  char Target[MAXPATH];
  PTListBoxData pListBox;
  TByContentTransfer();        // constructor
};


//
// Search By Content Dialog
//
class TByContentDialog : public TDialog {
  public:
    TByContentDialog(PTWindowsObject pParent); // constructor
    virtual void SetupWindow();
    virtual BOOL CanClose();
    static TByContentTransfer ByContentData;     // transfer data
};
```

LISTING 12.3

find.cpp

```cpp
#define WIN31
#define STRICT
#include <owl.h>
#include <listbox.h>
#include "resource.h"
#include "dialog.h"

//
// the Find App class
//
class TFindApp : public TApplication {
  public:
    TFindApp(LPSTR name, HINSTANCE hInstance, HINSTANCE hPrevInstance,
      LPSTR lpCmdLine, int nShow) :
      TApplication(name, hInstance, hPrevInstance, lpCmdLine, nShow)
    {
      return;
    }
    void InitInstance();
    virtual void InitMainWindow();
};

//
// the Find Window Class
//
class TFindWindow : public TWindow {
  public:
    // constructor
    TFindWindow(PTWindowsObject pParent, LPSTR pTitle);
    // window class members
    LPSTR GetClassName() {
      return "TFindWindow";
    }
    void GetWindowClass(WNDCLASS& rWndClass);
    // message handlers
    virtual void CMQuit(RTMessage msg) =
      [CM_FIRST + CM_Quit];
    virtual void CMSrchForName(RTMessage msg) =
      [CM_FIRST + CM_ForName];
    virtual void CMSrchForSize(RTMessage msg) =
      [CM_FIRST + CM_ForSize];
    virtual void CMSrchForText(RTMessage msg) =
      [CM_FIRST + CM_ForText];
    virtual void CMAbout(RTMessage msg) =
      [CM_FIRST + CM_About];
};

// Find App, routine initialization
void TFindApp::InitInstance()
{
  TApplication::InitInstance();
  HAccTable = LoadAccelerators(hInstance, "ACCELTABLE");
}
```

LISTING 12.3

find.cpp (Continued)

```cpp
// Find App, create the main window
void TFindApp::InitMainWindow()
{
  MainWindow = new TFindWindow(NULL, "Find Files");
}


// Find Window, constructor
TFindWindow::TFindWindow(PTWindowsObject pParent, LPSTR pTitle) :
  TWindow(pParent, pTitle)
{
  AssignMenu("FindMenu");
  return;
}


// create a Windows class for the Find Window
void TFindWindow::GetWindowClass(WNDCLASS& rWndClass)
{
  TWindow::GetWindowClass(rWndClass);
  rWndClass.hIcon = LoadIcon(GetApplication()->hInstance, "IDI_FindApp");
  if (rWndClass.hIcon == NULL) {
    MessageBox(HWindow, "Bad Icon Load", "icon", MB_ICONSTOP);
    rWndClass.hIcon = LoadIcon(0, IDI_APPLICATION);
  }
}


//
// Handle the QUIT menu item
//
void TFindWindow::CMQuit(RTMessage /*msg*/)
{
  PostQuitMessage(0);
}


//
// Handle the Search by Name menu item
//
void TFindWindow::CMSrchForName(RTMessage /*msg*/)
{
  GetApplication()->ExecDialog(new TByNameDialog(this));
}


//
// Handle the Search by Size menu item
//
void TFindWindow::CMSrchForSize(RTMessage /*msg*/)
{
  GetApplication()->ExecDialog(new TBySizeDialog(this));
}


//
// Handle the Search for Content menu item
//
void TFindWindow::CMSrchForText(RTMessage /*msg*/)
```

LISTING 12.3

find.cpp (Continued)

```cpp
{
  GetApplication()->ExecDialog(new TByContentDialog(this));
}


//
// Make an About dialog
//
void TFindWindow::CMAbout(RTMessage /*msg*/)
{
  GetApplication()->ExecDialog(new TDialog(this, "AboutDialog"));
}


//
// WIN MAIN
//
int PASCAL WinMain(HINSTANCE hInstance, HINSTANCE hPrevInstance,
  LPSTR lpCmdLine, int nShow)
{
  TFindApp findApp("Find Application", hInstance, hPrevInstance,
    lpCmdLine, nShow);
  findApp.Run();
  return findApp.Status;
}
```

LISTING 12.4

bycontnt.cpp

```cpp
#define STRICT
#define WIN31
#include <owl.h>
#include <listbox.h>
#include <edit.h>
#include <stdio.h>
#include "resource.h"
#include "dialog.h"

void TByContentDialog::SetupWindow()
{
  TDialog::SetupWindow();
  DlgDirList(HWindow, "*.*", IDD_LB_Drivc, 0, 0xc000);
}


//
// return TRUE if the dialog has text in the filename control
BOOL TByContentDialog::CanClose()
{
  if (TDialog::CanClose() == False)
    return False;

  PTEdit pEdit = (PTEdit)ChildWithId(IDD_TE_Value);
```

LISTING 12.4

bycontnt.cpp (Continued)

```cpp
  if (pEdit == NULL) {
    MessageBox(HWindow, "Can't find edit control",
      "CanClose", MB_ICONEXCLAMATION);
    return True;
  }

  char buf[MAXPATH];
  *buf = 0;
  pEdit->GetText(buf, MAXPATH);
  if (*buf == 0) {
    MessageBox(HWindow, "Please enter a search target or Cancel",
      "", MB_ICONEXCLAMATION);
    return False;
  }
  return True;
}

//
// TByContentDialog constructor
//
TByContentDialog::TByContentDialog(PTWindowsObject pParent) :
  TDialog(pParent, "ByContentDialog")
{
  // order must match order of TByContentTransfer struct
  new TEdit(this, IDD_TE_Value, MAXPATH);
  new TListBox(this, IDD_LB_Drive);
  TransferBuffer = &ByContentData;
}

// static transfer buffer for TForNameDialog
TByContentTransfer TByContentDialog::ByContentData;

//
// Initialize TByContentDialog transfer buffer
//
TByContentTransfer::TByContentTransfer()
{
  memset(Target, 0, MAXPATH);
  pListBox = new TListBoxData;
}
```

LISTING 12.5

byname.cpp

```cpp
#define STRICT
#define WIN31
#include <owl.h>
#include <listbox.h>
#include <edit.h>
#include <stdio.h>
```

LISTING 12.5

byname.cpp (Continued)

```cpp
#include "resource.h"
#include "dialog.h"

void TByNameDialog::SetupWindow()
{
  TDialog::SetupWindow();
  DlgDirList(HWindow, "*.*", IDD_LB_Drive, 0, 0xc000);
}

//
// return TRUE if the dialog has text in the filename control
BOOL TByNameDialog::CanClose()
{
  if (TDialog::CanClose() == False)
    return False;

  PTEdit pEdit = (PTEdit)ChildWithId(IDD_TE_Name);
  if (pEdit == NULL) {
    MessageBox(HWindow, "Can't find edit control",
      "CanClose", MB_ICONEXCLAMATION);
    return True;
  }

  char buf[MAXPATH];
  static const char bad[] = " \t/\\:;";
  int i = 0;
  *buf = 0;
  pEdit->GetText(buf, MAXPATH);
  if (*buf == 0) {
    MessageBox(HWindow, "Please enter a filename or Cancel",
      "", MB_ICONEXCLAMATION);
    return False;
  }

  while(bad[i]) {
    if (strchr(buf, bad[i])) {
      MessageBox(HWindow, "Illegal character in filename",
        "", MB_ICONEXCLAMATION);
      return False;
    }
    i++;
  }
  return True;
}
```

LISTING 12.5

byname.cpp (Continued)

```cpp
//
// TByNameDialog constructor
//
TByNameDialog::TByNameDialog(PTWindowsObject pParent) :
  TDialog(pParent, "ByNameDialog")
{
  // order must match order of TByNameTransfer struct
  new TEdit(this, IDD_TE_Name, MAXPATH);
  new TListBox(this, IDD_LB_Drive);
  TransferBuffer = &ByNameData;
}

// static transfer buffer for TByNameDialog
TByNameTransfer TByNameDialog::ByNameData;

//
// Initialize TByNameDialog transfer buffer
//
TByNameTransfer::TByNameTransfer()
{
  memset(FileName, 0, MAXPATH);
  pListBox = new TListBoxData;
}
```

LISTING 12.6

bysize.opp

```cpp
#define STRICT
#define WIN31
#include <owl.h>
#include <listbox.h>
#include <edit.h>
#include <radiobut.h>
#include <stdio.h>
#include <ctype.h>
#include "resource.h"
#include "dialog.h"

void TBySizeDialog::SetupWindow()
{
  TDialog::SetupWindow();
  DlgDirList(HWindow, "*.*", IDD_LB_Drive, 0, 0xc000);
```

LISTING 12.6

bysize.cpp (Continued)

```cpp
}

//
// return TRUE if the dialog has text in the filename control
BOOL TBySizeDialog::CanClose()
{
  if (TDialog::CanClose() == False)
    return False;

  PTEdit pEdit = (PTEdit)ChildWithId(IDD_TE_Size);
  if (pEdit == NULL) {
    MessageBox(HWindow, "Can't find edit control",
      "CanClose", MB_ICONEXCLAMATION);
    return True;
  }

  char buf[MAXPATH];
  *buf = 0;
  pEdit->GetText(buf, MAXPATH);
  if (*buf == 0) {
    MessageBox(HWindow, "Please enter a file size or Cancel",
      "", MB_ICONEXCLAMATION);
    return False;
  }
  if (!isdigit(buf[0])) {
    MessageBox(HWindow, "Size should be numeric",
      "", MB_ICONEXCLAMATION);
    return False;
  }
  return True;
}

//
// TBySizeDialog constructor
//
TBySizeDialog::TBySizeDialog(PTWindowsObject pParent) :
  TDialog(pParent, "BySizeDialog")
{
  // order must match order of TForSizeTransfer struct
  new TRadioButton(this, IDD_RB_Less, 0);
  new TRadioButton(this, IDD_RB_Same, 0);
  new TRadioButton(this, IDD_RB_More, 0);
  new TEdit(this, IDD_TE_Size, MAXPATH);
  new TListBox(this, IDD_LB_Drive);
```

LISTING 12.6

bysize.cpp (Continued)

```
  TransferBuffer = &BySizeData;
}


// static transfer buffer for TForNameDialog
TBySizeTransfer TBySizeDialog::BySizeData;


//
// Initialize TForSizeDialog transfer buffer
//
TBySizeTransfer::TBySizeTransfer()
{
  memset(FileSize, Ø, MAXPATH);
  BtnLess = BtnMore = FALSE;
  BtnSame = TRUE;
  pListBox - new TListBoxData;
}
```

LISTING 12.7

find.rc

```
#include "resource.h"
#include "find.mnu"
#include "find.ico"
#include "about.dlg"
#include "byname.dlg"
#include "bysize.dlg"
#include "bycontnt.dlg"
```

LISTING 12.8

bycontnt.dlg

```
ByContentDialog DIALOG 59, 32, 142, 1Ø7
STYLE DS_MODALFRAME | WS_POPUP | WS_CAPTION | WS_SYSMENU
CAPTION "Search for Text in Files"
BEGIN
  LTEXT "Search&Target:", -1, 6, 17, 45, 8,
    WS_CHILD | WS_VISIBLE,
  EDITTEXT IDD_TE_Value, 54, 15, 8Ø, 12,
    ES_LEFT | WS_CHILD | WS_VISIBLE |
    WS_BORDER | WS_TABSTOP
  LTEXT "&DiskDrive:", -1, 6, 36, 42, 8,
    WS_CHILD | WS_VISIBLE,
  CONTROL "", IDD_LB_Drive, "LISTBOX",
```

LISTING 12.8

bycontnt.dlg (Continued)

```
       LBS_NOTIFY | WS_CHILD | WS_VISIBLE | WS_BORDER |
       WS_VSCROLL | WS_TABSTOP, 6, 49, 60, 53
   PUSHBUTTON "Cancel", IDCANCEL, 95, 60, 39, 14,
       WS_CHILD | WS_VISIBLE | WS_TABSTOP
   DEFPUSHBUTTON "OK", IDOK, 95, 82, 39, 14,
       WS_CHILD | WS_VISIBLE | WS_TABSTOP
END
```

LISTING 12.9

byname.dlg

```
ByNameDialog DIALOG 85, 33, 142, 107
STYLE DS_MODALFRAME | WS_POPUP | WS_CAPTION | WS_SYSMENU
CAPTION "Search for Named Files"
BEGIN
  LTEXT "File&Name:", -1, 6, 17, 38, 8,
     WS_CHILD | WS_VISIBLE
  EDITTEXT IDD_TE_Name, 45, 15, 89, 12, ES_LEFT |
     WS_CHILD | WS_VISIBLE | WS_BORDER | WS_TABSTOP
  LTEXT "&DiskDrive:", -1, 6, 36, 42, 8,
     WS_CHILD | WS_VISIBLE
  LISTBOX, IDD_LB_Drive, 6, 49, 60, 53, LBS_NOTIFY |
     WS_CHILD | WS_VISIBLE | WS_BORDER |
     WS_VSCROLL | WS_TABSTOP,
  PUSHBUTTON "Cancel", IDCANCEL, 95, 60, 39, 14,
     WS_CHILD | WS_VISIBLE | WS_TABSTOP
  DEFPUSHBUTTON "OK", IDOK, 95, 82, 39, 14,
     WS_CHILD | WS_VISIBLE | WS_TABSTOP
END
```

LISTING 12.10

bysize.dlg

```
BySizeDialog DIALOG 81, 25, 142, 104
STYLE DS_MODALFRAME | WS_POPUP | WS_CAPTION | WS_SYSMENU
CAPTION "Search for Files by Size"
BEGIN
  LTEXT "File&Size:", -1, 6, 17, 38, 8,
     WS_CHILD | WS_VISIBLE
  EDITTEXT IDD_TE_Size, 41, 15, 39, 12, ES_LEFT |
     WS_CHILD | WS_VISIBLE | WS_BORDER | WS_TABSTOP
  LTEXT "&DiskDrive:", -1 ,6, 42, 42, 8,
     WS_CHILD | WS_VISIBLE
```

LISTING 12.10

bysize.dlg (Continued)

```
LISTBOX IDD_LB_Drive, 6, 57, 6Ø, 43, LBS_NOTIFY |
  WS_CHILD | WS_VISIBLE | WS_BORDER | WS_VSCROLL | WS_TABSTOP
CONTROL "&Match", -1, "BUTTON", BS_GROUPBOX |
  WS_CHILD | WS_VISIBLE | WS_GROUP, 85, 3, 53, 5Ø
CONTROL "&Less Than", IDD_RB_Less,
  "BUTTON", BS_AUTORADIOBUTTON |
  WS_CHILD | WS_VISIBLE | WS_TABSTOP, 89, 13, 47, 12
CONTROL "&Exactly", IDD_RB_Same,
  "BUTTON", BS_AUTORADIOBUTTON |
  WS_CHILD | WS_VISIBLE | WS_TABSTOP, 89, 25, 47, 12
CONTROL "M&ore Than", IDD_RB_More,
  "BUTTON", BS_AUTORADIOBUTTON |
  WS_CHILD | WS_VISIBLE | WS_TABSTOP, 89, 37, 47, 12
PUSHBUTTON "Cancel", IDCANCEL, 96, 62, 39, 14,
  WS_CHILD | WS_VISIBLE | WS_GROUP | WS_TABSTOP
DEFPUSHBUTTON "OK", IDOK, 96, 84, 39, 14,
  WS_CHILD | WS_VISIBLE | WS_TABSTOP
END
```

LISTING 12.11

about.dlg

```
AboutDialog DIALOG 85, 47, 125, 91
STYLE DS_MODALFRAME | WS_POPUP | WS_CAPTION | WS_SYSMENU
CAPTION "About Find Files"
BEGIN
  CTEXT "Stage 4 Find Files", -1, 15, 1Ø, 95, 8,
    WS_CHILD | WS_VISIBLE
  CTEXT "By Name, by Size, by Content.", -1, 12, 27, 1ØØ, 9,
    WS_CHILD | WS_VISIBLE
  CTEXT "Copyright \251 1993\nby Kaare Christian", -1,
    1Ø, 42, 1Ø4, 18, WS_CHILD | WS_VISIBLE
  DEFPUSHBUTTON "OK", IDOK, 45, 67, 34, 14,
    WS_CHILD | WS_VISIBLE | WS_TABSTOP
END
```

LISTING 12.12

find.mnu

```
FindMenu MENU
BEGIN
  POPUP "&File"
  BEGIN
    MENUITEM "E&xit\tAlt+F4", CM_Quit
  END
  POPUP "&Search"
  BEGIN
    MENUITEM "For File by &Name...\tAlt+N", CM_ForName
    MENUITEM "For File by Si&ze...\tAlt+Z", CM_ForSize
    MENUITEM "For File Containing &Text...\tAlt+T", CM_ForText
  END
  POPUP "&Help"
  BEGIN
    MENUITEM "&About...", CM_About
  END
END
ACCELTABLE ACCELERATORS
BEGIN
  VK_F4, CM_Quit, VIRTKEY, ALT
  "z", CM_ForSize, ASCII, ALT
  "n", CM_ForName, ASCII, ALT
  "t", CM_ForText, ASCII, ALT
END
```

13 ASSEMBLING AN OWL APPLICATION

A WINDOWS APPLICATION IS A WITCH'S BREW—A BIT OF THIS, A PINCH OF THAT, and a long time simmering. In this chapter I want to add the ingredients to the caldron, stir, and then finally emerge with a functional version of Find Files. The major ingredients are the Find Files Stage 4 framework that I completed in Chapter 12, plus the DOS-based search engine, which is discussed in Appendix A.

Unlike the lucky witch, who merely chants incantations while stirring, I have to develop a few new components so that the basic components will fit together to form the Find Files application. The two major new ingredients are a dialog box to display the names of the files that are found by the search, and a new dialog box to cancel the search. These two components will be discussed shortly.

Find Files Stage 5: Putting It Together

I've tried to present the Find Files application so that each stage builds slowly and steadily on the previous one. But now it's time to pull it all together, and this step will be larger than any of the previous ones. In broad summary, Stage 5 incorporates the following enhancements:

- The TTreeSearch classes from the findem application are hooked into the Stage 4 dialogs.

- A member function is added to the application class to allow the Windows message loop to continue to operate during a long compute-intensive chore.

- A modeless dialog is developed to allow control over a compute-intensive task.

- A modeless dialog is developed to store the names of the found files.

Although change is the theme of Stage 5, there are a few things that don't change: the menu resource, the four dialog resources, the accelerator table, and the three C++ classes for managing the dialogs. Yes, it's nice to have some things that can be left alone.

Canceling a Compute-Bound Task

When you're running the DOS findem program, you can always strike Ctrl-C to cancel an ongoing search. When DOS detects a Ctrl-C (or Ctrl-Break) during program execution it notifies the program, and if the program doesn't have a Ctrl-C handler, it will terminate. But things aren't so simple in Windows. Most Windows programs that have operations that you might want to cancel display a dialog box with a Cancel button. If you click the Cancel button, then the operation that's in progress will be stopped.

I created a Cancel dialog box for the Find Files application to enable the user to cancel a pending search. Then I decided to get additional mileage from my Cancel dialog, so I made it possible for it to display file names. This provides some feedback as the search progresses. The Cancel dialog box is shown in Figure 13.1.

FIGURE 13.1

The Cancel dialog box of the Find Files application. In this figure, the search has progressed to a file named mciseq.drv.

It's trivially easy to create a dialog resource that contains a Cancel button, and then to display that resource on the screen as a modeless dialog. But such a simple scheme doesn't really solve the problem, because it doesn't provide an easy way for the other routines in the program to know when the Cancel dialog has been canceled.

My approach is to derive a TCancel dialog class from OWL's TDialog class. Then I create a public interface consisting of static member functions. This means that routines in any part of my program can access the current Cancel dialog box without explicitly using a global pointer to the Cancel dialog box object. (Of course the public interface routines do access the Cancel dialog box object using a static pointer, but that's okay because they are members of the TCancel class.) Here's the definition of the TCancel class, which also appears in the cancel.h file:

```
class TCancelBox : public TDialog {
  public:
    TCancelBox(PTWindowsObject pParent);
    static BOOL IsDone()
      { return bDone; }
    static void SafeSayMessage(char *msg)
      { if (!bDone) pCancelBox->SayMessage(msg); }
    static void SafeCloseWindow()
      { if (!bDone) pCancelBox->CloseWindow(IDCANCEL); }
  protected:
```

```
    void SayMessage(char *msg);
    virtual void ShutDownWindow()
      { bDone = True; TDialog::ShutDownWindow(); }
    static TCancelBox* pCancelBox;
    static BOOL bDone;
};
```

The TCancel class houses a static Boolean value that specifies whether the Cancel button has been pressed. Because the Boolean value is static, it can be interrogated at any time, even after the dialog box has vanished from the screen. To make this a bit more foolproof, I protect the actual Boolean variable and instead provide a public static member function to return the status. This ensures that the actual Boolean value will only be changed by the TCancel dialog box's own member functions. (It is set by the TCancel constructor to False, and it is set by ShutDownWindow(), which is called automatically as the dialog box is canceled, to True.) You can see the TCancel constructor by looking at the cancel.cpp file. (The Cancel dialog box resource is shown in the cancel.dlg file.)

Using the TCancel dialog box to display the file names as they are being processed presents a similar problem. How can you make it easy for a routine in one part of your code to access a specific control in a dialog that it didn't create? What's more, the dialog box may or may not be present on the screen. Again, the answer was to create a static member function to handle the chore. In the TCancel dialog, I provide a public static routine called SafeSayMessage() that places a message in the TCancel dialog box's static text control.

SafeSayMessage() simply makes sure that the Cancel dialog box is still active, by checking the bDone Boolean. If the dialog is still active, SafeSayMessage() calls the TCancel class's SayMessage() to actually place the message into the Cancel dialog box's IDD_ST_Cancel static text control. SayMessage() uses the ChildWithID() function to get a pointer to the control object, and it uses SetText() to actually pour the message (the file name) into the control. For details refer to the cancel.cpp file.

Keeping the Message Loop Rolling

The TCancel class, discussed in the preceding section, is an ordinary OWL component. It starts with OWL's TDialog class, and then adds a small amount of functionality, to produce a useful object. As you can tell from my discussion or from the cancel.h and filelist.h files, there's nothing remarkable about TCancel.

But if you think for a moment about how the Cancel dialog is used, you might discover a serious problem. How can it operate if some task is monopolizing the computer? First, here's some background. What normally happens in Windows software is that an application receives a message from Windows, it responds to that message, and then it waits for the next message. The assumption underlying this design is that it doesn't take very long for the application to manage each message. If an application stops asking for messages, then Windows is literally out of the loop, and operations such as using the mouse to click a button control aren't possible.

The solution is to keep the message loop operating, even when a traditional, long-running compute- or I/O-bound operation is in progress. Within the OWL framework, there are two ways to perform a long-running computation:

- In your application class, provide an IdleAction() member function that performs a snippet of the task each time it is called. The TApplication class calls the virtual IdleAction() function whenever there is spare processing time. Like message handling functions, IdleAction() shouldn't operate for long periods, but it is ideal for long-running tasks that can be divided into discrete parcels that individually aren't very long-running.

- Keep the message loop running from within your long-running task. In a traditional C application, you would do this by calling Windows's Peek-Message() function, as described in all of the standard Windows references. This basic approach can be used in an OWL application, but you need to handle the resulting messages in an OWL-compatible manner.

I originally planned to implement the first approach, using the IdleAction() function, in the Find Files application. But I encountered several problems. Using IdleAction() is best suited for tasks that are easily partitioned into independent chunks. But how do you search, say, the next ten files? It would certainly be possible to take the findem program, presented in Appendix A, and modify it to browse piecemeal through the disk. Unfortunately this would be a difficult change, because you would need to develop a data structure to keep track of the progress of the search, allowing the search to progress in discrete chunks.

Therefore I decided to implement the second approach, keeping the message loop running from within the search routines. The first thing I did was examine Borland's own message loop code, which is found in the procedure called MessageLoop() in the applicat.cpp file in the OWL source directory. Borland's code is a simple while(TRUE) style loop. All I did was take the code out of the infinite loop and move it into a function called PollMessages() that I made a member of my TFindApp class.

The one thing inside PollMessages that needs special treatment is the WM_QUIT message. In Borland's original MessageLoop() code, the WM_QUIT message terminates the infinite loop, causing MessageLoop() to return, which in turn sets in motion the sequence of actions that terminate the application. When you are in the body of PollMessages(), simply returning won't bring about this same series of actions. Therefore inside my PollMessages() function I do the following in response to the WM_QUIT message:

- Shut down the ongoing search, by calling the TCancel class's SafeShutdownWindow() function. (This is an easy, automatic way of pressing the Cancel button of the Cancel dialog.)

- Send another WM_QUIT message to the application, because PollMessages() has already consumed the current WM_QUIT message.

- Drop out of PollMessages(), as there probably isn't much more that needs to be done, but more importantly I don't want the current activation of PollMessages() to get the WM_QUIT message that I just posted.

Here's my PollMessages() function:

```
void TFindApp::PollMessages()
{
  int i = 100;
  MSG Message;
  PTApplication pApp = GetApplicationObject();
  if (!pApp)
    return;
  while (i--) {
    if (PeekMessage(&Message, 0, 0, 0, PM_REMOVE)) {
      if (Message.message == WM_QUIT) {
        PostQuitMessage(0); // replace msg in queue
        TCancelBox::SafeShutdownWindow();
        break;
      }
      if (!ProcessAppMsg(&Message)) {
        TranslateMessage(&Message);
        DispatchMessage(&Message);
      }
    }
    else   // No message waiting.
      break;
  }
}
```

Unfortunately, the version of PollMessages() that I developed for Find Files may not be exactly right for your own Windows application, because you may need a slightly different response to the WM_QUIT message.

Displaying File Stats in a Modeless Dialog

As I discussed when I first described the Find Files application in Chapter 11, I'm trying to be more educational than practical. In a more polished version of Find Files, I would probably implement a scrolling window to store and display the list of files that meet the search criteria. But for Find Files the idea is to build the application from a minimal set of components, so I'm instead using a modeless dialog box to store the file-name list. The dialog consists solely of a list box control and a button to close the dialog. It's modeless so that it will remain on screen after the conclusion of the search, which means that you can display several search result dialogs on the screen at once.

Here is the definition of the TFileList class from the filelist.h file.

```
class TFileList : public TDialog {
  public:
    TFileList(PTWindowsObject pParent);
    virtual ~TFileList()
    {
      pFileList = 0;
    }
    static void SafeAddString(char *s)
    {
      if (pFileList) {
```

```
          int i = pFileList->pFileListBox->AddString(s);
          if (i >= 0)
            pFileList->pFileListBox->SetSelIndex(i);
      }
   }
   static void SafeSetCaption(LPSTR title)
   {
     if (pFileList)
       pFileList->SetCaption(title);
   }
 protected:
   void SetupWindow();
   static TFileList *pFileList;
   PTListBox pFileListBox;
   RECT rctPrev;  // position of previous dialog
};
```

The TFileList member functions are shown in the filelist.cpp file, and the dialog resource for the file list dialog is in the filelist.dlg file. Figure 13.2 shows the Find Files application with the file list dialog box that contains the names of all the .BAT files on my disk.

FIGURE 13.2

The Find Files application searching for .BAT files

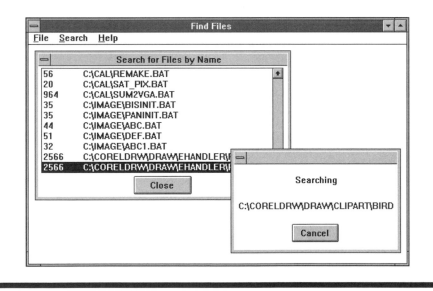

The TFileList class, like the TCancel class, contains a static data pointer to the current dialog box object. This static pointer is used by the static member functions of the TFileList class whenever they want to access the current TFile-List object. This organization presumes that there will only be one active (meaning currently accepting entries) file list box at a time. If necessary, we could extend this scheme to allow multiple active file list boxes.

The public interface of the TFileList class consists of the constructor and destructor, plus the SafeAddString() and SafeSetCaption() member functions. The static SafeAddString() function has two roles: to make it possible to add strings to a dialog for which you may not have a handle, and to make sure that the dialog is visible and operational before adding the strings. Similarly, the static TFileList member function SafeSetCaption() adds a caption to the current file list dialog box.

When a dialog box appears on the screen, it is displayed at the location specified in its dialog box resource. This can be a problem for a modeless dialog. If you display one dialog box on the screen, and then display a second, the second will exactly overlay the first. I alleviated this problem by making sure that one file list dialog won't step on top of the previous one. The solution comes in two parts. The first part is in the constructor, which notices if a previous file list dialog exists, and if it does, saves its location in the member variable named rctPrev. Here's the constructor for the TFileList class.

```
TFileList::TFileList(PTWindowsObject pParent) :
  TDialog(pParent, "FileListDialog")
{
  // save position of previous file list dialog
  memset(&rctPrev, 0, sizeof(RECT));
  if (pFileList)
    GetWindowRect(pFileList->HWindow, &rctPrev);
  // set up global pointer and create list box obj.
  pFileList = this;
  pFileListBox = new TListBox(this, IDD_LB_FileList);
  return;
}
```

The second part of the solution occurs in the SetupWindow() member function, which calls Windows's MoveWindow() function to move the new dialog box below and to the right of the existing dialog.

```
void TFileList::SetupWindow()
{
  TDialog::SetupWindow();
  // move down, right from existing window
  if (rctPrev.top || rctPrev.left) {
    int x = rctPrev.left + 20;
    int y = rctPrev.top + 20;
    int w = rctPrev.right - rctPrev.left;
    int h = rctPrev.bottom - rctPrev.top;
    MoveWindow(HWindow, x, y, w, h, 1);
  }
}
```

The reason for a two-step approach is that during construction of a dialog box object the Windows part of the dialog box doesn't yet exist, so it can't be moved. That's why OWL provides the SetupWindow() virtual member function. It lets you provide last-minute adjustments just before a window appears on the screen. (SetupWindow() is also used in the three search dialogs, to fill the disk drive list box with a list of the available disk drives.)

Adding the TTreeSearch Classes

All of the searching functionality of the Find Files application is found in the TTreeSearch class hierarchy. A DOS version of the TTreeSearch hierarchy is discussed in Appendix A. In this section I am going to describe how these classes were modified to fit into the anxiously waiting Find Files framework.

The simplest changes were rearrangements of the code:

- The TTreeSearch class definitions were moved into a header file called search.h.

- The code for the TTreeSearch classes was moved into a source file called search.cpp.

- The DOS main() and usage() functions were eliminated.

The other changes are more substantive and interesting and require more discussion. These changes address integrating the TTreeSearch classes with the Cancel and file list modeless dialogs, and as necessary inserting calls to my Poll-Messages() function.

Hooking up the TTreeSearch dialogs to the Cancel and file list modeless dialogs was straightforward:

1. In the TTreeSearch constructor, I called OWL's MakeWindow() function (from the TApplication hierarchy) to create the Cancel and file list dialog boxes.

2. In the constructors of the classes derived from TTreeSearch I called TFileList::SafeSetCaption() to set the file list dialog's caption. (Note that this relies on C++'s clearly defined order of construction—base classes first.)

3. In the TTreeSearch class's print() function I called TTreeSearch::-SafeAddString() to add the file-name citations to the file list dialog.

4. In the TTreeSearch destructor, I called TCancelBox::SafeCloseWindow() to remove the Cancel dialog from the screen. Note that I don't close the file list dialog; it remains on the screen at the conclusion of the search.

5. In the TTreeSearch class's Search() routine I placed a call to TCancel-Box::SafeSayMessage() so directory names would be displayed in the Cancel box as each was searched. I also placed a call to the routine in the TByContentSearch class's checkFile() procedure, so that file names would be displayed during the much slower search for text operation.

6. In the Search() procedure, and in the TByContentSearch class's check-File() procedure, I placed calls to the TCancelBox::IsDone() routine, so that search could be abandoned if the user pressed the Cancel button. Similarly, these routines call the PollMessages() function, so that the message loop continues to operate.

The last item in the preceding list hides a few hours of fine-tuning. You need to activate the message loop often enough to keep the program responsive, but not so often as to degrade the search performance. Similarly, you need to check for cancellation often, but not so often that performance suffers. In the TTreeSearch class's Search() procedure I eventually decided to perform these chores once for each directory that I examined (by calling Search() recursively), and once for each file that I checked (by calling a derived class's checkFile() procedure). Additionally, because the search for text is so slow compared with the file size or file name searches, I had to add calls to IsDone() and PollMessages() in the main search loop. This does slow down a content search, but it is a necessary overhead if the goal is to induce Find Files to be a good Windows citizen.

Overall, my strategy of integrating a DOS-based search engine into my Windows framework worked very well. It wasn't very hard under DOS to get the search engine to operate properly, and it wasn't very hard to integrate the working engine into the Windows framework. Although I've listed a dozen or more changes that I made to integrate the search engine into the Windows framework, in practice it was just a few hours of work. Certainly the bulk of a Windows development project must be done using Windows, but many applications contain a core set of functions that you can develop in whatever environment you choose, before adding them to your Windows application.

Stage 5 Source Code

The listings that follow present the source code files for Find Files Stage 5 that are new or that have changed since Stage 4. Table 13.1 lists all of the components of Find Files and specifies where they can be located in this book. Of course on the accompanying disk, all of the Find Files Stage 5 files are in the find.5 directory. Figure 13.3 shows the relationships of the Find Files Stage 5 development files, and Figure 13.4 shows the class hierarchy diagram for the Find Files Stage 5 application. And finally, Figure 13.5 shows the project window of BCW, so you can see which files are listed in the project.

TABLE 13.1

The Find Files Stage 5 Source Code Files

File	Listing	Stage 5 Summary
resource.h	13.1	Slightly changed. New #defines for two new resource identifiers.
find.h	13.2	New. The classes are modifications of those found in Stage 4 find.cpp.
search.h	13.3	Modified class definitions from the findem application.
dialog.h	12.2	Unchanged from Stage 4.
cancel.h	13.4	New.
filelist.h	13.5	New.
find.cpp	13.6	Expanded.
search.cpp	13.7	Modified version of the findem application.
cancel.cpp	13.8	New.

TABLE 13.1

The Find Files Stage 5 Source Code Files (Continued)

File	Listing	Stage 5 Summary
filelist.cpp	13.9	New.
bycontnt.cpp	12.4	Unchanged from Stage 4.
byname.cpp	12.5	Unchanged from Stage 4.
bysize.cpp	12.6	Unchanged from Stage 4.
find.rc	13.10	Slightly changed. New #include statements for the new resources.
cancel.dlg	13.11	New.
filelist.dlg	13.12	New.
bycontnt.dlg	12.8	Unchanged from Stage 4.
byname.dlg	12.9	Unchanged from Stage 4.
bysize.dlg	12.10	Unchanged from Stage 4.
about.dlg	12.11	Unchanged from Stage 4, except the "Stage 4" label was changed to "Stage 5."
find.mnu	12.12	Unchanged from Stage 4.
find.ico	11.3	Unchanged from Stage 2.

FIGURE 13.3

The Find Files Stage 5 application. Source files are shown shaded, while files supplied with OWL or files produced by the compilers are shown unshaded.

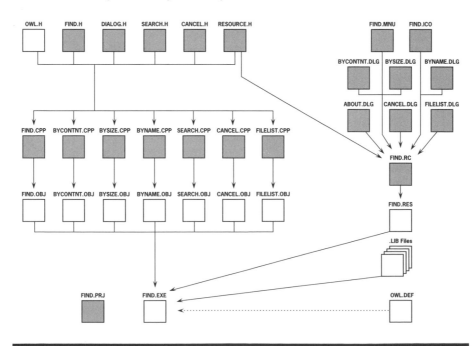

FIGURE 13.4

The Find Files Stage 5 class hierarchy diagram. Classes developed for the Find Files application are shown shaded.

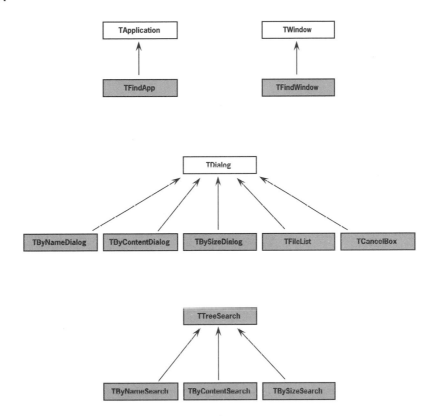

FIGURE 13.5

The BCW environment, showing the project for Find Files Stage 5

LISTING 13.1

resource.h

```
//
// Find App Resource Constants
//

// Menu Items
#define CM_Quit         101   // File menu
#define CM_ForName      111   // Search menu
#define CM_ForSize      112
#define CM_ForText      113
#define CM_About        114   // Help menu

// Dialog Controls
#define IDD_LB_Drive    120   // TListBox for all three
#define IDD_TE_Name     121   // TEdit file name for byName
#define IDD_TE_Size     122   // TEdit file size for bySize
#define IDD_TE_Value    123   // TEdit search target for
                              // byContent
#define IDD_RB_Less     124   // TRadioButton < for bySize
#define IDD_RB_Same     125   // TRadioButton = for bySize
#define IDD_RB_More     126   // TRadioButton > for bySize
#define IDD_ST_Cancel   127   // TStaticText in Cancel dialog
#define IDD_LB_FileList 128   // List box in file list dialog
```

LISTING 13.2

find.h

```
//
// the Find App class
//
class TFindApp : public TApplication {
  public:
    TFindApp(LPSTR name, HINSTANCE hInstance, HINSTANCE hPrevInstance,
      LPSTR lpCmdLine, int nShow) :
      TApplication(name, hInstance, hPrevInstance, lpCmdLine, nShow)
    {
      return;
    }
    void InitInstance();
    virtual void InitMainWindow();
    void PollMessages();
};

//
// the Find Window Class
//
class TFindWindow : public TWindow {
  public:
```

LISTING 13.2

find.h (Continued)

```
    // constructor
    TFindWindow(PTWindowsObject pParent, LPSTR pTitle);

    // window class members
    LPSTR GetClassName() {
      return "TFindWindow";
    }
    void GetWindowClass(WNDCLASS& rWndClass);

    // message handlers
    virtual void CMQuit(RTMessage msg) =
      [CM_FIRST + CM_Quit];
    virtual void CMSrchForName(RTMessage msg) =
      [CM_FIRST + CM_ForName];
    virtual void CMSrchForSize(RTMessage msg) =
      [CM_FIRST + CM_ForSize];
    virtual void CMSrchForText(RTMessage msg) =
      [CM_FIRST + CM_ForText];
    virtual void CMAbout(RTMessage msg) =
      [CM_FIRST + CM_About];
};
```

LISTING 13.3

search.h

```
//
// Search through a file system tree for files
//
class TTreeSearch {
  public:
    TTreeSearch(PTWindowsObject pParent, char drive);
    virtual ~TTreeSearch();
    void Search();
  protected:
    virtual int checkFile(struct ffblk& ff) = 0;
    void print(struct ffblk& ff);
    char filePattern[13];
    int startDisk;
    char startPath[MAXPATH];
};

//
// Search for files with specific names
//   (DOS wildcards ok)
//
class TByNameSearch : public TTreeSearch {
  public:
    TByNameSearch(PTWindowsObject pParent, char drive, char *nm);
  protected:
    int checkFile(struct ffblk& ff);
```

LISTING 13.3

search.h (Continued)

```
};

//
// Search for files with specific sizes
//
class TBySizeSearch : public TTreeSearch {
  public:
    enum matchType { lessThan, equalTo, moreThan };
    TBySizeSearch(PTWindowsObject pParent, char drive, long siz, matchType t);
  protected:
    int checkFile(struct ffblk& ff);
    long siz;
    matchType match;
};

//
// Search for files that contain the target text
//
class TByContentSearch : public TTreeSearch {
  public:
    TByContentSearch(PTWindowsObject pParent, char drive, char *targ);
    ~TByContentSearch()
    {
      if (target) delete target;
      if (target2) delete target2;
      if (buf) delete buf;
    }
  protected:
    int checkFile(struct ffblk& ff);
    char *target;
    char *target2;
    char *buf;
    int len;
};
```

LISTING 13.4

cancel.h

```
//
// A dialog box to cancel an operation.
// It also contains a static text control to display
//    status messages.
//
class TCancelBox : public TDialog {
  public:
    TCancelBox(PTWindowsObject pParent);
    static BOOL IsDone()
      { return bDone; }
    static void SafeSayMessage(char *msg)
```

LISTING 13.4

cancel.h (Continued)

```
      { if (!bDone) pCancelBox->SayMessage(msg); }
    static void SafeCloseWindow()
      { if (!bDone) pCancelBox->CloseWindow(IDCANCEL); }
  protected:
    void SayMessage(char *msg);
    virtual void ShutDownWindow()
      { bDone = True; TDialog::ShutDownWindow(); }
    static TCancelBox* pCancelBox;
    static BOOL bDone;
};
```

LISTING 13.5

filelist.h

```
//
// A dialog box to contain file names
//
class TFileList : public TDialog {
  public:
    TFileList(PTWindowsObject pParent);
    virtual ~TFileList()
    {
      pFileList = Ø;
    }
    static void SafeAddString(char *s)
    {
      if (pFileList) {
        int i - pFileList->pFileListBox->AddString(s);
        if (i >= Ø)
          pFileList->pFileListBox->SetSelIndex(i);
      }
    }
    static void SafeSetCaption(LPSTR title)
    {
      if (pFileList)
        pFileList->SetCaption(title);
    }
    void SetupWindow();
  protected:
    static TFileList *pFileList;
    PTListBox pFileListBox;
    RECT rctPrev;  // position of previous dialog
};
```

LISTING 13.6

find.cpp

```cpp
#define WIN31
#define STRICT
#include <owl.h>
#include <listbox.h>
#include "resource.h"
#include "dialog.h"
#include "cancel.h"
#include "filelist.h"
#include "search.h"
#include "find.h"

// Find App, routine initialization
void TFindApp::InitInstance()
{
  TApplication::InitInstance();
  HAccTable = LoadAccelerators(hInstance, "ACCELTABLE");
}

// Find App, create the main window
void TFindApp::InitMainWindow()
{
  MainWindow = new TFindWindow(NULL, "Find Files");
}

//
// Run the message loop for a while
//
void TFindApp::PollMessages()
{
  int i = 100;
  MSG Message;
  PTApplication pApp = GetApplicationObject();
  if (!pApp)
    return;
  while ( i--) {
    if (PeekMessage(&Message, 0, 0, 0, PM_REMOVE)) {
      if (Message.message == WM_QUIT) {
        PostQuitMessage(0); // replace msg in queue
        TCancelBox::SafeShutdownWindow();
        break;
      }
      if (!ProcessAppMsg(&Message)) {
        TranslateMessage(&Message);
        DispatchMessage(&Message);
      }
    }
    else   // No message waiting.
      break;
  }
}

// Find Window, constructor
TFindWindow::TFindWindow(PTWindowsObject pParent,
```

LISTING 13.6 ▌

find.cpp (Continued)

```cpp
    LPSTR pTitle) :
  TWindow(pParent, pTitle)
{
  AssignMenu("FindMenu");
  return;
}

// create a Windows class for the Find Window
void TFindWindow::GetWindowClass(WNDCLASS& rWndClass)
{
  TWindow::GetWindowClass(rWndClass);
  rWndClass.hIcon =
    LoadIcon(GetApplication()->hInstance, "IDI_FindApp");
  if (rWndClass.hIcon == NULL) {
    MessageBox(HWindow, "Bad Icon Load", "icon", MB_ICONSTOP);
    rWndClass.hIcon = LoadIcon(0, IDI_APPLICATION);
  }
}

//
// Handle the QUIT menu item
//
void TFindWindow::CMQuit(RTMessage /*msg*/)
{
  PostQuitMessage(0);
}

//
// Handle the Search by Name menu item
//
void TFindWindow::CMSrchForName(RTMessage /*msg*/)
{
  if (GetApplication()->ExecDialog(new TByNameDialog(this)) == IDOK) {
    char buf[10];
    TByNameDialog::ByNameData.pListBox->GetSelString(buf, 10, 0);
    char drive = 0;
    if (*buf)
      drive = buf[2];
    TByNameSearch *s =
      new TByNameSearch(this, drive,
        TByNameDialog::ByNameData.FileName);
    s->Search();
    delete s;
  }
}

//
// Handle the Search for size menu item
//
void TFindWindow::CMSrchForSize(RTMessage /*msg*/)
{
  if (GetApplication()->ExecDialog(new TBySizeDialog(this)) == IDOK) {
    char buf[10];
```

LISTING 13.6

find.cpp (Continued)

```cpp
    char drive = Ø;
    TBySizeTransfer& val = TBySizeDialog::BySizeData;
    val.pListBox->GetSelString(buf, 1Ø, Ø);
    if (*buf)
      drive = buf[2];
    TBySizeSearch::matchType m;
    if (val.BtnLess == True)
      m = TBySizeSearch::lessThan;
    else if (val.BtnSame == True)
      m = TBySizeSearch::equalTo;
    else
      m = TBySizeSearch::moreThan;
    TBySizeSearch *s =
      new TBySizeSearch(this, drive, atol(val.FileSize), m);
    s->Search();
    delete s;
  }
}


//
// Handle the Search for Text menu item
//
void TFindWindow::CMSrchForText(RTMessage /*msg*/)
{
  if (GetApplication()->ExecDialog(new TByContentDialog(this)) == IDOK) {
    char buf[1Ø];
    char drive = Ø;
    TByContentTransfer& val = TByContentDialog::ByContentData;
    val.pListBox->GetSelString(buf, 1Ø, Ø);
    if (*buf)
      drive = buf[2];
    TByContentSearch *s =
      new TByContentSearch(this, drive, val.Target);
    s->Search();
    delete s;
  }
}


//
// The About dialog
//
void TFindWindow::CMAbout(RTMessage /*msg*/)
{
  GetApplication()->ExecDialog(new TDialog(this, "AboutDialog"));
}


//
// WIN MAIN
//
int PASCAL WinMain(HINSTANCE hInstance, HINSTANCE hPrevInstance,
  LPSTR lpCmdLine, int nShow)
```

LISTING 13.6

find.cpp (Continued)

```
{
  TFindApp findApp("Find Application", hInstance, hPrevInstance,
    lpCmdLine, nShow);
  findApp.Run();
  return findApp.Status;
}
```

LISTING 13.7

search.cpp

```
#include <dir.h>
#include <dos.h>
#include <string.h>
#include <ctype.h>
#include <stdio.h>
#define STRICT
#define WIN31
#include <owl.h>
#include <listbox.h>
#include "search.h"
#include "cancel.h"
#include "resource.h"
#include "filelist.h"
#include "find.h"

void SearchMenu(BOOL enable)
{
  HWND hWin =
    GetApplicationObject()->MainWindow->HWindow;
  HMENU hMenu = GetMenu(hWin);
  WORD enb = enable ? MF_ENABLED : MF_GRAYED;
  EnableMenuItem(hMenu, CM_ForName, MF_BYCOMMAND | enb);
  EnableMenuItem(hMenu, CM_ForSize, MF_BYCOMMAND | enb);
  EnableMenuItem(hMenu, CM_ForText, MF_BYCOMMAND | enb);
}

//
// TTreeSearch constructor
//
TTreeSearch::TTreeSearch(PTWindowsObject pParent, char drive)
{
  // gray the search menu
  SearchMenu(False);
  // init search pattern
  strcpy(filePattern, "*.*");
  // Start modeless dialogs
  GetApplicationObject()->MakeWindow(new TFileList(pParent));
  GetApplicationObject()->MakeWindow(new TCancelBox(pParent));
  // move to root dir of search disk
  startDisk = getdisk();
  getcwd(startPath, MAXPATH);
  if (drive)
```

LISTING 13.7

search.cpp (Continued)

```
    setdisk(drive - 'a');
  chdir("\\");
}

//
// TTreeSearch destructor
//
TTreeSearch::~TTreeSearch()
{
  // return to starting directory and drive
  setdisk(startDisk);
  chdir(startPath);
  // get rid of cancel modeless dialog
  TCancelBox::SafeCloseWindow();
  // restore search menu
  SearchMenu(True);
  return;
}
void TTreeSearch::Search()

{
    struct ffblk ff;
    int done;
    // first descend into directories
    done = findfirst("*.*", &ff, FA_DIREC);
    while (!done && !TCancelBox::IsDone()) {
      if (ff.ff_attrib & FA_DIREC) {
        if (strcmp(ff.ff_name, ".") && strcmp(ff.ff_name, "..")) {
          chdir(ff.ff_name);
          Search();  // recursion . . .
          chdir("..");
        }
      }
      done = findnext(&ff);
      // keep message loop running
      ((TFindApp *)GetApplicationObject())->PollMessages();
    }

    // now ordinary files
    char dirname[MAXPATH];
    getcwd(dirname, MAXPATH);
    TCancelBox::SafeSayMessage(dirname);
    done = findfirst(filePattern, &ff, Ø);
    while (!done && !TCancelBox::IsDone()) {
      if (checkFile(ff))
        print(ff);
      done = findnext(&ff);
      // keep message loop running
      ((TFindApp *)GetApplicationObject())->PollMessages();
    }
}
```

LISTING 13.7

search.cpp (Continued)

```
//
// Print a line for a found file
//
void TTreeSearch::print(struct ffblk& ff)
{
   static char dirname[MAXPATH];
   static char buf[MAXPATH+15];
   getcwd(dirname, MAXPATH);
   int last = strlen(dirname) - 1;
   if (dirname[last] == '\\')
     dirname[last] = 0;
   sprintf(buf, "%ld\t%s\\%s", ff.ff_fsize, dirname, ff.ff_name);
   TFileList::SafeAddString(buf);
}


//
// TByNameSearch constructor
//
TByNameSearch::TByNameSearch(PTWindowsObject pParent,
  char drive, char *nm) :
    TTreeSearch(pParent, drive)
{
  strcpy(filePattern, nm);
  TFileList::SafeSetCaption("Search for Files by Name");
}


//
// For TByNameSearch, all files match because of pattern supplied
//   to constructor.
int TByNameSearch::checkFile(struct ffblk& /*ff*/)
{
  return 1;
}


//
// TBySizeSearch constructor
TBySizeSearch::TBySizeSearch(PTWindowsObject pParent,
  char drive, long s, matchType t) :
    TTreeSearch(pParent, drive),
    siz(s),
    match(t)
{
  TFileList::SafeSetCaption("Search for Files by Size");
  return;
}


//
// TBySizeSearch -- implement file size criteria
//
int TBySizeSearch::checkFile(struct ffblk& ff)
{
    switch(match) {
      case lessThan:
```

LISTING 13.7

search.cpp (Continued)

```cpp
      if (ff.ff_fsize < siz)
          return 1;
    break;
      case equalTo:
    if (ff.ff_fsize == siz)
          return 1;
    break;
      case moreThan:
    if (ff.ff_fsize > siz)
          return 1;
    break;
  }
  return 0;
}


//
// TByContentSearch constructor
//
TByContentSearch::TByContentSearch(PTWindowsObject pParent,
  char drive, char *targ) :
    TTreeSearch(pParent, drive)
{
  len = strlen(targ);
  buf = new char[len + 1];
  target = new char[len + 1];
  target2 = new char[len + 1];
  strcpy(target, targ);
  strcpy(target2, targ);
  strupr(target);
  strlwr(target2);
  buf[len] = 0;
  TFileList::SafeSetCaption("Search for Files by Content");
}

//
// TByContent criteria -- open file and search
//
int TByContentSearch::checkFile(struct ffblk& ff)
{
  if (TCancelBox::IsDone())
    return 0;
  TCancelBox::SafeSayMessage(ff.ff_name);
  FILE *fin = fopen(ff.ff_name, "rb");
  if (!fin)
    return 0;
  int cnt = 0;
  int ch;
  char t1 = *target;
  char t2 = *target2;
  len = strlen(target) - 1;
  // Avoid subr calls in this inner loop:
  // getc is a macro
  // fseek will only be called when 1st char of search is
```

LISTING 13.7

search.cpp (Continued)

```cpp
      // in the target buffer
      while((ch = getc(fin)) != EOF) {
        if (ch == t1 || ch == t2) {
          int n;
          char *p = buf;
          for(n=0; n<len; n++) // read into buf
            *p++ = getc(fin);
          // do a strnicmp() operation
          char *pt1;
          char *pt2;
          int matched;
          pt1 = target + 1;
          pt2 = target2 + 1;
          matched = 1;
          for(p=buf,n=0; n<len && matched; n++) {
            if (*p != *pt1 && *p != *pt2)
              matched = 0;
            p++;
            pt1++;
            pt2++;
          }
          if (matched) { // found!
            fclose(fin);
            return 1;
          }
          if (feof(fin)) {
            fclose(fin);
            return 0;
          }
          // restart search, but only go back if 1st char is in buf
          for(n=0; n<len; n++)
            if (buf[n] == t1 || buf[n] == t2) {
              fseek(fin, (len-n), SEEK_CUR);
              break; // out of inner for, restarts search
            }
        } // if
        if (cnt++ % 2000 == 0) {
          // keep message loop running
          ((TFindApp *)GetApplicationObject())->PollMessages();
          if (TCancelBox::IsDone())
            break;
        } // if
      } // while
      fclose(fin);
      return 0;
}
```

LISTING 13.8

cancel.cpp

```
#define WIN31
#define STRICT
#include <owl.h>
#include <static.h>
#include "cancel.h"
#include "resource.h"

// display a modeless cancel box on the screen
// static data
TCancelBox* TCancelBox::pCancelBox = Ø;
BOOL TCancelBox::bDone = True;

//
// constructor
//
TCancelBox::TCancelBox(PTWindowsObject pParent) :
  TDialog(pParent, "CancelDialog")
{
  bDone = False;
  pCancelBox = this;
  new TStatic(this, IDD_ST_Cancel, 4Ø);
}

void TCancelBox::SayMessage(char *msg)
{
  ((PTStatic)ChildWithId(IDD_ST_Cancel))->SetText(msg);
}
```

LISTING 13.9

filelist.cpp

```
//
// File Dialog Stuff
//
#define STRICT
#define WIN31
#include <owl.h>
#include <listbox.h>
#include "resource.h"
#include "filelist.h"

// TFileList static pointer to active list box
TFileList *TFileList::pFileList = Ø;
```

LISTING 13.9

filelist.cpp (Continued)

```cpp
//
// TFileList constructor
//
TFileList::TFileList(PTWindowsObject pParent) :
  TDialog(pParent, "FileListDialog")
{
  // save position of previous file list dialog
  memset(&rctPrev, 0, sizeof(RECT));
  if (pFileList)
    GetWindowRect(pFileList->HWindow, &rctPrev);
  // set up global pointer and create list box obj.
  pFileList = this;
  pFileListBox = new TListBox(this, IDD_LB_FileList);
  return;
}


//
// Initialize the window
//   (don't pop up on top of previous.)
//
void TFileList::SetupWindow()
{
  TDialog::SetupWindow();
  // move down, right from existing window
  if (rctPrev.top || rctPrev.left) {
    int x = rctPrev.left + 20;
    int y = rctPrev.top + 20;
    int w = rctPrev.right - rctPrev.left;
    int h = rctPrev.bottom - rctPrev.top;
    MoveWindow(HWindow, x, y, w, h, 1);
  }
}
```

LISTING 13.10

find.rc

```
#include "resource.h"
#include "find.mnu"
#include "find.ico"
#include "about.dlg"
#include "byname.dlg"
#include "bysize.dlg"
```

LISTING 13.10

find.rc (Continued)

```
#include "bycontnt.dlg"
#include "cancel.dlg"
#include "filelist.dlg"
```

LISTING 13.11

cancel.dlg

```
CancelDialog DIALOG 72, 40, 127, 66
STYLE DS_MODALFRAME | WS_POPUP | WS_CAPTION | WS_SYSMENU | WS_VISIBLE
CAPTION ""
BEGIN
  CTEXT "Searching", -1, -1, 8, 129, 8,
    WS_CHILD | WS_VISIBLE | WS_GROUP
  CTEXT "", IDD_ST_Cancel, -2, 28, 131, 8,
    WS_CHILD | WS_VISIBLE | WS_GROUP
  PUSHBUTTON "Cancel", IDCANCEL, 45, 46, 36, 14,
    WS_CHILD | WS_VISIBLE | WS_TABSTOP
END
```

LISTING 13.12

filelist.dlg

```
FileListDialog DIALOG 18, 18, 194, 101
STYLE DS_MODALFRAME | WS_POPUP | WS_VISIBLE | WS_CAPTION | WS_SYSMENU
CAPTION "Files"
BEGIN
  CONTROL "", IDD_LB_FileList, "LISTBOX",
    LBS_NOTIFY | LBS_USETABSTOPS |
    WS_CHILD | WS_VISIBLE | WS_BORDER | WS_VSCROLL, 3, 2, 187, 79
  DEFPUSHBUTTON "Close", IDOK, 74, 85, 45, 14,
    WS_CHILD | WS_VISIBLE | WS_TABSTOP
END
```

Find Files Stage 5B: Borland Custom Controls

The dialog boxes and controls in Find Files Stage 5 are attractively presented, but to many people they look old-fashioned and plain. Most newer Windows applications use more stylish controls, such as those developed by Borland for their own Windows applications. In this section I want to show how I modified the Find Files application to create Stage 5B, where the B stands for Borland Windows Custom Controls. (I thought of calling it Stage 5BWCC, but that seemed too long-winded.)

Perhaps surprisingly, there really isn't much difference between using a custom control library such as BWCC versus using the controls built into Windows. For the custom controls, the functionality is provided in a third-party dynamic link library (DLL), while the logic for the standard Windows controls is built into Windows. But this is mostly a difference without a distinction, because in both cases all you have to do is place the controls in a dialog resource, and then build appropriate OWL control and dialog classes to interact with the dialog boxes.

You can see the BWCC version of the Find Files application in Figure 13.6, which shows the Search for Files by Size dialog, and in Figure 13.7, which shows the Find Files application during that search.

FIGURE 13.6

The Find Files Stage 5B Search for Files by Size dialog

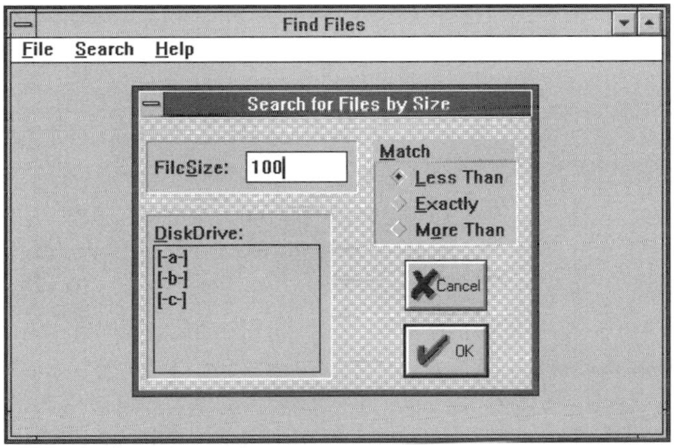

FIGURE 13.7

Find Files Stage 5B during a search for files whose size is less than 100 bytes

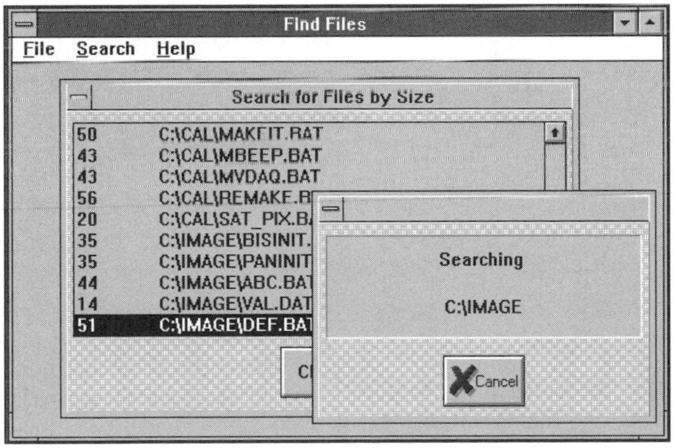

Switching to Borland Windows Custom Controls

It took me about two hours to convert Find Files Stage 5 to Stage 5B. Most of that time was spent in Resource Workshop adjusting the six dialog boxes, which are part of the diagram in Figure 13.3.

Here are some of the notes that I took during the conversion:

- bwcc.h was included into find.cpp.

- bwindow.h was included into find.cpp and search.cpp.

- The TFindWindow class was based on the TBWindow class, instead of on the TWindow class. The result was a gray main window, instead of a white main window.

- A call was added to BWCCGetVersion() to the TFindApp class's Init-MainWindow() function. This ensures that the custom control's DLL is accessible.

- Resource Workshop was used to assign the Window class BorDlg to all the dialogs. (In Resource Workshop, double click the dialog frame to activate the Window Style dialog, and then enter BorDlg in the Class field.)

- All of the control types were changed to their BWCC analogs. You can insert BWCC controls by using the menu Control-Custom option to pop up the New Custom Control dialog, or you can pick up the BWCC controls from the right column of the Tools palette.

- Gray boxes for grouping related controls were added to most of the dialogs. This was necessary only to make things look right; it had no effect on functionality. This step was included because in an ordinary dialog, you can place controls near each other to imply grouping. (For example, you can place a static text control next to an edit control, and the spatial layout makes it clear that the static text is a label for the edit control.) But with the BWCC controls you need to use a gray group box to provide visual grouping for related controls. You'll notice that in the About dialog I placed a gray box around the three static text controls that contain the About information. Figure 13.8A shows the Stage 5B About dialog without the gray box, and Figure 13.8B shows it with the gray box. For style guidance, look carefully at the dialogs in BCW and Resource Workshop.

- A speed bump (a horizontal or vertical line with a 3-D aspect) was placed into the About dialog, to separate the OK button from the static text controls.

- In Stage 5 the button identifier IDOK was used for the Close button of the TFileList class. This didn't work when I switched to the BWCC controls, because Borland assumed that a button with an ID of IDOK should have a check mark and the legend OK. Therefore I created a new dialog button ID called IDD_BB_Close and added it to resource.h. Then I created a handler for the Close button in the TFileList class. The new button message handler, called DlgClose(), simply calls the Ok() handler of the TDialog class.

■ bwcc.lib, which is found in the /borlandc/lib directory, was added to the project file.

FIGURE 13.8

(A) The Stage 5B About dialog without a gray group box to group the three static text controls; (B) The Stage 5B About dialog, using a gray group box to group the static text controls

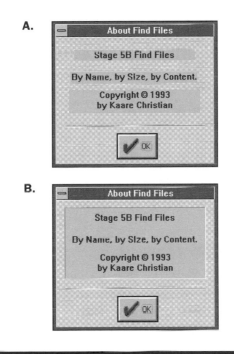

Stage 5B Source Code

The Stage 5B source code is nearly the same as Stage 5, so I'm not going to duplicate the unchanged listings. Instead I'm only going to provide listings for files that changed significantly. For files that have changed slightly, the changes are specified in detail in Table 13.2, which also tells you where in this book to find every component of the Stage 5B application. Of course on the disk every file for Stage 5B is found in the find.5b directory.

The file organization of Find Files Stage 5B (shown in Figure 13.9) is the same as Stage 5, except that Stage 5B must be linked to the file bwcc.lib, which contains the BWCC code. The class hierarchy of Stage 5B (shown in Figure 13.10) is the same as Stage 5, except that the TFindWindow class is now based on TBWindow.

TABLE 13.2

The Stage 5B Find Files Source Code Files

File	Listing	Stage 5B Summary
resource.h	13.13	Slightly changed since Stage 5. New #define for the Close button identifier of the File List dialog.
find.h	13.2	Slightly changed since Stage 5. The TFindWindow class in 5B is derived from TBWindow, not TWindow as in Stage 5. (The listing is not repeated in this section because the change is so small.)
search.h	13.3	Unchanged from Stage 5.
dialog.h	12.2	Unchanged from Stage 4.
cancel.h	13.4	Unchanged from Stage 5.
filelist.h	13.14	Slightly changed since Stage 5 to include a handler for the Close button. (Note that filelist.cpp isn't affected by this change, because the handler is specified in the class definition.)
find.cpp	13.6	Slightly changed since Stage 5: New #includes for bwindow.h and bwcc.h; TWindow changed to TBWindow in two places; BWCCGetVersion() called from the TFindApp class's InitMainWindow() function. (The listing is not repeated in this section because the changes are so small.)
search.cpp	13.7	Slightly changed since Stage 5. New #include for the bwindow.h header file. (The listing is not repeated in this section because the change is so small.)
cancel.cpp	13.8	Unchanged since Stage 5.
filelist.cpp	13.9	Unchanged since Stage 5.
bycontnt.cpp	12.4	Unchanged from Stage 4.
byname.cpp	12.5	Unchanged from Stage 4.
bysize.cpp	12.6	Unchanged from Stage 4.
find.rc	13.10	Unchanged from Stage 5.
about.dlg	13.15	Revised for BWCC controls.
cancel.dlg	13.16	Revised for BWCC controls.
filelist.dlg	13.17	Revised for BWCC controls.
bycontnt.dlg	13.18	Revised for BWCC controls.
byname.dlg	13.19	Revised for BWCC controls.
bysize.dlg	13.20	Revised for BWCC controls.
find.mnu	12.12	Unchanged from Stage 4.
find.ico	11.3	Unchanged from Stage 2.

FIGURE 13.9

The file organization of Find Files Stage 5B

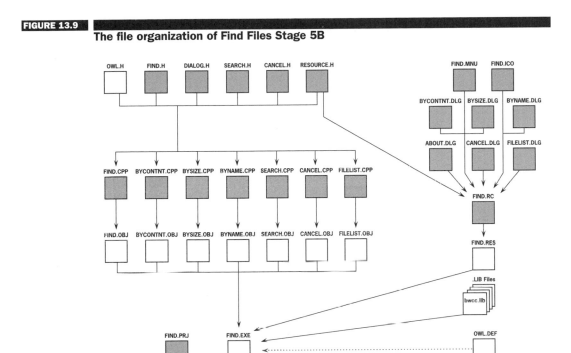

LISTING 13.13

resource.h

```
//
// Find App Resource Constants

//
// Menu Items
#define CM_Quit         101  // File menu
#define CM_ForName      111  // Search menu
#define CM_ForSize      112
#define CM_ForText      113
#define CM_About        114  // Help menu


// Dialog Controls
#define IDD_LB_Drive     120  // TListBox for all three
#define IDD_TE_Name      121  // TEdit filename for byName
#define IDD_TE_Size      122  // TEdit filesize for bySize
#define IDD_TE_Value     123  // TEdit search target for byContent
#define IDD_RB_Less      124  // TRadioButton < for bySize
#define IDD_RB_Same      125  // TRadioButton = for bySize
#define IDD_RB_More      126  // TRadioButton > for bySize
#define IDD_ST_Cancel    127  // TStaticText in Cancel dialog
#define IDD_LB_FileList  128  // List box in File List dialog
#define IDD_BB_Close     129  // TBButton Close button in FileListBox
```

FIGURE 13.10

The class hierarchy of Find Files Stage 5B

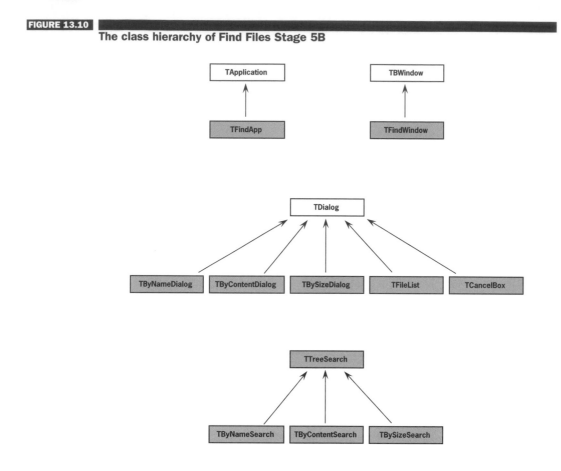

LISTING 13.14

filelist.h

```
//
// A dialog box to contain file names
//
class TFileList : public TDialog {
  public:
    TFileList(PTWindowsObject pParent);
    virtual ~TFileList()
    {
      pFileList = Ø;
    }
    static void SafeAddString(char *s)
    {
      if (pFileList) {
        int i = pFileList->pFileListBox->AddString(s);
        if (i >= Ø)
```

LISTING 13.14 ▇▇▇▇▇▇▇▇▇▇▇▇▇▇▇▇▇▇▇▇▇▇▇▇▇▇▇▇▇▇▇▇▇▇▇▇▇▇

filelist.h (Continued)

```
        pFileList->pFileListBox->SetSelIndex(i);
    }
  }
  static void SafeSetCaption(LPSTR title)
  {
    if (pFileList)
      pFileList->SetCaption(title);
  }
  virtual void DlgClose(RTMessage msg) =
    [ ID_FIRST + IDD_BB_Close ]
  {
    Ok(msg);
  }
protected:
  void SetupWindow();
  static TFileList *pFileList;
  PTListBox pFileListBox;
  RECT rctPrev;  // position of previous dialog
};
```

LISTING 13.15 ▇▇▇▇▇▇▇▇▇▇▇▇▇▇▇▇▇▇▇▇▇▇▇▇▇▇▇▇▇▇▇▇▇▇▇▇▇▇

about.dlg

```
AboutDialog DIALOG 85, 47, 125, 99
STYLE DS_MODALFRAME | WS_POPUP | WS_CAPTION | WS_SYSMENU
CLASS "BorDlg"
CAPTION "About Find Files"
BEGIN
  CTEXT "Stage 5B Find Files", -1, 15, 10, 95, 8,
    WS_CHILD | WS_VISIBLE | WS_GROUP
  CTEXT "By Name, by Size, by Content.", -1, 12, 27, 100, 9,
    WS_CHILD | WS_VISIBLE | WS_GROUP
  CTEXT "Copyright \251 1993\nby Kaare Christian",
    -1, 11, 41, 103, 18,
    WS_CHILD | WS_VISIBLE | WS_GROUP
  CONTROL "OK", IDOK, "BorBtn", BS_DEFPUSHBUTTON |
    WS_CHILD | WS_VISIBLE | WS_TABSTOP, 48, 75, 40, 20
  CONTROL "", 101, "BorShade", 1 |
    WS_CHILD | WS_VISIBLE, 7, 6, 111, 56
  CONTROL "", 102, "BorShade", 2 |
    WS_CHILD | WS_VISIBLE, 7, 69, 111, 2
END
```

LISTING 13.16

cancel.dlg

```
CancelDialog DIALOG 72, 4Ø, 127, 74
STYLE DS_MODALFRAME | WS_POPUP | WS_CAPTION | WS_SYSMENU | WS_VISIBLE
CLASS "BorDlg"
CAPTION ""
BEGIN
  CTEXT "Searching", -1, 3Ø, 1Ø, 65, 8,
    WS_CHILD | WS_VISIBLE | WS_GROUP
  CTEXT "", IDD_ST_Cancel, 4, 28, 118, 8,
    WS_CHILD | WS_VISIBLE | WS_GROUP
  CONTROL "", 129, "BorShade", 1 |
    WS_CHILD | WS_VISIBLE, 3, 5, 121, 39
  CONTROL "Cancel", IDCANCEL, "BorBtn", BS_PUSHBUTTON |
    WS_CHILD | WS_VISIBLE | WS_TABSTOP, 47, 5Ø, 32, 2Ø
END
```

LISTING 13.17

filelist.dlg

```
FileListDialog DIALOG 18, 18, 194, 114
STYLE DS_MODALFRAME | WS_POPUP | WS_VISIBLE | WS_CAPTION | WS_SYSMENU
CLASS "BorDlg"
CAPTION "Files"
BEGIN
  CONTROL "", IDD_LB_FileList, "LISTBOX",
    LBS_NOTIFY | LBS_USETABSTOPS |
    WS_CHILD | WS_VISIBLE | WS_BORDER | WS_VSCROLL, 3, 5, 188, 79
  CONTROL "Close", IDD_BB_Close, "BorBtn", BS_PUSHBUTTON |
    WS_CHILD | WS_VISIBLE | WS_TABSTOP, 81, 89, 32, 2Ø
END
```

LISTING 13.18

bycontnt.dlg

```
ByContentDialog DIALOG 59, 32, 142, 1Ø7
STYLE DS_MODALFRAME | WS_POPUP | WS_CAPTION | WS_SYSMENU
CLASS "BorDlg"
CAPTION "Search for Text in Files"
BEGIN
  LTEXT "Search&Target:", -1, 6, 17, 48, 8,
    WS_CHILD | WS_VISIBLE | WS_GROUP
  EDITTEXT IDD_TE_Value, 6Ø, 15, 74, 12, ES_LEFT |
    WS_CHILD | WS_VISIBLE | WS_BORDER | WS_GROUP | WS_TABSTOP
  LTEXT "&DiskDrive:", -1, 9, 38, 42, 8,
    WS_CHILD | WS_VISIBLE | WS_GROUP
  CONTROL "", IDD_LB_Drive, "LISTBOX", LBS_NOTIFY |
    WS_CHILD | WS_VISIBLE | WS_TABSTOP | WS_BORDER |
    WS_VSCROLL, 9, 48, 6Ø, 53
  CONTROL "Cancel", IDCANCEL, "BorBtn", BS_PUSHBUTTON |
```

LISTING 13.18

bycontnt.dlg (Continued)

```
      WS_CHILD | WS_VISIBLE | WS_TABSTOP, 91, 48, 32, 2Ø
    CONTROL "OK", IDOK, "BorBtn", BS_PUSHBUTTON |
      WS_CHILD | WS_VISIBLE | WS_TABSTOP, 91, 76, 32, 2Ø
    CONTROL "", 121, "BorShade", 1 |
      WS_CHILD | WS_VISIBLE, 3, 11, 135, 19
    CONTROL "", 122, "BorShade", 1 |
      WS_CHILD | WS_VISIBLE, 3, 37, 71, 64
END
```

LISTING 13.19

byname.dlg

```
ByNameDialog DIALOG 85, 33, 142, 112
STYLE DS_MODALFRAME | WS_POPUP | WS_CAPTION | WS_SYSMENU
CLASS "BorDlg"
CAPTION "Search for Named Files"
BEGIN
  LTEXT "File&Name:", -1, 6, 17, 38, 8,
    WS_CHILD | WS_VISIBLE | WS_GROUP
  EDITTEXT IDD_TE_Name, 45, 15, 89, 12, ES_LEFT |
    WS_CHILD | WS_VISIBLE | WS_BORDER | WS_GROUP | WS_TABSTOP
  LTEXT "&DiskDrive:", -1, 8, 43, 42, 8,
    WS_CHILD | WS_VISIBLE | WS_GROUP
  CONTROL "", IDD_LB_Drive, "LISTBOX", LBS_NOTIFY |
    WS_CHILD | WS_VISIBLE | WS_TABSTOP | WS_BORDER |
    WS_VSCROLL, 9, 53, 65, 49
  CONTROL "Cancel", IDCANCEL, "BorBtn", BS_PUSHBUTTON |
    WS_CHILD | WS_VISIBLE | WS_TABSTOP, 97, 49, 32, 2Ø
  CONTROL "OK", IDOK, "BorBtn", BS_PUSHBUTTON |
    WS_CHILD | WS_VISIBLE | WS_TABSTOP, 97, 78, 32, 2Ø
  CONTROL "", 122, "BorShade", 1 |
    WS_CHILD | WS_VISIBLE, 4, 1Ø, 133, 23
  CONTROL "", 123, "BorShade", 1 |
    WS_CHILD | WS_VISIBLE, 4, 4Ø, 76, 64
END
```

LISTING 13.20

bysize.dlg

```
BySizeDialog DIALOG 6Ø, 27, 151, 1Ø4
STYLE DS_MODALFRAME | WS_POPUP | WS_CAPTION | WS_SYSMENU
CLASS "BorDlg"
CAPTION "Search for Files by Size"
BEGIN
  LTEXT "File&Size:", -1, 6, 15, 38, 8,
```

LISTING 13.20

bysize.dlg (Continued)

```
        WS_CHILD | WS_VISIBLE | WS_GROUP
    EDITTEXT IDD_TE_Size, 41, 13, 39, 12, ES_LEFT |
        WS_CHILD | WS_VISIBLE | WS_BORDER | WS_GROUP | WS_TABSTOP
    LTEXT "&DiskDrive:", -1, 6, 4Ø, 42, 8,
        WS_CHILD | WS_VISIBLE | WS_GROUP
    CONTROL "", IDD_LB_Drive, "LISTBOX", LBS_NOTIFY |
        WS_CHILD | WS_VISIBLE | WS_TABSTOP | WS_BORDER |
        WS_VSCROLL, 6, 49, 63, 47
    LTEXT " &Match", -1, 9Ø, 9, 54, 8,
        WS_CHILD | WS_VISIBLE | WS_GROUP
    CONTROL "", -1, "BorShade", BSS_GROUP |
        WS_CHILD | WS_VISIBLE | WS_GROUP, 9Ø, 17, 55, 32
    CONTROL "&Less Than", IDD_RB_Less, "BorRadio", BS_AUTORADIOBUTTON |
        WS_CHILD | WS_VISIBLE, 96, 18, 47, 1Ø
    CONTROL "&Exactly", IDD_RB_Same, "BorRadio", BS_AUTORADIOBUTTON |
        WS_CHILD | WS_VISIBLE, 96, 28, 47, 1Ø
    CONTROL "M&ore Than", IDD_RB_More, "BorRadio", BS_AUTORADIOBUTTON |
        WS_CHILD | WS_VISIBLE, 96, 38, 47, 1Ø
    CONTROL "Cancel", IDCANCEL, "BorBtn", BS_PUSHBUTTON |
        WS_CHILD | WS_VISIBLE | WS_TABSTOP, 1Ø1, 54, 32, 2Ø
    CONTROL "OK", IDOK, "BorBtn", BS_PUSHBUTTON |
        WS_CHILD | WS_VISIBLE | WS_TABSTOP, 1Ø1, 79, 32, 2Ø
    CONTROL "", 121, "BorShade", 1 |
        WS_CHILD | WS_VISIBLE, 3, 9, 81, 2Ø
    CONTROL "", 123, "BorShade", 1 |
        WS_CHILD | WS_VISIBLE, 3, 37, 71, 63
END
```

Find Files Stage N: Improvements

Find Files was designed primarily as a learning tool. It's a way for me to introduce you to OWL and Windows. It wasn't designed to be the ultimate application, but rather a tractable application that you could understand. I hope it has served well in that role. But now Find Files is ready for another role, serving as a basis for further development. If you really want to understand Windows development you have to step up to the keyboard and start working. Here are some ideas for extending Find Files:

- **Search for dates or times**. Use the TBySizeDialog class as a model for the new dialog, and use the TBySizeSearch class as a model for the search class.

- **Put the file names in the Cancel dialog**. Currently, the Cancel dialog only shows the current directory. It might be nice to add a field so you can also see the file name.

- **Search through only a part of a file system**. Currently Find Files only examines entire disks. Using Borland's TFileDialog as a model, you could change the three search dialogs to allow the user to select a particular directory on a drive, so that parts of disk drives can be searched. You'll also need to make tiny changes to the TTreeSearch constructor so that the search starts in the right place.

- **Speed up the text search**. The "Findem Source Code" section of Appendix A presents some ideas for speeding up the text search.

- **Enable the user to copy file names from the file list dialog to the Clipboard**. This would let you import the file names into other applications, which would occasionally be useful.

- **Execute a windows app by double clicking on a found file name**. This capability is found in Windows's File Manager.

- **Use a nicer format and display more information in the file list dialog box**. File dates would be nice. Even better might be a set of buttons on the dialog allowing you to select from several formats! This would be easiest if you abandoned the file list dialog and instead crafted your own window for file-name display.

- **Put more information about the search in the file list dialog box title**. Currently, each TTreeSearch derived constructor puts a generic message in the file list dialog box title. It would be nice to also specify what is being sought. Thus instead of Search for Files by Size, you would have Search by Name for *.bat Files, and so on.

I'm sure you can think of many other enhancements that would make the Find Files application more useful.

PAINTING THE WINDOW

THE FIND FILES APPLICATION PRESENTED IN CHAPTERS 11, 12, AND 13 IS AN unusual Windows application, because all of its output appears in dialog boxes. True, most Windows applications have dialog boxes, but rarely are they the only way that an application conveys information. It is much more common for an application to paint its own main window or windows, so that information is presented according to the application's needs.

I started my tutorial on OWL and Windows with an application that uses dialog boxes for output. When it comes to dialog boxes, Windows is able to do most of the work without your intervention because dialog boxes are so alike. What differs from one dialog to another is the selection, size, placement, and order of the controls, and most of these issues can be addressed in the dialog box resource.

But when we look at traditional applications that display information in their own main window, we find that the variation from one application to another is much more fundamental; some applications look like documents, others look like drawings, others look like paintings, others look like tables, and many applications combine these things. This tremendous variety shifts the management burden from Windows to you, because you have to specify in great detail just how you want the window to behave.

There are numerous secondary tasks that you must do to make an application's window behave as you wish, but the primary one is to paint the window. Painting the window is Windows jargon for displaying information on the window. Painting is central partly because display of information on a window is the main interface between an application and the user, but also because so many facilities of Windows are related to the painting operation.

Blake Stage 1: Painting the Window

I've decided to illustrate painting the window by writing an application that displays part of William Blake's poem "Auguries of Innocence" in a window. As with the Find Files application, I'm going to develop the Blake application in several stages.

- Stage 1; Directory: blake.1: Display the poem in a window.

- Stage 2; Directory: blake.2: Provide for a choice of fonts and draw a title.

- Stage 3; Directory: blake.3: Add scrolling capability.

- Stage 4; Directory: blake.4: Improve the scrolling and enable selection of lines of text by using the mouse.

Also as I did in the Find Files application, I'm struggling to keep the application simple enough to serve an educational role, while trying to show a realistic use of Windows's facilities. Stage 1 of the Blake application merely demonstrates Windows's paint paradigm; by Stage 4 you'll see the basis of an interactive Windows application.

The Graphics Device Interface

Windows's Graphics Device Interface, which is usually called the GDI, is the output side of Windows. It's a set of functions and conventions that allow a Windows program to display output. GDI is used both for output to the screen, and for output to a printer, and it dictates the graphical file formats that are often used by Windows applications. In addition, GDI isn't limited to those things that are obviously "graphical," it also manages all output of text. GDI doesn't address multimedia output, such as output of audio or video.

The reason for GDI is to provide a uniform graphical interface so that Windows programs don't need to manage low-level graphical details. Of course GDI does enable an application to learn about the physical characteristics of the display or printer, so that programs are able to adapt their output to specific devices. GDI also provides a measure of protection, because it ensures that each program's output is restricted to the region of the screen that is owned by that program. (Like other aspects of Windows's security, this is an aid, not a panacea; GDI also provides facilities that allow a program to write anywhere on the screen.)

Somewhat surprisingly, OWL does very little to help with GDI. There aren't any OWL classes that relate to GDI needs, even though it's not hard to imagine what such classes might accomplish. Perhaps OWL has avoided GDI needs because while GDI programming is often complex, that complexity is usually local, meaning it is confined to a screenful or two of code. GDI programming can also be very dangerous, because applications will fail if you don't scrupulously follow GDI's rules for managing GDI resources.

The Device Context

In part GDI is a set of functions that perform graphical operations. But it's also a way of organizing drawing information, such as the current output color, the current coordinate system, and so on. This information is stored in a Windows data structure called a *device context*.

A device context is a repository, a storage region for information about how drawing operations should be performed. Each device context contains information about

- The selected coordinate system

■ The selected font, pen (used for line drawing), and brush (used for area filling)

■ The selected output settings, such as the text color, the background color, the drawing mode, polygon fill mode, and so on

But additionally a device context is a permission, a passport of sorts that you use to gain access to a specific device. You must get a handle for a device context before you can perform any output operations.

Figure 14.1 shows the relationship between an application, the GDI, and device contexts. Some GDI functions, such as the SetTextColor() function, control settings stored in the device context. These functions, which are symbolized by the two-headed arrow in Figure 14.1 from the application through the GDI, down to the device contexts, don't directly produce output. Other GDI functions, such as TextOut(), cause the GDI to retrieve information from the device context, which is used to specify the characteristics of the output. This path is indicated in Figure 14.1 by the arrow from the application, through the GDI, that ends at the output devices, with a branch path leading up through the GDI from the DCs.

FIGURE 14.1

Overview of the GDI components

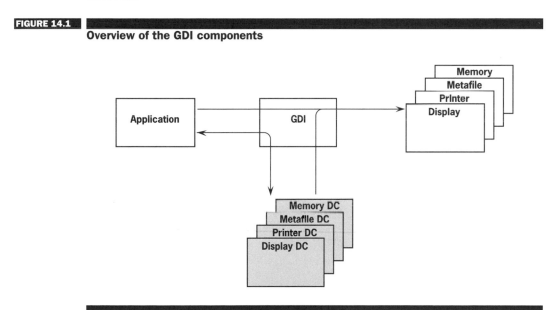

When you first get a device context all of the settings are set to their default values. Before you use the device context for output, you may want to change some of these default settings. The reason that Windows maintains a device context is to make it easier to produce output. When you write text to the output, you don't need to specify its color because that information is stored in the device context. Similarly, when you draw a line you don't need to specify a pen, because the pen characteristics are stored in the device context. This approach may take some accommodation on your part if you're used to a graphics system that requires full specification of the parameters for each output statement. Table 14.1 lists the attributes stored in a device context, together with a list of the GDI functions that are used to change or inspect each setting. See the next section, "GDI Coordinate Systems," for details.

TABLE 14.1

Device Context Attributes and GDI Functions That Change or Inspect DC Attributes

Device Context Attribute	Default Value	Set Attribute	Get Attribute	Drawing Functions Affected
Font	SYSTEM_FONT	SelectObject()	SelectObject() GetObject() GetTextFace() GetTextMetrics()	T
Text color	Black	SetTextColor()	GetTextColor()	T
Intercharacter spacing	0	SetTextCharacterExtra()	GetTextCharacterExtra()	T
Text alignment	TA_LEFT TA_TOP	SetTextAlign()	GetTextAlign()	T
Text justification	0	SetTextJustification()		T
Pen	BLACK_PEN	SelectObject()	SelectObject() GetObject()	L A
Pen position	(0, 0)	MoveTo()	GetCurrentPosition()	L
Drawing mode	R2_COPY_PEN	SetROP2()	GetROP2()	L A
Brush	WHITE_BRUSH	SelectObject()	SelectObject() GetObject()	A B
Brush origin	(0, 0)	SetBrushOrg()	GetBrushOrg()	A B
Polygon filling mode	ALTERNATE	SetPolyFillMode()	GetPolyFillMode()	A
Bitmap	None	SelectObject()	SelectObject() GetObject()	
Stretching mode	BLACKONWHITE	SetStretchBltMode()	GetStretchBltMode()	B
Background color	White	SetBkColor()	GetBkColor()	T L A
Background mode	OPAQUE	SetBkMode()	GetBkMode()	T L A
Color palette	DEFAULT_PALETTE	SelectPalette()	SelectPalette() GetPaletteEntries()	T L A
Clipping region	None	SelectObject() IntersectClipRect() ExcludeClipRect() SelectClipRgn() OffsetClipRgn() ExcludeUpdateRgn()	SelectObject() GetClipRect()	T L A B
Mapping mode	MM_TEXT	SetMapMode()	GetMapMode()	T L A B

TABLE 14.1

Device Context Attributes and GDI Functions That Change or Inspect DC Attributes (Continued)

Device Context Attribute	Default Value	Set Attribute	Get Attribute	Drawing Functions Affected
Viewport origin	(0,0)	SetViewportOrg() OffsetViewportOrg()	GetViewportOrg()	T L A B
Viewport extents	(1,1)	SetViewportExt() SetMapMode()	GetViewportExt()	T L A B
Window origin	(0,0)	SetWindowOrg()	GetWindowOrg()	T L A B
Window extents	(1,1)	SetWindowExt() SetMapMode()	GetWindowExt()	T I A B

The right column uses the codes T, L, A, and B to indicate the following groups of GDI drawing functions:

T   Text functions, including TextOut(), ExtTextOut(), and TabbedTextOut()

L   Line drawing functions, including LineTo(), Arc(), and PolyLine()

A   Area functions, including Chord(), Rectangle(), RoundRectangle(), Polygon(), PolyPolygon(), Ellipse(), DrawFocusRect(), Chord(), Pie(), FloodFill(), and ExtFloodFill()

B   Bitmap functions, including BitBlt(), PatBlt(), and StretchBlt()

Device contexts are a Windows resource that you must manage very carefully. What you usually do is get a specific device context from Windows, change its default settings to the settings that you prefer, use it for output, and then release it so that its ownership reverts to Windows. Windows has a very limited set of device contexts, and disaster will quickly follow if you forget to release device contexts as soon as you're done with them.

There are two common ways to get a device context for a window. The first way is to use BeginPaint() when your program is responding to a WM_PAINT message. You can use the device context while you are responding to the WM_-PAINT message, but at the conclusion of your painting you must use the End-Paint() function to release the paint device context to Windows. When you're not responding to the WM_PAINT message, you can get a device context by calling the GetDC() function, and then release it by calling the ReleaseDC() function. Both of these uses of device contexts are shown in the Blake application.

There are several other ways to obtain device contexts that I don't plan to cover in the Blake application. These include

■ GetWindowDC() to get a device context for the entire window, including the title, menu, border, and scroll bars. This contrasts with the device context returned by GetDC(), which just covers the client part of the window. (The client area is discussed in the next section.) The device context is released by calling ReleaseDC().

- CreateDC() to get a device context for a whole device, such as the display or a printer. The device context is released by calling DeleteDC().

- CreateIC() to get a device context for a whole device that is used for information purposes, not for writing. The device context is released by calling DeleteDC().

- CreateCompatibleDC() to get a device context for a memory device. The device context is released by calling DeleteDC().

- CreateMetaFile() to get a device context for sending GDI commands to a file. The device context is released by calling CloseMetaFile().

Information on these additional ways to get a device context can be found in the standard Windows references and tutorials.

I've been talking about getting a device context, but to be more accurate I should say "getting a handle to a device context." The device context itself is maintained internally by Windows. When you get a device context what you really get is its handle, which is a small number that you use in subsequent GDI function calls to refer to that device context. The Windows data type of a device context handle is HDC.

Here's a snippet of code that gets a device context, draws a diagonal line, and then releases the device context:

```
HDC dc = GetDC(HWindow);
MoveTo(dc, Ø, Ø);
LineTo(dc, 1ØØ, 1ØØ);
ReleaseDC(HWindow, dc);
```

More complete, realistic device context code will be shown in the four stages of the Blake application.

GDI Coordinate Systems

Coordinates are a fundamental part of any graphical system. Windows makes it easy for you to work in whatever coordinate system you choose, so long as your coordinate system is rectangular, aligned with the axes of the device, and your coordinates can be expressed using 16-bit integers.

First, some basic terminology:

- A *pixel* is an addressable point on the display.

- A *window* is a rectangular region of the display.

- The *client area* of a window is the part of a window that an application customarily uses for output. It's what is left over after setting aside space for the window border, window title, menu bar, scroll bars, and so on.

- *Device coordinates* are in units of pixels. They are also called *display coordinates*.

- *Logical coordinates* are in whatever units you choose, although the default units are pixels. Logical coordinates are used to interact with a device context.

- A *viewport* is similar to a window, but it always uses device coordinates. You'll only encounter viewports when you're setting up a coordinate system, when you're managing scrolling, and in certain settings where Windows is telling you about the window, such as when Windows is telling you the position of a mouse click.

The terminology reveals a lot of complexity. Let me try to explain why things are this complex. First, recognize that in Windows there are three sets of coordinate systems: the device coordinates, the viewport coordinates, and the window coordinates.

When a Windows program is sending output to a window, it uses logical coordinates to specify sizes and positions. Logical coordinates work with whatever scaling and origin you want. Scaling refers to how much size is meant by a given number. For example, a coordinate of 100 might refer to 100 pixels, 1 millimeter, 1 inch, or some other value. The origin refers to where the point (0,0) is located. Three common locations for the origin are the top-left corner of the window, which is its default location; the bottom-left corner, which corresponds to the graphs you made in grade school; and the center of the window. But as I just mentioned, an application can choose its own coordinate system for a window.

But what does Windows do with your logical coordinates? It can't access the screen using logical coordinates directly, because the video driver needs to be told which pixels to modify; the video driver doesn't understand inches or millimeters. So to actually perform output, Windows needs to convert your logical coordinates into device coordinates. But Windows doesn't transform the window coordinates directly to screen locations because windows can be placed anywhere on the screen. So instead Windows performs an intermediate transformation to a viewport. In a viewport, the units of the coordinates are always in pixels. This makes it easy to display the information directly on the screen. You may find it easiest to think of a viewport as a scrap of note paper, and imagine that it is Windows's job to paste these note papers onto the surface of the actual display screen. The Windows coordinate transformations are shown in Figure 14.2.

You don't need to worry much about viewports, just as you usually don't need to think much about screen coordinates, but there are a few times when viewport coordinates are important. The first is when you're telling Windows about your window's coordinate system. (If you use the predefined coordinate systems you don't need to specify anything about the viewport, but when you use Windows's two roll-your-own mapping modes, MM_ISOTROPIC and MM_ANISOTROPIC, you need to specify some aspects of the viewport.) The second reason you might need to work with viewport coordinates concerns scrolling, which is usually accomplished by moving the viewport origin. A third situation where you need to work with viewport coordinates is when you're getting messages from Windows about positions of things in the window. For example, the WM_LBUTTONDOWN message encodes the mouse's position in device coordinates. When you get a mouse position message you should usually call DPtoLP()—Windows's device points to logical points function—in order to translate to your own coordinate system.

FIGURE 14.2

The Windows coordinate transformations. Window coordinates have whatever scale has been selected by the programmer. Viewport coordinates always work with the unit of pixels, although the viewport origin can always be specified by the programmer.

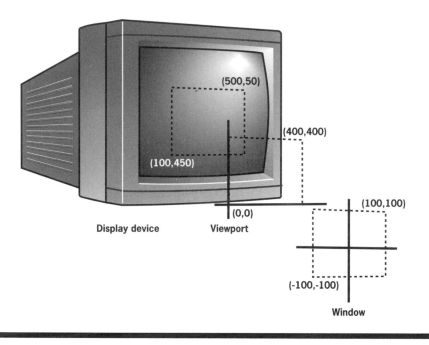

I've already mentioned two of the Windows mapping modes, MM_ISOTROPIC and MM_ANISOTROPIC. There are actually eight mapping modes, which are detailed in Table 14.2. The default mapping mode is MM_TEXT, and it's the only one I use in the examples in this chapter. The five mapping modes that let you specify coordinates using units of measure, MM_TWIPS, MM_LOMETRIC, MM_HIMETRIC, MM_LOENGLISH, and MM_HI-ENGLISH, are used when you need a coordinate system that is device independent. Output produced with these mapping modes will operate the same on different displays, and will even scale properly when output is to a printer, which typically has much higher resolution than a display. The two remaining mapping modes, MM_ISOTROPIC and MM_ANISOTROPIC, are used when you want complete control of the coordinate system. In Chapter 16, these two mapping modes are discussed further, and the MM_ISOTROPIC mode is used in an application.

TABLE 14.2

Windows's Mapping Modes

Mapping Mode	Logical Units	Orientation	Comments
MM_TEXT	Pixel		The default mapping mode. The name MM_TEXT comes from the orientation of the coordinate system, with Y increasing downward, which is the common coordinate system on text displays. The window and viewport extents are set to (1,1) and cannot be changed.
MM_TWIPS	1/20 pt.		Twip is a Windows term that means 1/20 point. (A point is a typographic term meaning approximately 1/72 inch.) The window and viewport extents are set by Windows and can't be changed.
MM_LOMETRIC	0.1 mm		The window and viewport extents are set by Windows and can't be changed.
MM_HIMETRIC	0.01 mm		The window and viewport extents are set by Windows and can't be changed.
MM_LOENGLISH	0.01 in.		The window and viewport extents are set by Windows and can't be changed.
MM_HIENGLISH	0.001 in.		The window and viewport extents are set by Windows and can't be changed.
MM_ISOTROPIC	Arbitrary but x equals y	Any	The units are the same in both the X and Y dimension, so that the aspect ratio of the drawing is always maintained. The window and viewport extents must be set by the application.
MM_ANISOTROPIC	Arbitrary	Any	The X and Y coordinate units are independently selectable, which means that the drawing's aspect ratio may not be preserved. The window and viewport extents must be set by the application.

You set the mapping mode for a device context using the SetMapMode() Windows function. The two arguments for SetMapMode() are a device context handle and one of the mapping mode names from Table 14.2.

In the computer graphics world, the word *extent* usually follows its dictionary meaning, which is the length or width of something. But be careful when you're dealing with Windows's window and viewport extents, because in Windows's usage the window and viewport extents don't refer to either width or height. Instead the two sets of extents control the scaling of coordinates from the window coordinate system to the viewport coordinate system. If the window X extent is 1 and the viewport X extent is 2, then coordinates are doubled when translating from window coordinates to viewport coordinates, and halved when translating from viewport to window. It's only the ratio of the extents that matters, as shown in Figure 14.3, which details the formulas used by Windows to translate from window coordinates to viewport coordinates and vice versa.

FIGURE 14.3

Windows coordinate translations

Window-to-Viewport Transformation

xView = xViewOrg + (xWin–xWinOrg) × (xViewExt/xWinExt)

yView = yViewOrg + (yWin–yWinOrg) × (yViewExt/yWinExt)

Viewport-to-Window Transformation

xWin = xWinOrg + (xView–xViewOrg) × (xWinExt/xViewExt)

yWin = yWinOrg + (yView–yViewOrg) × (yWinExt/yViewExt)

It might be tempting to determine the width of a viewport by calling the GetViewportExt() function, but it doesn't work. A viewport is simply a coordinate system, and its width is infinite. The GetViewportExt() function returns the numerators of the X and Y window-to-viewport scaling factors. You should call GetClientRect() to get the size of the client rectangle in device coordinates. If you have Windows logical coordinates and want to translate to device coordinates, then call LPtoDP() (logical points to device points). To convert in the opposite direction, use DPtoLP().

The window and viewport origins are often used by applications. As a general guideline, you should set the window origin when you truly want to control the location of the window coordinate system's origin, while you often use the viewport origin to implement scrolling.

The WM_PAINT Message

I would like to digress for a moment to talk about the WM_PAINT message. I think it is important for you to understand all the subtleties of WM_PAINT, even though as an OWL programmer you will usually avoid the difficulties by using Paint() in order to paint your window. So let's first cover the background by learning the traditional rules for responding to WM_PAINT, and then in the next section we'll examine OWL's Paint() procedure, which is the proper home for your painting logic.

Windows sends the WM_PAINT message to an application whenever that application's window needs to be repainted. Remember, it is a Windows application's obligation to keep track of what it has displayed on its window, so that it can repaint the window at any time.

There are several things that are unique about the WM_PAINT message. First, it is a low-priority message that always finds its way to the end of the message queue. This means that your application gets all its other messages before it gets the WM_PAINT message. The reason is that painting should be done last, after as many changes as possible, which are often triggered by other messages.

Another unusual aspect of the WM_PAINT message is that simply taking it from the queue doesn't remove it from the queue. Instead, the act of completing the painting by calling EndPaint() is what actually removes WM_PAINT from the queue. No other Windows message has this odd characteristic.

When an application receives a WM_PAINT message it should paint its window. The first step is to retrieve a device context for the window by calling BeginPaint(). Then the device context is used to update the window, and then finally EndPaint() is used to complete the process. Traditional C programmers are warned to be careful to only call BeginPaint() when responding to a WM_-PAINT message, because its use at any other time can be disastrous.

The WM_PAINT message is sent to an application whenever part of its window becomes invalid. Invalid is a descriptive way of saying that its contents are no longer up-to-date. Sometimes Windows loses track of what should be in a window and asks the application to redraw. But more often an application invalidates its own window when it realizes that it needs to make changes. For example, suppose that in a text editor or word processor the user strikes the PgDn (page down) key to advance to the next page. The proper way to handle this in a Windows application is to update the current file location variable, and then to invalidate the window. This schedules the window for a redraw. (The wrong way to handle the PgDn key press would be to redraw the window within the handler for the PgDn key. As much as possible, you should only paint the window in response to the WM_PAINT message.)

The standard way to invalidate the window is to use the InvalidateRect() function. InvalidateRect() takes three arguments: the window handle, a pointer to a RECT containing the boundaries of the invalid area, and a BOOL indicating whether the invalid rect must be erased. If the whole window is invalid, then you can specify NULL instead of supplying a pointer to a RECT struct. Here's typical code that invalidates a whole window:

```
InvalidateRect(HWindow, NULL, TRUE);
```

Stage 4 of the Blake application shows how you can increase performance by only invalidating those parts of a window that have changed. (See the WMLButtonDown() procedure in the blake.h file, later in this chapter under "Stage 4 Source Code.")

When you invalidate part of a window, then Windows automatically uses the invalid rectangle as a clipping rectangle. This means that output generated using the device context returned by BeginPaint() will be clipped to the invalid rectangle. Any output destined for areas outside the invalid rect will be discarded.

OWL's Paint() Procedure

When you use OWL you usually don't need to provide a message handler for the WM_PAINT message, because OWL's TWindow class includes one named WMPaint() that is sufficient. Instead you control window painting by defining the virtual function named Paint() in your application's window class. Here's the typical sequence of events that occur in an OWL application to paint the window:

1. The WM_PAINT message arrives and results in activation of the TWindow class's WMPaint() member function.

2. The WMPaint() function calls BeginPaint() to get the window's device context, it adjusts the device context's viewport origins if the scroll bars are active, and then it calls Paint().

3. The application's window class should implement the Paint() procedure and use it to repaint the window. Paint() is passed the handle to the device context returned by BeginPaint(), plus a reference to the PAINTSTRUCT initialized by BeginPaint().

4. Your application's window class's Paint() function performs the window painting.

5. When Paint() returns, the WMPaint() message handler releases the device context and signals the completion of the update by calling EndPaint().

Using the Paint() member function to paint the window is advantageous partly because it is a single function that is called whenever the WM_PAINT message arrives. Slightly more importantly, OWL automatically calls Begin-Paint() before calling Paint(), and then automatically calls EndPaint() after your Paint() routine returns. Thus all you need to do is provide your own version of Paint() that does the painting.

You'll see another benefit of using the OWL approach, overloading the Paint() function, in Stage 3 of the Blake application, which shows how to implement scrolling. OWL facilitates scrolling by adjusting the coordinate system before Paint() is called, which lets you implement scrolling with very little effort.

I've already described the first parameter of Paint(), which is a handle to the window's device context. The second parameter is a reference to a PAINTSTRUCT structure. There are three members of PAINTSTRUCT that you might want to use inside Paint():

- hdc—An HDC that contains the handle of the device context

- rcPaint—A RECT that contains the window's invalid rectangle

- fErase—A BOOL that is TRUE if Windows has erased the invalid rectangle of the window

The PAINTSTRUCT's hdc parameter is redundant (it's the same as the HDC passed as Paint()'s first argument), but the other two are occasionally useful. The rcPaint RECT struct is useful because it lets Paint() know what part of the window is invalid. And as I mentioned above, the invalid part of the window is also the window's clipping rectangle. You can always paint the whole window and let Windows take care of the clipping, but sometimes you can gain performance by only producing output that lies within the clipping rectangle. (The PAINTSTRUCT contains additional fields that are not intended for use by the applications programmer; consider them to be private.)

Overview of the Blake Application

The Blake Stage 1 application is a far more capable and complete Windows program than the Find Files Stage 1 application. Blake Stage 1 contains a menu, an About dialog, and an icon, plus code (explained shortly) to paint the main window. Blake Stage 1 is simple, but useful and complete. The appearance of Blake Stage 1 is shown in Figure 14.4, which shows two copies executing, plus a third version iconized (so you can see the Blake icon). In the left Blake window the poem is clipped to fit inside, while the right window is large enough to display the whole first verse of the poem.

FIGURE 14.4

The Blake Stage 1 application. The Blake icon is shown at the bottom left of the screen.

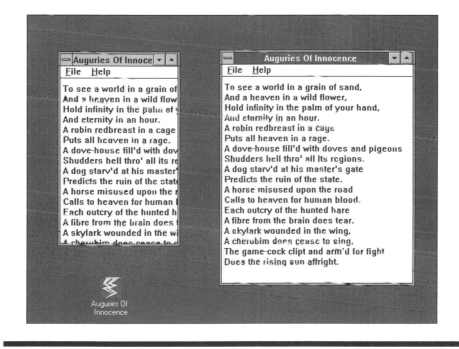

You will find the source code for each stage of the Blake application at the end of each respective section.

The file blake.h contains definitions of two classes: the TBlakeApp class and the TBlakeWindow class. The TBlakeApp class, which is derived from OWL's TApplication class, consists solely of a constructor and an InitMainWindow() function; it's unremarkable and won't be discussed further.

The TBlakeWindow class is derived from OWL's TWindow class. It consists of

- the constructor
- the GetClassName() and GetWindowClass() functions for establishing a unique window class

- the CMQuit() and CMAbout() member functions for handling the two menu bar choices

- the Paint() member function

It's the Paint() function that we're interested in examining closely; the other aspects of the TBlakeWindow class should already be familiar from your close encounter with the Find Files application.

Blake's Stage 1 Paint() Function

I'm going to examine the Blake Stage 1 application's Paint() procedure line by line, so we can see exactly what it does. This will provide a basis for understanding the progressively more complex Paint() procedures that we'll encounter in the next three stages of Blake. If you want to see the whole Paint() procedure without my commentary, look for it later in the middle of Listing 14.3.

First, the Paint() function header.

```
void TBlakeWindow::Paint(HDC PaintDC, PAINTSTRUCT & /*ps*/)
```

As promised, the Paint() function is passed two parameters, a handle for a device context and a reference to a PAINTSTRUCT struct. The PAINTSTRUCT isn't used, so the name of the PAINTSTRUCT parameter is commented out to avoid compilation warnings.

Next we have the declaration of the local variables. The first variable is hInstance, which is initialized by the hInstance data member of the application object:

```
HINSTANCE hInstance = GetApplication()->hInstance;
```

The reason for having a local variable store the instance handle is to simplify the appearance of the code that loads the lines of the poem.

The second initialized variable is named txtExtent:

```
DWORD txtExtent = GetTextExtent(PaintDC, "1", 1);
```

The txtExtent variable is initialized by calling GetTextExtent(), a native Windows function that returns the size of its text. Its three parameters are a handle to a device context, a string of text, and the length of the string. If you look in the Windows API reference manual, you'll discover that GetTextExtent() returns a DWORD (a Windows unsigned long data type) that contains the height of the text in the high word and the width of the text in the low word. These values are then used to initialize the local variables ht, x, and y.

```
int ht = HIWORD(txtExtent);
int x = LOWORD(txtExtent)/2;
int y = ht/2;
```

The x and y variables will be used to position each line of text. X is initialized to half the width of the character "1", and y is initialized to half the height, so that the text will be moved down and right from the window border by half the size of a character. (X and y could have been initialized to zero, but then the poem text would be drawn too close to the top and left window edges.) The ht variable is initialized to the height of a character, and it will be used to increment the y drawing position after each line is drawn. Figure 14.5 shows how these variables are used to draw the text in the Blake application.

FIGURE 14.5

The top-left corner of the Blake application's window shows how text is positioned. The variables x and y are initialized to half the width and height of a character in the current font, and the first line is drawn. Then y is incremented by the ht of a line before drawing each additional line.

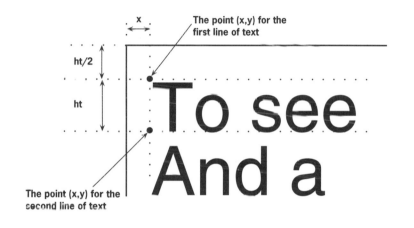

The last two local variables are

```
char line[100];
int i;
```

The line and i variables are used to fetch the lines of the first verse of Blake's poem "Auguries of Innocence."

Here is the loop that actually retrieves the lines of the poem and displays them in the window.

```
for(i=0; i< IDS_nStrings; i++) {
  line[0] = '\0'; // in case LoadString() fails
  LoadString(hInstance, IDS_Body+i, line, sizeof(line));
  TextOut(PaintDC, x, y, line, strlen(line));
  y += ht;
}
```

As you should be able to see, the for loop iterates once for each line of the poem. To make things as simple as possible, the header file resource.h contains an identifier IDS_nStrings that specifies the number of lines in the poem. The actual lines of the poem are stored as Windows string resources. Each string resource has a number that you pass to the LoadString() Windows function. Load-String() accesses the resource, and stores the text in the buffer whose address is passed as the third argument.

I could have stored the text of Blake's poem in a text file, and then just read the file, or I could have simply initialized an array of strings with the poem text. I decided to store the text as string resources because it was slightly simpler than storage in a separate data file, and because string resources don't consume space in the data segment, unlike an initialized array. As you can see both from blake.str (Listing 14.7, below) and from the above code, I don't use a unique resource identifier for each line of the poem, but instead I identify the first line using a named numeric identifier, and then I increment from that point forward. This is common usage when you have a group of related string resources.

The third line of the for loop calls TextOut() to output the text to the window. Like most GDI output functions, TextOut() requires a device context handle as its first argument. The next two arguments to TextOut() are the (x,y) position of the text. As mentioned above, x and y are initialized to slightly offset the text from the top-left edge of the window, and then y is incremented by the line height after each line of output. The last two arguments to TextOut() are a pointer to the line of text and the number of characters in the line.

It's important in the Paint() procedure to attend to both what is stated directly and what is left unstated. What's explicit, if you look at the code, is that a succession of string resources are displayed on the window at locations increasing in y. But what font is used? What color is the text? What size, what style? The answers to these questions are found in Table 14.1, which lists the default characteristics of a device context. In Blake Stage 1 nothing about the device context was altered, so all of the defaults are in effect. If you look in Table 14.1, you'll discover that the default font is the SYSTEM_FONT, that the default text color is black, and the default background color is white. You'll see how these settings can be modified in Blake Stage 2.

Stage 1 Source Code

Listings 14.1 through 14.8 contain all of the source code for the Blake application. Figure 14.6 shows the file organization of the Blake application, while Figure 14.7 shows its simple class hierarchy. In both figures the shaded elements are specific to the Blake application, while the unshaded elements are standard Windows or OWL components.

FIGURE 14.6

The files used to construct the Blake application. Files created for the application are shown shaded, while standard OWL files or files produced by the compilers are shown unshaded.

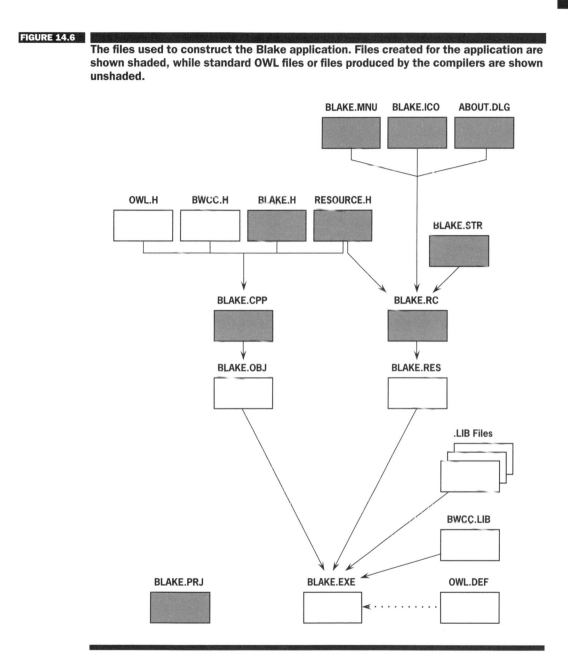

FIGURE 14.7

The class hierarchy of the Blake application. The shaded files are classes of the Blake application, while the unshaded classes are standard OWL components. The full OWL class hierarchy is not shown.

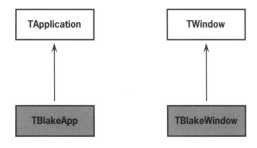

LISTING 14.1

blake.h

```
//
// the Blake Application class
//
class TBlakeApp : public TApplication {
  public:
    TBlakeApp(LPSTR name, HINSTANCE hInstance, HINSTANCE hPrevInstance,
      LPSTR lpCmdLine, int nShow) :
      TApplication(name, hInstance, hPrevInstance, lpCmdLine, nShow)
    {
      return;
    }
    virtual void InitMainWindow();
};

//
// the Blake Window class
//
class TBlakeWindow : public TWindow {
  public:
    // constructor
    TBlakeWindow(PTWindowsObject pParent, LPSTR pTitle);

    // window class members
    LPSTR GetClassName() {
      return "TBlakeWindow1";
    }
    void GetWindowClass(WNDCLASS& rWndClass);

    // Paint the window
    void Paint(HDC PaintDC, PAINTSTRUCT& ps);

    // message handlers
    virtual void CMQuit(RTMessage msg) =
```

LISTING 14.1

blake.h (Continued)

```
      [CM_FIRST + CM_Quit];
   virtual void CMAbout(RTMessage msg) =
      [CM_FIRST + CM_About];
};
```

LISTING 14.2

resource.h

```
//
// Blake App Resource Constants
//

// Menu Items
#define CM_Quit    101  // File menu
#define CM_About   114  // Help menu

// Strings
#define IDS_Title  50
#define IDS_Body   51
#define IDS_nStrings 18
```

LISTING 14.3

blake.cpp

```
#include <string.h>
#define STRICT
#define WIN31
#include <owl.h>
#include <bwcc.h>
#include "resource.h"
#include "blake.h"

//
// Blake App, create the main window
//
void TBlakeApp::InitMainWindow()
{
  char title[100];
  BWCCGetVersion();
  LoadString(hInstance, IDS_Title, title, sizeof(title));
  MainWindow = new TBlakeWindow(NULL, title);
}

//
// Blake Window, constructor
//
TBlakeWindow::TBlakeWindow(PTWindowsObject pParent, LPSTR pTitle) :
  TWindow(pParent, pTitle)
{
  AssignMenu("BlakeMenu");
  return;
```

LISTING 14.3

blake.cpp (Continued)

```cpp
}

//
// create a Windows class for the Blake Window
//
void TBlakeWindow::GetWindowClass(WNDCLASS& rWndClass)
{
  TWindow::GetWindowClass(rWndClass);
  rWndClass.hIcon = LoadIcon(GetApplication()->hInstance, "BlakeIcon");
  if (rWndClass.hIcon == NULL) {
    MessageBox(HWindow, "Bad Icon Load", "icon", MB_ICONSTOP);
    rWndClass.hIcon = LoadIcon(0, IDI_APPLICATION);
  }
}

//
// Paint
//
void TBlakeWindow::Paint(HDC PaintDC, PAINTSTRUCT & /*ps*/)
{
  HINSTANCE hInstance = GetApplication()->hInstance;
  DWORD txtExtent = GetTextExtent(PaintDC, "1", 1);
  int ht = HIWORD(txtExtent);
  int x = LOWORD(txtExtent)/2;
  int y = ht/2;
  char line[100];
  int i;
  for(i=0; i< IDS_nStrings; i++) {
    line[0] = '\0'; // in case LoadString() fails
    LoadString(hInstance, IDS_Body+i, line, sizeof(line));
    TextOut(PaintDC, x, y, line, strlen(line));
    y += ht;
  }
}

//
// handle the quit menu command
//
void TBlakeWindow::CMQuit(RTMessage /*msg*/)
{
  PostQuitMessage(0);
}

//
// handle the about menu command
//
void TBlakeWindow::CMAbout(RTMessage /*msg*/)
{
  GetApplication()->ExecDialog(new TDialog(this, "AboutDialog"));
}
//
// WIN MAIN
//
```

LISTING 14.3

blake.cpp (Continued)

```
int PASCAL WinMain(HINSTANCE hInstance, HINSTANCE hPrevInstance,
  LPSTR lpCmdLine, int nShow)
{
  TBlakeApp blakeApp("Blake Application", hInstance, hPrevInstance,
    lpCmdLine, nShow);
  blakeApp.Run();
  return blakeApp.Status;
}
```

LISTING 14.4

blake.rc

```
#include "resource.h"
#include "blake.ico"
#include "blake.mnu"
#include "about.dlg"
#include "blake.str"
```

LISTING 14.5

blake.mnu

```
BlakeMenu MENU
BEGIN
  POPUP "&File"
  BEGIN
    MENUITEM "E&xit\tAlt+F4", CM_Quit
  END
  POPUP "&Help"
  BEGIN
    MENUITEM "&About...", CM_About
  END
END
```

LISTING 14.6

about.dlg

```
AboutDialog DIALOG 72, 35, 125, 100
STYLE DS_MODALFRAME | WS_POPUP | WS_CAPTION | WS_SYSMENU
CLASS "BorDlg"
CAPTION "About Blake"
BEGIN
  CTEXT "Stage 1 Blake", -1, 15, 11, 95, 8,
    WS_CHILD | WS_VISIBLE
  CTEXT "Copyright \251 1993\nby Kaare Christian",
    -1, 11, 25, 104, 18, WS_CHILD | WS_VISIBLE
  DEFPUSHBUTTON "OK", IDOK, 45, 82, 34, 14,
```

LISTING 14.6

about.dlg (Continued)

```
    WS_CHILD | WS_VISIBLE | WS_TABSTOP
  CONTROL "", 101, "BorShade", 1 |
    WS_CHILD | WS_VISIBLE, 8, 6, 109, 70
  CTEXT "Auguries of Innocence\nBy William Blake\n1757 - 1827",
    -1, 25, 46, 74, 24, WS_CHILD | WS_VISIBLE | WS_GROUP
END
```

LISTING 14.7

blake.str

```
STRINGTABLE LOADONCALL MOVEABLE DISCARDABLE
BEGIN
  IDS_Title,   "Auguries Of Innocence"
  IDS_Body+0,  "To see a world in a grain of sand,"
  IDS_Body+1,  "And a heaven in a wild flower,"
  IDS_Body+2,  "Hold infinity in the palm of your hand,"
  IDS_Body+3,  "And eternity in an hour."
  IDS_Body+4,  "A robin redbreast in a cage"
  IDS_Body+5,  "Puts all heaven in a rage."
  IDS_Body+6,  "A dove-house fill'd with doves and pigeons"
  IDS_Body+7,  "Shudders hell thro' all its regions."
  IDS_Body+8,  "A dog starv'd at his master's gate"
  IDS_Body+9,  "Predicts the ruin of the state."
  IDS_Body+10, "A horse misused upon the road"
  IDS_Body+11, "Calls to heaven for human blood."
  IDS_Body+12, "Each outcry of the hunted hare"
  IDS_Body+13, "A fibre from the brain does tear."
  IDS_Body+14, "A skylark wounded in the wing,"
  IDS_Body+15, "A cherubim does cease to sing."
  IDS_Body+16, "The game-cock clipt and arm'd for fight"
  IDS_Body+17, "Does the rising sun affright."
END
```

LISTING 14.8

blake.ico

```
BlakeIcon ICON
BEGIN
  '00 00 01 00 01 00 20 20 10 00 00 00 00 00 E8 02'
  '00 00 16 00 00 00 28 00 00 00 20 00 00 00 40 00'
  '00 00 01 00 04 00 00 00 00 00 80 02 00 00 00 00'
  '00 00 00 00 00 00 00 00 00 00 00 00 00 00 00 00'
  '00 00 00 00 80 00 00 80 00 00 00 80 80 00 80 00'
  '00 00 80 00 80 00 80 80 00 00 80 80 80 00 C0 C0'
```

LISTING 14.8

blake.ico (Continued)

```
'CØ ØØ ØØ ØØ FF ØØ ØØ FF ØØ ØØ ØØ FF FF ØØ FF ØØ'
'ØØ ØØ FF ØØ FF ØØ FF FF ØØ ØØ FF FF FF ØØ DD DD'
'DD DD BB 99 DD DD DD DD DD DD DD DD DD DD DD DD'
'DD DD DB BB 99 DD DD DD DD DD DD DD DD DD DD DD'
'DD DD DD DB BB 99 9D DD DD DD DD DD DD DD DD DD'
'DD DD DD DD BB BB B9 9D DD DD DD DD DD DD DD DD'
'DD DD DD DD DD BB BB B9 9D DD DD DD DD DD DD DD'
'DD DD DD DD DD DB BB BB B9 99 DD DD DD DD DD DD'
'DD DD DD DD DD DD 9B BB BB BB 99 DD DD DD DD DD'
'DD DD DD DD DD 99 BB BC BB BB BB 99 DD DD DD DD'
'DD DD DD DD 99 BB BC CB BB BB BD DD DD DD DD DD'
'DD DD DD 99 BB BB CB BB BB BD DD DD DD DD DD DD'
'DD DD 99 BB BB BC BB BB BD DD DD DD DD DD DD DD'
'DD 99 BB BB BC CB BB BB DD DD DD DD DD DD DD DD'
'99 BB BB BB CB BB BB DD DD DD DD DD DD DD DD 99'
'BB BB BB CC BB BB DD DD DD DD DD DD DD DD D9 BB'
'BB BB BC BB BB B9 9D DD DD DD DD DD DD DD DD DD'
'BB BB BB BB BB BB B9 9D DD DD DD DD DD DD DD DD'
'DD BB BB BB BB BB BB B9 9D DD DD DD DD DD DD DD'
'DD DD D9 BB BD BB BB BB B9 99 DD DD DD DD DD DD'
'DD D9 9B BB BB BC CC BB BB BB 99 DD DD DD DD DD'
'D9 9B BB BB BC CC BB BB BB BB BB 99 9D DD DD D9'
'9B BB BB BC CC BB BB BB BB BB 99 9D DD DD DD 9B'
'BB BB BB BB BB BB BB BB 99 99 DD DD DD DD DD D9'
'BB BB CC BB BB BB B9 99 DD DD DD DD DD DD DD D9'
'BB BB BC CB BB BB BB 99 DD DD DD DD DD DD DD DD'
'9B BB DB CC BB BB BB BD 9D DD DD DD DD DD DD DD'
'9B BB BB BC CB BB BB BB B9 9D DD DD DD DD DD DD'
'D9 BB BB BB CC CB BB BB BB D9 DD DD DD DD DD DD'
'D9 BB BB BB BB CC BB BB BB BB 9D DD DD DD DD DD'
'DD 9B BB BB BB BC CB BB BB BB B9 9D DD DD DD DD'
'DD 9B BB BB BB BB CC BB BB BB BB B9 DD DD DD DD'
'DD D9 BB BB BB BB BB BB BB BB BB 99 DD DD DD'
'DD D9 BB BB BB BB BB BB BB BB BB BB 9D ØØ ØØ'
'ØØ ØØ ØØ ØØ ØØ ØØ ØØ ØØ ØØ ØØ ØØ ØØ ØØ ØØ ØØ ØØ'
'ØØ ØØ ØØ ØØ ØØ ØØ ØØ ØØ ØØ ØØ ØØ ØØ ØØ ØØ ØØ ØØ'
'ØØ ØØ ØØ ØØ ØØ ØØ ØØ ØØ ØØ ØØ ØØ ØØ ØØ ØØ ØØ ØØ'
'ØØ ØØ ØØ ØØ ØØ ØØ ØØ ØØ ØØ ØØ ØØ ØØ ØØ ØØ ØØ ØØ'
'ØØ ØØ ØØ ØØ ØØ ØØ ØØ ØØ ØØ ØØ ØØ ØØ ØØ ØØ ØØ ØØ'
'ØØ ØØ ØØ ØØ ØØ ØØ ØØ ØØ ØØ ØØ ØØ ØØ ØØ ØØ ØØ ØØ'
'ØØ ØØ ØØ ØØ ØØ ØØ ØØ ØØ ØØ ØØ ØØ ØØ ØØ ØØ ØØ ØØ'
'ØØ ØØ ØØ ØØ ØØ ØØ ØØ ØØ ØØ ØØ ØØ ØØ ØØ ØØ'
```
END

Blake Stage 2: Using GDI Objects

Painting the window using only the default device context settings is not the best way to take advantage of Windows. Now it's time to learn how to alter the device context defaults, which means learning about GDI objects, so that you can exercise finer control over the drawing process.

To illustrate the general technique, I've decided to add font selection to the Blake application, to use more than a single font, and to draw a line in the window to emphasize the poem's title. These aren't big changes, but they do introduce a big change in programming perspective and technique.

If you examine Table 14.1, which lists device context attributes, you'll discover that there are really two sorts of device context attributes. The first kind of attribute is a simple value, such as the value for the background color, or the value for the window origin. Well, the window origin is actually two values, but still it is a very simple element. Most of these simple attributes are managed by feeding a number or two into a Windows function, usually a function with the prefix "Set." For example, the background color is specified using the SetBk-Color() function and the window origin is specified using the SetWindowOrg() function. Most simple values can be retrieved using "Get" functions, such as GetBkColor() and GetWindowOrg().

The second kind of device context attribute is much more complex, meaning that a single attribute specifies a group of related settings. For example, a Pen has a size, a color, and a style. Device context attributes that encompass multiple settings are called GDI objects. All of the GDI objects are listed in Table 14.3.

There are two slightly different ways to acquire a GDI object. The first way is to create the object, using one of the Create functions listed in Table 14.3. When you create a GDI object it is stored and manipulated by Windows, although you own it. The second way to get a GDI object is to ask Windows for a handle to one of its stock (meaning standard) GDI objects. Table 14.3 specifies which GDI objects can be acquired using Windows's GetStockObject() function, and the right column of Table 14.3 specifies the stock object identifiers for each type of GDI object.

Like other Windows resources, GDI objects must be managed very carefully, or unexpected, undesired behavior will occur. And when you misuse GDI objects the "failure" usually occurs a long time after the abuse, so such bugs can be difficult to isolate. The best defense against these bugs is a clear and reliable coding style that follows the rules that I'm about to describe.

First, let me sketch the general approach to using GDI objects. In almost all cases, your code for working with GDI objects will use the following blueprint:

- Create a GDI object (or get a stock GDI object).

- Select it into a device context, and save the handle of the previous object.

- Use the device context.

- Select the previous object into the device context.

- Delete the GDI object (except don't bother to delete a stock GDI object).

TABLE 14.3

GDI Objects

GDI Object	Creation/Acquisition Functions	Major Attributes and Stock Objects
Pens	CreatePen() CreatePenIndirect() GetStockObject()	Attributes: style, size, color. Stock objects: BLACK_PEN, WHITE_PEN, NULL_PEN.
Brushes	CreateSolidBrush() CreateHatchBrush() CreatePatternBrush() CreateBrushIndirect() CreateDIBPatternBrush() GetStockObject()	Attributes: style, color, hatching, bitmap. Stock objects: BLACK_BRUSH, DKGRAY_BRUSH, LTGRAY_BRUSH, NULL_BRUSH, WHITE_BRUSH.
Bitmaps	CreateBitmap() CreateCompatibleBitmap() CreateDiscardableBitmap() CreateDIBitmap() CreateBitmapIndirect() LoadBitmap()	Attributes: width, height, number of planes, number of bits per plane, plus additional information as specified by a BITMAPINFOHEADER struct for DI (device indepen- dent) bitmap.
Fonts	CreateFont() CreateFontIndirect() GetStockObject()	Attributes: width, height, escapement, orientation, weight, italics, underline, strikeout, character set, out- put characteristics, pitch, font family, font face name. Stock objects: ANSI_FIXED_FONT, ANSI_VAR_FONT, DEVICE_DEFAULT_FONT, OEM_FIXED_FONT, SYSTEM_FONT, SYSTEM_FIXED_FONT.
Palettes	CreatePalette() GetStockObject()	Attributes: the entries for the color palette. Stock objects: DEFAULT_PALETTE.
Regions	CreateRectRgn() CreateRectRgnIndirect() CreateEllipticRgn() CreateEllipticRgnIndirect() CreatePolygonRgn() CreatePolygonRgnIndirect() CreateRoundRgn()	Attributes: the size and shape of the region.

Now let me get more concrete, and recast the above blueprint in C pseudo-code. First, when you want to use a GDI object you often create two GDI object handles:

```
HGDIOBJ hGDIOBJ;
HGDIOBJ hOldGDIOBJ;
```

One handle will be for the object you create, and the other will save the handle of the object (of the same type) that was previously selected into the device context.

Next, create a GDI object using one of the Create... functions and save the handle of the created object:

```
hGDIOBJ = CreateSomething( . . . parameters . . . );
```

Simply creating a GDI object doesn't put it into action. To do that you must use the SelectObject() Windows function to specify that the object should be used in a device context. SelectObject() returns a handle for the previous object of the same type:

```
hOldGDIOBJ = SelectObject(hDC, hGDIOBJ);
```

At this point you can use the device context and its newly selected GDI object. When you are through using the device context you should reselect the device context's original GDI object (of the same type):

```
SelectObject(hDC, hOldGDIOBJ);
```

The final step is to delete the created GDI object, so that Windows is informed that it won't be used again. This enables Windows to free its resources.

```
DeleteObject(hGDIOBJ);
```

The two important rules to glean from this discussion are that you should always

- Deselect your GDI objects from their device context before you delete them

- Delete every GDI object that you create (use Windows's DeleteObject() function, not C++'s delete operator!)

There are two circumstances when these rules can be amended. The first is when you get a stock GDI object. You needn't delete a stock object, although in Windows version 3.0 and later it is harmless to delete a stock object. (In prior versions of Windows it was a serious error to delete a stock object.) The second exception is when a window has its own device context, which is specified by ORing the value CS_OWNDC into the window style. In an OWL application you usually do this by ORing CS_OWNDC into the style member of the WND-CLASS struct that is passed to your window class's GetWindowClass() procedure. (Be sure to call the TWindow class's GetWindowClass() before changing any element of the WNDCLASS struct.)

GDI Fonts

The GDI interface can manage four separate types of fonts:

- *Raster fonts*　Raster fonts operate quickly because the font file contains the bitpatterns for each character. Most display devices include several raster fonts, such as SYSTEM_FONT and SYSTEM_FIXED_FONT, so that standard window title and menu text can be output efficiently.

■ *Stroke fonts* Stroke fonts should only be used for output to devices that don't support bitmap operations, such as pen plotters. They work, in a technical sense, on a display or raster printer, but the resulting text is thin and unattractive.

■ *TrueType fonts* TrueType fonts are scalable, outline fonts. This means that they have high quality at any point size. TrueType fonts are only available in Windows version 3.1 and later.

■ *Device fonts* Device fonts really aren't managed by GDI, but instead are the device's responsibility. They include fonts that are resident in a printer, fonts that are added to a printer using font cartridges, and fonts that aren't directly supported by Windows, such as Adobe Type 1 fonts.

You can create a font and get its handle using the CreateFont() or Create-FontIndirect() functions. Both of these functions require detailed information about the font that you want to use. Some of the information that you need will be what you would expect, such as the name of the font, while other information requires more typographic expertise. The Blake Stage 2 application's Paint() function, which I will cover in detail soon, shows basic usage of the CreateFont() function.

Note that by creating a font, we don't mean actually drawing the outlines for every character in the font. In Windows lingo, creating a font simply informs Windows that you want to use a specific size, orientation, weight, and so on of one of the fonts that is in its repertoire. In this book, we'll entrust font design to the font foundaries.

One of the limitations of the Blake Stage 2 application is that the font names it uses are built into the application. This works for Windows 3.1 and higher because they always contain the three fonts that are used by Blake. But a better approach is to ask Windows for a list of available fonts, and then present that list to the user. This lets your application access all the fonts on your user's computer.

There are two ways to let the user of your application choose from a list of fonts. The first way is to use the ChooseFont() function, which is available only in Windows 3.1 and later. ChooseFont() creates the Select a Font dialog shown in Figure 14.8. This is a complete and convenient way to provide for font selection in your application. You can see exactly how to produce the Select a Font dialog in Borland's TTFont example application. Also, note that ChooseFont() is documented in Volume III of the Windows API reference supplied by Borland.

The second way to provide font selection in an application is to interrogate Windows for a list of available fonts. I find this technique less attractive now that we have ChooseFont(), but its advantage is that it works with Version 3.0 of Windows. You can see all the details in the font.cpp file in Borland's GDIDemo example application.

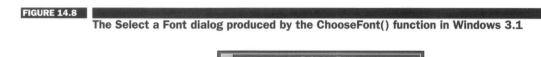

FIGURE 14.8

The Select a Font dialog produced by the ChooseFont() function in Windows 3.1

GDI Pens and Brushes

GDI pens and brushes are GDI objects that are used for graphical output. Brushes are used to fill the interiors of most filled objects, while Pens are used to draw lines and to draw the outlines of filled objects. The characteristics of GDI pens and brushes are listed in Table 14.1.

Pens are relatively simple. They have only three characteristics: size, color, and line style.

The Blake Stage 2 Font Menu

The new aspect of Blake Stage 2 is its ability to select the font used to display the poem. In the Blake application I kept things very simple by providing three font selection choices: Times New Roman, Arial, and Courier New. Because these are TrueType fonts, Blake is limited to running on Windows 3.1 systems. However, because these fonts are supplied with all copies of Windows 3.1 the Blake application will run on any 3.1 computer.

The TBlakeWindow class was augmented with three message handlers to respond to menu selections from the Font menu. Since all three are nearly the same, I'm only going to discuss the CMArial() handler.

```
//
// Arial menu selection
void TBlakeWindow::CMArial(RTMessage /*msg*/)
{
  CurFont = "Arial";
  CheckMenuItem();
  InvalidateRect(HWindow, NULL, TRUE);
}
```

The CMArial handler performs three functions: It sets the TBlakeWindow class's CurFont pointer to the name of the font Arial, it calls the CheckMenu-Item() member function to place a check mark next to Arial in the Font menu, and it causes the window to be redrawn by calling InvalidateRect(). The other two Font menu item handlers are the same, except for the name of the font that they select.

The TBlakeWindow class's CheckMenuItem() member function checks the menu item of the currently selected font and makes sure that the other two selections are unchecked.

```
void TBlakeWindow::CheckMenuItem()
{
  HMENU hMenu = GetMenu(HWindow);
  WORD chkT = MF_UNCHECKED;
  WORD chkA = MF_UNCHECKED;
  WORD chkC = MF_UNCHECKED;
  switch(CurFont[0]) {
    case 'T': chkT = MF_CHECKED; break;
    case 'A': chkA = MF_CHECKED; break;
    case 'C': chkC = MF_CHECKED; break;
  }
  ::CheckMenuItem(hMenu, CM_TRoman, MF_BYCOMMAND | chkT);
  ::CheckMenuItem(hMenu, CM_Arial, MF_BYCOMMAND | chkA);
  ::CheckMenuItem(hMenu, CM_Courier, MF_BYCOMMAND | chkC);
}
```

There are several reasonable strategies, but the approach that I chose was to set the check mark status of all three menu items each time that CheckMenu-Item() is called. The other common strategy is to remember the old selection, so it can be unchecked, and then place a check mark near the new selection.

The work in the TBlakeWindow class's CheckMenuItem() member function is done by the Windows CheckMenuItem() function. The C++ compiler can distinguish between these two functions, even though they have the same name, by their argument types. But to make things clearer I placed the :: scope resolution operator in front of the calls of the Windows functions. Some people advocate placing the :: scope resolution operator in front of all calls to global functions in C++ code, but to me that seems excessive. However in this case use of the scope resolution operator is a good idea because it helps clarify the code.

Windows's CheckMenuItem() requires three parameters: a handle for the menu, an indicator for which menu item should be altered, and a code indicating the action. The code indicates both how the menu item should be displayed (MF_CHECKED or MF_UNCHECKED) plus how the menu item is identified. You can specify a menu item either by its ordinal position in the menu, or by the command ID value that it sends when it is selected. I used the MF_BYCOM-MAND code because I supplied the menu command ID as the second argument.

If you supply the item's ordinal position you should instead use the MF_BYPO-SITION code. The CheckMenuItem() code shown here is very similar to the EnableMenuItem() requests found in the SearchMenu() function in the Find Files application. See the top of Listing 13.7 (search.cpp in Find Files Stage 5).

The Blake Stage 2 Paint() Function

The Blake Stage 2 Paint() function differs from Stage 1 in its creation and use of three GDI objects. These GDI objects are a handle to a 15 point font, a handle to a 20 point bold font, and a handle to a 3 pixel wide pen. The 20 point bold font and the pen are used to draw the title of William Blake's poem centered above the poem text. You can see how these resources are used in Figure 14.9, which shows the Blake Stage 2 application.

FIGURE 14.9

Three instances of the Blake Stage 2 application. The window on the left shows the full first verse of Blake's poem in Times New Roman; the window on the upper right shows part of the verse in Arial; and the window on the bottom right shows part of the verse in Courier New, with the Font menu pulled down to show the check mark on the Courier New menu item.

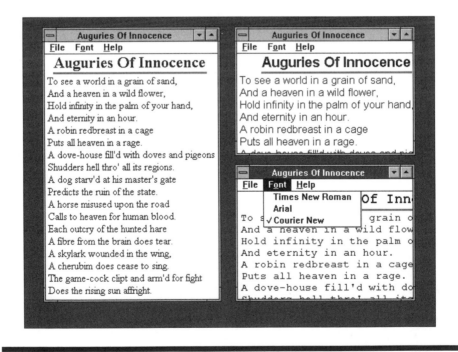

Since the most important new feature in Stage 2 is the creation and use of the resources, let me start my discussion of the Stage 2 Paint() procedure by examining the creation of the font used in the body of the poem. (The complete source code of Paint() appears in the "Stage 2 Source Code" section later in this chapter.) Fonts are usually specified in points, where a point is a typographic term representing approximately 1/72 inch. Often 10 or 12 point fonts are used for the body of a book. So first let's detour for a moment to think about what size of font we want.

It's important to use some absolute measure for font sizes, because they must be legible. On a VGA a 20 pixel font is easily readable, but on other displays a 20 pixel font size isn't a good choice. Table 14.4 shows the height of a 20 pixel font on several common graphics devices. As you can see in Table 14.4, a 20 pixel character would be over half an inch tall on a CGA, but too tiny to be legible on a laser printer.

TABLE 14.4

Pixel Sizes on Different Devices

Device	Vertical Pixels	Typical Height	Vertical Pixels/Inch	Height of a 20 Pixel Character
CGA display	200	6 in.	33	0.6 in.
EGA display	350	6 in.	58	0.34 in.
VGA display	480	6 in.	80	0.25 in.
Super VGA	600	6 in.	100	0.20 in.
300 DPI laser printer	2400	8 in.	300	0.066 in.
600 DPI laser printer	4800	8 in.	600	0.033 in.

The solution is to make your code more device independent. One way is to use one of the fixed-size mapping modes, such as the MM_TWIPS mode, but that may be more effort than is justified. An easier solution is to find out more about the display device, so you can make more informed size selections. In Windows you do this with the GetDeviceCaps() function. GetDeviceCaps() can return about 25 separate pieces of information about the device; consult the Windows API reference manual citation for GetDeviceCaps() for a full list.

For producing figures with a constant size, the two useful device capabilities are LOGPIXELSX and LOGPIXELSY, which are the pixels per inch in the X and Y directions. Actually, these two capabilities refer to a logical inch, not to a true physical inch. A logical inch is an inch that is inflated to account for the poor resolution of the early PC display adapters. On an EGA, the logical inch is inflated about 40 percent, while it is accurate on a laser printer. This inflation makes it possible for 10 and 12 point fonts, which are easily readable on paper, to also be readable on a video display.

In the Blake Stage 2 application I used the LOGPIXELSY capability to determine how many pixels lie in a vertical inch. By dividing that value by 72 I computed the number of pixels in a typographic point ($1/72$ in.). Here's the declaration of the dPixPerPoint variable:

```
double dPixPerPoint = GetDeviceCaps(PaintDC, LOGPIXELSY) / 72.0;
```

If you multiply dPixPerPoint times the desired size of something in points, you'll get the size in pixels.

Now that we know how to work with device independent sizes, let's look at the CreateFont() call to Windows that creates the 15 point font used for the body of the poem:

```
HFONT BodyFont = CreateFont(15*dPixPerPoint,
    Ø, Ø, Ø,       // ht,wid,esc,ori
    Ø, Ø, Ø, Ø,    // wt,ital,ul,so
    ANSI_CHARSET, OUT_DEFAULT_PRECIS,
    CLIP_DEFAULT_PRECIS, DEFAULT_QUALITY,
    DEFAULT_PITCH, CurFont);
```

The above call to CreateFont() has only two parameters that matter, the first and the last. All the other parameters are set to their default value, and you should consult the Windows API reference for more information on these parameters. The two important parameters are the first, which is the height of the font in logical units, and the last, which is the name of the font. Since Blake uses the default device context coordinate system, which operates in pixels, the number used for the height will specify the height in pixels. That's why I multiplied the desired height in points, 15, times dPixPerPoint, to produce the height in pixels.

The declaration of the bold font for the poem title is the same, except that a 20 point font is created and I set the font weight to 700, which is the value suggested by the Windows API reference manual, for creating a bold font.

The third object created in the Blake Stage 2 Paint() procedure is a pen for drawing a heavy line under the title.

```
HPEN hPen = CreatePen(PS_SOLID, 3, RGB(128, 128, 128));
```

There are two things about the pen that can cause problems. The first is its fixed size, 3 pixels. This will work reasonably on most displays, but it would be a poor choice for most printers. This difficulty would be easy to fix by specifying its size in points and then multiplying by dPixPerPoint to convert to pixels. The second potential problem is the color of the pen. I used Windows's RGB function to specify a color by specifying its red, green, and blue components. The range for each component is 0 to 255. I specified 128 for each color, which is a medium gray.

But what if the window background is gray? If it is, then the pen will be invisible. One other way to choose colors is to use the GetSysColors() function, which will return the color for one of the predefined interface elements. These colors are usually distinct from one another. This solution will be discussed further under "The Blake Stage 4 Paint() Function," later in this chapter. Another solution is to compare your desired color with the current window background color. This is a little tricky because colors that aren't identical numerically may be indistinguishable to the eye. The general problem veers directly into psychophysics and perception, but a simple solution is to compute the three-dimensional distance between the pen color and the background color. Here's the formula for calculating the 3-D distance between two RGB colors:

$$dist = \sqrt{(R_{pen} - R_{bkg})^2 + (G_{pen} - G_{bkg})^2 + (B_{pen} - B_{bkg})^2}$$

If the color values range from 0 to 255, the distance will range from 0 to 441, with 0 meaning identical and 441 meaning maximally different. (The maximum distance is 441 because it is the square root of $255^2 + 255^2 + 255^2$.) A reasonable minimum distance to require is 100 if you want to make sure that two colors are easily distinguishable.

The next problem in Blake Stage 2 is where to draw the poem title. What I want to do is draw the title centered above the body of the poem. But how wide is the poem? It's hard to know the width until it's been drawn once. What I decided to do was to leave room for the title, and then draw it after drawing the body of the poem. While drawing the poem body, I measured the length of each line so I could find the widest line. But even skipping over the title presents a small problem—how tall is the title? The solution to this is to select the title font into the PaintDC device context, measure the height of some typical text, and then add some space for the underlining. Thus I arrived at the following code whose sole purpose is to leave a blank area at the top of the window for eventual use by the title of the poem:

```
// leave room for poem title in the window
// (can't draw it now, don't know the width yet)
OldFont = (HFONT)SelectObject(PaintDC, HeadFont);
txtExtent = GetTextExtent(PaintDC, "a", 1);
y = HIWORD(txtExtent) + 6;   // + 6 for the underlining
```

The other important aspect of this code is that it keeps track of what font was originally selected in the device context. Remember that the old font must be reselected into the device context before we release the device context and before we delete the GDI object that we have created.

Now let's look at the setup for actually drawing the poem. The first step is to select the correct font into the device context, and then to find out the size of things in that font. Here's the setup code:

```
// body of the poem
SelectObject(PaintDC, BodyFont);
txtExtent = GetTextExtent(PaintDC, "1", 1);
ht = HIWORD(txtExtent);
x = LOWORD(txtExtent)/2;
```

Except for the SelectObject() call that tells Windows to use the font that we've specified for the poem body, the above code looks just like the corresponding code in Blake Stage 1.

The next step is the loop that writes the strings to the device context:

```
for(i=0; i< IDS_nStrings; i++) {
  int w, n;
  line[0] = '\0'; // in case LoadString() fails
  LoadString(hInstance, IDS_Body+i, line, sizeof(line));
  n = strlen(line);
  w = x + GetTextExtent(PaintDC, line, n);
  if (w > nMaxWidth)
    nMaxWidth = w;
  TextOut(PaintDC, x, y, line, strlen(line));
  y += ht;
}
```

This code is also similar to the corresponding code in Blake Stage 1, except that the width of each string is measured, so that we determine the width of the widest line.

Now that the body of the poem has been drawn, it is time to return to the title. There are a few chores to perform: select the title font into the PaintDC device context, measure the width of the title, and compute the X position of the title based on its width and the width of the widest line from the poem. Here's the code that performs these chores:

```
// place poem title in the window, centered above
// the body of the poem
SelectObject(PaintDC, HeadFont);
LoadString(hInstance, IDS_Title, line, sizeof(line));
txtExtent = GetTextExtent(PaintDC, line, strlen(line));
x = (nMaxWidth - (int)LOWORD(txtExtent)) / 2; // center
TextOut(PaintDC, x, 0, line, strlen(line));
y = HIWORD(txtExtent) + 3;
```

The last drawing in the Blake Stage 2 Paint() procedure is to underline the title. That's pretty easy, as shown by the following code.

```
// underline poem title
OldPen = (HPEN)SelectObject(PaintDC, hPen);
MoveTo(PaintDC, x, y);
LineTo(PaintDC, x+(int)LOWORD(txtExtent), y);
```

Note that I am careful to save the handle of the PaintDC's original pen, as it must be restored at the end of Paint().

The last task of the Blake Stage 2 Paint() procedure is to clean up all the GDI resources. All the created resources must be deleted, and the PaintDC device context must be restored to its original state. Here is the Paint() code that performs these chores:

```
// cleanup
SelectObject(PaintDC, OldFont);
SelectObject(PaintDC, OldPen);
DeleteObject(BodyFont);
DeleteObject(HeadFont);
DeleteObject(hPen);
```

Note that I selected the original GDI objects back into the PaintDC before I deleted the GDI objects that I created in the beginning of Paint(). The order matters. Also recall that when I talk about deleting a GDI object, I'm using Windows jargon, where delete means use the DeleteObject() Windows function, not C++ jargon, where delete means the delete operator.

Stage 2 Source Code

Table 14.5 summarizes the changes in Stage 2 of the Blake application, and it specifies where you can find the listing for each file in the application. You'll notice these changes specifically in Listings 14.9–14.12. I've chosen to repeat only four of the eight Blake source files, because the other four are unchanged (or only trivially changed). Figures 14.6 and 14.7, which documented the file and class organization of the Blake Stage 1 application, are also valid for Blake Stage 2, so they aren't repeated here.

TABLE 14.5

Blake Stage 2 Listings

File	Listing	Stage 2 Summary
blake.h	14.9	The TBlakeWindow class has a new SetupWindow() member function; there are new message handlers for the Font menu items, and there is a CheckMenuItem() procedure for managing check marks on the Font menu.
resource.h	14.10	Contains new identifiers for the Font menu.
blake.cpp	14.11	New message handlers to manage the Font menu selections; a new CheckMenuItem() procedure for checking items in the Font menu, and a more interesting Paint() procedure.
blake.rc	14.4	Unchanged since Stage 1.
blake.mnu	14.12	Contains a new Font menu.
about.dlg	14.6	Unchanged since Stage 1, except that the label "Stage 1" is changed to "Stage 2."
blake.str	14.7	Unchanged since Stage 1.
blake.ico	14.8	Unchanged since Stage 1.

LISTING 14.9

blake.h

```
//
// the Blake Application class
//
class TBlakeApp : public TApplication {
  public:
    TBlakeApp(LPSTR name, HINSTANCE hInstance, HINSTANCE hPrevInstance,
      LPSTR lpCmdLine, int nShow) :
      TApplication(name, hInstance, hPrevInstance, lpCmdLine, nShow)
    {
      return;
    }
    virtual void InitMainWindow();
};


//
// the Blake Window class
//
class TBlakeWindow : public TWindow {
  public:
    // constructor
    TBlakeWindow(PTWindowsObject pParent, LPSTR pTitle);

    // window class members
    LPSTR GetClassName() {
      return "TBlakeWindow2";
    }
    void GetWindowClass(WNDCLASS& rWndClass);

    // last-minute init
    void SetupWindow()
    {
      CheckMenuItem();
    }

    // Paint the window
    void Paint(HDC PaintDC, PAINTSTRUCT& ps);

    // message handlers
    virtual void CMQuit(RTMessage msg) =
      [CM_FIRST + CM_Quit];
    virtual void CMAbout(RTMessage msg) =
      [CM_FIRST + CM_About];
    virtual void CMTRoman(RTMessage msg) =
      [CM_FIRST + CM_TRoman];
    virtual void CMArial(RTMessage msg) =
      [CM_FIRST + CM_Arial];
    virtual void CMCourier(RTMessage msg) =
      [CM_FIRST + CM_Courier];

    // manage check marks on the menu bar
    void CheckMenuItem();

  protected:
```

LISTING 14.9

blake.h (Continued)

```
    LPSTR CurFont;
};
```

LISTING 14.10

resource.h

```
//
// Blake App Resource Constants
//

// Menu Items
#define CM_Quit       101  // File menu
#define CM_About      102  // Help menu
#define CM_TRoman     103  // Font Times Roman
#define CM_Arial      104  // Font Arial
#define CM_Courier    105  // Font Courier

// Strings
#define IDS_Title     50
#define IDS_Body      51
#define IDS_nStrings  18
```

LISTING 14.11

blake.cpp

```
#include <string.h>
#define STRICT
#define WIN31
#include <owl.h>
#include <bwcc.h>
#include "resource.h"
#include "blake.h"

//
// Blake App, create the main window
//
void TBlakeApp::InitMainWindow()
{
  char title[100];
  BWCCGetVersion();
  LoadString(hInstance, IDS_Title, title, sizeof(title));
  MainWindow = new TBlakeWindow(NULL, title);
}

//
// Blake Window, constructor
//
```

LISTING 14.11

blake.cpp (Continued)

```cpp
TBlakeWindow::TBlakeWindow(PTWindowsObject pParent, LPSTR pTitle) :
  TWindow(pParent, pTitle),
  CurFont("Times New Roman")
{
  AssignMenu("BlakeMenu");
  return;
}


//
// create a Windows class for the Blake Window
//
void TBlakeWindow::GetWindowClass(WNDCLASS& rWndClass)
{
  TWindow::GetWindowClass(rWndClass);
  rWndClass.hIcon = LoadIcon(GetApplication()->hInstance, "BlakeIcon");
  if (rWndClass.hIcon == NULL) {
    MessageBox(HWindow, "Bad Icon Load", "icon", MB_ICONSTOP);
    rWndClass.hIcon = LoadIcon(0, IDI_APPLICATION);
  }
}


//
// Paint
//
void TBlakeWindow::Paint(HDC PaintDC, PAINTSTRUCT & /*ps*/)
{
  HINSTANCE hInstance = GetApplication()->hInstance;
  HFONT OldFont;
  HPEN OldPen;
  DWORD txtExtent;
  char line[100];
  int i, ht, x, y;
  int nMaxWidth = 0;
  double dPixPerPoint = GetDeviceCaps(PaintDC, LOGPIXELSY) / 72.0;

  HFONT BodyFont = CreateFont(15*dPixPerPoint, 0, 0, 0, // ht,wid,esc,ori
    0, 0, 0, 0, // wt,ital,ul,so
    ANSI_CHARSET, OUT_DEFAULT_PRECIS,
    CLIP_DEFAULT_PRECIS, DEFAULT_QUALITY,
    DEFAULT_PITCH, CurFont);

  HFONT HeadFont = CreateFont(20*dPixPerPoint, 0, 0, 0, // ht,wid,esc,ori
    700, 0, 0, 0, // wt,ital,ul,so
    ANSI_CHARSET, OUT_DEFAULT_PRECIS,
    CLIP_DEFAULT_PRECIS, DEFAULT_QUALITY,
    DEFAULT_PITCH, CurFont);

  HPEN hPen = CreatePen(PS_SOLID, 3, RGB(128, 128, 128));

  // leave room for poem title in the window
  // (can't draw it now, don't know the width yet)
  OldFont = (HFONT)SelectObject(PaintDC, HeadFont);
  txtExtent = GetTextExtent(PaintDC, "a", 1);
```

LISTING 14.11

blake.cpp (Continued)

```cpp
    y = HIWORD(txtExtent) + 6;

    // body of the poem
    SelectObject(PaintDC, BodyFont);
    txtExtent = GetTextExtent(PaintDC, "1", 1);
    ht = HIWORD(txtExtent);
    x = LOWORD(txtExtent)/2;
    for(i=0; i< IDS_nStrings; i++) {
      int w, n;
      line[0] = '\0'; // in case LoadString() fails
      LoadString(hInstance, IDS_Body+i, line, sizeof(line));
      n = strlen(line);
      w = x + GetTextExtent(PaintDC, line, n);
      if (w > nMaxWidth)
        nMaxWidth = w;
      TextOut(PaintDC, x, y, line, strlen(line));
      y += ht;
    }

    // place poem title in the window, centered above
    // the body of the poem
    SelectObject(PaintDC, HeadFont);
    LoadString(hInstance, IDS_Title, line, sizeof(line));
    txtExtent = GetTextExtent(PaintDC, line, strlen(line));
    x = (nMaxWidth - (int)LOWORD(txtExtent)) / 2; // center
    TextOut(PaintDC, x, 0, line, strlen(line));
    y = HIWORD(txtExtent) + 3;

    // underline poem title
    OldPen = (HPEN)SelectObject(PaintDC, hPen);
    MoveTo(PaintDC, x, y);
    LineTo(PaintDC, x+(int)LOWORD(txtExtent), y);

    // cleanup
    SelectObject(PaintDC, OldFont);
    SelectObject(PaintDC, OldPen);
    DeleteObject(BodyFont);
    DeleteObject(HeadFont);
    DeleteObject(hPen);
}

//
// handle the quit menu command
//
void TBlakeWindow::CMQuit(RTMessage /*msg*/)
{
    PostQuitMessage(0);
}

//
// handle the about menu command
//
void TBlakeWindow::CMAbout(RTMessage /*msg*/)
```

LISTING 14.11 ■■■

blake.cpp (Continued)

```cpp
{
  GetApplication()->ExecDialog(new TDialog(this, "AboutDialog"));
}

//
// Times menu selection
void TBlakeWindow::CMTRoman(RTMessage /*msg*/)
{
  CurFont = "Times New Roman";
  CheckMenuItem();
  InvalidateRect(HWindow, NULL, TRUE);
}

//
// Arial menu selection
void TBlakeWindow::CMArial(RTMessage /*msg*/)
{
  CurFont = "Arial";
  CheckMenuItem();
  InvalidateRect(HWindow, NULL, TRUE);
}

//
// Courier menu selection
void TBlakeWindow::CMCourier(RTMessage /*msg*/)
{
  CurFont = "Courier New";
  CheckMenuItem();
  InvalidateRect(HWindow, NULL, TRUE);
}

//
// manage the check marks in the Font menu
//
void TBlakeWindow::CheckMenuItem()
{
  HMENU hMenu = GetMenu(HWindow);
  WORD chkT = MF_UNCHECKED;
  WORD chkA = MF_UNCHECKED;
  WORD chkC = MF_UNCHECKED;
  switch(CurFont[0]) {
    case 'T': chkT = MF_CHECKED; break;
    case 'A': chkA = MF_CHECKED; break;
    case 'C': chkC = MF_CHECKED; break;
  }
  ::CheckMenuItem(hMenu, CM_TRoman, MF_BYCOMMAND | chkT);
  ::CheckMenuItem(hMenu, CM_Arial, MF_BYCOMMAND | chkA);
  ::CheckMenuItem(hMenu, CM_Courier, MF_BYCOMMAND | chkC);
}

//
// WIN MAIN
//
```

LISTING 14.11

blake.cpp (Continued)

```
int PASCAL WinMain(HINSTANCE hInstance, HINSTANCE hPrevInstance,
  LPSTR lpCmdLine, int nShow)
{
  TBlakeApp blakeApp("Blake Application", hInstance, hPrevInstance,
    lpCmdLine, nShow);
  blakeApp.Run();
  return blakeApp.Status;
}
```

LISTING 14.12

blake.mnu

```
BlakeMenu MENU
BEGIN
  POPUP "&File"
  BEGIN
    MENUITEM "E&xit\tAlt+F4", CM_Quit
  END
  POPUP "F&ont"
  BEGIN
    MENUITEM "Times New Roman", CM_TRoman
    MENUITEM "Arial", CM_Arial
    MENUITEM "Courier New", CM_Courier
  END
  POPUP "&Help"
  BEGIN
    MENUITEM "&About...", CM_About
  END
END
```

Blake Stage 3: Scrolling the Window

Scrolling is a desirable feature in most Windows applications, because the information that you are presenting is often too large to fit in a window. Windows provides some help for scrolling—it has scroll bar controls that are endowed with some intelligent behavior—but Windows also leaves much of the work to you. Or rather, Windows leaves much of the work to OWL. Borland's OWL class library contains a TScroller class that can handle most of the details of scrolling.

OWL's TScroller Class

The TScroller class is designed to manage much of the work of scrolling. But it is up to you to specify the X and Y scrolling ranges, and to specify how much the window should scroll for each request to scroll one line. Once these parameters have been specified, scrolling will happen automatically because OWL's TWindow class, which has a pointer to a TScroller object, will make sure that the TScroller object is involved in window painting.

But the Blake Stage 3 application has one small difficulty with this approach: It doesn't know how large an area is occupied by the poem until it has drawn the poem. And, the size of the poem changes when the poem is drawn in a different font. This problem means that Blake Stage 3 informs the TScroller object too late about the size of the scroll area, which causes some extra display redrawing. I'll repair this feature in Stage 4, where I'll also add the ability to select individual lines of the poem using the mouse. But for now let's just get a working program that scrolls, and then we'll worry about refinement later.

First, as usual, some terminology. I'm sure you've used scroll bars in a Windows application, but do you know all of the terms? The handle in the middle that you can drag is called the *thumb*, the arrows at either end are called, well, the arrows. Figure 14.10 shows the Blake Stage 3 application with labels on the vertical scroll bar.

FIGURE 14.10

The parts of a scroll bar

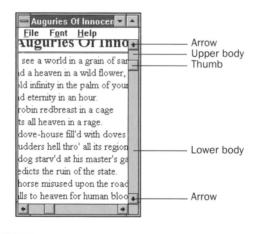

When you use the mouse to press any area on the scroll bar, Windows sends either the WM_VSCROLL or WM_HSCROLL message. The word parameter (wParam) codes exactly what you pressed, as shown in Figure 14.11. When you release the mouse button, a completion message is also sent. Also note that as you are dragging the thumb a succession of SB_THUMBTRACK messages are sent. I'm mentioning these messages so that you have a general understanding of what's happening, but if you use OWL's TScroller class, you usually won't need to pay attention to these individual messages.

FIGURE 14.11

The wParam codes of the WM_VSCROLL and WM_HSCROLL messages. The figure doesn't show the SB_TOP and SB_BOTTOM wParam codes, which indicate scrolling to the extreme of the scroll bar.

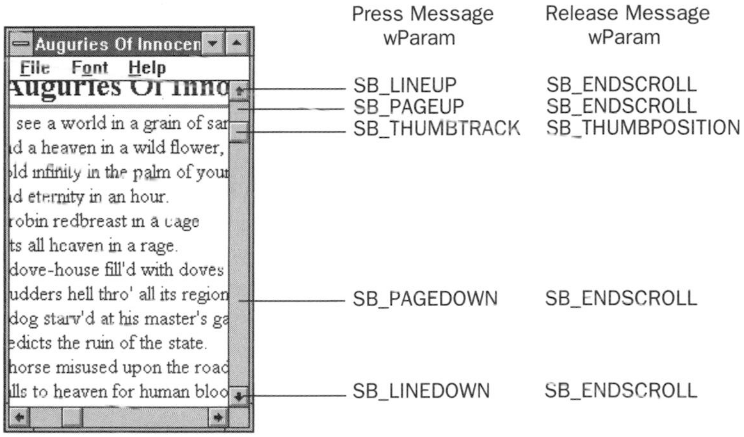

	Press Message wParam	Release Message wParam
	SB_LINEUP	SB_ENDSCROLL
	SB_PAGEUP	SB_ENDSCROLL
	SB_THUMBTRACK	SB_THUMBPOSITION
	SB_PAGEDOWN	SB_ENDSCROLL
	SB_LINEDOWN	SB_ENDSCROLL

Adding Scrolling to Blake

There are just a few things that you need to do to add scrolling to enable the Blake application to have a scrolling window. The first two chores are performed by the constructor, which changes the window style to support scrolling, and also creates the TScroller object that manages most of the scrolling details. Here is the Stage 2 TBlakeWindow constructor:

```
TBlakeWindow::TBlakeWindow(PTWindowsObject pParent, LPSTR pTitle) :
  TWindow(pParent, pTitle),
  CurFont("Times New Roman"),
  nPixWidth(Ø),
  nPixHeight(Ø),
  nXunit(1Ø),
  nYunit(1Ø)
{
  AssignMenu("BlakeMenu");
  Attr.Style |= WS_VSCROLL | WS_HSCROLL;
  Scroller = new TScroller(this, nXunit, nYunit, Ø, Ø);
}
```

The two important scrolling-related lines are in the body of the constructor. The first ORs-in WS_VSCROLL and WS_HSCROLL to the Style field of the attribute. This lets the window have scroll bars. The second is the creation of a new TScroller object, whose address is assigned to the Scroller member of the TWindow class. When Scroller is non-null, the TWindow class assumes it points at a TScroller object, and it uses that object to implement scrolling. The TScroller object is constructed with five arguments: a pointer to the window being scrolled; the X and Y scroll units, which specify how many pixels to scroll each time a scroll-one-line message is received; and the X and Y scroll ranges. The X and Y scroll ranges are set to zero because when the TBlakeWindow is constructed it isn't known how much space will be occupied by the poem, so it's not possible to know the scrolling range. Thus the scrolling range must be set later. (In an application where the size of the active region were known, it would be specified when the scroller was created. In Blake the size of the poem isn't known until the poem is drawn, and the size changes when the font changes.)

The Blake Stage 3 TBlakeWindow constructor also shows that the TBlake-Window class has some new data members. These include nPixWidth and nPix-Height, which store the size of the drawing (in pixels), plus nXunit and nYunit, which store the X and Y scroll units discussed above. The X and Y scroll units are arbitrarily set to 10, because scrolling the window in 10 pixel increments looks about right. A less arbitrary selection would relate the scroll units to the line size and the average character width.

As I've just mentioned, the TBlakeWindow constructor doesn't set the scrolling range because it doesn't know how large the poem will be. That's why the TBlakeWindow has a function called AdjustScroller(). AdjustScroller() is called whenever the TBlakeWindow's Paint() procedure notices that the poem has changed size. Other than keeping track of the poem height and width and calling AdjustScroller() when they change, Paint() is unchanged, and I'm not going to talk about it here. See Listing 14.14 for the details. But it is worthwhile to examine AdjustScroller().

```
void TBlakeWindow::AdjustScroller()
{
  RECT r;
  GetClientRect(HWindow, &r);
  Scroller->SetRange((nPixWidth - (r.right - r.left))/nXunit + 1,
    (nPixHeight - (r.bottom - r.top))/nYunit + 1);
}
```

The AdjustScroller() function is actually called from two places in the Blake application. I've mentioned the first place, Paint(), which calls Adjust-Scroller() when the size of the poem changes. AdjustScroller() is also called from the WMSize() member function, which is activated (in response to the WM_SIZE message) each time the size of the window changes.

A Keyboard Interface to Scrolling

The changes already outlined provide a perfectly good mouse-controlled scrolling capability for the Blake Stage 3 application. But what about the keyboard? Different applications have different requirements, so there isn't a uniform way to use the keyboard for scrolling. In the Blake application I decided to make the keypad's up and down arrows do the same thing as clicking on the scroll bar's arrows, and I decided to make the PgUp and PgDn keys do the same thing as clicking on the body of the scroll bar. The Home and End keys scroll to the extremes of the range.

The key to creating a keyboard interface is to catch the WM_KEYDOWN message. In the Blake application the WMKeyDown() member of TBlakeWindow handles the WM_KEYDOWN messages. The WMKeyDown() function gets a virtual key code in WParam and an assortment of flag bits in LParam. (The virtual key codes are listed in Windows.h.) In the Blake application's WMKeyDown() function the key codes in the message's WParam are compared with the keypad's arrow, PgUp, PgDn, Home, and End keys. When a match is detected, Windows's SendMessage() function is called to send an appropriate scroll bar message to the window.

For example, when WMKeyDown() detects the VK_END key, it executes the following code:

```
SendMessage(HWindow, WM_VSCROLL, SB_BOTTOM, 0L);
```

Because the keyboard interface receives keyboard messages and then reissues these messages as scroll bar messages, it doesn't add much complexity to the Blake application. The full code of the TBlakeWindow application's WMKeyDown() function is shown in blake.cpp.

Stage 3 Source Code

Table 14.6 summarizes the changes in the Blake Stage 3 application, and it specifies where you can find the listing for each file in the application. You'll notice these changes specifically in Listings 14.13 and 14.14. I've repeated only two of the eight Blake source files, because the other four are unchanged (or only trivially changed). Figures 14.6 and 14.7, which documented the file and class organization of the Blake Stage 1 application, are also valid for Blake Stage 3, so they aren't repeated here.

TABLE 14.6

Blake Stage 3 Listings

File	Listing	Stage 3 Summary
blake.h	14.13	The TBlakeWindow class has new data and function members to assist with scrolling.
resource.h	14.10	Unchanged since Stage 2.
blake.cpp	14.14	The TBlakeWindow class has a new AdjustScroller() function to set the scrolling range, a new WMSize() function to manage window size changes, new data members to record the active window size and scrolling units, and slight changes to the constructor and Paint() to accommodate scrolling.
blake.rc	14.4	Unchanged since Stage 1.
blake.mnu	14.12	Unchanged since Stage 2.
about.dlg	14.6	Unchanged since Stage 1, except that the label "Stage 1" is changed to "Stage 3."
blake.str	14.7	Unchanged since Stage 1.
blake.ico	14.8	Unchanged since Stage 1.

LISTING 14.13

blake.h

```
//
// the Blake Application class
//
class TBlakeApp : public TApplication {
  public:
    TBlakeApp(LPSTR name, HINSTANCE hInstance, HINSTANCE hPrevInstance,
      LPSTR lpCmdLine, int nShow) :
      TApplication(name, hInstance, hPrevInstance, lpCmdLine, nShow)
    {
      return;
    }
    virtual void InitMainWindow();
};


//
// the Blake Window class
//
class TBlakeWindow : public TWindow {
  public:
    // constructor
    TBlakeWindow(PTWindowsObject pParent, LPSTR pTitle);

    // window class members
    LPSTR GetClassName() {
      return "TBlakeWindow3";
    }
    void GetWindowClass(WNDCLASS& rWndClass);

    // last-minute init
    void SetupWindow()
    {
      CheckMenuItem();
    }

    // Paint the window
    void Paint(HDC PaintDC, PAINTSTRUCT& ps);

    // menu message handlers
    virtual void CMQuit(RTMessage msg) =
      [CM_FIRST + CM_Quit];
    virtual void CMAbout(RTMessage msg) =
      [CM_FIRST + CM_About];
    virtual void CMTRoman(RTMessage msg) =
      [CM_FIRST + CM_TRoman];
    virtual void CMArial(RTMessage msg) =
      [CM_FIRST + CM_Arial];
    virtual void CMCourier(RTMessage msg) =
      [CM_FIRST + CM_Courier];

    // handle the size message
    void WMSize(TMessage &msg) =
      [WM_FIRST + WM_SIZE];
```

LISTING 14.13

blake.h (Continued)

```
      // provide a keyboard interface for scrolling
      void WMKeyDown(TMessage &msg) =
        [WM_FIRST + WM_KEYDOWN];

    protected:
      // manage check marks on the menu bar
      void CheckMenuItem();

      // adjust the TScroller
      void AdjustScroller();

      LPSTR CurFont;   // name of cur font
      int nPixHeight;  // height of drawing
      int nPixWidth;   // width of drawing
      int nXunit;      // X scroll step
      int nYunit;      // Y scroll step
  };
```

LISTING 14.14

blake.cpp

```
#include <string.h>
#include <stdio.h>
#define STRICT
#define WIN31
#include <owl.h>
#include <bwcc.h>
#include "resource.h"
#include "blake.h"

//
// Blake App, create the main window
//
void TBlakeApp::InitMainWindow()
{
  char title[100];
  BWCCGetVersion();
  LoadString(hInstance, IDS_Title, title, sizeof(title));
  MainWindow = new TBlakeWindow(NULL, title);
}

//
// Blake Window, constructor
//
TBlakeWindow::TBlakeWindow(PTWindowsObject pParent, LPSTR pTitle) :
  TWindow(pParent, pTitle),
  CurFont("Times New Roman"),
  nPixWidth(0),
  nPixHeight(0),
  nXunit(10),
```

LISTING 14.14

blake.cpp (Continued)

```
  nYunit(1Ø)
{
  AssignMenu("BlakeMenu");
  Attr.Style |= WS_VSCROLL | WS_HSCROLL;
  Scroller = new TScroller(this, nXunit, nYunit, Ø, Ø);
}


//
// create a Windows class for the Blake Window
//
void TBlakeWindow::GetWindowClass(WNDCLASS& rWndClass)
{
  TWindow::GetWindowClass(rWndClass);
  rWndClass.hIcon = LoadIcon(GetApplication()->hInstance, "BlakeIcon");
  if (rWndClass.hIcon == NULL) {
    MessageBox(HWindow, "Bad Icon Load", "icon", MB_ICONSTOP);
    rWndClass.hIcon = LoadIcon(Ø, IDI_APPLICATION);
  }
}


//
// Tell the scroller the new settings
//
void TBlakeWindow::AdjustScroller()
{
  RECT r;
  GetClientRect(HWindow, &r);
  Scroller->SetRange((nPixWidth - r.right)/nXunit + 1,
    (nPixHeight - r.bottom)/nYunit + 1);
}


//
// Paint
//
void TBlakeWindow::Paint(HDC PaintDC, PAINTSTRUCT & /*ps*/)
{
  HINSTANCE hInstance = GetApplication()->hInstance;
  HFONT OldFont;
  HPEN OldPen;
  DWORD txtExtent;
  char line[1ØØ];
  int i, ht, x, y;
  int nMaxWidth = Ø;
  double dPixPerPoint = GetDeviceCaps(PaintDC, LOGPIXELSY) / 72.Ø;

  HFONT BodyFont = CreateFont(15*dPixPerPoint, Ø, Ø, Ø, // ht,wid,esc,ori
    Ø, Ø, Ø, Ø, // wt,ital,ul,so
    ANSI_CHARSET, OUT_DEFAULT_PRECIS,
    CLIP_DEFAULT_PRECIS, DEFAULT_QUALITY,
    DEFAULT_PITCH, CurFont);

  HFONT HeadFont = CreateFont(2Ø*dPixPerPoint, Ø, Ø, Ø, // ht,wid,esc,ori
    7ØØ, Ø, Ø, Ø, // wt,ital,ul,so
```

LISTING 14.14

blake.cpp (Continued)

```
    ANSI_CHARSET, OUT_DEFAULT_PRECIS,
    CLIP_DEFAULT_PRECIS, DEFAULT_QUALITY,
    DEFAULT_PITCH, CurFont);

  HPEN hPen = CreatePen(PS_SOLID, 3, RGB(128, 128, 128));

  // leave room for poem title in the window
  // (can't draw it now, don't know the width yet)
  OldFont = (HFONT)SelectObject(PaintDC, HeadFont);
  txtExtent = GetTextExtent(PaintDC, "a", 1);
  y = HIWORD(txtExtent) + 6;

  // body of the poem
  SelectObject(PaintDC, BodyFont);
  txtExtent = GetTextExtent(PaintDC, "1", 1);
  ht = HIWORD(txtExtent);
  x = LOWORD(txtExtent)/2;
  for(i=0; i< IDS_nStrings; i++) {
    int w, n;
    line[0] = '\0'; // in case LoadString() fails
    LoadString(hInstance, IDS_Body+i, line, sizeof(line));
    n = strlen(line);
    w = x + GetTextExtent(PaintDC, line, n);
    if (w > nMaxWidth)
      nMaxWidth = w;
    TextOut(PaintDC, x, y, line, n);
    y += ht;
  }

  // scroll range
  if (y != nPixHeight || nMaxWidth != nPixWidth) {
    nPixHeight = y;
    nPixWidth = nMaxWidth;
    AdjustScroller();
  }

  // place poem title in the window
  SelectObject(PaintDC, HeadFont);
  LoadString(hInstance, IDS_Title, line, sizeof(line));
  txtExtent = GetTextExtent(PaintDC, line, strlen(line));
  x = (nMaxWidth - (int)LOWORD(txtExtent)) / 2; // center
  TextOut(PaintDC, x, 0, line, strlen(line));
  y = HIWORD(txtExtent) + 3;

  // underline poem title
  OldPen = (HPEN)SelectObject(PaintDC, hPen);
  MoveTo(PaintDC, x, y);
  LineTo(PaintDC, x+(int)LOWORD(txtExtent), y);

  // cleanup
  SelectObject(PaintDC, OldFont);
  SelectObject(PaintDC, OldPen);
  DeleteObject(BodyFont);
```

LISTING 14.14

blake.cpp (Continued)

```
  DeleteObject(HeadFont);
  DeleteObject(hPen);
}

//
// handle the quit menu command
//
void TBlakeWindow::CMQuit(RTMessage /*msg*/)
{
  PostQuitMessage(Ø);
}

//
// handle the about menu command
//
void TBlakeWindow::CMAbout(RTMessage /*msg*/)
{
  GetApplication()->ExecDialog(new TDialog(this, "AboutDialog"));
}

//
// Times font selection
void TBlakeWindow::CMTRoman(RTMessage /*msg*/)
{
  CurFont = "Times New Roman";
  CheckMenuItem();
  InvalidateRect(HWindow, NULL, TRUE);
}

//
// Arial font selection
void TBlakeWindow::CMArial(RTMessage /*msg*/)
{
  CurFont = "Arial";
  CheckMenuItem();
  InvalidateRect(HWindow, NULL, TRUE);
}

//
// Courier font selection
void TBlakeWindow::CMCourier(RTMessage /*msg*/)
{
  CurFont = "Courier New";
  CheckMenuItem();
  InvalidateRect(HWindow, NULL, TRUE);
}

//
// Window resized, revisit the scroll settings
void TBlakeWindow::WMSize(TMessage &msg)
{
  TWindow::WMSize(msg);
  if (msg.WParam != SIZEICONIC)
```

LISTING 14.14

blake.cpp (Continued)

```
    AdjustScroller();
}

//
// Key Down Message - keyboard interface for scrolling
//
void TBlakeWindow::WMKeyDown(TMessage &msg)
{
  UINT key = msg.WParam;
  switch(key) {
    case VK_HOME:
      SendMessage(HWindow, WM_VSCROLL, SB_TOP, ØL);
      SendMessage(HWindow, WM_HSCROLL, SB_TOP, ØL);
      break;
    case VK_END:
      SendMessage(HWindow, WM_VSCROLL, SB_BOTTOM, ØL);
      break;
    case VK_PRIOR:
      SendMessage(HWindow, WM_VSCROLL, SB_PAGEUP, ØL);
      break;
    case VK_NEXT:
      SendMessage(HWindow, WM_VSCROLL, SB_PAGEDOWN, ØL);
      break;
    case VK_UP:
      SendMessage(HWindow, WM_VSCROLL, SB_LINEUP, ØL);
      break;
    case VK_DOWN:
      SendMessage(HWindow, WM_VSCROLL, SB_LINEDOWN, ØL);
      break;
    case VK_LEFT:
      SendMessage(HWindow, WM_HSCROLL, SB_LINEUP, ØL);
      break;
    case VK_RIGHT:
      SendMessage(HWindow, WM_HSCROLL, SB_LINEDOWN, ØL);
      break;
  }
}

//
// place check marks in the Font menu
// to show current selection
//
void TBlakeWindow::CheckMenuItem()
{
  HMENU hMenu = GetMenu(HWindow);
  WORD chkT = MF_UNCHECKED;
  WORD chkA = MF_UNCHECKED;
  WORD chkC = MF_UNCHECKED;
  switch(CurFont[Ø]) {
    case 'T': chkT = MF_CHECKED; break;
    case 'A': chkA = MF_CHECKED; break;
    case 'C': chkC = MF_CHECKED; break;
  }
```

LISTING 14.14

blake.cpp (Continued)

```
  ::CheckMenuItem(hMenu, CM_TRoman, MF_BYCOMMAND | chkT);
  ::CheckMenuItem(hMenu, CM_Arial, MF_BYCOMMAND | chkA);
  ::CheckMenuItem(hMenu, CM_Courier, MF_BYCOMMAND | chkC);
}

//
// WIN MAIN
//
int PASCAL WinMain(HINSTANCE hInstance, HINSTANCE hPrevInstance,
  LPSTR lpCmdLine, int nShow)
{
  TBlakeApp blakeApp("Blake Application", hInstance, hPrevInstance,
    lpCmdLine, nShow);
  blakeApp.Run();
  return blakeApp.Status;
}
```

Blake Stage 4: Using the Mouse in a Window

In Stage 4 of the Blake application I'm going to overcome two limitations of Blake Stage 3. The first limitation is obvious: Blake Stage 3 doesn't show how the mouse can be integrated into an interactive Windows application. Programming for the mouse isn't magic, but there are a few things that you must consider.

The second problem with Blake Stage 3 won't be apparent to you unless you actually run the application. When the application first appears on the screen, it draws the window once, and then completely redraws the window. This presents a flickery appearance; it doesn't look right. When I first noticed this I was puzzled, but then I realized what was happening. The TScroller object was causing the second draw of the screen. I will explain the problem and present the solution in the "Smart Scrolling" section.

Using the Mouse

Most aspects of working with a mouse are handled for you by Windows. Windows responds to the input data from the mouse, it moves the mouse cursor, and it will automatically switch from one cursor to another as the mouse passes over different types of windows. When you press one of the mouse buttons, release a mouse button, or even move the mouse, Windows sends a mouse message to the window under the mouse. If you want your window to work with the mouse you must respond to these messages.

In the Blake Stage 4 application I want to use the mouse to select individual lines of the poem. Thus whenever the left button is pressed I want to highlight the line under the pointer. In more specific terms, I plan to respond to the WM_-LBUTTONDOWN message, note the mouse's Y position, translate the Y position into a specific line of the poem, and then draw the poem so that the line is highlighted.

Handling the WM_LBUTTONDOWN message is very simple. Here's the prototype of the TBlakeWindow class's WMLButtonDown() member function:

```
void WMLButtonDown(TMessage &msg) =
  [WM_FIRST + WM_LBUTTONDOWN];
```

When the WMLButtonDown() handler gets activated, the WParam and LParam of the msg struct will be filled in with information about the mouse event. You can find all the details in the citation for the WM_LBUTTON-DOWN message in the Windows API reference manual. The parameter that I need for the Blake Stage 4 application is the mouse's Y position, which is encoded in the high word of the LParam. (X is in the low word, flag bits are in the word param.)

The Y value that is passed to the handler is in device coordinates, so we must call DPtoLP() to convert to logical coordinates. But DPtoLP() requires a device context, which means that first we must call GetDC() to create a device context. Here's where things get slightly tricky. GetDC() creates a default device context. We need to ensure that the coordinate part of the device context used in the WMLButtonDown() procedure matches the coordinate system used during painting. If they don't agree, mouse clicks will be wildly misinterpreted. (In WMLButtonDown() we don't need to make the device context's colors, and so on, match those of the paint device context.)

We don't need to worry about the mapping mode, because both the WML-ButtonDown() device context and Paint() device context will use the default MM_TEXT mapping mode. But their viewport origins may differ because of scrolling. Remember that before calling Paint() the TWindow class's WMPaint() message handler will take care of scrolling. It calls the TScroller's BeginView() function to do the scrolling, and then TScroller::BeginView() implements the scrolling by setting the device context's viewport origin. Therefore the WML-ButtonDown() function must also call the TScroller class's BeginView(). Here is the beginning of the WMLButtonDown() handler, where these operations are performed. (The full text of WMLButtonDown() appears in resource.h.)

```
HDC hDC = GetDC(HWindow);
if (Scroller)
  Scroller->BeginView(hDC, ps);
DPtoLP(hDC, (LPPOINT)&msg.LP, 1);
int y = msg.LP.Hi;
int YOrg = (int)HIWORD(GetViewportOrg(hDC));
ReleaseDC(HWindow, hDC);
```

The next chore that WMLButtonDown() tackles is conversion of the Y position from the mouse click into an index that specifies which line of the poem must be highlighted. That's mostly a matter of simple geometry and arithmetic, which is performed by the following code:

```
if (y > nTitleHt)
  newKeyString = (y - nTitleHt) / nLineHt;
```

The nTitleHt is the position of the start of the text, and nLineHt is the height of a line of text. These Stage 4 TBlakeWindow class member variables are set by the SizePoem() function, which will be discussed shortly. For now, it's enough to know that they are set before the poem is drawn, which means long before the WMLButtonDown() procedure will be called. These values are depicted graphically in Figure 14.12.

FIGURE 14.12

The nTitleHt and nLineHt values calculated by the SizePoem() function

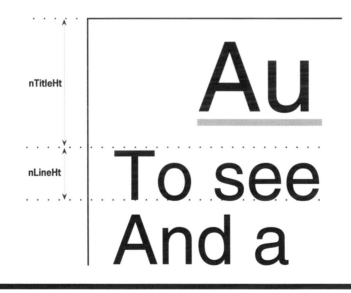

In my first version of this routine I ended the routine at this point by invalidating the whole window. That worked, but redrawing the whole poem just to change the highlight looked clumsy. Even on a fast machine, it was obvious that the whole window was being redrawn to make a small change. Therefore I went back to the keyboard and crafted the following code, which invalidates only the changed parts of the window. Remember you need to make two changes: You must unhighlight the previously selected text, and then highlight the new selection. In the following code, newKeyString is the index of the newly selected line, and nKeyString is a member of the TBlakeWindow class that stores the index of the selected line.

```
RECT r;
if (nKeyString >= 0) {    // redraw old selection
```

```
    GetClientRect(HWindow, &r);
    r.top = YOrg + nTitleHt + nKeyString * nLineHt;
    r.bottom = r.top + nLineHt;
    InvalidateRect(HWindow, &r, FALSE);
  }
  if (newKeyString >= 0) {    // draw new selection
    GetClientRect(HWindow, &r);
    r.top = YOrg + nTitleHt + newKeyString * nLineHt;
    r.bottom = r.top + nLineHt;
    InvalidateRect(HWindow, &r, FALSE);
  }
  nKeyString = newKeyString;
```

The reason for calling GetClientRect() in each of the if statements is to get the left and right members of the rect r. Then the top and bottom members are set manually with regard to the origin of the viewport, whose Y component is stored in YOrg. The result of invalidating only the changed part of the window is that the redraw operation looks smoother.

Smart Scrolling

Using OWL's TScroller class is a great simplifier; it makes short work of managing the details of scrolling. But it isn't a perfect solution for all needs. The problem that I encountered is that the TScroller object wants to know the size of the scrolling region at the outset. That's a tough requirement for the Blake application, because it doesn't know the size of the poem display until it has drawn the poem. That's why in Blake Stage 2 the window flickered. First the window was drawn with the TScroller's concept of scroll regions set to 0. Then the TScroller was told the real size of the scroll region, using the SetRange() member function, and the TScroller object then forced a screen redraw.

The solution to this dilemma is to be somewhat smarter about sizes. First, consider that the size is only unknown when the application first starts to execute, or when it switches to a new font. At either of these times it is okay to set the scroll region size, because the window is about to be redrawn anyway. But how can we set the scroll region size before it's painted? The solution is to create a function whose sole job is to compute the size of the poem. Then you can compute the poem size before it's drawn, which means that there won't be any flicker.

Calculating the size of the poem is not much work. The code can be modeled on the Paint() procedure, although much of the detail will fall away. Here's the Stage 4 code for calculating the size of the poem:

```
void TBlakeWindow::SizePoem()
{
  HDC ClientDC = GetDC(HWindow);
  HINSTANCE hInstance = GetApplication()->hInstance;
  HFONT OldFont;
```

```
DWORD txtExtent;
char line[100];

HFONT BodyFont = BlakeFont(ClientDC, 15, FALSE);
HFONT HeadFont = BlakeFont(ClientDC, 20, TRUE);

// calculate size of poem title
OldFont = (HFONT)SelectObject(ClientDC, HeadFont);
txtExtent = GetTextExtent(ClientDC, "1", 1);
nTitleHt = HIWORD(txtExtent) + 6;

// calculate size of the body of the poem
SelectObject(ClientDC, BodyFont);
line[0] = '\0'; // in case LoadString() fails
LoadString(hInstance, IDS_Body+IDS_Longest, line, sizeof(line));
txtExtent = GetTextExtent(ClientDC, line, strlen(line));
nLineHt = HIWORD(txtExtent);
nPixWidth = LOWORD(txtExtent);
nPixHeight = nTitleHt + IDS_nStrings * nLineHt;
AdjustScroller();  // scroll range

// cleanup
SelectObject(ClientDC, OldFont);
DeleteObject(BodyFont);
DeleteObject(HeadFont);
ReleaseDC(HWindow, ClientDC);
}
```

It should be easy for you to see that the SizePoem() code has been culled from Paint() and then simplified. One simplification is to replace the call to CreateFont(), which entailed specifying 14 parameters, with a call to Blake-Font(). BlakeFont() just wants to know the size in points and whether the font will be bold, plus a handle to the device context so it can convert points to pixels. Another simplification is that I've added an identifier to resource.h called IDS_Longest, which specifies which string is the longest string. SizePoem() could check every string and find the longest, but why bother if we already know which is the longest. Once the size has been computed, AdjustScroller() is called to specify the size of the scroll region. Yes, this may schedule a redraw of the poem, but SizePoem() is only called when a redraw is inevitable.

There are four places in the code that call SizePoem(). The first three are the message handlers for the three font menu items. Each of these handlers points the CurFont pointer at the name of the new font, then calls SizePoem(), and then invalidates the entire window. The other place where SizePoem() is called is in the TBlakeWindow class's SetupWindow() function, which is called just before the window is drawn for the first time. As advertised, SizePoem() is only called when the window is about to be redrawn.

The Blake Stage 4 Paint() Function

The Blake Stage 4 Paint() procedure isn't radically different from Stage 3, so I won't discuss it line by line. In functionality, Stage 4 Paint() differs from Stage 3 in that it must be able to highlight a line of the poem, but it no longer needs to keep track of the poem size. Thus Stage 4 has both more and less to do, making it about the same length as Stage 3.

Because of the need to highlight lines of the poem, Blake Stage 4 Paint() uses the ExtTextOut() function to display text. The advantage of ExtTextOut() for this use is that it will fill an entire rectangle with the background, instead of just the background in back of the output text. This is important when you want a line's highlight to extend the full width of the window, as shown in Figure 14.13. If TextOut() had been used instead of ExtTextOut(), the highlight shown in Figure 14.13 would have stopped at the end of the word "hour."

FIGURE 14.13

The Blake Stage 4 application

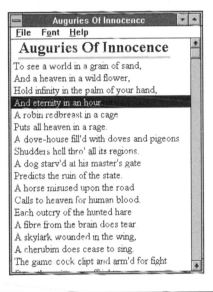

Here is the code from Blake Stage 4 that prepares the RECT for the call to ExtTextOut():

```
GetClientRect(HWindow, &r);
r.top = y;
r.bottom = y + nLineHt;
r.right -= (int)LOWORD(GetViewportOrg(PaintDC));
```

The call to GetClientRect() is used to set the left and right members of the RECT r, while the desired Y position and the height of a line are used to set the top and bottom members. If there is horizontal scrolling, you need to extend the rect to the right by the amount of the scrolling.

Each line of the poem is output using the window's default colors except for the selected line. For that specific line the colors are set to highlight the line. This action is performed by the following few lines of code:

```
if (i == nKeyString) {  // switch to hilite color
  SetBkColor(PaintDC, GetSysColor(COLOR_HIGHLIGHT));
  SetTextColor(PaintDC, GetSysColor(COLOR_HIGHLIGHTTEXT));
}
ExtTextOut(PaintDC, x, y, ETO_OPAQUE, &r, line,
  strlen(line), Ø);
if (i == nKeyString) {  // switch back to normal color
  SetBkColor(PaintDC, GetSysColor(COLOR_WINDOW));
  SetTextColor(PaintDC, GetSysColor(COLOR_WINDOWTEXT));
}
```

The SetBkColor() and SetTextColor() functions are used to set the colors used by the PaintDC for text output. For the highlighted line, the colors are set to COLOR_HIGHLIGHT and COLOR_HIGHLIGHTTEXT, using the GetSys-Color() procedure to look up those two colors in Windows's system color table. This means that if you choose a different color scheme, the colors used by Blake Stage 4 will change. After the highlighted line is displayed, the colors are reset to the defaults, which are COLOR_WINDOW and COLOR_WINDOWTEXT. You can find a complete listing of the names for all the colors in the system color table in the citation for the GetSysColor() function in the Windows API reference.

One other change in Blake Stage 4 Paint() is that the output of the poem title occurs first, before the output of the body of the poem. This is possible because the poem has been measured, using SizePoem(), before Paint() is called. I think this is a nice change, because it lets the code in Paint() follow a more natural order.

Stage 4 Source Code

Stage 4 uses the same resources as the earlier stages, so they won't be repeated. Listings 14.15, 14.16, and 14.17 are confined to the blake.h, resource.h, and blake.cpp files. You can consult Table 14.7 for a guide to where all the listings used to build Blake Stage 4 can be found.

William Blake—poet, printer, artist, seer—never imagined that one of his poems would be used to illustrate Windows programming. For some more fun with Blake, you might try

- Using Choose Font() to provide better font selection
- Adding file input so multiple poems can be displayed
- Allowing multiple line selections using the mouse
- Adding clipboard operations

I hope you've enjoyed Blake!

TABLE 14.7

Blake Stage 4 Listings

File	Listing	Stage 4 Summary
blake.h	14.15	Slightly changed.
resource.h	14.16	Contains a new identifier that specifies which line of the poem is the longest, so the size can be calculated without browsing through the whole poem.
blake.cpp	14.17	The TBlakeWindow class has a new SizePoem() function to measure the size of the poem, and a new BlakeFont() function to create a font.
blake.rc	14.4	Unchanged since Stage 1.
blake.mnu	14.12	Unchanged since Stage 2.
about.dlg	14.6	Unchanged since Stage 1, except that the label "Stage 1" is changed to "Stage 4"
blake.str	14.7	Unchanged since Stage 1.
blake.ico	14.8	Unchanged since Stage 1.

LISTING 14.15

blake.h

```cpp
//
// the Blake Application class
//
class TBlakeApp : public TApplication {
  public:
    TBlakeApp(LPSTR name, HINSTANCE hInstance, HINSTANCE hPrevInstance,
      LPSTR lpCmdLine, int nShow) :
      TApplication(name, hInstance, hPrevInstance, lpCmdLine, nShow)
    {
      return;
    }
    virtual void InitMainWindow();
};

//
// the Blake Window class
//
class TBlakeWindow : public TWindow {
  public:
    // constructor
    TBlakeWindow(PTWindowsObject pParent, LPSTR pTitle);

    // window class members
    LPSTR GetClassName() {
      return "TBlakeWindow4";
    }
    void GetWindowClass(WNDCLASS& rWndClass);

    // last-minute init
```

LISTING 14.15 ■■■

blake.h (Continued)

```
    void SetupWindow();

    // Paint the window
    void Paint(HDC PaintDC, PAINTSTRUCT& ps);

    // message handlers
    virtual void CMQuit(RTMessage msg) =
      [CM_FIRST + CM_Quit];
    virtual void CMAbout(RTMessage msg) =
      [CM_FIRST + CM_About];
    virtual void CMTRoman(RTMessage msg) =
      [CM_FIRST + CM_TRoman];
    virtual void CMArial(RTMessage msg) =
      [CM_FIRST + CM_Arial];
    virtual void CMCourier(RTMessage msg) =
      [CM_FIRST + CM_Courier];

    // handle the size message
    void WMSize(TMessage &msg) =
      [WM_FIRST + WM_SIZE];

    // provide a keyboard interface for scrolling
    void WMKeyDown(TMessage &msg) =
      [WM_FIRST + WM_KEYDOWN];

    // handle mouse clicks
    void WMLButtonDown(TMessage &msg) =
      [WM_FIRST + WM_LBUTTONDOWN];

  protected:
    // manage check marks on the menu bar
    void CheckMenuItem();

    // calculate the size of poem
    void SizePoem();

    // adjust the TScroller
    void AdjustScroller();

    // Create a font in the given size, boldness
    HFONT BlakeFont(HDC hDC, int ptsiz, BOOL bold);

    // DATA members
    LPSTR CurFont;  // name of cur font
    int nPixHeight; // height of drawing
    int nPixWidth;  // width of drawing
    int nXunit;     // X scroll step
    int nYunit;     // Y scroll step
    int nTitleHt;   // height of Title area of poem
    int nLineHt;    // height of each line
    int nKeyString; // which string s.b. hilited
};
```

LISTING 14.16

resource.h

```
//
// Blake App Resource Constants
//

// Menu Items
#define CM_Quit      101  // File menu
#define CM_About     102  // Help menu
#define CM_TRoman    103  // Font Times Roman
#define CM_Arial     104  // Font Arial
#define CM_Courier   105  // Font Courier

// Strings -- stored in blake.str
#define IDS_Title    50  // id of title line
#define IDS_Body     51  // id of first line of innocence
#define IDS_nStrings 18  // how many strings in blake.str
#define IDS_Longest   6  // longest string in blake.str
```

LISTING 14.17

blake.cpp

```cpp
#include <string.h>
#include <stdio.h>
#define STRICT
#define WIN31
#include <owl.h>
#include <bwcc.h>
#include "resource.h"
#include "blake.h"

//
// Blake App, create the main window
//
void TBlakeApp::InitMainWindow()
{
  char title[100];
  BWCCGetVersion();
  LoadString(hInstance, IDS_Title, title, sizeof(title));
  MainWindow = new TBlakeWindow(NULL, title);
}

//
// Blake Window, constructor
//
TBlakeWindow::TBlakeWindow(PTWindowsObject pParent, LPSTR pTitle) :
  TWindow(pParent, pTitle),
  CurFont("Times New Roman"),
  nPixWidth(0),
```

LISTING 14.17

blake.cpp (Continued)

```
  nPixHeight(Ø),
  nXunit(1Ø),
  nYunit(1Ø),
  nKeyString(-1)
{
  AssignMenu("BlakeMenu");
  Attr.Style |= WS_VSCROLL | WS_HSCROLL;
  Scroller = new TScroller(this, nXunit, nYunit, Ø, Ø);
}

//
// create a Windows class for the Blake Window
//
void TBlakeWindow::GetWindowClass(WNDCLASS& rWndClass)
{
  TWindow::GetWindowClass(rWndClass);
  rWndClass.hIcon = LoadIcon(GetApplication()->hInstance, "BlakeIcon");
  if (rWndClass.hIcon == NULL) {
    MessageBox(HWindow, "Bad Icon Load", "icon", MB_ICONSTOP);
    rWndClass.hIcon = LoadIcon(Ø, IDI_APPLICATION);
  }
}

//
// last-minute setup of the window
void TBlakeWindow::SetupWindow()
{
  CheckMenuItem();
  SizePoem();
}

//
// private util to create a font for the Blake app
//
HFONT TBlakeWindow::BlakeFont(HDC hDC, int siz, BOOL bold)
{
  double dPixPerPoint = GetDeviceCaps(hDC, LOGPIXELSY) / 72.Ø;
  return CreateFont(siz*dPixPerPoint, Ø, Ø, Ø,      // ht,wid,esc,ori
    bold == TRUE ? 7ØØ : Ø, Ø, Ø, Ø, // wt,ital,ul,so
    ANSI_CHARSET, OUT_DEFAULT_PRECIS,
    CLIP_DEFAULT_PRECIS, DEFAULT_QUALITY,
    DEFAULT_PITCH, CurFont);
}

//
// Tell the scroller the new settings
//
void TBlakeWindow::AdjustScroller()
{
  RECT r;
  GetClientRect(HWindow, &r);
  Scroller->SetRange((nPixWidth - r.right)/nXunit + 1,
    (nPixHeight - r.bottom)/nYunit + 1);
```

LISTING 14.17

blake.cpp (Continued)

```cpp
}

//
// Calculate Poem Size
//
void TBlakeWindow::SizePoem()
{
  HDC ClientDC = GetDC(HWindow);
  HINSTANCE hInstance = GetApplication()->hInstance;
  HFONT OldFont;
  DWORD txtExtent;
  char line[100];

  HFONT BodyFont = BlakeFont(ClientDC, 15, FALSE);
  HFONT HeadFont = BlakeFont(ClientDC, 20, TRUE);

  // calculate size of poem title
  OldFont = (HFONT)SelectObject(ClientDC, HeadFont);
  txtExtent = GetTextExtent(ClientDC, "1", 1);
  nTitleHt = HIWORD(txtExtent) + 6;

  // calculate size of the body of the poem
  SelectObject(ClientDC, BodyFont);
  line[0] = '\0'; // in case LoadString() fails
  LoadString(hInstance, IDS_Body+IDS_Longest, line, sizeof(line));
  txtExtent = GetTextExtent(ClientDC, line, strlen(line));
  nLineHt = HIWORD(txtExtent);
  nPixWidth = LOWORD(txtExtent);
  nPixHeight = nTitleHt + IDS_nStrings * nLineHt;
  AdjustScroller();  // scroll range

  // cleanup
  SelectObject(ClientDC, OldFont);
  DeleteObject(BodyFont);
  DeleteObject(HeadFont);
  ReleaseDC(HWindow, ClientDC);
}

//
// Paint
//
void TBlakeWindow::Paint(HDC PaintDC, PAINTSTRUCT & /*ps*/)
{
  HINSTANCE hInstance = GetApplication()->hInstance;
  HFONT OldFont;
  HPEN OldPen;
  HBRUSH OldBrush;
  DWORD txtExtent;
  char line[100];
  int i, x, y;

  HFONT BodyFont = BlakeFont(PaintDC, 15, FALSE);
  HFONT HeadFont = BlakeFont(PaintDC, 20, TRUE);
```

LISTING 14.17

blake.cpp (Continued)

```cpp
    HPEN hPen = CreatePen(PS_SOLID, 3, GetSysColor(COLOR_SCROLLBAR));

    // place poem title in the window
    OldFont = (HFONT)SelectObject(PaintDC, HeadFont);
    LoadString(hInstance, IDS_Title, line, sizeof(line));
    txtExtent = GetTextExtent(PaintDC, line, strlen(line));
    x = (nPixWidth - (int)LOWORD(txtExtent)) / 2; // center
    TextOut(PaintDC, x, Ø, line, strlen(line));
    y = HIWORD(txtExtent) + 3;

    // underline poem title
    OldPen = (HPEN)SelectObject(PaintDC, hPen);
    MoveTo(PaintDC, x, y);
    LineTo(PaintDC, x+(int)LOWORD(txtExtent), y);
    y += 3;

    // body of the poem
    SelectObject(PaintDC, BodyFont);
    txtExtent = GetTextExtent(PaintDC, "1", 1);
    x = LOWORD(txtExtent)/2;
    for(i=Ø; i< IDS_nStrings; i++) {
      RECT r;
      line[Ø] = '\Ø'; // in case LoadString() fails
      LoadString(hInstance, IDS_Body+i, line, sizeof(line));
      // calculate rect for the line
      GetClientRect(HWindow, &r);
      r.top = y;
      r.bottom = y + nLineHt;
      r.right -= (int)LOWORD(GetViewportOrg(PaintDC));
      if (i == nKeyString) {  // switch to hilite color
        SetBkColor(PaintDC, GetSysColor(COLOR_HIGHLIGHT));
        SetTextColor(PaintDC, GetSysColor(COLOR_HIGHLIGHTTEXT));
      }
      ExtTextOut(PaintDC, x, y, ETO_OPAQUE, &r, line,
        strlen(line), Ø);
      if (i == nKeyString) {  // switch back to normal color
        SetBkColor(PaintDC, GetSysColor(COLOR_WINDOW));
        SetTextColor(PaintDC, GetSysColor(COLOR_WINDOWTEXT));
      }
      y += nLineHt;
    }

    // cleanup
    SelectObject(PaintDC, OldFont);
    SelectObject(PaintDC, OldPen);
    DeleteObject(BodyFont);
    DeleteObject(HeadFont);
    DeleteObject(hPen);
}

//
// handle the quit menu command
//
```

LISTING 14.17

blake.cpp (Continued)

```
void TBlakeWindow::CMQuit(RTMessage /*msg*/)
{
  PostQuitMessage(0);
}

//
// handle the about menu command
//
void TBlakeWindow::CMAbout(RTMessage /*msg*/)
{
  GetApplication()->ExecDialog(new TDialog(this, "AboutDialog"));
}

//
// Times font selection
void TBlakeWindow::CMTRoman(RTMessage /*msg*/)
{
  CurFont = "Times New Roman";
  CheckMenuItem();
  SizePoem();
  InvalidateRect(HWindow, NULL, TRUE);
}

//
// Arial font selection
void TBlakeWindow::CMArial(RTMessage /*msg*/)
{
  CurFont = "Arial";
  CheckMenuItem();
  SizePoem();
  InvalidateRect(HWindow, NULL, TRUE);
}

//
// Courier font selection
void TBlakeWindow::CMCourier(RTMessage /*msg*/)
{
  CurFont = "Courier New";
  CheckMenuItem();
  SizePoem();
  InvalidateRect(HWindow, NULL, TRUE);
}

//
// Window resized, revisit the scroll settings
void TBlakeWindow::WMSize(TMessage &msg)
{
  TWindow::WMSize(msg);
  if (msg.WParam != SIZEICONIC)
    AdjustScroller();
}

//
```

LISTING 14.17

blake.cpp (Continued)

```cpp
// Key Down Message - keyboard interface for scrolling
//
void TBlakeWindow::WMKeyDown(TMessage &msg)
{
  UINT key = msg.WParam;
  switch(key) {
    case VK_HOME:
      SendMessage(HWindow, WM_VSCROLL, SB_TOP, ØL);
      SendMessage(HWindow, WM_HSCROLL, SB_TOP, ØL);
      break;
    case VK_END:
      SendMessage(HWindow, WM_VSCROLL, SB_BOTTOM, ØL);
      break;
    case VK_PRIOR:
      SendMessage(HWindow, WM_VSCROLL, SB_PAGEUP, ØL);
      break;
    case VK_NEXT:
      SendMessage(HWindow, WM_VSCROLL, SB_PAGEDOWN, ØL);
      break;
    case VK_UP:
      SendMessage(HWindow, WM_VSCROLL, SB_LINEUP, ØL);
      break;
    case VK_DOWN:
      SendMessage(HWindow, WM_VSCROLL, SB_LINEDOWN, ØL);
      break;
    case VK_LEFT:
      SendMessage(HWindow, WM_HSCROLL, SB_LINEUP, ØL);
      break;
    case VK_RIGHT:
      SendMessage(HWindow, WM_HSCROLL, SB_LINEDOWN, ØL);
      break;
  }
}


//
// Mouse clicks in the window
//
void TBlakeWindow::WMLButtonDown(TMessage &msg)
{
  int newKeyString = -1;
  PAINTSTRUCT ps;
  RECT r;
  HDC hDC = GetDC(HWindow);
  if (Scroller)
    Scroller->BeginView(hDC, ps);
  DPtoLP(hDC, (LPPOINT)&msg.LP, 1);
  int y = msg.LP.Hi;
  int YOrg = (int)HIWORD(GetViewportOrg(hDC));
  ReleaseDC(HWindow, hDC);
  if (y > nTitleHt)
    newKeyString = (y - nTitleHt) / nLineHt;
  if (nKeyString >= Ø) {     // redraw old selection
    GetClientRect(HWindow, &r);
```

LISTING 14.17

blake.cpp (Continued)

```
      r.top = YOrg + nTitleHt + nKeyString * nLineHt;
      r.bottom = r.top + nLineHt;
      InvalidateRect(HWindow, &r, FALSE);
    }
    if (newKeyString >= 0) {    // draw new selection
      GetClientRect(HWindow, &r);
      r.top = YOrg + nTitleHt + newKeyString * nLineHt;
      r.bottom = r.top + nLineHt;
      InvalidateRect(HWindow, &r, FALSE);
    }
    nKeyString = newKeyString;
}


//
// place check marks in the Font menu
// to show current selection
//
void TBlakeWindow::CheckMenuItem()
{
  HMENU hMenu = GetMenu(HWindow);
  WORD chkT = MF_UNCHECKED;
  WORD chkA = MF_UNCHECKED;
  WORD chkC = MF_UNCHECKED;
  switch(CurFont[0]) {
    case 'T': chkT = MF_CHECKED; break;
    case 'A': chkA = MF_CHECKED; break;
    case 'C': chkC = MF_CHECKED; break;
  }
  ::CheckMenuItem(hMenu, CM_TRoman, MF_BYCOMMAND | chkT);
  ::CheckMenuItem(hMenu, CM_Arial, MF_BYCOMMAND | chkA);
  ::CheckMenuItem(hMenu, CM_Courier, MF_BYCOMMAND | chkC);
}


//
// WIN MAIN
//
int PASCAL WinMain(HINSTANCE hInstance, HINSTANCE hPrevInstance,
  LPSTR lpCmdLine, int nShow)
{
  TBlakeApp blakeApp("Blake Application", hInstance, hPrevInstance,
    lpCmdLine, nShow);
  blakeApp.Run();
  return blakeApp.Status;
}
```

OWL AND THE MULTIPLE DOCUMENT INTERFACE

MANY OF THE LATEST WINDOWS APPLICATIONS ARE WINDOWS MULTIPLE DOCument Interface (MDI) applications. Such applications include word processors that allow you to view and work with several document windows, spreadsheets that support multiple sheet and graphics windows, and graphics programs that provide several drawing windows. Most readers of this book will be especially familiar with two particular MDI applications: Borland's BCW programming environment and their Resource Workshop resource editor.

MDI allows the main window of an application to contain one or more child windows. Each child window can have its own behavior; in essence each child window presents a complete user interface. But the application also allows the windows to work together, to share a menu bar, to be linked so that actions in one child window affect other child windows, and so on. It's this synergy between the child windows that makes it better to use two document windows in an MDI word processor than to run two separate instances of an SDI (single document interface) word processor.

MDI is such an important aspect of creating a productive user interface that support for MDI is built into Windows. This built-in support is important partly because the common behavior of MDI applications makes them easier to use, and partly because the functionality provided by Windows makes it easier to develop MDI applications.

MDI Behaviors

My example of MDI programming is the Duet application. As its name implies, Duet is comprised of two types of child window. The reason for having two types of child window is that it provides a rich environment for showing how child windows interact with the frame window. Duet is a more realistic example of MDI programming than either of the examples provided with Borland C++, but it isn't so complex as to be opaque.

The Duet application in Figure 15.1 shows most of the aspects of an MDI application. As you can see from Figure 15.1, child windows can have a system menu control and min/max controls. However, child windows can't have a menu; instead child windows share the menu of the frame window. This is where some of the complexity of MDI elbows through to the programmer, but menu management is clearly illustrated by the Duet application. As you can also see in Figure 15.1, child windows can be iconified.

FIGURE 15.1

Elements of MDI applications

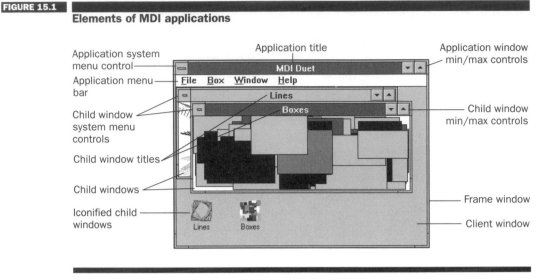

The terms frame window and client window will be discussed in the "MDI Components" section.

When a child window is maximized, several things happen automatically to produce the result shown in Figure 15.2. The most obvious event is that the child window enlarges to fill the area that's available. The other events center around the menu and title bars:

- The title of the child window is appended to the application title.

- The child window's system menu control is placed at the left end of the application's menu bar.

- The child window's minimize/maximize control is placed on the far right of the application's menu bar.

As you can see from the above list, the menu in an MDI application is a dynamic entity. You've just seen the two most obvious changes—when a child window is maximized, its system menu control and its min/max control are placed on the ends of the application menu bar. Now let's focus for a moment on the changes that occur in an MDI application's menu.

- Whenever there are no child windows, the application's menu bar should display a minimal menu that presents only those selections that are always necessary. This is shown for the Duet application in Figure 15.3.

- When a child window is created, the menu bar should be updated to show the menu selections appropriate for that child. See Figure 15.4.

- If more than one kind of child window exists, the menu bar should be redrawn each time a new type of child window is activated. See Figure 15.5.

FIGURE 15.2

The Duet application when a Boxes child window is maximized

Application system
menu control

Application title   Child window title

Application
menu bar

Application window
min/max controls

Child window
system menu
control

Child window
min/max control

Maximized child
window

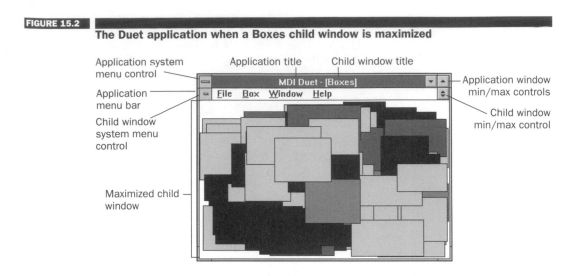

FIGURE 15.3

The Duet application, showing the simple menu bar that is present whenever there are no child windows. The File menu has been activated to show three choices—creating either of the child window types or exiting.

FIGURE 15.4

When a Lines child window is created, the menu bar is updated to contain Line and Window selections

FIGURE 15.5

When there are several types of child windows, the menu should always show the choices that apply to the active child window. Here we see that a Boxes child window is active, and the menu bar now contains a Box menu for selections related to a Boxes child window.

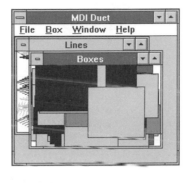

■ When child windows are present, the menu bar should usually contain a Window menu, as shown in Figures 15.4 and 15.5. Windows will automatically append a list of the child windows to this menu, and it will identify the current child menu with a check mark. This menu should usually contain the standard menu selections Cascade, Tile, and Arrange Icons, as shown in Figure 15.6. The logic to perform these tasks is present in Windows, although it is the developer's responsibility to make the connection between the menu selection and this built-in functionality. The "Implementing the Window Menu Selections" section later in this chapter discusses these options as well as Close All.

FIGURE 15.6

Most MDI applications contain menu choices that relate to all of the child windows such as Cascade and Tile, plus a Window menu that contains a list of the child windows

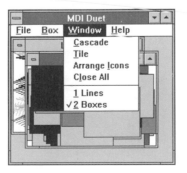

Menu bar management is important to creating an intuitive MDI application. Windows does a lot of the grunt work, but it's up to you to be the general who issues clear orders to the troops.

MDI Components

Windows implements MDI using three types of windows. The first type of window is a child window. A child window contains a document or drawing, and it behaves in many ways like a normal application window. In OWL programming you usually implement child windows by deriving your own window class from OWL's TWindow class.

The second type of window used to implement MDI is the frame window. For an MDI application the frame window is the application window. For example, it's the frame window's icon that is usually displayed when an MDI application is iconified, it's the frame window that controls the application's menu, and so forth. In an OWL application you derive your own application window class from OWL's TMDIFrame class. OWL's TMDIFrame class is derived from TWindow.

The client window is the third type of window in an MDI application. I imagine the client window to be a village elder, who steps in to offer assistance whenever a child window has a life crisis. Client windows are involved when child windows are created, when they are minimized or maximized, and when the focus switches from one child to another. OWL provides the TMDIClient class, which is derived from TWindow, to further hone the behavior of client windows. The services provided by TMDIClient are important in OWL applications, but you probably won't need to derive a class from TMDIClient. Figure 15.7 shows the relationships between frame, client, and child windows.

FIGURE 15.7

In an MDI application, the frame window is the application window. The client window, which is responsible for much of the MDI behavior, is a child of the frame window. The child windows, which are the visible windows containing documents or other application information, are offspring of the client window.

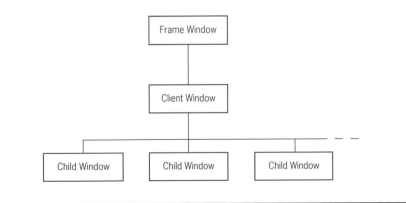

Although the window relationships shown in Figure 15.7 apply to an MDI application constructed using OWL, you should also keep in mind how the OWL classes are interconnected. Figure 15.8 shows how pointers are used in the OWL classes. First, let's look at child-to-parent linkage. Remember that the TWindowsObject class contains a data member named Parent that is either NULL or points at the class's parent TWindowsObject. In an MDI application, each child window's Parent pointer points at the application's TMDIFrame object. Similarly, the single client window's Parent pointer points at the application's TMDIFrame object. (If you use the Parent pointer to access a member of the TWindow or TMDIFrame class, then you'll have to use a cast, because Parent is a PTWindowsObject type.)

FIGURE 15.8

In an OWL multiple document application, each child window object's Parent pointer, and the TMDIClient object's Parent pointer, points at the application's TMDIFrame object. The TMDIFrame object can use its ClientWnd pointer to access the TMDIClient object, and it can use its list of child windows, provided by the TWindowsObject base class, to access the child window objects.

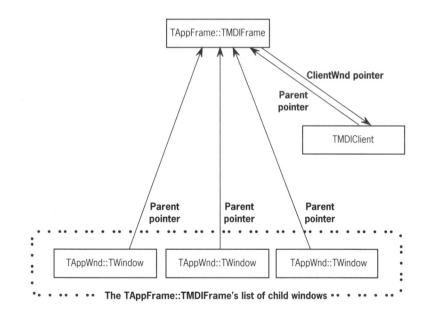

Parent-to-child linkages let the application's TMDIFrame object access the child window objects and the TMDIClient object. The child window objects are accessed using the list of child windows that is maintained by every class that is derived from TWindowsObject. The TMDIClient object is created by the TMDIFrame class's constructor, and a pointer to it is stored in the ClientWnd pointer. You should usually access the ClientWnd pointer via the public function GetClient() because GetClient() guarantees read-only access.

The TMDIFrame Class

If you read the standard Windows references on creating an MDI application, you'll find that much of the magic revolves around three C structs: CREATE-STRUCT, CLIENTCREATESTRUCT, and MDICREATESTRUCT. When you use OWL you won't need to worry about these three interlocking data structures because that level of detail is managed automatically. Similarly, if you read about creating an MDI child window you'll learn that the procedure is very different from the procedure for creating an ordinary window. Again, OWL shields you from these low-level details.

But there are other aspects of an MDI application that you need to handle yourself. The most important of these is the menu bar. MDI menus are dynamic, but you need to manage the dynamism. It's tempting to use the TWindow class's AssignMenu() function to control the menu, but it isn't MDI aware and it won't work properly in an MDI application. Later in this chapter I'll present a function called SetMenu() that will make it easy for you to manage menus in an MDI application.

The TMDIFrame class is the basis for creating an MDI application using OWL. It performs the special processing needed to create a client window, and it contains some logic for managing child windows. Actually, most of TMDI-Frame's logic for child windows is knowing how to delegate the responsibility to the client window, which actually does the work.

I'm first going to discuss the TMDIFrame class from the perspective of an application containing a single type of child window, using Borland's MDIApp example program to illustrate the details. Then in the second half of this chapter I'll demonstrate more realistic MDI programming techniques using the Duet application that you've already glimpsed in Figures 15.1 through 15.6.

Deriving Classes from TMDIFrame

All MDI applications that use Borland's OWL library should derive their main window class from the TMDIFrame class. Then in your application class's Init-MainWindow() function you should create a single instance of your main window object. Except for using TMDIFrame as a base instead of TWindow, this is standard OWL usage.

The TMDIFrame class has more specialized constructors than TWindow, because TMDIFrame is always used to create the main window of an MDI application. Your own main window class's constructor must mention TMDIFrame in its initialization list, and it must specify the main window's title and the name of the main window's initial menu bar. The body of the constructor should usually initialize the TMDIFrame class's ChildMenuPos variable, which specifies which of the menu bar pop-ups should be used to list the child window names.

In typical MDI applications most functionality resides in the child windows. The practical implication is that most MDI applications don't extend the TMDI-Frame class very far. The most important feature that you must add to your main window class is the ability to create child windows. If you have only one type of child window, you can replace the TMDIFrame class's InitChild() procedure so that it creates your own flavor of child window. That's what is done in Borland's

MDIApp example, and I'll show you the details in the "Creating MDI Child Windows" section. If you have more than one type of child you are on your own, but I'll show how it's done in the second half of this chapter.

Implementing the Window Menu Selections

Most MDI applications have a menu selection called Window that gives you access to the child windows. (This was shown earlier in Figures 15.1–15.2, and 15.4–15.6.)The Window menu usually offers the following standard selections:

- Cascade, which allows you to display all of the child windows arranged somewhat like a hand of cards in a poker game. The child windows will be large but overlapped. The standard shortcut key is Shift+F5.

- Tile, which displays all the child windows in a checkered fashion. The child windows won't be overlapped. The standard shortcut key is Shift+F4.

- Arrange Icons, which makes a tidy row of the child icons near the bottom of the main window.

Additionally in most applications created using OWL the following choice will be available:

- Close All, which will attempt to close all of the child windows. The child windows' CanClose() function will be interrogated for all the children, and they will all be closed only if all of them can be closed. If any child window's CanClose() returns False, usually because the window contains unsaved data, none will be closed.

Following these standard selections many applications place their own selections. For example, BCW places the Message and Project selections on its Window menu so you have an easy way to get to these two key windows.

Following all of the application's own part of the Window menu, which usually means the part of the Window menu specified in the menu resource, there is a list of child window names that is maintained by Windows. Each child window is identified by a number, and the active child is indicated by a check mark. Figure 15.6 showed the Window menu of the Duet application, and Figure 15.9 shows the misnamed MDI Children menu of Borland's MDIApp example, which is that application's Window menu. (It's misnamed, in my opinion, because it should be called the Window menu.)

As you can probably tell from the above discussion, there are actually two separate things that intersect in the Window menu. The first is that the standard menu selections in the Window menu need to invoke standard behavior. The second is that the client window needs to have a handle to the Window menu, so that it can add, subtract, and modify entries for the child windows as they are respectively created, destroyed, and activated.

First, let's look at the menu resource for Borland's MDIApp program, which is shown in Listing 15.1.

FIGURE 15.9

The MDI Children menu of Borland's MDIApp example application

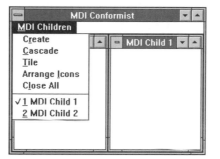

LISTING 15.1

mdiapp.rc from Borland's MDIApp program

```
// ObjectWindows - (C) Copyright 1992 by Borland International
#include "windows.h"
#include "owlrc.h"
MDIMenu MENU
BEGIN
  POPUP "&MDI Children"
    BEGIN
    MENUITEM "C&reate",  CM_CREATECHILD,
    MENUITEM "&Cascade", CM_CASCADECHILDREN,
    MENUITEM "&Tile", CM_TILECHILDREN,
    MENUITEM "Arrange &Icons", CM_ARRANGEICONS,
    MENUITEM "C&lose All", CM_CLOSECHILDREN,
    END
END
```

Let's first look at the menu items for Cascade, Tile, and Arrange Icons. These three standard selections are identified by the IDs CM_CASCADE-CHILDREN, CM_TILECHILDREN, and CM_ARRANGEICONS. These IDs are important, because if you look in OWL's mdi.h header file you'll find that they invoke the CMCascadeChildren(), CMTileChildren(), and CMArrangeIcons() member functions of the TMDIFrame class. Wherever you use these predefined OWL IDs you'll need to include the file owlrc.h.

The process for implementing the Close Children window menu selection is the same—if you have a menu item whose ID is CM_CLOSECHILDREN then it will automatically invoke the TMDIFrame class's CMCloseChildren() function. But from that point forward the process is a little different, because OWL itself (not Windows) implements the Close Children function. For example, if you look at the Program Manager or File Manager applications, written by Microsoft and presumably not written using OWL, you'll find that their Window menu doesn't include a Close Children selection. If you look at BCW, which was written by Borland, you'll find that its Window menu does include Close Children.

The second aspect of managing your application's Window menu gives the application's client window a handle to the Window menu, so it knows which menu to modify when child windows are created, destroyed, and activated. If your MDI application has only a single menu, which is possible but not realistic, then all you need to do is assign a value to ChildMenuPos in the constructor of your main window class. As the MDIFrame window is initializing, it uses the ChildWindowPos variable to give the client window a handle to the application's window menu. The leftmost menu selection is numbered 0, the next is numbered 1, and so forth. So if your application's window menu is the leftmost menu selection, which is the case in Borland's MDIApp program, then ChildMenuPos can be set to 0.

The problem with this scheme is that it only provides for a static menu structure. Every time the menu structure changes, the client window needs to know, so that it can continue to update the application's menu bar. Unfortunately the OWL class library makes no provision for dynamic menus, so I'll cover this topic in more detail later in this chapter.

Creating MDI Child Windows

I mentioned already that the only thing that you are required to provide in your MDI application's main window class is some way to create child windows. Usually there will be selections in your application's File menu that create child windows. For example, in Borland's MDIApp program the Create menu selection creates a child window. Here's the full sequence of events that occurs when you select the Create menu item in the MDIApp application:

1. Windows sends a WM_COMMAND message to the frame window, specifying the menu ID CM_CREATECHILD.

2. OWL handles this message by invoking the TMDIFrame class's CMCreateChild() function. CMCreateChild() calls CreateChild().

3. CreateChild() contains a single line of code:

   ```
   return GetModule()->MakeWindow(InitChild());
   ```

4. InitChild() creates a new child window object. Here's the definition of InitChild() from the TMyMDIFrame class, which is the main window class of Borland's MDIApp application:

   ```
   PTWindowsObject TMyMDIFrame::InitChild()
   {
     char ChildName[14];

     wsprintf(ChildName, "MDI Child %d", ChildNum++);
     return new TWindow(this, ChildName);
   }
   ```

5. The module's MakeWindow() function takes the pointer to the new TWindow object, performs validity checking, and then creates the window by calling Create(). This is the standard procedure for associating a window with a TWindow object.

In a simple MDI application that contains only one type of child window, you can hook into this five-step process quite easily by supplying your own Init-Child() in your main window class. In more complex applications you will need to supply equivalent code for one or more of the above steps.

The Duet MDI Application

Duet is an MDI application that contains two types of child window: one that draws a pattern of lines, and one that draws a collection of filled rectangles. There are two aspects of Duet that make it a more interesting and realistic MDI example than the simplistic examples supplied with OWL. The first is that Duet has three menus that are displayed in synchrony with the activation and deactivation of the child windows. One of the menus is used when no children exist; the second is used when a line child is active; and the third is used when a box child is active. The second interesting aspect of Duet is that it bypasses the TMDIFrame's restrictive conventions for creating child windows, and instead implements its own scheme for child window creation.

Duet's Icons

Since each MDI child window behaves much like an application's main window, each type of MDI child should have its own icon. To associate an icon with a child window you need to do exactly what you do with a true main window—create a unique window class and register that class so that Windows knows the class characteristics. This should be familiar territory so I won't bother to show the GetClassName() and GetWindowClass() member functions of each of the child window classes. The two child window icons are visible in Figure 15.1.

Don't forget that the true main window class, which is the TDuetFrame class in the Duet application, also needs its own icon and its own GetClassName() and GetWindowClass() functions. (The Duet application's icons are visible in the About dialogs that appear later in this chapter.)

Child Creation

Because the Duet application contains two types of child windows, I decided to completely avoid the InitChild() path that is suggested by the OWL documentation. OWL's InitChild() function assumes that you'll have only a single type of child window, and there's no elegant way to extend it to support multiple child windows. So instead I borrowed the necessary code from OWL, to make my own routines to create the child windows.

Duet's File menu contains two choices for creating child menus, the New Line Window menu item and the New Box Window item. These two menu items have the IDs CM_LineWin and CM_BoxWin. My TDuetFrame class contains the CMLineWin() and CMBoxWin() member functions that are activated by these two menu selections.

Here is the source of the CMLineWin() function:

```
void TDuetFrame::CMLineWin(RTMessage /*m*/)
{
  GetModule()->MakeWindow(new TLineWindow(this));
}
```

CMLineWin() is simply a compression of the three routines, CMCreate-Child(), CreateChild(), and InitChild(), that OWL's TMDIFrame uses to create a child window. My CMBoxWin() function is the same as CMLineWin(), except that it creates a new TBoxWindow object.

Menu Management

The Duet application contains three menus, which are shown in Figure 15.10. MainMenu is visible whenever there aren't any child windows, while LineMenu and BoxMenu are displayed when their respective child windows are active.

FIGURE 15.10

The three Duet menus

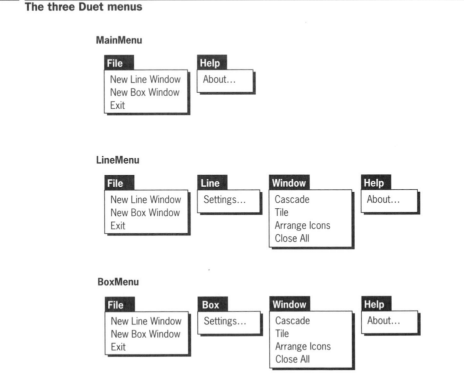

I'll first focus on the strategy for switching from one menu to another, and then we'll look at the mechanics of the actual switch from one menu to another in an MDI application. Keep in mind the following characteristics of the WM_-MDIACTIVATE message, which is the key message for managing menus in an MDI application:

- When child windows are activated and deactivated they receive the WM_MDIACTIVATE Windows message. For deactivation, the wParam is 0, while for activation its value is 1.

- When you create a child window, it receives the WM_ACTIVATE message with wParam set to 1. This message occurs very late in the creation process, after both Create() and SetupWindow() are called.

- When you switch from one child to another the first child receives WM_MDIACTIVATE with wParam set to 0 (deactivate), and then the next receives the message with wParam set to 1.

- When you close a child window, it receives the WM_ACTIVATE message with wParam set to 0.

There are several strategies that you can use to manage the menus, but in my opinion the simplest is the following:

- When the application starts, display the main menu. Yes, this is a no-brainer.

- When a child window receives WM_MDIACTIVATE with wParam set to 1, check to see if the current menu is correct. If the menu isn't correct, it switches to the correct menu.

- The frame window object keeps track of the number of child windows. When the last child window is destroyed, the frame window object switches to the main menu. (An alternative way to revert to the main menu when the last child window is destroyed is to switch to the main menu on every child window deactivation. This is too much busywork for my taste, because almost all of the switches to the main menu will immediately be undone by a subsequent activation of a child window, which will display its own menu.)

The simplest part of this scheme is to display the main menu when the application starts. This chore is performed by the TDuetFrame constructor, which passes the name of the main menu to the TMDIFrame constructor.

The next simplest part of the strategy is the child window's handling of the WM_MDIACTIVATE message. Here is the message handler for the TLine-Window class. (The TBoxWindow handler is the same, except that it switches to BoxMenu.)

```
void TLineWindow::WMMDIActivate(RTMessage m)
{
  if (m.WParam == 1) // activate
    if (*((TDuetFrame *)Parent)->GetMenuName() != *LineMenuName)
```

```
    ((TDuetFrame *)Parent)->SetMenu(LineMenuName, LineMenuChildPos);
  TWindow::WMMDIActivate(m);
}
```

GetMenuName() is a function from the TDuetFrame class that returns a pointer to the name of the menu. The above code only looks at the first character of the name, but that's enough because in Duet all of the menu names have different first characters. But this clearly isn't a general solution; it doesn't account for menu names that have the same first character, and it doesn't account for menu resources that are identified by a number.

The last line of the TLineWindow class's WMMDIActivate() function calls the base class's WMMDIActivate(). Whenever you override an OWL function, you should consult the OWL manual to see if the base class version needs to be called from within your own version. (If you look up WMMDIActivate() in your OWL manual, you'll discover their requirement to call the base class version at the end of the derived class's version.)

The TDuetFrame class's GetMenuName() procedure's trivial source code appears at the end of this chapter in the duet.h file, and I'll discuss SetMenu() in detail later in this section. LineMenuName is a string, defined in resource.h, that contains the name of the menu. LineMenuChildPos, also defined in resource.h, specifies the position of the Window menu.

The Duet application should revert to the main menu whenever the last child window is closed. The strategy is for the child window constructors and destructors to notify the frame window, so it can keep count of the children. Here are the constructors and destructors of the TLineWindow class:

```
// constructor
TLineWindow::TLineWindow(PTWindowsObject pParent) :
  TWindow(pParent, "Lines")
{
  ((TDuetFrame*)Parent)->ChildBirth();
}


// destructor
TLineWindow::~TLineWindow()
{
  if (TDuetFrame::IsValid())
    ((TDuetFrame *)Parent)->ChildDeath();
}
```

The constructor calls the parent class's ChildBirth() procedure while the destructor calls ChildDeath(). ChildBirth() simply increments the TDuetFrame class's nChildren variable, while ChildDeath() decrements nChildren. When the number of children drops to zero, ChildDeath() calls SetMenu() to revert to the main menu. The TBoxWindow constructors and destructors follow the same plan.

In the child window's constructor, the TDuetFrame's ChildBirth() procedure is called unconditionally, because when a child window is born the application's frame window is sure to exist. But at the other end of an application's life we must be more careful. When you close a TMDIFrame window, the TMDIFrame object deletes the associated TMDIClient object, which leads to the closure of the child windows. By the time the children are closed, their parent TDuetFrame object, which is pointed at by their Parent pointers, no longer exists! Therefore I created a static variable called isValid in my TDuetFrame class that is set to one in the TDuetFrame constructor and to zero in its destructor. In my child window destructors I use the IsValid() function, which returns the isValid variable, to make sure there is a parent MDI frame window object before notifying it of the child's demise.

The SetMenu() Procedure

I've just explained when I switch the menus, so now it's time to discuss exactly how they are switched. First, let's think about what needs to be done. You might be surprised that there are actually two separate chores. The first chore is the obvious: switching to a new menu. However, the second chore is equally important: managing the menu resources.

There are two general approaches to managing the application's menu resources. The first approach is to load all of the menus at the outset. This is simple, and it might be an acceptable strategy in an application with just a few menus. The second approach is to only load the menu resources as they are needed. I prefer this strategy because it makes better use of memory, and because it is consistent with the usual Windows approach, to hold onto resources only when they are being used.

The TDuetFrame class's SetMenu() procedure needs to know two things to switch to a new menu. First, it must know the name of the menu resource. My version of SetMenu() only allows string names, but it could be adapted to accept numeric identifiers. Second, SetMenu() must know the position of the Window menu. Remember that the MDI client window uses the Window menu to append the names of the child windows, so that you can switch to a specific child by selecting it from the Window menu. The MDI client window's additions to the Window menu are shown in Figure 15.6 for the Duet application and in Figure 15.9 for Borland's MDIApp application.

The code inside SetMenu() reflects the chores outlined above. First the Menu member of Attr (a TWindowAttr struct) is set to point at the new name. This part of the SetMenu() code was borrowed from Borland's AssignMenu() procedure from the TWindow class. Before switching the menus, SetMenu() gets a handle for the existing menu. Then the menus are switched, by sending the WM_MDISETMENU message to the client window. Then the menu bar is redrawn, and the old menu is destroyed. Here's the code for SetMenu().

```
void TDuetFrame::SetMenu(LPSTR menuName, int childPos)
{
  ChildMenuPos = childPos;
  if (HIWORD(Attr.Menu))
```

```
   farfree(Attr.Menu);
 Attr.Menu = _fstrdup(menuName);
 HMENU OldMenu = GetMenu(HWindow);
 HMENU FrameMenu = LoadMenu(GetModule()->hInstance, menuName);
 HMENU WinMenu = GetSubMenu(FrameMenu, ChildMenuPos);
 DWORD handles = MAKELONG(FrameMenu, WinMenu);
 if (ClientWnd)
   SendMessage(ClientWnd->HWindow, WM_MDISETMENU, 0, handles);
 DrawMenuBar(HWindow);
 DestroyMenu(OldMenu);
}
```

The code for managing the menu resources is straightforward. At the beginning of SetMenu() a handle to the current menu is acquired using GetMenu().

```
HMENU OldMenu = GetMenu(HWindow);
```

Then at the end of SetMenu() the old menu is destroyed.

```
DestroyMenu(OldMenu);
```

The only subtlety is to delay the destruction until after the new menu is completely installed, which explains why DestroyMenu() is the last line of SetMenu(). The installation of a new menu in the Duet MDI applications starts by loading a menu from the application's menu resources.

```
HMENU FrameMenu = LoadMenu(GetModule()->hInstance, menuName);
```

Next we need to get a handle for what we've been calling the Window menu, the submenu that is used to record the comings and goings of the child windows. This is easily accomplished with the Windows function called GetSubMenu(), which returns the handle of a submenu, given a menu handle and the index of the desired submenu.

```
HMENU WinMenu = GetSubMenu(FrameMenu, ChildMenuPos);
```

The next step is to get ready for sending the WM_MDISETMENU message to the client window. If you look up the WM_MDISETMENU message in the Windows API reference, you'll discover that it wants the handles of the new menu, and its Window submenu, in the low and high words of lParam. We can build a long comprised of these two handles using Windows's MAKELONG macro.

```
DWORD handles = MAKELONG(FrameMenu, WinMenu);
```

The last step is to actually send the WM_MDISETMENU message to the client window.

```
if (ClientWnd)
  SendMessage(ClientWnd->HWindow, WM_MDISETMENU, 0, handles);
```

As a formality I check the ClientWnd pointer to make sure there is a client window object, but this test affords little real protection. (If the client window doesn't exist, much worse difficulties are lurking nearby.)

The last step is to call DrawMenuBar() to redraw the application's menu bar.

```
DrawMenuBar(HWindow);
```

The SetMenu() procedure that I've just discussed is a general solution for the problem of switching menus in an MDI application, but it's not a general solution for the problem of switching menus. Ironically, my SetMenu() suffers the opposite problem from Borland's AssignMenu(): My SetMenu() doesn't work in an ordinary (non-MDI) application!

MDI Command Message Passing

In an MDI application the command messages are first routed to the active child window, and then routed to the child's parent, the TMDIFrame window. This gives the child the first opportunity to handle the message, but it also lets the frame window serve as a message handler for any messages not handled by the child.

I've illustrated this message handling procedure in the Duet application's About() procedures. Notice that all three window classes in Duet—TDuet-Frame, TBoxWindow, and TLineWindow—have an About() procedure that is hooked up to the CM_About menu selection. All three Duet menus have an About menu item that is hooked up to the CM_About command ID, so it is always possible in Duet to ask for an About dialog box.

When there isn't an active child, either because there are no child windows or because all the child windows are iconified, then the CM_About command is passed directly to the frame window, which handles it by displaying the main About dialog, as shown in Figure 15.11. If a TLineWindow child is active when the About menu selection is made, then it gets first rights to the CM_About command, and it responds by displaying its own About dialog, as shown in Figure 15.12. Similarly, when a TBoxWindow is active, it displays its own About dialog, as shown in Figure 15.13.

We should also consider the two simpler possibilities, commands that are handled by the frame window but not by the child, and those that are handled by the child and not by the parent. The File and Window submenus contain menu selections that are handled exclusively by the frame window. Because neither of Duet's child windows handles any of these selections, all of these menu selections are managed by the frame window.

The Boxes and Lines submenus, which are only present when a TLineWindow and TBoxWindow child is active, respectively, show the opposite behavior. These menu handlers are only present in the children. If you have child windows, but all the children are iconified, then you'll be able to make a selection from the Line or Box menu, but that selection won't do anything because the frame window doesn't contain these message handlers.

FIGURE 15.11

The Duet application's About dialog. Because both child windows are iconified, the CM_About command ID is passed directly to the TDuetFrame window, which displays the application's About dialog.

FIGURE 15.12

The TLineWindow's About dialog. Because a TLineWindow child is active, it gets to handle the CM_About command.

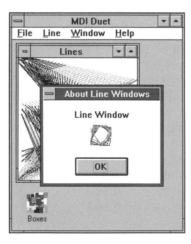

The TBoxWindow's About dialog. Because a TBoxWindow child is active, it gets to handle the CM_About command.

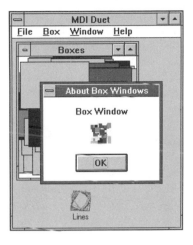

Paint() in the TBoxWindow and TLineWindow Classes

The Duet application's two child windows draw geometric patterns in their Paint() procedures. Although these simple graphical algorithms don't have anything to do with MDI, I'd like to briefly describe the logic.

TLineWindow draws 500 lines. The initial endpoints are the top-left and bottom-right corners of the client window. For each successive line the endpoints are moved by a fixed amount, much like the bouncing ball in the seminal video game Pong. When an endpoint moves out of the client rectangle, the increment is adjusted to produce the opposite direction of movement, and the endpoint is moved back inside the client rect. This endpoint logic is performed by the BoundsCheck() function, which is an inline function. Moving this tedious code into an inline function makes Paint() less cluttered and the visual regularity of the four calls to BoundsCheck() makes errors less likely. Notice that the first two parameters to BoundsCheck() are passed by reference, so they can be modified within BoundsCheck().

TLineWindow's Paint() procedure changes the color every 20 lines. I chose to use the system colors as my palette, by using the GetSysColor() procedure. Alternatively I could have specified colors directly using Windows's RGB macro. The decision to switch colors every 20 lines was arbitrary. Groups of 20 looked nice; changing color every time I drew a new line looked too busy.

The other thing to notice about TLineWindow's Paint() procedure is that it is careful to manage the pen resources. Paint() needs to create a new pen each time it switches color. The switch is done in the following sequence:

1. The current pen's handle is saved.

2. The new pen is created by calling CreatePen().

3. The new pen is selected into the paint device context.

4. The previous pen is deleted.

Careful attention to creation and deletion of GDI objects is always necessary.

The TBoxWindow class draws a sequence of 150 randomly placed, randomly colored boxes. The logic for picking a position for each rectangle is placed in the PickCoords() inline function. PickCoords() needs to be called twice for each box—once to pick a pair of X coordinates, and once to pick a pair of Y coordinates.

The logic in PickCoords() is slightly tricky. Let's say we're randomly choosing a pair of X coordinates. First a coordinate is chosen that lies in the given X range. If that coordinate is to the left of center, meaning its value is less than half the range, then it is used as the coordinate of the left side of the rectangle. If the picked coordinate is on the right half of the client window, then it is used as the right coordinate of the rectangle. This logic, which is repeated for the Y dimension, assures that the box will reside completely inside the client rectangle.

The TBoxWindow class's Paint() procedure uses a new brush object for each rectangle. This approach is easy to code, because it follows the plan established in the TLineWindow class. A more appropriate choice might be to create a set of six or eight brushes, and simply cycle through them during the drawing loop. I don't know if this would noticeably reduce the drawing time, but it would certainly eliminate nearly 150 calls to GetSysColor(), CreateSolidBrush(), and DeleteObject().

Duet Source Code

The complete Duet application source code, except for the source code for its icon resources, is presented in this section (see Listings 15.2–15.9). The Duet application is a relatively simple MDI application, but like many Windows applications it comprises many lines of code and is stored in many files. The file organization of Duet is shown in Figure 15.14, and its class hierarchy is shown in Figure 15.15. Table 15.1 shows where you can find every listing in the Duet application.

There are several ways that you could improve the Duet application. If you just want to have more control over the displays, you might want to create dialog boxes to control the characteristics of each of the two child windows. Duet already contains placeholders for these dialogs in the Settings() functions in each child window class. You might want the user to be able to specify line thicknesses, colors, rectangle borders, the number of elements that are drawn, and the like, using these dialogs.

If you want to make an addition that is more related to MDI programming, you could consider adding a new type of child window. Or suppose you want to make the menu structure more complex. For example, you might want each child window to have both short and long menus, to accommodate both novice and expert users. Have fun.

FIGURE 15.14

The file organization of the Duet application

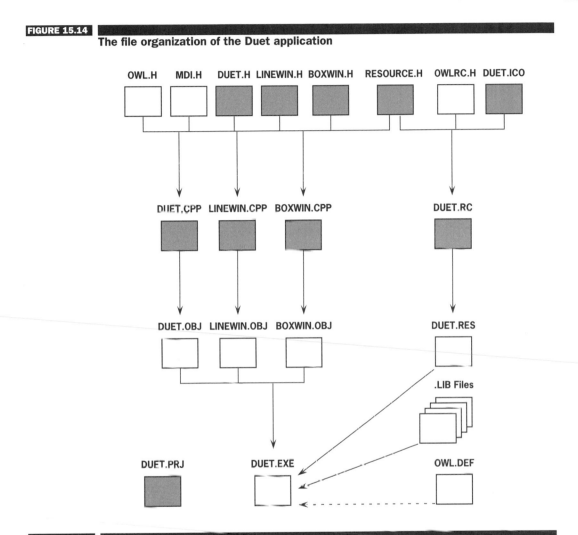

TABLE 15.1

The Duet Application Source Code

File	Listing
duet.h	15.2
resource.h	15.3
linewin.h	15.4
boxwin.h	15.5
duet.cpp	15.6
linewin.cpp	15.7
boxwin.cpp	15.8

FIGURE 15.15

The class hierarchy of the Duet application

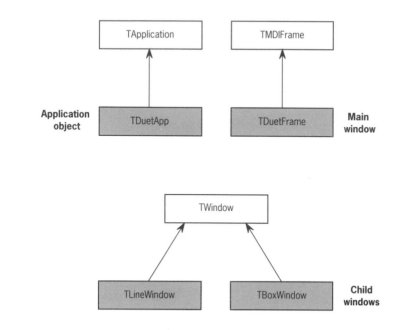

LISTING 15.2

duet.h

```
//
// Define a TApplication descendent
//
class TDuetApp : public TApplication {
  public:
    TDuetApp(LPSTR name, HINSTANCE hInstance,
      HINSTANCE hPrevInstance, LPSTR lpCmd,
      int nCmdShow) :
      TApplication(name, hInstance, hPrevInstance, lpCmd, nCmdShow)
    {
      return;
    }
    virtual void InitMainWindow();
};

// Define a TMDIFrame descendent
class TDuetFrame : public TMDIFrame {
  public:
    TDuetFrame(LPSTR ATitle);
    ~TDuetFrame()
    {
      isValid = Ø;
    }

    // return the class name for win class registration
```

LISTING 15.2

duet.h (Continued)

```
    LPSTR GetClassName() {
      return "TDuetFrameWindow";
    }

    // specify the window class info
    void GetWindowClass(WNDCLASS& rWndClass)
    {
      TWindow::GetWindowClass(rWndClass);
      rWndClass.hIcon = LoadIcon(GetApplication()->hInstance,
        "DuetAppIcon");
    }

    // Menu Switching
    void SetMenu(LPSTR name, int childPos);
    const LPSTR GetMenuName()
    {
      return HIWORD(Attr.Menu) ? Attr.Menu : "?";
    }
    void ChildBirth() { nChildren++; }
    void ChildDeath()
    {
      if (!--nChildren)
        SetMenu(MainMenuName, MainMenuChildPos);
    }

    // MDI Frame menu bar handlers
    void About(RTMessage) =
      [ CM_FIRST + CM_About ];
    void CMLineWin(RTMessage) =
      [ CM_FIRST + CM_LineWin ];
    void CMBoxWin(RTMessage) =
      [ CM_FIRST + CM_BoxWin ];
    void Quit(RTMessage) =
      [ CM_FIRST + CM_Quit ];

    // static function to return TRUE if frame exists
    static int IsValid() { return isValid; }

  protected:
    int nChildren;
    static int isValid;
};
```

LISTING 15.3

resource.h

```
//
// resource IDs
//
#define CM_LineWin      100  // File menu
#define CM_BoxWin       101
```

LISTING 15.3

resource.h (Continued)

```
#define CM_Quit          102
#define CM_LineDialog    103   // Line menu
#define CM_BoxDialog     104   // Box menu
#define CM_About         105   // Help menu


//
// Menu Names
#define MainMenuName  "MainMenu"
#define LineMenuName  "LineMenu"
#define BoxMenuName   "BoxMenu"


//
// Position of the child (WINDOW) menus
#define MainMenuChildPos 0
#define BoxMenuChildPos  2
#define LineMenuChildPos 2
```

LISTING 15.4

linewin.h

```
//
// A TWindow child class
// for filling the window with lines
//
class TLineWindow : public TWindow {
  public:
    TLineWindow(PTWindowsObject pParent) :
      TWindow(pParent, "Lines")
    {
      ((TDuetFrame*)Parent)->ChildBirth();
    }
    ~TLineWindow()
    {
      if (TDuetFrame::IsValid())
        ((TDuetFrame *)Parent)->ChildDeath();
    }

    // return the class name for win class registration
    LPSTR GetClassName() {
      return "TLineWindow";
    }

    // specify the window class info
    void GetWindowClass(WNDCLASS& rWndClass)
```

LISTING 15.4
linewin.h (Continued)

```
  {
    TWindow::GetWindowClass(rWndClass);
    rWndClass.hIcon = LoadIcon(GetApplication()->hInstance,
      "LineWinIcon");
  }

  void Paint(HDC PaintDC, PAINTSTRUCT& ps);
  void WMMDIActivate(RTMessage m);

  // TLineWindow menu selections
  void About(RTMessage) =
    [ CM_FIRST + CM_About ];
  void Settings(RTMessage) =
    [ CM_FIRST + CM_LineDialog ];
};
```

LISTING 15.5
boxwin.h

```
//
// A TWindow child class
// for filling the window with boxes
//
class TBoxWindow : public TWindow {
  public:
    TBoxWindow(PTWindowsObject pParent) :
      TWindow(pParent, "Boxes")
    {
      ((TDuetFrame *)Parent)->ChildBirth();
      srand((unsigned)time(0));
      seed = rand();
    }
    ~TBoxWindow()
    {
      if (TDuetFrame::IsValid())
        ((TDuetFrame *)Parent)->ChildDeath();
    }

    // return the class name for win class registration
    LPSTR GetClassName() {
      return "TBoxWindow";
    }

    // specify the window class info
```

LISTING 15.5

boxwin.h (Continued)

```cpp
    void GetWindowClass(WNDCLASS& rWndClass)
    {
      TWindow::GetWindowClass(rWndClass);
      rWndClass.hIcon = LoadIcon(GetApplication()->hInstance,
        "BoxWinIcon");
    }

    void Paint(HDC PaintDC, PAINTSTRUCT& ps);
    void WMMDIActivate(RTMessage m);

    // TBoxWindow menu selections
    void About(RTMessage) =
      [ CM_FIRST + CM_About ];
    void Settings(RTMessage) =
      [ CM_FIRST + CM_BoxDialog ];

  protected:
    int seed;  // to restart random number
    static const int nAvgBoxHt;
    static const int nAvgBoxWid;
};
```

LISTING 15.6

duet.cpp

```cpp
#include <stdlib.h>
#include <alloc.h>
#include <string.h>
#define WIN31
#define STRICT
#include <owl.h>
#include <mdi.h>
#include "resource.h"
#include "duet.h"
#include "boxwin.h"
#include "linewin.h"

//
// Application Object constructor - build main window
//
void TDuetApp::InitMainWindow()
{
  MainWindow = new TDuetFrame("MDI Duet");
}

//
// MDI Frame static variable
int TDuetFrame::isValid = 0;
```

LISTING 15.6

duet.cpp (Continued)

```cpp
//
// MDI Frame constructor
//
TDuetFrame::TDuetFrame(LPSTR ATitle) :
  TMDIFrame(ATitle, MainMenuName),
  nChildren(0)
{
  ChildMenuPos = MainMenuChildPos;
  isValid = 1;
}

//
// switch to a new menu
//
void TDuetFrame::SetMenu(LPSTR menuName, int childPos)
{
  ChildMenuPos = childPos;
  if (HIWORD(Attr.Menu))
    farfree(Attr.Menu);
  Attr.Menu = _fstrdup(menuName);
  HMENU OldMenu = GetMenu(HWindow);
  HMENU FrameMenu = LoadMenu(GetModule()->hInstance, menuName);
  HMENU WinMenu = GetSubMenu(FrameMenu, ChildMenuPos);
  DWORD handles = MAKELONG(FrameMenu, WinMenu);
  if (ClientWnd)
    SendMessage(ClientWnd->HWindow, WM_MDISETMENU, 0, handles);
  DrawMenuBar(HWindow);
  DestroyMenu(OldMenu);
}

//
// New Line Window
void TDuetFrame::CMLineWin(RTMessage /*m*/)
{
  GetModule()->MakeWindow(new TLineWindow(this));
}

//
// New Box Window
void TDuetFrame::CMBoxWin(RTMessage /*m*/)
{
  GetModule()->MakeWindow(new TBoxWindow(this));
}

//
// Quit
void TDuetFrame::Quit(RTMessage /*m*/)
{
  PostQuitMessage(0);
}

//
```

LISTING 15.6

duet.cpp (Continued)

```cpp
// Duet Frame About dialog
void TDuetFrame::About(RTMessage /*m*/)
{
  GetApplication()->ExecDialog(new TDialog(this, "AboutDialog"));
}

//
// Run the MDIApp
int PASCAL WinMain(HINSTANCE hInstance, HINSTANCE hPrevInstance,
  LPSTR lpCmd, int nCmdShow)
{
  TDuetApp DuetApp ("DuetApp", hInstance, hPrevInstance,
    lpCmd, nCmdShow);
  DuetApp.Run();
  return (DuetApp.Status);
}
```

LISTING 15.7

linewin.cpp

```cpp
#include <stdlib.h>
#define WIN31
#define STRICT
#include <owl.h>
#include "resource.h"]
#include "duet.h"
#include "linewin.h"

//
// Helper fn for the TLineWindow Paint() function
inline void BoundsCheck(int& c, int& inc, int lo, int hi)
{
  c += inc;
  if (c < lo || c > hi) {
    inc = - inc;
    c += inc;
  }
}

//
// Draw lines
// Endpoint bounces like a Pong ball
void TLineWindow::Paint(HDC PaintDC, PAINTSTRUCT& /*ps*/)
{
  const int nLines = 500;
  HPEN hOldPen, hPen;
  RECT r;
  GetClientRect(HWindow, &r);
  int xs = r.left, ys = r.top;      // src
  int xd = r.right, yd = r.bottom; // dest
  int dxs = 4, dys = 2;             // src inc
  int dxd = -5, dyd = -1;           // dest inc
```

LISTING 15.7

linewin.cpp (Continued)

```cpp
    int i;
    int color = 0;

    hPen = CreatePen(PS_SOLID, 1, GetSysColor(color++));
    hOldPen = (HPEN)SelectObject(PaintDC, hPen);

    for(i=0;i<nLines; i++) {
      if (i % 20 == 0) {
        COLORREF c;
        do {
          if (color > COLOR_BTNTEXT)
            color = 0;
          c = GetSysColor(color++);
        } while(c == GetBkColor(PaintDC));
        HPEN hPrevPen = hPen;
        hPen = CreatePen(PS_SOLID, 1, c);
        SelectObject(PaintDC, hPen);
        DeleteObject(hPrevPen);
      }
      MoveTo(PaintDC, xs, ys);
      LineTo(PaintDC, xd, yd);
      BoundsCheck(xs, dxs, r.left, r.right);
      BoundsCheck(xd, dxd, r.left, r.right);
      BoundsCheck(ys, dys, r.top, r.bottom);
      BoundsCheck(yd, dyd, r.top, r.bottom);
    }
    SelectObject(PaintDC, hOldPen);
    DeleteObject(hPen);
}

//
// Activation/Deactivation of a Line window
void TLineWindow..WMMDIActivate(RTMessage m)
{
  if (m.WParam == 1) // activate
    if (*((TDuetFrame *)Parent)->GetMenuName() != *LineMenuName)
      ((TDuetFrame *)Parent)->SetMenu(LineMenuName, LineMenuChildPos);
  TWindow::WMMDIActivate(m);
}

//
// TLineWindow About menu
void TLineWindow::About(RTMessage /*m*/)
{
  GetApplication()->ExecDialog(new TDialog(this, "LineAboutDialog"));
}

//
// TLineWindow Settings menu
void TLineWindow::Settings(RTMessage /*m*/)
{
  MessageBox(HWindow, "Settings TK", "Line Win", MB_ICONINFORMATION);
}
```

LISTING 15.8

boxwin.cpp

```cpp
#include <stdlib.h>
#define WIN31
#define STRICT
#include <owl.h>
#include "resource.h"
#include "duet.h"
#include "boxwin.h"

inline void PickCoords(int& c1, int& c2, int range, int var)
{
  c1 = random(range);
  if (c1 > range/2) {
    c2 = c1;
    c1 = c2 - (var + random(var));
  } else
    c2 = c1 + var + random(var);
}

const int TBoxWindow::nAvgBoxHt = 40;
const int TBoxWindow::nAvgBoxWid = 60;

//
// Draw Boxes
// Endpoint bounces like a Pong ball
void TBoxWindow::Paint(HDC PaintDC, PAINTSTRUCT& /*ps*/)
{
  const int nBoxes = 150;
  HBRUSH hOldBrush, hBrush;
  RECT r;
  GetClientRect(HWindow, &r);
  int x1, x2, y1, y2;
  int i;
  int color = 0;

  COLORREF BkColor = GetBkColor(PaintDC);
  srand(seed); // always restart from the same point

  hBrush = CreateSolidBrush(GetSysColor(color++));
  hOldBrush = (HBRUSH)SelectObject(PaintDC, hBrush);

  for(i=0;i<nBoxes; i++) {
    COLORREF c;
    do {
      if (color > COLOR_BTNTEXT)
        color = 0;
      c = GetSysColor(color++);
    } while(c == BkColor);
    HBRUSH hPrevBrush = hBrush;
    hBrush = CreateSolidBrush(c);
    SelectObject(PaintDC, hBrush);
    DeleteObject(hPrevBrush);
    PickCoords(x1, x2, r.right, nAvgBoxWid);
    PickCoords(y1, y2, r.bottom, nAvgBoxHt);
```

LISTING 15.8

boxwin.cpp (Continued)

```cpp
      Rectangle(PaintDC, x1, y1, x2, y2);
   }
  SelectObject(PaintDC, hOldBrush);
  DeleteObject(hBrush);
}


//
// Activation/Deactivation of a Box window
void TBoxWindow::WMMDIActivate(RTMessage m)
{
  if (m.WParam == 1) // activate
    if (*((TDuetFrame *)Parent)->GetMenuName() != *BoxMenuName)
      ((TDuetFrame *)Parent)->SetMenu(BoxMenuName, BoxMenuChildPos);
  TWindow::WMMDIActivate(m);
}


//
// TBoxWindow About menu
void TBoxWindow::About(RTMessage /*m*/)
{
  GetApplication()->ExecDialog(new TDialog(this, "BoxAboutDialog"));
}


//
// TBoxWindow Settings menu
void TBoxWindow::Settings(RTMessage /*m*/)
{
  MessageBox(HWindow, "Settings TK", "Box Win", MB_ICONINFORMATION);
}
```

LISTING 15.9

duet.rc

```
#include <windows.h>
#include <owlrc.h>
#include "resource.h"
#include "duet.ico"


MainMenu MENU
BEGIN
    POPUP "&File"
    BEGIN
        MENUITEM "New &Line Window", CM_LineWin
        MENUITEM "New &Box Window", CM_BoxWin
        MENUITEM "&Exit", CM_Quit
    END
    POPUP "&Help"
    BEGIN
        MENUITEM "About...", CM_About
```

LISTING 15.9

duet.rc (Continued)

```
        END
END

LineMenu MENU
BEGIN
    POPUP "&File"
    BEGIN
        MENUITEM "New &Line Window", CM_LineWin
        MENUITEM "New &Box Window", CM_BoxWin
        MENUITEM "&Exit", CM_Quit
    END
    POPUP "&Line"
    BEGIN
        MENUITEM "Settings...", CM_LineDialog
    END
    POPUP "&Window"
    BEGIN
        MENUITEM "&Cascade", CM_CASCADECHILDREN
        MENUITEM "&Tile", CM_TILECHILDREN
        MENUITEM "Arrange &Icons", CM_ARRANGEICONS
        MENUITEM "C&lose All", CM_CLOSECHILDREN
    END
    POPUP "&Help"
    BEGIN
        MENUITEM "About...", CM_About
    END
END

BoxMenu MENU
BEGIN
    POPUP "&File"
    BEGIN
        MENUITEM "New &Line Window", CM_LineWin
        MENUITEM "New &Box Window", CM_BoxWin
        MENUITEM "&Exit", CM_Quit
    END
    POPUP "&Box"
    BEGIN
        MENUITEM "Settings...", CM_BoxDialog
    END
    POPUP "&Window"
    BEGIN
        MENUITEM "&Cascade", CM_CASCADECHILDREN
        MENUITEM "&Tile", CM_TILECHILDREN
```

LISTING 15.9

duet.rc (Continued)

```
        MENUITEM "Arrange &Icons", CM_ARRANGEICONS
        MENUITEM "C&lose All", CM_CLOSECHILDREN
    END
    POPUP "&Help"
    BEGIN
        MENUITEM "About...", CM_About
    END
END


AboutDialog DIALOG 45, 22, 91, 79
STYLE DS_MODALFRAME | WS_POPUP | WS_CAPTION | WS_SYSMENU
CAPTION "About MDI Duet"
BEGIN
  CTEXT "MDI Demonstration", -1, 8, 7, 75, 1Ø,
    WS_CHILD | WS_VISIBLE | WS_GROUP
  CTEXT "Copyright \251 1993\nby Kaare Christian",
    -1, 1Ø, 21, 71, 18, WS_CHILD | WS_VISIBLE | WS_GROUP
  ICON "DuetAppIcon", -1, 13, 41, 16, 16,
    WS_CHILD | WS_VISIBLE
  ICON "LineWinIcon", -1, 38, 41, 16, 16,
    WS_CHILD | WS_VISIBLE
  ICON "BoxWinIcon", -1, 62, 41, 16, 16,
    WS_CHILD | WS_VISIBLE
  DEFPUSHBUTTON "OK", IDOK, 25, 61, 41, 14,
    WS_CHILD | WS_VISIBLE | WS_TABSTOP
END


BoxAboutDialog DIALOG 45, 22, 91, 65
STYLE DS_MODALFRAME | WS_POPUP | WS_CAPTION | WS_SYSMENU
CAPTION "About Box Windows"
BEGIN
  CTEXT "Box Window", -1, 8, 7, 75, 1Ø,
    WS_CHILD | WS_VISIBLE | WS_GROUP
  ICON "BoxWinIcon", -1, 37, 2Ø, 16, 16,
    WS_CHILD | WS_VISIBLE
  DEFPUSHBUTTON "OK", IDOK, 25, 44, 41, 14,
    WS_CHILD | WS_VISIBLE | WS_TABSTOP
END


LineAboutDialog DIALOG 45, 22, 91, 64
STYLE DS_MODALFRAME | WS_POPUP | WS_CAPTION | WS_SYSMENU
CAPTION "About Line Windows"
BEGIN
  CTEXT "Line Window", -1, 8, 7, 75, 1Ø,
```

LISTING 15.9

duet.rc (Continued)

```
     WS_CHILD | WS_VISIBLE | WS_GROUP
   ICON "LineWinIcon", -1, 37, 19, 16, 16,
     WS_CHILD | WS_VISIBLE
   DEFPUSHBUTTON "OK", IDOK, 25, 44, 41, 14,
     WS_CHILD | WS_VISIBLE | WS_TABSTOP
END
```

16 WINDOWS L-SYSTEMS

IN CHAPTER 6 I DISCUSSED ARISTID LINDENMAYER'S L-SYSTEMS, AND I SHOWED how you could develop a DOS program for displaying L-systems by creating a few simple data structures based on Borland's container class library. In Chapter 6 my example L-systems were drawn using Borland's BGI graphics facility, which is a simple graphics library for DOS.

The examples in Chapter 6 served their purpose, demonstrating the Borland class library, but they proved unsatisfying for several reasons because of their use of BGI graphics and their simplistic user interface. L-systems, which are usually interpreted graphically, can best be presented in a fully graphic environment such as Windows. In addition, the menu-based, dialog-based, multiple-document-capable Windows environment is ideal for creating an exploratory environment, so that you can create new L-systems and see how they behave. Yes, there is a lot of fun in this chapter.

But the major focus of this chapter isn't enjoyment of L-systems, but rather the full development of Windows programming techniques using the OWL class library. The L-system application, shown in Figure 16.1, is the most complete Windows example in this book. More than any other example, the L-system application demonstrates realistic Windows/OWL programming. It's not a full Windows spreadsheet, database, or word processor, and it's not 50,000+ lines of production code. But it is a complete and useful Windows application that serves both as an example for learning about Windows programming and as an environment for exploring L-systems.

The L-system Application's Organization

As you can see from Figure 16.1, the L-system application is a Windows MDI application. Therefore its organization is similar to any MDI application. It contains

- An application class, TLsysApp, which is derived from TApplication

- A frame window class, TLsysFrame, which is derived from TMDIFrame

- A single type of child window, TLsysWindow, which is derived from TWindow

These classes and the other classes in the L-system application are shown in Figure 16.2.

FIGURE 16.1

The L-system application, showing all eight built-in L-systems

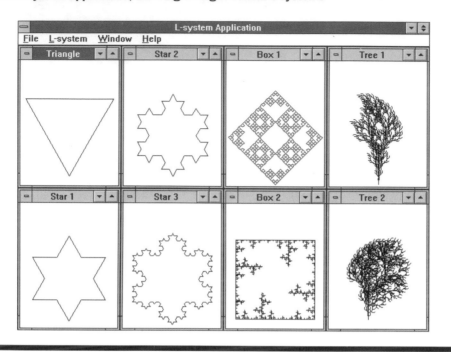

Most of the Windows aspect of the L-system application resides in the TLsysWindow class. It is responsible for invoking the dialogs that are used to control an L-system, it contains the code to produce the eight built-in L-systems shown in Figure 16.1, and it contains the logic for reading and writing files, so that L-system descriptions can be stored permanently. Of course TLsysWindow itself doesn't know how to calculate an L-system; instead it contains an instance of an L-system object that manages L-system details.

Figure 16.2 reveals that the L-system application contains four dialog classes:

- The Settings dialog lets you specify the L-system's seed, rule, and the number of iterations.

FIGURE 16.2

The class hierarchy of the L-system application. Standard OWL classes are unshaded, and the details of the OWL class hierarchy are not shown.

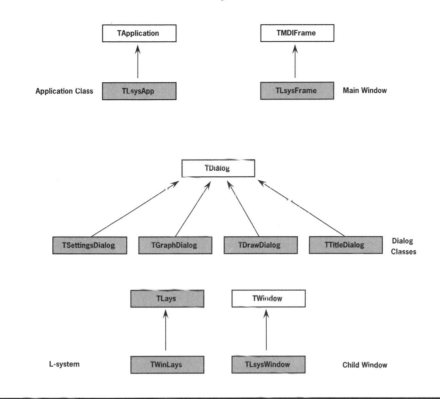

- The Graphing dialog lets you specify the L-system's graphical interpretation: the X and Y position, the initial angle (Theta), the turning angle (Delta), and the length of each segment (Length).

■ The Drawing dialog lets you specify the L-system's color and the width of the pen used to draw the L-system.

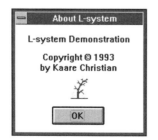

■ The Title dialog lets you specify the window title.

These four dialogs will be discussed in greater detail under "L-systems Dialogs," later in this chapter.

There are three additional L-system dialogs that aren't recorded in Figure 16.2:

■ An About dialog

■ A File Open dialog that is implemented by OWL's TFileDialog class

```
┌─────────────────────────────────────────────────────┐
│ ▭                    File Open                         │
├─────────────────────────────────────────────────────┤
│ File̲name:  [*.lsy            ]        ┌──────────┐    │
│ Directory:  c:\borlandc\kaare\winlsys │    OK    │    │
│ F̲iles:              D̲irectories:      └──────────┘    │
│ ┌──────────────┐   ┌──────────────┐   ┌──────────┐    │
│ │box1.lsy      │   │[..]          │   │  Cancel  │    │
│ │david.lsy     │   │[-a-]         │   └──────────┘    │
│ │              │   │[-b-]         │                   │
│ │              │   │[-c-]         │                   │
│ │              │   │              │                   │
│ │              │   │              │                   │
│ │              │   │              │                   │
│ └──────────────┘   └──────────────┘                   │
└─────────────────────────────────────────────────────┘
```

■ A File Save As dialog that is implemented by OWL's TFileDialog class

```
┌─────────────────────────────────────────────────────┐
│ ▭                   File Save As                       │
├─────────────────────────────────────────────────────┤
│ File̲name:  [star1.lsy        ]        ┌──────────┐    │
│ Directory:  c:\borlandc\kaare\winlsys │    OK    │    │
│ D̲irectories:                          └──────────┘    │
│ ┌──────────────┐                      ┌──────────┐    │
│ │[..]          │                      │  Cancel  │    │
│ │[-a-]         │                      └──────────┘    │
│ │[-b-]         │                                      │
│ │[-c-]         │                                      │
│ │              │                                      │
│ │              │                                      │
│ │              │                                      │
│ └──────────────┘                                      │
└─────────────────────────────────────────────────────┘
```

The About dialog is omitted from Figure 16.2 because it isn't implemented using its own class, and the two file dialogs are omitted because they are standard OWL components.

Like most MDI applications, the L-system application contains two menus. A brief menu is displayed when there are no child windows

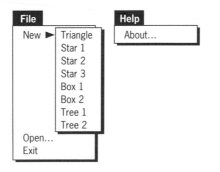

and a full menu is presented when child windows exist.

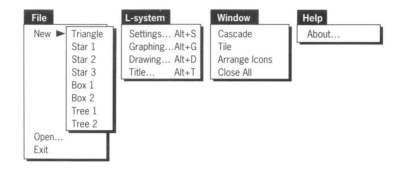

Note that the File-New menu selection invokes a second-level pop-up menu that allows you to select a particular type of L-system for the new window.

The L-system application is assembled from many source files, as shown in Figure 16.3. I placed all of the dialog classes in separate source and header files, even though the dialog classes are relatively simple. In a break from the practice in the preceding chapters, I've placed all the menu and dialog resources for the L-system application into the lsys.rc resource file. However, the application's icon resource is stored in a separate file, and the File dialog resources are standard OWL components that are stored in OWL's filedial.dlg.

Figure 16.3 shows the eight .CPP source code files used to create the L-system application. Five of these files—charray.cpp, setdlg.cpp, graphdlg.cpp, drawdlg.cpp, and titledlg.cpp—have obvious roles, which you should be able to guess based on their names. But the three other .CPP files—lsysapp.cpp, lsysw.cpp, and lsyswin.cpp—are much easier to confuse. Let me briefly mention each of these files so that you'll know exactly how the program is organized:

- The lsysapp.cpp file contains the two classes that are the basis of the L-system application: TLsysApp and TLsysFrame. Most functionality in these two classes relates to Windows and to MDI, not to L-systems. The lsysapp.cpp file is described in the section "The L-system Application."

- The lsysw.cpp file contains the TWinLsys class. The TWinLsys class is a Windows version of the L-system class from Chapter 6. It knows how to calculate an L-system using the seed and the rule, it stores the L-system text, and it knows how to graph an L-system using a Windows device context. The lsysw.cpp file is described in the section "An L-system Class for Windows."

- The lsyswin.cpp file contains the L-system application's MDI child window class, TLsysWindow. The TLsysWindow class, which is derived from TWindow, invokes the main dialogs, it contains the dialog box transfer buffers, it saves and restores L-system parameters, and it contains a TWinLsys object that actually houses the L-system. The lsyswin.cpp file is described in the section "An L-systems Window Class."

FIGURE 16.3

The L-system application's source code files. Standard OWL and Windows files, and files produced during compilation, are unshaded. Standard C library include files are not shown.

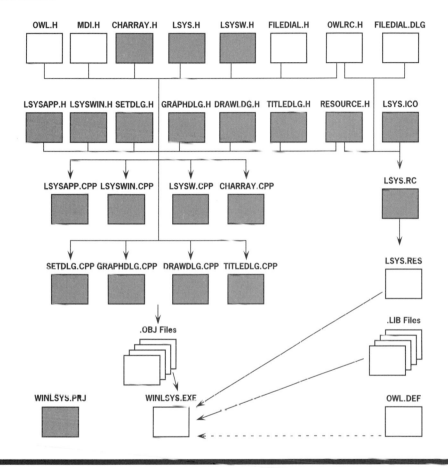

Figure 16.2 and subsequent illustrations reveal that the L-system application contains many components, but these graphics don't accurately portray the character of the application. Overall, the L-system application contains about four parts borrowed code and only one part new code. The borrowed code includes MDI components from Chapter 15, the L-system implementation from Chapters 5 and 6, and file dialog boxes from OWL. The new code is mostly related to the dialog boxes: the dialog box classes and the glue code that implements the changes specified by the dialogs. The dialog box code is voluminous, but straightforward.

The L-system Application

The standard part of the L-system application is its application class and its frame window class. These two classes are not the most interesting part of the application, but rather they are the framework that supports the application.

The TLsysApp class is a standard application class. It consists of just three functions—a constructor, the InitMainWindow() function, and the InitInstance() function. These three functions should be familiar to you from the previous chapters on OWL.

The TLsysFrame class is the L-system application's frame window class. Like all frame window classes, its primary responsibility is child window creation. In the TLsysFrame class, child windows are created in two ways, either by reading the L-system parameters in from a file, or by creating one of eight standard L-systems. In both cases the initial child window creation occurs in a TLsysFrame function (Open() and DefCommandProc(), respectively), and then the newly created child window object completes the creation, either by reading the parameters from a file or by using one of the eight sets of standard parameters to create one of the eight standard L-systems. Both of these processes are discussed later in this chapter: Reading from a file is discussed in the "File Open Dialog" section and creating one of the eight standard L-systems is discussed in the "Handling Similar Menu Selections" section.

The TLsysFrame class, which is defined in Listing 16.1 and whose full source code appears in Listing 16.2, contains several components from the Duet application in Chapter 15. The SetMenu() function, which was discussed extensively in Chapter 15, appears unchanged, as do the much simpler ChildBirth() and ChildDeath() procedures. Like the TDuetFrame class, the TLsysFrame class maintains a count of the number of active children, and it switches back to the main menu when the last child is destroyed. Again like the TDuetFrame class, the TLsysFrame class has a static flag called isValid that indicates whether the frame window object exists. The flag is set to True in the constructor, to False in the destructor, and it is tested using the static member function IsValid().

LISTING 16.1

lsysapp.h

```
//
// Define a TApplication descendent
//
class TLsysApp : public TApplication {
  public:
    TLsysApp(LPSTR name, HINSTANCE hInstance,
      HINSTANCE hPrevInstance, LPSTR lpCmd,
      int nCmdShow) :
      TApplication(name, hInstance, hPrevInstance, lpCmd, nCmdShow)
    {
      return;
    }
    virtual void InitMainWindow();
    void InitInstance();
```

LISTING 16.1 ■

lsysapp.h (Continued)

```
};

// Define a TMDIFrame descendent
class TLsysFrame : public TMDIFrame {
  public:
    TLsysFrame(LPSTR ATitle);
    ~TLsysFrame()
    {
      isValid = 0;
    }

    // return the class name for win class registration
    LPSTR GetClassName() {
      return "TLsysFrameWindow";
    }

    // specify the window class info
    void GetWindowClass(WNDCLASS& rWndClass)
    {
      TWindow::GetWindowClass(rWndClass);
      rWndClass.hIcon = LoadIcon(GetApplication()->hInstance,
        "LsysAppIcon");
    }

    // Menu Switching
    void SetMenu(LPSTR name, int childPos);
    const LPSTR GetMenuName()
    {
      return HIWORD(Attr.Menu) ? Attr.Menu : "?";
    }
    void ChildBirth() { nChildren++; }
    void ChildDeath()
    {
      if (!--nChildren)
        SetMenu(MainMenuName, MainMenuChildPos);
    }

    // Lsys Frame menu bar handlers
    void Open(RTMessage) =
      [ CM_FIRST + CM_FILEOPEN ];
    void About(RTMessage) =
      [ CM_FIRST + CM_About ];

    // static function to return TRUE if frame exists
    static int IsValid() { return isValid; }

    // route CM_NewTriangle ... to NewLsysWin()
    void DefCommandProc(RTMessage m);
```

LISTING 16.1

lsysapp.h (Continued)

```
protected:
   int nChildren;
   static int isValid;
};
```

LISTING 16.2

lsysapp.cpp

```
#include <stdlib.h>
#include <alloc.h>
#include <string.h>
#include <math.h>
#include <dir.h>
#define WIN31
#define STRICT

#include <owl.h>
#include <mdi.h>
#include <filedial.h>

#include "resource.h"
#include "lsysapp.h"
#include "lsysw.h"
#include "setdlg.h"
#include "drawdlg.h"
#include "graphdlg.h"
#include "lsyswin.h"

//
// Application Object constructor - build main window
//
void TLsysApp::InitMainWindow()
{
  MainWindow = new TLsysFrame("L-system Application");
}

//
// Lsys Frame static variable
int TLsysFrame::isValid = 0;

//
// Lsys Frame constructor
//
TLsysFrame::TLsysFrame(LPSTR ATitle) :
  TMDIFrame(ATitle, MainMenuName),
  nChildren(0)
{
  ChildMenuPos = MainMenuChildPos;
  isValid = 1;
}
```

LISTING 16.2

lsysapp.cpp (Continued)

```cpp
// L-system App, routine initialization
void TLsysApp::InitInstance()
{
  TApplication::InitInstance();
  HAccTable = LoadAccelerators(hInstance, "ACCELTABLE");
}

//
// switch to a new menu
//
void TLsysFrame::SetMenu(LPSTR menuName, int childPos)
{
  ChildMenuPos - childPos;
  if (HIWORD(Attr.Menu))
    farfree(Attr.Menu);
  Attr.Menu = _fstrdup(menuName);
  HMENU OldMenu = GetMenu(HWindow);
  HMENU FrameMenu = LoadMenu(GetModule()->hInstance, menuName);
  HMENU WinMenu = GetSubMenu(FrameMenu, ChildMenuPos);
  DWORD handles = MAKELONG(FrameMenu, WinMenu);
  if (ClientWnd)
    SendMessage(ClientWnd->HWindow, WM_MDISETMENU, 0, handles);
  DrawMenuBar(HWindow);
  DestroyMenu(OldMenu);
}

//
// handle CM_NewTriangle ... menu commands
void TLsysFrame::DefCommandProc(RTMessage m)
{
  if (m.WParam >= CM_NewTriangle && m.WParam <= CM_NewTree2) {
    TLsysWindow *p = new TLsysWindow(this);
    if (GetModule()->MakeWindow(p))
      p->CannedLsys(m.WParam);
  } else
    TWindow::DefCommandProc(m);
}

//
// handle the open message
void TLsysFrame::Open(RTMessage /*msg*/)
{
  char tmp[MAXPATH];

  _fstrcpy(tmp, "*.lsy");
  if (GetModule()->ExecDialog(
    new TFileDialog(this, SD_FILEOPEN, tmp, GetModule())
    ) == IDOK) {
    TLsysWindow *p = new TLsysWindow(this);
    if (GetModule()->MakeWindow(p)) {
      if (p->Read(tmp) == FALSE)
        delete p;
```

LISTING 16.2

lsysapp.cpp (Continued)

```
      }
    }
}

//
// Lsys Frame About dialog
void TLsysFrame::About(RTMessage /*m*/)
{
  GetApplication()->ExecDialog(new TDialog(this, "AboutDialog"));
}

//
// Run the L-system app
int PASCAL WinMain(HINSTANCE hInstance, HINSTANCE hPrevInstance,
  LPSTR lpCmd, int nCmdShow)
{
  TLsysApp LsysApp ("L-system Application",
    hInstance, hPrevInstance, lpCmd, nCmdShow);
  LsysApp.Run();
  return (LsysApp.Status);
}
```

An L-system Class for Windows

Before discussing the Windows aspects of the L-system application, let me discuss how I modified the DOS-based L-system code in Chapters 5 and 6 to work in a Windows MDI application. There are three components from these chapters that I borrowed to create the Windows L-system application:

- **lsys2.h**   This file contains all of the L-system logic. Lsys2.h uses templates, which means that there is no corresponding .CPP file. In the Windows L-system application I use the class in lsys2.h as a basis for the new TWinLsys class. In Chapter 6 lsys2.h is shown in Listing 6.4. It is used without modification in this chapter, so I'm not going to repeat the listing. However I have placed the file with the other L-system application files in the winlsys directory on the accompanying disk, and I've changed its name to lsys.h.

- **charray.h**   This file contains the definition of the CharArray class, which is used to store the L-system text. The CharArray class was first presented in Chapter 5 and is shown in Listing 5.4. It is used unchanged in the L-system application and its listing isn't repeated here. I've placed a copy of charray.h into the winlsys directory.

- **charray.cpp**   This file contains the full source code of the CharArray class. It is shown in Listing 5.5 and its listing is not repeated here. I've placed a copy of charray.cpp into the winlsys directory.

All other source code files in the L-system application are detailed in Table 16.1, which helps you find the L-system application listings.

TABLE 16.1

The L-system Listings

File Name	Listing Number
lsysapp.h	16.1
lsysapp.cpp	16.2
lsysw.h	16.3
lsysw.cpp	16.4
lsyswin.h	16.5
lsyswin.cpp	16.6
setdlg.h	16.7
setdlg.cpp	16.8
graphdlg.h	16.9
graphdlg.cpp	16.10
drawdlg.h	16.11
drawdlg.cpp	16.12
titledlg.h	16.13
titledlg.cpp	16.14
resource.h	16.15
lsys.rc	16.16

When I was planning the L-system application, I considered two different ways of using the Chapter 6 L-system code. My first idea was to modify the Chapter 6 code, so that it used Windows graphics routines instead of Borland's BGI (DOS-based) graphics routines. As I mentioned in Chapter 6, the L-system code uses only the line drawing function of BGI, so modifying it for Windows would not be difficult. The drawback is that I would then have two very similar versions of the L-system code, which in the long run can be a maintenance headache.

The second idea was to derive a Windows L-system class from my DOS L-system class. This uses C++'s strength, inheritance, to avoid duplication of code. Unfortunately, the DOS L-system class includes BGI output statements, so there isn't a clean way to derive a Windows version that doesn't reference BGI functions.

The best solution conceptually would probably be to start with a generic L-system class, which means one without any graphics output capability, and then from that class derive both DOS and Windows L-system classes. I didn't

choose this approach in Chapter 6 for two reasons. First, I didn't want to introduce another layer of classes in what was already becoming a complex class. And
second, I was hesitant to introduce a second software layer into the drawing
loop, which is very performance sensitive in all L-systems work.

The solution I chose was to use the existing L-system code without change.
The technical problem with this solution is that the existing code references the
line() procedure from the BGI library. Therefore I created a dummy line() procedure so that I could compile the L-system code. Then I derived a new TWinLsys
class from the existing code, using Windows GDI primitives. The TWinLsys class
contains a new draw() routine which is passed a handle to a device context, plus
it contains a new graph() routine which actually uses the specified device context
for output. Listing 16.3 contains the lsysw.h header file and Listing 16.4 contains
the short source code for the class. Note that the definitions of the draw() and
graph() functions in Listing 16.4 are modeled closely on the corresponding functions in lsys.h (Listing 6.4).

LISTING 16.3

lsysw.h

```
//
// L-system class for Windows
//

// this null line() lets us compile lsys.h w/out error
inline void line(int x, int y, int x2, int y2)
{
}

#include "lsys.h"
typedef LSystem<double, 10> LSys;

//
// TWinLsys
//
class TWinLsys : public LSys {
  public:
    // Windows version of draw()
    void draw(HDC dc, int x0, int y0);

  protected:
    // Windows version of graph()
    void graph(double x, double y, int theta);

    // saved hDC used by graph()
    HDC hDc;
};
```

LISTING 16.4

lsysw.cpp

```cpp
//
// L-System implementation
//
#include <math.h>

#define WIN31
#define STRICT

#include "windows.h"
#include "lsysw.h"
//
// public drawing interface
void TWinLsys::draw(HDC dc, int x0, int y0)
{
  hDc = dc;
  system.rewind();
  graph(x0, y0, CacheSize);
}


//
// recursive drawing routine
//
void TWinLsys::graph(double x, double y, int theta)
{
  int ch;
  double x1, y1;
  while((ch - system.getch()) != -1) {
    if (ch == 'F') { // step and draw
      if (theta >= 0 && theta <= 2*CacheSize) {
        x1 = x + cosDist[theta];
        y1 = y + sinDist[theta];
      } else {
        // not in cache -- do calculation
        double th = theta0 + (theta-CacheSize) * delta;
        x1 = x + dist * cos(th);
        y1 = y + dist * sin(th);
      }
      MoveTo(hDc, x, y);
      LineTo(hDc, x1, y1);
      x = x1;
      y = y1;
    } else if (ch == '-')
      theta--;
    else if (ch == '+')
      theta++;
    else if (ch == '[')
      graph(x, y, theta);
    else if (ch == ']')
      return;
  }
}
```

An L-systems Window Class

The TLsysWindow class is the heart of the Windows side of the L-system application. Its responsibilities include storing the L-system object, handling the WM_PAINT message by setting up the device context for the L-system's draw() procedure, file read and write operations so that L-systems can be stored on the disk, and the menu message handlers to start the dialogs.

The TLsysWindow class implements a child window in the L-system application, which is an MDI application. Thus it follows closely the form of the TBoxWindow and TLineWindow classes from Chapter 15. In the TLsysWindow class, whose definition is shown in Listing 16.5 and whose source is in Listing 16.6, the following procedures are taken almost verbatim from Chapter 15: the constructor, the destructor, GetClassName(), GetWindowClass(), and WMMDIActivate(). Therefore they won't be discussed in this chapter.

LISTING 16.5 ▆▆▆▆▆▆▆▆▆▆▆▆▆▆▆▆▆▆▆▆▆▆

lsyswin.h

```
//
// A TWindow child class
// for drawing an L-system graphic
//
class TLsysWindow : public TWindow {
  public:
    TLsysWindow(PTWindowsObject pParent);

    ~TLsysWindow()
    {
      if (TLsysFrame::IsValid())
        ((TLsysFrame *)Parent)->ChildDeath();
    }
    // return the class name for win class registration
    LPSTR GetClassName() {
      return "TLsysWindow";
    }

    // specify the window class info
    void GetWindowClass(WNDCLASS& rWndClass)
    {
      TWindow::GetWindowClass(rWndClass);
      rWndClass.hIcon = LoadIcon(GetApplication()->hInstance,
        "LsysAppIcon");
    }

    void Paint(HDC PaintDC, PAINTSTRUCT& ps);

    void WMMDIActivate(RTMessage m);

    // TLsysWindow menu selections
    void Save(RTMessage) =
      [ CM_FIRST + CM_FILESAVE ];
```

LISTING 16.5

lsyswin.h (Continued)

```
    void SaveAs(RTMessage) =
      [ CM_FIRST + CM_FILESAVEAS ];
    void SettingsDialog(RTMessage) =
      [ CM_FIRST + CM_LsysDialog ];
    void GraphDialog(RTMessage) =
      [ CM_FIRST + CM_GraphDialog ];
    void DrawDialog(RTMessage) =
      [ CM_FIRST + CM_DrawDialog ];
    void TitleDialog(RTMessage) =
      [ CM_FIRST + CM_TitleDialog ];

    // create specific l-systems
    void CannedLsys(int id);

    // prepare an lsys for drawing, using
    // the values stored in the 3 transfer bufs
    void Prepare();

    // file I/O
    int Read(char *filename);
    void Write(char *filename);

  protected:

    // the L-system object
    TWinLsys *lsys;

    // transfer buffers for the dialogs
    TSettingsTransfer settingsBuf;
    TGraphTransfer graphBuf;
    TDrawTransfer drawBuf;

    // drawing parameters
    int nColor;
    int nPenWidth;
    int nX, nY;
    // the filename
    char FileName[MAXPATH];
};
```

LISTING 16.6

lsyswin.cpp

```
#include <stdlib.h>
#include <math.h>
#include <dir.h>
#include <iomanip.h>

#define WIN31
#define STRICT

#include <owl.h>
#include <filedial.h>
```

LISTING 16.6

lsyswin.cpp (Continued)

```cpp
#include "resource.h"
#include "lsysw.h"
#include "lsysapp.h"
#include "setdlg.h"
#include "graphdlg.h"
#include "drawdlg.h"
#include "titledlg.h"
#include "lsyswin.h"

//
// TLsysWindow child window constructor
//
TLsysWindow::TLsysWindow(PTWindowsObject pParent) :
  TWindow(pParent, "L-system"),
  nColor(ID_RB_Red),
  nPenWidth(1),
  nX(500),
  nY(100)
{
  _fstrcpy(FileName, "");
  ((TLsysFrame*)Parent)->ChildBirth();
  lsys = new TWinLsys;
}


//
// Draw L-system
//
void TLsysWindow::Paint(HDC PaintDC, PAINTSTRUCT& /*ps*/)
{
  RECT r;
  GetClientRect(HWindow, &r);

  SetMapMode(PaintDC, MM_ISOTROPIC);
  SetWindowExt(PaintDC, 1000, 1000);
  SetViewportExt(PaintDC, r.right, -r.bottom);
  SetViewportOrg(PaintDC, 0, r.bottom);

  HPEN hPen, hOrigPen;
  COLORREF c;
  switch(nColor) {
    case ID_RB_Red: c = RGB(255, 0, 0); break;
    case ID_RB_Green: c = RGB(0, 255, 0); break;
    case ID_RB_Blue: c = RGB(0, 0, 255); break;
    default:
    case ID_RB_Black: c = RGB(0, 0, 0); break;
  }

  POINT p;
  p.x = nPenWidth;
  p.y = 0;
  DPtoLP(PaintDC, &p, 1); // pen width in logical coords
  hPen = CreatePen(PS_SOLID, p.x, c);
  hOrigPen = (HPEN)SelectObject(PaintDC, hPen);
```

LISTING 16.6

lsyswin.cpp (Continued)

```
  lsys->draw(PaintDC, nX, nY);

  SelectObject(PaintDC, hOrigPen);
  DeleteObject(hPen);
}

//
// Activation/Deactivation of an Lsys window
void TLsysWindow::WMMDIActivate(RTMessage m)
{
  if (m.WParam == 1) // activate
    if (*((TLsysFrame *)Parent)->GetMenuName() != *LsysMenuName)
      ((TLsysFrame *)Parent)->SetMenu(LsysMenuName, LsysMenuChildPos);
  TWindow::WMMDIActivate(m);
}

//
// TLsysWindow Settings dialog
void TLsysWindow::SettingsDialog(RTMessage /*m*/)
{
  int res = GetApplication()->ExecDialog(
    new TSettingsDialog(this, &settingsBuf));
  if (res == IDOK) {
    lsys->setRules(settingsBuf.Seed, settingsBuf.Rule);
    lsys->rewrite(settingsBuf.GetIterations());
    InvalidateRect(HWindow, NULL, TRUE);
  }
}

//
// TLsysWindow Graphing Parameters dialog
void TLsysWindow::GraphDialog(RTMessage /*m*/)
{
  int res = GetApplication()->ExecDialog(
    new TGraphDialog(this, &graphBuf));
  if (res == IDOK) {
    lsys->setDrawing(atof(graphBuf.Theta),
      atof(graphBuf.Delta), atof(graphBuf.Length));
    nX = atoi(graphBuf.X);
    nY = atoi(graphBuf.Y);
    InvalidateRect(HWindow, NULL, TRUE);
  }
}

//
// TLsysWindow Drawing Parameters dialog
void TLsysWindow::DrawDialog(RTMessage /*m*/)
{
  int res = GetApplication()->ExecDialog(
    new TDrawDialog(this, &drawBuf));
  if (res == IDOK) {
    nColor = drawBuf.GetColor();
    nPenWidth = drawBuf.GetPenWidth();
```

LISTING 16.6

lsyswin.cpp (Continued)

```cpp
      InvalidateRect(HWindow, NULL, TRUE);
  }
}

//
// TLsysWindow Title Dialog
void TLsysWindow::TitleDialog(RTMessage /*m*/)
{
  char titleBuf[TitleLength];
  int res = GetApplication()->ExecDialog(
    new TTitleDialog(this, titleBuf));
  if (res == IDOK)
    SetCaption(titleBuf);
}

//
// Use the settingsBuf and graphBuf transfer
// buffers to ready an L-system for drawing
void TLsysWindow::Prepare()
{
  lsys->setRules(settingsBuf.Seed, settingsBuf.Rule);
  lsys->rewrite(settingsBuf.GetIterations());
  lsys->setDrawing(atof(graphBuf.Theta),
    atof(graphBuf.Delta), atof(graphBuf.Length));
  nX = atoi(graphBuf.X);
  nY = atoi(graphBuf.Y);
}

//
// Some specific L-systems
void TLsysWindow::CannedLsys(int id)
{
  switch(id) {
    case CM_NewTriangle:
      settingsBuf.Assign("F", "F++F++F", 1);
      graphBuf.Assign(500, 100, 60, 60, 900);
      SetCaption("Triangle");
      break;
    case CM_NewStar1:
      settingsBuf.Assign("F++F++F", "F-F++F-F", 1);
      graphBuf.Assign(500, 75, 60, 60, 250);
      SetCaption("Star 1");
      break;
    case CM_NewStar2:
      settingsBuf.Assign("F++F++F", "F-F++F-F", 2);
      graphBuf.Assign(500, 100, 60, 60, 80);
      SetCaption("Star 2");
      break;
    case CM_NewStar3:
      settingsBuf.Assign("F++F++F", "F-F++F-F", 3);
      graphBuf.Assign(500, 40, 60, 60, 30);
      SetCaption("Star 3");
      break;
```

LISTING 16.6

lsyswin.cpp (Continued)

```cpp
      case CM_NewBox1:
        settingsBuf.Assign("F-F-F-F", "FF-F-F-F-FF", 3);
        graphBuf.Assign(500, 20, 135, 90, 25);
        SetCaption("Box 1");
        break;
      case CM_NewBox2:
        settingsBuf.Assign("F-F-F-F", "FF-F--F-F", 4);
        graphBuf.Assign(100, 100, 90, 90, 10);
        SetCaption("Box 2");
        break;
      case CM_NewTree1:
        settingsBuf.Assign("F", "FF+[F-F]-[-F+F+F]", 4);
        graphBuf.Assign(500, 25, 90, 30, 18);
        SetCaption("Tree 1");
        break;
      case CM_NewTree2:
        settingsBuf.Assign("F", "FF-[-F+F+F]+[+F-F-F]", 4);
        graphBuf.Assign(400, 100, 90.0, 30, 16);
        SetCaption("Tree 2");
        break;
  }

  Prepare();
  InvalidateRect(HWindow, NULL, TRUE);
}

//
// File Save
void TLsysWindow::Save(RTMessage msg)
{
  if ( !*FileName )
    SaveAs(msg);
  else
    Write(FileName);
}

//
// File Save As
void TLsysWindow::SaveAs(RTMessage /*msg*/)
{
  char TmpName[MAXPATH];
  char OldName[MAXPATH];
  char tmp[MAXPATH + 20];
  OFSTRUCT TmpOfStruct;

  _fstrcpy(OldName, FileName);
  if ( *FileName )
    _fstrcpy(TmpName, FileName);
  else
    TmpName[0] = '\0';
  if ( GetModule()->ExecDialog(
    new TFileDialog(this, SD_FILESAVE, TmpName, GetModule())) == IDOK)
```

LISTING 16.6

lsyswin.cpp (Continued)

```cpp
  {
    if ( OpenFile(TmpName, &TmpOfStruct, OF_EXIST) != -1 )
    {
      wsprintf(tmp, "Replace Current \"%s\"?", (LPSTR)TmpName);
      if ( MessageBox(HWindow, tmp, "File Changed",
                        MB_YESNO | MB_ICONQUESTION) == IDNO )
      {
        _fstrcpy(FileName, OldName);
        return;
      }
    }
    _fstrcpy(FileName, TmpName);
    Write(FileName);
  }
}


//
// File Write
void TLsysWindow::Write(char *file)
{
  ofstream s;
  s.open(file);
  if (!s) {
    char temp[MAXPATH+2Ø];
    wsprintf(temp, "Can't create \"%s\".", file);
    MessageBox(HWindow, temp, "File Creation Error",
      MB_ICONINFORMATION);
    return;
  }

  s << Title << endl
    << settingsBuf.Seed << endl
    << settingsBuf.Rule << endl
    << settingsBuf.GetIterations() << endl
    << graphBuf.X << endl
    << graphBuf.Y << endl
    << graphBuf.Theta << endl
    << graphBuf.Delta << endl
    << graphBuf.Length << endl;

  s.close();
}

//
// File Read
int TLsysWindow::Read(char *file)
{
  int ret = TRUE;
  char temp[MAXPATH+2Ø];
  ifstream s;

  s.open(file);
  if (!s) {
```

LISTING 16.6

lsyswin.cpp (Continued)

```
    wsprintf(temp, "Can't open \"%s\".", file);
    MessageBox(HWindow, temp, "File Open Error",
      MB_ICONINFORMATION);
    FileName[0] = '\0';
    return FALSE;
  }
  _fstrcpy(FileName, file);

  char title[TitleLength];
  int iterations;
  char seed[TextLength];
  char rule[TextLength];

  s.getline(title, sizeof(title));
  s.getline(seed, sizeof(seed));
  s.getline(rule, sizeof(rule));
  s >> iterations
    >> setw(sizeof(graphBuf.X))
    >> graphBuf.X
    >> setw(sizeof(graphBuf.Y))
    >> graphBuf.Y
    >> setw(sizeof(graphBuf.Theta))
    >> graphBuf.Theta
    >> setw(sizeof(graphBuf.Delta))
    >> graphBuf.Delta
    >> setw(sizeof(graphBuf.Length))
    >> graphBuf.Length;

  SetCaption(title);
  settingsBuf.Assign(seed, rule, iterations);

  if (!s) {
    wsprintf(temp, "Error reading \"%s\".", file);
    MessageBox(HWindow, temp, "File Read Error",
      MB_ICONINFORMATION);
    ret = FALSE;
  }

  s.close();

  Prepare();
  return ret;
}
```

Handling Menu Selections

In Chapter 15 I talked about how menu selections can either be handled by a child window or by the frame window. The active child gets first crack at menu selections, but menu selections not handled by the child are passed to the frame window. The L-system application contains 20 menu selections, which are handled as summarized in Table 16.2. Note that the menu IDs referenced in Table 16.2 refer to the definitions in resource.h. Also note that the menu resources are defined in lsys.rc. The code for resource.h and lsys.rc is shown later in this chapter under "The L-system Application Resources."

Probably the most surprising aspect of Table 16.2 is the difference between how the File Open and File New commands are handled, and how the File Save and File Save As commands are handled. The two menu selections for creating an L-system child window go to the TLsysFrame object, which creates the window object, and then uses that window object's member functions (Read() for the File Open command; CannedLsys() for the File New command) to complete the window's initialization with a specific L-system. The two Save menu selections are handled directly by the child window object. The reason for the difference is that child window creation is the responsibility of the frame window, while saving data is best done by the individual child window object.

TABLE 16.2

Handling the L-system Application's Menu Selections

Menu ID	Handled By
CM_NewTriangle CM_NewStar1 CM_NewStar2 CM_NewStar3 CM_NewBox1 CM_NewBox2 CM_NewTree1 CM_NewTree2	The eight menu items that create a new built-in L-system are initially handled by the TLsysFrame class's DefCommandProc() function. It creates a TLsysWindow child window object, and then it calls that object's CannedLsys() function to actually create the specified L-system.
CM_FILEOPEN	The File Open menu selection is handled by the TLsysFrame class's Open() procedure. It first creates a File Open dialog to get a file name. Then it creates a TLsysWindow child window object, and then calls that object's Read() procedure to read in the L-system description from that file.
CM_FILESAVE	The File Save menu selection is handled by the active TLsysWindow child window object's Save() function. It calls the object's SaveAs() function if there isn't a current file name for the L-system, or it calls Write() if there is a current file name.
CM_FILESAVEAS	The File Save As menu selection is handled by the active TLsysWindow child window object's SaveAs() function. It first creates a Save As dialog, and then it calls Write() to save the L-system characteristics.
CM_EXIT	The exit menu selection is passed to the frame window, where it is handled by the TWindowsObject class's CMExit() procedure.
CM_LsysDialog CM_GraphDialog CM_DrawDialog CM_TitleDialog	These four requests to create dialog boxes are handled by the active TLsysWindow child window object. In each case, it creates the requested dialog. If the dialog is closed by pressing OK, then the specified changes are conveyed to the window's L-system object, and the window is redrawn.
CM_CASCADECHILDREN CM_TILECHILDREN CM_ARRANGEICONS CM_CLOSECHILDREN	These four Window menu selections are handled by the TMDIFrame class.

The TLsysWindow Class's Paint()

The Paint() procedure in the L-system application is different from the Paint() procedures in the other examples in this book, because it doesn't contain any drawing commands. Instead its role is to prepare the paint device context for output, and then let the L-system object perform its own output operations.

If you look at Paint() from Listing 16.6, you'll see that it actually performs just four chores:

1. It changes the coordinate system to a 1000 by 1000 isotropic system.

2. It creates a new pen in the specified size and color.

3. It asks the window's L-system object to draw itself.

4. It restores the paint DC's original pen and deletes the new pen.

The last three steps are routine and I won't comment further, but the isotropic coordinate system is an interesting topic.

Isotropic Coordinates   The L-system application uses isotropic coordinates so that the shape of the drawings is independent of the window size or shape. I decided to use a standard coordinate system orientation, in which the origin is in the lower left of the window, and I decided to have both the X and Y axis range from 0 to 1000.

The isotropic mapping mode allows you to specify three aspects of the window coordinate system:

■ The coordinate range. The X and Y may have different ranges.

■ The direction of the axes. The X axis is always horizontal, but X may increase either to the right, which is usual, or to the left. The Y axis is always vertical, but Y may increase downward or upward.

■ The location of the origin.

However, the isotropic mapping mode constrains you so that your logical units on each axis have the same physical size. If you draw a rectangle that is the same number of units high as it is wide, then it will be a square. In contrast, the anisotropic mapping mode doesn't constrain the logical units on each axis to represent the same physical dimension. In the anisotropic mapping mode, if a rectangle is the same number of logical units high as it is wide, all we can say is that it's a rectangle; it needn't be a square.

The usual approach to creating an isotropic coordinate system is to specify the desired window coordinate range by calling SetWindowExt(), and then pass the dimensions of the client area to SetViewportExt(). Remember, it's only the ratio of the extents that matters, not their individual values. Here's the code from the beginning of the TLsysWindow class's Paint() procedure that specifies the coordinate range and the direction of the axes:

```
RECT r;
GetClientRect(HWindow, &r);
```

```
SetMapMode(PaintDC, MM_ISOTROPIC);
SetWindowExt(PaintDC, 1000, 1000);
SetViewportExt(PaintDC, r.right, -r.bottom);
```

The negative sign in the Y extent parameter of SetViewportExt() reverses the direction of the Y axis, so that Y increases upward. You could also specify a "Y increasing upward" axis by using a negative Y window extent, and a positive Y viewport extent. All that really matters is that the ratio be negative.

Since we haven't set either the window or the viewport origin, the origin of the window coordinate system is in the upper left of the window, producing the coordinate system shown in Figure 16.4.

FIGURE 16.4

An isotropic window coordinate system. The window is shaded, the axes are drawn to the length of 1000, 1000. Mapping mode: MM_ISOTROPIC; Window extents: 1000, 1000; Viewport coordinates: client rect width, –client rect height; viewport and window origins: 0, 0.

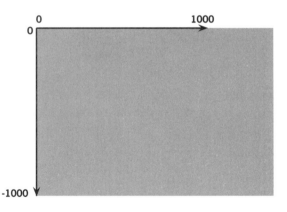

So that you fully understand this, let's go through the math. In Chapter 14 I presented the formulas for translating window coordinates to viewport coordinates. Here they are again:

$$xView = xViewOrg + (xWin - xWinOrg) \times \frac{xViewExt}{xWinExt}$$

$$yView = yViewOrg + (yWin - yWinOrg) \times \frac{yViewExt}{yWinExt}$$

Since in the current example both window and viewport origins are zero, the above equations can be simplified.

$$xView = xWin \times \frac{xViewExt}{xWinExt}$$

$$yView = yWin \times \frac{yViewExt}{yWinExt}$$

If we fill in the window and viewport extents already specified, we get the following:

$$xView = xWin \times \frac{r.right}{1000}$$

$$yView = yWin \times \frac{-r.bottom}{1000}$$

If the window (logical) coordinates are (0, 0), then the viewport equations will also be (0, 0), the top left of the window. In Figure 16.4, the window happens to be wider than it is tall. Thus the mapping is really controlled by the Y values, because there is extra room for the X values. Thus if you vary Y coordinates from 0 to –1000, you'll move from the top of the window to the bottom. If you vary X from 0 to 1000, you'll move from the left edge over toward the right edge. But you won't get to the right edge, because 1000 logical units in the X direction is the same distance as 1000 units in the Y direction. In Figure 16.4 the window is approximately a fifth wider than it is high, so you need an X coordinate of about 1200 to reach the right edge.

Figure 16.5 shows how the coordinate systems would be arranged if the window were taller than it is wide. The scaling would be controlled by X, location 1000 in X would be at the right edge of the window, while location –1000 in Y would be above the bottom of the window.

Figures 16.4 and 16.5 show the logical coordinate system after the window extents have been specified, but before the viewport origin has been specified. Here's the next line of the TLsysWindow class's Paint() procedure, which specifies the viewport origin:

```
SetViewportOrg(PaintDC, Ø, r.bottom);
```

After executing this final coordinate system setup command, the paint device context's coordinate system origin is in the lower left of the window, as shown in Figure 16.6.

FIGURE 16.5

An isotropic window coordinate system. The characteristics are the same as Figure 16.4 except that the window is taller than it is wide.

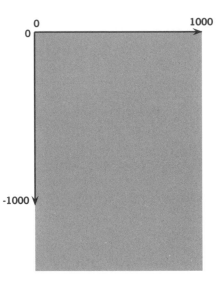

FIGURE 16.6

An isotropic window coordinate system. The window is shaded, the axes are drawn to the length of 1000, 1000. Mapping mode: MM_ISOTROPIC; Window extents: 1000, 1000; Viewport coordinates: client rect width, –client rect height; viewport origin: 0, client rect height; window origin: 0, 0.

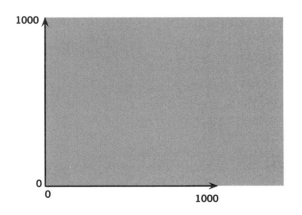

Again let's go over the numbers. Here are the equations that govern the window-to-viewport mapping when both extents and the viewport origin have been set as was just described:

$$xView = xWin \times \frac{r.right}{1000}$$

$$yView = r.bottom + yWin \times \frac{-r.bottom}{1000}$$

If we plug the logical coordinates (0, 0) into these equations, we'll produce the viewport coordinates (0, r.bottom). As we wanted, the origin is in the lower-left corner. If we use the logical coordinates (0, 1000), we can calculate the viewport coordinates (0, 0), the top-left corner of the client area.

Anisotropic Coordinates The anisotropic mapping mode is the same as the isotropic, except that the X and Y coordinates are independent. By *independent* I mean that X and Y logical units aren't constrained to represent the same physical dimension. Independent means 100 logical units in the X direction might not be the same distance as 100 logical units in the Y direction. The difference between the two is best illustrated by Figures 16.7A and 16.7B. Figure 16.7A shows the Box 2 L-system displayed in an isotropic coordinate system, while Figure 16.7B shows the same L-system but in an anisotropic coordinate system. Figure 16.7B was produced by recompiling the L-system application with the paint DC's mapping mode set to MM_ANISOTROPIC. In Figure 16.7A, 1000 logical units in the Y direction is the same size as 1000 logical units in the X direction. However, in Figure 16.7B 1000 logical units in Y is the height of the client area, while 1000 units in X is the width of the client area. Figure 16.8 shows the coordinate system used by the L-system application when the mapping mode is set to MM_ANISOTROPIC.

The impression from Figures 16.7A and 16.7B might be that the anisotropic mapping mode makes the aspect ratio of the window dictate the aspect ratio of the drawing. This happens to be true in the L-system application, but it can be avoided. You can use the size of the client rectangle plus the device's pixels per inch in X and Y directions to discover the aspect ratio of the window, and then use that information to devise a coordinate system that's appropriate for your own needs.

L-systems Dialogs

One of the nicest parts of the L-system application is its set of four dialogs: the Settings dialog, the Graphing dialog, the Drawing dialog, and the Title dialog. These four dialogs allow you to specify the L-system parameters, so that you can modify the supplied L-systems and create your own L-systems. These four dialogs are invoked by the message handler functions in the TLsysWindow class, and they were shown earlier in this chapter in the section "The L-system Application's Organization."

FIGURE 16.7

(A) A square L-system drawn in the L-system application's usual isotropic coordinate system; (B) The same square L-system drawn in an anisotropic coordinate system

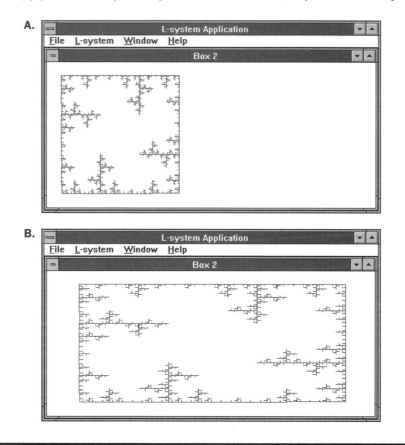

When you create dialog classes based on OWL's TDialog class, you should usually specify a transfer buffer so that dialog box settings can be saved when a dialog terminates, and then used to initialize the dialog the next time it is invoked. In Chapter 13 I suggested that you make the transfer buffer a static member of your dialog class, so that the transfer buffer is available even after the dialog box object is destroyed.

But the L-system application is an MDI application, and each child window needs to maintain its own set of L-system characteristics. This implies that the dialog box transfer buffers should be stored in the child window objects, instead of being housed as static members of the dialog classes. Note that if a dialog stored something that pertained to all of the child windows, then it might be appropriate for the application to have a single copy of the transfer buffer, instead of having one copy of the transfer buffer for each child window.

FIGURE 16.8

An anisotropic 1000 by 1000 coordinate system. Note that the axis lengths match the size of the window, unlike Figures 16.7A and 16.7B, in which the axes were the same length.

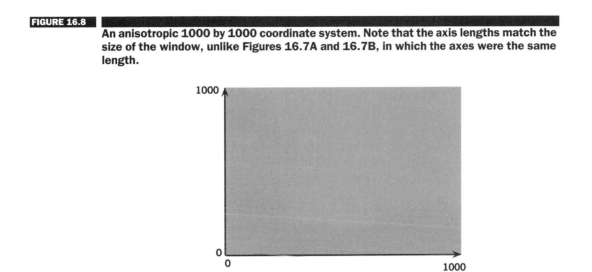

The transfer buffers for the L-system application contain all the information needed to draw the L-system. Therefore they aren't just used to initialize the dialogs. They are also used for file input and output operations, and they are used by the TLsysWindow class's CannedLsys() procedure when it initializes an L-system. The values stored in the transfer buffers are used to control the L-system object in the Prepare() function of the TLsysWindow class.

The Settings Dialog

The Settings dialog allows you to specify the seed, rule, and the number of iterations of an L-system. The seed and the rule are specified using two edit controls, while the number of iterations is specified using a set of six radio buttons.

The TSettingsDialog class, which is defined in Listing 16.7, implements the Settings dialog. It contains just three members: a constructor, the CanClose() function, and the CheckEditControl() function. CanClose() calls CheckEdit-Control() to make sure that each of the two edit controls contains text. This is a very minimal check, but a good first step. A more comprehensive check might look for characters other than the allowable characters (F, +, –, [, and]), and for unbalanced brackets. Those improvements are left for the reader.

LISTING 16.7

setdlg.h

```
#define nIterations 6

//
// N.B. Order must match order in TSettingsDialog constr.
struct TSettingsTransfer {
  char Seed[TextLength];
```

LISTING 16.7 ▮▮▮▮▮▮▮▮▮▮▮▮▮▮▮▮▮▮▮▮▮▮▮▮▮▮▮▮▮▮▮▮▮▮▮▮▮▮

setdlg.h (Continued)

```
  char Rule[TextLength];
  ushort Iterations[nIterations];

  TSettingsTransfer();            // constructor
  int GetIterations();
  void Assign(char *seed, char *rule, int it);
};

//
// L-system Settings dialog
//
class TSettingsDialog : public TDialog {
  public:
    TSettingsDialog(PTWindowsObject pParent,  // constructor
      TSettingsTransfer *t);
    int CheckEditControl(int id, char *name);
    virtual BOOL CanClose();
};
```

The TSettingsTransfer struct is the transfer buffer for the Settings dialog. It contains three data members that store the dialog box settings, plus three member functions. One member of the TSettingsTransfer struct is a constructor, to ensure that the struct is initialized. The other two member functions are for convenience: the Assign() function assigns a value to all three data members of the struct, and the GetIterations() function returns the iteration count. The Assign() function simply makes it easier to assign values to all three data members; it's used nine times by the TLsysWindow class. The GetIterations() function makes it easy to find out how many iterations have been requested. In the dialog box the iterations are specified using six radio buttons. Thus in the dialog's transfer buffer there is an array of six unsigned shorts. GetIterations() looks through the array to find the active radio button, and then returns the corresponding iteration count. Both of these functions are detailed in Listing 16.8.

LISTING 16.8 ▮▮▮▮▮▮▮▮▮▮▮▮▮▮▮▮▮▮▮▮▮▮▮▮▮▮▮▮▮▮▮▮▮▮▮▮▮▮

setdlg.cpp

```
#define STRICT
#define WIN31

#include <owl.h>
#include <radiobut.h>
#include <edit.h>
#include <string.h>

#include "resource.h"
#include "setdlg.h"
//
// Make sure edit control exists and has content
```

LISTING 16.8

setdlg.cpp (Continued)

```cpp
int TSettingsDialog::CheckEditControl(int id, char *name)
{
  char buf[TextLength];

  // check existence of edit control
  PTEdit pEdit = (PTEdit)ChildWithId(id);
  if (pEdit == NULL) {
    wsprintf(buf, "Can't find %s control", name);
    MessageBox(HWindow, buf,
      "CanClose", MB_ICONEXCLAMATION);
    return True;
  }

  // make sure it has something in it
  *buf = 0;
  pEdit->GetText(buf, TextLength);
  if (*buf == 0) {
    wsprintf(buf, "Please enter a %s or Cancel", name);
    MessageBox(HWindow, buf,
      "CanClose", MB_ICONEXCLAMATION);
    return False;
  }

  return True;
}

//
// return TRUE if the dialog has text in the file-name control
BOOL TSettingsDialog::CanClose()
{
  if (TDialog::CanClose() == False)
    return False;

  if (CheckEditControl(ID_ET_Seed, "Seed") == False)
    return False;

  if (CheckEditControl(ID_ET_Rule, "Rule") == False)
    return False;

  return True;
}

//
// TSettingsDialog constructor
//
TSettingsDialog::TSettingsDialog(PTWindowsObject pParent,
  TSettingsTransfer *transfer) :
  TDialog(pParent, "SettingsDialog")
{
  // order must match order of TSettingsTransfer struct
  new TEdit(this, ID_ET_Seed, TextLength);
  new TEdit(this, ID_ET_Rule, TextLength);
  for(int i = 0; i<nIterations; i++)
```

LISTING 16.8 ■■

setdlg.cpp (Continued)

```
    new TRadioButton(this, ID_RB_Iter1+i, 0);
  TransferBuffer = transfer;
}


//
// Initialize TSettingsDialog transfer buffer
//
TSettingsTransfer::TSettingsTransfer()
{
  Assign("F", "FF-[-F+F+F]+[+F-F-F]", 4);
}


//
// Get the iteration count
int TSettingsTransfer::GetIterations()
{
  for(int i = 0; i<nIterations; i++)
    if (Iterations[i])
        return i+1;
  return 1; // should not happen!
}


//
// Assign a value to the TSettingsDialog transfer buffer
void TSettingsTransfer::Assign(char *seed, char *rule, int it)
{
 memset(Iterations, FALSE, sizeof(Iterations));
 if (it < 1 || it > nIterations)
   Iterations[0] = 0;
 else
   Iterations[it-1] = TRUE;
 strcpy(Seed, seed);
 strcpy(Rule, rule);
}
```

The Graphing Dialog

The Graphing dialog lets you specify the graphical interpretation of the L-system.
It contains edit controls that let you specify the L-system's initial position and orientation, plus controls to specify the turning angle and the length of each line segment. Remember that each L-system is displayed in a 1000 by 1000 region, with
the origin in the lower-left corner of the region. I discussed how L-systems are interpreted graphically in Chapter 6, but the ideas are also well illustrated in Figure 16.9, which shows one of the tree L-systems with Delta set to, from left to
right, 15, 30, and 45 degrees.

FIGURE 16.9

A tree L-system drawn with different turning angles. Delta is set to 15 degrees in the left window, 30 in the middle, and 45 in the right.

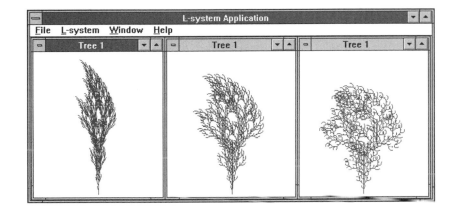

The TGraphDialog class, which is shown in Listings 16.9 and 16.10, has the same three functions as the TSettingsDialog: a constructor, the CanClose() function, and the CheckEditControl() function. The most significant difference is that the TGraphDialog class's CheckEditControl() function makes sure that each edit control contains, or at least starts with, a number. Again this is minimal checking, but it's better than nothing. Improved checking might specify numeric ranges for each control, and it might look at each character in the edit control, not just the first. Again, these improvements are left to the reader.

LISTING 16.9

graphdlg.h

```
//
// N.B. Order must match order in TGraphDialog constr.
struct TGraphTransfer {
  char X[NumberLength];
  char Y[NumberLength];
  char Theta[NumberLength];
  char Delta[NumberLength];
  char Length[NumberLength];
  TGraphTransfer();          // constructor
  void Assign(int x, int y, double th0, double dth,
    int incr);
};


//
// L-system Graphing dialog
//
class TGraphDialog : public TDialog {
  public:
    TGraphDialog(PTWindowsObject pParent,  // constructor
```

LISTING 16.9

graphdlg.h (Continued)

```
        TGraphTransfer *t);
     int CheckEditControl(int id, char *name);
     virtual BOOL CanClose();
};
```

LISTING 16.10

graphdlg.cpp

```cpp
#include <ctype.h>
#include <string.h>

#define STRICT
#define WIN31

#include <owl.h>
#include <edit.h>

#include "resource.h"
#include "graphdlg.h"
//
// check edit control to make sure it exists
// and it starts with a digit
int TGraphDialog::CheckEditControl(int id, char *name)
{
  char buf[TextLength];

  // check existence of edit control
  PTEdit pEdit = (PTEdit)ChildWithId(id);
  if (pEdit == NULL) {
    wsprintf(buf, "Can't find %s control", name);
    MessageBox(HWindow, buf,
      "CanClose", MB_ICONEXCLAMATION);
    return True;
  }

  // make sure it has something in it
  *buf = 0;
  pEdit->GetText(buf, TextLength);
  if (*buf == 0) {
    wsprintf(buf, "Please enter a %s or Cancel", name);
    MessageBox(HWindow, buf,
      "CanClose", MB_ICONEXCLAMATION);
    return False;
  }

  // make sure it starts with a digit
  if (!isdigit(*buf) && *buf != '-' && *buf != '+') {
    wsprintf(buf, "Please enter a numeric %s or Cancel", name);
    MessageBox(HWindow, buf,
      "CanClose", MB_ICONEXCLAMATION);
```

LISTING 16.10

graphdlg.cpp (Continued)

```cpp
      return False;
  }

  return True;
}

//
// return TRUE if the dialog can be closed
BOOL TGraphDialog::CanClose()
{
  char buf[TextLength];

  if (TDialog::CanClose() == False)
    return False;

  if (CheckEditControl(ID_ET_X, "X value") == False)
    return False;

  if (CheckEditControl(ID_ET_Y, "Y value") == False)
    return False;

  if (CheckEditControl(ID_ET_Theta, "Theta") == False)
    return False;

  if (CheckEditControl(ID_ET_Delta, "Delta") == False)
    return False;

  if (CheckEditControl(ID_ET_Length, "Length") == False)
    return False;

  return True;
}

//
// TGraphDialog constructor
//
TGraphDialog::TGraphDialog(PTWindowsObject pParent,
  TGraphTransfer *transfer) :
  TDialog(pParent, "GraphDialog")
{
  // order must match order of TGraphTransfer struct
  new TEdit(this, ID_ET_X, NumberLength);
  new TEdit(this, ID_ET_Y, NumberLength);
  new TEdit(this, ID_ET_Theta, NumberLength);
  new TEdit(this, ID_ET_Delta, NumberLength);
  new TEdit(this, ID_ET_Length, NumberLength);
  TransferBuffer = transfer;
}

//
// Initialize TGraphDialog transfer buffer
//
TGraphTransfer::TGraphTransfer()
```

LISTING 16.10

graphdlg.cpp (Continued)

```
{
  Assign(500, 100, 90.0, 22.5, 12);
}

//
// Assign values to the fields of the TGraphTransfer struct
void TGraphTransfer::Assign(int x, int y, double th0, double dth,
    int incr)
{
  itoa(x, X, 10);
  itoa(y, Y, 10);
  gcvt(th0, 3, Theta);
  gcvt(dth, 3, Delta);
  itoa(incr, Length, 10);
}
```

The Drawing Dialog

The Drawing dialog lets you specify the color and the width of the pen used to draw the L-system. Both selections are made using sets of four radio buttons. The four color choices are Red, Green, Blue, and Black, while the four pen width choices are 1, 2, 4, and 8 pixels. You might want to implement a more sophisticated system for color selection, which is a task that is left for you, the reader.

Unlike the Settings and Graphing dialogs, the Drawing dialog doesn't have a CanClose() member function. That's because the dialog only contains two sets of radio buttons, and it always contains valid settings. If the dialog contained an edit control it would probably need a CanClose() member function, because edit controls are often empty or contain invalid text. Thus the TDrawDialog class's only member function is its constructor.

The transfer buffer for the dialog contains two arrays of unsigned shorts to store the contents of the dialog's two sets of radio buttons. The transfer buffer struct contains three member functions: a constructor, the GetColor() function, and the GetPenWidth() function. The GetColor() and GetPenWidth() functions examine their respective arrays of button data to see which radio button has been depressed. Like the GetIterations() member function of the TSettings-Transfer class, they make it convenient to access the button information. The source code for the Drawing dialog is in Listings 16.11 and 16.12.

LISTING 16.11

drawdlg.h

```
#define nColors 4
#define nPens 4

//
// N.B. Order must match order in TDrawDialog constr.
```

LISTING 16.11

drawdlg.h

```
struct TDrawTransfer {
  ushort Colors[nColors];
  ushort Pens[nPens];

  TDrawTransfer();   // constructor
  int GetColor();    // get color
  int GetPenWidth(); // get pen size
};

//
// L-system Drawing dialog
//    (color and pen width)
//
class TDrawDialog : public TDialog {
  public:
    TDrawDialog(PTWindowsObject pParent,  // constructor
      TDrawTransfer *t);
};
```

LISTING 16.12

drawdlg.cpp

```
#define STRICT
#define WIN31

#include <owl.h>
#include <radiobut.h>

#include "resource.h"
#include "drawdlg.h"

//
// TDrawDialog constructor
//
TDrawDialog::TDrawDialog(PTWindowsObject pParent,
  TDrawTransfer *transfer) :
  TDialog(pParent, "DrawDialog")
{
  int i;
  // order must match order of TDrawTransfer struct
  for(i = 0; i<nColors; i++)
    new TRadioButton(this, ID_RB_Red+i, 0);
  for(i = 0; i<nPens; i++)
    new TRadioButton(this, ID_RB_Pen1+i, 0);
  TransferBuffer = transfer;
}

//
// Initialize TDrawDialog transfer buffer
//
TDrawTransfer::TDrawTransfer()
{
```

LISTING 16.12

drawdlg.cpp (Continued)

```
    memset(this, 0, sizeof(TDrawTransfer));
    Colors[0] = TRUE;
    Pens[0] = TRUE;
}

//
// extract color id from transfer buffer
int TDrawTransfer::GetColor()
{
  for(int i = 0; i<nColors; i++)
    if (Colors[i])
      return ID_RB_Red + i;
  return ID_RB_Red;
}

//
// extract pen size from transfer buffer
int TDrawTransfer::GetPenWidth()
{
  static int size[nPens] = { 1, 2, 4, 8 };
  for(int i = 0; i<nPens; i++)
    if (Pens[i])
      return size[i];
  return 1;
}
```

The Title Dialog

The Title dialog is the simplest dialog in the L-system application. It has only one control, other than the usual OK and Cancel buttons. The only member of the Title dialog is the constructor.

The Title dialog is unusual because it doesn't have a permanent transfer buffer. Even though there isn't a transfer buffer, the transfer mechanism is used. The constructor of the TTitleDialog is passed the address of a temporary character buffer. It fills that buffer with the current window title, and then uses it as a transfer buffer. When the dialog is closed by pressing OK, the new title is used as the window title by calling OWL's SetCaption() function. Thus OWL stores the dialog settings while the dialog is closed. The source for the Title dialog is shown in Listings 16.13 and 16.14.

LISTING 16.13

titledlg.h

```
//
// Set the window title
//
class TTitleDialog : public TDialog {
```

LISTING 16.13

titledlg.h (Continued)

```
public:
  TTitleDialog(PTWindowsObject pParent,  // constructor
    char *transfer);
};
```

LISTING 16.14

titledlg.cpp

```
#define STRICT
#define WIN31

#include <owl.h>
#include <edit.h>
#include <string.h>

#include "resource.h"
#include "titledlg.h"

//
// TSettingsDialog constructor
//
TTitleDialog::TTitleDialog(PTWindowsObject pParent,
  char *transfer) :
  TDialog(pParent, "TitleDialog")
{
  // order must match order of TSettingsTransfer struct
  new TEdit(this, ID_ET_Title, TitleLength);
  _fstrcpy(transfer, Parent->Title);
  TransferBuffer = transfer;
}
```

File Dialogs

File dialogs are an important part of most applications' user interface. People expect to be able to navigate through the file system using a file dialog, and they expect that file dialogs will work in the standard manner. From a programmer's perspective, a file dialog is much like a mini-application because of the rich interactions between the three major controls—the Filename edit control, and the Files and Directories list-box controls.

The L-system application contains File Open and File Save As dialogs so that L-system specifications can be stored in files. I implemented both of these dialogs using OWL's TFileDialog class. (See the respective illustrations under "The L-system Application's Organization," earlier in this chapter.) When you use the TFileDialog class you need to include the OWL header file filedial.h into the source files that create file dialog boxes, and you need to include the files owlrc.h and filedial.dlg into your .RC file. All three of these files are stored in the OWL include directory.

File Open Dialog

The L-system application's File Open dialog is created by the TLsysFrame class's Open() procedure. Open() belongs to the frame window class because the file open operation, if successful, will lead to the creation of a new child window, and child window creation is a prime responsibility of the frame window. In the L-system application it isn't possible to read a stored L-system description for use in an existing child window, so child windows don't have an open function. But in many MDI applications both the frame and the child windows will have open functionality—the frame will implement open by creating a child, while the child implements open by reading in new data.

Here is the source of the Open() function from the TLsysFrame class (Listing 16.2):

```
void TLsysFrame::Open(RTMessage /*msg*/)
{
  char tmp[MAXPATH];
  _fstrcpy(tmp, "*.lsy");
  if (GetModule()->ExecDialog(
    new TFileDialog(this, SD_FILEOPEN, tmp, GetModule())
    ) == IDOK) {
    TLsysWindow *p = new TLsysWindow(this);
    if (GetModule()->MakeWindow(p)) {
      if (p->Read(tmp) == FALSE)
        delete p;
    }
  }
}
```

The file dialog constructor needs four parameters: a pointer to the parent window object, either SD_FILEOPEN or SD_FILESAVEAS to indicate the dialog type, a character buffer to store the file name, and a pointer to the application's module object (the module part of the application object). If the dialog is closed by pressing OK, then the Open() procedure makes a TLsysWindow object and then asks that object to read in an L-system description from a file by calling that object's Read() procedure.

File Save and File Save As Dialog

The File Save As capability of the L-system application resides completely in the TLsysWindow class. When the File Save As menu selection is made, the TLsysWindow class's SaveAs() procedure is activated. The SaveAs() function in the L-system application was closely based on Borland's SaveAs() function in their TFileWindow class. Here's the source for SaveAs() (from Listing 16.6):

```
void TLsysWindow::SaveAs(RTMessage /*msg*/)
{
  char TmpName[MAXPATH];
  char OldName[MAXPATH];
  char tmp[MAXPATH + 20];
  OFSTRUCT TmpOfStruct;
  _fstrcpy(OldName, FileName);
```

```
  if ( *FileName )
    _fstrcpy(TmpName, FileName);
  else
    TmpName[Ø] = '\Ø';
  if ( GetModule()->ExecDialog(
    new TFileDialog(this, SD_FILESAVE, TmpName, GetModule()))
    == IDOK)
  {
    if ( OpenFile(TmpName, &TmpOfStruct, OF_EXIST) != -1 )
    {
      wsprintf(tmp, "Replace Current \"%s\"?", (LPSTR)TmpName);
      if ( MessageBox(HWindow, tmp, "File Changed",
                          MB_YESNO | MB_ICONQUESTION) == IDNO )
      {
        _fstrcpy(FileName, OldName);
        return;
      }
    }
    _fstrcpy(FileName, TmpName);
    Write(FileName);
  }
}
```

If the File Save As dialog is closed by pressing OK, then SaveAs() checks to see if the file exists. If so, a message box is displayed to ask the user if the existing file should be overwritten. This checking could be done elsewhere, or it could be omitted, depending on the needs of the specific application. In the L-system application, the Write() routine that actually does the output doesn't return any status or do anything more than minimal checking. This is fine for the L-system application, in part because parameter files are so small that disk write errors or other I/O errors are unlikely, and partly because the amount of work lost in the event of a failure is probably small. In other applications there would be a different set of concerns that would likely lead to a different level of vigilance.

The Save As dialog is one of the weaker components of the OWL library. The problem is that it doesn't display a list of file names, which makes it hard to see if the file name that you're choosing is one that's already in use. The Save As dialogs in both BCW and Resource Workshop show you the files in the selected output directory, and they both are implemented using Borland Windows Custom Controls. You can implement both of these features by extending the supplied TFileDialog class, but you shouldn't have to.

Reading and Writing L-system Parameters

The L-system parameter files are read and written using the iostream library. This class library, which was discussed in Chapter 7, makes it easy to create text files for storing data. I originally wrote the TLsysWindow class's Read() and Write() procedures using the C standard I/O library, because I thought it might be easier for most readers to understand. But the code, especially the file read code, quickly escalated in size and complexity. Plus, I kept making simple mistakes. After an hour or so of frustration, I switched to the iostream library. In just a few minutes that code had shrunk by half and was working perfectly.

The file write code is very simple:

```
void TLsysWindow::Write(char *file)
{
  ofstream s;
  s.open(file);
  if (!s) {
    char temp[MAXPATH+20];
    wsprintf(temp, "Can't create \"%s\".", file);
    MessageBox(HWindow, temp, "File Creation Error",
      MB_ICONINFORMATION);
    return;
  }
  s << Title << endl
    << settingsBuf.Seed << endl
    << settingsBuf.Rule << endl
    << settingsBuf.GetIterations() << endl
    << graphBuf.X << endl
    << graphBuf.Y << endl
    << graphBuf.Theta << endl
    << graphBuf.Delta << endl
    << graphBuf.Length << endl;
  s.close();
}
```

Write() places one parameter, which it gleans from the dialog box transfer buffers, on each line of the file. For example, here is the parameter file that is written when you create a new Box 1 L-system and then save those parameters in a file:

```
Box 1
F-F-F-F
FF-F-F-F-FF
3
500
20
135
90
25
```

Read() is harder, which is pretty common because when you are reading a file you must be more alert to errors. When you're reading, almost anything can, and sometimes will, go wrong. The first three lines of an L-system parameter file contain text strings. I decided to use the iostream library's getline() function to read in these lines, because ordinary iostream extraction into a character array stops when whitespace is encountered. (Only the L-system caption is expected to contain whitespace, but it's certainly possible for both the seed and the rule to have whitespace.) After the three strings are input using getline(), ordinary extraction operations are used to read the numeric parameters. Here's the source code for Read() (from Listing 16.6):

```
//
// File Read
int TLsysWindow::Read(char *file)
{
  int ret = TRUE;
  char temp[MAXPATH+2Ø];
  ifstream s;
  s.open(file);
  if (!s) {
    wsprintf(temp, "Can't open \"%s\".", file);
    MessageBox(HWindow, temp, "File Open Error",
      MB_ICONINFORMATION);
    FileName[Ø] = '\Ø';
    return FALSE;
  }
  _fstrcpy(FileName, file);
  char title[TitleLength];
  int iterations;
  char seed[TextLength];
  char rule[TextLength];
  s.getline(title, sizeof(title));
  s.getline(seed, sizeof(seed));
  s.getline(rule, sizeof(rule));
  s >> iterations
    >> setw(sizeof(graphBuf.X))
    >> graphBuf.X
    >> setw(sizeof(graphBuf.Y))
    >> graphBuf.Y
    >> setw(sizeof(graphBuf.Theta))
    >> graphBuf.Theta
    >> setw(sizeof(graphBuf.Delta))
    >> graphBuf.Delta
    >> setw(sizeof(graphBuf.Length))
    >> graphBuf.Length;
  SetCaption(title);
  settingsBuf.Assign(seed, rule, iterations);
  if (!s) {
    wsprintf(temp, "Error reading \"%s\".", file);
    MessageBox(HWindow, temp, "File Read Error",
      MB_ICONINFORMATION);
    ret = FALSE;
  }
  s.close();
  Prepare();
  return ret;
}
```

After all the parameters are checked the ifstream object's status is tested. If a failure has occurred, then Read() will return False. This helps guard against absurd L-system descriptions, which are likely to cause serious problems when they are computed or drawn. If read errors don't occur, then the Prepare() function is called to pull the L-system characteristics out of the dialog transfer buffers and install them in the TLsysWindow object's L-system object, and then Read() returns True.

Handling Similar Menu Selections

Many applications contain a group of related menu selections that are so similar they should all be handled in a single function. For example, in the L-system application the File-New menu selection pops up a list of eight standard L-system types. These eight menu selections all need almost the same thing, so it makes sense to manage all of them in a single function (see Table 16.2).

In traditional C Windows programs this type of need is easily handled by lumping together the set of menu IDs in a single case statement of the switch statement that handles menu selections. And of course in OWL it can be handled by creating individual message handler functions for each menu selection, and then making each of those handlers call a common function. Ick!

A better way to handle related menu selections in an OWL application is to override the DefCommandProc() function. DefCommandProc() is the member of the TWindowsObject class that is called to manage Windows command messages that aren't otherwise handled by specific message handlers. If you override DefCommandProc() you can get control when any message occurs that isn't specifically handled elsewhere. Thus if you want to respond to a group of menu selections, all you need to do is create your own DefCommandProc() that picks out those particular messages. Like other message handlers, DefCommandProc() is passed a reference to a TMessage struct.

Here's the DefCommandProc() function from the TLsysFrame class that manages all eight new window requests.

```
void TLsysFrame::DefCommandProc(RTMessage m)
{
  if (m.WParam >= CM_NewTriangle && m.WParam <= CM_NewTree2) {
    TLsysWindow *p = new TLsysWindow(this);
    if (GetModule()->MakeWindow(p))
      p->CannedLsys(m.WParam);
  } else
    TWindow::DefCommandProc(m);
}
```

If you look in the Windows API manual for the WM_COMMAND message, you'll find that the wParam of the message contains the menu item ID. That's why the if statement compares m.WParam with the range of the eight CM_New… commands (see resource.h, Listing 16.15). If the message does correspond to one of those commands, a new TLsysWindow child window object is created and then that object's CannedLsys() procedure is called to initialize the selected L-system. If the command isn't one of the eight CM_New… commands, then the base class's DefCommandProc() function is called. This second step is very important; you can't simply turn off default command processing when you want to step in to process a few specific messages.

OWL's TWindowsObject class also contains the DefWndProc() for window messages, DefNotificationProc() for all notification messages, and DefChildProc() for child window messages.

The L-system Application Resources

The L-system application contains a large, but by now familiar, set of resources as shown in Table 16.3. There are two menus, four dialog boxes, an icon, and an accelerator table. Listings 16.15 and 16.16 show the code for resource.h and lsys.rc. The source code for the icon isn't displayed, and the source code for the two file dialog boxes isn't displayed because it is a standard part of OWL. You can look in filedial.dlg in the OWL include directory if you want to see the details.

TABLE 16.3

Windows L-system Resources

Resource Name	Resource Type	File	Listing
MainMenu	MENU	lsys.rc	16.16
LsysMenu	MENU	lsys.rc	16.16
AboutDialog	DIALOG	lsys.rc	16.16
GraphDialog	DIALOG	lsys.rc	16.16
SettingsDialog	DIALOG	lsys.rc	16.16
DrawDialog	DIALOG	lsys.rc	16.16
TitleDialog	DIALOG	lsys.rc	16.16
SD_FILEOPEN	DIALOG	filedial.dlg	None
SD_FILESAVE	DIALOG	filedial.dlg	None
ACCELTABLE	ACCELERATORS	lsys.rc	16.16
LsysApplcon	ICON	lsys.ico	None

LISTING 16.15

resource.h

```
//
// Resource IDs
//

//
// Menu IDs
//
// Lsystem menu
#define CM_LsysDialog    100
#define CM_GraphDialog   101
#define CM_DrawDialog    102
#define CM_TitleDialog   103
// Help menu
```

LISTING 16.15

resource.h (Continued)

```
#define CM_About        1Ø4
// File-New menu
#define CM_NewTriangle  1Ø5
#define CM_NewStar1     (CM_NewTriangle+1)
#define CM_NewStar2     (CM_NewTriangle+2)
#define CM_NewStar3     (CM_NewTriangle+3)
#define CM_NewBox1      (CM_NewTriangle+4)
#define CM_NewBox2      (CM_NewTriangle+5)
#define CM_NewTree1     (CM_NewTriangle+6)
#define CM_NewTree2     (CM_NewTriangle+7)

//
// Menu Names
#define MainMenuName "MainMenu"
#define LsysMenuName "LsysMenu"

//
// Position of the child (WINDOW) menus
#define MainMenuChildPos Ø
#define LsysMenuChildPos 2

//
// LsysDialog IDs
#define ID_ET_Seed   121
#define ID_ET_Rule   122
#define ID_RB_Iter1  13Ø
#define ID_RB_Iter2  131
#define ID_RB_Iter3  132
#define ID_RB_Iter4  133
#define ID_RB_Iter5  134
#define ID_RB_Iter6  135

//
// GraphDialog IDs
#define ID_ET_X      14Ø
#define ID_ET_Y      141
#define ID_ET_Theta  142
#define ID_ET_Delta  143
#define ID_ET_Length 144

//
// DrawDialog IDs
#define ID_RB_Red    15Ø
#define ID_RB_Green  151
#define ID_RB_Blue   152
#define ID_RB_Black  153
#define ID_RB_Pen1   16Ø
#define ID_RB_Pen2   161
#define ID_RB_Pen4   162
#define ID_RB_Pen8   163

// TitleDialog IDs
#define ID_ET_Title  17Ø
```

LISTING 16.15

resource.h (Continued)

```
// text lengths
#define TextLength     128
#define TitleLength    32
#define NumberLength   16
```

LISTING 16.16

lsys.rc

```
#include <windows.h>
#include <owlrc.h>
#include <filedial.dlg>
#include "resource.h"
#include "lsys.ico"

MainMenu MENU
BEGIN
    POPUP "&File"
    BEGIN
        POPUP "&New"
        BEGIN
            MENUITEM "Triangle", CM_NewTriangle
            MENUITEM "Star 1", CM_NewStar1
            MENUITEM "Star 2", CM_NewStar2
            MENUITEM "Star 3", CM_NewStar3
            MENUITEM "Box 1", CM_NewBox1
            MENUITEM "Box 2", CM_NewBox2
            MENUITEM "Tree 1", CM_NewTree1
            MENUITEM "Tree 2", CM_NewTree2
        END

        MenuItem  "&Open...", CM_FILEOPEN
        MenuItem  SEPARATOR
        MenuItem  "E&xit", CM_EXIT
    END

    POPUP "&Help"
    BEGIN
        MENUITEM "&About...", CM_About
    END

END

LsysMenu MENU
BEGIN
    POPUP "&File"
    BEGIN
        POPUP "&New"
        BEGIN
            MENUITEM "Triangle", CM_NewTriangle
            MENUITEM "Star 1", CM_NewStar1
```

LISTING 16.16

lsys.rc (Continued)

```
            MENUITEM "Star 2", CM_NewStar2
            MENUITEM "Star 3", CM_NewStar3
            MENUITEM "Box 1", CM_NewBox1
            MENUITEM "Box 2", CM_NewBox2
            MENUITEM "Tree 1", CM_NewTree1
            MENUITEM "Tree 2", CM_NewTree2
        END

        MenuItem  "&Open...", CM_FILEOPEN
        MenuItem  "&Save", CM_FILESAVE
        MenuItem  "Save &As...", CM_FILESAVEAS
        MenuItem  SEPARATOR
        MenuItem  "E&xit", CM_EXIT
    END

    POPUP "&L-system"
    BEGIN
        MENUITEM "&Settings...\tAlt+S", CM_LsysDialog
        MENUITEM "&Graphing...\tAlt+G", CM_GraphDialog
        MENUITEM "&Drawing...\tAlt+D", CM_DrawDialog
        MENUITEM "&Title...\tAlt+T", CM_TitleDialog
    END

    POPUP "&Window"
    BEGIN
        MENUITEM "&Cascade", CM_CASCADECHILDREN
        MENUITEM "&Tile", CM_TILECHILDREN
        MENUITEM "Arrange &Icons", CM_ARRANGEICONS
        MENUITEM "C&lose All", CM_CLOSECHILDREN
    END

    POPUP "&Help"
    BEGIN
        MENUITEM "&About...", CM_About
    END

END

AboutDialog DIALOG 45, 22, 100, 83
STYLE DS_MODALFRAME | WS_POPUP | WS_CAPTION | WS_SYSMENU
CAPTION "About L-system"
BEGIN
  CTEXT "L-system Demonstration", -1, 7, 7, 86, 10,
    WS_CHILD | WS_VISIBLE | WS_GROUP
  CTEXT "Copyright \251 1993\nby Kaare Christian",
    -1, 14, 21, 71, 18,
    WS_CHILD | WS_VISIBLE | WS_GROUP
  ICON "LsysAppIcon", -1, 42, 41, 16, 16,
    WS_CHILD | WS_VISIBLE
  DEFPUSHBUTTON "OK", IDOK, 29, 63, 41, 14,
    WS_CHILD | WS_VISIBLE | WS_TABSTOP
END
```

LISTING 16.16

lsys.rc (Continued)

```
GraphDialog DIALOG 33, 34, 136, 77
STYLE DS_MODALFRAME | WS_POPUP | WS_CAPTION | WS_SYSMENU
CAPTION "L-system Graphing Parameters"
BEGIN
  RTEXT "&X:", -1, 4, 9, 26, 8, SS_RIGHT |
    WS_CHILD | WS_VISIBLE | WS_GROUP
  CONTROL "", ID_ET_X, "EDIT", ES_RIGHT |
    WS_CHILD | WS_VISIBLE | WS_BORDER | WS_TABSTOP,
    34, 7, 36, 12
  RTEXT "&Y:", -1, 73, 9, 12, 8, SS_RIGHT |
    WS_CHILD | WS_VISIBLE | WS_GROUP
  CONTROL "", ID_ET_Y, "EDIT", ES_RIGHT |
    WS_CHILD | WS_VISIBLE | WS_BORDER | WS_TABSTOP,
    89, 7, 36, 12
  RTEXT "&Theta:", -1, 4, 26, 26, 8, SS_RIGHT |
    WS_CHILD | WS_VISIBLE | WS_GROUP
  CONTROL "", ID_ET_Theta, "EDIT", ES_RIGHT |
    WS_CHILD | WS_VISIBLE | WS_BORDER | WS_TABSTOP,
    34, 24, 36, 12
  RTEXT "&Delta:", -1, 4, 43, 26, 8
  CONTROL "", ID_ET_Delta, "EDIT", ES_RIGHT |
    WS_CHILD | WS_VISTBLE | WS_BORDER | WS_TABSTOP,
    34, 41, 36, 12
  RTEXT "&Length:", -1, 4, 60, 26, 8
  CONTROL "", ID_ET_Length, "EDIT", ES_RIGHT |
    WS_CHILD | WS_VISIBLE | WS_BORDER | WS_TABSTOP,
    34, 58, 36, 12
  PUSHBUTTON "Cancel", IDCANCEL, 92, 34, 30, 14,
    WS_CHILD | WS_VISIBLE | WS_TABSTOP
  PUSHBUTTON "OK", IDOK, 92, 56, 30, 14,
    WS_CHILD | WS_VISIBLE | WS_TABSTOP
END

SettingsDialog DIALOG 31, 31, 165, 79
STYLE DS_MODALFRAME | WS_POPUP | WS_CAPTION | WS_SYSMENU
CAPTION "L-system settings"
BEGIN
  LTEXT "&Seed:", -1, 5, 5, 22, 8,
    WS_CHILD | WS_VISIBLE | WS_GROUP
  CONTROL "", ID_ET_Seed, "EDIT", ES_LEFT | ES_AUTOHSCROLL |
    WS_CHILD | WS_VISIBLE | WS_BORDER | WS_TABSTOP,
    5, 15, 96, 12
  LTEXT "&Rule:", -1, 5, 31, 21, 8,
    WS_CHILD | WS_VISIBLE | WS_GROUP
  CONTROL "", ID_ET_Rule, "EDIT", ES_LEFT | ES_AUTOHSCROLL |
    WS_CHILD | WS_VISIBLE | WS_BORDER | WS_TABSTOP,
    5, 41, 96, 12
  CONTROL "&Iterations", 106, "button", BS_GROUPBOX |
    WS_CHILD | WS_VISIBLE, 109, 8, 50, 45
  CONTROL "&1", ID_RB_Iter1, "BUTTON", BS_AUTORADIOBUTTON |
    WS_CHILD | WS_VISIBLE | WS_TABSTOP, 115, 19, 17, 12
  CONTROL "&2", ID_RB_Iter2, "BUTTON", BS_AUTORADIOBUTTON |
    WS_CHILD | WS_VISIBLE | WS_TABSTOP, 115, 29, 17, 12
```

LISTING 16.16

lsys.rc (Continued)

```
    CONTROL "&3", ID_RB_Iter3, "BUTTON", BS_AUTORADIOBUTTON |
      WS_CHILD | WS_VISIBLE | WS_TABSTOP, 115, 39, 17, 12
    CONTROL "&4", ID_RB_Iter4, "BUTTON", BS_AUTORADIOBUTTON |
      WS_CHILD | WS_VISIBLE | WS_TABSTOP, 137, 19, 17, 12
    CONTROL "&5", ID_RB_Iter5, "BUTTON", BS_AUTORADIOBUTTON |
      WS_CHILD | WS_VISIBLE | WS_TABSTOP, 137, 29, 17, 12
    CONTROL "&6", ID_RB_Iter6, "BUTTON", BS_AUTORADIOBUTTON |
      WS_CHILD | WS_VISIBLE | WS_TABSTOP, 137, 39, 17, 12
    PUSHBUTTON "Cancel", IDCANCEL, 45, 6Ø, 33, 14,
      WS_CHILD | WS_VISIBLE | WS_TABSTOP
    PUSHBUTTON "OK", IDOK, 87, 6Ø, 33, 14,
      WS_CHILD | WS_VISIBLE | WS_TABSTOP
END

DrawDialog DIALOG 31, 31, 11Ø, 82
STYLE DS_MODALFRAME | WS_POPUP | WS_CAPTION | WS_SYSMENU
CAPTION "L-system drawing"
BEGIN
  CONTROL "&Color", 1Ø6, "button", BS_GROUPBOX |
    WS_CHILD | WS_VISIBLE | WS_GROUP, 1Ø, 5, 42, 52
  CONTROL "&Red", ID_RB_Red, "BUTTON", BS_AUTORADIOBUTTON |
    WS_CHILD | WS_VISIBLE | WS_TABSTOP, 13, 14, 36, 12
  CONTROL "&Green", ID_RB_Green, "BUTTON", BS_AUTORADIOBUTTON |
    WS_CHILD | WS_VISIBLE | WS_TABSTOP, 13, 24, 36, 12
  CONTROL "&Blue", ID_RB_Blue, "BUTTON", BS_AUTORADIOBUTTON |
    WS_CHILD | WS_VISIBLE | WS_TABSTOP, 13, 34, 37, 12
  CONTROL "Blac&k", ID_RB_Black, "BUTTON", BS_AUTORADIOBUTTON |
    WS_CHILD | WS_VISIBLE | WS_TABSTOP, 13, 44, 37, 12
  CONTROL "&PenWidth", -1, "button", BS_GROUPBOX |
    WS_CHILD | WS_VISIBLE | WS_GROUP, 59, 5, 42, 52
  CONTROL "&1", ID_RB_Pen1, "BUTTON", BS_AUTORADIOBUTTON |
    WS_CHILD | WS_VISIBLE | WS_TABSTOP, 62, 14, 36, 12
  CONTROL "&2", ID_RB_Pen2, "BUTTON", BS_AUTORADIOBUTTON |
    WS_CHILD | WS_VISIBLE | WS_TABSTOP, 62, 24, 36, 12
  CONTROL "&4", ID_RB_Pen4, "BUTTON", BS_AUTORADIOBUTTON |
    WS_CHILD | WS_VISIBLE | WS_TABSTOP, 62, 34, 37, 12
  CONTROL "&8", ID_RB_Pen8, "BUTTON", BS_AUTORADIOBUTTON |
    WS_CHILD | WS_VISIBLE | WS_TABSTOP, 62, 44, 37, 12
  PUSHBUTTON "Cancel", IDCANCEL, 18, 62, 33, 14,
    WS_CHILD | WS_VISIBLE | WS_TABSTOP
  PUSHBUTTON "OK", IDOK, 59, 62, 33, 14,
    WS_CHILD | WS_VISIBLE | WS_TABSTOP
END

TitleDialog DIALOG 41, 31, 92, 51
STYLE DS_MODALFRAME | WS_POPUP | WS_CAPTION | WS_SYSMENU
CAPTION "Set L-system Title"
BEGIN
  LTEXT "Title:", -1, 9, 9, 24, 8,
    WS_CHILD | WS_VISIBLE | WS_GROUP
  EDITTEXT ID_ET_Title, 35, 7, 47, 12, ES_LEFT | ES_AUTOHSCROLL |
    WS_CHILD | WS_VISIBLE | WS_BORDER | WS_TABSTOP
  PUSHBUTTON "Cancel", IDCANCEL, 9, 3Ø, 3Ø, 14,
```

LISTING 16.16

lsys.rc (Continued)

```
    WS_CHILD | WS_VISIBLE | WS_TABSTOP
  DEFPUSHBUTTON "OK", IDOK, 52, 30, 30, 14,
    WS_CHILD | WS_VISIBLE | WS_TABSTOP
END

ACCELTABLE ACCELERATORS
BEGIN
  "s", CM_LsysDialog, ASCII, ALT
  "g", CM_GraphDialog, ASCII, ALT
  "d", CM_DrawDialog, ASCII, ALT
  "t", CM_TitleDialog, ASCII, ALT
END
```

Extending the L-system Application

L-systems are enjoyable. Besides the pleasure I experienced building the L-system application, I've also enjoyed trying to see what happens as I make changes to L-systems. Being able to save L-system parameters in a file is great, because it allows me to save my work. But there are several additional things that would make the L-system application even better:

- Printing L-system graphics

- Saving the actual L-system graphic in a file

- Copying the L-system graphic into the Clipboard

- Adding labels to the output, so that each L-system is documented on screen

- Allowing more than one L-system to be displayed in each window

Each of these additions, except perhaps the last, is a relatively simple extension of the existing code. Have fun!

APPENDIX A
SEARCHING FOR FILES

The core of the Find Files application, which is discussed in Chapters 11, 12, and 13, is a search engine that finds files anywhere in a single disk drive according to one of three criteria: the file's name, the file's size, or the file's text content. In this appendix I'm going to describe the original DOS based version of the file search engine. Chapter 13 shows how this engine was incorporated into the Find Files Stage 4 framework to produce the Find Files Stage 5 application.

I chose to develop this search engine as a DOS application, but using a structure that would make it easy to move the core engine into my Windows framework. I selected this approach because, for certain core functions—searching, sorting, file system manipulations, and the like—it's easier to work in the DOS environment than in Windows.

The TTreeSearch Classes

I must confess that my first design for the search engine was simply to write three separate search procedures, one for each criterion. But as I started to implement this design, I realized that the three search routines had a lot in common. For all three searches, I used an approach similar to the following:

- For each subdirectory in the current directory, change to that directory and then call Search().

- For each file, test to see if it meets the specified criteria.

What's different about each search is the test. Therefore I reworked my design to take advantage of the common search tasks. In my final design I used a hierarchy of classes. The base class, called TTreeSearch, implements the above strategy in a member function called Search(). For each ordinary file, Search() calls checkFile() to see if the match criteria are satisfied, while for each subdirectory Search() calls itself to search that directory. The three derived classes implement the three search styles (see Figure A.1). In each derived class the checkFile() virtual member function is defined to implement one of the search strategies.

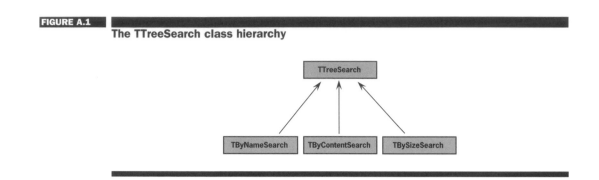

FIGURE A.1

The TTreeSearch class hierarchy

Findem Source Code

If you've ever used the DOS functions findfirst() and findnext(), you probably won't find much of interest in the findem source code. For those who may not have used DOS's find twins, let me briefly describe them. Findfirst() and findnext() are used to search through directories for files that meet some criteria. For example, you can find all the subdirectories, all the hidden files, all the files whose names begin with an A, and so on.

Your first step is to call findfirst() with a bitmask indicating what types of files interest you, plus a file name, possibly containing DOS wildcards, that indicates what names interest you. If you're looking, say, for directories, the mask will probably indicate directories and the file name will probably be "*.*". But if you're looking for files whose name begins with A, the mask will probably indicate ordinary files and the file name will likely be "a*.*".

If findfirst() finds any files, it returns information about them and also returns a True status. This allows you to call findnext(), repeating until the set of files is exhausted. The TTreeSearch classes use findfirst() and findnext() twice in the Search() procedure. In the first instance, the find duo is looking for directories, and each time one is encountered Search() is called recursively. In the second instance, the find duo is looking for ordinary files, and for each file Search() calls checkFile() to see if the file matches the criteria. As mentioned already, checkFile() is a virtual member that is defined in the three derived classes to implement the individual search strategies.

The findem.cpp source code is shown in Listing A.1. The findem source is organized, like most R+D code, into a single file: first the class definitions, then the member function definitions, then a small main() to exercise the classes. In Find Files Stage 5, findem.cpp was split into two files, search.h and search.cpp, and the main() and usage() functions were left behind.

LISTING A.1

findem.cpp

```cpp
#include <stdio.h>
#include <dir.h>
#include <dos.h>
#include <string.h>
#include <ctype.h>
#include <stdlib.h>

//
// Search through a file system tree for files
//
class TTreeSearch {
  public:
    TTreeSearch()
      { strcpy(filePattern, "*.*"); }
    virtual ~TTreeSearch()
      { return; }
    void Search();
  protected:
    virtual int checkFile(struct ffblk& ff) = 0;
    void print(struct ffblk& ff);
    char filePattern[13];
};

//
// Search for files with specific names
//   (DOS wildcards ok)
//
class TByNameSearch : public TTreeSearch {
  public:
    TByNameSearch(char *nm);
  protected:
    int checkFile(struct ffblk& ff);
};

//
// Search for files with specific sizes
//
class TBySizeSearch : public TTreeSearch {
  public:
    enum matchType { lessThan, equalTo, moreThan };
    TBySizeSearch(long siz, matchType t);
  protected:
    int checkFile(struct ffblk& ff);
    long siz;
    matchType match;
};

//
// Search for files that contain the target text
//
class TByContentSearch : public TTreeSearch {
  public:
    TByContentSearch(char *targ);
```

findem.cpp (Continued)

```cpp
      ~TByContentSearch()
      {
        if (target) delete target;
        if (target2) delete target2;
        if (buf) delete buf;
      }
  protected:
      int checkFile(struct ffblk& ff);
      char *target;
      char *target2;
      char *buf;
      int len;
};

//
// The generic search-through-a-file-system routine
//   (calls checkFile() for customized criteria)
//
void TTreeSearch::Search()
{
    struct ffblk ff;
    int done;
    // first descend into directories
    done = findfirst("*.*", &ff, FA_DIREC);
    while (!done) {
        if (ff.ff_attrib & FA_DIREC) {
    if (strcmp(ff.ff_name, ".") && strcmp(ff.ff_name, "..")) {
      printf("Directory %s\n", ff.ff_name);
      chdir(ff.ff_name);
      Search();  // recursion . . .
      chdir("..");
    }
        }
        done = findnext(&ff);
    }
    // now ordinary files
    done = findfirst(filePattern, &ff, 0);
    while (!done) {
        if (checkFile(ff))
    print(ff);
        done = findnext(&ff);
    }
}

//
// Print a line for a found file
//
void TTreeSearch::print(struct ffblk& ff)
{
    static char dirname[MAXPATH];
    getcwd(dirname, MAXPATH);
    printf("%s\\%s\n", dirname, ff.ff_name);
}
```

findem.cpp (Continued)

```cpp
//
// TByNameSearch constructor
//
TByNameSearch::TByNameSearch(char *nm)
{
  strcpy(filePattern, nm);
}


//
// For TByNameSearch, all files match because of pattern supplied
//  to constructor.
int TByNameSearch::checkFile(struct ffblk& /*ff*/)
{
  return 1;
}


//
// TBySizeSearch constructor
TBySizeSearch::TBySizeSearch(long s, matchType t) :
  siz(s), match(t)
{
  return;
}


//
// TBySizeSearch -- implement file size criteria
//
int TBySizeSearch::checkFile(struct ffblk& ff)
{
  switch(match) {
    case lessThan:
      if (ff.ff_fsize < siz)
        return 1;
      break;
    case equalTo:
      if (ff.ff_fsize == siz)
        return 1;
      break;
    case moreThan:
      if (ff.ff_fsize > siz)
        return 1;
      break;
  }
  return 0;
}


//
// TByContentSearch constructor
//
TByContentSearch::TByContentSearch(char *targ)
{
  len = strlen(targ);
  buf = new char[len + 1];
```

findem.cpp (Continued)

```
  // store both upper- and lowercase target
  target = new char[len + 1];
  target2 = new char[len + 1];
  strcpy(target, targ);
  strupr(target);
  strcpy(target2, targ);
  strlwr(target2);
  buf[len] = 0;
}


//
// TByContent criteria -- open file and search
//
int TByContentSearch::checkFile(struct ffblk& ff)
{
  int ch;
  char t1 = *target;
  char t2 = *target2;
  FILE *fin;
  fin = fopen(ff.ff_name, "rb");
  if (!fin)
    return 0;

#ifdef SlowWay
  while((ch = getc(fin)) != EOF) {
    if (ch == t1 || ch == t2) {
      fseek(fin, -1L, SEEK_CUR);
      if ((fread(buf, len, 1, fin) == 1) &&
       !strnicmp(buf, target, len)) { // found!
        fclose(fin);
        return 1;
      }
      if (!feof(fin))
        fseek(fin, -(len-1L), SEEK_CUR);
    }
  }
#else
  len = strlen(target) - 1;
  while((ch = getc(fin)) != EOF) {
    if (ch == t1 || ch == t2) {
      // read in the potential match string
      int n;
      char *p = buf;
      for(n=0; n<len; n++)
        *p++ = getc(fin);
      // do a strnicmp() operation
      char *pt1;
      char *pt2;
      int matched;
      pt1 = target + 1;
      pt2 = target2 + 1;
      matched = 1;
      for(p=buf,n=0; n<len && matched; n++) {
```

findem.cpp (Continued)

```
            if (*p != *pt1 && *p != *pt2)
              matched = 0;
            p++;
            pt1++;
            pt2++;
          }
          // return if found
          if (matched) { // found!
            fclose(fin);
            return 1;
          }
          // return if eof
          if (feof(fin)) {
            fclose(fin);
            return 0;
          }
          // restart search, but only go back if 1st char is in buf
          for(n=0; n<len; n++)
            if (buf[n] == t1 || buf[n] == t2) {
              fseek(fin,  (len-n), SEEK_CUR);
              break; // out of inner for, restarts search
            }
      }
    }
#endif
  fclose(fin);
  return 0;
}

// print a usage message
int usage()
{
  printf("Usage:\n");
  printf(" findem -n name | Search for files by name\n");
  printf(" findem -eq n   | Search for files of size n\n");
  printf(" findem -lt n   | Search for files smaller than n\n");
  printf(" findem -gt n   | Search for files larger than n\n");
  printf(" fintem -t text | Search for text in files\n");
  return -1;
}


//
// DOS main to exercise TTreeSearch classes
//
int main(int c, char **v)
{
  if (c != 3)
    return usage();
  TTreeSearch *srch;
  if (!stricmp("-n", v[1]))
    srch = new TByNameSearch(v[2]);
  else if (!stricmp("-t", v[1]))
    srch = new TByContentSearch(v[2]);
```

LISTING A.1

findem.cpp (Continued)

```
else if (!stricmp("-eq", v[1]))
  srch = new TBySizeSearch(atoi(v[2]), TBySizeSearch::equalTo);
else if (!stricmp("-lt", v[1]))
  srch = new TBySizeSearch(atoi(v[2]), TBySizeSearch::lessThan);
else if (!stricmp("-gt", v[1]))
  srch = new TBySizeSearch(atoi(v[2]), TBySizeSearch::moreThan);
else
  return usage();
srch->Search();
return 0;
}
```

The checkFile() routine of the TByContentSearch class is the most complex routine in the findem application. The reason is efficiency. On my fast development machine the original text scanning algorithm in the TByContentSearch class's checkFile() routine worked acceptably. But when I tried the program on some older, slower PCs I found that I had a performance problem. This original code is bracketed by the #ifdef SlowWay conditional in the code. The most obvious problem with the original code is that the inner loop had too many subroutine calls. Therefore I reworked the code to avoid subroutine calls as much as possible, producing the more complicated version that appears in the second part of the #ifdef SlowWay conditional. I've left the original in place, partly as documentation and partly so that I can compare the two when questions arise.

In my testing on a 20 MHz 386 machine with a moderately fast ESDI disk system, the "fast" version operates in half the time of the "slow" version. Thus the additional complexity is clearly worthwhile. On my fast machine the difference is much less, because on a fast PC both versions are limited by the disk I/O speed. One lesson here is that you shouldn't optimize until you find a problem. Another lesson is that it's easier to optimize if you have a working routine to start from. But perhaps the most important lesson is that C++ doesn't stand in the way of optimal code. The object-oriented features of C++ can help you produce code efficiently, but its C origins also enable you to produce efficient code.

Is there still room for improvement in the performance of the checkFile() routine of the TByContentSearch class? Yes, I'm sure there is. One idea is to hand-optimize the assembly language produced by the compiler. I've often attained 50–100 percent improvements by careful hand coding. Another idea is to replace the stdio input routines with specialized routines. Borland's stdio library is already well tuned, but it is more general than needed here, and I suspect that for this application faster file I/O could be attained. A more drastic improvement would be to replace this simplistic, linear search method with a more sophisticated search method. I'll leave that as an exercise for the reader!

APPENDIX B
CONSTRUCTORS AND VIRTUAL BASE CLASSES

When a class is an ordinary base, not a virtual base, then the constructors of the derived control which base class constructors are invoked. That's the usual situation. But when a class is a virtual base, things are much less straightforward because there are many derived classes, each with equal claim on the base class. Since the virtual base should only be initialized once, we need a rule to specify which derived class actually controls the activation of a virtual base's constructor. The solution adopted by C++ is to let the class of the actual object, sometimes called the *most derived class,* be in charge.

For example, if Z has, via many twisty turns, a virtual base called A, then it is up to Z's constructors to control which of A's constructors are invoked. If A has a default constructor and a Z constructor doesn't explicitly refer to A in its initialization list, then A's default constructor will be used. However, and here's the surprise, if A only has argument-taking (nondefault) constructors, then Z must explicitly select one of A's constructors. This can be very surprising, especially if Z and A are widely separated in the inheritance tree.

Although the rule is that the most derived class is in control, by implication every derived class's constructors must specify which of A's constructors to use, because you can't know which of the derived classes will actually be created during runtime. Thus if A has only argument-taking constructors, every class having A as a virtual base, no matter how distant, must explicitly provide constructors that invoke A constructors in their initialization lists.

The last surprise follows directly from all the others. If you have a class hierarchy with A as a virtual base, then only the initialization of A specified by the most derived class will be used; all the others will be skipped. I'm uncomfortable with this feature of C++ because when you look at the code you see initializations that may or may not be performed. If a B object is created, then its initialization of virtual base A will be used. But if class C is derived from B, and a C object is created, then B's initialization of virtual base A will be skipped, and C's will be used instead. You must understand this feature to use the Turbo Vision library, because it contains several virtual base classes that require arguments.

APPENDIX C:

WHAT'S ON THE DISK

Table C.1 lists the zipped files that appear on the disk that accompanies this book. Each zipped archive contains the source code files for a single example program in the book. For the Blake and Find Files applications, I've included archive files for each stage of the applications, as discussed in the book. Each of these archives is installed into its own directory on your hard disk.

TABLE C.1

The Disk Contents

batch.zip	charray.zip	find4.zip	qstring.zip	tvview.zip
blake1.zip	dosfind.zip	find5.zip	sets.zip	tvview2.zip
blake2.zip	duet.zip	find5b.zip	tvdial1.zip	unzip.bat
blake3.zip	find1.zip	install.bat	tvdial2.zip	viewer.zip
blake4.zip	find2.zip	lsys.zip	tvmenu.zip	winlsys.zip
calc.zip	find3.zip	priqueue.zip	tvnull.zip	

The zipped-up version of the source code on the disk takes up about 250k, while the expanded version is about 700k. But when everything is compiled, your storage requirements will balloon to about 28Mb, mostly because of the enormous .SYM files that store precompiled headers.

Disk Installation

Your first decision is where to install the source. The path names in the project files assume that the book's source code is installed in a subdirectory of the \borlandc directory. I suggest that you create the directory \borlandc\bccdisk to store the contents of the disk.

I realize that some people may not be able to place this book's disk contents into a subdirectory of the \borlandc directory. Some people have already filled the drive on which Borland C++ is stored, others access \borlandc via a network, and others don't ever merge separate distributions. If you place the disk's code elsewhere, you will need to adjust the paths in all of the project files. The IDE's

Options-Directories menu selection will let you specify the paths to the compiler, and the project file itself will let you specify the paths to owl.def and to bwcc.lib.

After you've created a directory for the book's source code disk you're ready to run the disk's install program. Install needs to be run from the floppy drive, and it needs to be told the location of the installation directory. Note that the install script doesn't make the installation directory, although it does check to be sure that the installation directory exists. Here's a typical installation dialog, assuming that A is your floppy drive:

```
C> mkdir \borlandc\bccdisk
C> A:
A> install c:\borlandc\bccdisk
. . . many messages as directories are created
        and files are unzipped . . .
A>
```

The installation script places about 25 subdirectories into the installation directory, and it also places a few batch files there. Thus it's not a good idea to install directly into a disk's root directory, or directly into the \borlandc directory.

Compilation

All the directories contain project files, so one option is simply to go to one of the source directories, start BC (for the DOS applications) or BCW (for the Windows applications), and compile manually. And if things go awry with the auto compilation that I'm about to describe, you should manually compile an application, so you can see what is set wrong. Usually the problem is bad path names in the Options-Directories dialog.

There are two batch files that help you compile—makeall.bat and makeone.bat. Makeall.bat compiles everything, by calling makeone.bat for each application. If you only want to compile some of the applications, you can comment out the unwanted applications from makeall.bat.

You can also compile things selectively using makeone.bat. Makeone.bat needs to be told which directory contains the application that you want to compile. Thus to compile the Windows L-system application, you would go to the directory containing this book's source (\borlandc\bccdisk is the default) and then type

```
makeone winlsys
```

For the directories that contain more than one project file, you must also tell makeone.bat the name of the project file.

There are also batch files for cleaning up the source code directories, which to me means removing all the object files, all the backup files, the executable files, the symbol table files, and so on. The cleanall.bat file cleans everything, while cleandir.bat cleans a single directory. You might want to modify cleandir.bat to meet your specific needs, such as not cleaning .EXE files, or only cleaning .SYM files.

List of Files

Table C.2 contains a list of the files that are created when you install the source code disk.

TABLE C.2 ▬▬▬▬▬▬▬▬▬▬▬▬▬▬▬▬▬▬▬▬▬▬▬▬▬

The Source Code Files Supplied with This Book

.batch files

./makeall.bat

./makeone.bat

./cleanall.bat

./cleandir.bat

./blake1 files

./blake1/blake.cpp

./blake1/about.dlg

./blake1/blake.h

./blake1/resource.h

./blake1/blake.ico

./blake1/blake.mnu

./blake1/blake1.prj

./blake1/blake.rc

./blake1/blake.str

./blake1/blake.res

./blake1/blake1.dsk

./blake2 files

./blake2/about.dlg

./blake2/blake.cpp

./blake2/blake.h

./blake2/blake.ico

./blake2/blake.mnu

./blake2/blake.rc

./blake2/blake.str

./blake2/blake2.prj

./blake2/resource.h

./blake2 files (Continued)

./blake2/blake.res

./blake2/blake2.dsk

./blake3 files

./blake3/about.dlg

./blake3/blake.h

./blake3/resource.h

./blake3/blake.ico

./blake3/blake.mnu

./blake3/blake3.prj

./blake3/blake.rc

./blake3/blake.str

./blake3/blake.res

./blake3/blake3.dsk

./blake3/blake.cpp

./blake4 files

./blake4/blake.cpp

./blake4/about.dlg

./blake4/blake.h

./blake4/resource.h

./blake4/blake.ico

./blake4/blake.mnu

./blake4/blake4.prj

./blake4/blake.rc

./blake4/blake.str

./blake4/blake.res

./blake4/blake4.dsk

./calc files

./calc/calc.cpp

./calc/calc.prj

./calc/calc.dsk

./charray files

./charray/charray.h

./charray/charray.cpp

./charray/main.cpp

./charray/charray.prj

./charray/charray.dsk

./charray/mem.cpp

./dosfind files

./dosfind/findem.cpp

./dosfind/findem.prj

./dosfind/findem.dsk

./duet files

./duet/duet.cpp

./duet/duet.prj

./duet/duet.h

./duet/duet.res

./duet/boxwin.h

./duet/duet.rc

./duet/linewin.cpp

./duet/duet.ico

./duet/boxwin.cpp

./duet/linewin.h

TABLE C.2

The Source Code Files Supplied with This Book (Continued)

./duet files (Continued)

./duet/duet.map

./duet/duet.dsk

./duet/resource.h

./find1 files

./find1/find.cpp

./find1/find.prj

./find1/find.dsk

./find2 files

./find2/find.cpp

./find2/find.prj

./find2/find.rc

./find2/find.res

./find2/find.dsk

./find3 files

./find3/find.cpp

./find3/resource.h

./find3/find.prj

./find3/find.rc

./find3/find.ico

./find3/find.res

./find3/find.dsk

./find4 files

./find4/bycontnt.cpp

./find4/byname.cpp

./find4/bysize.cpp

./find4/find.cpp

./find4/dialog.h

./find4/resource.h

./find4 files (Continued)

./find4/find.prj

./find4/find.rc

./find4/about.dlg

./find4/bycontnt.dlg

./find4/byname.dlg

./find4/bysize.dlg

./find4/find.ico

./find4/find.res

./find4/find.mnu

./find4/find.dsk

./find5 files

./find5/bycontnt.cpp

./find5/byname.cpp

./find5/bysize.cpp

./find5/cancel.cpp

./find5/filelist.cpp

./find5/find.cpp

./find5/search.cpp

./find5/cancel.h

./find5/dialog.h

./find5/filelist.h

./find5/find.h

./find5/resource.h

./find5/search.h

./find5/find.prj

./find5/find.rc

./find5/about.dlg

./find5/bycontnt.dlg

./find5/byname.dlg

./find5/bysize.dlg

./find5/cancel.dlg

./find5 files (Continued)

./find5/filelist.dlg

./find5/find.ico

./find5/find.res

./find5/find.mnu

./find5/find.dsk

./find5b files

./find5b/bycontnt.cpp

./find5b/byname.cpp

./find5b/bysize.cpp

./find5b/cancel.cpp

./find5b/filelist.cpp

./find5b/find.cpp

./find5b/search.cpp

./find5b/cancel.h

./find5b/dialog.h

./find5b/filelist.h

./find5b/find.h

./find5b/resource.h

./find5b/search.h

./find5b/find.prj

./find5b/find.rc

./find5b/about.dlg

./find5b/bycontnt.dlg

./find5b/byname.dlg

./find5b/bysize.dlg

./find5b/cancel.dlg

./find5b/filelist.dlg

./find5b/find.ico

./find5b/find.res

./find5b/find.mnu

./find5b/find.dsk

TABLE C.2	

The Source Code Files Supplied with This Book (Continued)

./winlsys files

./winlsys/lsyswin.h

./winlsys/lsysw.h

./winlsys/charray.h

./winlsys/charray.cpp

./winlsys/lsysw.cpp

./winlsys/lsysapp.cpp

./winlsys/lsys.h

./winlsys/resource.h

./winlsys/lsysapp.h

./winlsys/lsyswin.cpp

./winlsys/drawdlg.h

./winlsys/lsys.rc

./winlsys/seldlg.cpp

./winlsys/winlsys.prj

./winlsys/winlsys.dsk

./winlsys/graphdlg.cpp

./winlsys/setdlg.h

./winlsys/lsys.ico

./winlsys/graphdlg.h

./winlsys/lsys.res

./winlsys/drawdlg.cpp

./winlsys/titledlg.cpp

./winlsys/titledlg.h

./winlsys/david.lsy

./winlsys/box1.lsy

≡ INDEX

■ TO RECEIVE 5¼-INCH DISK(S)

The Ziff-Davis Press software contained on the $3\frac{1}{2}$-inch disk included with this book is also available in $5\frac{1}{4}$-inch format. If you would like to receive the software in the $5\frac{1}{4}$-inch format, please return the $3\frac{1}{2}$-inch disk with your name and address to:

Disk Exchange
Ziff-Davis Press
5903 Christie Avenue
Emeryville, CA 94608

■ END-USER LICENSE AGREEMENT

READ THIS AGREEMENT CAREFULLY BEFORE BUYING THIS BOOK. BY BUYING THE BOOK AND USING THE PROGRAM LISTINGS, DISKS, AND PROGRAMS REFERRED TO BELOW, YOU ACCEPT THE TERMS OF THIS AGREEMENT.

The program listings included in this book and the programs included on the diskette(s) contained in the package on the opposite page ("Disks") are proprietary products of Ziff-Davis Press and/or third party suppliers ("Suppliers"). The program listings and programs are hereinafter collectively referred to as the "Programs." Ziff-Davis Press and the Suppliers retain ownership of the Disks and copyright to the Programs, as their respective interests may appear. The Programs and the copy of the Disks provided are licensed (not sold) to you under the conditions set forth herein.

License. You may use the Disks on any compatible computer, provided that the Disks are used on only one computer and by one user at a time.

Restrictions. You may not commercially distribute the Disks or the Programs or otherwise reproduce, publish, or distribute or otherwise use the Disks or the Programs in any manner that may infringe any copyright or other proprietary right of Ziff-Davis Press, the Suppliers, or any other party or assign, sublicense, or otherwise transfer the Disks or this agreement to any other party unless such party agrees to accept the terms and conditions of this agreement. This license and your right to use the Disks and the Programs automatically terminates if you fail to comply with any provision of this agreement.

U.S. GOVERNMENT RESTRICTED RIGHTS. The disks and the programs are provided with **RESTRICTED RIGHTS**. Use, duplication, or disclosure by the Government is subject to restrictions as set forth in subparagraph (c)(1)(ii) of the Rights in Technical Data and Computer Software Clause at DFARS (48 CFR 252.277-7013). The Proprietor of the compilation of the Programs and the Disks is Ziff-Davis Press, 5903 Christie Avenue, Emeryville, CA 94608.

Limited Warranty. Ziff-Davis Press warrants the physical Disks to be free of defects in materials and workmanship under normal use for a period of 30 days from the purchase date. If Ziff-Davis Press receives written notification within the warranty period of defects in materials or workmanship in the physical Disks, and such notification is determined by Ziff-Davis Press to be correct, Ziff-Davis Press will, at its option, replace the defective Disks or refund a prorata portion of the purchase price of the book. **THESE ARE YOUR SOLE REMEDIES FOR ANY BREACH OF WARRANTY.**

EXCEPT AS SPECIFICALLY PROVIDED ABOVE, THE DISKS AND THE PROGRAMS ARE PROVIDED "AS IS" WITHOUT ANY WARRANTY OF ANY KIND. NEITHER ZIFF-DAVIS PRESS NOR THE SUPPLIERS MAKE ANY WARRANTY OF ANY KIND AS TO THE ACCURACY OR COMPLETENESS OF THE DISKS OR THE PROGRAMS OR THE RESULTS TO BE OBTAINED FROM USING THE DISKS OR THE PROGRAMS AND NEITHER ZIFF-DAVIS PRESS NOR THE SUPPLIERS SHALL BE RESPONSIBLE FOR ANY CLAIMS ATTRIBUTABLE TO ERRORS, OMISSIONS, OR OTHER INACCURACIES IN THE DISKS OR THE PROGRAMS. THE ENTIRE RISK AS TO THE RESULTS AND PERFORMANCE OF THE DISKS AND THE PROGRAMS IS ASSUMED BY THE USER. FURTHER, NEITHER ZIFF-DAVIS PRESS NOR THE SUPPLIERS MAKE ANY REPRESENTATIONS OR WARRANTIES, EITHER EXPRESS OR IMPLIED, WITH RESPECT TO THE DISKS OR THE PROGRAMS, INCLUDING BUT NOT LIMITED TO, THE QUALITY, PERFORMANCE, MERCHANTABILITY, OR FITNESS FOR A PARTICULAR PURPOSE OF THE DISKS OR THE PROGRAMS. IN NO EVENT SHALL ZIFF-DAVIS PRESS OR THE SUPPLIERS BE LIABLE FOR DIRECT, INDIRECT, SPECIAL, INCIDENTAL, OR CONSEQUENTIAL DAMAGES ARISING OUT THE USE OF OR INABILITY TO USE THE DISKS OR THE PROGRAMS OR FOR ANY LOSS OR DAMAGE OF ANY NATURE CAUSED TO ANY PERSON OR PROPERTY AS A RESULT OF THE USE OF THE DISKS OR THE PROGRAMS, EVEN IF ZIFF-DAVIS PRESS OR THE SUPPLIERS HAVE BEEN SPECIFICALLY ADVISED OF THE POSSIBILITY OF SUCH DAMAGES. NEITHER ZIFF-DAVIS PRESS NOR THE SUPPLIERS ARE RESPONSIBLE FOR ANY COSTS INCLUDING, BUT NOT LIMITED TO, THOSE INCURRED AS A RESULT OF LOST PROFITS OR REVENUE, LOSS OF USE OF THE DISKS OR THE PROGRAMS, LOSS OF DATA, THE COSTS OF RECOVERING SOFTWARE OR DATA, OR THIRD-PARTY CLAIMS. IN NO EVENT WILL ZIFF-DAVIS PRESS' OR THE SUPPLIERS' LIABILITY FOR ANY DAMAGES TO YOU OR ANY OTHER PARTY EVER EXCEED THE PRICE OF THIS BOOK. NO SALES PERSON OR OTHER REPRESENTATIVE OF ANY PARTY INVOLVED IN THE DISTRIBUTION OF THE DISKS IS AUTHORIZED TO MAKE ANY MODIFICATIONS OR ADDITIONS TO THIS LIMITED WARRANTY.

Some states do not allow the exclusion or limitation of implied warranties or limitation of liability for incidental or consequential damages, so the above limitation or exclusion may not apply to you.

General. Ziff-Davis Press and the Suppliers retain all rights not expressly granted. Nothing in this license constitutes a waiver of the rights of Ziff-Davis Press or the Suppliers under the U.S. Copyright Act or any other Federal or State Law, international treaty, or foreign law.